ActionScript™ 3.0
Bible

ActionScript™ 3.0 Bible

Published by
Wiley Publishing, Inc.
10475 Crosspoint Boulevard
Indianapolis, IN 46256
www.wiley.com

Copyright © 2008 by Wiley Publishing, Inc., Indianapolis, Indiana

Published simultaneously in Canada

ISBN: 978-0-470-13560-0

Manufactured in the United States of America

10 9 8 7 6 5 4 3 2 1

Library of Congress Cataloging-in-Publication Data

Braunstein, Roger, 1981–
　ActionScript 3.0 bible / Roger Braunstein, Mims H. Wright, Joshua J. Noble.
　　　p. cm.
　ISBN 978-0-470-13560-0 (pbk.)
　1. Flash (Computer file) 2. ActionScript (Computer program language) 3. Computer animation. 4. Web
sites — Design. I. Wright, Mims H., 1979– II. Noble, Joshua J., 1977– III. Title.
　TR897.7.B793 2007
　006.6'96—dc22

2007032141

ActionScript™ 3.0 Bible

Roger Braunstein

Mims H. Wright

Joshua J. Noble

BICENTENNIAL
1807
WILEY
2007
BICENTENNIAL

Wiley Publishing, Inc.

About the Authors

Roger Braunstein was recently knighted the director of technology at Your Majesty in New York City. He lives in and rides his bike around Brooklyn, which provides him with limitless opportunity for adventure and misadventure. He likes all sorts of things — including films, cooking, 8-bit music, and summer. You'd have to ask him for a more complete list. He tries desperately to learn far more than is possible, but he realizes that the journey is in the trying. Roger is usually embarrassed about the state of his web page at `http://partlyhuman.com/`.

Mims H. Wright (yes, that's his real name) was born a curious Southern boy in Mississippi. Transplanted to Boulder, Colorado, at the unstable age of thirteen, he was spared from a teen life filled with shaggy hair and polo shirts. Adept at finding order in chaos and vice versa, he followed his passion for design and upon graduation from high school went to an art college to avoid any real responsibility. During the Internet boom, he joined the ranks of nerdy twenty-somethings to get his piece of the pie only to find that not only was there no pie left but it wasn't very tasty after all. After returning to school for safety, he helped develop the newly formed interactive design program at the University of Colorado.

In 2002, he moved to New York and took a job as a Production Artist where he was awarded for his performance and quickly became the go-to guy for Flash design and development. Since then, he's worked with a wide range of clients from "mom and pop" to "evil empire" and, with a strong sense of irony, has achieved veteran status before the age of thirty.

Mims presently resides in Brooklyn, New York, where he makes web sites for cash. He is also an amateur international racecar driver. His blog on ActionScript development can be found at `http://mimswright.com/blog`.

Joshua J. Noble lives in Buenos Aires, Argentina. He studies up on his Spanish, Chinese, C, Erlang, and Ruby in his free time; watches soccer; reads as many newspapers as he can; goofs around with computer vision libraries; and plays with mini-controllers. He has worked with ActionScript for four years in various companies and capacities.

Credits

Executive Editor
Chris Webb

Development Editor
Adaobi Obi Tulton

Technical Editors
Corey Szopinski
Mark Llobrera
Mark Walters

Copy Editors
Nancy Rapoport
Travis Henderson

Editorial Manager
Mary Beth Wakefield

Production Manager
Tim Tate

**Vice President and
Executive Group Publisher**
Richard Swadley

Vice President and Executive Publisher
Joseph B. Wikert

Project Coordinator, Cover
Lynsey Osborn

Compositor
Happenstance Type-O-Rama

Illustrator
Oso Rey, Happenstance Type-O-Rama

Proofreaders
Sossity Smith
Martine Dardignac
Kathryn Duggan

Indexer
Melanie Belkin

Anniversary Logo Design
Richard Pacifico

Acknowledgments

This book was, above all, a team effort. My coauthors, editors, and the team at Wiley all deserve a huge cheer. Thanks to Mims for being amazingly organized and driven. Joey, I'll never understand how you managed to make time for the book, but it's so much better for your experience and contributions. Thank you. Josh, you've been a pleasure to work with and I thank you for effortlessly taking on a hero's task. To our editor Chris Webb, thank you for the incredible opportunity, and for backing us up along the whole journey. Adaobi Obi Tulton, your gifts to this book went way above and beyond your title of editor. You were a motivator, an organizer, a manager, and a friend. We couldn't have done this without you. To our technical editors, Mark Walters, Corey Szopinski, and Mark Llobrera, thank you for your eagle eyes and your invaluable suggestions. Thanks to Schematic for supporting me far more than I expected possible. I also thank all my coworkers at Schematic for being mentors and great friends, in particular Robert Reinhardt, Danny Patterson, and Joey Lott. Thanks for the wisdom and guidance you continually impart and the doors you opened for me. Thanks to my friends and family for enduring my occasional self-isolation and other antisocial behaviors. Last but far from least, thanks to my parents for cheering me on when I needed it most, and for giving me the most important gifts.

— *Roger Braunstein*

Rewriting *ActionScript Bible* from scratch was a huge undertaking that required the help of several people. I'd like to thank our editors at Wiley, Chris Webb and Adaobi Obi Tulton; our tech editors, Corey Szopinksi, Mark Walters, and Mark Llobrera; and of course, the other authors. To Roger, you've been a great friend and a great partner to work with on this project and all the others. I hope for more chances in the future. To my family and friends whom I repeatedly blew off while writing and who suffered my sleep-deprived irritability, thank you for your patience. Thanks to Schematic for being flexible with my writing schedule and for allowing me to work on this. Thanks to my blog readers and colleagues who helped hash out sticky issues. Thanks to the Flash CS3 prerelease testers and to everyone at Adobe for making these awesome products more awesomer. Shouts-out to JS, JM, KH, DS, DW, JN, CS, JC, CD, NW, LW, VH, MW, JY, DP, JB, SP, CZ, AC, WJ, *and you!*

Most important, I thank Robert Reinhardt and Joey Lott for passing the torch to us. It will surely change my life.

— *Mims H. Wright*

Thanks to Chris Webb and Adaobi Obi Tulton and to Corey Szopinksi, Mark Walters, and Mark Llobrera for tech editing, and to Joey, Roger, and Mims for asking me to contribute. It's been a blast.

I'd like to thank Morgan Schwartz for so patiently walking me through the fine art of Flash Remoting, and PHP and MySQL so many years ago and teaching me about the joys of tweaking scripts and servers, and that it's not the tools that matter so much as what you do with them. I'd also like to thank Abey George for teaching so much about Flex and Object Oriented Development, about how to keep your cool on a deadline, and finally about what it means to write beautiful code and think clearly.

—Joshua J. Noble

Contents at a Glance

Contents

Contents

Contents

Contents

Contents

Contents

Contents

Contents

Contents

Introduction

Hello! Welcome to *ActionScript 3.0 Bible*. This book aims to be a comprehensive resource on all things ActionScript 3.0. You can use it as an instructional textbook, as a reference book, or both. This book introduces concepts used in ActionScript 3.0 with both background information and real-world examples to enrich your understanding. Armed with the knowledge contained herein, you will be able to bring your ideas to life with ActionScript 3.0, whether they are applications, web sites, presentations, games, toys, art, or experiments.

ActionScript 3.0 is the language used in a range of tools developed by Adobe, including Flash CS3, Flex 2 and 3, and AIR (formerly Apollo). This book's coverage remains agnostic as to the tool you choose to use. It does not cover topics specific to Flash CS3 or Flex 2, but it does cover the topics common to both. When the various tools handle something differently, we let you know how. Accordingly, this is the right book to help you learn how to program for any of these tools.

In addition, ActionScript 3.0 is based on web standards. It implements a draft of the ECMAScript edition 4 language specification, as well as E4X and DOM level 3 events. This means that learning ActionScript 3.0 will prepare you to program in other ECMAScript languages, particularly new versions of JavaScript.

ActionScript and the *Flash Bible* Series

ActionScript 3.0 is the third major incarnation of the ActionScript language. Previously, ActionScript was used primarily to develop Flash content. Now ActionScript is being applied in an increasing variety of contexts, and it is a mature technology in its own right. *ActionScript 3.0 Bible* was written with this in mind, while additional offerings from Wiley provide focused training for the tools that use ActionScript 3.0.

The *Flash Bible* series continues with *Adobe Flash CS3 Professional Bible* (Reinhardt and Dowd, 2007). Rely on *Adobe Flash CS3 Professional Bible* to learn the ins and outs of the latest version of Flash, such as using the timeline, the library, and drawing tools. The *Flash Bible* series can get you started with ActionScript, but it is not a comprehensive reference for programming topics in Flash. If you plan on using Flash to develop your ActionScript projects, we recommend using *Adobe Flash CS3 Professional Bible* as a complement to this book.

Wrox Press, a Wiley imprint, offers a series of books on Adobe Flex. If you are using ActionScript 3.0 with Flex, we recommend complementing our book with *Professional Adobe Flex 2* (Tretola et al, 2007) or the upcoming *Professional Adobe Flex 3* (Tretola et al, 2008).

The Wrox imprint also offers several books on Adobe AIR that can complement our book if you are developing desktop applications using ActionScript 3.0 and AIR. We recommend the upcoming titles *Adobe AIR Instant Results* (Leuchner et al, 2007) and *Professional AIR* (Freedman et al, 2007).

Who Should Read This Book

If you're interested in developing web sites and applications using Flex Builder or tapping into the powerful programming features of Flash CS3, *ActionScript 3.0 Bible* is for you. This book walks you through ActionScript 3.0, from the basics of the language through powerful new advanced features.

If you want to learn the new features of Adobe Flash CS3 Professional or learn how to use the Flash software, this book may not be right for you. It does not cover the Flash authoring tool, nor will it tell you how to set up your Flash files or where to find the correct commands and tools. To learn more about this tool, see the recommended books in the preceding section.

If you want to develop applications using Flex, note that although this book provides you with the necessary prerequisite — a solid grounding in ActionScript 3.0 — it does not cover the Flex framework or MXML. To learn more about this technology, see the recommended books in the preceding section.

> **NOTE** The Flex framework is a predefined library of components that are commonly used in Flash application development. This framework utilizes and is built in ActionScript 3.0, but it is not covered in this book.

Whether or not you have experience with previous versions of ActionScript, this book is appropriate for you. Even more so than ActionScript 2.0, ActionScript 3.0 requires an object-oriented approach, and this book includes a primer on object-oriented programming. You will find all you need in order to get up-to-speed on object-oriented programming in a very short time. Regardless of your skill level or experience, this book provides what you need to learn and use ActionScript 3.0.

This book does pay special attention to differences between ActionScript 2.0 and 3.0, so if you are upgrading your brain matter, we will help. We highlight topics that have changed in this latest version of ActionScript. These notes will help make sure you don't miss any of the differences, subtle or not.

How This Book Is Organized

The phrase "ActionScript 3.0," as commonly used, refers to both a programming language and the Flash Player 9 API, or Application Programming Interface. Mastering ActionScript 3.0 the *language* will let you write programs, but it's the Flash Player API — a library of classes and functions that are available to all ActionScript 3.0 programs — that will let you create programs that you can see, that move, that react to the keyboard and mouse, that play video and sound, that connect to the

Internet, and more. In addition, there are topics associated with programming in ActionScript that you will deal with by necessity that aren't parts of the language or the API, such as debugging. All of the subject matter of the ActionScript 3.0 language, the Flash Player 9 API, and related topics are covered in discrete parts of this book. The parts group similar topics and related functionality. The parts are further divided into chapters, each of which focuses on a single topic.

We think this book works well from front to back, but after learning the language in Part I, you can jump around as you desire to the topic that you'd like to learn about. Some topics may require knowledge of preceding chapters, but these are cross-referenced for your benefit.

Part I: Getting Started with ActionScript 3.0

Part I of this book, consisting of Chapters 1 through 5, is designed to get all readers up to the same level. This part teaches you what ActionScript 3.0 is all about and how to use the language. By the end of this part, you should be able to write programs in ActionScript 3.0. You will learn:

- About ActionScript 3.0: what it is, what it's for, what's new
- ActionScript 3.0, the language
- Programming basics: expressions, variables, operators, functions, scope
- Object-oriented programming: classes, interfaces, inheritance, composition

If ActionScript 3.0 is your first programming language, make sure you read all of Part I; however, everyone should read Chapter 1, "Introducing ActionScript 3.0."

If you have experience with other object-oriented programming languages, you should read Part I to get a feel for the syntax and features of the language. If you are an ActionScript 2.0 veteran, you should also read this part in full, paying close attention to the information called out in the text as "New in AS3."

After Part I and a bit of practice, readers new to ActionScript and readers with experience should be equally prepared to tackle the rest of the book.

Part II: Working with ActionScript 3.0 Objects

Part II covers the data structures in ActionScript 3.0 that you will use most commonly, including how they are implemented in ActionScript and what you can do with them. The following data structures are covered:

- Strings
- Numbers, dates, and math
- Arrays
- Objects
- XML
- Regular expressions

Part III: Working with the Display List

Part III covers the ground you'll need to start making programs that have a visual aspect. The fundamentals introduced here are used frequently in other parts of the book. You will learn about:

- Display lists: used by Flash Player to handle the display of visual objects
- The display classes used to create visuals and how they are related
- Using graphics created in Flash or external images in an ActionScript 3.0 project
- Printing
- Displaying and interacting with text

Part IV: Understanding the Event Framework

Part IV provides the fundamentals for writing interactive software by introducing events. This is a key topic that will be used in many other parts. You will learn about:

- What events are, how they work, how to use them
- How to create your own events
- Using events to react to the mouse and keyboard
- Using the Timer class and its events to control ActionScript over time

Part V: Working with Error Handling

Part V gives you the tools you need to write rock-solid programs in ActionScript 3.0, including:

- An introduction to errors: the Error class, try blocks, and asynchronous errors
- Using the debugger to track down, understand, and eliminate bugs in your code
- Strategies for handling errors

Part VI: Working with External Data

In Part VI, you learn about using information from sources outside the program, including:

- Getting data and images from the Internet, and navigating to other destinations
- Communicating with a server, and some of the many ways of sending information back and forth
- Storing and retrieving information saved on the user's computer
- Uploading and downloading files

Part VII: Enriching Your Program with Sound and Video

Part VII explains how to add multimedia capabilities to your program, including:

- Loading, playing, and controlling sounds and music
- Video: your options with Flash Player, loading, streaming, and playing video
- Using input from a user's camera and microphone

Part VIII: Programming Graphics and Motion

In Part VIII, you learn how to use ActionScript 3.0 to generate visuals and make them move, including:

- Adding filters to and modifying colors of existing graphics
- Drawing lines and shapes from scratch
- Animating objects

Part IX: Working with Binary Data

Part IX shows you how to use ActionScript code to read, write, store data, and communicate, in binary.

Part X: Deploying Your Program

The final part discusses running your application in the real world, including:

- Placing your program into a web site in a standards-compliant way
- Communicating with JavaScript to affect the containing web site
- Communicating between different programs running at the same time

Conventions and Features

Many different organizational and typographical features throughout this book have been designed to help you get the most from the information.

Callouts

Throughout this book you will see sections "called out" from the main text. We use these special notes to bring important information to your attention, or to add context and optional additions to the main discussion.

CAUTION Cautions provide information about things to watch out for, whether simply inconvenient or potentially hazardous to your data or systems.

TIP Tips generally are used to provide information that can make your work easier — special shortcuts or methods for doing something easier than the norm.

NOTE Notes provide additional, ancillary information that is helpful, but somewhat outside of the current presentation of information.

NEW IN AS3 These notes call out topics that are different in ActionScript 3.0 from those in previous ActionScript languages. If you are skilled in another version of ActionScript, these notes will help you migrate painlessly. In cases where chapters cover classes and features completely new to ActionScript 3.0, this icon is not used. Instead, the introduction to the chapter will let you know that the feature is all-new.

Code Formatting and Conventions

ActionScript code is used heavily throughout this book. Text that appears in code or is for use in code is presented in a monospace font, like `Object`.

In addition, example code is included in two ways: as longer blocks that provide more complete examples and as brief snippets.

Longer examples are often included that are self-contained, complete programs. These examples can be assembled and run without writing any addional code, following the steps in the "Running Code in This Book" section later in this Introduction. These examples are provided to show code in the context of a real-world task. Although the task is usually very small, it should illustrate the utility of the topic and demonstrate how the ActionScript code would interact with other related code.

Examples always have at least one full class, and at least one class that extends `Sprite`. A short example would look like this:

```
package com.wiley.as3bible {
    import flash.display.Sprite;
    public class HelloWorld extends Sprite {
        public function HelloWorld() {
            trace("Hello World!");
        }
    }
}
```

Snippets, on the other hand, are short blocks of code, even as small as a single line. These are prevalent throughout the book. Snippets don't have the necessary structural code to be launched and compiled by themselves but rather illustrate lines of code that could be added to a larger program. They are succinct, including only the important content and leaving out the context. The text around snippets will let you know what they are meant to accomplish. In general, we recommend that you read snippets and use them to enhance your understanding.

Frequently, snippets illustrate what certain code will do by outputting some values with `trace()`. Look for this output in the Console panel of Flex Builder or in the Output panel of Flash. A comment after `trace()` shows the expected output. The following is a snippet:

```
var a:int = 1;
var b:int = 1;
trace(a + b); //2
```

As you use the book, we recommend you simply read the snippets but interact with the larger examples — modify them to do different things, play with them to see if they break, add onto them to make them yours. Getting hands-on with code is the best way to learn it.

What's on the Companion Web Site

This book's companion web site can be found at `www.wiley.com/go/as3bible/`. There, you can download the larger examples featured in this book and find links to resources the authors provide.

Minimum Requirements

You can read this book without touching a computer, but we recommend performing your own exercises and using frequently what you learn. To build ActionScript 3.0 code, you need one of the following:

- **Adobe Flex Builder 2 (or greater)** (Mac OS X 10.4.7 or greater; Windows XP SP2, Windows 2000 Server Professional, Windows Server 2003 or greater)

- **Adobe Flash CS3** (Mac OS X 10.4.8 or greater; Windows XP SP2 or Windows Vista or greater)

- **Adobe Flex 2 (or greater) Software Development Kit (SDK)** (Mac OS X 10.4.x; Windows 2000, XP, Server 2003; Red Hat Enterprise Linux 3; SUSE 10; Solaris 9; or greater)

At the time of this writing, Flex Builder 2 and Flash CS3 are available for 30-day trials or purchase. The Flex 2 SDK is available for free; additionally, Adobe has announced its intention to make the Flex 2 SDK open source by the end of 2007. You can learn more about this announcement at `http://labs.adobe.com/wiki/index.php/Flex:Open_Source:FAQ`.

To run your creations, you will need Flash Player 9 or greater, available for free and supported on Windows, Mac OS X, Linux, and Solaris.

Please see the following URLs for more detailed software and hardware requirements:

```
www.adobe.com/products/flex/productinfo/systemreqs/
www.adobe.com/products/flash/systemreqs/
www.adobe.com/products/flashplayer/productinfo/systemreqs/
```

Running Code in This Book

This section explains, step by step, how to get examples from this book running so you can experiment with them. Depending on the tool you are using, there are different steps to running the code from this book. We demonstrate with Adobe Flex Builder 2 and Adobe Flash CS3 Professional.

First, let's take a look at how to run a complete example. You can recognize examples because they are full classes that extend Sprite (you'll learn about classes in Chapter 3). They may also contain more than one class. Let's say we're trying to run the following example:

```
package com.wiley.as3bible
{
    import flash.display.Sprite;
    import flash.text.TextField;
    import flash.text.TextFormat;
    public class Example extends Sprite
    {
        public function Example()
        {
            var tf:TextField = new TextField();
            tf.multiline = true;
            tf.wordWrap = true;
            tf.width = stage.stageWidth;
            tf.height = stage.stageHeight;
            tf.text = "Congratulations! You just ran an "
                    + "example from the ActionScript 3.0 Bible!";
            var format:TextFormat = new TextFormat();
            format.font = "_sans";
            format.size = 42;
            tf.setTextFormat(format);
            addChild(tf);

            trace("Done!");
        }
    }
}
```

Adobe Flash CS3 Professional

First, you need to create a folder on your hard drive to store and run the example from. The following steps all take place inside this folder, wherever you decide to put it.

You can either type the code or retrieve it from the book's companion site. Larger examples will have their code available for download as described in the "What's on the Companion Web Site" section. If you have the files available already, drop them into this folder, or follow these steps to create the file anew:

1. Launch Flash and create a new ActionScript file by navigating to File ⇨ New and selecting ActionScript File, as shown in Figure I-1. Type or paste in the contents of the example in the editor that Flash opens.

FIGURE I-1

Create a new ActionScript file.

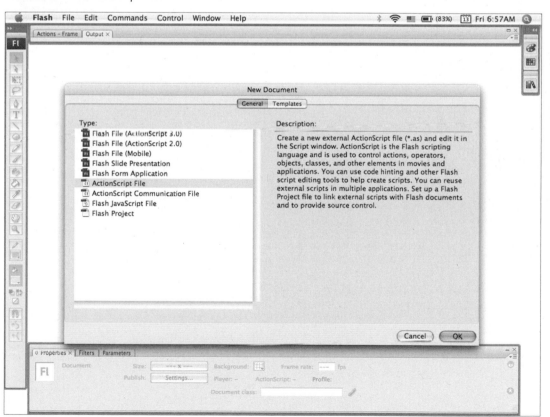

2. Save the file in the path specified by its class name (you learn how to do this in Chapter 3). This class is `com.wiley.as3bible.Example`, so we'll put it in the folder under the subfolders com/wiley/as3bible and name it Example.as. You can use the operating system or the Save File dialog box to create the intermediary folders as necessary. Getting the name and location of the class correct is essential. In Figure I-2, note that the file is going in the correct path.

FIGURE I-2

Save the ActionScript file with the proper name.

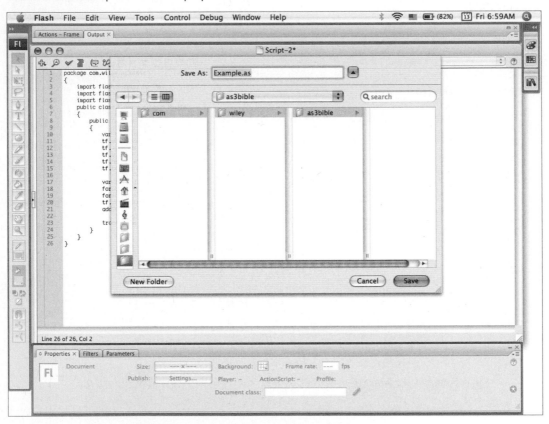

You must repeat this step for every file if the example has multiple class files.

3. To create a new Flash file that will run the code, again use File ➪ New. This time, create a Flash File (ActionScript 3.0), as shown in Figure I-3.

4. Before you do anything else, save this file in the folder you created for the example. Don't place it in any of the subdirectories like com/. You can give it any name you like. In Figure I-4, we named the file ExampleRunner.fla. By saving the FLA in the correct location, you ensure that it can find the classes it's supposed to use.

FIGURE I-3

Create a new Flash file.

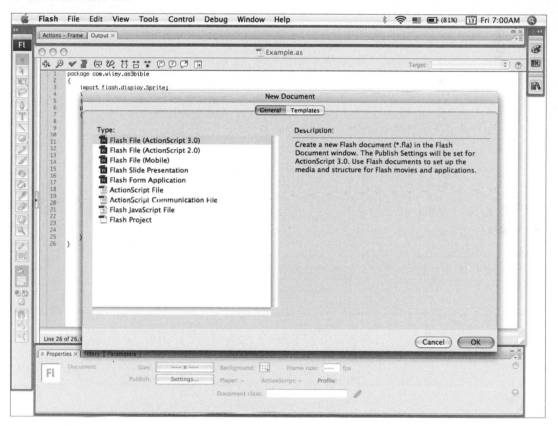

FIGURE I-4

Save the Flash file.

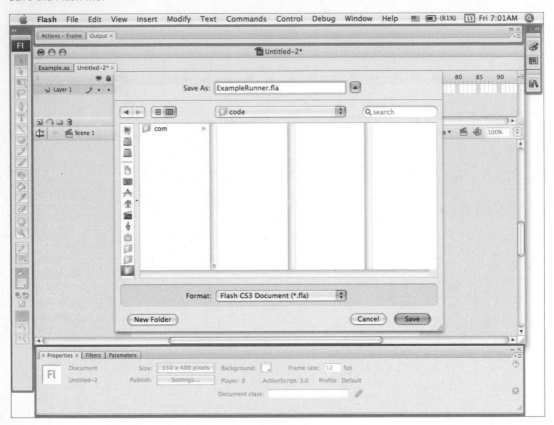

5. Each example has a main class. If the example is a single class, the main class is the entire example. Otherwise, it is listed first. The main class always extends `Sprite`.

   Once you've determined which class is the main class, enter this class's fully qualified name (see Chapter 3) into the Document Class input box in the Properties panel. If this panel is not visible, you can show it by selecting Window ➪ Properties ➪ Properties in the menu. In this case, the main class or document class is `com.wiley.as3bible.Example`, as we entered in Figure I-4.

   If the Flash file and the ActionScript files aren't saved in the correct places with the correct names, you will see the following warning message: "A definition for the document class could not be found in the classpath, so one will be automatically generated in the SWF file upon export." If you see this warning, ensure that all open files have been saved and are in the correct location.

FIGURE I-5

Set the Document Class.

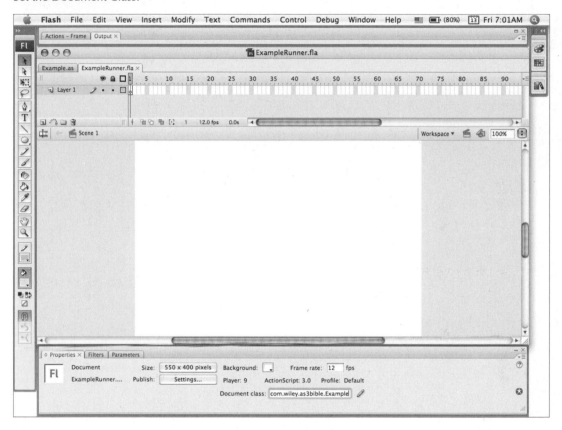

The Document Class in Flash is the class that will be associated with the stage when the SWF runs. Whatever is on the stage will become part of that class, and whatever you do to that class will affect the stage. When you add the `TextField` in the `Example` class, it's being added to the stage because the stage is, in effect, an `Example` instance now. You learn all about the display list in Part III.

The setup of the example is complete. To see the results of the example code, invoke Control ➪ Test Movie. You can see the `Example` class and its output in Figure I-6. Note that the output of the `trace()` statement in `Example` appears in the Output panel. Many examples in this book only trace out information, so check the Output panel if you don't see anything when you test the example code.

FIGURE I-6

The example in action

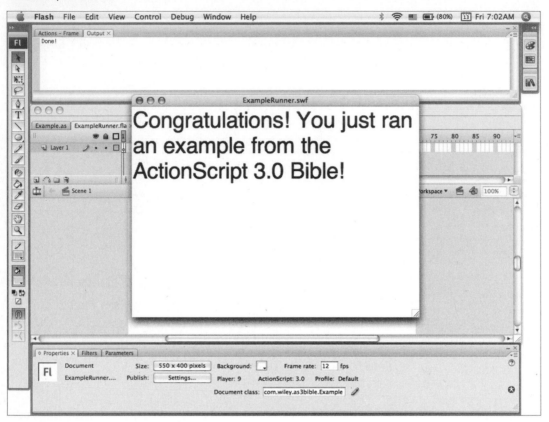

Once you have the example set up, you can modify the ActionScript files within Flash, save your changes, and run Test Movie again to try out your own code.

Running a Snippet

You may also wish to run snippets of code contained in this book. Many snippets are merely expository and will not run by themselves, but you can fill in the blanks and run them, or create your own code that uses the snippet. Others will run by themselves with no modifications. By following these steps, you can run blocks of code that aren't contained in a class.

1. Create a new Flash File (ActionScript 3.0), as shown previously in Figure I-3. You don't need to save it in any particular place.

2. Select the first frame on the timeline. If you can't see the timeline, select Window ⇨ Timeline from the menu. Type the code you want to run into the Actions panel. If you can't see the Actions panel, select Window ⇨ Actions. In Figure I-7, you can see the correct place to add your code. Make sure that the Actions panel is associated with the first frame of a layer. For example, in Figure I-7 the layer is called Layer 1, so the tab on the Actions Panel reads "Layer 1 : 1," and a small "a" appears on the first frame in the timeline. If you try to place code elsewhere, you may encounter errors.

FIGURE I-7

Entering snippet code in a frame action

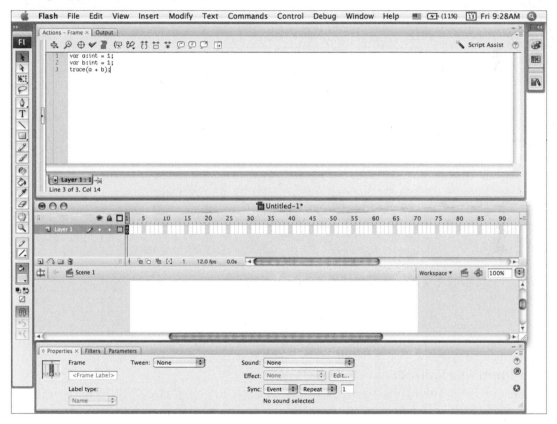

Frequently, necessary code for running the snippets has been omitted. You may have to add import statements or other code when attempting to run expository snippets.

Adobe Flex Builder 2

You can build examples from this book using Adobe Flex Builder 2 or greater. You can type the examples from the book, or copy them from the book's companion site.

First, you should create a new project for the example.

1. Launch Flex Builder and create a new ActionScript project (File ➪ New ➪ ActionScript Project). Follow the wizard and name the project whatever you like. It will help to name the project something other than the main class name. In Figure I-8, we have created an ActionScript project called ExampleProject. The wizard creates a main class for us this time, called ExampleProject.

FIGURE I-8

A new ActionScript project created by the Flex Builder New Project Wizard

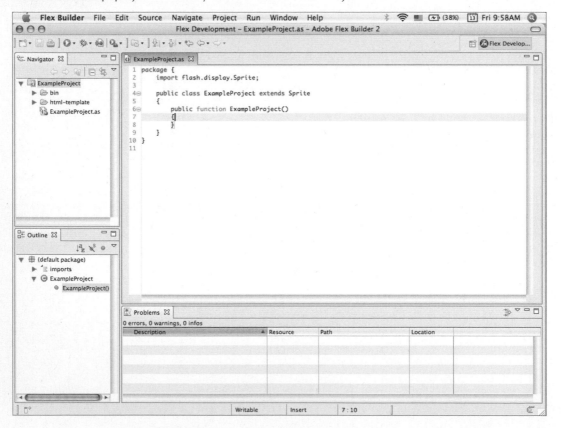

Flex Builder likes to have the main class, or Application, in the default package. (See Chapter 3 for more information on packages.) Therefore, if the example you want to run is in the default package, you can skip the following steps by choosing the name of the example class as the name of the project and replacing the empty class that the wizard leaves for you with the example's main class.

2. If the example's main class is in another package, such as com.wiley.as3bible, create a new ActionScript file (File ⇨ New ⇨ ActionScript Class) and supply the wizard with the information it needs. You can see a completed New Class Wizard in Figure I-9. The package name is com.wiley.as3bible, the class's name is Example, and it extends flash.display.Sprite.

FIGURE I-9

Creating the Example class

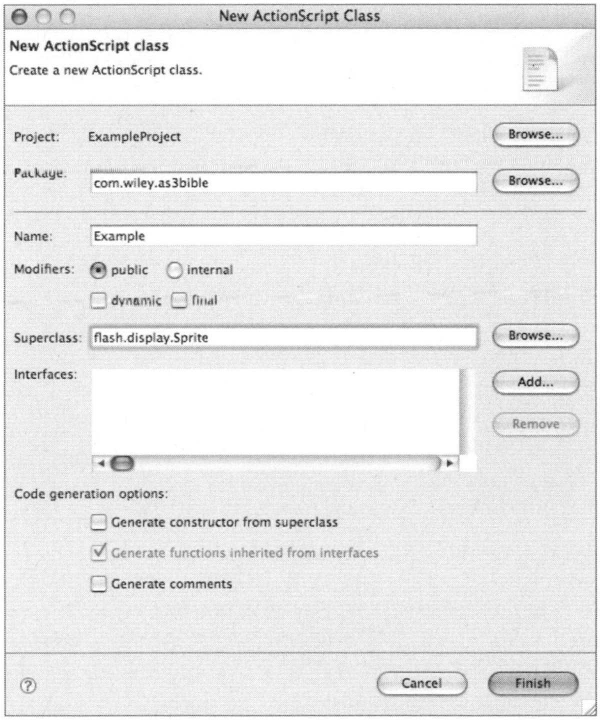

Now you can fill out the skeleton provided by the class wizard. Alternately, if you have the files already, you can drop them into the project directory in the correct location. After you do so, they should appear in the Navigator view in Flex Builder.

The `Example` class isn't in the default package, so Flex Builder won't let you run it directly. To quickly bypass this problem, just add the line

```
addChild(new Example());
```

to the constructor of the application class, in this case `ExampleProject`. Additionally, make sure to import the class `Example` from `com.wiley.as3bible`, or if you use auto-completion on the word `Example`, you should automatically get the import.

Again, if the example exists in the default package, simply use the application class as the main class, and you won't need to add another file or this code.

To run the application from Flex Builder, start a new debugging session. This way, you will see output from the `trace()` statements in the example, should there be any. You can start a new debugging session by choosing Run ➪ Debug ➪ ExampleProject, or whatever you named your project.

By default, Flex Builder will launch the example in your web browser. In order to debug this, you must have the debugging version of Flash Player installed in the browser it uses. However, you also have the option of running the application in Flash Player. Open the project's properties by right-clicking the project's name in the Navigator or choosing Project ➪ Properties in the menu. Choose the ActionScript Compiler section, uncheck Generate HTML wrapper file, and click OK. After performing these steps, Flex Builder should run your application in the standalone Flash Player.

For More Information

The steps presented in the preceding section should get you as far as editing and running code and are presented to help you follow along with the examples in the book. For more information on how to use Flex Builder 2 and greater or Adobe Flash CS3 Professional, we recommend you check the documentation that came with these products, as well as the books suggested earlier.

Where to Go from Here

Armed with the knowledge herein, you should be equipped to program in ActionScript 3.0. Countless doors open when you can implement your ideas in code, and there's no way we can tell you what your newfound knowledge could help you do. That's up to you. We strongly encourage you to work on projects aligned with your interests. You learn best by doing, and you do more when you do what you enjoy. So dream up an application, an animation, a simulation, or an installation and make it happen. Find some freelance jobs that sound enticing and bid for them. Challenge yourself, and keep *ActionScript 3.0 Bible* by your side for reference.

Once you are comfortable programming in ActionScript 3.0, give the book to a new AS3 disciple and move on with your own learning! The field of programming is wonderfully wide. You can dive deeper: learn about algorithms, data structures, object-oriented design, design patterns, architecture, or software development practices. You can enhance your ActionScript 3.0 skills: learn Flex or AIR. You can make things realistic: learn computer graphics techniques, physics, animation, or algorithmic art. You can learn more about programming by learning a different kind of language. You can focus on server communication. There's no end to the possibilities.

You can find resources for further reading and inspiration at the book's companion site, `www.wiley.com/go/as3bible/`. If you wish, you can also take the time to send Wiley and the authors your impressions and feedback on Wiley's site.

Part I

Getting Started with ActionScript 3.0

Chapter 1

Introducing ActionScript 3.0

ActionScript 3.0 is vastly new and different and at the same time remarkably familiar for those who have worked with ActionScript 2.0. ActionScript 3.0 is new because it's built from the ground up, based on a new edition of the ECMA specification, and runs in a new virtual machine (AVM2). Yet despite all the newness of ActionScript 3.0, it is still similar enough to ActionScript 2.0 that those who have previously worked with Flash will find their footing without much difficulty.

In this chapter we look at what ActionScript is, where you can use it, and the specifics of what's new to ActionScript 3.0.

IN THIS CHAPTER

Introduction to ActionScript 3.0

Understanding where to use ActionScript

Summary of new features of ActionScript 3.0

What Is ActionScript?

Presumably, if you're reading this book, you already have a general sense of what ActionScript is, but further clarification will help you to better understand how to build content using ActionScript. In a nutshell, ActionScript is a programming language that is used to create content for Flash Player. You can use tools such as Flash CS3 Professional or Flex Builder to create content using other tools and technologies such as drawing tools, library symbols, timelines, and MXML. However, ActionScript can be used either as a complement to these things or in place of these things in order to create Flash content. ActionScript is often necessary when you want to create Flash applications that are highly dynamic, responsive, reusable, and/or customizable. Here's just a short list of the many things you can accomplish using ActionScript:

- Loading images
- Playing audio and video

3

- Drawing programmatically
- Loading data such as XML files
- Responding to user events such as mouse clicks

Where Can You Use ActionScript?

At the time of this writing there are two primary ways to work with ActionScript: building Flash applications using Flash authoring (Flash CS3) or building Flex or ActionScript applications using Flex Builder 2. There is no black-and-white rule for when or why to use one authoring toolset over the other. Rather, there is a large gray area of overlap between the two. A helpful way to decide which toolset is most appropriate for you is simply to consider what workflow you're more accustomed to using. If you are most comfortable using drawing tools and timelines, then Flash CS3 is likely the best option. On the other hand, Flex Builder 2 is good for those who feel most comfortable writing code in a robust IDE (integrated development environment) and don't feel comfortable with the animation metaphors used by Flash CS3. With all that said, there is no reason that you couldn't use both authoring toolsets for building applications. The good news in this case is that ActionScript 3.0 is identical regardless of which toolset you use. We have made an effort to write this book in such a way that you can use the examples with either Flash CS3 or Flex Builder.

If you are using Flex Builder 2 (note that we don't discuss the Flex framework in this book) to create applications using ActionScript then you are forced to use strict object-oriented design, meaning that the main entry point for your application must be a class (more on classes in Chapter 3). This is not so for Flash CS3. If you are using Flash CS3, then you have the option to place your ActionScript code on keyframes on a timeline. While this is not inherently wrong, it is troublesome if the goal is to write good code that is maintainable and adheres to best practices. For this reason, in this book we advocate for the use of a document class if you are using Flash CS3, and all the examples in this book use document classes. In Flash CS3, the document class is the analog to the main class in a Flex Builder 2 project. By using a document class you will be learning the most scalable way to write ActionScript 3.0 code in Flash CS3, and what you learn will easily translate if you use Flex Builder 2 at any time.

What's New in ActionScript 3.0?

As mentioned earlier in this chapter, ActionScript 3.0 has a whole lot of new features. You'll learn about all the details in the chapters that follow, but here is an overview of the key new features.

Display List

In ActionScript 2.0, there were three basic types of objects that could be displayed: movie clips, buttons, and text fields. These types didn't inherit from a common source, meaning polymorphism didn't work for these display types. Furthermore, instances of these display types always had a fixed, parent-child relationship with other instances. For example, to create a movie clip you had to create that movie clip as a child of an existing movie clip. It was not possible to move a movie clip from one parent to another.

In ActionScript 3.0 there are many new display types. In addition to the familiar types such as movie clips, buttons, and text fields, you'll now find new types such as shapes, sprites, loaders, bitmaps, and more. All display types in ActionScript 3.0 inherit from `flash.display.DisplayObject`, meaning you can use polymorphism. Furthermore, and perhaps most important, display type objects in ActionScript 3.0 can be created independent of any other display type object, and these objects can be placed as children of other display objects and even moved from one parent container. In other words, you can create a text field in ActionScript 3.0 simply by calling the constructor as part of a new statement, and that text field will exist independent of any parent container object.

```
var text:TextField = new TextField();
```

You can then add the text field to a parent container at any time. The following example illustrates this with a display object called `container`, which could be a sprite or any other display object container type:

```
container.addChild(text);
```

 In the preceding example, `container` is used as a generic variable name that would presumably refer to an object created elsewhere in the code.

The hierarchy of parent containers and their children is known as the *display list* in ActionScript 3.0.

Runtime Errors

ActionScript 3.0 provides many new runtime errors. This is an important new feature because it allows you to diagnose problems much more quickly. In ActionScript 2.0, when an error occurred at runtime it would frequently occur silently, and it would be difficult for you as the developer to determine what the problem was. With improved runtime errors and error reporting in the debug player it is now much easier to debug ActionScript 3.0 applications than it was with ActionScript 2.0.

Runtime Data Types

Strict typing in ActionScript 2.0 was only used by the compiler, not at runtime. At runtime, all ActionScript 2.0 types are dynamic. However, in ActionScript 3.0, strict typing is preserved at runtime as well. The advantage is that now runtime data mismatches are reported as errors, and application performance and memory management is improved as a result of preserved typing at runtime.

Method Closures

In ActionScript 3.0 all methods have proper method closures, which means that a reference to a method always includes the object from which the method was originally referenced. This is important for event handling, and it stands in stark contrast to method closures in ActionScript 2.0. In

ActionScript 2.0, when you reference a method, the object from which the method is referenced does not persist. This causes problems most notably when adding event listeners. In ActionScript 2.0, a delegate is often used as a solution. However, in ActionScript 3.0 delegates are not necessary.

Intrinsic Event Model

In ActionScript 3.0, the event model is built right in to the core language. The `flash.events` `.EventDispatcher` class is the base class for many native ActionScript classes, including all the display object types. This means that there is one standard way to dispatch and handle events in ActionScript 3.0.

Regular Expressions

Regular expressions are a powerful way to find substrings that match patterns. Although regular expressions have long been built into sister languages such as JavaScript, regular expressions were never a part of ActionScript until now. ActionScript 3.0 includes an intrinsic `RegExp` class, which allows you to run regular expressions natively in Flash Player.

E4X

E4X is short for ECMAScript for XML, and it is a new way to work with XML data in ActionScript. Although you can still work with XML as you did in ActionScript 2.0 by traversing the DOM, E4X allows you to work with XML in a much more natural and intuitive manner.

Summary

- ActionScript 3.0 is a new language with enough similarities to ActionScript 2.0 to make the learning curve low.

- You can use ActionScript 3.0 just as you used ActionScript 2.0 (in classes or on the time-line), though the preferred usage of ActionScript 3.0 is in classes using object-oriented principles.

- ActionScript 3.0 introduces a lot of new features, including a new way to manage display types, runtime error handling, runtime data types, method closures, an intrinsic event model, regular expressions, and a new way of working with XML.

Chapter 2

Understanding ActionScript 3.0 Language Basics

S o you want to be an ActionScript coder? Great! This chapter will get you started with the basic syntax and structure of the language. If you have worked with other programming languages, some of the topics covered will be familiar territory for you. However, even if you are an experienced ActionScript 2.0 user, you will find a few subtle differences in this version of ActionScript so we recommend that you read through.

IN THIS CHAPTER

Defining variables and constants

Applying operators and functions

Assigning core data types

Working with scope

Using techniques to effectively comment your code

Using Variables

Back in high school, I used to argue with my algebra teacher that the subject matter would never be useful in the real world. Even though I have yet to simplify a polynomial outside of the classroom, I have to admit I was wrong. ActionScript 3.0 is built entirely around the use of variables just like the *x* and *y* variables in an algebra problem.

A variable is a representation of a number, string of characters, or some other value that can change values the way the *x* variable in algebra represents a number that may have any value. You might think of variables as containers used to hold pieces of information. In ActionScript, variables contain chunks of information known as objects for the time during which your program is running. They allow your program to temporarily hold on to that information and behave differently depending on what the information is. Variables are used in nearly every aspect of programming. You may also hear variables referred to as properties when they are part of a class.

Anatomy of a variable declaration

Defining your own variables is easy. Let's take a look at a typical variable declaration and step through its different parts in the list that follows:

```
var food:String;
food = "pizza";
```

- `var`: All variables are defined by using the `var` keyword followed by the name of the variable. This is different from previous versions of ActionScript where the `var` keyword was optional.

- `food`: This is the name of the variable. This can be any word or string of letters and numbers beginning with either a letter or an underscore. By convention, we recommend naming your variables using descriptive words in camel case and starting with a lower-case letter. For example, `mainCourse = "pizza";`.

- `:String`: This defines the data type or the type of information that the variable can hold. The word `String` could be replaced with any class or interface name. We'll talk more about data types later in this chapter.

- `food = "pizza";`: This statement sets the value of `food` to the word "pizza" using the `=` (assignment) operator. The quotes around the word pizza signify that this is text rather than a variable called pizza.

Variables can also be declared and assigned a value in a single line:

```
var drink:String = "Root beer";
```

You can even declare several variables on a single line:

```
var breakfast:String, lunch:String, dinner:String;
```

After a variable is defined, it can be used to replace the use of its value. For example:

```
trace("My favorite food is " + food);
// displays "My favorite food is pizza"
```

Constants in this changing world

ActionScript 3.0 introduces a special kind of variable called a *constant*. Constants define values that don't change during the course of your program. This is great for values that either never change or that you want to protect from change. For example, if you wanted to store the boiling point of water in Fahrenheit, you could write the following:

```
const BOILING_POINT:int = 212;
```

As you can see, this looks a lot like a variable declaration but with the `var` keyword replaced with `const`. Constant statements can be defined only at the beginning of a class with the other properties or in the constructor for a class. Attempting to assign a new value to a constant anywhere else will result in an error.

Constants are used extensively in the ActionScript 3.0 API, especially in the `flash.errors` and `flash.events` packages. By convention, constant names are written in all caps with words separated by underscores.

Taking it literally

Aside from variables and values returned from functions, you will also use literals in your code. The term literal refers to any value that is explicitly included in the code at the time that it's compiled. They offer a convenience when dealing with complex data types. Following is a list of the different types of values that you can include directly in your code:

- Number (including `int` and `uint`) values like `42`, `-100`, `98.6`
- Boolean values `true` and `false`
- Strings written with single or double quotes, as in `"Lorem ipsum"`
- The special empty values `void`, `null`, and `undefined`
- Array literals that use square brackets such as `["Monday"`, `"Wednesday"`, `"Friday"]`
- Generic objects defined using the curly bracket syntax such as `{name:"Alita"`, `likesSpaghetti:true}`

ActionScript 3.0 introduces two new literals that can be included directly into code for defining regular expressions and XML objects:

- Regular expressions enclosed in forward slashes, as in `/href="(.*)"/`
- Elements written in XML such as `<person><name first="Mims"` `last="Wright" /></person>`

XML and regular expressions are covered in more detail in Chapters 10 and 11 respectively.

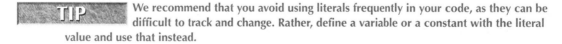 We recommend that you avoid using literals frequently in your code, as they can be difficult to track and change. Rather, define a variable or a constant with the literal value and use that instead.

Using Access Controls

When working with classes, you'll use an additional word written before the variable (or function) declaration, such as:

```
private var lunchtime:Date;
```

This is called the *access control attribute*. It indicates whether the variable or function will be available to classes other than the one in which the object is defined. We'll talk more about classes and what all of this means later on.

Four keywords are defined in ActionScript 3.0 for defining access. They are:

- `public`: This indicates that a variable or method is available to all classes that attempt to access it. That is, any code can access a variable or call a method if it is marked with this keyword.

- `private`: Private variables and methods can be accessed only by the class in which they are defined. Attempting to access these methods or variables anywhere outside of the class where they are defined will result in a compile-time error. This also includes child classes. Unlike ActionScript 2.0, child classes no longer have access to private members. Instead you should use the `protected` keyword, which we discuss in a moment.

- `internal`: Internal objects are neither public nor private. They are available only to classes within the same class package as the class where the object is defined. That is, any class that has the same package declaration (e.g., `package com.wiley.bible {...}`) will be able to call the method or access the variable.

  This is the default access control namespace for all objects in ActionScript 3.0.

- `protected`: Protected is similar to internal in that it limits access to certain other classes; however, protected classes can be accessed only by classes that extend the functionality of the class (subclasses).

NEW IN AS3   ActionScript 2.0 also has access control attributes, but they are limited to only `public` and `private`. Furthermore, the amount of access allowed for AS2's `private` keyword is equivalent to the new `protected` keyword. AS3's `private` keyword is stricter than AS2's `private` keyword because it is not inherited.

Because there were no runtime data types in ActionScript 2.0, the `private` keyword is not always honored and sometimes, private objects can be accessed from outside of the class. In ActionScript 3.0, this will cause a runtime error in strict mode.

AS2 did not require you to use these access controls. While these keywords are not required in AS3, the compiler gives you a warning if you do not provide one.

ActionScript 3.0 also introduces the concept of custom namespace attributes, but we get into that more in Chapter 3.

Introducing Scope

All variables and functions defined in ActionScript exist in a certain scope. This scope is defined as the area in which the object can be accessed and in which the value is defined. To understand this, we'll use the analogy of levels of government.

In most countries, the national government deals with issues affecting the entire country such as tax law, and local governments deal with local issues such as funding for a certain town's school. National governments aren't equipped to handle local issues and vice versa. In most cases the national laws are used except when overridden by a local law.

Scope works in much the same way. Objects operate in a particular scope depending on how and where they are defined. Generally speaking, the more broadly defined objects are used except when replaced by local versions. Let's take a look at the different types of scope that we'll be dealing with.

Types of scope

Scope can be either *global* or *local*. Objects in the global scope can be accessed from anywhere in the code whereas objects in local scopes can be accessed only through the object where they are defined.

Global scope

Anything defined on the root timeline in a Flash movie or outside of a function or class is in the global scope. These objects can be accessed from any other scope. However, defining objects in the timeline is discouraged and most of the time you will be working with local scope.

Local scope

Local scope is a bit more complicated. There are several layers of localized access (or subscopes) depending on how the object is defined.

Class level (static) variables and methods

The most broadly defined local objects are the *static* (or class level) variables and methods. These objects exist in the class level scope; in other words, they belong to the class itself rather than the instances of the class.

These object are defined using the `static` keyword such as:

```
package {
    public class ScopeTest {
        public static var foo:String = "bar";
    }
}
```

They are accessed by using the class name followed by the object name. For example:

```
trace(ScopeTest.foo); // Displays: bar
```

The code defined in a class can make use of these variables and methods without using the class name to access them, but all instances of the class will share the same static values. Because classes are available anywhere (as long as they are imported and public), class variables are as good as global.

Instance level variables and methods

Classes can also define variables and methods that exist in each instance of the class. Most of the variables or methods that you work with will be in this scope:

```
package {
    public class ScopeTest {
        public static var foo:String = "bar";

        public var answer:Number = 42;
    }
}
```

Unlike static variables, the instance variables will be independent for each instance of the class.

When accessing instance variables, you would use the name of the instance followed by a dot and then the name of the variable:

```
var myTest:ScopeTest = new ScopeTest();
trace(myTest.answer) //Displays: 42
```

NOTE   All instance variables are released from memory automatically when the instance itself is deleted. However, these variables might stay in memory if they are referenced by other objects. If memory management is an issue for your program, make sure all references to classes and their members are removed before attempting to delete them.

Function-level variables and functions

Finally, objects can be defined within a function. Each function creates a temporary scope that exists for the duration of the time that it is running. Variables defined within a function can be used to store values temporarily and are deleted after the function completes. In the following example, the variable message is defined only during the execution of the showGreeting() function.

```
package {
    public class ScopeTest {
        public static var foo:String = "bar";

        public var answer:Number = 42;

        public function showGreeting():void {
            var message:String = "Hello, world!";
            trace(message);
        }
```

```
      }
  }

  var myTest:ScopeTest = new ScopeTest();
  myTest.showGreeting(); // Displays: Hello, world!
  trace(myTest.message); // undefined
```

Variables defined within functions won't be available until the function is executed. Variables defined in the class can be accessed from within the function, but not the other way around.

Parameters of a function are always treated as though they are defined within the function scope.

Functions can also be defined within functions. This is sometimes known as nesting functions. These nested functions will be available only as support to the function in which it's nested.

Block-level variables

Some programming languages allow you to define variables within blocks, such as for loops, that exist in an even more localized scope than the function level scope. It's important to note that ActionScript does not support this level of scope — function level is the most localized scope.

The scope chain

The scope chain, shown in Figure 2-1, is an internal device that is created to manage variable scope during function execution.

When a variable is referenced, the Flash Player starts with the most recent function called and checks for variable declarations. If the value isn't found in the most local scope, it moves up one level to the parent function that called the function and checks there. This process continues until the scope chain has been checked all the way up to the global scope.

Overriding variables

As stated before, objects defined in more localized scopes will always override objects defined in more global scopes. Instance variables are also available in the function scope but anything defined using the var keyword will create a new localized instance in the scope where it is defined. Here's an example:

```
  package {
    public class Local {
      public var a:String = "instance";
      public var b:String = "instance";

      public function method():void {
        var a:String = "function";
        b = "function";
        trace(a);
        trace(b);
      }
    }
  }
```

FIGURE 2-1

Example of a scope chain

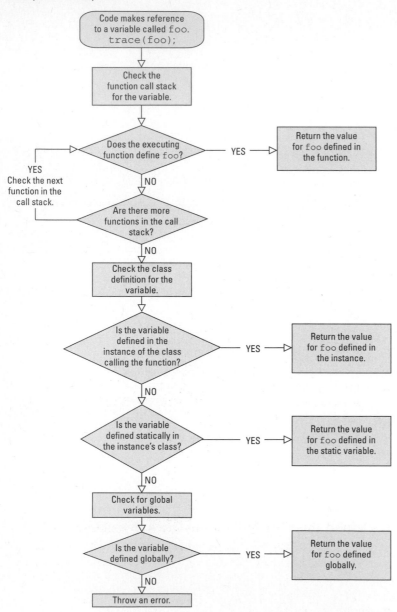

Notice that within the function called `method`, you're defining a string called `a` by using the `var` keyword, and also using the string called `b` without using `var`.

```
var myLocal:Local = new Local();
trace(myLocal.a); // Displays: instance
trace(myLocal.b); // Displays: instance

myLocal.method(); // Displays: function
                                   function

trace(myLocal.a); // Displays: instance
trace(myLocal.b); // Displays: function
```

In the case of `a`, the function defines its own variable, called `a`, which defines a function-level variable that temporarily overrides the instance variable `a`. However, with `b`, the instance variable is used within the function (because the `var` keyword wasn't used) and is overwritten with the new value `"function"`.

In order to be more explicit about which variable you're using, we recommend that you use the `this` keyword when referring to an instance variable with the same name as a function variable:

```
public function setFoo (foo:String):void {
    this.foo = foo;
}
```

In this case, the instance variable called `foo` will be overwritten with the value passed into the method.

Working with scope

It's great to know all of these rules about scope, but what should you do with the information? Normally, it's best to define a variable in the most localized scope as possible. Local variables are garbage collected more easily so they reduce overhead, but that doesn't mean you should always strive to use function variables when it's not appropriate.

The simplest way to answer this question is to think about how you plan to use the object you're creating. Ask yourself who needs to know about the object you're creating.

Does the variable pertain to the class or to an instance of a class?

Static variables are useful because they are available from almost anywhere. Using them can be tempting, but it might be better to think of whether the variable applies to the class or to an instance. For example, if you're modeling a `LiterSizedBottle` class with two properties, `capacity` and `contents`, how would each variable be used?

The capacity of a liter-sized bottle will be the same for all liter-sized bottles — one liter. Therefore, `capacity` should be a class variable.

The contents, on the other hand, could vary from bottle to bottle. One might hold water, while another might hold an industrial-strength cleaning product. contents should be an instance variable.

Will I need this object after the function is complete?
Do I need to save changes to this variable?

When determining whether to use function-level or instance-level scope, you might ask yourself the preceding question. Generally speaking, if you find yourself using the same variable in two different functions, you might want to define it as an instance variable. Whenever a value needs to be stored within the object after the function is done executing, an instance variable should be used.

Introducing the Data Types

ActionScript 3.0 is a typed, object-oriented language. That means that every object (variable) is assigned a data type, which refers to the type of data that can be stored inside it. The data type helps the compiler and the Flash Player know what type of value to expect. It can be used to set the type of a variable or a function's parameter or return type.

Declaring types

In order to declare the data type of a variable, we use the colon operator right after the name of the variable. This tells the compiler that only values with the same data type as declared may be stored in the variable.

```
var x:Number;
var name:String = "Mims";

x = 42;    // No problem
x = -13;   // No problem
x = 3.141; // No problem
x = "foo"; // Throws compile time error!
x = name;  // Throws compile time error!
```

Because x is defined with the type Number, a string value like "foo" can't be added. The compiler checks all the incoming data types to make sure they're compatible. If a problem is encountered, the compiler throws an error.

Why would you want to throw an error? Sometimes errors can be a good thing. Imagine what would have happened if there were no error. The value of x would suddenly be a string. Then next time you tried to use it as a number, the results wouldn't make sense ("foo" * 8.5 = ???). Keeping data types intact helps your code to be more predictable and stable.

NOTE In most cases, the data type is the same as the class that an object is an instance of. However, the data type may also be a parent class (superclass) that the object's class inherits from or an interface that it implements. For example, the `flash.display.Sprite` class inherits from several other classes and interfaces. A variable that holds a Sprite object could use any of the following classes or interfaces as its data type: `Object`, `EventDispatcher`, `IEventDispatcher`, `DisplayObject`, `DisplayObjectContainer`, `InteractiveObject`, or `IBitmapDrawable`. So the following is perfectly acceptable:

```
var mySprite:Sprite = new Sprite();
var myDisplayObject:DisplayObject = mySprite;
```

A variable's data type defines the type of data that it's acceptable to store within the variable. While all Sprites are DisplayObjects, not all DisplayObjects are Sprites. So the following would not work:

```
var mySprite:Sprite = new DisplayObject(); // TypeError!
```

Using untyped variables with the wildcard (*) data type

Occasionally, you may need to store a value in a variable without knowing what type of data it will hold. For this, AS3 allows the use of a wildcard (*) data type. The * denotes that a data type is unknown until runtime (dynamic) or will accept more than one type of data (e.g., both strings and numbers). The wildcard is very useful when creating functions that behave differently depending on the data type of its parameters.

 AS3 uses the * data type for untyped variables. This was done in AS2 by omitting the data type.

You should exercise caution when using these types because strong type checking will not be available for these variables and your results may be unpredictable.

Working with Operators

Operators are built-in function-like commands that operate on one or more values. You are probably already familiar with most of the operators because many of them are used in math equations. Most of the operators are some kind of symbol (such as +) but some are words (such as `return`). Unlike functions, operators never need parentheses to function — not even the operators that are words.

Unary vs. binary operators

Some operations are applied to a single argument such as the increment operator (++). These are the unary operators. Others require two arguments to function such as the plus operator (+). These are called binary operators. There is also a single trinary operator, which takes three arguments that will be discussed later in this chapter. It's important to provide the correct number of arguments when using operators, which isn't very difficult because they're fairly self-explanatory (you can't add something to nothing).

Order of operations

Operators follow a certain order of operations. That is, certain operators are processed before others. This is so that mathematical functions will behave in a manner that is consistent with calculators and the laws of arithmetic. In general, more complex operations will be executed first followed by simpler operations.

ActionScript executes operations in more or less the following order:

1. Expressions contained within parentheses are executed starting with the most deeply nested working outward.

2. The results of functions are evaluated assuming all their arguments are evaluated.

3. The multiplication, division, and modulus operators (*, /, %) are given equal weight and executed from left to right.

4. The addition and subtraction operators (+, -) are given equal weight and executed from left to right.

Parentheses can be used to group expressions so that they will be evaluated first before moving on to other operations. For example:

```
trace(3 + 4 * 5); // Displays : 23
trace((3 + 4) * 5); // Displays: 35
```

Some commonly used operators

Here are some operators that you're likely to see but may not be familiar with.

Arithmetic (+, -, *, /)

These need no explanation except that multiplication is written as a * instead of × and division is written as / instead of ÷.

Modulo (%)

The modulo operator returns the remainder after a division operation. It divides the first number by the second and returns the leftover portion only.

```
0 % 3 // 0
1 % 3 // 1
2 % 3 // 2
3 % 3 // 0
4 % 3 // 1
5 % 3 // 2
6 % 3 // 0
...
```

Increment (++) and decrement (−−)

These operators add or subtract 1 from the number they're used on. These are unary operators so they require only one argument:

```
var x:Number = 5;
x++; // 6
x--; // 5
```

When the increment or decrement is placed before the operand, the 1 is added immediately before other variables are processed.

Compound Assignment operators (+=, -=, *=, /=, and %=)

The compound assignment operators provide a shorthand solution to performing arithmetic on numbers and reassigning the answer to the number. For instance += will add the value on the right to the value on the left and reassign the value on the left to the answer.

```
x += 1;
```

is the same as writing

```
x = x + 1;
```

The following code shows more examples of these compound operators.

```
var x:Number = 0;

x += 5; // x = 5
x -= 3; // x = 2
x *= 3; // x = 6
x /= 2; // x = 3
x %= 3; // x = 0
```

A chart of all the operators and their uses can be found in the AS3 documentation (http://livedocs.adobe.com/flex/2/langref/operators.html).

Making Logical Choices with Conditionals

What good would it be if your programs and functions always executed the exact same way every time you ran them? Essentially, the element of choice over how to act under different circumstances would be lost. That's where *conditionals*, or decision-making points in your code, come into play. Conditionals, such as the if statement, enable you to evaluate the truth of a logical expression, which lets you program different outcomes for the different results.

All conditional statements deal with *Boolean* values. Booleans, named for the mathematician George Boole, are simple logical objects that can have only one of two values, either true or false. Any logical expression, such as the operators used in the following examples, should produce Boolean results, which will allow them to be evaluated by conditionals.

If statements

The most commonly used type of conditional is the `if` statement. An `if` statement allows you to execute a piece of code only *if* a certain condition is met: if this is true, then do that.

```
if (logical expression) {
    // code to execute if the expression is true
}
```

Here's an example. This statement checks to see if the value of `weather` is equal to the string `"rain"` and if so, it calls the made-up function `bringUmbrella`. You might read this aloud as "If the weather is rainy, then bring an umbrella."

```
if (weather == "rain") {
    bringUmbrella();
}
```

 `{}` are optional for statements with only one line but we recommend that you always use brackets for the sake of consistency.

Equality (==)

In the preceding example, the `if` keyword is followed by the logical expression to evaluate in parentheses. Notice that there are two equal signs and not just one. This double equal sign is known as the equality operator (==). It checks to see whether the value on the left is equal to the value on the right. This is quite different from the single equal sign operator (=), which sets the variable on the left to the value on the right. The double equal sign is a logical comparison operator, which means it evaluates to a single result, either true or false. In this case, we're checking to see if the value for `weather` is equal to the string `"rain"`.

TIP Using the single equal sign instead of a double equal sign in a comparison statement can cause confusing and unexpected results. This is a very common mistake for developers in all programming languages. Luckily, changes to the compiler have been made to help automatically identify this error. Regardless of those improvements, be very careful to check your comparison statements thoroughly.

After the logical expression, we have the block of code that will be executed if the expression is found to be true. In this case, we're calling a function called `bringUmbrella()`. If weather is anything but rainy, this block of code will not be run.

Testing other comparisons

The `if` keyword can be used to evaluate more than simple equality. ActionScript includes many other types of comparison operators and logical operators, which you can use alone or combine into more complex types of comparisons.

Greater than (>) and less than (<)

Besides checking for equality, you can compare whether a value is less than or greater than another number by using the corresponding operators, < and >. The following code says "If the rainfall is more than 0, then the weather is rainy."

```
if (rainfall > 0) { weather = "rain" }
```

You can also use less than or equal to (<=) and greater than or equal to (>=), as follows:

```
var x:int = 0;

var a:int = -1;
var b:int = 0;
var c:int = 1;

trace(x <= a); // Displays: false
trace(x >= a); // Displays: true
trace(x <= b); // Displays: true
trace(x >= b); // Displays: true
trace(x <= c); // Displays: true
trace(x >= c); // Displays: false
```

Not equal to (!=)

Adding an exclamation point before a bit of logic will evaluate the opposite of the expression. This is known as the not operator (!). Similarly, ActionScript includes a not equal to operator (!=) which, as you might imagine, checks to see if the value on the left is not equal to the value on the right:

```
if (weather != "sun") { bringUmbrella(); }
```

This statement calls the bringUmbrella() function if it is *not* sunny outside. Another way of writing this would be to use the not operator to negate an equality:

```
if (!(weather == "sun")) { bringUmbrella(); }
```

This line of code functions identically to the one above.

And (&&) and Or (||) operators

If you wish to string together multiple conditions, you might try nesting or duplicating your if statements together like this:

```
if (weather == "rain")  { bringUmbrella(); }
if (weather == "sleet") { bringUmbrella(); }
if (weather == "snow")  { bringUmbrella(); }

if (weather != "rain")  {
   if (weather != "sleet") {
      if (weather != "snow") { leaveUmbrella(); }
   }
}
```

As you can see, this takes a lot of effort to write. Luckily, ActionScript uses two logical operators that allow us to combine multiple conditions into a single if statement. They are And (&&) and Or (||). With the And operator, all conditions must be true in order for the code to be executed. You might say "If this and that are true, then do something."

With the Or operator, any condition that is true will cause the code to be executed. It basically says, "If this or that is true, then do something."

Let's rewrite our example from above using And and Or.

```
if (weather == "rain" || weather == "sleet" || weather == "snow") {
   bringUmbrella();
}

if (weather != "rain" && weather != "sleet" && weather != "snow") {
   leaveUmbrella();
}
```

Checking for null values

When you're working with objects that could be null in AS3, it's important to check whether the value is null before attempting to access methods or properties of the object (failure to do so can result in a runtime error). Checking for null is very simple:

```
if (weather != null) { checkWeather(); }
```

If the weather is not null, the checkWeather() method is called. You can also use the following code to achieve the same result.

```
if (weather) { checkWeather(); }
```

The value for weather will be converted into its Boolean equivalent before being evaluated. With objects, anything that is defined will return true, whereas null or undefined values return false. This way of checking is easier to write but is less reliable because it can cause different results depending on the data type of the object you're checking.

Using other Boolean values

Functions that return Boolean values can also be used in conditional statements. Some such functions are defined by AS3, but you can create your own as well. As a convention, these functions usually are named in a way that sounds like the logic they check for by starting with the word "is" or "has," such as the isNaN() (is not a number) function, which returns true if the argument passed is not a Number, int, uint, or a string representation of a number such as "5".

```
if (isNaN(temperature)) { updateTemp(); }
```

if..else

By adding the `else` keyword, you can add an additional block of code that will be executed only if the condition is *not* met. The example that follows could be read as "If it's raining, then bring an umbrella; otherwise, leave the umbrella behind."

```
if (weather == "rain") {
   bringUmbrella();
} else {
   leaveUmbrella();
}
```

You can also add another `if` statement that will be checked only if the first `if` statement isn't true. The statement that follows says "If it's raining, then bring an umbrella, but if it's snowing, then bring a coat. If it's not raining or snowing and it's sunny out, then bring sunscreen."

```
if (weather == "rain") {
   bringUmbrella();
} else if (weather == "snow"){
   bringCoat();
} else if (weather == "sun") {
   bringSunscreen();
}
```

switch

If you need to test the condition of something against several possible outcomes, as in our last example when we were testing for rain, snow, and sun, it might be best to use a `switch` statement. A *switch* is like a giant `if..else` statement that tests a single expression against several possible outcomes. You can check for any number of different *cases* or possible outcomes for the expression you're evaluating and even define a *default* behavior in case none of the cases match.

Notice that `break` statements are used after each case. The `break` statement tells the conditional statement or loop to cancel the rest of its operation without going any further. Unlike the `if` statement, which executes code in a block enclosed with curly braces (`{}`), when working with switches, you must include `break` after each `case` to prevent the code from continuing to the next case.

```
switch (weather) {
   case "rain" :
      bringUmbrella();
   break;

   case "snow" :
   bringCoat();
   break;

   case "sun" :
      bringSunscreen();
   break;

   default :
      bringBook();
}
```

This is equivalent to writing:

```
if (weather == "rain") {
  bringUmbrella();
} else if (weather == "snow") {
  bringCoat();
} else if (weather == "sun") {
  bringSunscreen();
} else {
  bringBook();
}
```

> **NOTE**   It's not required, but we recommend that you use the `default` keyword to define a case that executes if none of the other cases in the switch statement match.

The conditional operator

The final method that you can use to check the truth of an expression is the conditional operator (`?:`). This operator looks a bit different from the other operators in that it has two separate parts and takes three operands (this is the only ternary operator in ActionScript). The conditional operator behaves similarly to the basic `if` statement.

```
(logical expression) ? if true : if false;
```

The conditional operator takes three expressions as operands. The first is a logical expression to evaluate for truth much like the expression passed into an `if` statement. This can be a comparison, a variable, a function call, or anything that can be evaluated as either true or false.

The logical expression is followed by a question mark, which is the first part of the operator. Immediately after the question mark is the expression that will be evaluated and returned if the logical statement is found to be true. This is followed with a colon, the second part of the operator, and finally, the expression to be returned if the first value was found to be false.

Here's a more practical example. This time, we check for hail:

```
(weather == "hail") ? bringMotorcycleHelmet() : bringStrawHat();
```

This is basically the same as writing:

```
if (weather == "hail") {
  bringMotorcycleHelmet();
} else {
  bringStrawHat();
}
```

You can also use the conditional operator to return values that can be stored in a variable. The following:

```
hatType = (weather == "hail") ? "helmet" : "straw";
```

will set `hatType` to `helmet` or `straw` depending on the value of `weather`.

A common implementation of this is to set a default value for an undefined variable:

```
weather = weather ? weather : "partly cloudy";
```

The preceding code might look a bit confusing but what it's doing is simple. It's checking to see if `weather` is defined and, if not, assigning the value of `"partly cloudy"`. Because most objects in ActionScript evaluate to `true` if they have a value and `false` if they are null or undefined, the code `weather ?` will evaluate to `true` if there is a definition and `false` otherwise. One of the two following expressions will be returned and assigned to the variable resulting in either:

```
weather = weather
```

which causes no changes, or assigning the default value of `"partly cloudy"`:

```
weather = "partly cloudy"
```

> **TIP** While conditional statements are much more compact to write, they are more difficult to read and understand quickly than `if` statements. You will have to use your best judgment when choosing between them.

Repeating Actions Using Loops

Loops are another control structure used for counting up or down or through a set of data. They allow you to repeat an action multiple types while writing the code only once. Just as conditional statements make our programs interesting by providing points of variation, so do loops make our program interesting by allowing us to perform operations that we wouldn't be able to do by hand. After all, isn't the computer supposed to be doing the work?

The uses for loops are endless. For example, you might want to read a list of 100 items, apply a calculation to every graphic on the screen, search through an array for a particular value, initialize every object in a list, or just write every letter from A to Z. The most common use for loops that you'll encounter is for stepping through every item in an array.

> **NOTE** An array is an ordered list of data. Arrays have a `length` property, which returns the number of items in the array.

Using for loops

There are a few different types of looping structures in ActionScript. Let's start with everyone's favorite, the for loop. If you've used C, Java, JavaScript, or almost any language, you are probably familiar with this structure.

A common for loop looks something like this:

```
for (var i:int = 1; i <= 100; i++) {
    // do some action
}
```

Yikes, that looks a little bit scary and, well, code-y, but really, it's not so bad. The trained eye will read this as follows. "For every integer from 1 up to and including 100, do some action." In other words, "Repeat some action 100 times."

Let's break it into sections:

- `for` — All for loops start with this word.
- `var i:int = 1;` — By itself, this doesn't look so bad. We're creating a new integer called i and setting it to 1. This will be the number that counts up during each loop. The i stands for iteration or index or integer. This c-an also be a `uint` or a `Number` and doesn't have to be named i, but it is a commonly used naming convention to always use i as the name of the counter.
- `i <= 100;` — The next snippet of code shows the conditions for the loop to continue running. This is like an `if` statement that asks "If i is less than my upper limit (100), keep on looping; otherwise, stop looping." The number 100 is arbitrary and should be replaced with whatever your upper limit is.
- `i++;` — This portion is called the iterator and it tells the `for` loop what to do at the end of each loop. You'll almost always use an increment operator (++) to add one to your counter variable. This is equivalent to saying `i = i + 1;`.
- `// do some action` — This is where you would place your code that gets executed during each iteration. You should know that the i variable will be available to you for this block of code, which can be very useful.

Let's take another very common example using arrays. Arrays are ordered sets of data. If you've never used arrays before, you can either jump ahead to Chapter 9 or just try to follow along. This code:

```
var myArray:Array = ["Andrew", "Ben", "Casey", "Daniel", ↩
"Elizabeth", "Frank", "Geoff"];
for (var i:int = 0; i < myArray.length; i++) {
    trace("Hello, " + myArray[i] + "!");
}
```

produces the output:

```
Hello, Andrew!
Hello, Ben!
Hello, Casey!
Hello, Daniel!
Hello, Elizabeth!
Hello, Frank!
Hello, Geoff!
```

In this example, we're looping through every item in an array of seven names and saying "hello" to each of them. This type of for loop is used all the time in ActionScript. In fact, nearly every array you create will be used in a for loop at some point in your code.

We're doing a couple of things differently here that weren't in the first example. First, we're starting the iterations with the number zero (`var i:int = 0;`). This is because array indexes start with the number zero. Also, we're counting up to the value for `myArray.length`. Because this value is the number of items in the array, we'll step through every item in `myArray`.

 **AS3 adds additional looping functions when working with Arrays. These are discussed in Chapter 9.**

Using for..in and for each..in

For loops can be useful for repeating an action multiple times, especially when the number of repetitions is known. However, you'll find that it's commonly necessary to iterate through every variable stored within an object such as all of the Product objects contained within a Catalog object. The next few sections will explain how to do this more efficiently.

for..in

The *for..in* loop uses the values stored in an object to iterate. So, for every object stored within another object, there will be one iteration.

It looks like this:

```
for (var element:String in targetObject) {
    // do some action
}
```

In this case, you could read this as "For every element within the object called `targetObject`, do some action", or "Act upon every object in the target object." `targetObject` is the object whose variables and functions we're looping through. The `element` variable is the name of the variable or function contained in `targetObject` as a string.

Let's take a look at a practical example. This loop takes weather (or any object) and shows the names and values of every property within it. The following code

```
var weather:Object = new Object();
weather.temp = 45;
weather.conditions = "rain";
weather.pressure = 970;
for (var element:String in weather) {
    trace(element + ": " + weather[element]);
}
```

produces the result:

```
conditions: rain
temp: 45
pressure: 970
```

for each..in

There is another variation on for..in that is new in ActionScript 3.0. It comes in the form

```
for each (var element:Object in targetObject) {
    // do some action
}
```

This is slightly different from the standard for..in loop because with for each..in you're handling the properties or functions within the targetObject directly. The element *is* the property rather than just the name of the property.

Let's look at the previous weather example again, this time using for each..in:

```
var weather:Object = new Object();
weather.temp = 45;
weather.conditions = "rain";
weather.pressure = 970;
for each (var element:Object in weather) {
    trace(element.toString());
}
```

With this method, you see the following results:

```
45
rain
970
```

Using while and do..while

The final type of loop that we'll look at is the while loop. While is a much more basic type of loop than for. You can use while when you need to say "As long as a certain condition is met, keep looping." Here's the basic structure:

```
while (condition == true) {
   // do some action
}
```

That's it. Inside the parentheses, put whatever conditional statement you want to test for. As long as the condition is true, the action will be continuously looped.

The following two loops are virtually identical:

```
for (var i:int = 0; i < 100; i++) {
   // Do some action
}

var i:int = 0;
while (i < 100) {
   // do some action
   i++;
}
```

While statements can be useful in situations where you need to loop without knowing when you'll stop looping, such as when you need to loop until a variable reaches a certain value but you don't know how many iterations it will take. For example, this loop adds random numbers together until the result surpasses 100:

```
var sum:Number = 0;
while (sum < 100) {
   trace(sum + " - not there yet.");
   var random:Number = Math.ceil(Math.random() * 10);
// create a random number between 0 and 10
   sum += random;
}
trace(sum + " - surpassed 100. END");
```

When we ran this, we got the following output. Yours will be different because random numbers are being used.

```
0 - not there yet.
3 - not there yet.
12 - not there yet.
21 - not there yet.
27 - not there yet.
32 - not there yet.
39 - not there yet.
```

```
49 - not there yet.
55 - not there yet.
64 - not there yet.
70 - not there yet.
80 - not there yet.
90 - not there yet.
92 - not there yet.
95 - not there yet.
104 - surpassed 100. END
```

do..while

The standard while loop comes in one other flavor — the *do..while* loop. The only difference here is that the check for the condition happens after the loop is complete instead of before. So that means there is always at least one iteration.

```
var sum:Number = 10;
do {
   sum += 40;
} while (sum < 10);
trace(sum + " - surpassed 10"); // Displays: 50 - surpassed 10
```

Using for vs. using while

Between `for` loops and `while` loops most developers choose `for` loops for most situations. You should certainly know about both and choose the one that makes the most sense for each situation. If you're not sure, just stick with `for` loops. Either can be used for most situations. Some would argue that `while` statements are better optimized. `for` statements are more compact and less likely to result in an infinite loop because they tend to count toward a well-defined upper limit.

Avoiding infinite loops

If any loop is allowed to continue running unchecked, you are likely to encounter an infinite loop. An infinite loop can occur any time there is no variation on the conditional causing it to be false. Infinite loops should always be avoided as they cause the Flash Player to hang and eventually crash. The following is a simple example of an infinite loop.

 Run this code at your own risk! It *will* crash Flash Player and maybe more.

```
while (true) {
   trace("desu");
}
```

Using break and continue

In some situations you may find that your loop is no longer useful or you've found the result you were looking for. In these cases you can use `continue` and `break` respectively.

continue

`continue` ceases to execute the current iteration of the loop and skips ahead to the next iteration.

Break

As mentioned before, `break` is a keyword that allows you to stop processing a loop or conditional.

Say you want to search through a `haystack` array to find an instance of the `Needle` class. If you dig up only `Hay`, you can use `continue` to skip to the next iteration until you've identified the needle, and then `break` the loop so that unnecessary repetitions are halted.

```
var needle:Needle = null;
for (var i:int = 0; i < haystack.length; i++) {
   var hay:* = haystack[i];
   if (!(hay is Needle)) { continue; }
   needle = Needle(hay);
   trace("I found the needle!");
   break;
}
```

Commenting Your Code

Comments are pieces of text that are not executed when the program is run. They are used to add notes to yourself or others who may work on your code. Although some beginning programmers shy away from using comments because it seems tedious or frivolous, it is a very good habit to get into. Comments can provide a quick explanation for what your code is doing, saving you the time and confusion of trying to interpret the code. When you are working with others, comments become a helpful tool for describing your intention to other programmers. More important, they can be useful for your own benefit if you haven't looked at a piece of code in a long time.

In this book, comments are used frequently in the code samples to add notes.

Types of comments

There are two types of comments in ActionScript, single line and block comments. They both work the same way, and either method will do. Typically, the single line comments are used for shorter comments and block comments are used for longer chunks of text.

Single line comment

You can create a single line comment by using two forward slashes (//). This converts the remaining text on a line of code into a comment. They can be useful for adding a note to a line in a function, as follows:

```
trace("Hello, " + name); // Displays: Hello, Mims
```

Block comments

Block comments allow you to comment out all text between a starting and an ending marker. Use /* to start your comment block and */ to end it. The compiler will ignore all text between the two markers.

```
/*
   This is an example
   of a multi-line
   block comment.
*/
```

This type of comment can be used in CSS files as well.

XML comments

A third type of comment you might encounter is an XML comment. This is a block comment that is used exclusively within XML code (including MXML). XML comments are started by <!-- and ended by -->. The string -- must not be included anywhere inside the start and end markers.

```
public var xml:XML = <people>
   <!--A list of developers-->
   <person name="Corey"/>
   <person name="Brian"/>
   <person name="Mark"/>
</people>;
```

There is no single line XML comment.

When to use comments

As you're starting out, it's not a bad idea to add comments anywhere that your code might not be completely self-explanatory, especially with algorithms that may be unfamiliar to you or other people. Comments can be great for adding notes to remind yourself of something. A very common comment is the word TODO. As in

```
// Calculates the area of a square.
// TODO : add a separate height and width to support rectangles.
public function calculateArea(width:Number):Number {
   return width * width;
}
```

They can also be used to *comment out* a line of code, which allows you to keep a line of code without it executing. The following code:

```
trace("hello world");
```

will display `hello world` while the following will display nothing:

```
//trace("hello world");
```

Self-commenting code

Many developers would argue that the best way to comment is by using *self-commenting code*. This simply means writing code that is completely self-evident by using descriptive words for all variable names and method names, using strongly typed and well-defined variables, and encapsulating complex functionality into easy-to-describe functions. This leads to less reliance on commenting. Self-commented code should ideally be understandable even by a non-programmer.

Summary

- ActionScript is based around the use of variables, which are essentially containers for holding data for the duration of your program.

- Each variable has a data type that defines the type of data that can be stored inside it. This helps the compiler and the Flash Player catch errors in your code.

- Selecting the right scope and access identifiers for your variables can allow you to control which other objects in your program can have access to a particular piece of information.

- You can add decision-making logic to your program through the use of `if` statements and other conditionals.

- Repeating the same code multiple times is simplified by using `for` and `while` loops. The new `for each..in` gives you easier access to the properties stored within a complex object.

- Commenting your code may seem tedious but it allows other coders to understand the purpose of your work at a quick glance. It may even help you — you never know when you'll have to go back to something you worked on weeks ago and make changes.

- Operators are like simplified functions used for common applications such as doing basic math and comparing Boolean values.

Chapter 3

Programming with Classes

Programming using classes is essential to take advantage of the full power of ActionScript 3.0. By using classes, you participate in object-oriented programming, a versatile way to think about and structure code. Objects are high-level building blocks, and classes are the constructs which define them. In this chapter you learn what constitutes a class, how classes relate to objects and other language constructs, and how to write a class in ActionScript 3.0.

Understanding Classes

To program using classes, you must understand what classes are. Classes perform multiple roles in object-oriented programming, and there are many ways to think about them. This section introduces these fundamental ideas.

Classes can model the real world

Classes often work best, and are easiest to think about, when they represent objects in the real world. You can, for example, create a class to represent a bicycle. That bicycle can have a color, a size, and two tires. You can pedal it, brake it, switch gears, and ring the bell. The bicycle has relationships with other real-world objects: your feet, the road surface, occasionally a bike pump. If we model the bicycle as a class, we can represent all of these, and carefully design it to interact with the other objects in the right ways. Let's call this class `Bicycle`. We will come back to the `Bicycle` class to describe concepts in class design throughout this chapter.

35

You can use classes throughout your program to model tangible objects within the world of your program, if you are modeling actual phenomena. However, classes perform equally well at representing abstract concepts and nonphysical objects. You might consider, for example, a table in a database as a class. Although nobody has actually seen a database table, or knows what it looks like or how it tastes, we can form a complete representation of it. We know everything that a table must do in its own world and all the properties that define it. Therefore, we can easily model it as a class.

When you become comfortable associating real-world objects with classes in your program, you will have the basics of object-oriented programming under your belt! You'll be modeling `Toast`, `Guitar`, `LaserGrenade`, and `FuzzyLobster` classes with aplomb.

Classes contain data and operations

The textbook definition of a class is a structure that contains both data and operations. Classical organization in object-oriented programming differs from procedural programming in which data and operations (variables and functions) mingle without supervision. Imagine placing the color of a bicycle next to the action of popping a water balloon next to the number of licks in a lollipop. You could make sense of procedural programs only if you were strict about imposing your own organization. Classes group the activities and properties associated with the same subject together, and impose order naturally. The color and speed of a bicycle, the actions of braking and pedaling appear together in a `Bicycle` class and the flavor and duration of a lollipop appear together in a `Lollipop` class.

> **NOTE**   Frame scripts and ActionScript 1.0 are examples of procedural programming. In procedural programming, code executes from top to bottom and can go into functions or procedures.

Binding the behaviors of an object together with its properties results in a self-contained, fully functional unit. In the same breath, we can talk about rotating the pedals of a bicycle, and the color of that bicycle. It's all the same bicycle.

Classes separate responsibilities

Classes can perform work. You use this when designing a program to determine how to split up the program's responsibilities. Say you are required to build a program that makes deliveries throughout the city. You have to handle the responsibilities of picking up an item, finding out its destination, determining the best route to that destination, handing off the package, and collecting a fee. The `Bicycle` class, then, is just one class in your program. When thinking about how to do a program with object-oriented design, you create classes to perform certain responsibilities. Here, a `Dispatcher` would be a natural choice for determining optimal routes, and a `Messenger` is needed to control the `Bicycle` and to handle the `Package`. By carefully analyzing the actions that need to be performed by your program, you can determine what classes are appropriate to use. With just a little more thought, the relationships between these classes become obvious as well.

Classes work well when they are small, specific units. If you end up with a class that takes care of many different responsibilities, it's usually possible and desirable to split it up into multiple classes. If you write a `Level` class that draws a centipede, player, and obstacles, and keeps track of the score, you've created the same kind of jumble as exists in a procedural program. Look instead at the nouns used in that description for your clues to what the classes could be: a `Centipede`, a `Player`, a `Stage`, and a `Score`.

Classes are types

Classes are used by ActionScript 3.0 as types. All `Bicycle` classes are of a type `Bicycle`. This isn't because of any complex self-reference but simply the nature of *names*. Bicycle is both a definition of a thing (has two wheels, gears, and so on), and the word you use to refer to that thing ("bicycle"). When you write out a class, first you declare its name and then you define it. When you use that class in the rest of your program, you only have to refer to it by name.

In ActionScript 3.0, the inverse is also true: all types are classes (except for interfaces, which you'll learn later in this chapter). In some languages, simple types like numbers are not represented by classes. These are called *base types*. In a language like this, 12 would have a type, say, `integer`, but no class associated with it. The type of 12 has a name, but no definition. There's nothing more you can learn about 12; there's no data contained in it or operations it can perform. However, in ActionScript 3.0, even numbers like 42 and Boolean values like `true` are represented by classes. They have data — at minimum, their own value — and operations. For example, you can ask a number like 12 to represent itself as a string by calling its `toString()` operation. In ActionScript 3.0, *every* value is described by a class.

Classes contain your program

With the new generation of tools that support ActionScript 3.0, it is encouraged that you write *all* of your code in classes. There is no functionality that can't be performed with the right objects acting together, and creating a set of classes that divide up all of the responsibilities of your program is what object-oriented design is all about.

This means that scripts attached to frames or symbols using the Flash authoring tool can be, and should be, written in appropriate classes rather than on the timeline. Even the initialization of your program can move out of the frames by associating a Document class to your Flash project.

In ActionScript, classes are stored in `.as` files. Most of the time, each class file contains a single class (although this is not a requirement as you will see later). ActionScript class files end in the file extension `.as`, for example, `Bicycle.as` might contain the code for the `Bicycle` class.

NOTE   The `.as` extension is used for ActionScript 1.0, 2.0, and 3.0. Accordingly, simply examining the filename will not tell you what language is contained in the file. ActionScript 3.0 files can be distinguished by the `package` block that surrounds the class definition.

The older practice of using `.as` files to store code snippets and load them using the `#include` directive is deprecated in AS3.

Understanding Terminology

Although classes are the cornerstone of object-oriented programming, there are other essential, related concepts. We've already touched on some, and we've tiptoed around others, for it's impossible to discuss object-oriented programming without this vocabulary.

Object

Object can have slightly different meanings in different contexts. An object is the basic unit of object-oriented programming. It is a self-contained thing that contains data and operations. Every object is defined by a class. For example, a bicycle object would be defined by the class `Bicycle`.

An object is concrete. A real bicycle has two wheels that make it a bicycle — a bicycle object has traits that make it a `Bicycle`. Any instance of `Bicycle` is a bicycle.

Typically, we use the word object to refer to an arbitrary object, one whose details we are not interested in. When the object has a specific type, sometimes we use the word *instance* instead, as in "this is an instance of the `Bicycle` class."

Objects are constructs that exist at runtime, while the program is running. You can write code to manipulate objects, but the objects don't actually exist until the code you wrote executes and creates them.

The word object can also refer to the class `Object`, which is the base class of all classes, the root of all type hierarchies. You can find more about this later in the chapter, and in Chapter 9.

Class

A *class* is a blueprint for an object. It defines the object in full: the data and operations of that object. You write classes before you run your program, and when your program is running, they are set in stone. An exception to this is dynamic classes, which are discussed later in this chapter. Otherwise, the only thing that a running program uses classes for is to create new objects, and to manipulate types.

Classes contain the code you write. When your program runs, it's an orchestrated production of objects, and that production is directed by the code in the classes.

Instance

An *instance* is a specific object created from a specific class. It may be used by itself or with the name of the class to specify the type of the instance, as in "an instance of the `FuzzyLobster` class." Instances are unique. When you point to one shiny red road bike screaming down the road, you can refer to an instance of `Bicycle`. Although there are other bicycles, and although there are other shiny red road bikes, that instance is one individual bike.

The word instance is related to the word *instantiate*. When you create a new instance of a `Bicycle`, perhaps with the code `new Bicycle()`, you are also instantiating a class.

Often, instance and object are used interchangeably. All instances are objects, although some static objects, like `Capabilities`, are not an instance of a class but the class itself. Usually, you deal with objects (like a particular bicycle) that are instances of a certain class. In most cases, object and instance are equally valid.

Type

The *type* of an object tells you what the object is. An object of type `Bicycle` is a bicycle. ActionScript 3.0 allows you to create variables with and without types. In other words, you can create both *statically typed* and *dynamically typed* code. Except where the situation requires it, all code in this book will use statically typed variables.

In statically typed code, types help you ensure that you only perform actions on the right kind of things. For example, if you want to do a wheelie on a bicycle, you might make sure that something is a bicycle before you try to pop a wheelie with it. Imagine the embarrassment you would have to endure if you were caught popping a wheelie on a strawberry, or the hospital bill you'd incur by popping a wheelie on a unicycle. When you write statically typed programs, the code itself can enforce these checks; your code will be incorrect if it uses incompatible types, and the compiler won't let you run the program. The assurance that types are correct is known as *type safety*.

Because ActionScript is object-oriented, the actual type of every object will be a class, and it is impossible to create an object with a type, whose type is not a class. (You can use objects as if they were compatible types and interfaces as you will read below in Manipulating Types, but their actual type will remain the class they were instantiated from.) From `Strings` to `ints`, objects' types are classes.

Understanding Encapsulation

By containing and controlling access to the data that represents it, an object can hide its implementation from the outside world. Outside that class, no other part of the program can see how it works internally. This principle is known as *encapsulation*.

Encapsulation is also described as *information hiding*. Classes should keep certain information pertaining to their implementation hidden from the outside. This practice is at work constantly in the real world. You don't need to know how a bicycle works to ride it, or understand the principles of electromagnetic wave propagation to use a microwave, or how the telephone system is structured to make a phone call. If you had to deal with the information that is hidden by the systems you use every day, you'd probably go completely insane. Encapsulation allows other objects in the program to be users of an object in the simplest way possible.

We also depend on the *interfaces* of systems to be able to use them. While there are some weird bikes out there, let's agree that bicycles have two pedals that you can apply rotation to, a handlebar to change direction, some manner of controls to change the gears, an indicator which shows what gear you're on, levers to squeeze and apply the brakes, and a button which rings the bell. This is the interface of the bicycle: everything about it that you can affect and inspect. It is all you need to know about to use a bicycle. Similarly, telephones expose an interface of 12 keys, and microwaves have several functions you can use to cook and reheat your food.

The black box principle

In the real world, you may be able to see the gears of a bicycle, see how the brakes work, and touch and modify parts of the bike we didn't mention in its interface. But in programming as in science, we deal with abstractions of reality. Our goal is to hide anything about an object that the user of that object does not have an explicit need to know or use. In the real world, hiding the brakes and the derailleur of a bike might cost more money or make it harder to repair, but when we're designing a program, we use encapsulation with the normal use of the object — in this case, riding the bicycle — in mind.

Hiding an object's implementation and only providing access to an interface you carefully design is known as the *black box principle*, illustrated in Figure 3-1. If the user wants to make some toast, you can provide them with a sealed black box with inputs and outputs. You put in a slice of bread, and you get toast. You don't need to know or care how the bread is transformed into toast. If some new, more efficient way of toasting arrives, you can get a new black box and it will still toast your bread, and you won't care.

FIGURE 3-1

A toaster. How does it work? Who cares?!

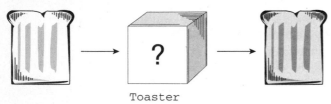

Toaster

Encapsulation and polymorphism

The prior example touches on another principle of object-oriented programming. If your goal is to get toast, you can be equally happy using a `HeatedResistorToaster` object or an `AcetyleneFlameToaster` object, as long as they both have a slot which accepts bread. Similarly, provided you know how to ride one kind of bike, you can quickly start riding your friend's bike, even if it's a mountain bike and your bike is a road bike. The principle being hinted at by this real-world equivalent is *polymorphism*, the ability of related classes to be substituted for each other.

More specifically, class instances may always be referred to by a type more general than their actual type. This means that both a RoadBike and a MountainBike may both be referred to as Bicycle, and the parts of their interfaces which belong to the more general Bicycle may be used on an instance of either. You can ride both RoadBikes and MountainBikes, if you just treat them as Bicycles and use the common Bicycle interface on them.

The ActionScript 3.0 language gives you tools to create objects that act as black boxes, hide their implementations, and provide sensible interfaces. But it doesn't require that you use the tools correctly: you can violate all these principles while writing legal code. As the programmer, you shoulder the responsibility for upholding these principles in classes you write. Keep the principles of encapsulation in mind, and this chapter will show you how to embody them in code.

Understanding Packages

Simply separating your code into classes isn't always enough to keep the code your program requires in order. Large software projects can contain lots of classes, hundreds or even thousands of them, which beg to be organized further into related groups. The functionality of Flash Player itself is exposed in dozens of classes, which are also grouped by function. For example, flash.net contains classes related to network access, and flash.geom contains classes that help with geometry.

flash.net and flash.geom are examples of *packages*. Packages are structures that group classes together, define the full name for the classes they contain, and add a level of access control. Packages can be nested arbitrarily deeply using dot notation, as these examples are.

When we refer to classes by their class name, for example, Rectangle, we may not be giving their full name. Because we find the Rectangle class in the flash.geom package, the class has what is known as a *fully qualified* name: flash.geom.Rectangle. In a conversation, once you establish that Roger means Roger Eliot Braunstein, and there's only one Roger in your story, you simply use the name Roger. The same principle applies to writing code.

Class uniqueness

Without packages to organize classes, we would find ourselves with the problem of uniqueness. Say your next project is a drawing tool written in ActionScript, and one of the shapes you have to allow users to draw is a rectangle. It would only be natural to start writing a Rectangle class to handle the display of Rectangle objects, but — imagining packages don't exist — there is already a Rectangle class in the Flash Player API, and it doesn't do what you need it to. (The flash.geom.Rectangle class stores the position and size of a rectangle. It does not draw anything.) You would be left with no option but to name your class something else, so you might grumble to yourself, name it `DrawingRectangle`, and move on. But after hundreds of such decisions, you might start running out of names.

Indulge one more hypothetical and imagine, that after much hard work on the drawing application, you decide to use a third-party ActionScript library to display dialog boxes. To your dismay, you realize that the authors of the library have their own class called `DrawingRectangle` for drawing buttons on the dialog box. Without packages, you have to find this and all the other name collisions between your code and theirs and resolve them, as well as rewriting any code that references a class whose name you changed.

An entire set of unique names is known as a *namespace*. Packages make it possible to create new namespaces. Packages give your classes rational names and enable you to share code with others without worrying about name collisions. As usual, this language feature doesn't bestow its benefits automatically. You have to be careful to use packages, and to name them well. Putting all your classes in a package named `classes`, for example, is not likely to guarantee that they will be unique. (Except for the fact that, hopefully, nobody else will make that mistake!)

The typical technique for guaranteeing a package's uniqueness is to piggyback on the uniqueness of domain names: you are likely to own a domain, or the work you're doing is likely going to end up hosted on one. If you were creating your drawing application for `http://www.example.com`, your `Rectangle` class might reside in the package `com.example.shapes`, so that its fully qualified class name is `com.example.shapes.Rectangle`. Core classes that are built into Flash Player, and the Flex framework classes are special cases, reserving the package names `flash` and `mx`. For example, the `MovieClip` class in AS3 is located in `flash.display`, so that its fully qualified class name is `flash.display.MovieClip`. This is the exception, not the rule. Even for throw-away code, placing your code in packages starting with your domain name in reverse is a good practice to get into.

> **NOTE** If you don't have a domain name and your work won't be hosted on one, you don't have to use the reverse domain name convention. The idea is simply to create something that is unique to you. You could use your full name, or a phone number, or make up a domain name that isn't likely to be used.

Hierarchy

Packages serve to organize classes into related groups. In the example class `com.example.shapes.Rectangle`, we have created a package for shape classes. We anticipate having to write other shapes, like `com.example.shapes.Circle`, so this package will keep them grouped together. If we were to support both two- and three-dimensional shapes, we could further group these with an intermediary package, keeping `com.example.shapes.twodimensional.Triangle` and `com.example.shapes.threedimensional.Cone` separate. Exercise the same heuristics you might apply when organizing files in your hard drive into directories to section off your code into cohesive groups.

Because packages serve to both guarantee uniqueness and provide organization, packages for both of these purposes are nested in a single path. As in the examples you've read already, place the organizational packages inside the uniqueness packages. So you would interpret `com.example` `.shapes.twodimensional.Triangle` as a triangle that's a two dimensional shape (organization) from the domain example.com (uniqueness).

This hierarchy is visible not just inside your code but on your file system. ActionScript classes must be located in nested folders whose names match the package they are contained in: `com` `.example.shapes.Rectangle` must be defined in the file `com/example/shapes/` `Rectangle.as` in your source directory. In Flash CS3 Professional, the default source directory is the same directory that your FLA resides in, though you can add other directories to your class-path in File ⇨ Publish Settings ⇨ ActionScript 3.0 Settings. In Flex Builder, the source directory can be set in your project's Properties ⇨ ActionScript Build Path ⇨ Main source folder.

NEW IN AS3 In ActionScript 2.0, a file's path alone defined a package. ActionScript 3.0 uses folders to organize packages in the same way, but also makes the package explicit with a package block declaring the package-scoped items.

Controlling visibility

Packages in ActionScript 3.0 impact the visibility of the items they contain. The listing below might be found in the file `com/example/shapes/Rectangle.as`.

```
package com.example.shapes
{
    public class Rectangle
    {
        // define Rectangle here.
    }
}
class SecretClass
{
    // define SecretClass here.
}
```

The first line declares a package, `com.example.shapes`. Notice how two classes are declared in this file, one inside the package block, matching the name of the file, and one outside the package block.

In any file, a maximum of one class may be made accessible to the world outside that file. This class must be contained in a `package` block, and it must be declared `public`. It is rare to write code outside of a `package` block, but this example illustrates the technique with the `SecretClass`. This technique may be used to simulate the effects of nested class definitions, which are available in Java but not ActionScript. `SecretClass` will only be accessible to other code inside the file `Rectangle.as`. Often, the out-of-package classes are helper classes for the public class in the file that the outside world never needs to know about. Even so, most of the time your class files will have a package block containing a single public class.

For code inside the `package` block like `Rectangle`, access modifiers — `public` in this example — can determine where the code is usable from. We go into depth on access modifiers later in the chapter.

Code allowed in packages

By far the most common configuration of an ActionScript 3.0 file is one public class contained in a package block. The class is named the same as the file, and the file's path corresponds to its package. While the single-class-per-file setup accounts for a vast majority of situations, variables, functions, and namespace declarations can also be contained inside packages.

All the same rules apply for files containing variables or functions in package blocks. There can only be one item per file visible to the outside world, whether that item is a class, variable, function, or namespace. The name of the file must match the name of the externally visible item. For example, you can write a file `com/example/shapes/DEFAULT_SIZE.as`:

```
package com.example.shapes
{
    public const DEFAULT_SIZE:int = 256;
}
```

This file declares a package-level constant that you could use in any other code, without tying the constant to a specific class.

An example package-level function might be written in `com/example/shapes/testShapes.as`:

```
package com.example.shape
{
    public function testShapes():void
    {
        trace("test the shapes here...");
    }
}
```

An example of a package-level function found in the Flash Player API is `flash.net.navigateToURL()`.

Using code from packages

In order to use code from a package, you must import the code using an `import` statement. By importing the classes (and variables and functions) that you use from other packages, you tell the compiler to go fetch the class definitions, and by virtue of the file path mirroring the package, you tell the compiler where to find those definitions as well. Without importing the code you need from other packages, the compiler will have no idea what you mean when you refer to `Rectangle`.

NEW IN AS3 The `import` statement should not be confused with the `#include` compiler directive from earlier versions of ActionScript. Imports provide a reference from one class to another while `#include` inserts actual code from an external file into your code. Be aware that `#include` is no longer supported in ActionScript 3.0.

When you refer to other classes in the same package, there is no need to import them. If you referred to the `Circle` class inside the `Rectangle` class, provided these were both located in the `com.example.shapes` package, you could do so without importing `Circle`, and vice-versa.

Import statements always appear inside the package block but before the class declaration in ActionScript 3.0 files. The following example is a class that demonstrates your ability to import and use code from the package you just created.

```
package
{
    import com.example.shapes.Rectangle;
    import com.example.shapes.DEFAULT_SIZE;
    import com.example.shapes.testShapes;

    public class PackagesTest
    {
        public function PackagesTest()
        {
            var r:Rectangle = new Rectangle();
            10 + DEFAULT_SIZE;
            testShapes();
        }
    }
}
```

In the example, you use three `import` statements, line after line, to import the class, constant, and function from the `com.example.shapes` package you have been working with. The `import` statements come inside the package block but outside the class block. Each import gives the fully qualified name of the item to import, even if it is not a class.

In this example, there is nothing after the `package` keyword. That's because this code defines a class in the *default package*. The fully qualified name of the class in the example is `PackagesTest`. Rather than think of this as no package, think of it as the root, or top-level, package. Adding classes to the default package is not recommended, as they lose the benefits of uniqueness, and the top level is already populated by core types of ActionScript 3.0. Nonetheless, it is important to note that even in files in the default package, the `package` block is required.

Additionally, you can ask the compiler to import all the classes in a particular package by using the wildcard operator (`*`) trailing the package name:

```
package
{
    import com.example.shapes.*;
```

```
public class PackagesTest
{
    public function PackagesTest()
    {
        var r:Rectangle = new Rectangle();
        10 + DEFAULT_SIZE;
        testShapes();
    }
}
}
```

> **NOTE**   Importing a class does not automatically include that class in your compiled SWF. You can import a class but never reference it, and it will not be added to your compiled project. For a class to be compiled and included, you must actually use it in executable code.

After classes have been imported using their fully qualified class names, they can be referred to by their class names alone. Using an `import` statement is analogous to explaining that when you say Roger in subsequent conversation, you mean Roger Eliot Braunstein. This applies equally to all types of imported code, as the previous example shows. The exception to this rule is when two classes with the same name have been imported from different packages. Their unique packages guarantee you can still use both, but when both are imported, you must always disambiguate references to the classes by using their full name. If you had also used the `Rectangle` class from `flash.geom`, our example would change:

```
package
{
    import com.example.shapes.Rectangle;
    import flash.geom.Rectangle;

    public class PackagesTest
    {
        public function PackagesTest()
        {
            var a:com.example.shapes.Rectangle =
                new com.example.shapes.Rectangle();

            var b:flash.geom.Rectangle =
                new flash.geom.Rectangle();
        }
    }
}
```

In this case, you would never gain the benefit of using just "`Rectangle`" to refer to a class. That reference would always be ambiguous between the two `Rectangle` classes imported. Similarly, if there were two Rogers at a party, you would have to use their full names when talking about them to keep them straight.

NEW IN AS3 In ActionScript 2.0, importing classes was not necessary to use them; you could use classes by their fully qualified name and skip importing them. In ActionScript 3.0, classes will not be accessible unless they are in the top level, they are in the same package as the code that uses them, or they have been imported.

Using Inheritance

Inheritance is one of the most powerful tools in the object-oriented toolbox, and in fact a primary motivation for the existence of OOP. It is a core feature of ActionScript 3.0 and other object-oriented languages.

Simply put, inheritance is a relationship between classes where one class builds on another. Think, for a moment, of Darwinian evolution. When an organism reproduces, its children inherit the essential attributes of their parents. A seagull will impart to its children two wings, two eyes, feathers, a beak: all the things that make it a seagull. This principle, laying the groundwork for Darwin, was proved by Gregor Mendel. However, a random mutation or a chance chromosomal configuration can result in the child having a new or modified attribute, like an extra-strong beak or a louder call, or even a third leg, as shown in Figure 3-2. Although the interesting part about Darwin's theory lies in the success of these children, the mechanics of passing on traits suffice to explain inheritance.

FIGURE 3-2

A child inherits traits from its parents, mutations and all.

Seagull   Seagull

ThreeLeggedSeagull

Inheritance in OOP is also a parent-child relationship. A child class, or *subclass*, inherits the attributes of its parent class, or *superclass*. Without any additional work, you can create a class that functions exactly like another class. Because of this, inheritance is a primary way to achieve code reuse. But there's no reason to create an identical copy of a class. Remember, a class is a template, and you can create many instances of it. Inheritance is useful when you use it to *extend* the abilities of an existing class.

Say you have a working Seagull class, which is about 2 lbs, able to squawk, fly, and eat sand crabs. For a while it's fun to watch your Seagulls go along their business, flying about carelessly. But soon you want a seagull that can do something more, a seagull that can be your friend. You want a seagull that can play soccer! Instead of creating a new class that includes all the Seagull code all over again, you can start by declaring a SoccerSeagull that inherits from Seagull. This creates a parent-child relationship and makes SoccerSeagull exactly like Seagull. The SoccerSeagull inherits both the attributes (being 2 lbs) and the operations — squawking, flying, etc. — of its superclass, Seagull, without rewriting a line of code. Now you can add new functionality, like playing soccer, to the class.

In the file SeagullInheritanceExample.as:

```
package
{
    import flash.display.Sprite;

    public class SeagullInheritanceExample extends Sprite
    {
        public function SeagullInheritanceExample()
        {
            var normalGull:Seagull = new Seagull();
            normalGull.fly();
            normalGull.squawk();

            var crazyGull:SoccerSeagull = new SoccerSeagull();
            crazyGull.fly();
            crazyGull.squawk();
            crazyGull.playSoccer();
        }
    }
}
```

In the file Seagull.as:

```
package
{
    /**
     * A normal seagull.
     */
    public class Seagull
    {
        public var weight:Number = 2;
```

```
        public function Seagull():void
        {
            trace("A new seagull appears.");
        }

        public function squawk():void
        {
            trace("The seagull says 'SQUAAA!'");
        }

        public function fly():void
        {
            trace("The seagull flies in a  lazy circle");
        }

        public function eat():void
        {
            trace("The seagull digs its beak into the sand, pulls up a tiny ↵
struggling crab, and swallows it in one gulp.");
        }
    }
}
```

In the file `SoccerSeagull.as`:

```
package
{
    /**
     * A seagull that has been trained to play soccer.
     */
    public class SoccerSeagull extends Seagull
    {
        public function playSoccer():void
        {
            trace("Incredibly, the seagull produces a miniature soccer ball ↵
and deftly kicks it into a goal.");
        }
    }
}
```

This code provides the classes for the `Seagull` class and the `SoccerSeagull` classes. Note that you use the `extends` keyword to declare the parent class which the class will inherit from, because a child class can *extend* the abilities of its superclass. The example also shows that no code is required for the `SoccerSeagull` subclass to inherit the functions `squawk()`, `fly()`, and `eat()` from its superclass.

Additionally, you can use inheritance to *override* some behavior of the parent. For example, if your seagulls are creating a lot of noise you might want to modify their squawking behavior. If you create a `QuietSeagull` that inherits from `Seagull`, the `QuietSeagull` will do everything a

`Seagull` does, including squawk. But you can specify attributes of the superclass that you want to modify, and provide new attributes in their place. So you could create a squawking behavior in `QuietSeagull` that squawks more quietly, or even modify it to make no noise!

Through all this, the original `Seagull` is untouched. You can still have original, classic Seagulls running about among their bizarre offspring. Inheriting a class does not in any way alter the class, but rather uses it as a starting point for a child class. Moreover, subclasses are still considered their superclass: a `SoccerSeagull` is still a `Seagull`. It doesn't stop being a `Seagull` just because it can play soccer, and it can still do all the things a `Seagull` always could. The example shows `crazyGull`, the `SoccerSeagull` instance, flying and eating just like a normal `Seagull` does.

Inheritance is a concept applicable to classes, not objects. So a `SoccerSeagull` subclass can inherit from the `Seagull` class, but a `Seagull` object, once created, can't change its class. In the same way, the properties of an object that are defined or changed at runtime won't be part of the subclass's instances. Put another way, if a seagull injured its foot, it might be affected for the rest of its life, but its children will not inherit that trait, or any other trait the parents acquired in the course of life. In the following example, the parent gains some weight, but we see that the new object inherits the default weight provided by the `Seagull` template rather than the runtime value of its parent.

```
package
{
    import flash.display.Sprite;
    public class SeagullInheritanceExample extends Sprite
    {
        public function SeagullInheritanceExample()
        {
            var gull:Seagull = new Seagull();
            gull.eat();
            gull.eat();
            gull.eat();
            gull.eat();
            gull.weight = 10; //gain some weight
            trace("The parent seagull's weight is", gull.weight); //10

            var childGull:SoccerSeagull = new SoccerSeagull();
            trace("The child seagull's weight is", childGull.weight); //2
        }
    }
}
```

Living things use a variety of reproductive practices, transferring their traits to their children in different ways. Humans have two parents, and inherit their characteristics based on the random ways in which chromosomes separate in the parents' ova and sperm, in which particular pair of cells meet and form a zygote, and on the ways in which dozens or hundreds of genes interplay to express a specific trait. More simple organisms like viruses make a direct copy of their DNA or RNA, so that their children inherit from only one parent. Inheritance in ActionScript 3.0 is this latter kind, called single inheritance. A class can only inherit from one class. In fact, if you don't specify a class to inherit from, your class will automatically extend the `Object` class, so all classes extend exactly one class (except `Object` itself). With single inheritance, you can draw a simple tree of classes, and you can trace any class back to `Object` with a simple list of classes. Things would get a lot more confusing if one class could inherit from multiple classes.

The whole list of classes that takes a class back to the root class, as shown in Figure 3-3, is called a class's *inheritance chain*.

FIGURE 3-3

Inheritance chain of the MovieClip class

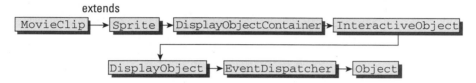

Structuring code with inheritance

The `MovieClip` class is a truly complex class, with several sets of duties and almost a hundred properties and methods. Important classes like these would quickly become a mess if it weren't for inheritance. Remember, one purpose of classes is isolating responsibility. With inheritance, you can ensure that those responsibilities are limited to the most specific possible interpretation of the class. All the more general responsibilities can be defined in a more general superclass.

Take the `Seagull` class, for example. Nowhere in its code did you have to define that it can lay an egg, that it has a beak and feathers, that it has two feet. These things are all true, of course, but they are really properties of birds. The `Seagull` class concerns itself with the specific responsibilities of a seagull: the way in which it flies, the kinds of food it eats, and its call. If you were to complete this example, you might have `Seagull` extend `Bird`, `Bird` extend `Vertebrate`, and `Vertebrate` extend `Animal`. Each class would be responsible for only its own specific set of traits. Your inheritance chain might look something like Figure 3-4.

FIGURE 3-4

Inheritance chain of a Seagull class

Does this idea sound familiar? We already have an inheritance-based system for classifying the living things around us, in which the most specific traits are described in a species, and the most generic traits are described in a kingdom. The real scientific classification for the Herring Gull we have been describing looks like Figure 3-5, just in Latin instead of monospace.

FIGURE 3-5

Scientific classification of a Herring Gull (*Larus argentatus*)

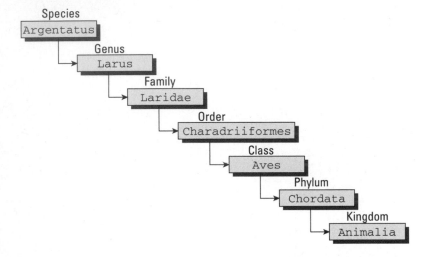

The most specific classification is the species, and the most generic is the kingdom. Usually the scientific classification is written from general to specific, but here it is diagrammed to be like an inheritance chain, with the class or animal in question appearing first, and revealing its more generic classifications.

A goal of your object-oriented designs should be to limit each class to one responsibility: managing itself. This sounds like circular reasoning, but really it's just an object-centric viewpoint. If you can create just the kinds of objects that are needed, they should be able to accomplish everything you desire. You can use inheritance to accomplish this. A `MovieClip`, as you will see in Chapter 12, is a `Sprite` with a timeline added, a `Sprite` is just a `DisplayObjectContainer` that can contain multimedia content, be drawn upon, and dragged, and so on. Using inheritance to create a family of classes which build on each other, you can make your code more modular, easier to modify, and simpler. One class, one responsibility.

Inheritance, types, and polymorphism

Inheritance gives rise to another important technique in the object-oriented toolbox: polymorphism. This technique is used to write decoupled code, enabling you to add functionality to your programs without the heartbreaking process of tearing apart code that's already written, tested, and tuned. The name *polymorphism* makes this property sound terribly complex, but armed with an understanding of inheritance, it is easily understood.

Polymorphism is the practice of treating subclasses like the classes they inherit from. You know that a `SoccerSeagull` is still a `Seagull`, and that an `AcetyleneFlameToaster` is still a `Toaster`. Both of these subclasses are able to do everything that their parents can, and this phenomenon is guaranteed by the mechanism of inheritance.

A typical usage of polymorphism is when you have a family of related objects that need to behave differently, and some functionality that doesn't care how they differ. This happens all the time. You don't need to know much about objects to store them, keep track of them, and arrange them. You don't need to know if a seagull plays soccer or not to see it fly. If all you want is toast you don't need to care about how the toaster does its job. In all of these cases, you could manipulate the objects as if they were more general types than they really might be.

The following example shows a seagull circus in action. This function, which could be part of a seagull trainer's repertoire, doesn't really care what kind of seagull is performing, since the trainer knows that all seagulls can fly and squawk.

```
package
{
    import flash.display.Sprite;

    public class SeagullPolymorphismExample extends Sprite
    {
        public function SeagullPolymorphismExample()
        {
            var normalGullBob:Seagull = new Seagull();
            var normalGullJoe:Seagull = new Seagull();
            var sportyGullFrank:Seagull = new SoccerSeagull();
            var strangeGullNed:Seagull = new ThreeLeggedSeagull();

            seagullShow(normalGullJoe, strangeGullNed, sportyGullFrank);
        }

        private function seagullShow(gull1:Seagull, gull2:Seagull, ↵
gull3:Seagull):void
        {
            gull1.fly();
            gull2.squawk();
            gull3.fly();

            gull1.squawk();
            gull2.fly();
            gull3.squawk();

            //get a treat for performing
            gull1.eat();
            gull2.eat();
            gull3.eat();
        }
```

```
        }
    }
```

The act can go on with any of the performers you created, since they are all seagulls. By creating the method seagullShow() so that its parameters are typed as instances of Seagull, you gain the ability to add all kinds of new Seagulls which can still participate in this show code without any modification. In fact, the example goes further here by putting the specialized seagulls into variables that hold the general type.

You will learn more about polymorphism when you look at interfaces later in this chapter, and when you learn how to get specific types out of generic variables when we discuss type manipulation.

Inheritance vs. composition

Inheritance is not the only technique you can use to augment classes with new abilities. Let's say you have a Kitchen class that does all the good things a kitchen does, like letting you fry, sauté, broil, parboil, and bake things, and wash and store dishes and cutlery. If your goal is to give people a place to live, you're going to need a lot more than that. So you can extend the Kitchen to add some sofas, beds, bathtubs, tables, mirrors, sinks, parking, maybe a fireplace. Now you have a specialized kind of Kitchen, say, a CrowdedKitchen, that people can live in. You can see immediately what's wrong with this example. A house isn't a special kind of kitchen, it is a structure with many kinds of rooms, including a kitchen. If you start adding these things to the Kitchen class, it really stops being what you might think of as a Kitchen.

Instead, let's build a House class that contains a Kitchen. When you have this House, you can continue to have all the convenience of a Kitchen just by accessing the Kitchen object inside it. You can continue to build out the House with lots of other rooms, adding in a Bedroom, Bathroom, LivingRoom, and Garage. Now you've created a composite class, a class that provides all the convenience of a Kitchen by *composition* instead of by *inheritance*. Following is a House class with a kitchen, living room, and any number of bedrooms:

```
package
{
    public class House
    {
        public var kitchen:Kitchen;
        public var livingroom:LivingRoom;
        public var bedrooms:Array;

        public function House(numberOfBeds:int)
        {
            kitchen = new Kitchen();
            livingroom = new LivingRoom();
            bedrooms = new Array();
            for (var i:int = 0; i < numberOfBeds; i++)
            {
                bedrooms[i] = new Bedroom();
            }
        }
    }
```

```
        }
```

There's another way you can use composition to build up additional functionality. When the president of a company asks a manager to get something done, the manager will tell her subordinates to do whatever parts of that task are necessary and then she will present the final result. The Manager needs to coordinate these actions with Employees that she oversees, and as far as the outside world is concerned, the Manager indeed composes the work of her Employees. But in the house example, the House simply provides access to the other classes it composed, whereas in this case the Manager *delegates* the activities to its constituent Employee objects. This method also provides better encapsulation, as the president of the company should not have to deal with the employees directly.

In the file Employee.as:

```
package
{
    public class Employee
    {
        public function doWork():int
        {
            //Each employee does one unit of work.
            return 1;
        }
    }
}
```

In the file Manager.as:

```
package
{
    public class Manager
    {
        protected var employees:Array;

        public function Manager(numberOfEmployees:int)
        {
            employees = new Array();
            for (var i:int = 0; i < numberOfEmployees; i++)
            {
                employees[i] = new Employee();
            }
        }

        public function delegateWork():int
        {
            var totalWork:int = 0;
            for each (var employee:Employee in employees)
            {
```

```
                    totalWork += employee.doWork();
                }
                return totalWork;
            }
        }
    }
```

And you can take this code for a spin in `Company.as`:

```
package
{
    public class Company
    {
        public function Company()
        {
            //The manager has ten employees.
            var manager:Manager = new Manager(10);
            //When you ask the manager to do work,
            var completedWork:int = manager.delegateWork();
            //You get the work of ten people.
            trace(completedWork); //10
        }
    }
}
```

Whether a class delegates responsibilities or simply aggregates objects, the class uses composition to add functionality instead of inheritance. The typical rule of thumb is: inheritance is an *is-a* relationship, and composition is a *has-a* relationship. An extra-loud seagull *is a* seagull, and a house *has a* kitchen.

This distinction is usually fairly clear, unmistakably so in these simple examples. But now and then there are ambiguous situations. The classic example is when you are creating a visual object. You can see your `IceCreamCone` class, but does that mean that your class should inherit from `Sprite` or should it merely contain a `Sprite`? (A `Sprite` is a visual object in ActionScript 3.0. You can learn more about it in Chapter 12.) In Flash CS3 Professional, the recommended way to get your movie up and running is to assign a class to the root document itself. This class, when you define it, extends the `DisplayObject` of your choice (for more information on `DisplayObjects`, please see Chapter 12). Similarly in Flex 2, your application starts with a class that must extend `Application`, also a view class. So there's some official sanction, if you needed it, to create view classes that extend display classes rather than composing them. However, you should still apply the test to your own code. Does your `IceCreamCone` *have* a visual component, or *is it* a visual component? If this class has other functionality, like storing a flavor, accepting toppings, and melting by degrees, it really isn't a display object but has one. We recommend creating view classes that only deal with the visual aspect of an object, and associating those with other classes that can deal with its functionality. This method is enshrined in the Model-View-Controller pattern, which you can learn more about from books such as *Advanced ActionScript 3.0 with Design Patterns* (Lott, Adobe Press, 2006) or *Head First Design Patterns* (Freeman, et. al., O'Reilly, 2004).

Preventing inheritance

In rare cases, you may want to ensure that the class you create is never, ever extended. The class might contain functionality that would be dangerous to modify. Another class might subclass yours, modify the behavior of one or more methods, and pass itself off as your class, since a subclass is also the type of its superclass. Of course, as the programmer, you ultimately have control over all the code going into your program, but when precompiled libraries are involved and projects get large, things can get out of control.

Even if malicious code is not your concern, you can use this ability to signify that the class just should not be extended, that the class performs its sole duty, and there is no possible extra duty it can conceivably take on. It can be your signal that the class works best with composition instead of inheritance.

For whatever reason you choose, you can make sure that nobody inherits your class by declaring it *final*. To declare a final class, simply add the `final` keyword to the class declaration.

NEW IN AS3 Final classes are a new feature of ActionScript 3.0.

NOTE The `final` keyword can come either before or after the access control attribute (in this case `public`). By convention, it is placed after.

```
package
{
    public final class Encrypter
    {
        public function encrypt(sourceText:String, key:String):String
        {
            //secure encryption algorithm goes here
        }
    }
}
```

Now if someone passes you an `Encrypter`, you can be sure that it's actually *this* `Encrypter`, and not a subclass like this impostor:

```
package
{
    public class MaliciousEncrypter extends Encrypter
    {
        override public function encrypt(sourceText:String, key:String):String
        {
            return sourceText; //mwa ha ha!
        }
    }
}
```

The `MaliciousEncrypter` class can pass itself off as an `Encrypter`, because it is a sub-class of `Encrypter`. However, it overrides the encryption algorithm to do nothing, defeating the security of an encryption class. However, as long as the `Encrypter` class is marked final, adding the `MaliciousEncrypter` class to your project will result in a compiler error. Extending `Encrypter` is forbidden as soon as you declare it `final`.

Extension is also prohibited on several classes that are built into the Flash Player API because their functionality is set in stone. For example, `flash.system.Security` works the way it works, and you should not be able to create your own implementation of the security system in Flash Player. Thus, `Security` is final.

Using Access Control Attributes with Classes

Access control attributes, or visibility modifiers, are keywords that are used with a piece of code to define who can access it. Most of the time, we use these with properties and methods of classes. In fact, all of the examples in this chapter thus far have already used them.

By having granular control over the visibility of different parts of our classes, we can determine our own level of encapsulation, giving us control over how classes look to the outside world. At the same time, you can use functions and achieve good code reuse, while making sure those functions are only used when you say they are.

We introduced access control attributes in Chapter 2; Table 3-1 summarizes them for your convenience.

TABLE 3-1

Access Control Attributes

Attribute	Meaning
`public`	Available to all code
`private`	Available only within the same class
`protected`	Available within the same class and subclasses
`internal`	Available to code within the same package
A custom namespace	Available where the custom namespace is opened or when the identifier is prefixed with the namespace

You've already seen the public attribute used before all of your class definitions. By making a class inside a package public, you enable that class to be used by the rest of the code in your program. In almost every case, you are writing a class so that everyone can use it, so putting public before class can become second nature.

Public and private

The public and private attributes are used to modify methods and properties of classes. Private variables and methods are typically used to allow a class to do internal work necessary to carry out the public requests made of it. Public variables and methods define what the class does. When you're designing a class you should think carefully about what your class should be able to do, and make those responsibilities public methods. For example, a toaster class should be able to take in some bread, and change the bread into toast.

```
package com.wiley.as3bible.kitchen
{
    public class HeatedResistorToaster extends Toaster
    {
        public function HeatedResistorToaster()
        {
            // initialize the toaster
        }

        public function toast(pieceOfBread:Bread):Bread
        {
            //do whatever we need to toast the bread
            return pieceOfBread;
        }
    }
}
```

The method toast() should be public because this is the core responsibility of a HeatedResistorToaster. Other code in your program should be able to use a toaster to toast bread. But you still need to add in the steps necessary that are going to toast that bread. The private variables and methods constitute the internal mechanics of the toaster that users of the toaster should not have to deal with.

```
package com.wiley.as3bible.kitchen
{
    public class HeatedResistorToaster extends Toaster
    {
        private var remainingToastSec:Number;
        private var insertedBread:Bread;
        private var resistor:Resistor;

        public function HeatedResistorToaster()
        {
```

```actionscript
        resistor = new Resistor();
        remainingToastSec = 0;
    }

    public function toast(pieceOfBread:Bread):Bread
    {
        insertedBread = pieceOfBread;
        startTimer(10);
        startCurrent(0.5);
        while (remainingToastSec > 0)
        {
            tick();
            remainingToastSec--;
        }
        stopTimer();
        stopCurrent();
        insertedBread = null;
        return pieceOfBread;
    }

    private function startTimer(toastDuration:Number):void
    {
        remainingToastSec = toastDuration;
    }

    private function startCurrent(currentAmps:Number):void
    {
        resistor.current = currentAmps;
    }

    private function tick():void
    {
        resistor.tick();
        insertedBread.toastiness += resistor.heat * 0.55667;
    }

    private function stopTimer():void
    {
        trace("The toaster sounds off a DING!");
    }

    private function stopCurrent():void
    {
        resistor.current = 0;
    }
    }
}
```

Now you've added a full algorithm to toast the bread. All these private functions and variables make up the way that heated resistor toasters make toast. First look at the properties you added.

The remainingToastSec variable represents the toaster's timer. When you put the bread in and start toasting, you shouldn't be able to fiddle with the time left, so remainingToastSec is private. The insertedBread variable keeps track of the bread inside the toaster to operate on. You can't mess with the bread inside the toaster after you plunge it in. The resistor is the wires or coils running inside the toaster that heat up and toast the bread. Messing with those could be dangerous! All these private variables are private because they represent either the state of the Toaster object or internal parts that are used in its business.

You also added several private methods to the class. These embody the steps that the machinery of the toaster follows to make bread into toast. If you were able to call startCurrent() from the outside, for example, you could force this toaster to unexpectedly become very hot, or if you were able to call startTimer() from the outside you could interrupt the toasting process.

The public properties and methods of a class make up its public interface. All non-public parts of the class are involved with its implementation. This is how access control enables you to practice encapsulation. The public interface of a HeatedResistorToaster is just a toast() method, but internally you see that it has a state and operations which help it do the toasting.

Protected

A drawback of private items is that they are not inherited by subclasses. So if the Toaster class had a private property finish that described its paint job, the HeatedResistorToaster would not be able to share it. We would have to add it again to the HeatedResistorToaster definition, and to any other class that derives from Toaster.

In the file com/wiley/as3bible/kitchen/Toaster.as:

```
package com.wiley.as3bible.kitchen
{
    public class Toaster
    {
        private var finish:String = "Reflective Silver";
    }
}
```

In the file com/wiley/as3bible/kitchen/HeatedResistorToaster.as:

```
package com.wiley.as3bible.kitchen
{
    public class HeatedResistorToaster extends Toaster
    {
        public function HeatedResistorToaster()
        {
```

```
                    trace(finish); //Compiler error! We don't have a finish.
                }
            }
        }
```

When you use inheritance to extend classes, and you want items in the superclass to be available to the subclass, use the protected attribute. A property or method declared as protected in a class will be available to any class that inherits from it.

NEW IN AS3 The protected **access control attribute is new to ActionScript 3.0. In ActionScript 2.0, the** private **attribute acted just like** protected **does in AS3. In other words,** private **is stricter in AS3 than AS2.**

To get the finish property to be available to Toaster's subclasses, you change its definition to protected. In the file com/wiley/as3bible/kitchen/Toaster.as:

```
package com.wiley.as3bible.kitchen
{
    public class Toaster
    {
        protected var finish:String = "Reflective Silver";
    }
}
```

In the file com/wiley/as3bible/kitchen/HeatedResistorToaster.as:

```
package com.wiley.as3bible.kitchen
{
    public class HeatedResistorToaster extends Toaster
    {
        public function HeatedResistorToaster()
        {
            trace(finish); //Reflective Silver
        }
    }
}
```

It's almost always a good idea to keep your classes open for extension. If, after you wrap up and deliver your toasting program, you find that you need more toasting power, you might decide to create a toaster class with multiple resistors. A quick way to do this would be to extend the HeatedResistorToaster class and add in a second resistor, modifying the startCurrent() and stopCurrent() methods to support two resistors. In order to do this, you would need to go back and make those methods protected instead of private. Whether private or protected, those methods are not available to classes outside the Toaster class hierarchy, so you haven't lost anything, but you needed to modify a class that you should have just been able to extend.

Unless you have a reason to hide a property or method from every class in the class hierarchy, or you're sure the class will never be extended, you should use `protected` over `private`. Using protected variables makes code easy to extend, even if you don't foresee a reason to right now. Use `protected` to encourage extension, and `final` to prohibit it.

> **TIP** The idea that you should be able to add on to your program without changing anything that's already written is a principle of object-oriented design called the *Open-Closed Principle*. According to the principle, code you write should be open for extension but closed for modification. This recognizes that code that's done means code that's been thought about, written, and tested. A lot of work has gone into it. It also recognizes that you should be able to add functionality to programs after you consider them "done," because even if you hate doing it, you always need to. Composition and inheritance are ways to add more functionality without touching code that already exists, and you should favor this to modifying completed, tested code.

Internal

The `internal` attribute is tied into the concept of packages. Frequently you have classes that need to work closely together, and sometimes have privileged access to each other: access that should not be generally open, but is acceptable within a certain group of classes. For example, in the toaster example, you had to modify the `toastiness` of the bread directly. But why would you need a toaster at all, if that attribute were publicly available? If `toastiness` were public, a `Bicycle` or a `Seagull` could go about toasting bread as if it were their business. This is definitely not desirable, but you have to have some way to change the properties of the bread. In this case, it might be a good idea to keep all the kitchenware classes in a `kitchen` package, including the `Bread` class, and to make `toastiness` an internal property. Now only kitchenware is allowed to modify the `toastiness` of bread.

In the file `com/wiley/as3bible/kitchen/Bread.as`:

```
package com.wiley.as3bible.kitchen
{
    public class Bread
    {
        internal var toastiness:Number = 0;
    }
}
```

Now you attempt to toast the bed from a non-kitchenware object. In the file `com/wiley/as3bible/bedroom/Pillow.as`:

```
package com.wiley.as3bible.bedroom
{
    import com.wiley.as3bible.kitchen.Bread;

    public class Pillow
    {
        public function Pillow()
```

```
        {
            var b:Bread = new Bread();
            b.toastiness = 20; //Compiler error! You can't do this!
        }
    }
}
```

Structuring packages in terms of modules or subsystems can help you add another level of organization above classes. When the `internal` attribute is used, you can hide implementation details of subsystems from outside, creating a kind of encapsulation for packages.

NEW IN AS3   The `internal` **access control attribute is a new addition to ActionScript 3.0.**

Namespaces

When you want even more control over who can access items, you can create a namespace. A namespace is a context in which names are unique, so we have already been creating namespaces, every time we write a new package. In this context, namespaces are used to collect arbitrary sets of functions, variables, and constants into one context regardless of where they are defined. Figure 3-6 shows a regular, controlled structure created by packages like `kitchen` and `bedroom`, and classes like `Pillow`, `Blender`, and `HeatedResistorToaster`. However, a namespace can contain whatever items you want. They let you break out of the order imposed by packages and classes, and overrule limitations of public, private, and protected access. In Figure 3-6, regardless of their natural grouping, seemingly unrelated methods like `Blender.puree()` and `Pillow.stuff()` can be grouped by creating a custom namespace like `foo`.

NOTE   **This type of namespace relates to which other classes can access a particular property or method. You may also use namespaces for XML. For more information about XML namespaces, see Chapter 10.**

NEW IN AS3   Namespaces and their use as access control modifiers are new to ActionScript 3.0.

There are three steps to gaining and sharing special access to items with namespaces. First, declare a new namespace. Second, determine what items belong in that namespace. For those items, use the namespace's name as a visibility modifier instead of `public`, `private`, `protected`, or `internal`. Third, in code that needs special access to the namespaced item, open the namespace that you created.

Creating your own namespace and using it as a visibility modifier for an item allows anyone who opens the namespace to access the item. It's like locking the item in a cupboard but leaving the key taped to it: it conveys the information that the item you are qualifying is meant only for certain uses, and requires you to be explicit that you are using it, but doesn't make it impossible to use.

FIGURE 3-6

A namespace collecting items in the same context regardless of their surrounding organization

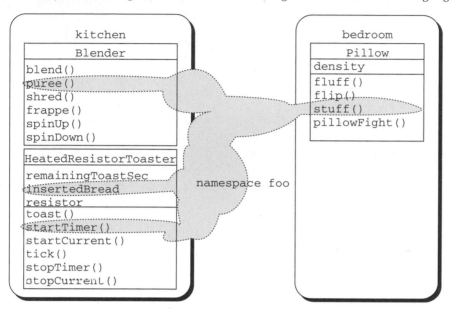

The Flex framework is an excellent example of the use of namespaces. Many of the properties and methods of classes in the framework are used by collaborating classes to help arrange them. However, these low-level functions should not be exposed to end users of the Flex components, so they are specified in the `mx_internal` namespace. When writing code that needs low-level control over components, you can dig deeper into the component classes simply by opening the `mx_internal` namespace and gaining access to the properties and methods.

You can create a new namespace with the `namespace` keyword. This item, too, must be able to be located from code that wishes to either put itself in the namespace or use code from the namespace. However, the namespace is usually used to allow communication between packages, so you would have to make the namespace itself public so that both packages can add their items to it.

```
package com.wiley.as3bible
{
    public namespace custom_namespace = "http://www.wiley.com/custom_namespace";
}
```

In this example, you define a namespace in its own file. Remember, this file should be named `com/wiley/as3bible/custom_namespace.as`. Now all code in this project should be able to use this namespace after importing it. The URL assigned to the namespace is optional. It allows the compiler to make sure that the namespace is truly unique by checking it against a presumably unique URL. Like package names, this is just a convention, and the URL is never fetched, nor does it have to really exist or contain anything at all.

To add items to this namespace, you simply use the namespace identifier as the access control attribute. First you have to import the namespace from its location in another package. When it is in the same package or the default package, this step is unnecessary.

```
package com.wiley.as3bible.package1
{
    import com.wiley.as3bible.custom_namespace;

    public class Class1
    {
        custom_namespace function sayHi():void
        {
            trace("Hi!");
        }
    }
}
```

NOTE The custom namespace is an alternative to the public, private, protected or internal namespaces. They cannot be used together.

Code in custom namespaces may also be unavailable to the rest of the class it is defined in, if that class does not open the namespace. For example, other methods in `Class1` would not be able to call `sayHi()`.

The following set of classes shows two ways to use methods defined in a namespace. In the file com/wiley/as3bible/package2/Class2.as:

```
package com.wiley.as3bible.package2
{
    public class Class2
    {
        import com.wiley.as3bible.package1.*;
        import com.wiley.as3bible.custom_namespace;

        use namespace custom_namespace;

        public function Class2()
        {
            var class1:Class1 = new Class1();
            class1.sayHi(); //Hi!
        }
    }
}
```

This class from `package2` is able to call the `sayHi()` method from a class in `package1`. The `use namespace` directive is like an `import` statement for namespaces. After opening the namespace with `use namespace`, all code in the class will be able to use items from that namespace.

```
package com.wiley.as3bible.package3
{
    public class Class3
    {
        import com.wiley.as3bible.package1.*;
        import com.wiley.as3bible.custom_namespace;

        public function Class3()
        {
            var class1:Class1 = new Class1();
            class1.custom_namespace::sayHi(); //Hi!
            class1.sayHi(); //Compiler error
        }
    }
}
```

This class from `package3` is also able to use the `sayHi()` method from `Class1`, without opening the namespace. To use items from a namespace on a per-case basis, qualify the item you wish to access with namespace followed by the name qualifier operator (`::`). We still have to import the namespace to be able to use it. Since the second attempted call to `sayHi()` doesn't qualify the namespace and the namespace isn't open, the compiler will keep you from accessing it.

Despite the detail given here, custom namespaces are infrequently needed. Like the Flex framework, namespaces might be best used for whole systems that have implementation details that should be hidden from most users when they are redistributed.

Using Methods in Classes

Through the examples in this chapter, you have already been exposed to dozens of methods, so let's formalize what you've already learned.

A method is a function that belongs to an object. (You learned about functions in Chapter 2.) Methods are used to carry out the responsibilities of the class they are declared on. They can take parameters and return values just like any other functions. Methods can be accessible to different sets of code based on the access modifier applied to them, and if none is specified, the default, `internal`, is used. Figure 3-7 shows all the different parts of a method declaration. This declaration is followed by the content of the method, which is a block of code enclosed in curly braces (`{}`) like any function's body.

FIGURE 3-7

Anatomy of a method declaration

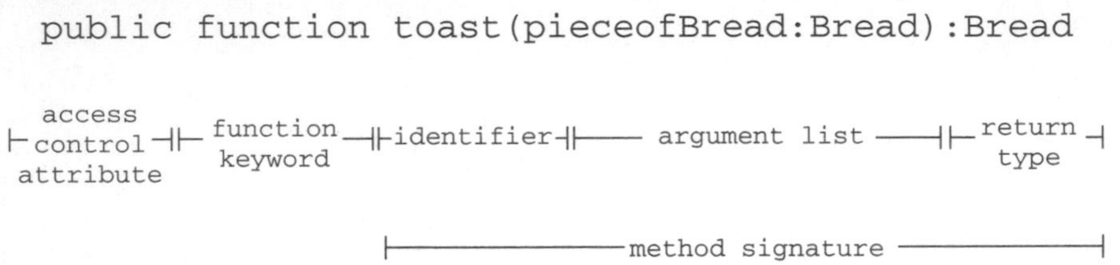

```
public function toast(pieceofBread:Bread):Bread
```

```
       access
      ├ control ┤├─ function ──┤├identifier┤├──── argument list ────┤├─ return ┤
      attribute      keyword                                          type

                    ├─────────────────── method signature ──────────────┤
```

It should be mentioned, briefly, that all coding conventions and styles are guidelines and not rules, and that they should be overall consistent. That having been said, methods are *verbs* and their names should be as well. The more descriptive a method name the better. If the verb has either a subject or adverbs, keep the verb first, as in `punchBear()`, which would punch a bear. Conventionally, you should use camel case for methods as you would variables, as discussed in Chapter 2.

Constructors

There is a special kind of method that you have also seen in many of the examples in this chapter. A *constructor* is a special method that executes when you create a new instance of the class with `new`. Its purpose is to initialize all the values of the object, create or retrieve collaborating objects where necessary, and put the object in a state where any of its public methods can be called without further ado.

Constructors are declared mostly like normal methods, except that:

- Constructors have the same name as the class they construct.
- There can only be one constructor per class. Omitting it is possible, in which case, the class will use an empty constructor.
- Constructors must use the `public` access control attribute.
- Constructors don't return anything, and don't specify a return type. However, you can think of the constructor as returning the newly created instance if it makes more sense that way, since the expression `new MyClass()` evaluates to the newly created instance of `MyClass`.

NEW IN AS3 In previous versions of ActionScript, the constructor could be declared `private`. In ActionScript 3.0, the constructor must always be `public`.

Take a look at the constructor from the `HeatedResistorToaster` class, from an earlier example:

```
public function HeatedResistorToaster()
{
    resistor = new Resistor();
    remainingToastSec = 0;
}
```

Note the lack of return type and return statement. The constructor sets the initial values for some of the state variables, and creates an object (`resistor`) that the class uses to do the toasting. If any public methods were called on the `HeatedResistorToaster` before this executed, they would generate runtime errors, because they all rely on the `resistor`, and the constructor would not have created it yet. Thankfully, we know that the constructor of a class runs as the class is instantiated, before you have the chance to call any methods on it. For any instance of any class, the constructor always runs first.

Constructors are allowed to take parameters like any other method, and those parameters are passed inside the parentheses in the new statement:

```
new SomeClass(12, "Helvetica", true);
```

There isn't much stylistic choice when it comes to constructors, since they inherit the name from their class. However, constructors should be the first method in a class listing. Usually when you write classes, the instance variables are grouped at the top, followed by the constructor, followed by public methods and finally non-public methods.

Using Properties in Classes

Properties, or instance variables, are variables that are part of an object. They can be used to store attributes of an object, or other objects it owns or is keeping track of. They can be defined like any other variable and they have the same access control attributes as methods. Constants are special properties that don't change values and are declared with the `const` keyword instead of `var`. Both constants and properties default to `internal` when no access control attribute is specified. Figure 3-8 illustrates the declaration of an instance variable.

FIGURE 3-8

A vivisected instance variable

```
internal var toastiness:Number = 0;
```

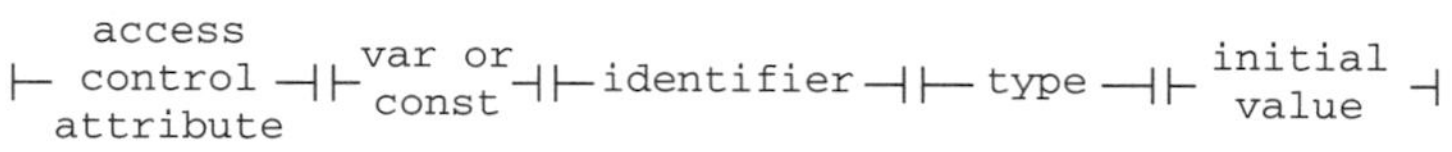

```
      access
   ├─ control ─┤├─ var or ─┤├─ identifier ─┤├─ type ─┤├─ initial ─┤
     attribute       const                                  value
```

The access control modifier, type, and initial assignment in a declaration like that in Figure 3-8 are all optional. Like methods, properties default to `internal` when another access control modifier is not specified.

Just like variables, properties are *nouns* and *adjectives* and should be named as such. They can be singular or plural. They should have descriptive names and be typed in camel case (see Chapter 2). Properties should be declared at the top of a class definition, before the constructor.

The choice to use initial values or not can be one of personal style. Any assignment that can be made at the declaration time of the property may also be made inside the constructor of the class with no ill effect. If initial values are used at all, they are typically used for Boolean properties, constant numbers and strings, and other simple values.

Accessors

In cases where the class is a simple datatype there is no shame in using public properties. For example, a point class that just collects three values is a good use of public properties:

```
package
{
    public class Point3d
    {
        public var x:Number;
        public var y:Number;
        public var z:Number;
    }
}
```

In general, however, public properties should be avoided in favor of accessors. Changing a property of an object by assigning directly to the property doesn't allow that object the opportunity to react to the change, and shifts the burden of updating the object to every other method which might need to know if the value has changed. It also doesn't give the object an opportunity to ensure the value assigned to its property is valid, so invalid input or code can easily trip up a perfectly working object.

Accessors fix this problem by allowing you to execute code when assignments are made to and when values are retrieved from an object. There are two kinds of accessors you can use in ActionScript 3.0, explicit and implicit.

Explicit accessors are normal functions that can retrieve and modify a property. There are no rules to explicit accessors, nor are they a special part of the language. They are typically implemented like this:

```
package com.wiley.as3bible.explicit
{
    public class Building
    {
```

```
//the height of the building in feet
private var _height:Number = 0;

public function setHeight(newHeight:Number):void
{
    if (!isNaN(newHeight) && newHeight >= 0
        && newHeight < Number.POSITIVE_INFINITY)
    {
        _height = newHeight;
        updateFloors();
    } else {
        throw new RangeError("Height must be finite and positive");
    }
}

public function getHeight():Number
{
    return _height;
}

private function updateFloors():void
{
    //Make sure the number of floors
    //jives with the height of the building
}
    }
}
```

The real, internal property is made to be private. One convention for handling properties with both a private version and public accessors is to name the private version of the property with a preceding underscore. Two normal methods are added to set and retrieve the property. These should be named setFoo() and getFoo() for the property named foo, and are appropriately called the setter and the getter.

In this example, the setter ensures that the attempted assignment is valid and only proceeds if it is. If an invalid assignment is attempted, the class throws a runtime error. For more on error handling, see Chapter 19. The setter also takes the opportunity to update the building's floors based on the new height. Otherwise, you would always have to be on your feet, checking that the two are in sync. By handling that at the only point it might happen, you can eliminate the problem.

Another thing you can do with accessors is to work with derived properties: values that aren't stored but are calculated on demand, masquerading as normal properties. For example, you could add to the Building class an accessor for the height of the building in inches:

```
public function getHeightInches():Number
{
    return getHeight() * 12;
}
```

When using explicit accessors, you must use method calls to manipulate the public properties of the class.

```
var b:Building = new com.wiley.as3bible.explicit.Building();
b.setHeight(100);
trace("The building is", b.getHeight(), "feet tall");
```

The second way to use accessors enables you to use dot notation as if the properties were public, but still intercept the assignment to do whatever you require. *Implicit accessors* are a special language feature and use the keywords get and set before the property names to define accessor functions. In other words, just add a space between set and height in the example:

```
package com.wiley.as3bible.implicit
{
    public class Building
    {
        //the height of the building in feet
        private var _height:Number = 0;

        public function set height(newHeight:Number):void
        {
            if (!isNaN(newHeight) && newHeight >= 0 ↵
                && newHeight < Number.POSITIVE_INFINITY)
            {
                _height = newHeight;
                updateFloors();
            } else {
                throw new RangeError("Height must be finite and positive");
            }
        }

        public function get height():Number
        {
            return _height;
        }

        private function updateFloors():void
        {
            //Make sure the number of floors
            //jives with the height of the building
        }

        public function get heightInches():Number
        {
            return height * 12;
        }
    }
}
```

Now to access the properties, you can use dot notation, and still reap the benefits of the range checking code:

```
var b:Building = new com.wiley.as3bible.implicit.Building();
b.height = 1000;
b.height = -12; //Error: Height must be finite and positive
```

> **TIP** You can also use implicit accessors to make a property read-only. Include a public implicit getter but omit the setter. The compiler will catch any attempts at setting the property from outside the class. In our `Building` example, the property `heightInInches` is, in addition to being derived, read-only.

> **NOTE** Implicit getters and setters are public by nature. You must always use the `public` keyword when defining them.

Avoid side effects

We just showed how to execute arbitrary code when a property assignment is made, but it's important that we issue a warning here. It's a good idea to use accessors to control access to properties and to ensure that a modified property has an immediate effect on anything that depends on it. However, when you call on an object to perform some task and in addition it performs something unrelated, this is known as a *side effect*, and although it is often convenient, it should generally be avoided. You should design your classes, methods, and properties so that they do what their names imply, and no more.

Methods as well as accessors can have side effects, so remember that setting values and performing actions should remain separate. It can be useful to be able to use implicit accessors to beef up handling of values, but don't use it to confuse adjectives with verbs.

Overriding Behavior

When using inheritance, sometimes you will want to make the child class do something that the parent class does, but differently. For example, you might want to make a `QuietSeagull`, which makes a much softer sound when it squawks. The superclass, or base class, of `Seagull`, already has a `squawk()` behavior, and by extending that class, your new subclass inherits that behavior.

Plain vanilla inheritance provides the new subclass with a starting point, which is all the public, internal, and protected properties and methods of the base class. But sometimes adding onto this starting point is not enough. Sometimes you have to change it.

You can *override* methods of a base class by using the `override` keyword. You can put this keyword before or after the access control attribute. Because you don't have access to them, you can't override any private methods from the superclass.

The `QuietSeagull` class might look something like this:

```
package
{
    public class QuietSeagull extends Seagull
    {
        override public function squawk():void
        {
            //A very polite seagull does not squawk,
            //despite what its parents may do.
            trace("...");
        }
    }
}
```

Now if you create several different kinds of seagull and ask them all to squawk, you'll find that the original Seagull, and all classes that extend it without overriding squawk(), act the same. But the QuietSeagull marches to the beat of his own very quiet drum:

```
var normalGull:Seagull = new Seagull();
var sportyGull:Seagull = new SoccerSeagull();
var quietGull:Seagull = new QuietSeagull();
normalGull.squawk(); //The seagull says 'SQUAAA!'
sportyGull.squawk(); //The seagull says 'SQUAAA!'
quietGull.squawk(); //...
```

You can only override methods of a class. You can't override properties, like the seagull's weight. However, by using accessors you can get around this. Because accessors are just methods, they can be overridden — even implicit accessors — to return a different value in the subclass. For example, you can convert the Seagull base class to expose its weight as an accessor rather than a public property, and override that. The side benefit is that the seagull's weight can become read-only, so that you can control the weight internally in response to eating and other behaviors, but disallow external modification of weight.

In the file Seagull.as:

```
package
{
    public class Seagull
    {
        public function get weight():Number
        {
            return 2;
        }

        public function squawk():void
        {
            trace("The seagull says 'SQUAAA!'");
        }
    }
```

```
        }
```

In the file `HungrySeagull.as`:

```
    package
    {
        public class HungrySeagull extends Seagull
        {
            override public function get weight():Number
            {
                return 1.5;
            }
        }
    }
```

Overriding methods is different from overloading methods. Overloading allows two methods to have the same name, if they have different argument lists. You can't do this in ActionScript 3.0. Overridden methods have to have the exact same signature as the original method. In ActionScript 3.0, you can only override methods.

Using the base class

When you override a function, you don't have to throw out everything that the base class did for you. You still have access to the non-private members and properties of the superclass, through the `super` object. Use `super` to add on to an existing method or call functionality in the superclass that has been overridden by other overrides.

You can create a very polite seagull that does everything a normal seagull does, but also apologizes afterwards. To make this work, you need to modify the main methods of a Seagull, but also to use the way they already work. Rather than copy that code, you depend on the superclass's implementation. This also means that changes in the implementation of methods on the base class will be reflected immediately in the subclasses.

```
    package
    {
        public class PoliteSeagull extends Seagull
        {
            override public function squawk():void
            {
                super.squawk();
                trace("The shy gull covers his mouth in shame.");
            }

            override public function fly():void
            {
                super.fly();
                trace("The gull lands and apologizes for blocking out the sun.");
            }
```

```
        override public function eat():void
        {
            trace("The gull apologizes to the animal it's about to eat.");
            super.eat();
        }
    }
}
```

The polite seagull example above shows that you can call the base class's methods, whether you call them before, after, or in the middle of the code you add.

```
var politeGull:Seagull = new PoliteSeagull(); //A new seagull appears
politeGull.eat();
/*The gull apologizes to the animal it's about to eat.
The seagull digs its beak into the sand, pulls up a tiny struggling crab,
and swallows it in one gulp.*/
```

The constructor, since it was not specified in this example, used a default constructor. You can see that a default constructor calls the superclass's constructor, because "A new seagull appears" is traced out. You can do something like overriding the constructor, but in fact, every class has a unique constructor. Instead of using the `override` keyword, just write your own constructor for the new class. Because it's a unique new method, the constructors of a superclass and a subclass can have completely different arguments, unlike overridden methods.

You see the superclass's constructor called in the above example because the default constructor consists of one line: a special function called `super()`. This method is bound to the superclass's constructor. You can use this method to control how the superclass's constructor gets called, but you can't prevent the superclass's constructor from being called. It must also be called in the first line of the constructor.

Using Static Methods and Properties

To recap, instance methods and instance properties are items that are defined in an object's class and exist in the object. A `Bicycle` class might have a property for the number of gears in the bike.

```
package
{
    public class Bicycle
    {
        private var _gears:Number;
        public function get gears():Number
        {
            return _gears;
        }

        public function Bicycle(numberOfGears:Number)
        {
```

```
            this._gears = numberOfGears;
        }
    }
}
```

This example uses accessors to good effect, enabling you to create a new `Bicycle` with any number of gears but never allowing you to change the number of gears once it is created. It does this by assigning the number of gears in the constructor and providing no setter for the property.

The concept here is that an instance variable, like `gears`, belongs to the particular instance. Each instance of `Bicycle` can have its own number of gears.

```
var eighteenSpeed:Bicycle = new Bicycle(18);
var fixedGear:Bicycle = new Bicycle(1);

trace(eighteenSpeed.gears); //18
trace(fixedGear.gears); //1
```

There are lots of other properties of a bicycle you could think of to make into instance variables, like the color of the bike, the size of the bike, or the kind of tires on the bike. There are some properties, however, that are part of the *definition* of a bicycle. All bicycles, by definition, have two wheels. These properties can be modeled by static variables.

Static variables

ActionScript 3.0 enables you to define methods and properties that belong to the class itself, rather than their instances. Since the number of wheels is part of the definition of a bicycle rather than a property of the bicycle itself, you can add this property to the class rather than the instance. This is called a class variable, or a static variable.

```
package
{
    public class Bicycle
    {
        public static var wheels:Number = 2;

        private var _gears:Number;
        public function get gears():Number
        {
            return _gears;
        }

        public function Bicycle(numberOfGears:Number)
        {
            this._gears = numberOfGears;
        }
    }
}
```

NOTE The static keyword can be written before or after the access control attribute. The convention is to write it after the visibility modifier as shown above.

By adding the static keyword, you are defining the variable wheels as part of the class instead of the instance. All Bicycle objects will now share the same wheels variable. Even if you create a fleet of a thousand bikes, they will all share this class variable and any changes to it will immediately affect all of the objects.

Now that wheels is a static variable, you use it differently. It belongs to the class Bicycle, so you use dot notation to access it from the class, not the instance!

```
var fixedGear:Bicycle = new Bicycle(1);
trace(fixedGear.wheels); //Wrong! Compiler error.
trace(Bicycle.wheels); //Right! 2
```

All of the normal access rules still apply, so you can only write Bicycle.wheels because wheels was defined as public. Remember that you can only see the Bicycle class because it, too, is public!

Code that goes inside the class can access the wheels variable without writing out Bicycle.wheels. Since it is in the same class as the static variable is defined in, the variable is in scope. However, many people think that it's good style to always reference static variables with their class names. This way, every time you reference a static variable it's quite clear that it's static and not an instance variable. Below you add code to the constructor of your Bicycle that uses the static variable.

```
package
{
    public class Bicycle
    {
        static public var wheels:Number = 2;

        private var _gears:Number;
        public function get gears():Number
        {
            return _gears;
        }

        public function Bicycle(numberOfGears:Number)
        {
            this._gears = numberOfGears;
            for (var i:int = 0; i < Bicycle.wheels; i++)
            {
                //Prepare a wheel.
            }
        }
    }
}
```

Static constants

When you think about it, since the number of wheels is part of the definition of a bicycle, the `wheels` variable should not only belong to the `Bicycle` class, it should be a constant as well. You can easily have static constants—constants that belong to the class instead of the instance.

```
package
{
    public class Bicycle
    {
        static public const WHEELS:Number = 2;

        //the rest of the class...
    }
}
```

In fact, it turns out that most values that must remain fixed must also remain fixed across all instances of a class. This is not a rule, but a common use. Things like terminal velocity, the melting point of lead, and the number of letters in the alphabet are constants, but also constants that can remain constant across instances, and which you would write as static. When a constant doesn't change between instances of a class, and when you need to be able to access a constant without constructing an instance of the class that owns it, use static constants.

Static constants also allow for some very useful techniques that are worth mentioning here.

String comparisons, and string parameters, can be very messy. Consider the following function that we might place in the `Bicycle` class:

```
package
{
    public class Bicycle
    {
        public function performTrick(trickName:String):void
        {
            switch (trickName)
            {
                case "wheelie":
                    //code goes here to wheelie
                    break;
                case "bunnyhop":
                    //code goes here to bunny hop
                    break;
                case "stoppie":
                    //code goes here to stoppie
                    break;
            }
        }
    }
}
```

This will perform the right kind of trick based on the name of the trick you pass it. The problem here is that if you misspell the trick accidentally, nothing will happen, which is disappointing. You might end up scratching your head, wondering where your error is, without realizing that there's no error except the spelling of the trick.

```
var stuntBike:Bicycle = new Bicycle();
stuntBike.performTrick("wheely"); //nothing happens
```

However, if we replace all the strings with constants:

```
package
{
    public class Bicycle
    {
        public static const WHEELIE:String = "wheelie";
        public static const BUNNYHOP:String = "bunnyhop";
        public static const STOPPIE:String = "stoppie";

        public function performTrick(trickName:String):void
        {
            switch (trickName)
            {
                case Bicycle.WHEELIE:
                    //code goes here to wheelie
                    break;
                case Bicycle.BUNNYHOP:
                    //code goes here to bunny hop
                    break;
                case Bicycle.STOPPIE:
                    //code goes here to stoppie
                    break;
            }
        }
    }
}
```

The compiler will catch that spelling mistake, since there is no WHEELY constant.

```
var stuntBike:Bicycle = new Bicycle();
stuntBike.performTrick(Bicycle.WHEELY); //compiler error
```

> **NOTE** If you use a development environment with code hinting such as Flex Builder 2, you can use the auto-completion features to help you find the valid trick name interactively.

This practice is used heavily in the events package, but can be used any time you need to compare against a special string. You can do even more with this case, however. Really, you'd like a trick to be its own type, which can have the values of wheelie, bunnyhop, or stoppie. Right now it's a String with special values defined in the Bicycle class, where arguably they don't belong.

Enumerations

A custom type you create which can only have certain discrete values is called an *enumeration*. ActionScript 3.0 does not have built-in support for enumerations, but they're easy enough to build. You could create a `Trick` class that enumerates the kinds of tricks the bike supports:

```
package
{
    public final class Trick
    {
        public static const WHEELIE:Trick = new Trick();
        public static const BUNNYHOP:Trick = new Trick();
        public static const STOPPIE:Trick = new Trick();
    }
}
```

This might seem odd at first, but `WHEELIE` is not only a static property of the `Trick` class, but an instance of `Trick` as well. By making the tricks instances of `Trick` and not just strings stored by `Trick`, you can type variables as `Tricks`. Now you can make sure that the parameter passed to the `performTrick()` function is a real `Trick`, not just some bogus string that may or may not be valid. All you have to do is change the signature of the function to accept a `Trick` parameter instead of a `String` parameter.

Enumeration classes are also ideal final classes. Because you're probably writing code based on the assumption that the enumeration only contains certain values, creating a subclass that adds values will prove a messy mistake. This is one of those cases in which modifying your original code is better than creating a subclass.

Static methods

Variables and constants aren't the only code that can belong to a class. There can also be methods that operate independently of any instance. These static methods must not access any instance variables, since they will be run by the class itself, possibly before the class is ever instantiated.

Static methods can be used in cases where you want to run some code before the object is actually created. In the following example, you replace a normal constructor with a static method. You can use this method to create new instances of the object.

```
package
{
    public class LimitedEdition
    {
        private static var editionsMade:int = 0;
        private static const MAX_EDITIONS:int = 20;

        private var serialNumber:int;

        public function LimitedEdition(serialNumber:int)
        {
```

```
            this.serialNumber = serialNumber;
        }

        public static function getOne():LimitedEdition
        {
            if (editionsMade++ < MAX_EDITIONS)
            {
                return new LimitedEdition(editionsMade);
            }
            return null;
        }

        public function toString():String
        {
            return "Limited Edition Object #" + serialNumber;
        }
    }
}
```

This object is a limited edition. Only 20 may be created, and they are indelibly branded with their serial number when they are created. A class variable and class constant are used to keep track of the number of instances made already and the total number of instances that can be made. Because the number of instances created is kept inside the class, it is intransient, able to exist inside LimitedEdition regardless of whether there are any LimitedEdition objects in existence. After the target number of editions has been created, the static creation method refuses to return a new one.

Just like a class variable, you call class methods by using dot notation on the class name. The getOne() static method is a function you call on the class to return an instance, and keep track of how many LimitedEdition instances have been created. In contrast, the toString() instance method is called on an instance to determine what your object will look like represented as a string:

```
for (var i:int = 0; i < 50; i++)
{
    var obj:LimitedEdition = LimitedEdition.getOne();
    trace(obj.toString());
}
/*
prints out:
Limited Edition Object #1
Limited Edition Object #2
Limited Edition Object #3
Limited Edition Object #4
Limited Edition Object #5
...
Limited Edition Object #19
```

```
Limited Edition Object #20
null
null
null
null
...
null
*/
```

This approach still has a weakness, though. Remember that one of the requirements of a constructor is that it's public. Therefore, you can't prevent the ability to create new instances by bypassing your static creator method and calling the constructor. This can be overcome by throwing an exception in the constructor or some clever trickery (you'll learn about exceptions in Chapter 19). The important thing about this example is that static methods can be used when there is no instance of the class to speak of, and these methods can work with other static variables and methods.

Another way that static methods are frequently used is to create utility classes. Utility classes are classes that aren't meant to be instantiated, and exist to group together some related functions, all of which are declared statically. Because of this, utility classes aren't really object-oriented, and if you rely on them too much you might end up programming procedurally instead of object-oriented.

A poster child for utility classes is the Math class, which you will explore in Chapter 7. Math provides a bunch of really useful mathematical functions all in one place, so it's a great utility. You would never create a new Math object, but you would definitely call its static method Math.pow(2, 10) to raise 2 to the 10th power or access the Math.PI static constant for the value of π.

Static accessors

You can create static implicit and explicit accessors, as well. Simply use the static keyword with your method names, and you can create static properties that are derived or read-only. Keep in mind, however, that static methods — accessors included — can't call non-static methods of the class.

Designing Interfaces

When you extend a base class, you have the opportunity to override any of its methods and provide new behavior. You also can't help but inherit all the existing methods and variables that aren't declared private. Inheritance is useful for augmenting existing classes with new functionality, but it has its drawbacks.

Being forced to start off with all the methods and properties of the superclass is a drawback. If you want a family of classes to perform the same kind task in radically different ways, it can be stifling to have to work around existing code.

You could work around this by having a relatively empty base class that your family of classes all extend. But then you are presented with another problem: this base class is a perfectly valid, although entirely ineffectual class. So the empty base class could be instantiated and used in your program, achieving nothing where something was undoubtedly expected.

You are also presented with the problem of multiple inheritance. Classes can only extend one other class. This enables you to create a class hierarchy in the shape of a tree and not an acid-induced spider web. Single inheritance makes sense when you're modeling your classes after whole, fully thought-out objects: an object can't be both a house and a hamburger, but an object *can* perform two different kinds of tasks. A tree belongs both to a class of objects that provides shelter and a class of objects that can yield food. It would be nice to be able to use the tree as a provider of food when you need food and use it as a provider of shelter when you need shelter.

What you're working towards is a completely abstract item that classes can implement in different ways, and that you can combine more than one of in one class. An *interface* fulfills these requirements. Interfaces are representations of a certain ability which don't say anything about how the ability will be carried out, but say how you will ask the ability to be carried out. Interfaces are not classes, and they can't be instantiated. They contain no code. Put another way, interfaces are contracts. When you choose to implement an interface, it's entirely up to you how to do it, but you must meet its specifications, and fulfill its contract. If inheritance is an "is a" relationship and composition is a "has a" relationship, then implementing an interface is a "can do" relationship.

This can be best explained in an example. This interface would be stored in a file called `IPowerable.as`:

```
package
{
    public interface IPowerable
    {
        function turnOn(volts:Number):void;
        function turnOff():void;
        function getPowerUse():Number;
    }
}
```

> **NOTE**   In ActionScript 3.0, type annotations — additions to the name of an item to indicate its usage or type — are not required, nor are they typically used. However, it remains customary to prefix interfaces with the letter `I` as in `IPowerable`.

No access control attribute is required on methods defined in an interface, because interfaces define the public interface to an object. The methods must by definition be public. Interfaces may not specify properties, but they may specify explicit or implicit accessor functions.

The interface `IPowerable` creates a promise of some kind of behavior. It specifies how things that can be powered will work with the outside world. The interface specifies a contract that the compiler guarantees will be followed in classes that choose to be `IPowerable`.

Classes that implement this interface can do much, much more than these three methods, but they are required to implement these three methods themselves.

Clearly the set of objects that can draw power can have very diverse behaviors. A lamp, for example, draws electricity and produces light:

```
package
{
    public class Lamp implements IPowerable
    {
        private var watts:Number;
        private var isOn:Boolean;

        public function Lamp(wattage:Number)
        {
            watts = wattage;
            isOn = false;
        }

        public function turnOn(volts:Number):void
        {
            isOn = true;
            trace("it gets brighter!");
        }

        public function turnOff():void
        {
            isOn = false;
            trace("it gets darker.");
        }

        public function getPowerUse():Number
        {
            return (isOn)? watts : 0;
        }
    }
}
```

The `Lamp` class fulfills the contract set out by the `IPowerable` interface by declaring the three methods in the interface with identical method signatures. The names of the parameters don't matter for a method's signature, but the types, order, and number of those parameters do. The `implements` keyword is used to make the class adhere to the interfaces that are specified. A class can both extend another class and implement an interface at once, but the `extends` section must come before the `implements` section.

You can create objects that implement the interface in very different ways. The toaster, for example, doesn't actually start drawing current until you put in a piece of toast and start toasting.

However, as far as `IPowerable` is concerned, as long as it can do `turnOn()`, `turnOff()`, and `getPowerUse()`, the object is an `IPowerable`.

```
package
{
    public class Toaster implements IPowerable
    {
        private var isOn:Boolean;
        private var isToasting:Boolean;

        public function turnOff():void
        {
            isOn = false;
            isToasting = false;
        }

        public function getPowerUse():Number
        {
            if (isToasting) {
                return 100;
            } else {
                return 0;
            }
        }

        public function turnOn(volts:Number):void
        {
            isOn = true;
        }

        public function toast(pieceOfBread:Bread):Bread
        {
            if (!isOn)
            {
                trace("nothing happens");
                return pieceOfBread;
            }
            trace("your bread gets toasty");
            isToasting = true;
            pieceOfBread.toastiness += 10;
            return pieceOfBread;
        }
    }
}
```

To use the `Lamp` and `Toaster` classes, we create and manipulate them like you normally would. But certain other classes just don't care what kind of appliance an object is, as long as it implements the `IPowerable` interface. Just like an interface is an agreement about how to use objects that implement it, the electrical system, too, is an interface. It says (in the United States) that as long as you insert a plug shaped like two prongs, you'll get 120 volts of current alternating at 60 Hz, and if the plug has a rounded pin below the prongs, you'll get a grounded connection. This is an agreement that would definitely fry everything you own if either appliance makers or electric companies decided to deviate from it. But because this interface is in place, you can take any electrical appliance you can think of and get electricity as easily and safely as sliding in a plug. Little agreements like this really do make the world go around, like the hundreds of protocols in use on the Internet today, our expectations about how to push buttons and tap keys, the common way you expect to use all kinds of cars. Interfaces allow systems to work together based on certain expectations of each other and not on their actual implementation.

Given this, we should be able to build a power strip that can power all your appliances at once. The power strip doesn't care what you plug into it, as long as what you plug into it is IPowerable. Lamps and Toasters may come from completely different families of classes, but with interfaces, we can treat any object in terms of what it *agrees to do*, rather than what it is.

```
package
{
    public class PowerStrip implements IPowerable
    {
        private var appliances:Array;

        public function PowerStrip()
        {
            appliances = new Array();
        }

        public function addAppliance(appliance:IPowerable):void
        {
            appliances.push(appliance);
        }

        public function turnOn(volts:Number):void
        {
            for each (var appliance:IPowerable in appliances)
            {
                appliance.turnOn(volts);
            }
        }

        public function turnOff():void
        {
            for each (var appliance:IPowerable in appliances)
            {
                appliance.turnOff();
            }
        }
```

```
        public function getPowerUse():Number
        {
            var powerDraw:Number = 0;
            for each (var appliance:IPowerable in appliances)
            {
                powerDraw += appliance.getPowerUse();
            }
            return powerDraw;
        }
    }
}
```

Furthermore, this power strip should be power-able itself, so we can encapsulate all of the appliances in one object. As far as the electrical system is concerned, the appliances in your house are one big appliance. This is great object-oriented stuff: you can aggregate many objects into one and utilize that single object, abstracting away the details of its constituents. Isn't it more convenient in real life to turn off a power strip than to individually turn off all of the things plugged into it?

Notice that in all the `for..each` loops, and in the `addAppliance()` function, you use `IPowerable` as a type. As long as you can agree that the object implements `IPowerable`, and limit yourself to the abilities that `IPowerable` specifically guarantees, there can't be any problem. This is what we mean by programming in terms of abilities instead of classes.

Now create a bunch of appliances and then test out the power strip.

```
var powerStrip:PowerStrip = new PowerStrip();
var heater:Heater = new Heater(10);
var toaster:Toaster = new Toaster();
var readingLamp:Lamp = new Lamp(25);
var overheadLamp:Lamp = new Lamp(60);
powerStrip.addAppliance(heater);
powerStrip.addAppliance(toaster);
powerStrip.addAppliance(readingLamp);
powerStrip.addAppliance(overheadLamp);
toaster.toast(new Bread()); //nothing happens
  powerStrip.turnOn(120);
  //it gets warmer! it gets brighter! it gets brighter!
trace(powerStrip.getPowerUse()); //1285
toaster.toast(new Bread()); //your bread gets toasty
trace(powerStrip.getPowerUse()); //1385
powerStrip.turnOff();
  //it gets cold. it gets darker. it gets darker.
```

Note that although it does adhere to the `IPowerable` interface, the `toaster` variable still holds a `Toaster` reference, and it can still use methods specific to `Toaster` like `toast()`. You don't lose anything by implementing the interface.

A class can implement multiple interfaces, like the earlier tree example. To implement multiple interfaces, just separate the interface names with commas, so the tree example might look like:

```
public class Tree extends Plant implements IShelterProvider, IFoodProvider
```

NOTE **Interface names often end in -able, since they describe an ability. However, sticking to this nomenclature can often end in awkward interface names, and we recommend that you drop it when it doesn't make sense.**

Interfaces can also extend other interfaces. For example, you might use this to create a category of objects that can be subscribed to as an event source in addition to the categorical ability. You could achieve this by extending the built-in `IEventDispatcher` interface. See more about event sources in Part IV.

The use of interfaces is encouraged by object-oriented designers because it keeps down dependencies between concrete classes. The more dependencies you create, the less opportunity you leave for yourself to change your program without impacting existing code, and less maintainable your code becomes as the web of interdependencies becomes exponentially thicker. As we've mentioned, interfaces allow you to address objects not in terms of what they are, but in terms of the minimum you need them to do, and this can give you micro control of how you deal with objects. Because objects can implement many interfaces, they can be one thing to one class and another thing to another class, as necessity dictates.

A principal rule of object-oriented design is "program to an interface, not an implementation." The usage of "interface" here does not necessarily mean `interface`, it could also mean a superclass or whatever is the most generic type that gives you the abilities you need at that time. Implementations change, but interfaces should not: we have laptops now that people wouldn't believe 10 years ago, but a time-traveler could take them back in time and demonstrate them perfectly, because the interface for drawing power has not changed, nor has the idea of typing on a keyboard and watching a display.

Manipulating Types

The type system enables you to refer to an object by its own class, by any of its superclasses, by any interface it implements, or by a combination of these. All of these potential types for an object are valid because by being more specific it must implement a superset of all the more general type's functionality. A `Square` is still a `Rectangle` because it is a specific kind of `Rectangle`, and it is a `Shape` because it is a very specific kind of `Shape`. It might also be an `IPointCollection` if it can provide a set of points that comprise its vertices. The point is that these aren't conversions: the class really is all of the things that it extends.

Because you can refer to a class by many names, you need ways to get between these types. You should be able to test at runtime if an object is an instance of a given class or implements a particular interface. You should be able to convert a specific type to a general type, and you should be able to attempt to convert general types to specific types, and we should even be allowed to attempt to convert types to unrelated types.

Type compatibility and coercion

Some types can be converted without any explicit action. Since any specific class is also a more general class, you can convert it to the more general type without writing any explicit code.

```
var square:Rectangle = new Square();
```

Again, this isn't really a conversion at all, but a renaming. These types are compatible. A Square is a Rectangle.

In addition, there are certain unrelated type conversions which ActionScript 3.0 knows how to make for you and will do so without asking. This is called coercion, or implicit type conversion. ActionScript 3.0 knows how to convert anything to a Boolean, for example, making the following kind of code tricks possible:

```
var array:Array = ["hello", "world"];
var obj:Object;
//Pull a value off the front of the array, set obj to that value,
//and check if obj converts to true or false. Stop the loop when
//the value converts to false. Null is returned by shift() when
//there are no more values in the array. Null converts to false.
while (obj = array.shift())
{
    trace(obj);
}
//hello
//world

var str:String = "";
//Set a default string if the string doesn't exist or is empty.
//Both empty strings and null values convert to false.
//Negating false gives you true so the conditional runs if
//the string is empty, giving it a default value instead.
if (!str) str = "Default";
trace(str); //Default

for (var i:int = 1; i < 4; i++)
{
    //Trace out the number (i) and whether it is odd or even.
    //i % 2 is the remainder when you divide it by two, always
    //a whole number. Any number converts to true, except 0
    //which converts to false. So when the remainder after
    //dividing by two is zero, the conditional is false.
    trace(i, (i % 2)? "odd" : "even");
}
//1 odd
//2 even
//3 odd
```

The first trick shows that any object is `true` but `null` is `false`. The second trick shows that an empty string is `false`. The third shows that an integer is `false` if it's 0 and `true` otherwise.

Similarly, ActionScript 3.0 uses an object's `toString()` method to automatically convert any object to a `String`, using the `Object` class's `toString()` method if no other class up the hierarchy defines it. Please see Chapter 9 for more about the `Object` class.

Other implicit type conversions are available to ActionScript 3.0 base types, but these are discussed in the chapters having to do with their types. For example, `XML` can convert to a `String` automatically when used in a string context.

Explicit type conversion

You can also induce type conversion. ActionScript 3.0 provides two kinds of checked cast that enable you to attempt to convert from one type to another. A cast attempts to fit a type into another type. If they are compatible, the conversion will continue, and the expression will result in the new type. The types of cast differ in how they act when the conversion fails.

Another bit of terminology is the *direction* of a cast. An upcast is a type conversion *up* the inheritance chain, toward the more general. This kind of cast is always successful, and, as you have seen, can be achieved implicitly, without a cast operation at all. A downcast is a type conversion *down* the inheritance chain, toward the more specific. Since you can't have any guarantee that a particular `Rectangle` is a `Square`, if you try to cast it without looking, the cast might fail.

FIGURE 3-9

Upcasting and downcasting

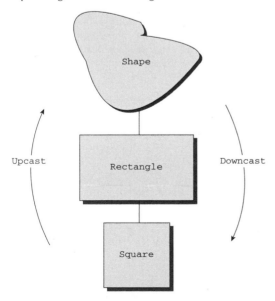

We will demonstrate these casts with a downcast, since it is likely to be unsuccessful, and you can see how the types of cast differ when the casts fail. The first kind of cast you can perform is safer and preferable in most cases. To cast a variable to a type, surround the name of the instance with parentheses and put the type name before it, as if you were calling its constructor but without the new operator:

```
var someShape:Shape = getRandomShape(); //get some unknown shape
Square(someShape); //treat it as a Square
```

In the above example, presume for the sake of argument that you have obtained a shape, but you don't know what kind of shape it is. This could happen when a method returns a general class rather than a specific one. This is represented with the method call getRandomShape().

If the conversion is not successful — in this case, if someShape was actually a Rectangle with different width and height — this cast will throw a TypeError. To learn more about how to handle these errors, and why they are your friend, see Chapter 19.

In order to capture the result of this cast, you probably want to store the result of the cast in a variable of the type you cast it to:

```
var mySquare:Square = Square(someShape);
```

The second kind of cast does not throw an error if the cast fails, but rather the cast will evaluate to null. An error is usually better, because as you test your program, you are immediately stopped where the cast fails, and not later, when this unexpected null causes some other error elsewhere and becomes a mysterious bug. That said, this kind of cast is achieved with the as operator, which treats the object on the left of the operator as if it were the class on the right.

```
var mySquare:Square = someShape as Square;
```

NEW IN AS3   In previous versions of ActionScript, there was only the constructor-style cast, but it behaved like the as-cast does in ActionScript 3.0, returning undefined when the type conversion was unsuccessful. In AS3, the new as-cast returns null on failure, and the constructor-style cast throws an error on failure.

One extremely common application of casting is when retrieving objects from a collection. Because ActionScript 3.0 does not support templates or generics, collections like Arrays simply store Objects, and when you retrieve values from these collections, they are returned as Objects, since ActionScript can make no guarantees as to the contents of the array. So whenever you must iterate over items from a collection, you can cast these items into the class you know they originally were. Because they come out as Object, this is always going to be a downcast unless you were storing Object instances.

Another benefit of the constructor-style cast is that it takes advantage of several intelligent conversion functions, which are cleverly disguised as cast operators. The top level of ActionScript 3.0 includes, among other top-level functions like trace() and isNaN(), several functions that when applied have exactly the same syntax as a cast. These functions behave just like a cast, too, but instead of failing to convert unrelated types, they perform an intelligent conversion. For example, the function XML() looks just like a cast to XML but will convert XML text in a String into an actual XML object, whereas a cast would fail.

```
var myXml:XML = XML("<root><party><time>Now</time> ↵
<location>Here</location></party></root>");
trace(myXml.party[0].time); //Now
```

Because these top-level functions act just like a cast (but more intelligent) and masquerade as cast operators, now that you know they exist you can blissfully ignore them. Keep using the constructor-style cast, and you will benefit automatically from a few conversion functions.

Determining types

To determine if an object is compatible with a class, you can use the is operator. This is a binary operator, not a function, so the syntax for using it is:

```
//get a shape from somewhere in the program
var someShape:Shape = getRandomShape();
if (someShape is Circle)
{
    (someShape as Circle).circumference;
}
```

Here, only circles have circumferences, so if you can determine that the shape is a Circle, you can then safely retrieve its circumference. Because the circumference property is only defined on instances of Circle, even though you know the someShape instance is in reality a Circle, you must convert its type to Circle before accessing Circle properties.

Also note that because you checked that the instance was a Circle type, there was no danger in performing the downcast, as you just checked its type compatibility in the line above it.

NEW IN AS3 The is operator is new to ActionScript 3.0, and replaces the instanceof operator from ActionScript 2.0.

It is important to note that is determines the compatibility of a type, not the exact type of the instance.

```
var s:Shape = new Square();
trace(s is Square); //true
trace(s is Rectangle); //true
```

There is actually a great deal more you can do with the type of objects, including determining the exact type of instances, and retrieving class references from the name of a class alone, but these topics, generally called *reflection*, are advanced techniques not covered in this chapter.

Creating Dynamic Classes

The last kind of class is saved for the end because it should be used rarely and with care. Dynamic classes are classes whose properties and methods can be changed, added, and removed at runtime. This works against the type system and many object-oriented principles, but it can be convenient for some needs.

You can create a dynamic class by adding the keyword `dynamic` to the class definition.

```
public dynamic class ShapeShifter
```

For a discussion of the benefits and properties of dynamic classes, see Chapter 9, the chapter about `Object`, everyone's favorite dynamic class. For most cases where you need a dynamic class, you might be satisfied by using an `Object` instance instead of an instance of a custom dynamic class.

Summary

- Classes are the templates for objects, the building blocks of your program.
- Objects have both data and operations.
- Classes should encapsulate their implementations and provide a simple interface.
- Classes are placed in packages, which structure and allow unique names for classes.
- Objects have a type, which is the class they are an instance of.
- All variables are objects, even numbers and Booleans.
- Objects have methods and properties, and classes can have static methods and static variables.
- You can use `public`, `private`, `protected`, `internal`, and custom namespaces to encapsulate and allow access to your objects.
- Classes can inherit from other classes, automatically inheriting public and protected properties and methods.
- Classes can only inherit from one other class, so all the classes can be drawn in a tree, and each class can have an inheritance chain up to the top of the tree.
- Classes should be closed for modification and open for extension.
- The public interface of a class is all of its public methods and properties, and is how the class appears to the outside world.
- Interfaces define a contract that classes can choose to follow to provide some ability.
- You can use interfaces as types, so that you can decouple your code from implementations.
- Types can be inspected, automatically coerced, or explicitly cast.

Chapter 4

Working with Methods and Functions

Now that you know all about creating variables, you probably want to start actually *doing* something with them. This is where methods and functions come in. Functions are reusable blocks of code that can be defined in your own classes and are frequently used throughout the ActionScript 3.0 API.

Functions allow you to organize your code into independent pieces of functionality. They can be used to return various results based on input you provide. Perhaps most important, functions can encapsulate behaviors and functionality within a class and provide a public interface to that functionality. This chapter covers ways to use functions and create your own from scratch.

If there's one thing to remember about ActionScript it's that *every variable and part of a class is an object.* Functions are no exception. While it might be strange to imagine, functions are instances of the Function class and contain their own methods and properties. In this chapter, we talk about how functions can be used as objects.

Understanding Functions

At the most basic level, a function is a piece of code that has been stored as a saved routine that can be run at will by writing out the function's name or *calling* the function. Every program you write will rely heavily upon functions.

Understanding the difference between methods and functions

You will hear both the words "method" and "function" (and sometimes even function closure) used to describe a reusable block of code. Although they are often used interchangeably, there is a slight difference. A method is any function defined within a class. Methods should be logically associated with the instance of the class and tend to act in conjunction with the object in which they're defined. For example, a Kitty class might define a function called meow(). In this case, meow() would be a method of the Kitty class.

The term "method" is a distinction in name only — in other words, methods do not have any additional abilities and there is no "method" keyword. Here's an example of how you might call a fictitious function:

```
addElementToGroup(myGroup, myElement);
```

Now here's the same function call if it were written as a method:

```
myGroup.addElement(myElement);
```

As you can see, the two calls are similar, but the latter is designed to act on the myGroup instance.

In this book we use both terms. We use "function" for general usage, but when describing functionality specific to a function defined within a class, we use the term "method." Because almost all functions in ActionScript are stored within classes, most of them are methods.

NEW IN AS3 Unlike AS2, which makes frequent use of the Delegate class, methods in AS3 are bound to the instances in which they are contained. They will execute as if they are being called from within that instance even if the function is passed into another scope. This ability of ActionScript 3.0 is known as a *method closure*.

Calling a function

Executing the code within a function or method is known as *calling* or *invoking*. Functions in ActionScript are called by using the function's name followed by a pair of parentheses (). Officially, these parentheses are known as the *call operator*.

Additional information can be passed on to your functions by adding *arguments* (also known as *parameters*) inside the parentheses and separated by commas. Some functions will have optional or required arguments. The number and type of values passed in must match the function definition, also called a *method signature*. Other functions require no arguments at all and are called by using an empty pair of parentheses.

These are both valid function calls:

```
trace("Hello world!");
addChild(mySprite);
```

> **TIP**   Be careful not to forget the parentheses operator when calling a function. Doing so will evaluate the function as a variable (an object of type `Function`) rather than executing the code within the function producing unexpected results. You will see later in the chapter how and when to use functions without the parentheses operator.

Calling functions vs. calling methods

When accessing methods within a particular instance, use the name of the containing object followed by a dot and then the method call. This is called *dot syntax*. You can think of this as calling a function within the context of the object.

```
var nameList:Array = new Array();
nameList.push("Daniel", "Julia", "Paul");
nameList.reverse();
trace(nameList); // Displays: "Paul", "Julia", "Daniel"
```

> **NOTE**   Some ActionScript statements or operators, such as `typeof` or `delete`, are not technically functions even though they appear to behave the same way. As such, you will not need to add parentheses around the arguments for these commands and won't be able to access Function methods and properties for these reserved words. Consequently, these operators, unlike most functions, exist globally and will be available anywhere in your code.

Creating Custom Functions

To create your own methods, you add function statements to your class declaration files. This is called *defining* or *declaring* a function. Let's take a look at how this is done.

Defining a function

Function statements share this basic structure:

```
public function doSomething(arg1:Object, arg2:Object):void {
    // the executed code goes here.
}
```

Let's break it down one word at a time.

- `public`: The access control attribute, which is usually a keyword such as `public`, `private`, or `internal`, is used to define whether other classes will be able to access the method. If you're defining a function outside of a package (such as on the timeline in Flash CS3), you should leave this part out. You should always define a namespace for your methods; however, for simplicity, some of the examples in this book may leave this out.

- `function`: Next is the `function` keyword. This is always required when defining a function just as `var` is always required when defining a variable.

- `doSomething`: Immediately after the `function` keyword is the name of your function. This is the command you will call when you want to run the function.

> **TIP**   The best function names are descriptive, describe an action, and can be read easily as though you were reading a sentence. A good rule of thumb is that your function name will start with a verb. For example, `button()` is not as useful as `drawButton()`. Likewise, the best variable names are usually nouns. Together, you can combine verb and noun to create a short sentence such as `snakeHandler.feed(python, mouse)`.

- `(arg1:Object, arg2:Object)` — Following the function name is the comma-separated list of arguments inside of a pair of parentheses. Each argument should be followed by a colon and the data type for the argument.

- `:void` — After the parentheses are another colon and the data type for the value the function returns. This is the value that will be returned by the function when it is done executing. In this case, the return type is `void` because the function doesn't have a return statement. We'll talk more about return types later in the chapter.

- `{...}` — All the code that is executed when the function is called is contained within the two curly braces `{}`. This is known as the *function body*.

All functions require the function keyword, the function name, the parentheses, and the function body. The rest of the areas are not required but that doesn't mean you shouldn't use them.

Passing parameters to your function

Functions become much more interesting, and much more useful, when you provide them with some external input. This can be achieved by adding *arguments*, also known as *parameters*, to your function definition. To do this, simply list one or more arguments within the parentheses of a function statement. The names you define here will be available at runtime as local variables that you can use to execute your code.

Not all functions will require parameters. Those functions will be invoked with nothing in between the parentheses.

Let's look at the example of finding the circumference of a circle:

```
function getCircumference(diameter:Number):Number {
    return Math.PI * diameter;
}
```

These parameter values can be rewritten as you see fit and exist in the local scope for the function. That is, they override any variables with the same name that might exist as properties of the class scope or global scope.

> **NEW IN AS3**   In strict mode, the number of arguments must match the function definition. This is different from previous versions of ActionScript where the symmetry between arguments in the function definition and function call is not enforced.

Passing by reference or by value

ActionScript 3.0 handles primitive data types and complex data types differently when it comes to passing values into a function. Primitive data types are passed *by value* — that is, their value is copied into the function leaving the original value intact and unchanged despite what may happen within the function. Complex data types, like `Array`, pass values *by reference*, which uses the actual object passed in instead of a duplicate. Incidentally, these rules apply to variable assignments, too.

If you use a computer, and I'm sure most of you do, you're likely to be aware of the difference between copying files or creating shortcuts (or aliases if you use Mac OS). As shown in Figure 4-1, passing by value is a lot like duplicating a file because the original file remains where it is, unchanged. Passing by reference is more like creating a shortcut to the original value. If you create a shortcut to a text file, open the shortcut, and edit it, your changes will be saved in the original file that you linked to.

FIGURE 4-1

Copying a file is like passing a parameter by *value*, whereas creating a shortcut is like passing a parameter by *reference*.

Passing by Value

Passing by Reference

The following is an example of passing by value. Notice that the original value doesn't change:

```
function limitPercentage(percentage:Number):Number {
    // ensure the percentage is less than 100
    percentage = Math.min(percentage, 100);

    // ensure the percentage is greater than 0
    percentage = Math.max(percentage, 0);

    return percentage;
```

```
    }

    var effort:Number = 110;
    var trimmedPercentage:Number = limitPercentage(effort);

    trace(effort, "%"); // Displays: 110%
    trace(trimmedPercentage, "%"); // Displays: 100%
```

The original value for `effort` put forth hasn't changed even though the `percentage` argument variable was reassigned during the course of the function.

The opposite is true for complex values. They are passed in *by reference*, meaning that the argument acts like a shortcut or link to the original value. Changes to the argument are reflected as changes directly on the value that was passed in. Most data types pass references to variable assignments. The following shows how `employee` is directly linked to the object passed in as a parameter.

```
    function capitalizeEmployeeName(employee:Object):void {
        if (employee.name != null) {
            employee.name = employee.name.toUpperCase();
        }
    }

    var person:Object = {name:"Peter Gibbons"};
    capitalizeEmployeeName(person);
    trace(person.name); // Displays: PETER GIBBONS
```

As you can see in this example, the name capitalization is happening directly on `employee`. That's because the `employee` value refers to the original copy of `person` — hence, the person's name is linked as well.

The following data types are passed by value:

```
    String
    Number
    int
    uint
    Boolean
    Null
    void
```

All other data types are passed by reference.

Setting default values

New in ActionScript 3.0, you have the ability to set default values for a method's arguments. To do this, simply add an equal sign (=) and the default value after an argument name, as follows:

```
    function showGreeting(name:String = "stranger"):void {
        trace("Hello, " + name + ", nice to meet you.");
    }
```

```
showGreeting("Mr. Whimsy"); // Displays: Hello, Mr. Whimsy, nice to meet you.
showGreeting(); // Displays: Hello, stranger, nice to meet you.
```

As you can see, in the second call, the name is replaced with the default value `"stranger"`.

There is one other rule to keep in mind when using default values. First, all arguments that have a default value are considered optional. As such, they must all be placed last in the order of arguments. So, the following code:

```
function storeAddress(name:String, zip:String = null, email:String)
```

is not valid because `email` is a required parameter and it appears after `zip`, which is not. The correct order would be:

```
function storeAddress(name:String, email:String, zip:String = null)
```

Using the rest argument (...)

ActionScript 3.0 adds a new feature called the *rest parameter* (...). The rest parameter is a symbol (...) that represents a variable number of arguments as an array followed by a name for that array. It is written as three dots followed by a name that will be used for the array containing the values. Adding a rest parameter to your function will allow you to make calls with as many parameters as you like. For example, if you want a function that adds together any quantity of numbers, you might use the rest parameter:

```
function sum(... numbers):Number {
    var result:Number = 0;
    for each (var num:Number in numbers) {
        result += num;
    }
    return result;
}

trace(sum(1,2,3,4,5)); // Displays: 15
```

The values passed in to the function are contained within the rest array called `numbers`. When you loop through the array, you are able to access each value.

CROSS-REF For more information on arrays, check out Chapter 8.

The rest parameter can also be used with other required parameters. The required parameters will have their own names as per usual and will exist independent of the rest array. Any additional parameters after the required ones will be stored in the rest array. Let's modify the previous example so that it requires at least one argument:

```
function sum(base:Number, ... numbers):Number {
    var result:Number = base;
    for each (var num:Number in numbers) {
        result += num;
```

```
    }
    return result;
}

trace(sum()); // throws a runtime error.
trace(sum(1,2,3,4,5)); // Displays: 15
```

Accessing the Arguments object

The Function class defines a single property, which is used to hold information about the data passed into the function during the function call. This property is called arguments. It is an object of the special data type arguments, which, though it behaves similarly to an array, is technically not an Array. Every function is an instance of the Function class and therefore has an arguments property.

 arguments **has been deprecated in ActionScript 3.0 but it remains to support legacy code. We recommend that you use the new rest parameter (. . .) instead.**

The rest parameter and the arguments object cannot be used together. Including the rest argument in your function will disable the arguments object.

Its usefulness is hampered in strict mode because strict mode requires you to provide the exact number of arguments defined in the function declaration. If you choose to use the arguments object, you may want to disable strict mode compiling.

Extracting values from the arguments property

The arguments property is very similar to the rest parameter in that it contains every parameter that is passed into the function as an ordered array. The main difference between the two is that all named arguments will be included in the arguments array as well as the unnamed arguments, whereas with the rest parameter, only the unnamed arguments are included.

Parameters passed into the function can be accessed through the square bracket syntax. The first parameter passed in will be at index 0, the second at index 1, and so on. The following example compiles correctly only with strict mode turned off:

```
function sum():Number {
    var result:Number = 0;
    for each (var num:Number in arguments) {
        result += num;
    }
    return result;
}

trace(sum(1,2,3,4,5)); // Displays: 15
```

NEW IN AS3 **Please note that the** arguments.caller **property is no longer available in ActionScript 3.0.**

Returning Results

Functions can do much more than simply run predefined code — that's only half of their purpose. Like mathematical functions, functions in ActionScript can calculate values based on variable input. This ability is extremely useful.

You can think of a function as being a factory that can convert raw materials into a finished product, as illustrated in Figure 4-2. In this case, the raw materials are the arguments that you pass into a function call and the finished product is the value that is returned by the function.

FIGURE 4-2

Functions, like factories, convert raw materials into a finished product.

Raw Materials   Factory   Product
(arguments)   (function)   (return value)

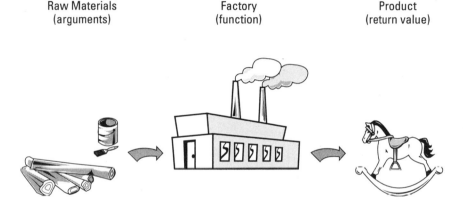

Returning a value using a return statement

In its simplest form, a return statement is the keyword `return` followed by the value that you wish to return. This value can be a primitive, a variable, the result of another function, or any other type of expression.

```
return someValue;
```

Notice that no parentheses are used in conjunction with the return statement. This is because it is not a function but rather an operator. You may see parentheses — like `return (someValue)` — used sometimes but they are not required.

In most situations, you'll want to manipulate the arguments within your function somehow and then return a new calculated value. This example calculates the circumference of a circle by taking a single variable, `diameter`, multiplying it by the mathematical constant pi, and returning the result as a number:

```
function getCircumference (diameter:Number):Number {
    var circumference:Number = diameter * Math.PI;
    return circumference;
}
trace(getCircumference(25)); // Displays: 78.53981633974483
```

As you can see, the getCircumference() method call can be used in a trace statement as if it were a variable. Results from a function with a return type can also be saved to a variable by putting the variable on the left side of the equal sign.

Whenever a return statement is executed in a function, the function ends and the rest of the code is not processed. Because of this, only a single value may be returned for each function. A return statement can also be used to end a function prematurely.

```
function getColor():String {
    var color:String = "Red";
    return color;
    color = "Blue";
    return color;
}

var color:String = getColor();
trace(color); // Displays: Red
```

This method will always return "Red" because the function code stops executing abruptly after the first return statement.

> **TIP** To return several values from a function you may want to create an object or, preferably, a custom class to hold all of your answers in a single variable.

```
return {firstName:"Paul", lastName:"Newman"};
```

Defining a return type for your function

When you define a data type for a variable, constant, or argument with the colon (:) after the object name, it indicates to the compiler what kind of information should be stored in the object. Functions are the same way.

All functions that define a *return type* must honor it by returning a value with a return statement that matches the data type. Conversely, all functions that use a return statement should have a return data type. A return type, like the data type attached to each argument, tells the compiler what kind of data to expect when the function returns a value.

> **TIP** Constructors are a special case. You might be tempted to use the class name as the return type for your constructor, but ActionScript dictates that you should leave the return type for all constructors blank—for example, public function MyClass() {...}.
>
> For more information on constructors, refer to Chapter 3.

TIP In AS3, strongly typing your variables and functions is not required, but it is highly recommended. You will find that your program performs faster by using runtime-type checking — not to mention, your code will be easier to read, debug, use, and reuse.

If you are unsure what type of data type you will be returning, you can use the wildcard data type (*), which represents untyped data. This will allow you to return any type of data.

In the example that follows, the type of data created is passed into the function call. As you can see, this function uses multiple return types, but only the first matching one will execute. The rest will never be encountered.

```
function createObject(type:String):* {
    switch (type) {
        case "Boolean": return new Boolean ();
        case "Number": return new Number ();
        case "String": return new String ();
        case "Array": return new Array ();
        default: trace("Unknown type"); return null;
    }
}
var myObject:* = createObject("Array");
myObject.push(1, 2, 3, 4, 5);

trace(myObject); //Displays: 1, 2, 3, 4, 5
```

The wildcard type can be very useful in certain circumstances but be careful not to overuse it. Most of your methods should have a specific data type.

Returning void

If you don't need your function to return anything, simply use a return type of void. No return statement is necessary for functions that return void.

```
function doNothing ():void {
    // Okay, I won't do anything.
}
```

Even though this example "does nothing," functions that don't return values are very common. Just because it doesn't return a value doesn't mean it can't execute useful code. In fact, a great number of functions in your code are likely to have no return statement. These are sometimes called *sub-procedures* — small, reusable blocks of code that serve to encapsulate frequently used tasks.

NEW IN AS3 As of ActionScript 3.0, the Void data type is written as void with a lowercase *V* to be more consistent with other languages. If you are used to developing in AS2, be careful to make this distinction and don't feel bad if you make a few mistakes at first.

Defining Functions Using Function Expressions

So far, we've looked at defining functions using a `function` statement. There is an alternative way to define functions; ActionScript also supports function expressions. With this technique, you would first define the function as a variable with a data type of `Function` and then set the value of the variable to a function expression.

```
var doSomething:Function = function (arg:Object):void {
                               // function code goes here.
                           }
```

Function expressions behave slightly differently than function statements. Table 4-1 compares some of the key differences.

TABLE 4-1

Differences Between Function Statements and Function Expressions

Function Statements	Function Expressions
Can be called at any point in the code regardless of where in the code the function is defined.	Like a variable declaration, is available only after the point in the code where the function is defined.
Easier to read.	Can be difficult and confusing to read.
Can be called as a method by using dot syntax.	In strict mode, cannot be called as a method. Instead, square bracket syntax is used.
Exists in memory as part of the object it's contained in.	Exists independently in memory. Good for "throw away" functions that don't need to be stored in memory for long.
Cannot be rewritten or deleted.	Can be reassigned a new value or deleted using the `delete` operator.

For most situations, we recommend that you use function statements exclusively rather than function expressions in your code. Their consistency and ease of use make them the superior choice. However, there are some situations where using a function expression can provide flexibility and usefulness that a function statement cannot. These may include:

- Functions that need to be used only once
- Functions defined within another function
- Attaching a method to a class's prototype
- Changing the functionality of a method at runtime
- Passing a function as an argument to another function

Accessing the Methods of a Superclass

As you learned in Chapter 3, ActionScript classes have the ability to extend (or subclass) the functionality of another class. The class extending the functionality is called the subclass and the class that is being extended is called the superclass. This concept is known as *inheritance*.

When creating a subclass, there is a special mechanism that can be used to access the methods of the superclass. This is the super keyword. The super keyword allows you to call upon or add to the existing methods defined in the superclass. When used by itself, it refers to the constructor function of the superclass. That is, it can be used to call all the code in the constructor function of the superclass, or parent class. This is the most common usage.

In this example, the code would be stored in MySprite.as:

```
package {
    import flash.display.*;
    public class MySprite extends Sprite{
        public function MySprite() {
            super();
            x = 100;
            y = 100;
        }
    }
}
```

In the previous example, super() is used to call all of the code in the constructor function for the Sprite class followed by setting the x and y values for MySprite to 100.

The super object can also be used to access the other methods of a superclass. Just use the syntax super.method() to call the method of the superclass. In the code that follows, we *override* the addChild() method of the Sprite class to trace the child object we're adding:

```
package {
    import flash.display.*;
    public class MySprite extends Sprite{
        override public ↵
function addChild(child:DisplayObject):DisplayObject {
            var addedChild:DisplayObject = super.addChild(child);
            trace("Just added child " + addedChild.toString());
            return addedChild;
        }
    }
}
```

By calling super.addChild(child), we're passing the child parameter to the superclass's addChild() method. The result is that the original addChild() code will be executed and the result passed to addedChild. Then the text equivalent of addedChild is displayed. Finally it is returned.

Overriding methods

You may have noticed in the previous example that the function signature for the `addChild()` method was preceded by the `override` keyword. This specifies that the function being defined overrides, or redefines, a method contained in the superclass.

The new method must have the exact same *signature* (list of function parameters, return type, and so on) as the overridden method. If you are unsure of the exact signature to use, refer to the documentation for the item in question.

NEW IN AS3 **The override keyword must be included before all overridden methods. Omitting it will cause a compile time error. Methods defined using either the `private` (and, in some cases, `internal`) keyword will not require the override keyword because they are not passed down to subclasses.**

Writing Recursive Functions

Sometimes a function will need to be called multiple times with input based on the previous call in order to return a value. This slightly tricky form of function design is known as *recursion*. Recursive functions are functions that call themselves within their own function body to create a result based on multiple levels of recursion. It is an advanced technique and may be confusing for beginning coders so you may want to skip over this and return if you ever need to learn more about it.

Here are some instances in which you would use a recursive function:

- When stepping through nested data such as an XML file or a property list.
- When calculating mathematical functions that rely on several iterations such as a factorial or statistical problem.
- Functions that require back-stepping to previous iterations or that steps through a complicated set of possible outcomes such as a maze solving algorithm.

Let's take a look at a simple, commonly used recursive function — factorial. In mathematics, the factorial function, usually written as a positive integer followed by an exclamation point (4!), is a function that calculates the product of all of the positive integers less than or equal to an integer. In other words, $3! = 3 \times 2 \times 1 = 6$. We could write this using a recursive function, as follows:

```
function factorial(i:uint) {
    if (i == 0) {
        return 1;
    } else {
        return (i * factorial(i - 1));
    }
}

trace(factorial(3)); // Displays : 6
```

What happens when you run this function? The original value 3 is passed in. The value 3 is greater than 0 so we skip over the first condition to the `else` statement. This returns i times the factorial of `i-1` (2). But before returning the value, the factorial statement kicks off for a second time using 2 as the parameter. Then the whole process repeats. `factorial(2)` returns `i * factorial(i-1)` (or 2 * the factorial of 1). This repeats until all of the integers are processed and the loop ends, finally sending all of the returned values to be multiplied together by the function.

Curing recursivitis

As you can see from the preceding example, working on recursive functions can quickly become confusing and hard to follow, which makes them tricky to troubleshoot. I call this feeling *recursivitis* (no, this is not a real medical term). One solution to this that I find helpful is to keep track of variables on a plain old fashioned sheet of paper by stepping through what would happen during each iteration. Given the preceding example, I might create a sheet like the one shown in Figure 4-3.

FIGURE 4-3

Curing recursivitis the old fashioned way

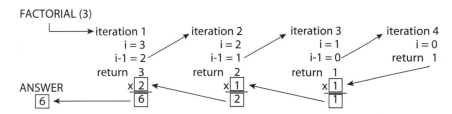

As you can see, with each iteration I'm keeping track of what changes by writing it down. It becomes much easier to follow this way. As things become more complex, you may find using the built-in debugger to be to your advantage. We cover the debugging tools in detail in Chapter 20.

While working with recursive functions, you are likely to encounter a *stack overflow* issue at least once. This problem occurs when a function has no mechanism that stops it from repeating forever. A related problem, *infinite loops*, can also happen when working with `for` and `while` loops and is covered in greater detail in the loop section in Chapter 2. The Flash Player has a built-in mechanism that stops any loop from repeating too many times. If your recursive function needs to repeat too many times, you may get an error such as this one.

```
Error: Error #1502: A script has executed for longer than the default timeout
period of 15 seconds.
```

Functions as Objects

I've said it before and I'll say it again: Almost everything in ActionScript is an object. Functions are no exception. Every function in ActionScript 3.0 is an instance of the Function class with properties and methods just like any other object. In this section we'll look at how this relationship can be exploited for your benefit.

function vs. Function

The word "function," written in lowercase, is the generic term that we've been using so far in this chapter to describe an executable block of code. Function, written in uppercase, is the Function class that all functions are instances of. Normally when you create a new instance of a class you would use the new keyword followed by the class name. However, because functions are such an integral and frequently used part of ActionScript, there are commands (like the function keyword) that are used instead of the new Function() statement.

 Technically, you can use new Function(), but it doesn't do very much except create an undefined function.

You are most likely to encounter the Function class by name when working with methods that require functions as input, or when creating functions by expression. For example, the method addEventListener() takes a function as a parameter. If you're not familiar with Events, don't worry about it. We're going to cover them in great detail in Part IV of this book. For now, let's look at what arguments it's expecting.

```
addEventListener(type:String, listener:Function):void
```

 addEventListener() accepts five arguments. I've included only the two required ones for the sake of simplicity.

As you can see, the second parameter expected by addEventListener() is a listener function. This is the function that will execute when the CLICK event is detected. If you want to pass a function into another function as an argument, simply use the passed in function name but leave off the parentheses (call operator).

```
function onClick(event:MouseEvent):void {
    // Handle click.
}
addEventListener(MouseEvent.CLICK, onClick);
```

 **TIP** Be careful here to leave the parentheses off. If you had written

```
addEventListener(MouseEvent.CLICK, onClick());
```

the onClick() would have executed and returned void, which would be passed in as your parameter (and void, of course, is not a function).

Methods and properties of the Function class

The Function class has few properties and methods. As a subclass of Object, it inherits all of the Object class's methods and properties such as toString(). In addition to these inherited values, the Function class defines its own methods and properties. We've already looked at arguments, the single property defined by Function. Let's take a look at the methods.

Function defines two methods, call() and apply(), which are meant to provide an alternative way to invoke the function. However, these functions do not behave the same way in ActionScript 3.0 as they did in ActionScript 2.0. In most cases, the thisObject is ignored completely. We recommend that you not use these methods. If you need to invoke methods not defined in a class, consider using flash.util.Proxy. For more information on proxies, check out the official ActionScript 3.0 documentation.

Summary

- Methods and functions are repeatable actions that execute blocks of code based on the input parameters that are passed in.

- Using the return operator, you can calculate and return values based on variable input with your functions.

- Like most other things in ActionScript 3.0, methods are objects. They belong to the Function class.

- Functions can be constructed using function statements or by assigning a value to an object of type Function using function expressions.

- The ... (rest) parameter can be used to access all the arguments of a function if the number of arguments is unknown or variable.

- The super and override keywords can be used by a subclass to add on to the functionality of a superclass's methods.

- Recursive functions allow you to loop an action and build upon the results that were generated from the previous call.

Chapter 5

Validating Your Program

N o matter how careful you are when writing code, you will almost certainly have one or two errors. Don't worry, it happens to everyone. In fact, even we, the authors of this very book, deal with errors every time we sit down to code. It's really nothing to be embarrassed about, and as you'll soon realize, being able to see error messages is a real blessing. Errors are your friends . . . well, sort of. Your goal should always be to strive for error-free code but error messages are the best way to tell when there's something wrong that you may not have noticed. Think of it like a spell-checker. Compiling your code and checking for errors frequently is the best way to catch problems before they multiply.

ActionScript 3.0 has added a significantly improved system for identifying and handling errors. Debugging your code, or working out the errors, is easier than ever. We'll talk more about errors and logging later on in the book but for now we'll focus on some of the most common bugs and how to fix them.

Introducing Errors

Errors are messages generated by the compiler or by the Flash Player that let you know when something has gone wrong.

NEW IN AS3 A new feature in the AS3 compiler allows you to set whether you want the compiler to interpret your code using *Strict mode* or not. Strict mode, the default setting, allows you to compile your code using more rigorous compile-time–type checking. It checks to see that all classes, methods, and properties are valid before allowing the program to compile — hence, it's more strict. This makes debugging much easier; however, it also prevents you from dynamically accessing members of non-dynamic objects. Non–Strict mode is much more like Flash 8's compiler, which did not have strict compile-time–type checking.

 All examples in this book should be compiled with Strict mode enabled unless otherwise noted.

Compile-time errors vs. runtime errors

There are two basic types of errors that you'll deal with when writing programs in ActionScript 3.0: compile-time errors and runtime errors.

Compile-time errors

Compile-time errors occur when you attempt to compile your SWF file. These types of errors usually indicate a syntactical mistake or a reference to a class that does not exist. You must fix these errors in order for your program to compile properly.

Runtime errors

A runtime error is one that occurs during the execution of your SWF file while the program is running. These usually arise from a problem that occurs after your program begins, such as a reference to an object that has been deleted. Runtime errors can cause unpredictable results in your program. Some may cause the program to crash; others may go unnoticed. Either way, it's important to address any errors you have in your program.

 In order to see runtime errors from your web browser, you can install the Debug version of the Flash Player available at: www.adobe.com/support/flashplayer/ downloads.html.

Warnings

Sometimes, the compiler will issue a warning. Warnings concern problems that won't prevent your code from compiling or functioning properly but should be fixed for the sake of clean, readable, consistent code. A common example is when you forget to add a data type to a variable or function return. It's a good idea to heed any warnings generated and fix them as though they were errors.

Getting feedback from Flash CS3 and Flex Builder

Flash CS3 and Flex Builder differ slightly when identifying errors. This should get you started with whichever software you use.

 Both Flash CS3 and Flex Builder have Debugging modes that offer more advanced troubleshooting tools. We're not covering those in this chapter, but they are discussed in Chapter 20.

Debugging in Flash CS3

In Flash CS3, the output window (for trace statements and runtime errors) is brought up automatically when you test your movie. If there are any compile errors, a compiler error window also
comes up.

I'll use this code snippet to test out the Compiler Errors window. There's an obvious problem with
this `trace()` call:

```
trase("im a gud spellar");
```

Compiling shows the Compiler Errors window with one error reported, as shown in Figure 5-1.
The window shows the location of the error either in an AS file or in a scene, layer, and frame in an
FLA file along with the line number. If you highlight the error and click the Go to Source button in
the bottom right, the cursor jumps to that location in the code. There's also a Description column
with the error code and description of the error, and a Source column showing the offending
line of code.

FIGURE 5-1

The Flash CS3's Compiler Errors window shows that there is no method called "trase."

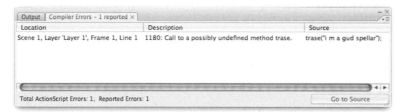

In addition to the Compiler Errors window is the Output window. This shows trace and logging
statements as well as errors that occur at runtime. Running this code:

```
var foo:Array = null;
foo.length;
```

produces the result shown in Figure 5-2. Again, this output shows the call stack that was executing
at the time of the error. Code that executes from the timeline will show the frame number as a
function in the call stack.

FIGURE 5-2

Flash CS3's Output window

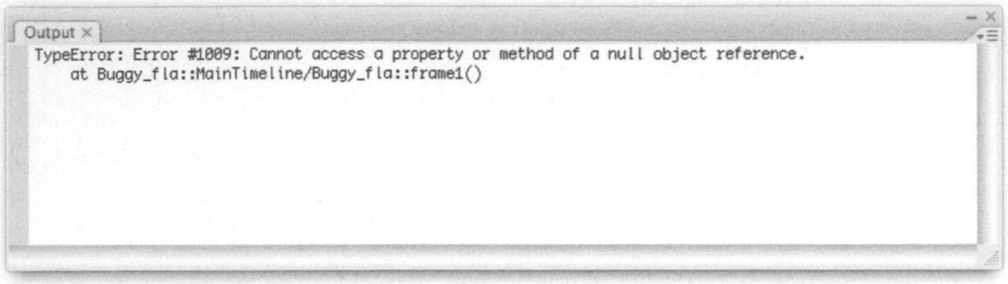

```
Output ×                                                           - ×
  TypeError: Error #1009: Cannot access a property or method of a null object reference.
      at Buggy_fla::MainTimeline/Buggy_fla::frame1()
```

Debugging in Flex Builder

One major advantage of using Flex Builder is its ability to notify you of problems in your code as they are written. Whenever you build your source code, markers will appear next to line numbers that contain compile-time errors. Hovering over these markers or opening the Problems view will show you more detailed information about the problem, as shown in Figure 5-3. You can click on the red reference markers next to the scroll bar on the right of your code or double-click on an item in the Problems view to jump to the line of code with the error.

FIGURE 5-3

Flex Builder showing the error line marker and its counterpart, the Problems view

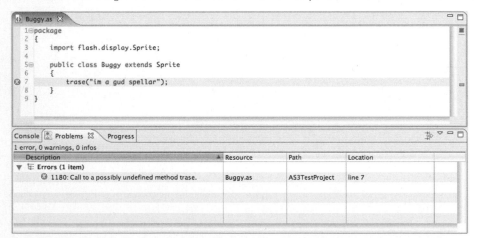

Warnings are reported in a similar way, but they use a yellow color code instead of red.

TIP   If Flex Builder is set to automatically build, you will see errors and warnings every time you save. You can toggle this feature under the Project ➪ Build Automatically menu item.

Similar to Flash CS3's Output window, Flex Builder also has a Console view, shown in Figure 5-4, that shows traces, logs, and errors when debugging.

Flex Builder showing a runtime error in the Console view

Fixing Errors

When a compile-time error is reported in a particular section of the code, a line number and file-name are given for reference. This is the best place to start when trying to fix the problems in your program. Go back to the line number where the error was found and look for typos or other mistakes that could have caused the error.

Runtime errors trace out the current *call stack*, a list of all of the functions that are in the process of being executed at the time of the failure. Studying the call stack will allow you to track back to the original function or functions that caused the problem. For example, consider the following code snippet, which causes a TypeError because nullSprite has no value:

```
package com.wiley.as3bible {
    import flash.display.Sprite;
    public class BuggySprite extends Sprite {
        public function BuggySprite () {
            var nullSprite:Sprite = null;
            updateLayout(nullSprite);
        }
        public function updateLayout(sprite:Sprite):void {
            moveSprite(sprite);
        }
```

```
public function moveSprite(sprite:Sprite):void {
    sprite.x = 100;
}
}
}
```

This code would produce the following error:

```
TypeError: Error #1009: Cannot access a property or method of a
null object reference.
    at BuggySprite/moveSprite()
    at BuggySprite/updateLayout()
    at BuggySprite$iinit()
```

NOTE   The `$iinit()` function refers to the constructor, in this case, `BuggySprite()`.

As you can see, both of the functions `BuggySprite()` and `updateLayout()` make calls to other functions within their function block. As such, they appear in the call stack above. This can help tremendously to find the original source of the problem. (In this case, the `null` assignment in the constructor was the issue.)

TIP   You may see several compiler errors at once; sometimes one error can be the cause for another. Don't jump around when fixing errors. Generally speaking, it's best to start from the first error on the list, fix it, save your files, and recompile. Many times, this will resolve more than one problem.

Common types of errors

Table 5-1 is a list of the more common errors that you are likely to encounter — especially if you're just starting out with ActionScript programming.

TABLE 5-1

A List of Commonly Found Errors and Their Remedies

Error Description	Possible Causes	Possible Solutions
TypeError: Error #1009: Cannot access a property or method of a null object reference.	Caused when an attempt is made to access properties or methods to an object that was never assigned a value or has been deliberately set to null. This is new to many ActionScript developers because previous versions did not treat this as an error.	Ensure that you properly define any objects whose methods or properties you need to access. Or you can add a check to your code to validate the object before calling methods on it. For example: `if (myArray != null) {` `    myArray.pop();` `}`

Error Description	Possible Causes	Possible Solutions
C1100: Assignment within conditional. Did you mean == instead of =?	This warning appears when an assignment (for example, a=b) is made within a conditional statement such as if.	This is one of the most common typos for developers in all programming languages. Because the assignment (=) and equality (==) operators are so similar, they are often confused. Make sure you're using the right one for the job. a = b means "Set a equal to b" a == b means "Is a equal to b?"

T1180: Call to a possibly undefined method _____.
Or
1119: Access of possibly undefined property _____ through a reference with static type _____.
Or
1120: Access of undefined property _____.
	These errors can appear when you attempt to call a function, get or set a variable, or access an object that does not exist. For example:
	var myArray:Array = new Array();
	myArray.washMyCar();
		Typos are a very common cause of these errors. Check through your code to make sure everything is spelled correctly. Remember that AS3 is case-sensitive so foo, Foo, and FOO are three different things.
		
		Make sure your variables are properly declared using a var statement before you attempt to use them. In AS2, the var was optional but it's required in AS3.
		
		Finally, make sure you're not trying to access a member of a class that does not exist. If necessary, check the documentation for the offending class to see if the property or method is valid.

1046: Type was not found or was not a compile-time constant: _____.	The class or interface you're trying to use couldn't be found. It might have been referenced incorrectly or might not exist at all.	This error is similar to the three we just mentioned. Check your code for typos around class names. Also, make sure you include import statements for any classes that aren't automatically imported. In AS3, even some of the built-in classes such as flash.display.Sprite need to be imported. Finally, check to make sure the filename and the name of the class are the same.

continued

TABLE 5-1 *(continued)*		
Error Description	**Possible Causes**	**Possible Solutions**
1067: Implicit coercion of a value of type _____ to an unrelated type _____. Or 1136: Incorrect number of arguments. Expected ___.	A call to a method was attempted with the wrong number of arguments (parameters) or with the wrong data type for one of the arguments.	If a function defines required arguments, the arguments passed to the function when it is called must match the function signature. That is, you must provide the correct number of arguments each with the data type that the function is expecting. This is a more strict rule than in previous versions of ActionScript. If you're not sure what arguments to use, check the documentation for the function you're trying to call.

Summary

- Errors happen all the time even for advanced programmers. Errors reported by Flash Player and the compiler are your best tool in making your code work better.

- Fix reported errors starting with the first one in the list and working your way down. Usually, fixing the first error makes it easier to fix the rest.

- Use the line numbers and the call stack provided with the errors to help identify the area of your code that is causing the problem.

- As you gain experience, you will become more familiar with common programming errors and will be able to catch them before they occur.

- For more info on errors and debugging, check out Part V of this book.

Part II

Working with ActionScript 3.0 Objects

Chapter 6

Using Strings

A string in Flash can be any piece of textual data from a letter to a word to several paragraphs. Strings might also contain or be exclusively made of numbers and other non-letter characters such as a phone number. ActionScript 3.0 provides several methods for working with, manipulating, searching, and converting strings. We cover some of the things you can do with strings in this chapter.

Working with string primitives

Most of what we've looked at so far have been string primitives or pieces of text surrounded by quotation marks added directly into the code. But as you learned in Chapter 2, everything in ActionScript 3.0 is an object, including strings. When you type a string like "Hello, world!" you're actually creating an instance of the String class. The String class offers a load of extra functionality beyond the capability to store text.

> **TIP**   While technically there is a difference between a string created with a new String() statement and a string created using a string literal, the compiler converts string literals into string objects automatically. Therefore the following code is perfectly valid:

```
"banana".length; // 6
```

Converting a string object to a primitive

Should the need arise, you can convert a string to its primitive equivalent by calling the valueOf() method. Actually, all objects have this ability. This may be useful when working with prototypes but, in common practice, this is rarely used.

```
var s:String = "Hello, world!";
trace(s); // Displays : Hello, world!
trace(s.valueOf()); // Displays : Hello, world!
```

IN THIS CHAPTER

Creating and editing strings

Combining multiple strings into a single string

Converting the case of a string

Altering the individual characters in a string

Chopping your string up into smaller parts

Converting objects to and from strings

123

Using escaped characters

String literals use quotes to tell the compiler that the text contained within them should be interpreted as a string. Whether you use single or double quotes doesn't matter, but how you use them does. Say you want to create a piece of text that contains quotes within it:

```
var s:String = 'Porky says "That's all folks!"';
```

Whichever type of quote mark is used first will be the type that the compiler looks for to end the string. This example would create an error in your code because it would be interpreted as a string `'Porky says "That'` followed by some extra gibberish code. In cases like this, you need to use escaped characters.

Escaped characters are a set of special pseudo-characters that are replaced by the compiler with real characters that may be difficult to type or would break the code. They are always preceded by a backslash. The escape characters for double and single quotes are `\"` and `\'` respectively. Here's an example:

```
var s:String = 'Bugs says \"What\'s up, doc?\"';
trace(s); // Bugs says "What's up, doc?"
```

Several escape characters are available to you. Another of the most useful ones is the newline character, `\n`, which is the equivalent of pressing the Enter key. The following:

```
var s:String = "Dear Mom,\nThings are swell. I miss you.\nLove,\nMims";
trace(s);
```

will display:

```
Dear Mom,
Things are swell. I miss you.
Love,
Mims
```

TABLE 6-1

A complete listing of all the escape sequences available to you

Escape Sequence	Resulting String
\b	Backspace character.
\f	Form feed character. This character advances one page and is rarely used.
\n	Newline character. Also known as line feed.
\r	Carriage return character.
	(Carriage return and newline are very similar. Technically, the newline advances the feed by one line while the carriage return brings the cursor back to the beginning of the line. In almost every case, you should just use newline.)
\t	Tab character.

Escape Sequence	Resulting String
\unnnn	Inserts a character with the four-digit hexadecimal Unicode code you specify — e.g., \u0416 is the Cyrillic character 'zhe' ( ).
\xnn	Inserts a character with the two-digit hexadecimal ASCII code you specify — e.g., \x9D is the yen sign character (¥).
\'	Single quote (') character.
\"	Double quote (") character.
\\	Backslash (\) character.

Converting to and from strings

Because strings are easily readable by humans, they are the preferred method for displaying information about other objects in Flash. For this reason, every object in ActionScript 3.0 implements the toString() method to display its value as a string.

Using toString

Say you want to display the current date using an instance of the Date class:

```
var now:Date = new Date();
trace("Today's date is " + now.toString());
// Displays: Today's date is Sat Nov 18 22:37:22 GMT-0500 2006
```

As you can see, the date is printed in the output as if it were a string. In fact, there are many situations where the toString() method is called automatically. This is a form of implicit conversion that's built into ActionScript. If you leave out the toString() method as in the following example, the trace() method will automatically call it on each parameter passed in.

```
trace(new Date()); // Displays: Sat Nov 18 22:37:22 GMT-0500 2006
```

Many classes, including ones you create, do not display much useful information by default when they are converted to strings using toString(). The default for most objects is to display the word "object" followed by their class name. For example:

```
trace(new Sprite()); // Displays : [object Sprite]
```

Fortunately, you can override this behavior in the classes you create to display whatever useful information you desire. Simply add a custom toString() method in your class definition that returns a string. Don't forget the override keyword!

Define the class in MySprite.

```
package com.wiley.as3bible {
    class MySprite extends flash.display.Sprite {

        override public function toString():String {
```

```
                    return ("MySprite (" + name + ") - x: " + x + ", y: " + y);
            }
        }
    }
```

In your main code (anywhere but the `MySprite` class) use the following:

```
var test:MySprite = new MySprite();
test.name = "foo";
test.x = 25;
test.y = 100;
trace(test); // Displays: MySprite (foo) - x: 25, y: 100
```

Much more helpful than tracing out only [`object MySprite`] isn't it? We recommend getting in the habit of defining a custom `toString()` method whenever you create a new class. It greatly improves the readability of your code during debugging.

Casting to a string

Now let's try something else — setting a string to today's date:

```
var now:Date = new Date();
var nowString:String = now; // Causes a compiler error.
```

What happened? Why doesn't this work? Shouldn't `now` be converted to a string implicitly? What's happening is that `nowString` is an object of type `String` and therefore is expecting a string object as its value. In cases like this one, the compiler is more strict about what's a string and what's not and we're forced to convert the object to a string manually.

```
var nowString:String = String(now);
```

This will convert the `Date` object to type `String` and return `now`'s string equivalent to be assigned to `nowString`. If you need to brush up, check out type conversions and casting in Chapter 3.

We could have also used the `toString()` method here as well:

```
var nowString:String = now.toString();
```

Converting strings into other types

The `String` class can also be converted into some other types fairly painlessly. Converting a string containing only numerical data is as easy as casting it as a `Number` object:

```
var shoeSize:String = "12";
var iq:Number = Number(shoeSize);
```

Be careful, however, to include numerical characters only. Trying to cast any other value will result in a nasty NaN (Not a Number) value being assigned instead:

```
var dialASong:Number = Number("(718) 387-6962");
trace(dialASong); // Displays : NaN
```

Adding strings and numbers can be confusing, too, because the compiler will convert the numbers to strings rather than the other way around.

```
var a:Number = 2 + "2";
trace(a); // Displays : 22
```

Converting strings to arrays

Converting a string to an array can be very useful, especially when processing responses that come from a server that can send only strings. For this, the `String` class has the `split()` method. The `split()` method takes two arguments. The first is the delimiter. This is the character, string, or regular expression used to divide up the different elements in the array. The second is optional and is the maximum number of elements in the new array. Here are three examples of the `split()` method in action:

```
var keywords:String = "people,new york,friends,picnic";
var tags:Array = keywords.split(",");
// tags = ["people", "new york", "friends", "picnic"]

var sentence:String = "The quick brown fox jumped over the lazy dog";
var words:Array = sentence.split(" ", 4); // limit to 4 elements.
// words = ["The", "quick", "brown", "fox"]

var state:String = "Mississippi";
var foo:Array = state.split("ss");
// foo = ["Mi", "i", "ippi"]
```

Combining strings

To join strings together, the `String` class provides the `concat` method, which takes any number of arguments (converting them to strings if necessary) and returns a new string with all of the arguments tacked onto the end of it.

```
var hello:String = "Good evening.";
var firstName:String = "Mims";
var greeting:String = hello.concat(" My name is ", firstName, ". Nice to meet ↵
you.");
trace(greeting); // Displays : Good evening. My name is Mims. Nice to meet you.
```

However, ActionScript also supports the addition (+) operator for text concatenation, which, you will likely find, is a much more practical way to join strings together.

```
var greeting:String = "Hello, my name is " + firstName + ". This is way ↵
easier!";
trace(greeting); // Displays: Hello, my name is Mims. This is way easier!
```

Converting the case of a string

To convert a string to the same text in uppercase, simply call the `toUpperCase()` method. As shown in the following example, this will return a new string object with the same letters switched to uppercase. The other non-letter characters will not be affected.

```
var cleanser:String = "Ajax";
var webTechnology:String = cleanser.toUpperCase();
trace(webTechnology); // Displays: AJAX
```

To switch to all lowercase, use `toLowerCase()` instead:

```
var loudText:String = "CAN YOU HEAR ME?"
var quietText:String = loudText.toLowerCase();
trace(quietText); // Displays: can you hear me?
```

NOTE Calling these methods does not change the case of the string itself but rather returns a new string with the case change. The original will stay the same. If you want to change the original you'll have to set its value to the result of the function. For example:

```
var alert:String = "error";
alert = alert.toUpperCase(); // alert = ERROR
```

Using `toUpperCase()` or `toLowerCase()` can be very helpful when you need to make sure that two strings are compared without regard to case, as when checking a password:

```
var inputPW:String = "HaXoR"
var storedPW:String = "haxor";
if (storedPW.toLowerCase() == inputPW.toLowerCase()) {
    trace("Login successful");
} else {
    trace("Login error");
}
// Displays : Login successful
```

Using the individual characters in a string

When working with strings, you may find the need to access a specific character in the string or know the total number of characters in the string. You might find it helpful to think of a string as being an array of single characters (this will probably sound familiar to those of you who have worked in the C programming language). While a string in ActionScript is not an array, it has some array-like properties. A string has indexes starting with 0 and counting up, each containing a single character. The following section describes ways to access the specific characters within a string.

Getting the number of characters in a string

To determine the number of characters a string object contains you can check its `length` property. This property works just like an array's `length` property.

```
var bigWord:String = "PNEUMONOULTRAMICROSCOPICSILICOVOLCANOCONIOSIS";
trace("Number of letters : ", bigWord.length); // Displays : 45
```

`length` is a read-only property, which means that you cannot change its value explicitly unless you add more characters to your string.

Getting a particular character

Unlike an array, you cannot access characters in a string using square bracket syntax:

```
var firstName:String = "Neal";
trace(firstName[1]);
```

This will produce an error.

To access the individual characters, use the `charAt()` method instead, which returns the character located at the specified index:

```
trace(name.charAt(1)); // Displays: e
```

Converting a character to a character code

Similarly, you can convert a character at a specified location into its ASCII character code by using `charCodeAt()`. This may be helpful when you need to work with a character's numerical equivalent instead of the character itself, for example when invoking a Key listener (discussed in Chapter 17).

```
var band:String = "Mötley Crüe";
trace(band.charCodeAt(1)); // Displays: 246 (character code for ö)
```

This code can be converted back into a letter by calling the static method `String.fromCharCode()`, which returns the converted character as a new `String` object.

```
var buttonPressed:Number = 88;
trace("User pressed ", String.fromCharCode(buttonPressed), " button.");
// Displays: User pressed X button.
```

For a list of ASCII character codes, check out the Wikipedia page `http://en.wikipedia.org/wiki/ASCII`.

Searching within a string

You may find the need to search within a string for a particular piece of text. For this, the `String` class provides several methods.

Searching by substring

A substring is any smaller portion of text within a String. For example, "def" is a substring of "abcdefghi". By using the `indexOf()` and `lastIndexOf()` methods, you can search for the first *index of* a substring, in other words, the first location of that substring within the text. They both operate the same way except `lastIndexOf()` starts from the end and works backward whereas `indexOf()` works from the first index forward. The function returns the index number of the substring or if it can't find anything, the number –1. Remember that string indexes are zero-based. Here we check the indexes of some of the names in a list:

```
var names:String = "Jenene, Jake, Jason, Joey, Jaya";
trace(names.indexOf("Jake"));    // Displays: 8
trace(names.lastIndexOf("J"));   // Displays: 27
trace(names.indexOf("Robert"));  // Displays: -1
```

The methods each take two parameters. The first is the substring to search for. The second is an optional parameter specifying the first index to start searching. The second parameter can be very useful if you want to find every instance of the substring. This example searches for the letter "a" in the story until it can't be found anymore:

```
var story:String = "It was a dark and stormy night...";
var pattern:String = "a";
var count:int = 0;
var startIndex:int = 0;
while (story.indexOf(pattern, startIndex) != -1) {
   count++;
   startIndex = story.indexOf(pattern, startIndex) + 1;
}
trace(count); // Displays : 4
```

 The `indexOf()` and `lastIndexOf()` methods have been added to the `Array` class in ActionScript 3.0.

Searching with Regular Expressions

ActionScript 3.0 updates the `String` class to incorporate these methods for searching its text with Regular Expressions that are much more powerful and flexible than the `indexOf` search. They include the following:

■ `search(pattern:*):int` — Functions similarly to `indexOf` in that it searches the string for any instances of the search criterion. The difference here is that you would use a

RegExp as an argument; however, search allows you to search for strings or other objects (which are first converted to strings). If nothing is found, it returns –1; otherwise, it returns the index of the first match.

- match(pattern:*):Array — To return all matches of a particular pattern as an array, use the match method. This will also accept strings or other objects as arguments.

- replace(pattern:*, replacement:Object):String — Searches the string for the pattern (usually a RegExp) and creates a new string that replaces each match with the replacement object (usually a String).

This is only a brief introduction to these methods. Because there is a lot to talk about when it comes to Regular Expressions, we've given them their own chapter. They are covered in greater detail in Chapter 11.

Chopping up your strings

Sometimes you may need to pull a smaller string out of a larger string. For example, you might want to find the first eight characters of a string or take everything after a colon. ActionScript offers three methods for doing this: slice(), substr(), and substring(). These functions are all very similar because they all basically return a substring of your string object. They vary only in the way they handle their two optional parameters.

```
slice(start:Number, end:Number):String
```

and

```
substring(start:Number, end:Number):String
```

are nearly identical. They both return all the characters between the indexes supplied by the start and end parameters. The only difference between them is that slice() can take negative values as parameters but substring() cannot. Negative values (such as –3) will count from the end of the string backward.

For both commands, if the end parameter is left out, the end of the string is used by default. If the start is left out, the beginning of the string is used by default.

The following example searches the string for a space character and uses its index to return the first word:

```
var address:String = "Fourscore and seven years ago...";
var firstSpace:int = address.indexOf(" ");
var firstWord:String = address.slice(0, firstSpace);
trace(firstWord); // Displays : Fourscore
var elipsis:String = address.slice(-3); // takes the last 3 characters.
trace(elipsis); // Display : ...
```

The substr() method is slightly different from slice() and substring(). Instead of taking an end index, this method uses a length parameter. It starts at the supplied start index and returns a string that is as many characters long as the number specified for the length parameter. For example:

```
trace(address.substr(4, 5)); // Displays : score
```

Because all of these methods behave very similarly in most situations, you should use whichever one makes the most sense to you. However, we recommend that you use slice() rather than substring() because it does more and is not as easy to confuse with substr().

Summary

- A string can be any piece of text. Quotation marks are used to identify strings from code that should be executed.

- The String class provides loads of additional functionality. All strings are instances of the String class even if they are string literals.

- Creating a custom toString() method in your classes will help you to understand the data contained within them when logging or using traces.

- Strings can be cut up and combined, and have individual characters accessed much like arrays.

- Strings in ActionScript are case-sensitive but converting cases is easy using the toUpperCase() and toLowerCase() methods.

- Searching strings and replacing text within strings is much easier now thanks to the new methods and regular expressions included in ActionScript 3.0.

Chapter 7

Working with Numbers and Math

IN THIS CHAPTER

Using number classes

Performing arithmetic and trigonometry

Working with dates and times

Without good support for numbers, there's not much you can program. It should be no surprise, then, that ActionScript 3.0 enables all kinds of numeric activity, from basic arithmetic to date and time handling. With the information in this chapter you can start making useful, interactive, and aesthetic computations.

Understanding Numeric Types

Using ActionScript, you can create numbers of different types. To understand how to use these, however, you must take a step back and look at the sets of numbers themselves, and what they represent. Later, you will review how different kinds of numbers are represented on modern computers. Knowing the implications of these implementation details can help the wary programmer understand which data types are appropriate in which situations, the limitations of the language, and common problems that might arise.

Sets of numbers

A number is a number is a number, right? Not so; there are several different types of numbers. These types of numbers are defined by the set of values that they can represent.

Most familiar might be the set of natural numbers, or $\mathbb{N}$. This contains whole numbers starting with zero: $\{0, 1, 2, 3, . . .\}$. These are the numbers you use to count discrete objects: "I have two parents." "There are four emergency exits on this aircraft." "This piano has 88 keys."

A superset of the natural numbers is the set of integers, represented by $\mathbb{Z}$. This set contains whole numbers both negative and positive: $\{\ldots, -2, -1, 0, 1, 2, \ldots\}$.

An even larger set is the set of real numbers, represented by $\mathbb{R}$. Real numbers include both rational numbers and irrational numbers — that is, numbers that can be represented by a fraction and those that can't. It's impossible to exhaustively list out any subset of them because between any two real numbers lie an infinite amount of other real numbers. Some examples, however, are –10, 6½, 3.14159265 . . ., and 4.4. (Of these examples, the number π, approximated by 3.14159265 . . ., is irrational. π, read "pi," can't be accurately represented with a fraction or decimal expansion.) Any number you can write with a fraction or a decimal is a real number. You can measure things such as distances, angles, pH, and pounds of cookies with real numbers.

Representing numbers

When you write down numbers, you are representing their values with digits. For instance, the concept of one hundred is a one followed by two zeros. But you could also express this as one hundred tick marks, 1×10^2, the Roman numeral *C*, or with ten rows of ten ones. With some imagination, you could come up with lots of different ways to represent a single number.

The common way we write numbers is in base 10, also known as decimal. In our system of writing, there are ten basic digits, *0* through *9*, and every place for a digit represents a factor of ten more than the place to its right. Thus, *342* is three hundreds plus four tens plus two ones.

When programming applications, you may find yourself using other bases, most likely base 16, also known as hexadecimal. In base 16, there are 16 basic digits, 0 through 9 followed by A, B, C, D, E, and F. A digit in each place represents 16 times the value of the digit to its right. The number written *12* in hexadecimal is one sixteen plus two ones: eighteen. But because the 0–9 digits look the same in both systems, there's no way to know whether a number written *12* is meant to be in hexadecimal, where it means sixteen, or decimal, where it represents twelve. To differentiate between hexadecimal and decimal notations, we typically precede hexadecimal numbers with *0x*. The number *0x2A* is two sixteens plus *A* (ten) ones, or *42* in decimal.

Why use hexadecimal? If you have tried talking to a computer, you would know computers don't understand decimal numbers. They understand only base 2, or binary, where the only digits are 0 and 1, and each place represents twice the value of the digit to the right of it. However, it takes a lot more space and effort to write in binary. For humans like us, that is. For example, *2007* is expressed in binary as *11111010111*. Hexadecimal is both compact and nicely compatible with binary. Each digit in base 16 is represented by four digits in base 2, because *16* is 2^4. So *2007* becomes *0x7D7*, much more compact despite the space taken up by *0x*. Hexadecimal is used in ActionScript 3.0 most frequently to write 32-bit color values, as shown in Figure 7-1.

Digital representations of numbers

Representing a number in a computer presents a unique set of challenges. First, computers represent everything as binary, and second, the way your CPU works sets limits on the number of binary digits that can be stored as a single value.

Unsigned integers

The simplest kind of number to represent digitally is a natural number. Natural numbers (positive whole numbers) are represented by *unsigned integers* on a computer.

The integer type in ActionScript 3.0 is 32 bits. This means that there are 32 places for binary digits. To understand the limit this imposes, consider a comparison to decimal numbers. The highest number you can write in base 10 with 3 digits is *999*, which is one less than *1,000* or 10^3. So the largest number you can write in base 2 with 32 digits is

    1111 1111 1111 1111 1111 1111 1111 1111

which is one less than

    1 0000 0000 0000 0000 0000 0000 0000 0000

or 2^{32}. This means that the biggest number you can represent with a 32-bit unsigned integer is $2^{32}-1$, which works out to *4,294,967,295* in base 10.

Four billion is a large number, to be sure, but it's not hard to imagine needing a bigger number, like the population of the world, or the number of hits some web sites get in a year. It is important to remember that numbers represented on your computer are limited. As we've just demonstrated, the maximum value of unsigned integers is limited directly by the size of the unsigned integer in memory — in ActionScript 3.0, it's 32 bits.

Signed integers

Integer numbers (whole numbers that might be either positive or negative) are represented by *signed integers* on a computer. The term "signed" refers to the fact that these numbers carry information about their sign, that is, whether they are positive or negative. Unsigned numbers, in contrast, do not carry any information about their sign. They do not say whether they are positive or negative. It is only through convention that we associate them with positive numbers, just as we expect maps to represent north as up.

But if all you have at your disposal to represent both positive and negative numbers are 32 binary digits, how do you represent both positive and negative numbers? The solution is both simple and clever. There are two signs, positive and negative. There are two values for one binary digit, *0* and *1*. So if you just reserve one of the 32 bits you have at your disposal for the sign, you can have 31 bits left to store the value of the number.

This tradeoff has an impact on the maximum absolute value that can be stored. If we reserve one bit for the sign, a signed integer will have 31 bits left to represent its absolute value. A binary number with 31 digits can only go up to $2^{31}-1$, or about 2 billion. By taking one binary digit away, you halve the maximum value. But wait! By adding a sign, you double the number of values that can be represented! Every number that was once an unsigned value (except zero) can now be two values, positive or negative. Signed integers, instead of going as high as unsigned integers, go half as high but equally as low. The minimum value of a 32-bit unsigned integer is *0*, but the minimum value of a 32-bit signed integer is *–2,147,483,648*.

The sign bit is stored as the most significant bit of the 32. But in addition to this, conventional languages such as ActionScript 3.0 use a trick to let the CPU add two numbers the same way regardless of their sign. This trick is called two's complement, and it involves counting backward in binary for the non-sign digits of negative numbers. For instance, a 4-bit signed integer for -1 would be *1111*, -2 would be *1110*, and so on. Then, adding a positive and a negative number is a normal binary addition, with the overflow ignored. We mention this because overflow in integer arithmetic is ignored, so if you are not careful with boundary cases, you can attain deceptively incorrect results as a result of an overflow. You must also be aware of this when using bit math with signed integers.

Floating-point numbers

Real numbers are represented by *floating-point* numbers on a computer. Just as scientific notation can represent a huge range of numbers concisely in the form $a \times 10^b$, floating-point numbers have an incredible range, and their accuracy is in proportion to the scale of the value itself. For example, 5.12×10^{-5} is an incredibly small and precise number, *0.0000512*, and 5.12×10^9 is a very large but imprecise number, *5,120,000,000*. However, both express sufficient precision for their own scale. You don't care about an error of a thousandth of a gram when measuring the weight of a planet, but you need that accuracy when measuring chemical compositions.

Floating-point numbers break up the available bits to store a sign, a significand, and an exponent. The significand in a floating-point number is its fractional part, the part that encodes the number to be scaled up or down, or *a* in the expression $a \times 2^b$. The exponent is the scale of the number, or *b* in the expression $a \times 2^b$. ActionScript 3.0 uses a standardized implementation of floating-point numbers defined by the IEEE Standard for Binary Floating-Point Arithmetic, or IEEE 754. In this implementation, both *a* and *b* are binary, and the base itself, as written previously, is 2.

The floating-point type in AS3, introduced in the material that follows, is a 64-bit double-precision IEEE 754 floating-point number. It reserves 52 bits for the fractional part and 11 bits for the exponent, with 1 bit left over for the sign. This size structure can represent incredibly small (in absolute value) and large numbers with a great amount of accuracy. It's impossible to represent all real numbers with perfect accuracy in a computer, so often floating-point numbers approximate rather than represent values, but the accuracy afforded by double-precision floating-point numbers should be sufficient for almost any task. Use floating-point numbers to represent real numbers and extremely large positive or negative numbers. The maximum value AS3 can represent with a double-precision floating-point number is about 1.8×10^{308}. It's incredibly difficult to give a number that big any perspective. For one measure, it's roughly 1,000,000,000,000,000,000,000,000,000,000,000,000, 000,000,000,000,000,000,000,000,000,000,000,000,000,000,000,000,000,000,000,000,000, 000,000,000,000,000,000,000,000,000,000,000,000,000,000,000,000,000,000,000,000,000, 000,000,000,000,000,000,000,000,000,000,000,000,000,000,000,000,000 times as many atoms exist in the visible universe.

Using Numbers in ActionScript

ActionScript 3.0 includes three base types for numbers, which reflect the three ways we covered to represent numbers digitally, allowing the programmer to choose the best number type for the task at hand. The number types include special values to keep your program from breaking in certain edge cases. Additionally, the language allows you to type numbers directly into code.

NEW IN AS3 Previous versions of ActionScript relied on a single type for all numeric values because floating-point numbers can represent both whole and fractional numbers. ActionScript 3.0 introduces types for signed and unsigned integers.

Number

The Number type is an IEEE 754 double-precision 64-bit floating-point number and, as such, can represent positive and negative numbers both whole and fractional. Numbers are applicable for almost any kind of measurement and are one of the principal workhorses of AS3.

The default value for an unassigned variable of type Number is NaN, which is defined in the section "Edge Cases" later in this chapter. Usually Numbers are assigned by setting them equal to a numeric literal, but the Number class also has a constructor, which will attempt to convert the object passed in to a number, and assign it to the new Number, as follows:

```
var n:Number;
trace(n); // NaN
n = 12;
trace(n); // 12
```

 **TIP** Assignment is the typical way to associate a value with a variable; it is rare to see a numeric type's constructor in use.

Use Numbers for any kind of measurement, values that might contain fractional parts, and for extremely large and small values.

int

An addition in ActionScript 3.0, the int type is a signed 32-bit integer. Despite its lowercase name, it is, like all types, a class. Like Number, int has a constructor that is rarely used. You can create a new int by merely typing a number literal. If you try to assign an int variable a non-whole number, the fractional part will be dropped. The default value for an unassigned int value is 0.

The performance of integer variables inside Flash Player is on the whole greater than that of floating-point numbers, so you can use integer number types for sections of code that need to be maximally optimized, and where fractional parts do not matter. The int type is perfect for counters, and is frequently found in for loops:

```
for (var i:int = 0; i < 1000; i++)
```

uint

Another new numeric type found in ActionScript 3.0, `uint` is an unsigned 32-bit integer. It, too, is a class and has a rarely used constructor. Like `int`, its default value is 0. In fact, `uint` is identical to `int` except in its range of values.

The `uint` type is used for bit math because its value is always a simple binary translation of the value, without any special encoding or rules like counting backward in two's complement. It provides unfettered access to all 32 bits of the value in memory. A good example of this is color values, illustrated in Figure 7-1, which pack information for transparency and amounts of red, green, and blue into a single 32-bit field.

FIGURE 7-1

A color value represented in a single uint

0 x F F A 0 A 0 A 0

      Alpha   Red   Green   Blue

The preceding value represents a solid gray. Because it uses all 32 bits, it can't be stored in a signed integer, which uses 1 bit for sign and leaves 31 bits for use.

CAUTION You should not use the `uint` type for integer numbers or counters because it is unable to represent negative numbers. Even if you know the integer you want to represent won't go under zero, it's a good idea to leave it signed. Otherwise it will be easy to make some simple errors. Use `uint`s for bit math and `int`s for all other integers.

Furthermore, it's good to remember that integers behave badly when they overrun their limits, wrapping over into the opposite sign for signed integers and between zero and the maximum value for unsigned integers, whereas `Number`s simply become less accurate as they increase radically. Don't use `int`s or `uint`s for values that have even a remote chance of exceeding their limits, or be sure to check these values. In general, use `Number` for all numeric types, as it is the most flexible.

Literals

Using number literals is simple. The easiest way to enter a number directly in code is to write it in normal decimal notation. Valid decimal literals include:

```
1337;
-4;
.8;
0.333;
-1.414;
```

As we briefly mentioned, you denote hexadecimal numbers by preceding them with *0x*. To interpret a number as hexadecimal in ActionScript code, you do the same thing:

```
var foo:uint = 0x12AB;
```

You can also use exponential notation to declare numbers. Exponential notation expresses a number as a real number times a power of ten. Typically this is seen in scientific notation, where the real number part is always between 1 and 10. This kind of representation lets you focus on the relative sizes of numbers without expressing them in a lengthy string of digits, especially for very small or very large numbers, such as 6.02×10^{23}. When writing exponential notation in code, you use the character e to represent the base, and to indicate that the value following it is the exponent. This same number, then, would be written as 6.02e23. The following are all valid exponential literals:

```
2.007e3; // 2007
1414e-3; // 1.414
1.9e+17; // 190,000,000,000,000,000
```

NEW IN AS3 In earlier versions of ActionScript, you could also enter literal numbers in base eight, or octal, by preceding them with an unnecessary 0. This feature is likely to have caused more inadvertent errors than triumphs for octal notation, and has been removed from ActionScript 3.0.

Edge cases

Each ActionScript type includes special values that are included in its possible range. These are extremely useful for preventing your program from producing errors when certain edge cases occur.

Not a number

The constant NaN represents "not a number," a non-numeric value included in the Number type. NaN is found in instances of Number that have not been assigned a value, or the failure of an attempted conversion. Mathematical operations with non-real or undefined results also yield NaN, such as the square root of *-1* or zero divided by zero.

Comparisons with NaN will always return false, and most mathematical operations on NaN result in NaN. To check if a number is defined, don't try to compare its value to NaN itself. Instead, use the top-level function isNaN(), as follows:

```
var n:Number;
trace(n); //NaN
trace(isNaN(n)); //true
trace(n == NaN); //false! That's why you use isNaN()
n = Number("this won't convert into a number");
trace(isNaN(n)); //true
n = 10;
trace(isNaN(n)); //false
```

 In previous versions of ActionScript, various errors could result in a Number being assigned either NaN or undefined. In ActionScript 3.0, Number instances can be only NaN or a real number, and never undefined or void.

Infinity

The Number type also has special constant values for positive and negative infinity, Number .POSITIVE_INFINITY and Number.NEGATIVE_INFINITY. If you end up with an infinite value, for instance by dividing a Number by zero, instead of an overflow or runtime error, the Number will take on one of the special infinite values. You can check infinite conditions through comparison, and the comparisons work as you might expect. Any non-infinite number is less than positive infinity and greater than negative infinity, although infinity equals itself.

```
var n:Number = 10 / 0;
trace(n); //Infinity
trace(n == Number.POSITIVE_INFINITY); //true
```

Minimum and maximum values

Not counting infinity, there are physical limits imposed on the size of numbers based on their implementation in the ActionScript Virtual Machine. For instance, you learned that 32-bit unsigned integers can go up to only $2^{31}-1$. These real limits are documented by the MAX_VALUE and MIN_VALUE static constants of all three number classes. The constants refer to the overall maximum and minimum possible values for int and uint. For Number, they refer to the largest positive finite number that can be represented, and the smallest nonzero, non-negative number that can be represented:

```
trace(uint.MIN_VALUE); //0
trace(uint.MAX_VALUE); //4294967295
trace(int.MIN_VALUE); //-2147483648
trace(int.MAX_VALUE); //2147483647
trace(Number.MIN_VALUE); //4.9406564584124654e-324
trace(Number.MAX_VALUE); //1.79769313486231e+308
```

NaN and Infinity are concepts that apply to the Number type only. Integers, signed and unsigned, don't have these fail-safes.

Manipulating Numbers

Numbers of all kinds in ActionScript 3.0 are flexible, and can serve whatever purpose you need them to. If this includes some type-bending, then all the better. Casting and conversion are easy in AS3.

Numeric conversions

You don't have to sweat it when you want to get an integer, but you are multiplying an integer and a floating-point number. Or when you want to add 0.1 to an integer and get the result as a floating-point number. ActionScript 3.0 automatically performs necessary conversions between floating-point and integer numbers in expressions based on the left-hand side of the expression: what type it will be assigned to or returned as. When it's not declared which type the expression should be evaluated as, expressions are upgraded to floating-point when any part of them results in a floating-point component:

```
var i:int = 3 * 2.04; //adding an int and a float, assigning to an int
trace(i); //6 (it's an int!)

var n:Number = i + 0.1; //adding an int and a float, assigning to a float
trace(n); //6.1 (it's a float!)

var x = 2 / 3;
//dividing an int and an int, upgraded to float since the result is
//not a whole number, and the left-hand side doesn't specify a type
trace(x); //0.6666666666666666 (it's a float!)
```

String conversions

Probably the most useful kind of conversions for numbers is to and from `Strings`. You can include numbers in messages, format them, and read them in from user input. Thankfully, this process is as simple as a cast, and in many cases can be handled automatically.

To convert a number to a string, you have a few options:

- Call the number's `toString()` method. This is the preferred way.
- Explicitly cast the number to a `String`. This actually calls the top-level `String()` conversion function, which will interpret the number as a string.
- Include the number variable in a string expression. This will implicitly convert the number to a `String`.

  ```
  for (var i:int = 99; i > 0; i--) {
      trace(i + " bottles of beer on the wall");
  }
  ```

- Call one of the special formatting methods on the number variable to print it to a string in a non-decimal notation. All three number types have methods `toExponential()`, `toFixed()`, and `toPrecision()`, for formatting the number in exponential and fixed-point notation.

When you want to get a number back from a string value, it's as easy as explicitly casting the string to a number type. To parse a number out of a string that might have other text in it, ignoring the other text, you can use the top-level `parseInt()` and `parseFloat()` functions to return integer and real number interpretations of the numeric content of a string. Also, `parseInt()` and `parseFloat()` allow you to interpret the text as a number in an arbitrary base. The following snippet compares approaches to converting strings into numbers:

```
trace(parseInt("3.14")); // 3
trace(int("3.14")); // 3
trace(parseFloat("3.14")); // 3.14
trace(Number("3.14")); // 3.14
trace(parseFloat("3.14 has a posse")); // 3.14
trace(Number("3.14 has a posse")); // NaN
trace(parseFloat("What's up 3.14?")); // NaN
```

The last line doesn't work because parseInt() and parseFloat() require the number to be the first thing in the string, which makes these functions a lot less useful.

Of these two approaches, I recommend using the explicit cast method. Because you really are changing types, a cast in your code looks better than calling a global function like parseInt().

CROSS-REF You can use regular expressions to easily parse out numbers from complex strings, and do a much better job than the parseInt() and parseFloat() functions. See Chapter 11 to learn about applying regular expressions.

Performing Arithmetic

ActionScript 3.0 supports all the basic arithmetic you'd find on any calculator, and expressions are written out as you might write them on paper. AS3 follows the correct order of operations, so

```
1 + 2 * 3
```

returns 7 as it should, instead of 9 if it simply operated left to right. Arithmetic and order of operations were introduced in Chapter 2. Table 7-1 summarizes the basic operators for arithmetic in AS3.

TABLE 7-1

Basic Arithmetic Operators

Operator	Meaning
a + b	The sum of a and b.
a * b	The product of a and b.
a - b	a minus b.
a / b	a divided by b.
a % b	a modulo b (the remainder of a / b).
-a	the negative of a (−1 times a).

Operator	Meaning
(a + b)	Evaluate subexpressions in parentheses first.
a++	Add 1 to a after evaluating the expression.
++a	Add 1 to a before evaluating the rest of the expression.
a--	Subtract 1 from a after evaluating the expression.
--a	Subtract 1 from a before evaluating the rest of the expression.

Combining operators with assignment will use the left-hand side of the expression as the first operand. For example,

```
a = a + 10;
```

can be more concisely written as

```
a += 10;
```

Beyond these simple operators, there are static methods in the Math utility class, as shown in Table 7-2, that enable you to perform more arithmetic.

TABLE 7-2

Math Class Arithmetic

Method Call	Returns
Math.pow(a, b)	a raised to the b power (a^b)
Math.exp(a)	e raised to the a power (e^a)
Math.floor(a)	a rounded down
Math.ceil(a)	a rounded up
Math.round(a)	a rounded to the nearest digit
Math.max(a, b, c...)	Maximum of the set a, b, c . . .
Math.min(a, b, c...)	Minimum of the set a, b, c . . .
Math.sqrt(a)	Square root of a
Math.abs(a)	Absolute value of a
Math.log(a)	Logarithm (base 10) of a
Math.ln(a)	Natural logarithm (base e) of a

Between built-in operators and the methods of the Math class, ActionScript 3.0 gives you a solid basis with which to make computations.

Performing Trigonometric Calculations

Also built into ActionScript 3.0 are trigonometric functions. Flash is so often employed to create interactive graphics, and these can rarely be done without a helping of trigonometry. Therefore, the `Math` utility class also includes the methods shown in Table 7-3.

TABLE 7-3

Math Class Trigonometry

Method Call	Returns
`Math.sin(a)`	Sine of an angle measuring a radians
`Math.cos(a)`	Cosine of an angle measuring a radians
`Math.tan(a)`	Tangent of an angle measuring a radians
`Math.asin(a)`	Angle in radians whose sine is a (arcsine of a)
`Math.acos(a)`	Angle in radians whose cosine is a (arccosine of a)
`Math.atan(a)`	Angle in radians whose tangent is a (arctangent of a)
`Math.atan2(y, x)`	Angle which, drawn from the origin, intersects the point (x, y) (arctangent of y/x)

In addition, the `Math` class includes the constant `Math.PI` for the number π, ratio of a circle's circumference to its diameter.

TIP All trig functions operate on radians, an angular unit in which 2π radians measure a full revolution. All display objects' rotations are measured in degrees, in which 360 degrees measures a full revolution. You can use the equality π radians = 180 degrees to translate between them easily:

```
valInRadians = valInDegrees / 180 * Math.PI;
valInDegrees = valInRadians / Math.PI * 180;
```

Generating Randomness

Incorporating elements of randomness into your program is an excellent way to simulate lifelike, unpredictable behavior. This can be applied to animate graphics for living creatures, or to create generative art, often producing real beauty from a chance arrangement. Altering subtly the appearance of your program with randomness is a common technique for evoking an organic, always-new feeling. Stochastic attributes can be applied to any quantifiable property, and in whatever degree you desire.

Given the many applications of chaos, generating some in ActionScript 3.0 is trivial.

```
Math.random();
```

This method generates a pseudorandom number between zero and 1. It could potentially be zero, but will never get as high as exactly 1 ($0 \leq n < 1$). In other languages, you may be required to set the seed value for the random number generator, but in ActionScript 3.0 this is not available or necessary.

> **NOTE** Pseudorandom numbers are determined by a series of repeatable steps a computer can execute. This means that they are not truly random. However, they have a random distribution and for almost every application are sufficient. For cryptographic applications you should consider writing your own random number routines and incorporating more chaotic variables into them, for instance sampling mouse movement or background noise from a microphone.

The `Math.random()` method generates unit random numbers only. More than likely, you will need the values to lie in a different range than zero to 1. Remember that the `Math.random()` function does not take arguments; you should scale the numbers to the desired range yourself. A simple formula for producing a random number between two values is presented here:

```
function randomInRange(min:Number, max:Number):Number {
    var scale:Number = max - min;
    return Math.random() * scale + min;
}
```

The fact that `Math.random()` returns a number between zero and 1 makes it easy to manipulate. Here, we simply multiply it by the size of the range and shift it up by the minimum value.

Manipulating Dates and Times

When we create applications that interface with the world at large, timing becomes a huge concern, if not the principal one. As individuals, we want to mark off the years since we were born, be on time for flights, plan a party for a specific time and day, know important events in our past and our history, and mark the passage of time. Time is a linear variable; we all experience it at the same rate forever. (Actually, we don't, but we'll save that for *Physics Bible*.) Therefore, we can represent time as a single number, measuring time with ever-increasing numbers. I could say, "I let my tea brew for 180 seconds," and you would understand that measurement of time. So, too, could any computer or simple pocket calculator because a number is just a number.

However, things get really complicated when we try to manipulate and communicate dates. We use a complex and fairly hacked-up system to break up time into cycles that synch up with earth's travel around the sun, its rotation, the location of the moon, seasons, and all kinds of events. This mess is called the Gregorian calendar. Times during the day have problems, too, as we use the angle of the sun to normalize our measurement, and are left with the same time being represented as different hours across the world: time zones. All of these we have become somewhat adept at manipulating mentally. I could tell you what month it was 50 days ago, but without a lot of thought, I couldn't tell you what day of the week it was. For both humans and computers, calculating dates requires knowledge of how our systems of measurement work.

ActionScript 3.0 knows all of these rules, and lets you manipulate times and dates in their common units, rather than simply as a raw number. There is one class in ActionScript 3.0 that represents a single moment in time, including both time and date information. This is the `Date` class.

Creating a date

Let's start using Dates by creating one that represents "right now," or more precisely, "the instant in which the Date object was created." The default use of the Date constructor will do just this.

```
var now:Date = new Date();
```

The Date constructor is one of the more versatile constructors in ActionScript 3.0. With it, you can construct not just Dates for right now, but Dates representing any point in time you pass in.

You can send the Date constructor a series of values for the year, month, day of the month, hour, minute, second, and millisecond to represent. You must include at least two parameters—at least the year and month—and all others will default to zero (the stroke of midnight the first day of the month).

```
var bday:Date = new Date(1981, 4, 12); // May 12, 1981 12:00:00AM
var timeOfWriting:Date = new Date(2007, 0, 28, 14, 36, 42, 16);
    // January 28, 2007 2:36:42.016PM
```

Hours are measured in 24-hour/military time, so they can range from 0 (12 a.m.) to 23 (11 p.m.).

CAUTION   You might notice that there's something fishy with the dates as entered in the preceding code. Certain units in the Date class are zero-indexed and certain units are one-indexed. While January is the first month, the Date class calls it zero. Properties are zero-indexed when they refer to named units, such as months (January, February, and so on) or days of the week (Monday, Tuesday, and so on). This way, you can use an array of the proper names to translate directly:

```
var daysOfWeek:Array = ["Sunday", "Monday", "Tuesday",
                        "Wednesday", "Thursday",
                        "Friday", "Saturday"];
trace(daysOfWeek[timeOfWriting.day]);
```

Using numbers for these properties of a date makes them abstract, so you can easily use this technique to apply the proper names for any language.

Months and days of the week are indexed from zero. Days of the month are indexed from one. Hours, minutes, seconds, and milliseconds are measured from zero. Years are measured from zero (AD 0).

A third way to create a Date object is by passing it a string representing a time. The string must contain a year, month, and day of the month, at minimum, and can contain more. If the Date constructor can't figure out how to get a date out of your string, it will create a new Date with an Invalid Date value, the equivalent of a NaN. The following lines all create valid dates:

NEW IN AS3   The capability of a Date object to parse dates out of strings is a convenient new feature of ActionScript 3.0.

```
new Date("1/28/2007"); // United States style MM/DD/YYYY
new Date("Sun Jan 28 2007");
new Date("28 Jan 2007");
new Date("Sun Jan 28 2007 3:16:12 PM");
```

The parsing function is only somewhat lenient, and is better suited for interpreting specifically computer-formatted dates than free-form human input. It's always a good idea to check a date's validity after constructing it from a string. You can check a date's validity by checking if its epoch time is a number (more on epoch time in the material that follows).

```
var invalid:Date = new Date("Yesterday");
trace(invalid); // Invalid Date
trace(isNaN(invalid.valueOf())); // true
```

There is one more form of the Date constructor that uses epoch time, so let's dive into that.

Epoch time

In simpler times, people didn't have Date classes or fancy laptops. Folks then, they had a big ol' heap of memory, and some simple types that stored some simple values. When they needed a time value — and people always needed a time value — they would rely on their old friend int. Remember that old tale about time just being a number? Well, it still can be, if you just measure it as time since something. So those folks did just that. They stored a time as a number of milliseconds since another time, and they put that number right in an int.

What was the time those folks measured against? It was the Epoch: midnight, January 1, 1970. But why that day? The epoch of what? This is the way time has always been represented in Unix, and that day was the birthday of Unix, or so they say. In fact, this kind of time measurement is usually referred to as Unix time, but because it is applied so widely now, we feel it more diplomatic to call it epoch time.

Of course, by putting that number in a signed int, they created a problem. Can you guess what it is? A 32-bit signed integer can represent only a time up to 2^{31} milliseconds before or after the epoch. That means dates before 1901 and dates after 2038 are out of the range of epoch time when stored in an int. In those simpler times, 2038 must have looked like a long way away, but for us, it might become a real problem.

In the present, epoch time is still a very useful tool. Because it's just a number, we can play with it freely, using arithmetic instead of bulky Date methods when it's more convenient. In order to selectively use epoch time, we have to be able to convert a Date object to an epoch time and back, and methods covered in the following section, "Accessing and Modifying a Date," will show how to do that. In addition to those methods that fit in with other means of modifying a Date, you can pass epoch time to the Date constructor to create a new Date instance from an epoch time.

```
var d:Date = new Date(0);
trace(d); // Wed Dec 31 16:00:00 GMT-0800 1969
```

In addition, if you want nothing to do with Date objects and just want to use epoch time, you can parse strings into dates without creating a new Date object by using the Date class's static parse() method.

```
trace(Date.parse("1/1/1970")); // 28800000
```

Did you notice something wrong with these examples? Get a different value when you execute them? Shouldn't the first one return January 1, 1970 and the second one zero? They would, if you lived on the Greenwich meridian.

Time zones

As you know, one of the complications of our way of measuring time is the separation of our globe into time zones, where the same instant is a different time at different longitudes. The Date class also takes this into account.

When you create a new Date object, ActionScript assumes you want it in your local time zone unless you specify a time zone, as in new Date("Jan 28 19:46:00 GMT-0500 2007"). Once you have a Date object, you can operate on it and reference it in either your local time zone or UTC.

UTC, or Coordinated Universal Time, is the same thing as GMT, Greenwich Mean Time, and is the "neutral" time zone. So if you want two people on different parts of the globe to agree on what to call a certain time, they can both reference it by the same time zone to call it the same time. That time zone is UTC or GMT, the time zone over the Greenwich meridian in Great Britain. So by referencing times with respect to UTC you can avoid geographical implications.

Because epoch time is measured relative to a specific instant, we need that reference point to be fixed. The epoch is not just January 1, 1970 at midnight, it's January 1, 1970, midnight at UTC. Therefore, if I am in Los Angeles using Pacific Time, GMT-0800, the *local* time of the epoch is at plus eight hours.

In the first example, we create a new Date object at the actual epoch time, but we print it out in our local time. For me, that's December 31, 1969 at 4 p.m. When it's midnight in UTC, it's 4 p.m. the previous day here in Pacific time. Your results may vary as you run the example from your local time zone.

In the second example, we create a new Date to represent January 1, 1970 in our local time. Epoch time is measured from January 1, 1970 UTC, so again the difference is eight hours, or *1000* ms/sec × *60* sec/min × *60* min/hr × *8* hr = *28,800,000* ms.

Accessing and modifying a date ·

Once you have a date stored in a Date variable, you can work with it in the natural units of time thanks to accessor methods and functions of the Date class. You can set or read any unit of time, in either UTC or in the local time zone. It's your choice whether to use the explicit accessors (methods) or implicit accessors (properties) to read and write these values.

NEW IN AS3 ActionScript 3.0 augments the Date object with implicit setters and getters for all the units of time that are already supported by explicit getters and setters.

For each property of a date and time listed in Table 7-4, the accessors are named as follows:

- get[*Property*]() to read the property from the Date object in local time
- getUTC[*Property*]() to read the property from the Date object in UTC
- set[*Property*]() to set the property in local time
- setUTC[*Property*]() to set the property in UTC
- [*property*] to read and/or write the property in local time
- [*property*]UTC to read and/or write the property in UTC

So for example, you can access hours of a date with any of the following:

```
date.hours;
date.hoursUTC;
date.hoursUTC = 20;
date.getHours();
date.setHours(5);
date.getUTCHours();
date.setUTCHours(20);
```

TABLE 7-4

Retrieving and Modifying Units of Time

Property	Use	Restrictions
milliseconds	Thousandths of a second (0–999)	
seconds	Seconds past the minute (0–59)	
minutes	Minutes past the hour (0–59)	
hours	Hour of the day (0–23)	
date	Day of the month (1–31)	
day	Day of the week (0–6)	Read-only (no setDay() or setUTCDay(), implicit accessors are read-only)
month	Month (0–11)	
fullYear	Unabridged year (1999 instead of 99)	
time	Milliseconds since January 1, 1970 UTC	No UTC version of accessors (this property is always relative to UTC)

Date arithmetic

To shift time, convert the Date object to an epoch time and use normal arithmetic to manipulate it in milliseconds. When you're done, you can write the new value into the existing Date with setTime().

This approach is recommended over directly setting units of the date as in the following:

```
date.setDate(date.getDate() + 1); // add one day(?)
```

because this approach leaves you as the programmer responsible for checking all kinds of boundary conditions such as leap years and different numbers of days in a month. This naïve example looks like it might break when it tries to assign 32 to the day of the month. Even though ActionScript saves you here, and actually does the right thing, it looks like a bug in your code and is considered bad style.

The exception to this rule is when the amount of time to be added is measured in a unit of time that might be dependent on special Gregorian rules. For example, you might want to add years by incrementing fullYear instead of adding 365 days to your Date. This figure for days a year is not entirely as accurate as using the fullYear setter would be, as it doesn't account for leap years.

Execution time

The function flash.utils.getTimer() returns the number of milliseconds since Flash Player was initialized. When it's not necessary to use a Date object, you can use getTimer(), typically to measure elapsed time while a program is executing.

NEW IN AS3 The getTimer() method was moved into the flash.utils package in ActionScript 3.0, so you must import it before using it. The Timer class and getTimer() are covered in more detail in Chapter 18.

This can be applied to either measure performance of your own application or the network, or to measure time as interactions take place with the user. Call getTimer() once before the event you wish to measure, and once after, and then take the difference to find the duration of the event.

Formatting a date

We are accustomed to seeing dates written out in lots of different ways. When generating text that include dates, we want control over how the dates will appear so that we can present date information in the most appropriate way.

FLEX FEATURE Flex 2.0 contains a DateFormatter class/tag, which lets you conveniently format dates with a formatting string.

You can format dates out-of-the-box with a single method call in a few ways. `Date` objects include a `toString()` method like every object, as well as several additional formatting methods, as shown in Table 7-5.

TABLE 7-5

Date Formatting Methods

Method	Includes	Example
`toDateString()`	Month, day, and year	Sun Jan 28 2007
`toDateLocaleString()`	Same as `toDateString()`	Sun Jan 28 2007
`toString()`	All information, 24h	Sun Jan 28 23:00:00 GMT-0800 2007
`toLocaleString()`	All information except time zone, 12h	Sun Jan 28 2007 11:00:00 PM
`toTimeString()`	Hours, minutes, seconds, time zone, 24h	23:00:00 GMT-0800
`toLocaleTimeString()`	Hours, minutes, seconds, 12h	11:00:00 PM
`toUTCString()`	All information relative to UTC, 24h	Mon Jan 29 07:00:00 2007 UTC

While these methods are useful to quickly print out date information, you can totally control the format of your dates with just a little bit more work, by gluing together the units you can access from the `Date` object itself, and whatever incidental formatting you need.

CROSS-REF For more information on formatting strings, see Chapter 6.

The following example uses custom formatting to display any date as `MM/DD/YYYY`:

```
function dateToMMDDYYYY(aDate:Date):String {
    var SEPARATOR:String = "/";

    var mm:String = (aDate.month + 1).toString();
    if (mm.length < 2) mm = "0" + mm;

    var dd:String = aDate.date.toString();
    if (dd.length < 2) dd = "0" + dd;

    var yyyy:String = aDate.fullYear.toString();
    return mm + SEPARATOR + dd + SEPARATOR + yyyy;
}
```

The example pads the month and date with leading zeros where necessary, and it shifts up the month field, which is otherwise zero-indexed, by one.

Summary

- There are three number types in ActionScript 3.0, each with different strengths.

- The value `NaN` represents invalid and unassigned numbers; a `Number` can be neither `undefined` nor `void`.

- Edge cases are handled by special constants in the number classes.

- You can operate on numbers with supported operators.

- Numbers can be typed directly in code in multiple notations.

- Numbers can be converted between numeric types, parsed from strings, and printed into strings.

- The `Math` utility class contains static methods for arithmetic and trigonometry.

- `Math.random()` generates pseudorandom numbers between zero and one.

- The `Date` class stores an instant in time.

- Epoch time stores an instant in time as a number.

- You can access and alter a `Date` instance using many units of time.

Chapter 8

Using Arrays

I n this chapter, we look at *arrays*. Arrays are a type of ordered set of data like a numbered list. By using an array, you can store any number of individual pieces of data in a single variable, which allows you to group values that should go together. The Array class also provides methods and properties that allow you to work with this set of data by editing it, searching through it, sorting it, and operating on the entire group. Arrays are used frequently in nearly all programming languages and ActionScript is no exception.

Arrays are the first complex data type that we study in Part II of this book. strings, numbers, Booleans, and the like are all primitive data types — which means they are the core building blocks of information and usually contain a single piece of immutable data of a specific type. Complex data types, on the other hand, are composites of the various primitive types.

Array Basics

As we said, arrays are a lot like a numbered list of items. Each item, or *element*, in an array has a location, or *index*. Unlike most numbered lists, indexes in an array start at 0 instead of 1. These indexes are used to look up elements in the array, as shown in Figure 8-1.

Using the Array constructor

Let's create our first array and fill it with information. For this, you're going to use the Array constructor.

```
var myArray:Array = new Array();
```

153

FIGURE 8-1

To visualize an array, think of a set of numbered cubbyholes, each containing a single item.

> **TIP**   Remember that a constructor is a function that creates an instance of a class. A constructor is always named after the class it constructs. To use a constructor, use the new keyword followed by the constructor name — for example, `new Array()`.

The previous code creates an empty array — an array with no items contained within it. Simply calling the `Array()` method with no arguments is the simplest form of the Array constructor. However, ActionScript provides two additional ways to use the constructor. If you want to call the constructor and assign values to it at the same time, simply pass the values you want to insert as arguments to the constructor:

```
var myThings:Array = new Array("coffee filters", "stapler", "Spin Doctors CD");
```

In this case, you create an array of your things and simultaneously fill it with some random stuff you might find in one of your desk drawers. We're filling this array with strings but arrays in ActionScript can contain any type of object:

```
var time:Date = new Date();
var currentTemp:Number = 56;
var currentConditions:String = "Light Showers";
var weatherReport:Array = new Array(time, currentTemp, currentConditions);
trace(weatherReport);
// Displays Sun Dec 3 17:02:16 GMT-0500 2006,56,Light Showers
```

In the previous example, we used the `trace()` statement to print out the contents of the array. This is by far the easiest method for finding out what values are stored in an array. The `trace()` statement prints the results of the `toString()` method for the array, which in turn prints the `toString()` value for all the elements contained within it. This is covered in more detail in the section "Converting Arrays to Strings."

The third and final way you can use the Array constructor allows you to specify the length of the new array. To use this, call the Array constructor and pass a single integer value to specify the length of the array. A new array is created with as many unassigned indexes as you ask for:

```
var topTen:Array = new Array(10);
// creates an array with 10 spaces.
```

In practice, this ability is not terribly useful. An array's length cannot be statically defined as it can in other languages such as Java. Instead, the length continues to change as you add or remove items from the array. This type of array is sometimes known as a vector. ActionScript arrays will allow you to add additional elements beyond the length that you specify. Therefore, defining a length is somewhat moot because the number is subject to change.

CAUTION If you pass a number to the Array constructor with the intent to add that number to the array, you may be disappointed. A single number will always create an empty array with that many spaces. Instead, you may want to use an array literal or add the values after you've called the constructor.

Creating an array by using an array literal

ActionScript provides a very useful way to create new arrays through the use of a type of shorthand called an *array literal*. As discussed in Chapter 2, a literal is a piece of data that can be written directly into the code without using variables, constructors, or other types of object-oriented structures. Numbers and strings have literals; array literals operate similarly.

To create an array literal, place any values that you would like to store in an array inside a set of square brackets ([ ]) separated by commas. For example:

```
[1,2,3]
```

The previous code is equivalent to:

```
new Array(1, 2, 3);
```

As you can see, the first one is quite a bit simpler to write. Of course, simply creating an array isn't very useful unless you plan to do something with it. Let's assign a value to a variable using an array literal:

```
var fibonacci:Array = [1, 1, 2, 3, 5, 8, 13, 21, 34, 55];
```

Likewise, you can create a new empty array by using an empty array literal:

```
var a:Array = [];
```

Literals are a quick and convenient way to create arrays.

Referencing values in an array

Now we've created some arrays a few different ways. Let's look at how you can access the values stored within an array. As we mentioned before, an array's values are stored in slots called indexes. Each index is numbered starting from 0 and counting up to one less than the length of the array. To look up a value, we'll use the array's name followed by the *array access* operator ([]) containing the index we want. Don't confuse this with an array literal, which is used by itself. The array access operator tells the array to return a specific element at the index you provide:

```
var animals:Array = ["newt", "vole", "cobra", "tortoise"];
trace(animals[2]); // Displays: cobra
```

By using `animals[2]` we're asking for the item stored at index 2 in the array. Accessing an element with the square bracket notation is like accessing a variable without a name. This square bracket notation can be used to write values to the array as well as retrieve them. Just place the array with the index number on the left side of an equals statement.

```
animals[0] = "salamander";
trace(animals); // Displays: salamander,vole,cobra,tortoise
```

Finding the number of items in an array

To find out how many elements are contained within an array, you can check the `length` property of the array as shown in the code that follows. `length` is a read-only property. You cannot set the length of an array without adding values to it or specifying the length in the Array constructor.

```
var veggies:Array = new Array();
trace(veggies.length); // Displays: 0
veggies = ["corn", "bok choy", "kale", "beet"];
trace(veggies.length); // Displays: 4
```

Remember that the indexes count up from 0 so the length is always one more than the last element in the array. In other words, `veggies[3]` is the last element in the list while `veggies[4]` is undefined.

Converting Arrays to Strings

When working with arrays, it is often helpful to be able to get a snapshot of the contents within it. By this point, you're probably familiar with the `toString()` method. This is implicitly called by functions, like trace, which allows you to quickly examine the contents. By default, arrays display a comma-separated list of values.

```
var names:Array = ["Jenene", "Josh", "Jac"];
trace(names); // Displays: Jenene,Josh,Jac
```

The `Array` class provides an alternative way to display its values as a string. By using the `join()` method, you can provide your own delimiter to separate the array's contents. You can use `join()` with your choice of string delimiter where you would have used `toString()`:

```
var menu:Array = ["eggplant parmesan", "chocolate", "fish tacos"];
trace("For dinner we're having " + menu.join(" and ") + ". Yum!");
// Displays: For dinner we're having eggplant parmesan and chocolate and fish
// tacos. Yum!
```

The commas are replaced by the word "and," making the sentence read a little more naturally.

 **TIP** **To create a string with no spaces or other characters between the array values, use the empty string:** `join("")`.

Adding and Removing Items from an Array

Adding elements to an array one index at a time is nice but as the number increases, it can be tricky to keep track of all those indexes. Luckily, you won't have to! The Array class provides methods for adding items to and removing items from your array without any regard to their index numbers. This functionality enables you to easily extend the contents of your array or work with it as a *stack* or a *queue*. We discuss what these do in a bit, but let's start with adding two or more arrays together through the use of concatenation.

Appending values to the end of your array with concat()

You've learned how to create individual arrays so let's take a look at how you might combine the contents of one array to another array. Naturally, the first thing you might try is adding the two arrays together:

```
var a:Array = [1,2,3];
var b:Array = [4,5,6];
var c:Array = a + b;
```

Running this code will result in the following runtime error:

```
TypeError: Error #1034: Type Coercion failed: cannot convert
"1,2,34,5,6" to Array.
```

What's happening here? The two arrays are complex data types so they're not appropriate values to use with the addition operator. Instead, they're automatically converted to strings, which are added together resulting in the string 1,2,34,5,6. This error occurs because we're attempting to assign a string value to a variable, c, which is expecting an array.

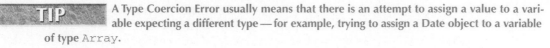

TIP A Type Coercion Error usually means that there is an attempt to assign a value to a variable expecting a different type — for example, trying to assign a Date object to a variable of type `Array`.

Instead of adding the two arrays together using the plus sign, you can use the `concat()` method, short for concatenate. This method creates a new array based on the array that calls the method and adds any number of objects you specify as parameters to the end of the new array. If you pass another array as a parameter, the contents of the array, rather than the array object itself, are added. The following example adds a to b and throws on a couple of extra numbers for fun:

```
var a:Array = [1,2,3];
var b:Array = [4,5,6];
var c:Array = a.concat(b, 7, "eight");

trace(a); // Displays: 1,2,3
trace(b); // Displays: 4,5,6
trace(c); // Displays: 1,2,3,4,5,6,7,eight
```

Notice that the original arrays, a and b, remain unchanged during this operation. The `concat()` method returns a brand new array that is based on the original but doesn't affect the original.

Applying stack operations push() and pop()

ActionScript includes interfaces for arrays that allow them to act as one of several different *data structures*, or sets of data organized in an efficient way. One such data structure is known as a *stack*. A stack is a list of data that is maintained in a first in/last out (FILO) manner. That is, the first piece of data added to the stack will stay there until all other pieces of data are removed.

It might be easiest to think of a stack as a Pez dispenser. Candy loaded in the top gets *pushed* down into the stack. When you lift the head, the last piece of candy that was loaded *pops* out of the front. The `Array` class provides methods that do the same thing with its elements.

Introducing `push()` and `pop()`. As with the Pez dispenser, values can be pushed onto the end of an array using the `push()` method and popped off of the end using the `pop()` method. Unlike most of the other methods that you've looked at, these two act directly on the array you call the method for rather than creating a new array. Let's take a look at this in action:

```
var pez:Array = new Array();
pez.push("cherry");
pez.push("orange");
pez.push("lemon");
pez.push("grape");

trace(pez); // Displays: cherry,orange,lemon,grape

var candy:String = String(pez.pop());
// We'll cast as String to make sure it's a String since array elements are ↵
initially untyped.
trace(candy); // Displays: grape
trace(pez);   // Displays: cherry,orange,lemon
```

Stacks are useful when your program needs to deal with new information as it comes in but retain the older information to refer back to it later. Imagine an alert system that displays a current threat level as a color. When the alert level rises, it might go from green to yellow and return to green when the threat has passed.

The push() method takes one or more objects as parameters and adds them all in order to the end of the array. That is, they are added to the last index of the array making these two statements identical:

```
myArray.push(myValue);
myArray[myArray.length] = myValue;
```

Whether you choose to use a formal stack structure or not, the push() method is a very quick and useful way to add elements to the end of your array without knowing what index number you intend to add it to.

The pop() method, conversely, takes no arguments. It removes and returns the last element of the array. There is no true equivalent to pop() because an array's elements may not be completely deleted via the array accessor ([ ]).

Applying queue operations shift() and unshift()

Similar to stacks are another type of data structure called *queues*. Queues are lists that work in a first in/first out (FIFO) fashion. This could be related to a line of people (or queue) waiting for tickets at the movie theater. The first person in line is the first person to get a ticket. The next person in line is next to buy and so on. Each time a person buys a ticket, the rest of the line *shifts* forward one space.

Arrays can also "push" elements on, and then "shift" them off using, you guessed it, the shift() method. Let's create the movie queue example using this technique:

```
var queue:Array = new Array();
queue.push("Anja");
queue.push("James");
queue.push("Will");
trace(queue);  // Displays: Anja,James,Will

var person:String = String(queue.shift());
trace(person); // Displays: Anja
trace(queue);  // Displays: James,Will
```

As you can see, the first person added to the list was the first person shifted off. The shift() method returns the value removed from the array.

If shifting is taking elements off of the front of the array, *unshifting* must be adding elements to the front of the array. Arrays can also call unshift() to add any number of elements to the front of the array just like push() adds elements to the end of an array.

```
queue.unshift("Jim", "Doro");
trace(queue); // Displays: Jim,Doro,James,Will
```

Queues can be very useful when you have a situation in which data needs to be processed in a first-come, first-served manner. A common example is loading several images from a server one at a time. You'll want the first image to load before moving on to the next, shifting each one until all the images are done loading.

 Stack and queue operations are not mutually exclusive. They can be used alone or together on any array.

Slicing, Splicing, and Dicing

In the previous section, you looked at adding to the front or back of your array. This is very useful but as you get more elements, you may want to be more selective about where you add or remove them. You may even want to work with a smaller subset of your array independently of the original. This portion of the chapter is all about working selectively with your array's elements.

Inserting and removing values with splice()

"Splice" usually means to join two things by interweaving them, such as pieces of film or rope. With an array, you can splice together two sets of elements using the `splice()` method. When you splice together film, you always have to destroy a single frame in order to get a clean transition. With an array, you have the option of deleting elements when you splice in new ones.

The `splice()` method takes two required parameters. The starting index, which is where the insertion or deletion will begin, and the delete count, which is the number of elements you wish to delete from the array or 0 if you don't want to delete any. You may also add any number of optional parameters, which are elements that will be added to the array at the start index. If any elements are removed from the array, they're returned by the `splice()` method.

Let's take a look at `splice()` in action:

```
var nobleGasses:Array = ["helium", "neon", "argon", "pentagon",
"xenon", "radon"];
var shapes:Array = nobleGasses.splice(3, 1, "krypton");

trace(nobleGasses);
// Displays : helium,neon,argon,krypton,xenon,radon
trace(shapes);
// Displays : pentagon
```

Working with a subset of your array with slice()

To extract a subset of your array to work on independently of the original array, you can use the `slice()` method. If you read Chapter 6, you may remember the `slice()` method for the `String` class. Slicing works pretty much the same way for the `Array` class. Just specify the start and end index (not inclusive) of the slice you want to create.

```
var metals:Array = ["iron", "copper", "gold", "silver",
"platinum", "tin", "chrome"];
var preciousMetals:Array = metals.slice(2,5);
trace(preciousMetals); // Displays: gold,silver,platinum
```

The slice() method also accepts negative numbers, which count from the end of the array rather than the beginning.

```
var metals:Array = ["iron", "copper", "gold", "silver", "platinum", "tin",
"chrome"];
var canMakingMetal:Array = metals.slice(-2,-1);
trace(canMakingMetal); // Displays: tin
```

CROSS-REF Also check out filter() and map() later in this chapter.

Iterating Through the Items in an Array

When working with arrays, you'll often want to perform an action using every element in the array. So far, we've looked at ways to create, add, and remove elements in an array; now let's look at how you can work with all of them.

Using a for loop

The most common way to access all the items in an array is by using a for loop. Furthermore, this is probably the most common way that a for loop is used. We covered repeating loops in Chapter 2; now you get a chance to put them into action.

When working with arrays, you're likely to see a for construct with this form:

```
for (var i:int = 0; i < myArray.length; i++) {
    trace(myArray[i]);
}
```

Let's take a look at what's going on here:

- for: The for keyword specifies that you want to create a loop.
- var i:int = 0: Create a new integer and set the initial value to zero. The i stands for iteration or index and represents a location in the array.
- i < myArray.length: This specifies that the loop should be repeated while the index is less than the length of the array.
- i++: After each loop, the index will use the iteration operator to count up by one.
- trace(myArray[i]): By using the value for i as it changes with the array accessor, you can trace out the value of every element in the array.

This is not the only way to loop through an array — for example, while loops can work as well. This is just the most common way.

Using the forEach() method

ActionScript 3.0 defines a new method of the `Array` class that provides an alternative to the traditional `for` loop called `forEach()`. This method skips the formality of a `for` loop and applies a function automatically to each element in an array. This function is passed in as a parameter and can be defined elsewhere in your class or passed in as a dynamic function using function expressions, as we discussed in Chapter 4.

The function used for a `forEach()` call takes three parameters. The first is the value of the element in the array, the second is the index of the element, and the third is the array itself. It should match the following function signature:

```
function functionName(element:*, index:int, array:Array):void
```

In this example, we're simply going to trace the values contained within the array using `forEach()`:

```
var subjects:Array = ["Art", "Science", "Math", "History"];

function traceArray(element:*, index:int, a:Array):void {
    trace("[" + index + "] = " + element);
}
subjects.forEach(traceArray);
```

This calls the `traceArray()` function on each element in the array producing the following result:

```
[0] = Art
[1] = Science
[2] = Math
[3] = History
```

The `forEach()` method allows you to conserve and reuse code for iterating through arrays. AS3 has added several other variations on this method to the `Array` class for automatically iterating through an array. You'll find the rest of these later on in the chapter in the section "Applying Actions to All Elements of an Array."

Searching for Elements

ActionScript 3.0 adds the capability to search an array for any value using the `indexOf()` and `lastIndexOf()` methods. You may already be familiar with these functions if you've worked with the `String` class as the methods for the `Array` class work exactly the same way. The method will return the index in the array containing the specified element. The following code shows how to get the indexes of the elements stored in an array. Notice that "Ocelot" doesn't exist and therefore returns a −1 for its index, indicating that the element could not be found.

```
var cats:Array = ["Cheetah", "Puma", "Jaguar", "Panther", "Tiger", "Leopard"];
trace(cats.indexOf("Leopard")); // Displays: 5
trace(cats.indexOf("Ocelot")); // Displays: -1
```

 **For more information on the** `indexOf()` **methods for strings, check out Chapter 6.**

Reordering Your Array

Arrays represent ordered sets of data much like a database does. Most times, the order will be based on the order that you add your data, or sometimes the order may not matter to you at all. Other times, you may want to order data based on other factors such as alphabetically, true or false, number of calories in a made-up `Food` object, fill color of a drawing, or number of points your player has in a video game. Fortunately, ActionScript provides an open-ended solution for sorting the values in an array into whatever order makes the most sense.

Flipping the order of your array using reverse()

One of the quickest ways to reorder your array is to reverse it — that is, flip the order so that the last is first and vice versa. To do this, use the `reverse()` method on your array:

```
var myArray:Array = [12,6,17,4,39];
myArray.reverse();
trace(myArray); // Displays: 39,4,17,6,12
```

This reorders the contents within the array on which it is called without creating a new array.

Using sorting functions

When sorting arrays in ActionScript, you're not just limited to numbers and alphabet, you can sort in whatever ways you see fit. The `Array` class has two methods that make this possible — `sort()` and `sortOn()`. The first will sort elements based on an algorithm you provide. The second uses properties of an object to sort. Both functions use an alphabetical search based on the string value of the array elements if none is provided.

For both of these functions, you'll need some data to sort. We're going to start with a custom `Book` class that contains the title, author, and publication date of a book.

```
package com.wiley.as3bible {
    public class Book {
        public var title:String;
        public var author:String;
        public var year:int;

        public function Book (title:String, author:String, year:int) {
            this.title = title;
            this.author = author;
            this.year = year;
        }
```

```
        public function toString():String {
            return '"' + title + '", ' + author + ' (' + year + ')';
        }
    }
}
```

We also need to start with some data. Let's assume that we've already created several book objects and added them to the array so that this:

```
trace(bookshelf.join("\n"));
```

will display this:

```
"Getting Things Done", Allen (2002)
"Cloudy with a Chance of Meatballs", Barrett & Barrett (1978)
"ActionScript 3.0 Bible", Braunstein, Wright, Lott & Noble (2007)
"Hamlet", Shakespeare (1601)
```

Now armed with a set of data, we can explore the sorting functions. We'll start with the `sort()` method. As already mentioned, using `sort()` with no additional parameters will sort the items by alphabet based on the object's string value. Because we've defined the `toString()` method for the `Book` class to print the book title, then author, then date, we should see the list sorted alphabetically. The following code:

```
bookshelf.sort();
```

reorders the array to produce this order:

```
"ActionScript 3.0 Bible", Braunstein, Wright, Lott & Noble (2007)
"Cloudy with a Chance of Meatballs", Barrett & Barrett (1978)
"Getting Things Done", Allen (2002)
"Hamlet", Shakespeare (1601)
```

Notice here that the `sort()` method makes changes to the array directly.

Now let's try creating a function for sorting this data. The functions that you write for the `sort()` method should follow this signature:

```
function sortFunction (valueA:*, valueB:*):Number
```

where *valueA* and *valueB* are two arbitrary values from the array. You'll want to set up your function to return a numeric result based on a comparison between the two values. Use the following rules to determine the results your function should generate:

- If *valueA* should come before *valueB*, return −1.
- If *valueB* should come before *valueA*, return 1.
- If *valueA* and *valueB* are equal, return 0.

You can use this system to sort the items based on any criteria you like. Let's try sorting the books by their date:

```
function byDate(valueA:Book, valueB:Book):Number {
    if (valueA.year == valueB.year) {return 0;}
    else if (valueA.year < valueB.year) {return -1;}
    else {return 1;}
}
bookshelf.sort(byDate);
```

The preceding function compares the `year` property of each `Book` object to see which one comes first, thus sorting the list from oldest to newest:

```
"Hamlet", Shakespeare (1601)
"Cloudy with a Chance of Meatballs", Barrett & Barrett (1978)
"Getting Things Done", Allen (2002)
"ActionScript 3.0 Bible", Braunstein, Wright, Lott & Noble (2007)
```

You can affect the way that it sorts by adding optional sort flags. These are stored as static constants in the `Array` class. To add these options, pass them in separated by "bitwise or" (`|`) operators after your sort function (in this case we'll sort by date). If you're not familiar with bitwise operations, don't worry about it. The following code will sort the elements in the array numerically (rather than using the string equivalent of the date, which is the default) and descending from the highest to lowest year.

```
bookshelf.sort(byDate, Array.NUMERIC | Array.DESCENDING);
```

produces the following result:

```
"ActionScript 3.0 Bible", Braunstein, Wright, Lott & Noble (2007)
"Getting Things Done", Allen (2002)
"Cloudy with a Chance of Meatballs", Barrett & Barrett (1978)
"Hamlet", Shakespeare (1601)
```

There are five such optional flags that you can pass to either `sort()` or `sortOn()`:

- CASEINSENSITIVE: Normally, sorting is case-sensitive. Using this flag will make the search ignore the case of letters.

- DESCENDING: Using this will cause the array to be sorted from highest to lowest.

- NUMERIC: If you're sorting only numbers, use this flag. Otherwise, numbers will be converted to their string equivalent before sorting occurs.

- RETURNINDEXEDARRAY: This flag will cause the sort function to return a sorted array without affecting the contents of the original array on which the sort method was called.

- UNIQUESORT: When this flag is set, the sorting method will abort and return 0 if any two elements are found to be equal to each other.

We looked at using `sort()` to compare elements using a function; now let's take a look at the `sortOn()` method, which allows you to automatically compare the properties of two elements. Rather than taking a sort function as an argument, the `sortOn()` method takes an array with one or more properties to use as sorting criteria. If a single property is passed in, the elements are sorted by that criterion. If more than one property is passed in, the elements are sorted primarily by the first property and then secondarily by the second property, and so on. Omitting the first parameter will sort the list alphabetically, just like the `sort()` method. Also, the optional parameters can be applied in the same manner as they are with the `sort()` method.

```
bookshelf.sortOn(["year"]);
```

This example sorts by year and is identical to the preceding `byDate()` example.

```
"Hamlet", Shakespeare (1601)
"Cloudy with a Chance of Meatballs", Barrett & Barrett (1978)
"Getting Things Done", Allen (2002)
"ActionScript 3.0 Bible", Braunstein, Wright, Lott & Noble (2007)
```

Applying Actions to All Elements of an Array

As you saw previously in the section "Iterating Through the Items in an Array," the `forEach()` method allows you to automatically iterate through an array and apply a function to each element. ActionScript 3.0 has added several additional methods for applying functions to the elements of the array, which we cover in this section.

NEW IN AS3   All of the functions in this section are new to ActionScript 3.0.

All of these methods take functions as parameters with the same signature as the `forEach()` method shown here. There is one subtle difference. The `every()`, `some()`, and `filter()` methods require functions that return a `Boolean` rather than `void`.

```
function functionName(element:*, index:int, array:Array):Boolean
```

Conditional processing with every(), some(), and filter()

The first set of methods you'll learn about are designed to allow you to check all values of an array for a certain condition that you specify. The `every()` method iterates over every element applying the function passed into it until one of the elements causes the function to return the Boolean value of false. The `some()` method works exactly the same way but, in its case, it stops when a value of `true` is reached. If the "stopper" value is reached, either method will return the last value processed. If the end of the array is reached without the stopper value being set off, the opposite value of the stopper value is returned — `true` in the case of `every()` and `false` in the case of `some()`. Which one you use depends on whether you want to check for `true` or `false`. Do you want to check if "every" element matches or if only "some" match?

Let's check out an example. Consider the following array and filtering functions:

```
var myArray:Array = [1,2,3,4,5];

function lessThanThree(elem:*, i:int, a:Array):Boolean {
    trace(i);
    return elem < 3;
}

function lessThanTen(elem:*, i:int, a:Array):Boolean {
    trace(i);
    return elem < 10;
}

function moreThanTen(elem:*, i:int, a:Array):Boolean {
    trace(i);
    return elem > 10;
}
```

We have an array with a few integers in it. Each of these functions simply traces out the index number that it's evaluating and then returns whether the element is "less than three," "less than ten," or "more than ten" respectively. Now let's see what happens when we apply some of these methods, starting with `every(lessThanThree)`:

```
trace(myArray.every(lessThanThree));
0
1
2
false
```

Checking `every()` evaluates each item up to three and then chokes and returns `false` because 3 < 3 is false. Now let's try the `some()` method.

```
trace(myArray.some(lessThanThree));
0
true
```

The `some()` call doesn't even get as far as three. It chokes at the first true value (0 < 3). Now let's try some examples where the functions run through every item:

```
trace(myArray.every(lessThanTen));
0
1
2
3
4
true
```

Every item in the list is less than 10 so they're all evaluated as `true`. Let's try again with the `some()` method with `moreThanTen`.

```
trace(myArray.some(moreThanTen));
0
1
2
3
4
false
```

Conversely, all of the values are *not* more than 10 so the `some()` function executes all the way through to the end.

 These two functions are nearly identical and could be used interchangeably. We suggest you pick the one that makes the most sense for you.

The `filter()` method, acts similarly to the previous two methods but adds a twist. Instead of searching for a Boolean stopper value, it always processes the entire array and then returns a new array containing all of the elements that resulted in a `true`:

```
var smallNumbers:Array = myArray.filter(lessThanThree);
trace(smallNumbers); // Displays: 1,2
```

Getting results with the map() method

The `map()` method takes a slightly different approach than `every()`, `some()` and `filter()`. A *map* is another type of data structure commonly used in functional programming languages that allows you to apply a function to every element of an array. The `map()` method in ActionScript 3.0 simulates this behavior by applying a method to every element in an array and returning a new array containing all of the results from each element's function. The following code demonstrates a map that returns the square of every element.

```
var myArray:Array = [1,2,3,4,5];

function getSquare(elem:*, i:int, a:Array):Number {
    if (isNaN(elem)) {
        return -1;
    } else {
        return elem * elem;
    }
}

var squaredArray:Array = myArray.map(getSquare);
trace(myArray);        // Displays: 1,2,3,4,5
trace(squaredArray); // Displays: 1,4,9,16,25
```

We use an `if` statement to check if the element is not a number using `isNaN()` because, of course, you cannot multiply a non-number. If it is a non-number, the function returns a –1; otherwise, it returns the number raised to the power of 2. The original array, myArray, is untouched and the new array, squaredArray, contains the results of the getSquare() function when it's applied to each element of myArray. This can be very useful when you need to gather results based on a large set of data.

Alternative Types of Arrays

There are other ways to access array data than the ones we've looked at so far. Some are simply techniques for using arrays and some are different classes.

Working with associative arrays

All types of dynamic objects in ActionScript, of which Array is one, allow you to create new variables stored within the object on-the-fly. You can then access these variables using the array accessor and passing a string rather than an index as a reference. These types of objects are known as associative arrays, lookup tables, or hashes. The following code demonstrates an associative array.

```
var lotto:Array = new Array(12, 30, 42, 6, 29, 75);
lotto.description = "This week's lotto picks.";
trace(lotto[3]); // Displays: 6
trace(lotto["description"]); // Displays: This week's lotto picks.
```

While these types of arrays are possible to create and may have been used frequently in previous versions of ActionScript, we suggest that you use an instance of the Object class, a dictionary, or ideally, a custom class, rather than an array for such applications. Here are some reasons why.

- Objects are designed for this type of use and offer the object initializer syntax.
- They have less overhead than Arrays because they do not contain methods for array manipulation.
- Values stored by name may not appear when iterating through all values in an array using a for loop.
- Values stored by name are not kept in any particular order, making the concept of an array as an ordered set of data untrue.
- Storing data dynamically in this way is not good object-oriented practice and makes debugging and type checking more difficult.

Using an object as a lookup key with dictionaries

ActionScript 3 adds a new type of array called a *dictionary*. The Dictionary class is actually a subclass of the Array class. You can find it in the flash.utils package. A dictionary is simply a type of array that uses an object rather than an index for looking up elements. This allows you to create a list of information that concerns several different objects that aren't necessarily related. In the following code, we'll create a dictionary to store information about the weather.

```
import flash.utils.*

var notes:Dictionary = new Dictionary();
var city:String = "New York City";
var currentConditions:String = "light showers";
var currentTemp:Number = 56;

notes[city] = "recorded at Central Park";
notes[currentTemp] = "Fahrenheit";
notes[currentConditions] = "70% chance of precipitation";


trace("Current Weather for", city, notes[city]);
trace("Current Temperature :", currentTemp, "degrees", notes[currentTemp]);
trace("Current Conditions :", currentConditions, "(", notes[currentConditions],
")");
```

This will display:

```
Current Weather for New York City recorded at Central Park
Current Temperature : 56 degrees Fahrenheit
Current Conditions : light showers ( 70% chance of precipitation )
```

Dictionaries are quick and easy solutions for this type of application but, like associative arrays, they are not always the most object-oriented way to store information. Consider using a static method or properties of a customized class for storing information instead.

Using Multidimensional arrays

No, multidimensional arrays are not some kind of time machine. All of the arrays we've looked at so far are single-dimensional arrays. That is, they have one index number each and represent a linear list of data — hence, one-dimensional. With a multidimensional array, however, you can store values using two or more indexes, which allows you to create data sets within data sets. Technically, a multidimensional array is not a different type of array but rather, it is a way to nest, or store arrays within each other, to create the effect of having a multidimensional lookup.

To create a multidimensional array, simply create an array as one of the elements of another array:

```
var grid:Array = new Array(new Array(1,2), new Array(3,4));
trace(grid[0][0]); // Displays: 1;
trace(grid[0][1]); // Displays: 2;
trace(grid[1][0]); // Displays: 3;
trace(grid[1][1]); // Displays: 4;
```

Suppose you want to store information in two dimensions — such as the locations of the pieces on a chessboard. Well, a chessboard is eight squares wide by eight squares high so it's 8 × 8. To store all of the values for this board you would need eight arrays each with a length of 8. Using a two-dimensional array, you could store this 2D grid-like data in one array. The following code sets up a new chessboard by creating several arrays within one array:

```
const k:String = "King";
const q:String = "Queen";
const b:String = "Bishop";
const n:String = "Knight";
const r:String = "Rook";
const p:String = "Pawn";
const o:String = "empty";

var chessBoard:Array = [

        [r,n,b,q,k,b,n,r],
        [p,p,p,p,p,p,p,p],
        [o,o,o,o,o,o,o,o],
        [o,o,o,o,o,o,o,o],
        [o,o,o,o,o,o,o,o],
        [o,o,o,o,o,o,o,o],
        [p,p,p,p,p,p,p,p],
        [r,n,b,q,k,b,n,r]
        ];

trace("Piece at (0,2) :", chessBoard[0][2]);
trace("Piece at (7,4) :", chessBoard[7][4]);
trace("Piece at (4,3) :", chessBoard[4][3]);
trace("Piece at (7,7) :", chessBoard[7][7]);
```

The following code will display:

```
Piece at (0,2) : Bishop
Piece at (7,4) : King
Piece at (4,3) : empty
Piece at (7,7) : Rook
```

What we've done in the previous example is create an 8 × 8 grid of data representing each space on a chessboard. Using constants to represent each piece and the array literal shorthand, we've added all the pieces to the board. To look up values, we look up the x and y coordinates as indexes. When we say `chessboard[7][4]` what we're really doing is saying get the value at the seventh index of the `chessboard` array, which in this case is another array. Then we're selecting the fourth index of the array that is returned. The shorthand looks conveniently like we're looking up numbers by two indexes instead of one.

You can use arrays like this one, or create even more complex three- or four- or seventeen-dimensional arrays whenever you need to deal with a complex geometric or cross-referential set of data.

Summary

- Arrays are ordered lists of data that use index numbers to look up values called elements.

- You can create new arrays by using the `Array` constructor or array literals `[]`.

- Create strings from array values using the `toString()` and `join()` methods.

- Access values within your array by using the array accessor operator (`[]`).

- Searching for a value within your array is easy with the new `indexOf()` method.

- Perform actions on every element in your array using `forEach()`, `map()`, `filter()`, `every()`, or `some()`.

- Insert values into your array or remove smaller chunks with `slice()` and `splice()`.

Chapter 9

Using Objects

All classes extend `Object` — it is the root of the ActionScript class hierarchy. Despite their inauspicious roots, `Objects` can be truly useful as a data structure. In Chapter 8, we show how arrays might be used to store associative data. In this chapter you see how to use `Objects` and other classes to store and retrieve this kind of information, and explore other situations where `Objects` are useful.

IN THIS CHAPTER

Using Objects and Dictionaries to manipulate associative arrays

Using Object as the root class

Applying Objects to common tasks

Working with Objects

The class `Object` is found at the root of all type hierarchies of all classes. In other words, every object in the ActionScript 3.0 world is an `Object`. The `Object` class by itself doesn't do much and, in fact, would easily be the simplest thing you could create, but for the interesting property that the `Object` class is one of the few classes that is *dynamic*.

Dynamic classes

Dynamic classes can be extended at runtime with new properties and methods. This means you can take the data and operations that define an object and rename them, rewire them, or add to them while the program is running. If Forrest Gump were a programmer, he might tell you that dynamic objects are like a box of chocolates: You never know what you're gonna get. This makes programming with dynamic classes usually a poor choice. If you were programming a dinner set as a dynamic class, some code you don't control could overwrite your `saltShaker` property to dispense habanero peppers, ruining a perfectly good meal. A chaotic world like that is no world to live in, so every class we write in this book is going to be *sealed*, or closed for modification at runtime. Without this guarantee we can't follow the principles of object-oriented design.

Classes are sealed by default, but you can create a dynamic (unsealed) class by using the keyword `dynamic` in front of your class definition:

```
public dynamic class UnsealedClass
```

However, combining this infinite expandability with an inherently empty class yields a perfect method of storage. This is how we come by `Object`s as a data type. Because we need its subclasses to be able to do almost anything, `Object` itself does almost nothing.

You can think of `Object`s as the clay from which all else in the ActionScript world is crafted. By creating classes, you sculpt a form in this clay and fire it, so that all objects like that one will have the same form. Or, as this chapter will show, you can choose to use the clay itself in its raw form, creating what you need for one time only. You don't need to know how `Object`s came to be, however, to use them. An `Object` can just be as simple as a storage place for properties.

Creating objects

You can create a new `Object` with its constructor. The `Object` constructor takes no parameters and makes an empty `Object`:

```
var o:Object = new Object();
```

`Object`, like `Number` and `String`, also has a literal form. You can create an `Object` from scratch with preset values simply by typing it in as a literal. The literal for `Object`s is a comma-separated list of name-colon-value pairs contained in curly braces:

```
var o:Object = {name: "Roger", hair: 0xff0000, hobbies: myHobbies};
```

Names of the properties don't need to be in quotes, and the values can be of any type. Values can also be references to other objects. In this example, we set the `hobbies` property of the object to a variable `myHobbies`. This doesn't copy the value of the variable into the object; it just stores a reference. If the hobbies stored in that variable are updated, retrieving the hobbies through the object will reference the same variable and have the latest information.

The properties of an object can be any string, including strings that aren't necessarily valid identifiers. This means you can store a property such as `99bottles` in an object, but you can't make a variable named `99bottles`, because identifiers aren't allowed to start with a number.

Accessing object properties

Like properties of any class instance, you can access the properties of an object using either dot notation or bracket notation. The difference, besides syntax, is that you can use dot notation only with property names that are also valid identifiers. You can use these methods to both read from and write to objects.

```
var shape:Object = new Object();
shape.name = "hexagon";
shape.sides = 6;
```

```
shape["color"] = 0x00ff00;
shape["stroke weight"] = 2;
shape["describe"] = function():String {return "A " + this.name;};
trace(shape.describe() + " has " + shape.sides + " sides.");
// Displays: A hexagon has 6 sides.
```

This example demonstrates that function objects, like any other type of data, can also be stored in an object instance. This is not a special case at all, but just another object stored away. Typing `shape.describe` or `shape["describe"]` refers to the function object stored as `describe`, and typing the parentheses invokes that function.

You might notice that the bracket notation looks just like array access, and we can use this "syntactic sugar" to use `Objects` as associative arrays.

toString()

There is one method defined on `Object` that you will find yourself using not just on `Objects` but on their subclasses. The `toString()` method is defined on `Object`, so it is available to all classes. It is used to represent the instance as a string. You might override this method in your own classes to provide a good string representation for messages and logging.

An implication of the `toString()` method is that storing a value in an `Object` with the name "toString" will override this function, so if this is likely, you might avoid calling `toString()` on `Objects` that might override this property.

Using Objects as Associative Arrays

An associative array is a data structure that stores items by index. It functions like a filing cabinet in that if you know the name of what you're looking for, you can find it by looking it up. The name, or the thing printed on the edge of the folders in your cabinet, is called a key, and the item itself, or the folder you find, is called a value. Associative arrays, like a filing cabinet, let you add a new folder, find a folder by its name, remove a folder from the cabinet, look to see if a folder by a certain name exists, and flip through all the folders in the cabinet. The essential action, however, is the lookup: storing values by name is what makes an associative array.

Associative arrays maintain a many-to-one relationship between keys and values. Each key refers to the same value every time, and this is essential. However, you could easily have one value that is filed under multiple keys. For example, you might want to create a long, thin `Noodle` object and store it under "Angel Hair," but also under "Cappellini." Both names refer to the same kind of pasta, and both keys can refer to the exact same value, an instance of `Noodle`.

You might also hear associative arrays referred to as hashes, hashtables, maps, or dictionaries. These are all names for the same kind of data type. The terms "hashtable," "hash," and "map" all refer to a particular way to implement this data structure in which a hash function is applied to the key to evenly distribute the values in memory and to later look them up. This is all handled inside the

ActionScript Virtual Machine, so for our purposes, we need to know only that an `Object` can be used as an associative array.

This kind of associative data is incredibly useful and is found all around us, in common programming situations, exposed to plain view on the Internet, and in metaphors for the real world we can use to structure code. Most search engines, for example, expose associative data to you right in the address. Consider the URL `www.google.com/search?q=hashtable&safe=active`. After the question mark (?) is an associative array of keys and values. The query is stored as the key q and its value is `hashtable` because we're searching for information on hashtables. The parameter for the search engine's content filtering feature is named `safe`, and its value is `active` because we don't want inappropriate results. Who knows what kind of lewd examples students in computer science courses might be posting right now? This example uses key-value pairs to represent parameters, as with any form on the Internet that uses `HTTP GET`. It's one key organizational technique to refer to complex data by reference, which is just what associative arrays do.

In the examples from the last section, we already demonstrated most of the necessary properties of an associative array with an `Object`. We stored and retrieved properties, or values, with dot and bracket notation. In this section, you see how to check for the existence of values, iterate through values, and remove values.

Comparing Arrays, Objects, and Dictionaries

Chapter 8 explained how to use an array to store associative arrays. We recommend that you use arrays only for numerically indexed data. Using an `Array` object creates the impression that the data can be accessed by numeric index and that useful `Array` methods such as `indexOf()` and `splice()` can be used. However, none of these methods apply to properties that are stored by key rather than index. You could create even more confusion by storing both values in an `Array` instance both by index and by associative key. Or consider the capability to store values with keys such as `12`. Using an array to access a property like that could confuse your code beyond use. Use `Objects` to store values by key, and use `Arrays` to store values by numeric index.

`Objects` are ideal for storing key-value pairs. Using bracket notation with an `Object` instance can look just like looking up an array index by number, so we can think of it like an `Array`, but without the confusion of it also supporting numerically indexed arrays.

NEW IN AS3   **ActionScript 3.0 introduces a new type of associative array called `Dictionary`. You can find it in the `flash.utils` package.**

Dictionaries can also be used to store key-value pairs. They have an important enhancement, however.

`Objects` use strings as keys. This is sufficient for most purposes, but say you need a quick-and-dirty way to annotate class instances with certain additional information. Strings may not always be sufficient for this purpose. For example, you might be meeting a bunch of new people at a party.

```
var guy1:Person = new Person("Roger");
var guy2:Person = new Person("Mims");
var girl1:Person = new Person("Ashley");
```

You're trying to remember stuff about each person, so you use an Object to store information by his or her name.

```
var notes:Object = new Object();
notes["Roger"] = "Likes games";
notes["Mims"] = "Super organized";
notes["Ashley"] = "Enjoys drawing";
```

This works, until you meet another person named Ashley! Suddenly, there's no way to keep track of both of them independently. Or heaven forbid, you might forget some of their names, but without the name you can't find anything.

```
var girl2:Person = new Person("Ashley");
```

This would be a perfect opportunity to use a Dictionary object. Dictionary objects can use objects themselves as keys. Instead of looking up a name, you would look up the entire person to get the value associated with that person.

```
import flash.utils.Dictionary;
var notes:Dictionary = new Dictionary();
notes[guy1] = "Likes games";
notes[guy2] = "Super organized";
notes[girl1] = "Enjoys drawing";
notes[girl2] = "Singer";
```

By using objects as keys, you can easily associate them with other data. A workaround for objects is to use a unique ID as a string key, but this is not always available, and it can be easier to simply store the object.

If you want to ensure that the objects you use as keys aren't kept around unnecessarily by a Dictionary object, you can pass true as the weakKeys parameter in the Dictionary constructor:

```
new Dictionary(true);
```

The value defaults to false. For more information, see the discussion on weak references in relation to event handling in Chapter 16.

Dictionarys follow the same syntax for all of the operations (inserting, deleting, setting and retrieving) as an Object, so the techniques you learn in this chapter for using Objects will also work with Dictionary instances.

Testing for existence

You can test for the existence of a key in an associative array either by performing a lookup or with the in operator.

NEW IN AS3 Use the in operator to test for existence of properties.

The in operator allows you to check on the existence of properties, methods, or values of an instance, as long as they are accessible. The operator returns a Boolean value. You can use the in operator to see if a key is associated with any value in an associative array:

```
var notes:Object = {Roger: "hereiam"};
"Roger" in notes; // Returns true
"Josh" in notes; // Returns false
```

You can use this operator to investigate instances of classes for methods and public properties, which they support, as well.

```
class Person
{
    public var name:String;
    private var SSN:Number;
    public function Person(name:String)
    {
        this.name = name;
    }
}
var sprite:Sprite = new Sprite();
trace("alpha" in sprite); // Displays true
trace("getChildAt" in sprite); // Displays true
var person:Person = new Person("Ben");
trace("name" in person); // Displays true
trace("SSN" in person); // Displays false
```

This example illustrates finding methods and properties in both built-in and custom classes, and shows that in respects the visibility of properties.

The old-school method of checking for existence by seeing if a lookup fails still works:

```
trace(notes["Josh"]); // Displays undefined
if (notes["Josh"])
{
    trace(notes["Josh"]);
} else {
    trace("I haven't met Josh yet.");
}
// Displays: I haven't met Josh yet.
```

NOTE This method can be a little dangerous because several values can be coerced to false. If you say that Josh is a zero (notes["Josh"] = 0), for example, the else branch executes. Either compare your lookups directly to undefined or use the in operator to be safe.

Removing properties

The `delete` operator can be used to remove key-value pairs from an associative array. Apply the `delete` operator to the value as you would look it up, and both the key and the value will be removed from the associative array:

```
var pastas:Object = {tortellini: 2, gemelli: 14, spaghetti: 9};
trace(pastas["spaghetti"]); // Displays 9
delete pastas["spaghetti"];
trace(pastas["spaghetti"]); // Displays undefined
```

The `delete` operator also works on dynamically added properties and methods of instances of dynamic classes.

> **NOTE** The `delete` **operator returns** `true` **if deletion succeeds. When using** `delete` **on an item in an** `Array`, **the** `length` **property is not updated. You cannot delete instance properties that are not dynamic, or local variables. To release objects, you can remove all references to them, for example by setting variables to** `null`.

Iterating

You can iterate through the key-value pairs of an object with the `for..in` and `for each..in` loops introduced in Chapter 2. Use the `for..in` loop when you need access to the keys and the `for each..in` loop when you are interested in the values only:

```
for (var name:String in notes)
{
    trace("Notes on " + name + ": " + notes[name]);
}
//Displays: Notes on Roger: Likes games... etc.
```

Here, the name is the key, and the notes we took on that person is the value.

Using Objects for Named Arguments

ActionScript 3.0 gives you added flexibility when passing parameters to functions. You can leave out arguments with default values and you can accept variable-length argument lists with the `...rest` operand. Every so often it might be necessary for a function to accept more than a handful of possible arguments, in which case identifying the argument's intention from its position in the argument list alone can be a memory exercise.

In these cases, when the number of parameters to the function is not the result of a design flaw, you might wish for named arguments. ActionScript 3.0 does not use named arguments, but an `Object` can be used as a variable argument list, using the keys as the arguments' names. Because you can't check the passed `Object` at compile time for correctness, it's best to only use an `Object` for named arguments which have defaults.

For example, the following code sets a particular line style in preparation to draw some strokes on a `Sprite`:

```
var sprite:Sprite = new Sprite();
var g:Graphics = sprite.graphics;
g.lineStyle(1, 0xff0000, 1, true, "none", "round", "round", 20);
g.lineStyle(1, 0xff0000, 1, true, LineScaleMode.NONE, CapsStyle.ROUND,
JointStyle.ROUND, 20);
```

The last two lines are identical. The function call is almost incomprehensible when we use plain strings for the three parameters near the end. When we use the static constants for these variables, the readability improves some. Let's pretend instead that we rewrote the `lineStyle()` function to take an `Object` parameter. The call might look very different:

```
g.lineStyle({
    thickness: 1,
    color: 0xff0000,
    alpha: 1,
    pixelHinting: true,
    scaleMode: LineScaleMode.NONE,
    caps: CapsStyle.ROUND,
    joints: JointStyle.ROUND,
    miterLimit: 20
});
```

This use of a one-time, or *anonymous*, object to name parameters can increase readability of your code, but at the cost of compile-time argument checking. We recommend that you use this approach sparingly.

Using Objects as Nested Data

By inserting `Object`s inside `Object`s, you can create nested tree-like structures. By using dot notation, it is easy to traverse deeply nested trees of `Object`s.

```
plants.veggies.underground.carrot;
```

XML as Objects

In ActionScript 1.0 and ActionScript 2.0, it was not uncommon to convert XML structures into `Object` trees for convenience because traversing XML could be somewhat unwieldy. With E4X, however, traversing XML is just as easy. Also, E4X lets you handle structured data with much more elegance and sophistication than nested `Object`s. We recommend always preferring XML for tree-structured data. Chapter 10 shows how to work with XML in depth.

JSON

The syntax used to declare `Object` literals is simple and efficient enough for most uses that it has been adopted by many web programmers as a lightweight alternative to XML. JavaScript interpreters simply have to `eval()` the string, which represents the structure to turn the string into the object it represents. Unfortunately, this trick doesn't work in ActionScript 3.0, as Flash Player does not compile or run ActionScript code at runtime. So E4X and lack of `eval()` interpretation are two good reasons to prefer XML for nested data.

If you must use JSON, however, Adobe provides a JSON parser in the corelib library available at `http://labs.adobe.com/wiki/index.php/ActionScript_3:resources:apis:libraries#corelib`.

Summary

- All classes extend `Object`.
- `Object` is an empty class that is dynamic.
- You can create and modify properties and methods of dynamic classes at runtime.
- `Object` and `Dictionary` both implement associative arrays.
- Associative arrays store key-value pairs. In `Objects`, the keys must be strings. In `Dictionarys`, they can be any object.
- Anonymous objects can be used to pass named arguments.
- JSON stores nested data in object literal syntax, but XML is more useful with E4X.

Chapter 10

Working with XML

P erhaps one of the most significant changes to ActionScript in version 3.0 is the introduction of E4X, a completely reworked system for handling XML data based on the ECMAScript standard. This allows programmers to work seamlessly with XML in their programs. With ActionScript 3.0, XML data can be written directly into code using XML literals, which are parsed automatically.

Getting Started with XML in ActionScript

XML is a type of markup language for structuring data hierarchically that is widely used and has countless applications. This book assumes a basic knowledge of XML's structure and syntax. If you are unfamiliar with XML, you may want to check out the W3C Schools XML Tutorial (www.w3schools.com/xml/) or the Wikipedia entry on XML (http://en.wikipedia.org/wiki/XML).

Although XML comes in many different flavors, all XML shares this basic structure:

```
<parentNode>
    <childNode attributeName="Attribute Value">
        Node Content
    </childNode>
</parentNode>
```

Data is contained within *nodes*, or *elements*, enclosed within start and end *tags*. Some elements contain *attributes* as name-value pairs within their start

IN THIS CHAPTER

Understanding XML and the new E4X system

Constructing XML objects using ActionScript

Accessing XML data using dot and at syntax

Filtering out the elements you need from an XML tree

Manipulating XML using built-in methods

Working with namespaces, comments, and processing instructions

tags, which contain additional information about the element. Some elements may contain *text nodes*, which contain data stored within an element. XML may also contain *namespace declarations*, *comments*, or *processing instruction* nodes.

Origins of E4X

If you've worked with Flash at any point over the last ten years, you probably don't think of the Flash platform as using open standards. However, ActionScript 3.0 is one of the most accurate implementations of the ECMAScript standard. The name E4X is a nickname for ECMAScript for XML, an implementation of the standard defined in ECMA-357. It's the same XML access standard that's used in JavaScript version 2.0.

The syntax for the new XML class is simple and intuitive for ActionScript developers. You may find it similar to the XPath standard or third-party XML tools for AS2. It provides a simplified short-hand notation that allows you to access specific nodes or sets of nodes by name or by index without complicated custom recursive functions. It also defines methods and properties for accessing all parts of the XML object including comments, namespaces, and processing instructions.

Working with XML literals

In addition to the new XML classes, AS3 adds support for XML Literals, or constant values that can be added to code and can be interpreted the same way strings and numbers are. This allows you to add XML data directly into your code without having to parse strings or load the data from external sources. Here's an example of an XML literal being assigned to an XML object. Notice that there is no constructor or quotes around the data — you can write XML directly into the code.

```
var employeeList:XML = <employeeList>
                    <employee>
                        <name first="Conan" last="O'Brien" />
                        <title>Host</title>
                    </employee>
                    <employee>
                        <name first="Andy" last="Richter" />
                        <title>Sidekick</title>
                    </employee>
                    <employee>
                        <name first="Max" last="Weinberg" />
                        <title>Band Leader</title>
                    </employee>
                </employeeList>;
```

The preceding example shows XML data being added directly to a variable called `employeeList`.

NOTE   AS3 provides the ability to load XML from external sources. However, for simplicity's sake we use literals for this chapter. To learn more about loading data from external sources, check out Chapter 22.

Using expressions within literals

You can also embed ActionScript code directly into your XML data by enclosing the code you wish to add in curly braces {}. This will allow you to fill a data set with dynamically generated values:

```
var squareLength:Number = 10;
var circleRadius:Number = 5;
var shapeData:XML = <shapeList>
                    <shape type="square" size={squareLength} />
                    <shape type="cicle" size={circleRadius} />
                </shapeList>;
trace(shapeData.toXMLString());
```

The last method, `toXMLString()`, converts the XML data stored in `shapeData` to the string equivalent, preserving the XML structure. This produces the following XML data:

```
<shapeList>
   <shape type="square" area="10" />
   <shape type="circle" area="5" />
</shapeList>
```

A brief introduction to E4X operators and syntax

E4X defines several different ways to access and edit the data within XML objects by using the methods of the `XML` and `XMLList` classes and by using a special set of operators for working with XML. Technically, the brackets around XML code are operators; the official name for the angle brackets is *XML literal tag delimiter*. There are many others but most of them are provided to help you create XML structures within your code.

We'll take a look at some of the more commonly used access operators. They are the *dot* (`.`), the *attribute identifier* (`@`), and the square brackets (`[]`). The dot enables you to access elements of your XML, the attribute identifier enables you to access the attributes of an element, and the square brackets enable you to access a property by name or index. In practice, these can be used in a way very similar to the dot used for properties and methods of an object and the brackets used in arrays.

In the following example, you can quickly find data nested deep within an XML tree.

```
var myXML:XML = <alpha>
                    <beta>
                        <charlie delta="echo">foxtrot</charlie>
                    </beta>
                    <beta>
                        <golf hotel="india">juliet</golf>
                    </beta>
                </alpha>;
trace(myXML.beta[1].golf);         // Displays: juliet
trace(myXML.beta[0].charlie.@delta); // Displays: echo
```

We discuss all of these operators (and their corresponding methods) in more detail in this chapter.

Understanding the XML classes

The new implementation of XML uses several classes that are new to ActionScript 3.0. Each class represents a different type of data that you will use when working with XML data. They are all located in the top level of the ActionScript API, which means you will not need an import statement to use them. Let's take a quick look at what each of these classes is used for.

XML

An XML object represents a portion of simple XML data such as an element, text node, comment, or processing instruction. Defining all these seemingly different nodes as XML objects allows you to use the methods for manipulating XML data on all of them without worrying about their type. Most times, you will see these values nested within elements to create complex values stored within a single variable. An example of a complex XML object containing a single element and a text node might be:

```
var myXML:XML = <message>Hello, world!</message>;
```

XMLList

An XMLList is a numbered set, very much like an array, of XML objects. The XML data contained within might be one or more XML objects, portions of XML objects, or individual nodes. Several of the XML class's methods, such as `children()`, will return results as XMLLists. XMLList shares many of the same methods as the XML class, enabling you to use most operations interchangeably. Like an array, XMLLists have indexes for each XML object within them and a `length()` method showing the total number of elements. Here is an example of an XMLList that contains several <item> nodes. Notice that the items in the XMLList exist next to each other without having a parent node (<list>) so the XMLList is a flat set of nodes rather than a hierarchy.

```
var list:XML = <list>
                    <item id="58" />
                    <item id="135" />
                    <item id="12" />
               </list>;
var items:XMLList = list.item;
trace(items);     // Displays: <item id="58" />
                  //           <item id="135" />
                  //           <item id="12" />
trace(items.length()); // Displays: 3
trace(items[1].toXMLString()); // Displays: <item id="135" />
```

Namespace

A Namespace object defines an XML namespace for your XML object. In XML, namespaces are used to define certain tags as being part of a group or a language. For example, all Flex 2 framework components are defined in the mx namespace and SOAP calls use the soap namespace. We'll discuss namespaces more later on in the chapter.

QName

A QName object represents the relationship between a qualified namespace URI and a local namespace identifier. In the case of the Flex framework, you would use it to couple the URI, www.adobe .com/2006/mxml, with the local identifier, mx. If this doesn't make any sense, don't worry about it for now. We discuss QNames when we get to namespaces later in the chapter.

> **NOTE** In AS3, the top-level XML classes handle XML data in an entirely new way; however, the older XML classes from previous versions of ActionScript are included for legacy support. The old XML class has been renamed to XMLDocument and is located in the flash.xml package to avoid confusion. We will not be covering legacy XML classes further in this chapter. For more information on the flash.xml package, you may want to look at the ActionScript 3.0 language reference.

Accessing Values with E4X

E4X provides you with ways to use the data in your XML files that are a huge improvement over firstChild() and nextSibling() methods from ActionScript 2.0.

Using the dot operator to access Elements

The dot operator is the simplest tool in your E4X arsenal and is best taught through example.

This code defines the XML for a list of movies. We'll use this code for the next several examples:

```
var movieList:XML = <movieList>
            <listName>My favorite movies</listName>
            <movie id="123">
                <title>Titus</title>
                <year>1999</year>
                <director>Julie Taymor</director>
            </movie>
            <movie id="456">
                <title>Rushmore</title>
                <year>1998</year>
                <director>Wes Anderson</director>
            </movie>
            <movie id="789">
                <title>Annie Hall</title>
                <year>1977</year>
                <director>Woody Allen</director>
            </movie>
        </movieList>;
```

Using the dot operator, you can access any of the movieList's elements. Simply write the name of the element you wish to access as if it were a property of the movieList object. Notice here that we omit the root element, <movieList>, from our path:

```
trace(movieList.listName); // Displays : My favorite movies
```

For elements with more than one of the same kind of node, such as <movie>, add a square bracket with an index number as you would if the value were stored in an array. Remember that the first <movie> tag will be at index 0.

```
trace(movieList.movie[1]);
// Displays : <movie id="456">
                <title>Rushmore</title>
                <year>1998</year>
                <director>Wes Anderson</director>
            </movie>
```

Dive further within this movie node by using more dot operators and element names:

```
trace(movieList.movie[0].title); // Displays : Titus
trace(movieList.movie[2].director);  // Displays : Woody Allen
```

You can also use this syntax to write new values to the XML:

```
movieList.movie[2].director = "Allen Konigsberg";
```

Using methods to access children

So far, you've looked at ways to access data by using operators. But the XML class offers several methods for extracting values as well. By using the child() method, you can get a particular set of children by name. The following two lines of code produce identical results:

```
trace(movieList.movie);
trace(movieList.child("movie"));
```

Using child(), you can search the element for any children with a given name. You can also use the children() method to get a child by index rather than node name.

```
trace(movieList.children()[0].toXMLString());
// Displays: <listName>My favorite movies</listName>
trace(movieList.children()[2].children()[0].toXMLString());
// Displays: <title>Rushmore</title>
```

If you're not sure what the particular index of a child node is, you can look it up using `childIndex()`. For example:

```
trace(movieList.movie[2].childIndex()); // Displays: 3
```

By using the `name()` method, you can get the node name of the child node you're accessing:

```
trace(movieList.children(1).name()); // Displays: movie
```

Finally, if you need to search for elements only while ignoring text nodes, comments, and processing directives, you can use `elements()`, which returns only elements. In this example, this method will function the same as `children()`.

Using the at operator to access attributes

To access attributes, you use a device similar to the child accessor called, that's right, the *attribute identifier*, which is written as an at sign (@). Use the at sign followed by the attribute name that you want to use:

```
trace(movieList.movie[0].@id); // Displays: 123
```

In addition to reading attribute values, you can also set them with this method:

```
movieList.movie[0].@id = 8675309;
```

If you wish to access all of the attributes for a tag, you can use an asterisk:

```
var myXML:XML = <foo a="1" b="2" c="3" />;
trace(myXML.@*.toXMLString()); // Displays: 1
                                             2
                                             3
```

Just as the dot operator has its method counterparts `child()` and `children()`, the @ operator has the `attribute()` and `attributes()` methods for accessing attributes by name or as an XML list respectively.

```
movieList.movie[1].attribute("id"); // 456
movieList.movie[2].attributes(); // 789
```

The preceding code is functionally identical to the following code:

```
movieList.movie[1].@id; // 456
movieList.movie[2].@*; // 789
```

Accessing text within an element

If an element contains only a text node, the `toString()` returns that text value automatically. Because the `toString()` method is called automatically when using `trace()`, this provides a quick way to display the value of the text node.

However, some elements will contain text as well as other child nodes, such as the following:

```
<messyElement>
    <junkNode />
    Text node
    <stuffNode>stuffNode's text node</stuffNode>
    Another text node
</messyElement>
```

To explicitly access the text node of an element you can use the `text()` method, which returns an XMLList of text nodes:

```
trace(movieList.movie[1].title.text()); // Displays: Rushmore
```

> **TIP** Be careful not to confuse `toString()` and `toXMLString()`. When you work with XML, `toString()` returns the value of a node (which might be empty) rather than the node itself, whereas `toXMLString()` returns the node as well as the text within it.

We discuss these methods further in the section "Converting to and from Strings."

Using the descendant accessor

One very powerful feature of E4X is the ability to directly access *descendant* nodes. A descendant is any node contained within a certain element or in any of that element's child nodes or in their child nodes, and so on. In other words, a descendant node is an element's child, grandchild, great-grandchild, great-great-grandchild, and so on.

By using the *descendant accessor operator*, which is written as a double dot (`..`), you can make a deep dive to the data you want without worrying about what the path to that data might be. This works with elements but also with attributes and other types of XML objects. In the following example, you get all the movie title tags in one fell swoop:

```
trace(movieList..title);
```

This displays the following:

```
<title>Titus</title>
<title>Rushmore</title>
<title>Annie Hall</title>
```

See how simple that was? The double dot is even more valuable when it comes to larger XML trees. Let's try another example and pull all of the attributes from the entire XML document:

```
trace(movieList..@*.toXMLString()); // Displays: 123
                                     //           456
                                     //           789
```

There is also a method form of this operator called `descendants()`. This function behaves the same way as the double dot:

```
trace(movieList.descendants("year").text().toXMLString());
// Displays: 1999
//           1998
//           1977
```

One thing you'll want to be aware of when using descendants is that all matches will be returned even if there are tags with the same name on different levels of the tree. In the following example, there is a <b> tag, which is a descendant of another <b> tag:

```
var foo:XML = <a>
                <b>
                  <c>
                    <b>foo</b>
                  </c>
                </b>
              </a>;
trace(foo..b.toXMLString());
```

This displays the following:

```
<b>
  <c>
    <b>foo</b>
  </c>
</b>
<b>foo</b>
```

As you can see, <b>foo</b> is returned twice, once as a descendant of the first <b> tag, and again on its own.

Accessing ancestors

If a descendant is a node or attribute contained within a particular element, then an *ancestor* must be a node that contains a particular element. While there is no shortcut operator to access an ancestor, the XML class has a `parent()` method that returns the next node up on the chain for a given XML object:

```
var title:XMLList = movieList.movie[1].title;
var director:XMLList = title.parent().director;
trace(title + " directed by " + director);
// Displays: Rushmore directed by Wes Anderson
```

Iterating through the children of an element

Let's say you need to perform an action on each of several XML items. For example, you may want to print out an inventory of all the <movie> items you have or maybe you'd like to create a list of new releases by sorting your movies by their release date. E4X makes this easy. Many of the functions we've mentioned, including the child access operator (.), return `XMLList` objects. As we briefly mentioned, XMLLists act like specialized arrays for holding pieces of XML. They have length and indexes just like an array. They can also be iterated through much like an array. The following shows a simple example of adding the names of the movies to an array and alphabetizing them:

```
var movieTitles:Array = new Array();
var movies:XMLList = movieList.movie;
for (var i:int = 0; i < movies.length(); i++) {
 movieTitles[i] = movies[i].title;
  }
movieTitles.sort();
trace(movieTitles); // Displays: Annie Hall,Rushmore,Titus
```

In addition, you can use the `for..in` or `for each..in` statements to iterate through an `XMLList`. The following code:

```
var movies:XMLList = movieList.movie;
for each (var movie:XML in movies) {
    movie.title = movie.title.toUpperCase();
}
trace(movies.title);
```

will display:

```
<title>TITUS</title>
<title>RUSHMORE</title>
<title>ANNIE HALL</title>
```

Filtering within XML

E4X also adds the powerful ability to filter your data on-the-fly by using the *XML parentheses filter operator ()*. When creating a path within an XML tree, you can add a search in the form of a

Boolean expression like the ones used in an `if` statement, to evaluate within two parentheses. Any nodes matching the terms of the search will be returned in an XMLList. The result is a very easy-to-use instant filtering tool. Let's look at a couple of examples. The first filters by the movie's `year` node, the second by the `id` attribute:

```
var classics:XMLList = movieList.movie.(year < 1990).title;
trace(classics); // Displays: <title>Annie Hall</title>
var idSort:XMLList = movieList.movie.(@id > 400).title;
trace(idSort);
// Displays: <title>Rushmore</title>
//           <title>Annie Hall</title>
```

You can filter by any variety of criteria as long as you keep in mind that the filter terms are evaluated in the scope of whatever node to which you've navigated. In this case, all of the examples are searching for matches within the `movieList.movie` XMLList. Here's an example that uses a string search on the director name:

```
var julieMovies:XMLList =
movieList.movie.(director.search("Julie") != -1).title;
trace(julieMovies); // Displays: Titus
```

Unlike some of the other operators we've discussed, there is no method equivalent of this filtering action.

Constructing XML objects

You can do more than just work from predefined XML values. The XML class also contains methods for adding to and modifying your data. You've already seen how you can change the values of individual nodes so let's look at some ways to combine chunks of XML objects together to make more complex ones.

Combining XML nodes

First, let's create a new XML element for a fourth movie to add to our list.

```
var anotherMovie:XML = <movie id="222">
                           <title>Tron</title>
                           <year>1982</year>
                           <director>Steven Lisberger</director>
                       </movie>;
```

This element, `anotherMovie`, uses the same format as the `movieList` movie elements that we've been working with but is not part of the `movieList` tree. We're going to look at some ways to add this movie to our list. The methods provided for combining XML nodes should be fairly straightforward.

Using + and += operators

Just like combining strings, you can add additional children to an XMLList using the + or += operators. This may be the simplest way to add data to an XML structure. The following code:

```
movieList.movie += anotherMovie;
trace(movieList);
```

displays:

```
<movieList>
  <listName>My favorite movies</listName>
  <movie id="123">
    <title>Titus</title>
    <year>1999</year>
    <director>Julie Taymor</director>
  </movie>
  <movie id="456">
    <title>Rushmore</title>
    <year>1998</year>
    <director>Wes Anderson</director>
  </movie>
  <movie id="789">
    <title>Annie Hall</title>
    <year>1977</year>
    <director>Woody Allen</director>
  </movie>
  <movie id="222">
    <title>Tron</title>
    <year>1982</year>
    <director>Steven Lisberger</director>
  </movie>
</movieList>
```

The new movie, Tron, is added to the end of the set of movie elements. This example used the += operator, which appends data to the variable itself. You can use the + operator as well. The following two lines produce identical results:

```
movieList.movie += anotherMovie;
movieList.movie = movieList.movie + anotherMovie;
```

The values that you add don't need to follow the same format as other elements in an XML object. You can use the + and += operators to add additional nodes to a specific element. In the following example, we add a <genre> tag to Annie Hall, and then add a new text node to that genre element. Running this code:

```
var annieHall:XML = movieList.movie[2];
annieHall.children += <genre></genre>;
```

```
annieHall.genre += "Comedy";
trace(annieHall);
```

displays:

```
<movie id="789">
    <title>Annie Hall</title>
    <year>1977</year>
    <director>Woody Allen</director>
    <genre>Comedy</genre>
</movie>
```

Using XML methods to combine values

If you need more control over exactly where you want your values to be added to an XML object, you can use the methods built into the XML class for adding values to other nodes. First, we look at appendChild(), which is analogous to the += operator and behaves the same way. You can use appendChild() to add a value to the end of an XML object or XMLList.

In the following example, we add <genre> tags to all of the remaining movies using appendChild():

```
movieList.movie[0].appendChild(<genre>Drama</genre>);
movieList.movie[1].appendChild(<genre>Comedy</genre>);
movieList.movie[3].appendChild(<genre>Sci-Fi</genre>);
trace(movieList.movie);
```

This produces the following result:

```
<movie id="123">
    <title>Titus</title>
    <year>1999</year>
    <director>Julie Taymor</director>
    <genre>Drama</genre>
</movie>
<movie id="456">
    <title>Rushmore</title>
    <year>1998</year>
    <director>Wes Anderson</director>
    <genre>Comedy</genre>
</movie>
<movie id="789">
    <title>Annie Hall</title>
    <year>1977</year>
    <director>Woody Allen</director>
    <genre>Comedy</genre>
</movie>
<movie id="222">
```

```
      <title>Tron</title>
      <year>1982</year>
      <director>Steven Lisberger</director>
      <genre>Sci-Fi</genre>
</movie>
```

Note that in the preceding example, we are able to append a child node directly onto a `movie` object without first accessing `children` as we did in the += example.

If adding to the end isn't what you're looking for, there are other ways to add values to your XML object. They are `prependChild()`, which adds to the beginning of an object, and `insertChildAfter()` and `insertChildBefore()`, which both allow you to specify the location at which you want to add. This example uses all of these options:

```
var example:XML = <example>
                      <b />
                      <d />
                      <f />
                  </example>;

example.appendChild(<g />);
trace(example);
//<example>
//    <b/>
//    <d/>
//    <f/>
//    <g/>
//</example>
example.prependChild(<a />);
trace(example);
//<example>
//  <a/>
//  <b/>
//  <d/>
//  <f/>
//  <g/>
//</example>
example.insertChildAfter(example.b, <c />);
trace(example);
//<example>
//    <a/>
//    <b/>
//    <c/>
//    <d/>
//    <f/>
//    <g/>
//</example>
example.insertChildBefore(example.f, <e />);
```

```
trace(example); .
//<example>
//    <a/>
//    <b/>
//    <c/>
//    <d/>
//    <e/>
//    <f/>
//    <g/>
//</example>
```

Removing XML nodes

Unlike adding nodes to an XML object, there are no methods for deleting XML nodes. Instead, you simply use the `delete` operator. This removes a specified element or value from the tree. Let us assume that I've grown tired of Woody Allen's neurotic musings and want him taken off of my list. Running the following code:

```
delete movieList.movie[2];
trace(movieList.movie);
```

displays:

```
<movie id="123">
    <title>Titus</title>
    <year>1999</year>
    <director>Julie Taymor</director>
    <genre>Drama</genre>
</movie>
<movie id="456">
    <title>Rushmore</title>
    <year>1998</year>
    <director>Wes Anderson</director>
    <genre>Comedy</genre>
</movie>
<movie id="222">
    <title>Tron</title>
    <year>1982</year>
    <director>Steven Lisberger</director>
    <genre>Sci-Fi</genre>
</movie>
```

The `delete` operator works for other types of nodes as well, such as attributes. In the following example, we remove all attributes from the movie *Tron*.

```
var tron:XML = movieList.movie[2];
delete tron.@*;
trace(tron); ·
```

```
// Displays: <movie> // Notice the id attribute is gone.
//              <title>Tron</title>
//              <year>1982</year>
//              <director>Steven Lisberger</director>
//              <genre>Sci-Fi</genre>
//           </movie>
tron.id = 222; // Adding the id attribute back.
```

Duplicating an XML object

As we discussed in previous chapters, only simple values are passed by value and all complex objects in ActionScript are passed by reference. XML is no exception to the rule. Setting a variable to be equal to another XML object will create a reference to the original object and any changes made to either variable will be reflected across both variables, which can sometimes cause unwanted results.

```
var template:XML = <person><name><first /><last /></name></person>;
var me:XML = template;
me.name.first = "Mims";
me.name.last = "Wright";
trace(template);
// Displays: <person>
//              <name>
//                 <first>Mims</first>
//                 <last>Wright</last>
//              </name>
//           </person>
```

For this reason, the copy() method creates a duplicate of the original XML object so that it can be passed by value rather than reference. This enables you to safely make changes to a new copy of the XML data without affecting the original data.

```
var template:XML = <person><name><first /><last /></name></person>;
var me:XML = template.copy();
me.name.first = "Mims";
me.name.last = "Wright";
trace(template);
// Displays:  <person>
//               <name>
//                  <first/>
//                  <last/>
//               </name>
//            </person>
trace(me);
```

```
// Displays: <person>
//              <name>
//                  <first>Mims</first>
//                  <last>Wright</last>
//              </name>
//          </person>
```

Replacing values in XML nodes

The child nodes of an XML object can be replaced all at once by using the `setChildren()` method. This replaces all the child nodes with the XML that you provide. In the following example, we change the movie Tron (which has the ID 222) first to an empty element, and then to The Science of Sleep:

```
movieList.movie.(@id == 222).setChildren(null);
trace(movieList.movie.(@id == 222).toXMLString());
// Displays: <movie id="222">null</movie>
movieList.movie.(@id == 222).setChildren(<title>The Science of Sleep</title> +
                                    <year>2006</year> +
                                    <director>Michel Gondry</director> +
                                    <genre>Romance</genre>);
trace(movieList.movie.(@id == 222).toXMLString());
// Displays: <movie id="222">
//              <title>The Science of Sleep</title>
//              <year>2006</year>
//              <director>Michel Gondry</director>
//              <genre>Romance</genre>
//          </movie>
```

A similar method, called `replace()`, allows you to replace a single node with a new XML object. The new XML object can be anything and doesn't need to use the same tag name as the element being replaced:

```
movieList.movie.(@id == 222).replace("genre", <category>Independent</category>);
trace(movieList.movie.(@id == 222).toXMLString());
// Displays: <movie id="222">
//              <title>The Science of Sleep</title>
//              <year>2006</year>
//              <director>Michel Gondry</director>
//              <category>Independent</category>
//          </movie>
```

For more information on the `setChildren()` and `replace()` methods, please consult the AS3 documentation.

Converting to and from Strings

XML objects are essentially made up of string data. Therefore, the most common type conversions that you'll be dealing with are converting strings to XML and XML to strings. These operations are very simple but there is added functionality that goes a little further than your typical `toString()`.

Converting strings to XML

Occasionally, you may find it necessary to convert string values to XML when working with data from a string-based source or an external text file. To do this, you can simply use the XML constructor to cast the text as XML data. You should be careful to use only well-formed XML text when casting. Failure to do so will result in a runtime error.

```
var dialog:String = "Lorem ipsum dolor sit amet";
var XMLString:String = "<dialog>" + dialog + "</dialog>";
var xml:XML = XML(XMLString);
trace(xml.text()); // Displays: Lorem ipsum dolor sit amet
```

Converting XML to strings

As you've seen so far throughout the chapter, you can use the traditional `toString()` method with XML objects to display their contents as strings. However, the XML class also contains the `toXMLString()` method, which behaves slightly differently.

The `toString()` method for XML objects will usually display the contents of an XML element including any tags. However, if the XML object in question contains only a single node — for example, `<foo>bar</foo>` — only the text value of the node will be returned, in this case, `"bar"`. The `toXMLString()` method, on the other hand, will always return the full XML tag and all values contained within an element. In this case, `toXMLString()` would return `"<foo>bar</foo>"`.

```
var meal:XML = <meal>
                  <name>Dinner</name>
                  <course number="1">
                     <item>Salad</item>
                  </course>
                  <course number="2">
                     <item>Potatoes</item>
                     <item temperature="Medium Rare">Steak</item>
                  </course>

               </meal>;

trace(meal.name); // Displays: Dinner
trace(meal.course[0]); // Displays: <course number="1">
```

```
//                     <item>Salad</item>
//              </course>
trace(meal.course[1].item[0].toXMLString()); // Displays: <item>Potatoes</items>
trace(meal.course[1].item[1].toString()); // Displays: Steak
trace(meal.course[1].item[1].@temperature.toXMLString()); // Displays: Medium
Rare
trace(meal..item.toString());
// Displays: <item>Salad</item>
//          <item>Potatoes</item>
//          <item temperature="Medium Rare">Steak</item>
```

Printing pretty

There are a few options when it comes to formatting the XML string that is created by the `toString()` and `toXMLString()` calls. The first is the `prettyPrinting` flag. When set, XML strings are automatically normalized, removing empty tags and extra whitespace. This flag affects all XML objects and is set to `true` by default.

```
var example:XML = <stooges>
                        <moe /><curly><larry>
    </larry>
                              </curly>
          </stooges>;
XML.prettyPrinting = false;
trace(example);
// Displays: <stooges><moe/><curly><larry/></curly></stooges>

XML.prettyPrinting = true;
trace(example);
// Displays: <stooges>
//              <moe/>
//              <curly>
//                 <larry/>
//              </curly>
//          </stooges>
```

Notice how some cleanup occurs automatically, removing most of the whitespace; however, things look much more structured with `prettyPrinting` enabled.

Setting the number of spaces per indentation

When you use the `prettyPrinting` feature, your text is automatically indented. The second static property you can set is `prettyIndent`. This is an integer specifying the number of spaces used for each level of indentation. The default value is 2. This setting is ignored when the `prettyPrinting` flag is set to `false`. The following code:

```
XML.prettyIndent = 0;
trace(example);
```

```
XML.prettyIndent = 8;
trace(example);
```

will display the text with 0 spaces per tab:

```
<stooges>
<moe/>
<curly>
<larry/>
</curly>
</stooges>
```

and then with 8 spaces per tab:

```
<stooges>
        <moe/>
        <curly>
                <larry/>
        </curly>
</stooges>
```

Normalizing text nodes

XML objects support multiple text nodes per element although, most times, only one text node is used per element. In the rare case that you might have more than one text node in a given element, you can use the `normalize()` method to clean up whitespace and combine these text nodes into a single, contiguous node. In the following example, we add a fourth Stooge to our list using a series of `appendChild()` calls.

```
// add "shemp" using 3 appendChild() calls
example.appendChild("sh");
example.appendChild("");
example.appendChild("emp");
trace(example.text().length()); // Displays : 3
trace(example.text().toXMLString());
//Displays: sh
//
//              emp
```

Notice that the length of the `text()` XMLList is 3 and three lines are printed when displaying this text. Normalizing will merge these three text nodes into one.

```
example.normalize();
trace(example.text().length()); // Displays : 1
trace(example.text().toXMLString()); // Displays: shemp
```

Keep in mind that most times, text nodes containing whitespace will exist with whitespaces intact as a single text node. Only in a situation where multiple text nodes are intentionally added, as in the preceding example, will the `normalize()` method be used.

Loading XML Data from External Sources

The subject of loading data from servers is much more involved than can be covered in a chapter on XML. Therefore, we discuss this in its own section later on in the book. However, in case you're really itching to try loading some data from a server, these are the basics of how it's done.

In the AS2 implementation of XML, the data was loaded through a method called by the XML class. However, in AS3, that functionality has been moved outside of the class to the `flash.net` package. In this example we use a `URLLoader` to load the XML file and then create an XML object from the data we've loaded.

```
import flash.net.*;

var myXML:XML;
var url:URLRequest = new URLRequest("http://www.your-domain.com/test.xml");
var loader:URLLoader = new URLLoader(url);
loader.addEventListener(Event.COMPLETE, onLoadComplete);

function onLoadComplete(event:Event):void {
   if (loader.data) {
      myXML = XML(loader.data);
   }
}
```

You can replace the URL in this example with the location of your data. When the loader is done loading, the `onLoadComplete()` function is called, which converts the data loaded by the loader into XML form. From this point, you can use `myXML` the same way we've used the other XML data in this chapter.

Gathering Meta-Information About XML Nodes

The XML class allows you to inspect some of the meta-information about the XML nodes you're working with. This can be useful when automating the processing of XML objects. You can use methods to find the type of node and the type of content a node contains, either simple or complex.

Finding node types

To determine the type of node that you're working with, you can use the `nodeKind()` method on the branch that you wish to inspect. The function returns a string that describes the kind of node. The string returned will be one of the following:

- `element`
- `attribute`

- text
- comment
- processing-instruction

TIP In order to work with comments or processing instructions, you must disable the ignorecomments or ignoreProcessingInstructions flags respectively. You can find more information about this later in the chapter.

The following example uses some XHTML code:

```
XML.ignoreComments = false;
XML.ignoreProcessingInstructions = false;
var XHTMLExample:XML = <html>
                        <head />
                        <body id="main">
                           Welcome!
                           <!-- Start PHP -->
                              <?php
                                 // execute some php code
                              ?>
                           <!-- End PHP -->
                        </body>
                      </html>;
trace(XHTMLExample.body.nodeKind()); // Displays: element
trace(XHTMLExample.body.@id.nodeKind()); // Displays: attribute
trace(XHTMLExample.body.text().nodeKind()); // Displays: text
trace(XHTMLExample.body.comments()[0].nodeKind()); // Displays: comment
trace(XHTMLExample.body.processingInstructions().nodeKind()); // Displays:
// processing-instruction
```

Determining the type of content in a node

Nodes that contain only a single text node or no content at all are said to have simple content. Nodes that contain other nodes are said to have complex content. To determine whether a node contains simple or complex content, you can use either hasComplexContent() or hasSimpleContent(). Either will do — just use whichever one makes more sense to you.

```
var contentTest:XML = <test>
                        <a />
                        <b>Lorem Ipsum</b>
                        <c>
                           <d />
                        </c>
                      </test>;
trace(contentTest.a.hasSimpleContent());  // Displays: true
trace(contentTest.b.hasSimpleContent());  // Displays: true
trace(contentTest.c.hasSimpleContent());  // Displays: false
trace(contentTest.d.hasComplexContent()); // Displays: false
```

Using Namespaces

Namespaces are a convention used in XML to help group XML elements and attributes into sets of similar functionality in much the same way that we use packages to group classes into sets that work together. XML files will use a namespace declaration that defines a name for the namespace and a unique identifier to differentiate it from other namespaces (this can be anything, but usually it's a URI of some kind):

```
<example xmlns:namespaceName="http://www.yoursite.com">
```

> **NOTE** The URI for an XML namespace doesn't have anything to do with a web site located there; it's strictly to provide a unique string. Generally, URIs are thought to be one-of-a-kind but so is the phrase "Grund staggle ipp brid hunf," which would work just as well.

To define a node as a member of a particular namespace, use the namespace name followed by a colon and then the name of your element or attribute.

```
<book xmlns:bible="http://www.wiley.com">
    <bible:chapter>Working with XML</bible:chapter>
</book>
```

Keep in mind that even if you've worked with XML in the past, you might not be familiar with XML namespaces (or more likely you've already worked with them without realizing it). Here are some tags with namespaces that you might recognize from RSS feeds, SOAP calls, and Adobe Flex:

```
<rss:channel />
<soap:Body />
<mx:Canvas />
```

Because the topic of why and when to use namespaces is so broad, we will not cover it in this book. However, if you're interested in learning more about the way namespaces work, you can check out the W3C Tutorial at www.w3schools.com/xml/xml_namespaces.asp.

> **TIP** XML namespaces and the Namespace class are completely unrelated to the namespace keyword, which is used in the construction of classes to allow specific access to a method or property of a class. You can find more on this type of namespace and the namespace keyword in Chapter 3.

Working with namespaces in ActionScript

Working with namespaces in E4X is a bit complicated when compared to the dot and at operators used to access elements and attributes. First let's look at the Namespace class. This class represents an XML namespace that is essentially just a namespace identifier or *prefix* (for example, rss, soap, mx) and the *namespace URI* (for example, http://www.wiley.com) and that's pretty much all that the class does. Creating a namespace is simple and can be done by passing either the prefix and the URI or just the URI to a namespace constructor. Consider that

```
var fooNamespace:Namespace = new Namespace("http://www.bar.com");
```

or

```
var fooNamespace:Namespace = new Namespace("foo", "http://www.bar.com");
```

produce the same results, a namespace object called `fooNamespace`, but the former will have a prefix value of `null` whereas the latter will have a prefix value of "`foo`". Unless you specifically need to work with the prefix, the URI is enough information to work with.

Namespace objects return their URI value by default when the `toString()` method is used:

```
trace(fooNamespace.toString()); // Displays: http://www.bar.com
```

Namespaces can also be created by using the `namespace()` method of the XML object. This method takes one string parameter, which is the prefix of one of the namespaces defined in your XML. Consider the following example data:

```
var example:XML = <example xmlns:test="http://foo.com">
                      <test:element>Lorem Ipsum</test:element>
                  </example>;
```

In this example, we're creating an XML tree that defines a namespace with the prefix of `test` and with the URI of `http://foo.com`. Now we'll use the `namespace()` method to access it:

```
var test:Namespace = example.namespace("test");
trace(test.prefix); // Displays: test
trace(test.uri); // Displays: http://foo.com
```

> **TIP**   Although technically the `namespace()` method will return a Namespace, we recommend that you use it to create a new Namespace object, as in the preceding code, and work from this object.

The `namespace()` method will attempt to return the namespace for whatever prefix you pass in as a parameter. If the prefix you pass is invalid, it will return `undefined`. If you omit the parameter altogether, the method will return the default namespace defined for the element.

Alternatively, you can use the `namespaceDelarations()` method to return an Array of all the namespaces defined for a given element.

```
var example:XML = <example xmlns:test="http://foo.com"
                           xmlns:mims="http://mimswright.com"
                           xmlns:roger="http://partlyhuman.com"
/>;
trace(example.namespaceDeclarations()[1]);
// Displays: http://mimswright.com
```

The `inScopeNamespaces()` method works similarly to `namespaceDeclarations()`. For more information on these, please consult the ActionScript 3.0 language reference.

Using the :: operator

E4X defines another operator for accessing nodes with namespaces: the double colon (::). You can use this in accordance with a namespace object to access nodes that have different namespaces than the default. Let's show this with our original example XML:

```
var example:XML = <example xmlns:test="http://foo.com">
                      <test:element>Lorem Ipsum</test:element>
                      <test:element test:attribute="Dolor Sit Amet" />
                  </example>;
var test:Namespace = example.namespace("test");
trace(example.test::element[0]); // Displays: Lorem Ipsum
```

The double colon tells ActionScript to access the element node from within the test namespace. This same syntax can be used to access attributes defined with namespaces:

```
trace(example.test::element[1].@test::attribute); // Displays: Dolor Sit Amet
```

When working frequently with a single namespace, you may want to try setting a default namespace rather than typing the name of the namespace over and over again. You can do this on a global scale by using the default xml namespace keyphrase (these three words work together as a single instruction):

```
default xml namespace = test;.
```

However, be cautious when using this because it changes the default namespace for all new XML objects.

Taking it further

The following are a few more methods dealing with XML namespaces, but for the sake of simplicity, they won't be covered in detail in this book. More information can be found in the AS3 language reference.

- addNamespace() and removeNamespace(): Allow you to add namespaces to your objects when dynamically constructing XML.

- setNamespace(): Sets the namespace of an XML object to the one you provide.

- localName(): Like the name() method, returns the node name for an element but in this case, the namespace prefix is omitted and only the local name is returned. For example, <foo:bar/>.localName() would return only "bar".

- setLocalName(): Likewise, sets the local name for an element with a namespace attached.

Working with Comments and Processing Instructions

Although they are not commonly used in ActionScript, the XML comment blocks and processing instructions included in your code are all considered nodes and therefore are included in your XML object when the data is parsed. If you should need to access these values, you can use the `comments()` method or the `processingInstructions()` method to get XMLLists of comments or processing instructions respectively.

Notice that the static properties `ignoreComments` and `ingnoreProcessingInstructions` both default to `true` and must be set to `false` in order for the `comments()` and `processingInstructions()` methods to work correctly. We discuss these flags later in the chapter.

```
XML.ignoreComments = false;
XML.ignoreProcessingInstructions = false;
var XHTMLExample:XML = <html>
                        <head />
                        <body id="main">
                          Welcome!
                          <!-- Start PHP -->
                            <?php
                                // execute some php code
                            ?>
                          <!-- End PHP -->
                        </body>
                      </html>;
trace(XHTMLExample.*.comments().length()); // Displays: 2
trace(XHTMLExample.body.comments().toXMLString());
// Displays: <!-- Start PHP -->
//           <!-- End PHP -->
trace(XHTMLExample.body.comments()[1].toXMLString());
// Displays: <!-- End PHP -->
trace(XHTMLExample.*.processingInstructions().toXMLString());
// Displays: <?php // execute some php code
//           ?>
```

How you use the comments and processing instructions could vary widely depending on your desired effect. For example, you may wish to manually parse the processing instructions into commands or output comments to a logging window. However, because this is fairly uncommon, we will not discuss these methods in further detail. For more information, refer to the ActionScript 3.0 documentation on the XML class.

Setting Options for the XML class

We've already looked at most of the various XML class level settings. They include:

- `ignoreWhitespace`
- `ignoreComments`
- `ignoreProcessingInstructions`
- `prettyPrinting`
- `prettyIndent`

The only one we've not yet covered is `ignoreWhitespace`. This flag, which defaults to `true`, determines whether text nodes consisting entirely of whitespace will be displayed. If set to `true`, whitespace will be ignored and the element containing the whitespace will be empty. You may want to set this value to `false` if it is important for you to maintain whitespace in your text nodes. For more information on this, please refer to the ActionScript 3.0 documentation.

All of these settings can be accessed as a group with the `settings()` static method, which returns an object containing the values for each of these variables:

```
trace(XML.settings().ignoreProcessingInstructions); // Displays: true
XML.ignoreProcessingInstructions = false;
trace(XML.settings().ignoreProcessingInstructions); // Displays: false
```

You can also get a list of all the default values for these properties by using the `defaultSettings()` static method. There is also a `setSettings()` static method that allows you to change the settings object to a new Object. Although this allows you to change all values for the various settings, we recommend setting the individual properties to change these values. The one exception is if you choose to use the `setSettings()` method in conjunction with the `defaultSettings()` method to reset all the settings to their defaults.

In the following example, we use the `defaultSettings()` object to reset an individual flag, `ignoreWhitespace`, and then reset all the settings to their defaults using `setSettings()`.

```
XML.ignoreWhitespace = XML.defaultSettings().ignoreWhitespace;
trace(XML.ignoreWhitespace); // Displays: true
XML.setSettings(XML.defaultSettings());
// All setting are returned to default
```

 Keep in mind that these settings are, for the most part, static properties and methods of the XML class and will affect all XML objects.

Summary

- E4X is the new, web-standardized way to work with XML data in ActionScript.

- You can create XML data directly in your code with E4X. These XML literals are interpreted as values just like strings and objects.

- Use the dot operator and the at operator to navigate through your XML tree. Values can be set and deleted using this syntax. Nearly all of the operators have method equivalents.

- Use the double dot operator (..) to search for an item within the entire XML object and all of its children.

- Filter XML data for items that match a particular set of criteria using a logical statement enclosed within two parentheses within an XML path.

- By using appendChild(), prependChild(), insertChildAfter(), and so on, you can add additional branches to your XML tree.

- Converting to and from strings can be achieved with the XML() constructor, and the toString() and toXMLString() methods.

- Work with namespaces by using the Namespace class and the namespace() method. Use the :: operator to access an element with a non-default namespace.

- Gather meta-information about an XML node or document using nodeKind() and hasComplexContent(), or by using the comments() and processingInstructions() methods.

- Global settings such as ignoreComments can be set using class properties or by accessing the settings() object of the XML class.

Chapter 11

Working with Regular Expressions

A lot of the work of programs is in getting and processing information from an outside source, no matter whether the source is a file, a web site, a service, a stored object, or user input. You have to extract or manipulate the information that the input contains, so ActionScript 3.0 gives you specialized tools for working with certain kinds of data. In Chapter 10, you saw that ActionScript 3.0 has a special syntax for dealing with XML data, so when you get XML from an external source, you can count yourself lucky and use E4X to interpret and manipulate it easily. A lot of the time you aren't so lucky, and the input you have to deal with uses a format ActionScript 3.0 doesn't support, or it's free-form. In order to help you deal with any kind of textual data, ActionScript 3.0 includes native support for regular expressions.

Introducing Regular Expressions

Regular expressions are fantastically cool. They are little programs inside your own program, written in their own very concise language. You can store them and use them over and over. You can use them to search through text, extract just the parts you want from a bigger piece of text, or replace parts of text.

With regular expressions, you can handle any kind of text with a regular grammar, from HTML to LaTeX, Markdown to DTDs. You can use them to create lexers, programs that break down a blob of text into discrete elements, like breaking an English sentence into words and punctuation. And you can use them to create parsers, programs that extract the meaning from text. ActionScript 3.0 contains built-in parsers for numbers, URL-encoded variables, and XML, enabling you to convert the string `"3.14"` to a `Number` type and the string `"<root><foo>bar</foo></root>"` to an XML type.

Most (application layer) protocols on the Internet use text to communicate. For example, your mail client probably talks to the server using POP, SMTP, and/or IMAP, using simple commands and responses such as `"LIST"`, `"RETR"`, and `"OK"`. Even your web browser uses simple textual commands such as `"GET /index.html"`. With sockets (introduced in Chapter 34), you can use regular expressions to help you talk to a variety of services on the Internet.

Quite a few languages have support for regular expressions, so you may have some experience with them. Regular expressions use the same syntax with very little variation between languages that use them, so they are a skill you can apply and re-apply.

Because regular expressions have been around for a long time without changing much, there is also an abundance of literature on them, if you wish to continue your studies beyond this chapter. You may want to start with *Beginning Regular Expressions* by Andrew Watt (Wrox, 2005).

NEW IN AS3 In previous versions of ActionScript, regular expressions were not part of the language, but you may have seen them used with custom classes written and made free to download by some very clever coders. Now that they are part of the language, they are implemented natively in Flash Player and should run much faster. Additionally, they can now be written literally and are accepted as parameters to built-in methods.

Writing a regular expression

Regular expressions in ActionScript 3.0 are instances of the `RegExp` top-level class. This means you don't have to `import` anything to use `RegExp` objects. Just like `Boolean` and `XML`, regular expressions can also be written as literals. Sometimes you will want to use the constructor and sometimes the literal form. Let's get started and look at the general form of a regular expression:

```
var re1:RegExp = /sunken treasure/g;
var re2:RegExp = new RegExp("sunken treasure", "g");
```

The preceding two lines create identical regular expressions, first as a literal, and then using the `RegExp` constructor. Both `re1` and `re2` are of type `RegExp`. The literal form of regular expressions is also consistent between ActionScript and other languages. In some languages the literal form executes the expression, whereas in ActionScript it only declares the expression. We're starting out with a very simple regular expression, one that searches for the text "sunken treasure" in every place that it might appear.

`RegExp` objects are built from the regular expression itself, in this case `sunken treasure`, and zero or more flags indicating how to apply the expression, in this case g. You'll learn more about how to construct expressions and what the flags mean in the course of this chapter.

Applying Regular Expressions

Before you start building complex expressions, let's find out how you can apply regular expressions. Once you know how regular expressions can be used, you'll expand your repertoire of regular expression techniques to achieve specific goals. With an understanding of how they are applied, your knowledge of building complex ones will have more meaning.

Earlier, we said that regular expressions can be used to lex and parse textual grammars. That's a high-level application. First you have to ask, what can you do with one regular expression?

String methods and RegExp methods

In these applications, you'll see that there are sometimes two ways to conduct the same kind of operation. The `String` class provides many functions that work with regular expressions, and the `RegExp` class provides functions that work with strings. Your decision on which to use might be based on functionality that only one of the functions provides, or it might be based on the structure of your code and what you wish to achieve.

For example, if you were searching a thousand strings for a specific substring, you might create one `RegExp` object to find the substring, and call `RegExp` methods on it, feeding it different `Strings` in a loop. If you were searching one string for a thousand different substrings, you might create one `String` object and call `String` functions on it, feeding it different `RegExp` objects.

As you see sets of functions that do similar things, think about these different cases and it will become clear which one to use in which case.

Testing

You can use regular expressions to test if some text matches a certain pattern. Particular regular expressions are often called "patterns" because they represent certain patterns of text. In our first example, this pattern was a simple phrase ("sunken treasure"), but the pattern can be quite complex, to the point that you can't describe it easily in English and the regular expression that describes it is preferable.

Testing can also be achieved by paying attention to the result of a find or match operation. By way of analogy, if we asked you how many raisins were in your cereal, your answer would clearly indicate to us if your cereal even contained raisins or not. Sneaky, right?

RegExp.test(str:String):Boolean

This method, when called on a regular expression, will run that expression on the passed string, and return simply whether the string matches the pattern at all.

```
var phoneNumberPattern:RegExp = /\d\d\d-\d\d\d-\d\d\d\d/;
trace(phoneNumberPattern.test("347-555-5555")); //true
trace(phoneNumberPattern.test("Call 800-123-4567 now!")); //true
trace(phoneNumberPattern.test("Call now!")); //false
```

The preceding example creates an expression for numbers formatted like XXX–XXX–XXXX. It shows that regular expressions can match patterns of text, more than just looking for substrings. When you run this expression, it looks inside all of the text for a match, so it finds the phone number in the second `test()`, even though there's other junk in the string.

Testing for existence of a pattern finds out only if that pattern exists. You don't know from this example what the phone number is, or where it appears in the text.

Locating

You can find a certain pattern inside a string, and use its location for other string operations, such as splitting up the string or inserting new text — although you'll see that these operations can often be performed in the same step. You can find the first place the pattern appears, or every place in which the pattern appears.

String.search(pattern:*):int

Call `search()` on a `String` to find the first occurrence of the pattern you pass it. You can pass it either a `String` or a regular expression: When passed a `String`, it just looks for that substring. This method searches from the beginning of the `String` to the end, starting at the beginning. If there are no matches, it returns –1, meaning this is another easy option for testing existence of a pattern.

```
var themTharHills:String = "hillshillshillsGOLDhills";
trace(themTharHills.search(/gold/i)); //15
```

This snippet sees if there is gold in them thar hills. Indeed, there is, starting at the fifteenth character: after three "hills," which have 5 characters each. If you were just searching for the lowercase string "gold," that would be too boring: You learned how to search for substrings in Chapter 6! Instead, we passed it a regular expression that matches any pattern of the letters g, o, l, and d in either case, using the flag for case-insensitivity, `i`. This matched the uppercase "GOLD." Not very well hidden, that gold. It would have also matched "gOLd," "GOLd," and all other 13 permutations of capitalizations.

RegExp.exec(str:String):Object

The `exec()` method of `RegExp` is a very useful one. You can use it to locate as well as identify patterns, and it plays very nicely with loops. First let's use it to locate a pattern:

```
var searchForGold:RegExp = /gold/gi;
var themTharHills:String = "hillsgoldhillshillsGOLDhills";

var result:Object = searchForGold.exec(themTharHills);
//TEST if there's gold in the hills
if (result) trace("There's gold in them thar hills!");
//LOCATE the gold
trace(result.index); //5
```

```
//look a second time
result = searchForGold.exec(themTharHills);
//output the second location
trace(result.index); //19
```

You can already see we're getting more intricate. Here we have created a regular expression that finds the word "gold" in any combination of uppercase and lowercase in the string you pass it. It is also configured to match all instances of the pattern.

In the second paragraph, we execute the regular expression once. The expression goes through the string from beginning to end, and stops when it finds the first match, the lowercase "gold" after the first "hill." The `exec()` method will return `null` if there are no (more) matches of the pattern; otherwise it returns an object with lots of useful data. First, we use this `Object` return in a `Boolean` context to see if there are any matches of the pattern. Remember that by finding out *where* the gold is, we know if there is gold at all. Also recall that when coercing types to `Boolean`s, complex objects will be `true` when they contain any value, that is, when they are not `null`.

Next we use the `index` property of the object `exec()` returned. As you might guess, this property contains the location in the string of the current match. This tells you where the first instance of the "gold" pattern appears in the text. Note that we said "current" match. `RegExp` objects maintain one bit of state information: They remember the last position they matched, so that you can repeatedly apply them to the same text.

In the third paragraph of the snippet, we run the expression again on the same string. It starts from the position of the first match and finds a second match: "GOLD." Running `exec()` with the same parameters gave us two different results, which means that `exec()` is a state-aware function.

Identifying

When we are looking for "gold," we know what we're looking for exactly and we're interested in where to find it. Many times you will be looking for text that matches a more arbitrary pattern, and the contents of the matching text is of equal or greater importance than its position in the source text.

RegExp.exec(str:String):Object

You just saw how to use this method to locate patterns in a string, so now let's use it to identify them. When the `exec()` method finds a match, the object it returns also includes the text which matched it. Let's use the phone number pattern from before to find the phone numbers in a big chunk of text:

```
var contactNumbers:String = ↵
    "Call us at one of these numbers.\n" + ↵
    "Los Angeles: 310-555-2910\n" + ↵
    "New York: 212-555-2499\n" + ↵
    "Boston: 617-555-7141";
var phoneNumber:RegExp = /\d{3}-\d{3}-\d{4}/g;
```

```
var result:Object;

while(result = phoneNumber.exec(contactNumbers))
{
    trace(result[0]); //prints out the phone numbers one by one
}
```

The snippet uses the same trick we just showed to loop through all the matches progressively. This time inside the loop, we trace out the matched text itself. The example will trace out the three phone numbers from the source text in order.

The `result` object returned by `exec()` contains indexed properties as well as named properties, and the first index, `result[0]`, contains the text that matched the pattern.

String.match(pattern:*):Array

The `match()` method of a `String` will return strings that match the pattern passed to it. If the pattern is set to search globally, it returns all matches; otherwise it returns the first one. It, too, will return `null` if there are no matches.

The differences between this method and `RegExp.exec()` are that this method is called on the text and not the pattern, that it only returns the matched text, and that it runs all at once, rather than in a loop.

```
var contactNumbers:String =
    "Call us at one of these numbers.\n" +
    "Los Angeles: 310-555-2910\n" +
    "New York: 212-555-2499\n" +
    "Boston: 617-555-7141";
var matches:Array = contactNumbers.match(/\d{3}-\d{3}-\d{4}/g);
if (matches)
{
    trace(matches.length); //3
    trace(matches[0]); //310-555-2910
}
```

The example checks to make sure there are any matches, and if there are, traces out the number of matches and the contents of the first matching string. As you know, there are plenty of ways to manipulate array data, so it can be more convenient to get all the matches as an `Array`, and then post-process it as necessary.

Extracting

Often, you will need to find information from a source text when it appears in a certain context. You can add this context to a regular expression and indicate that certain parts of the pattern are to be captured for later use. Just as you can express the pattern you are looking for as extremely specific (the word "gold") or generic ("three numbers, a dash, three numbers, a dash, four numbers"), you can include any kind of context as well as any kind of pattern to capture out of the context:

```
var contactNumbers:String =
    "Call us at one of these numbers.\n" +
    "Los Angeles: 310-555-2910\n" +
    "New York: 212-555-2499\n" +
    "Boston: 617-555-7141";
var nyPhone:RegExp = /New York: (\d{3}-\d{3}-\d{4})/;
var matches:Array = contactNumbers.match(nyPhone);
trace(matches[1]); //212-555-2499
```

This snippet creates an expression for text that follows the pattern of "New York: XXX-XXX-XXXX." By including "New York:" in the expression, we know it's only going to match the New York phone number, and only if it is followed by a phone number in that format.

However, in the snippet we are concerned only with the actual number that we should call to get the New York office. We don't want "New York: " to come back, only the number itself, but on the other hand, we need to limit the expression so that it matches only the New York number. We achieve this by surrounding the number part of the expression in parentheses. This creates a capturing group. Any parts of the expression in parentheses like this will be specifically extracted for every match of the full expression.

Capturing groups are part of the expression itself, but you still need to run the regular expression to access these captures in a match.

String.match(pattern:*):Array

In the preceding snippet, we used `String.match()` to extract the captured group. However, the behavior of `match()` can be tricky here, so be careful.

When the expression passed to `match()` has the global flag set, `match()` will return an array of all the substrings that match the pattern. It will not give you any of the captures.

When you use `match()` with an expression that does not have the global flag set, it returns an array containing the first matching substring, followed by all the capture groups in the expression for that match. This is the case in the preceding snippet. The expression does not have the global flag set, and `match()` returns an array where the first entry is the matching substring `"New York: 212-555-2499"`, and the second entry (`matches[1]`) is the part of the expression that was captured, `"212-555-2499"`.

Because of this tricky difference, if you need to use capture groups, you might do well to stick to the by-now familiar function we revisit in the following section.

RegExp.exec(str:String):Object

Let's modify this program so that we can get both the names and the numbers for every office in the list in one fell swoop. We'll add them to an associative array so we can look up numbers such as `contacts["New York"]`.

Let's step back for just a second and be explicit. With this example, we're parsing arbitrary text with a specific format into a data structure that we can conveniently use in other code. That's pretty useful!

```
var contacts:Object = new Object();

var contactText:String =
    "Call us at one of these numbers.\n" +
    "Los Angeles: 310-555-2910\n" +
    "New York: 212-555-2499\n" +
    "Boston: 617-555-7141";
var officeAndPhone:RegExp = /^([\w\s]+): (\d{3}-\d{3}-\d{4})/gm;

var result:Object;
while (result = officeAndPhone.exec(contactText))
{
    contacts[result[1]] = result[2];
}

trace(contacts["New York"]); //212-555-2499
trace(contacts["Boston"]); //617-555-7141
```

The expression got a little more complex in this example, but don't worry about it just yet. The expression matches the start of a line, a series of letters and spaces (which is captured), a colon and a space, and then a sequence of 3-3-4 digits (which is captured). It is set to match globally (meaning we couldn't use `String.match()` if we wanted to see the captured groups), and it is treated as a multiline string. We'll get into the details of how to build expressions like this shortly.

We use the `RegExp.exec()` method again, and its multipurpose returned object. The object contains the matched expression in the first indexed property, followed by all the captures for that match. So we use the first capture (the name of the office) as the key, and the second capture (the phone number) as the value, adding them into our associative array `contacts` as we go. When the expression runs out of matches, the loop terminates and we can successfully test looking up phone numbers in the `contacts` object by name.

Replacing

Once you have the ability to match patterns in text, replacing those patterns with desired text is a simple enough leap.

String.replace(pattern:*, repl:Object):String

You might recognize this function, as well, from Chapter 6. We can use this method with a string pattern and a string replacement object to perform a basic substitution:

```
var quote:String = "I did it for the money and the drugs.";
quote = quote.replace("money", "learning experience");
quote = quote.replace("drugs", "sleep deprivation");
trace(quote);
//I did it for the learning experience and the sleep deprivation.
```

Now that's closer to the truth! Remember that the `replace()` method returns the modified `String`, rather than modifying it in place, so we assign the result back to `quote` to immediately apply the replacements.

Now let's try replacing a pattern with a string:

```
var document:String = "My name is John Doe, SSN 123-45-6789," +
    "I live at 120 Birch st...";
var ssn:RegExp = /\d{3}-\d{2}-\d{4}/g;
document = document.replace(ssn, "<SSN REMOVED>");
trace(document);
//My name is John Doe, SSN <SSN REMOVED>, I live at 120 Birch st...
```

The example here searches for all patterns that look like a social security number (SSN), and sanitizes the document so that it contains no SSNs, but indicates that they have been removed.

If you have capture groups inside your expression, when replacing text you can use the captured text inside the replacement string. For example, let's change all instances of "my name is _____" to "_____ is my name."

```
var introduction:String =
"My name is Roger; but I'll have you know MY name is Henry!";
trace(introduction.replace(/my name is (\w+)/gi, "$1 is my name"));
//Roger is my name; but I'll have you know Henry is my name!
```

We have to search for the whole pattern "my name is _____" because we'll be modifying that phrase. However, of particular interest to us is the name itself, so we capture that. By using variables named $1, $2, and so on up to $99, in the replacement string, the first, second, and ninety-ninth captured groups will be re-substituted into the text that replaces the match.

To make replacing text even sweeter, you can pass `String.replace()` a replacement function instead of a replacement string. The function will be passed the matching text, all the captured groups for that match, and the full string in context, and you can make whatever kind of replacement you want. For instance, you could make sure that the authors' names always appear capitalized properly:

```
var authors:RegExp = /roger|mims|joey|josh/gi;
var fixCaps:Function = function fixCaps(...args):String
{
    var match:String = String(args[0]);
    return match.charAt(0).toUpperCase() + match.substr(1).toLowerCase();
}

var text:String = "ROGER told mIms that JoEY and JoSH were in Boston.";
trace(text.replace(authors, fixCaps));
//Roger told Mims that Joey and Josh were in Boston.
```

You can do all kinds of things with custom substitutions, such as encoding particularly secret bits of information in an otherwise innocuous stream of text.

Splitting

You can use regular expressions to break up text. This is useful when you are trying to interpret text that uses a delimiter to denote breaks between data.

String.split(delimiter:*, limit:Number = 0x7fffffff):Array

This method was introduced in Chapter 6 to split up text into its constituents. The delimiter parameter may also be a regular expression. You can use this to allow for more flexibility in the delimiter. In this example, a haiku is split up into phrases with slashes. However, we can't be entirely sure if the author will include spaces around the slashes, so we allow for whitespace on either side by splitting on a regular expression:

```
var haiku:String =
"Oh ActionScript three/ you make coding delightful / I think you are neat.";

var lineDelimiter:RegExp = /\s*\/\s*/;
var lines:Array = haiku.split(lineDelimiter);

for (var i:int = 0; i < lines.length; i++)
{
    trace(i, lines[i]);
}
//0 Oh ActionScript three
//1 you make coding delightful
//2 I think you are neat.
```

The first and second delimiters in the example have different formats, but the regular expression catches them both. Additionally, by interpreting the whitespace as part of the delimiter, it is not included in the split-up substrings. As you can see, all three lines print out without extra whitespace in the beginning.

Constructing Expressions

By now, you've seen many examples of what regular expressions can be used for. We've also come across a few instances of patterns that need further explanation. This section covers the building blocks of regular expressions and the flags that they can be used with.

Each expression is actually a mini-program that can be run on a string input. In general, it steps through the string from start to end, trying to match up the current part of the expression with the current part of the string, as you can see in Figure 11-1.

FIGURE 11-1

Stepping through a regular expression

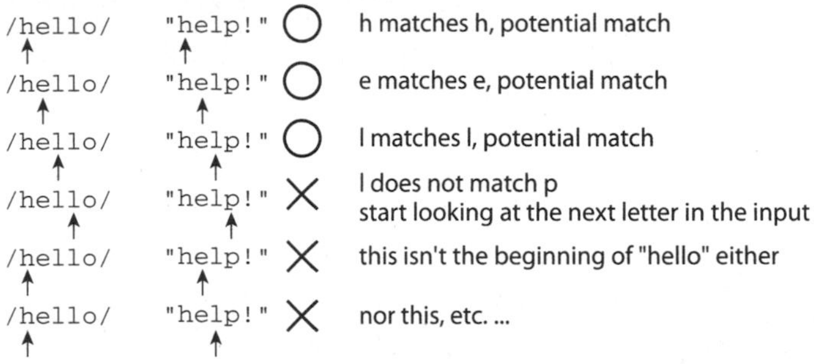

Normal characters

When you type letters in an expression, they will match those letters in the same sequence, as shown in examples throughout this chapter. You can type any letter or number, and some punctuation:

```
trace("am i thinking what you're thinking?".match(/think/g));
//think,think
trace("rub a dub dub, three men in a tub".match(/ub/g));
//ub,ub,ub,ub
```

Dot character

The period (.) has a very important meaning in regular expressions. It will match *any* character, with one exception, the newline character. If the dotall flag is set, "." will truly match any character, including newlines. The section on flags that follows explains why.

Escaped characters

There are two reasons to escape certain characters. In the language of regular expressions, many punctuation characters have special meanings. And escaped characters let you include characters that may be difficult to type or see in an expression.

We first introduced character escaping in Chapter 6. To escape a character, simply preface it with a backslash (\). This goes for the backslash character as well. To type a backslash, you must prefix it with a backslash:

```
trace("c:\\windows\\"); //c:\windows\
```

You can't go wrong by escaping any character you type in a regular expression that is not an alphanumeric character (a–z, A–Z, and 0–9):

```
var re:RegExp = /I have a \$5 bill \& his\/her ID card\./;
```

At a minimum, you must escape the following characters to ensure that they will be interpreted literally:

```
^ $ \ . * + ? ( ) [ ] { } |
```

The forward slash is added to this list, of course, if you are declaring a regular expression literally, as the forward slash acts as the beginning and end of the expression.

There are also several escape characters that are written with a sequence but represent a different character than the character after the slash. These are summarized in Table 11-1.

TABLE 11-1

Escape Sequences

Type this	Get this
\b	Backspace
\f	Form feed. This ejected the page currently in the printer back in the day.
\n	Newline, aka "LF." The line separator on Unix machines and Mac OS X is \n.
\r	Carriage return, aka "CR." The line separator on Windows is \r\n and on old Mac OS is \r.
\t	Tab.
\u*nnnn*	The Unicode character with character code *nnnn* in hexadecimal. For example, \u20ac is character U+20AC, the Euro sign (€).
\x*nn*	The ASCII character with the character code *nn* in hexadecimal. For example, \xa3 is ASCII character 0xA3, the pound sign (£).

Dealing with newlines on text that might come from different systems can be incredibly frustrating. Please keep the different possible line endings, as well as the encoding of the input text, in mind. See more on international regular expressions later in the chapter.

Metacharacters and metasequences demystified

You may see the words "metacharacter" and "metasequence" when reading about regular expressions. These terms sound fairly impressive, but they have a very simple meaning.

Both of these terms refer to any part of the pattern that has a special meaning in regular-expression-speak. A metacharacter is one single character that is not interpreted literally, such as *, whereas a metasequence is a sequence of characters that is not interpreted literally, such as \s or [a-z]. The asterisk does not mean "match an asterisk," and \n does not mean "match a backslash followed by the letter n." Escaped characters, therefore, are one kind of metasequence.

Character classes

Regular expressions allow you to conveniently match a whole set of possible characters with a single metasequence. There are several sequences that look like escaped characters but actually represent a whole range of characters.

The first example that used this matched a phone number. Let's look at this expression in a little more detail:

```
var phoneNumberPattern:RegExp = /\d\d\d-\d\d\d-\d\d\d\d/;
```

Each instance of \d matches any single digit, meaning that except for the dashes, every character in the match must be either a 0, 1, 2, 3, 4, 5, 6, 7, 8, or 9. You can easily remember this sequence because "d" is for "digit."

If you want to find any character that's *not* a digit, you can use the inverse of that character class, \D. The lowercase version matches digits; the uppercase matches non-digits.

There are three helpful shorthand character classes: \d for digits, \w for word characters, and \s for whitespace; and another three capitalized for their inverses: \D for non-digits, \W for non-word characters, and \S for non-whitespace. The details of these are summarized in Table 11-2.

You can also create your own groups of character classes. Simply place the letters that you want to match inside square brackets:

```
trace("the cat sat on the mat".match(/[msc]at/g)); //cat,sat,mat
```

You don't need to separate the letters with anything, and their order doesn't matter. Keep in mind that even though the metasequence for the character class ([msc]) is longer than one character, it matches one character. It says "look for a character that is an m, s, or c." You can also use ranges with the dash character (-), and you can have multiple ranges in one character class, as well as combine ranges with single characters:

```
trace("abcdefghijklmnopqrstuvwxyz".match(/[a-cmx-z]/g)); //a,b,c,m,x,y,z
```

Finally, you can invert a character class by using a caret (^) immediately after the open bracket ([). The whole sequence, then, will match a character that is *not* in the specified set:

```
trace("roger dodger".match(/[^oge\s]/g)); //r,r,d,d,r
```

In the preceding snippet, we find any letter that is not an o, g, e, or any kind of whitespace. Notice that we used a shorthand character class inside a character class. This, too, is possible.

Because the characters [, -, and] have special meaning in character classes, if you wish to include these in a set, you must escape them. The caret may be included literally without escaping, as long as it does not appear first, in which case it will be interpreted to mean the inverse of the set.

TABLE 11-2

Character Classes

Character	Meaning
[...]	A character in the set (...).
[^...]	A character not in the set (...).
[x-y]	Any character that lies between x and y, inclusive.
\w	Word characters. Equivalent to [a-zA-Z0-9_].
\W	Non-word characters. Equivalent to [^a-zA-Z0-9_].
\s	Whitespace characters: tab, space, newline, carriage return. Equivalent to [\t\n\r\ ] (note the space before the right bracket).
\S	Non-whitespace characters. Equivalent to [^\t\n\r\ ].
\d	Decimal digit characters. Equivalent to [0-9].
\D	Non-digit characters. Equivalent to [^0-9].
.	Any character (except newline when dotall flag is not set).

Quantifiers

Regular expressions allow you to specify not just kinds of characters that match, but how many of them to match. Matching a specific number of characters is a useful ability, but even more useful is to discard arbitrary amounts of noise between two items you are interested in matching.

```
trace(/\w+:\s*\$\d+/.test("soup:          $40")); //true
```

The preceding snippet makes good use of the plus quantifier (+). It is placed after the part of the pattern it is to quantify, and like all quantifiers, it changes the number of that subpattern that may appear in the text to qualify as a match. The plus symbol means "one or more," so the preceding pattern reads "one or more letters, a colon, some or no whitespace, a dollar sign, and one or more digits," which the test string indeed matches.

To match an optional character or sequence, use the question mark quantifier (?). The expression will then match text that has the subpattern zero or one time:

```
var betterPhoneNumber:RegExp = /\(?\d{3}\)?-?\d{3}-?\d{4}/;
trace(betterPhoneNumber.test("(703)555-1234")); //true
trace(betterPhoneNumber.test("310-555-1515")); //true
trace(betterPhoneNumber.test("7245559090")); //true
```

Here, we upgrade our phone regular expression to make all the dashes optional, and to allow parentheses around the area code. Remember that we must escape the parentheses in this expression to interpret them literally.

To match any number of a character or sequence, including none at all, you can use the star (*) quantifier. This modifies the preceding part of the pattern to match zero or more times:

```
trace("a thousand thousandss!".match(/thousands*/g)); //thousand,thousandss
```

In this snippet, the "s" character can either not appear or appear any number of times. No matter how many s's are put at the end of "thousands," it will continue to match.

As you've already seen a number of times, you can also specify an exact quantity for the subpattern to appear in. In the phone number regular expressions earlier in the chapter, we match exactly the right number of digits. We can write expressions to match an exact number, a minimum number, or a specific range of acceptable numbers. These options are summarized with the quantifier characters in Table 11-3.

TABLE 11-3

Quantifiers

Quantifier	Meaning
*	Zero or more; any number
?	Zero or one; optional
+	One or more; required
{n}	Exactly n times
{n,}	At least n times; n or more times
{n,m}	Between n and m times, inclusive

As we mentioned at the beginning, without any quantifiers, the expression expects to match exactly one of each constituent.

Anchors and boundaries

There are a few regular expression symbols that help you anchor parts of the expression to interesting parts of the input text. All of these are different from the kinds of metacharacters and meta-sequences you've seen so far in that they match a position rather than a character.

You can specify where the beginning and end of a string or line is supposed to appear within a pattern by using the ^ and $ anchors, respectively. When the multiline flag is set, these anchors match the beginning and end of any line; without the flag, they match the beginning and end of the entire string.

Let's revisit the contact parsing expression from the last section:

```
var contactText:String =
    "Call us at one of these numbers.\n" +
    "Los Angeles: 310-555-2910\n" +
    "New York: 212-555-2499\n" +
    "Boston: 617-555-7141";
var officeAndPhone:RegExp = /^([\w\s]+): (\d{3}-\d{3}-\d{4})/gm;
```

By setting the multiline flag on this expression and anchoring to the beginning of the line, we ensure that the "name: phone number" pairs are found on every new line. In this case, if we had two sets of name/phone pairs on one line, only the first one would match because the pattern matches only when it appears at the beginning of a line. We could furthermore disqualify that kind of line entirely by insisting that the line end right after the phone number:

```
var officeAndPhone:RegExp = /^([\w\s]+): (\d{3}-\d{3}-\d{4})$/;
trace(officeAndPhone.test(">>>New York: 212-555-2499")); //false
trace(officeAndPhone.test("New York: 212-555-2499 (fax)")); //false
```

These two test cases fail to match the pattern because they both contain garbage before and after the pattern, where the pattern specifies that it fills up the entire string. Anchoring your pattern to both the beginning and end of a string/line is a common technique.

Because these symbols match positions rather than characters, they are *zero-width*: when the regular expression is moving through the pattern and one of these anchors matches, it doesn't move to the next character in the string. When the "h" in /hello/ matched the "h" in "help!" in Figure 11-1, we moved on to the next character in the string and the pattern. When we match, for example, the beginning of a string with ^, we don't move to the next character in the string.

Additionally, you can use a metasequence that represents a word boundary. The anchor \b will match in a position between word characters and non-word characters (as defined by \w and \W). This matches both the beginning and the end of words. The benefit to this character is that it is zero-width.

```
var usingBoundary:RegExp = /\bzarflax\b/i;
var noBoundary:RegExp = /zarflax/i;

var garbage:String = "asndzarflaxhtewio";
trace(usingBoundary.test(garbage)); //false
trace(noBoundary.test(garbage)); //true

var dialogue:String = "Nice try, Zarflax!";
```

```
trace(usingBoundary.test(dialogue)); //true
trace(noBoundary.test(dialogue)); //true

var fakingBoundary:RegExp = /\Wzarflax\W/i;
trace(garbage.match(fakingBoundary)); //null
trace(dialogue.match(fakingBoundary)); // Zarflax!
```

In the second paragraph of this snippet, we see that not using word boundaries will match the word "zarflax" even when it is contained within garbage, which in this case is a false positive. Adding the boundaries makes the garbage string not match. In the third paragraph, we test against the intended usage. Both with and without boundaries, the word is found.

In the final paragraph of the snippet, you can see why using a zero-width word anchor is different than including the surrounding non-word characters in the pattern itself. Doing so makes the garbage string not match because there is no instance of "zarflax" that has non-word characters before and after it in the garbage string. So far so good — we've eliminated the false positive. But when we attempt to match the pattern in the dialogue string, we end up picking up the non-word characters we required "zarflax" to be surrounded in as part of the pattern. The benefit of \b here is that it matches a word boundary without consuming it into the pattern.

Table 11-4 summarizes the anchors available to regular expressions in ActionScript 3.0.

TABLE 11-4

Anchors and Boundaries

Anchor	Meaning
^	Beginning of the string, or beginning of a line when the multiline flag is set
$	End of the string, or end of a line when the multiline flag is set
\b	Word boundary; after a non-word character and before a word character
\B	Not a word boundary; between two word characters or between two non-word characters

Alternation

Using a pipe (|) character in a regular expression allows you to match multiple alternatives. You saw this at play earlier in the expression

```
var authors:RegExp = /roger|mims|joey|josh/gi;
```

You can use one pipe to allow two options, or multiple pipes to allow many options. This example will match the name of any of the authors.

This can be even more useful when you can specify parts to allow alternates instead of alternating the entire expression. You do this with groups.

Groups

Grouping can be used for several purposes. You've already seen that it can be used to capture information out of a specific context, using the pattern at large to match the entire format, and the group to make the text we're really interested in available after the match.

Use parentheses around part of the pattern to make a group out of it. This kind of group is a *capturing group* because it is captured for later use.

If you want to include parentheses in your expression, to match actual parentheses in the input text, you must escape the parentheses. Use \ (to match an open parenthesis and \ ) to match a close parenthesis.

We can also use groups as the container for alternates or repetition:

```
var rhymes:RegExp = /\b(tr|r|sp|b)a(c|s)e\b/gi;
var str:String = "trace() the race to the orbiting base in outerspace";
trace(str.match(rhymes)); //trace,race,base
```

This example goes further than a character class could. The (c|s) alternate could be replaced by [cs], but the beginning of the rhyming words can be two letters when you use alternates like this. In fact, an alternate can be any pattern, not just these simple letter sequences.

The two groups in this expression act as a scope for the alternates. If any of the alternates in the first group are fulfilled, the string and regular expression both advance to the next character. So you can look at the group as a subpattern, a single special kind of match that is self-contained.

Using groups for scoping purposes also allows you to apply quantifiers to subpatterns, as in the following example:

```
trace("the cat goes mew meow mewmew meow!".match(/(meo?w\s*)+/));
//mew meow mewmew meow,meow
```

This pattern tries to match any kind of cat language, crafting a pattern to match a single word, and then requiring one or more instances of that whole pattern. The second argument in the returned array "meow" is included because, as you might recall, when calling match() without the global flag, it also returns the captured groups. In this case there is only one capturing group, but it is repeated, so when the matching is finished, that capture includes the last instance of the subpattern to be captured. The first argument is still the matching text in its entirety. You can see that the expression has successfully extracted all cat language from the string.

Understanding Regular Expression Flags

Flags modify the interpretation of a regular expression. We've already used flags extensively in the examples in this chapter. This section covers these flags and their effects in detail. The default is for all of these flags to be off — that is, an expression with no flags set has all of the flags off, and you turn them on by adding them to the expression.

To recap, flags can be specified when the expression is created, either after the final slash in a literal RegExp, or as the second parameter of the RegExp() constructor. The following snippet activates all five available flags, first using a literal and then the constructor:

```
/foo/gimsx;
new RegExp("foo", "gimsx");
```

The two expressions above are equivalent. The flags in a regular expression may appear in any order.

Global

The global flag g allows the expression to be used repeatedly on the source text until there are no more matches. When it is not set, the expression will return the first match.

This flag applies to String.match(), String.replace(), RegExp.test(), and RegExp.exec(). In String.match(), the global flag determines whether the method returns an array of the first match and captured groups (when it is not set), or an array of all matches (when it is set). In String.replace(), the flag determines whether the first match is replaced (when it is not set), or all matches are replaced (when it is set). In RegExp.test() and RegExp.exec(), if the global flag is set, the expression continues to match from the nth character in the source text, where n is the expression's lastIndex property. This property is set after every match so that you can use a loop to progressively step through all matches with RegExp.test() or RegExp.exec() when the global flag is set. If the global flag is not set, these methods match the first occurrence by starting matching at the first character.

The flag does not need to be set to run String.split(). This method uses the limit passed in the second parameter to determine how many times the delimiter pattern may match. By default (when no limit parameter is passed), the string will be split as many times as necessary, up to an implausibly large number.

Ignore case

The ignore case flag, i, will match characters regardless of their case. This means that /a/i will match A or a. This flag affects all the methods we have covered.

We saw this flag used in the example where we fixed words with incorrect capitals:

```
var authors:RegExp = /roger|mims|joey|josh/gi;
```

This way, the expression matched "Joey" as well as "rOgER."

TIP Turning on the ignore case flag can make your expressions much more tolerant. This could be dangerous or extremely helpful depending on your intent. When parsing natural language like English text, the meaning of the words is usually more important than the capitalization. When dealing with URLs or file paths, servers and operating systems are frequently case sensitive and it's important to preserve case.

Multiline

The multiline flag, m, changes the behavior of the ^ and $ anchors in the expression. When the multiline flag is off, these metacharacters anchor to the first and last character of the entire text. When the flag is set, they will match at the beginning and end of every line. This flag affects the behavior of the expression regardless of the method using it.

This flag can be really useful when parsing strings that contain multiple lines (no surprise there). The same effects can generally be reached by splitting the input text into an array of lines and then processing each line independently:

```
var contacts:Object = new Object();
var contactText:String =
    "Call us at one of these numbers.\n" +
    "Los Angeles: 310-555-2910\n" +
    "New York: 212-555-2499\n" +
    "Boston: 617-555-7141";
var officeAndPhone:RegExp = /^([\w\s]+): (\d{3}-\d{3}-\d{4})/;

var lines:Array = contactText.split(/\n/);
var line:String;
for each (line in lines)
{
    var result:Array = line.match(officeAndPhone);
    if (result)
    {
        contacts[result[1]] = result[2];
    }
}
```

We could simplify this code by using the multiline flag:

```
var contacts:Object = new Object();
var contactText:String =
    "Call us at one of these numbers.\n" +
    "Los Angeles: 310-555-2910\n" +
    "New York: 212-555-2499\n" +
    "Boston: 617-555-7141";
var officeAndPhone:RegExp = /^([\w\s]+): (\d{3}-\d{3}-\d{4})/gm;

var result:Object;
while (result = officeAndPhone.exec(contactText))
{
    contacts[result[1]] = result[2];
}
```

By using the multiline and global flags, the same expression can match multiple times, even though the source text spans across several lines.

Dotall

The dotall flag, s, changes the behavior of the dot metacharacter. When the flag is not set, the dot (.) matches any character but a newline character. When the flag is set, the dot (.) matches every possible character including newlines.

You can think of this mode as *single-line mode* because that evokes s much better than dotall, and because it can be used to treat a string with multiple lines as one long string that happens to have \n characters in it. With the s flag on and the m flag off, the regular expression no longer maintains the illusion for you that the input string is partitioned into lines. You can see the dotall flag's effect in the following snippet:

```
var lines:String = "hello,\n cruel world!";
trace(lines.match(/hello.*world/)); //null
trace(lines.match(/hello.*world/s)); //hello,
                                 // cruel world
```

The first match() in this snippet operates on the assumption that you don't want your pattern to be broken by a line break unless you explicitly include one. The second match() allows anything to be in the .* subpattern, even newlines.

> **TIP** Be very careful with .*. This pattern is greedy and can eat more of the input text than you desired. With s on, it could eat its way across lines and to the very end. You can be more cautious with a lazy pattern. The next section of this chapter explains this in detail.

Extended

The extended flag, x, is included in an attempt to mitigate the general illegibility of regular expressions. Making dense, amazingly complex regular expressions that do the same work as dozens of lines of code is, we can speak from experience, very rewarding, but when it comes time to explain your code to someone else or even to remember what you wrote six months ago, you might see the other edge of the sword.

The extended flag lets you mitigate this clutter by adding in whitespace anywhere in the expression, which will not be literally interpreted unless it is escaped. When the flag is off, a space in a regular expression means "match a space in the source text in this position": the whitespace is taken literally.

Unfortunately, adding whitespace can do only so much for the understandability of your expressions. It's a good idea to briefly say what an expression does in a comment adjacent to it when the expression is complicated:

```
//find those complete words which rhyme with base: space, trace, race.
var rhymes:RegExp = /\b (tr|r|sp|b) a (c|s) e \b/gix;
```

Retrofitting the rhyme example with whitespace makes it a tad more legible.

Table 11-5 recaps the regular expression flags ActionScript 3.0 supports.

TABLE 11-5

Regular Expression Flags

Flag character	RegExp property	Behavior when flag is set
g	global	Don't stop after first match.
i	ignoreCase	All alphabetical comparisons are case-insensitive.
m	multiline	^ and $ anchors match beginning and end of lines.
s	dotall	. matches newline.
x	extended	Whitespace in expression is ignored unless escaped.

Constructing Advanced Expressions

In this chapter, we introduced a lot of information in a short space. The regular expression techniques discussed thus far should serve for a great majority of your text manipulation challenges. We did, however, leave out a few points about regular expressions, which build on the foundations we laid earlier.

If you are learning regular expressions for the first time, it might be helpful to return to this section after you've implemented a few regular expressions of your own and become comfortable with the way they work.

Greedy and lazy matching

The + and * quantifiers can be difficult to tame. You might have run into this before if you have attempted to parse HTML, as the expression below is intended to. (If the HTML is valid XHTML, you should use E4X for this and spare yourself the headache.)

```
//match <, (the tag name), any other stuff till >, >, (the inner text),
//then </, (a tag name), and >.
var getTag:RegExp = /< (\w+) \s* [^>]* > (.*) <\/ (\w+) >/x;
var parts:Array;

var htmlFragment1:String = '<li>item 1</li>';
parts = htmlFragment1.match(getTag);
trace("nodeName:", parts[1]); //nodeName: li
trace("innerHtml:", parts[2]); //innerHtml: item 1

var htmlFragment2:String = '<li>item 1</li><li>item 2</li>';
parts = htmlFragment2.match(getTag);
trace("nodeName:", parts[1]); //nodeName: li
trace("innerHtml:", parts[2]); //innerHtml: item1</li><li>item 2
```

The `getTag` expression works fine for a single tag. We want to be able to apply the expression over and over to pull out several tags in a row, but there's a problem. The `.*` in the middle of the expression keeps eating up everything until the last close tag. When the regular expression program sees the first closed tag that matches the last part of the expression, the `.*` remains in control. Its meaning, "any characters," certainly applies to `</li>` as well, so the `.*` in the pattern matches everything possible without preventing the rest of the expression from matching. The subexpression lets go before the last `</li>` so that the full expression can still match.

This behavior is called greedy matching because the subexpression, which has one of these quantifiers, will greedily match as far as it can into the string. By default, all regular expression quantifiers are greedy. If we could make the `.*` in the middle of our expression less greedy, the end of the regular expression might be able to match the first `</li>` instead of the last one, so that the whole expression matches only one `li` tag, the intended behavior.

Thankfully, there are more polite versions of these quantifiers. By adding a question mark to the quantifiers, we can make them match lazily instead of greedily. Lazily matching subexpressions will stop matching at the first opportunity to match the rest of the expression rather than the last. With the addition of this character, we can fix our regular expression:

```
//match <, (the tag name), any other stuff till >, >, (the inner text),
//then </, (a tag name), and >.
var getTag:RegExp = /< (\w+) \s* [^>]* > (.*?) <\/ (\w+) >/gx;
var htmlFragment:String = '<li>item 1</li><li>item 2</li>';
var parts:Array;
while(parts = getTag.exec(htmlFragment))
{
    trace("nodeName:", parts[1]);
    trace("innerHtml:", parts[2]);
}
//nodeName: li
//innerHtml: item 1
//nodeName: li
//innerHtml: item 2
```

Notice that the only difference in the regular expression (besides applying it globally) is the change from `.*` to `.*?`, which does the trick to match only until the first end tag.

You can use these lazy quantifiers any time you want to match a very general pattern between two specific patterns, without accidentally including the ending pattern in the middle. Useful lazy quantifiers include `*?` and `+?`, although you can make any quantifier lazy.

Backreferences

Throughout this chapter, you have seen how to use capturing groups to store particular subexpressions and use them in code. Regular expressions also allow you to use the captured groups inside the same expression they are captured with.

You use a backreference, as it is called, by referring to the ordinal number of the matching group, like using $1 through $99 in `String.replace()`, except backreferences use backslashes instead of dollar signs: \1 through \99. The text that matched the captured group is used as the subexpression where the backreference appears instead of the literal characters \1. This snippet demonstrates:

```
var re:RegExp = /\b (\w{3}) \b  .*?  \b \1 \b /ix;
var testString:String = "far, farther fetched free fun fetched fun free";
trace(testString.match(re)); //fun fetched fun,fun
```

The preceding regular expression finds the first three-letter word, which appears at least twice in the text. It uses a group to capture a three-letter word, .*? to keep matching through the rest of the string, and finally a backreference to assert that the word is repeated later in the string. Because it uses the word boundary anchor \b, it also ensures that the second time the captured three letters appear, they are in a single word. This disqualifies the word "far," which appears as part of the word "farther." If the expression matches at all, the first repeated three-letter word will be stored in the first captured group.

Lookahead and non-capturing groups

There are different kinds of groups that can be used for interesting purposes.

Non-capturing groups

When you want to use a group for alternation or a quantifier, but the actual contents of the group are not as important to your expression, you can reduce the amount of unnecessarily captured groups by making a group that does not capture: a *non-capturing group*. This is achieved with the following syntax:

```
(?:...)
```

where your grouped subexpression takes the place of the ellipsis. For example:

```
var re:RegExp = /(?:i|you|he|she|it|we|they) likes? to (\w+)/i;
var match:Object = re.exec("We like to party.");
trace(match[1]); //party
```

This expression finds what it is that someone likes to do. It uses a group to allow for several different subjects. However, the first group is non-capturing, so it does not interfere with the verb, which is captured in the first position.

 When using a non-capturing group, the contents of the group will still be available to backreferences.

Positive lookahead groups

Beyond non-capturing groups there are also zero-width groups: groups that will try to match the source string without moving ahead in the pattern. ActionScript 3.0 regular expressions have a *positive lookahead group*, or a *zero-width positive lookahead assertion*. When you use the syntax

```
(?=...)
```

you ensure that the pattern represented by the ellipsis would match, if you tried to. However, it doesn't perform the match, so that after the lookahead group, you're still talking about the same location in the source text as before it. This is unlike most metasequences you've seen so far, which will match and then continue on through the source text. Recall that anchors such as ^ and \b are also zero-width.

```
var re:RegExp = /\b (?:\w{3}) \b  (?= .*?  \b \1 \b) \s* (\w+) /x;
var testString:String = "far, farther fetched free fun fetched fun free";
trace(testString.match(re)); //fun fetched,fetched
```

Here we modified a prior snippet to find the word *after* the first three-letter word that repeats. The large lookahead in the middle looks ahead to see if there is, after a sequence of characters, another instance of the three-letter word matched. If this lookahead fails (if there is no duplication of the three-letter word just found) then the potential match immediately fails and the next bit of source text is considered. When the lookahead succeeds, as it does with "fun," it must have examined the source text through the second instance of the word "fun." But when the lookahead group matches positively, the regular expression restores the current position in the source text to the position that was already being considered when the expression encountered the lookahead group: after the word boundary after the first "fun." Then, the remainder of the expression is considered. After a lookahead group matches, the pointer in the expression is at the end of the lookahead group in the expression, but the pointer in the source text hasn't moved. It's zero-width. Thus, when the match continues at \s*, the source continues after the first "fun," and achieves our goal of getting the word after the first repeated three-letter word.

Incidentally, the snippet also uses a non-capturing group to find the three-letter word because the goal of our search is no longer the word, but the word immediately following. This way, the only captured group is "fetched," the solution to the puzzle. You can also see that the entire match "fun fetched" does not include text up to the second instance of "fun," even though that source text was examined by the lookahead.

Negative lookahead groups

In addition, we have negative lookahead groups, which like their brethren, do not advance the portion of the string being considered, and do not capture. The difference, of course, is that they assert that the pattern inside them would *not* be matched at the current position. To write a negative lookahead group, use the syntax

```
(?!...)
```

with your subexpression in place of the ellipsis.

Named groups

Another way to mitigate the jumble that can arise from complex applications of regular expressions is to assign names to capturing groups, rather than referring to them by their ordinal. Names are more descriptive than numbers, and as we can name variables descriptively in ActionScript, so can we assign names to capturing groups to clarify code dealing with regular expressions.

To create a named group, use the format

```
(?P<name>...)
```

where *name* is the name you will use to refer to the group if it is captured, and the expression to be captured replaces the ellipsis. See a summary of all the kinds of groups in Table 11-6.

NOTE Named groups are an extension to ECMAScript. They are used in ActionScript 3.0, but not ECMAScript/Javascript.

Named groups are applicable only to methods that would otherwise return the matched groups in an array: `RegExp.exec()` and `String.match()`. The names cannot be used in metasequences, either as backreferences or in `String.replace()`. When named groups are used, the captured groups are returned from these methods both in their ordinal position and by their named property.

Let's say that you want to create a method that will convert *From:* e-mail headers into a more readable format. Sometimes these headers will come with both the sender's real name and e-mail address, in the format "Roger Braunstein <roger@partlyhuman.com>". If this is the case, you want to present the field as the sender's name, hyperlinked to send e-mail to the correct address when clicked:

```
package
{
import flash.display.Sprite;

public class EmailParser extends Sprite
{
    public function EmailParser()
    {
        //run the test when we start
        test();
    }

    public function makeFromLink(fromField:String):String
    {
        //a from address with a name takes the format:
        //(some stuff, perhaps in quotes, which is the name),
        //perhaps some whitespace, <,
        //(some stuff with an @, which is the address), >
        var findHeader:RegExp = ↵
                /"? (?P<name>.+?) "? \s* < (?P<email>.+@.+) >/x;
        var match:Object = fromField.match(findHeader);
        if (match)
```

```
    {
        return '<a href="mailto:' + match.email + '">' ↵
            + match.name + '</a>';
    }
    //if this is not the format of the header, don't mess with it
    return fromField;
    }

    private function test():void
    {
        trace(makeFromLink('"Roger Braunstein" <roger@partlyhuman.com>'));
        //<a href="mailto:roger@partlyhuman.com">Roger Braunstein</a>
    }
    }
}
```

The class uses named capturing groups to refer to `match.name` instead of `match[1]`, making the code more self-explanatory.

TABLE 11-6

Kinds of Groups

Metasequence	Meaning
`(foo)`	Match "foo" and capture it.
`(?:foo)`	Match "foo."
`(?=foo)`	Continue only if "foo" would match here.
`(?!foo)`	Continue only if "foo" would fail to match here.
`(?P<bar>foo)`	Find "foo" and capture it with name *bar*.

International concerns

When you use regular expressions to deal with accented and non-English text, keep these tips in mind:

- Regular expressions, like strings, may contain UTF-8 encoded characters in the code itself. They will match corresponding characters in the input text.

- While there is a metasequence for Unicode characters, you may type them directly into the expression.

- The shorthand character classes include only the English alphabet. For example, \w includes only *a* through *z*. No accented characters are included.

- When using the ignore case flag (i), only the characters *a* through *z* act as case-insensitive. For example, *é* will not match *É*, even with the ignore case flag set.

Using the RegExp Class

In the examples in this chapter, you have seen regular expressions written as literals. However, using regular expressions as RegExp objects enables you to apply some useful techniques and gain important insight.

Building dynamic expressions with String operations

Keep in mind that if you use the RegExp constructor to create expressions, you can pass in an arbitrary String for the source of the pattern. This means that you can, using String manipulation, programmatically craft a pattern to fit the situation at hand:

```
package
{
import flash.display.Sprite;
public class RemoveLetters extends Sprite
{
    public function RemoveLetters()
    {
        //run the test when we start
        test();
    }

    private function test():void
    {
        trace(removeLetters("catch", "cathy catnaps in cathay"));
        //y nps in y
    }

    public function removeLetters(inWord:String, fromWord:String):String
    {
        return fromWord.replace(new RegExp("[" + inWord + "]", "gi"), "");
    }
}
}
```

The preceding example removes all letters found in a word from another bit of text. It does so by turning your blacklisted-letters string into a character class, dynamically generating the regular expression that will remove all offensive letters.

RegExp public properties

Whether a RegExp object was created with the RegExp constructor or a literal, you can access the public properties that RegExp defines to recall information about the expression.

Keep in mind that all of these properties save one are read-only. They are defined at construction time and not modified subsequently:

- `source:String`: The expression's source text.
- `dotall:Boolean`: Whether the dotall (s) flag is set.
- `extended:Boolean`: Whether the extended (x) flag is set.
- `global:Boolean`: Whether the global (g) flag is set.
- `ignoreCase:Boolean`: Whether the ignore case (i) flag is set.
- `multiline:Boolean`: Whether the multiline (m) flag is set.
- `lastIndex:Number`: The index of the character in the input text where the pattern should next begin matching. This property is read-write. This state variable affects only `RegExp.exec()` and `RegExp.test()`, and is set by these methods when (progressively) matching a pattern with the global flag set.

Summary

- Regular expressions may be used to parse regular grammars and loose human input.
- Regular expressions are used to test, locate, identify, extract, replace, and split text.
- Regular expressions are a compact language defined by normal text, metacharacters, and metasequences.
- Flags change the behavior of regular expressions.
- Often you have to choose between a String method and a RegExp method to achieve the same goal.
- You can match characters, alternates, classes of characters, and groups, in whatever quantity you specify.
- Quantifiers are greedy unless you make them lazy.
- Anchors can match a position rather than text.
- Groups can be made to not capture, to be zero-width, and to have names.
- Case insensitivity and word characters work only as advertised with English letters from *a* to *z*.

Part III

Working with the Display List

Chapter 12

Understanding the Flash Player 9 Display List

One of the biggest updates between ActionScript 2.0 and Action-Script 3.0 and Flash 8 and Flash 9 is the way that you can create new graphics and handle the graphics you've already created. In order to fully understand the differences between ActionScript 2.0 and ActionScript 3.0, you need to look at the following commonplace code:

```
var myMovieClip:MovieClip = ↵
    _root.attachMovie(libraryNameString);
```

You want to create a movie that has some drawings in it, so you create a reference to what you've just attached to the Stage, and use that to call methods and access properties of what we've just attached. Seems a little strange right? As it should. What ActionScript 3.0 enables you to do is instantiate and work with the clips in a far more streamlined way. Although to the practiced ActionScript 2.0 developer much of what you're about to look at will seem very strange, it will ultimately make your life better in deep and wonderful ways. So say good-bye to `createEmptyMovieClip()`, you're going to get a whole new way to program all of your graphics in Flash.

Display List

The display list has been around for a while. You could always access all the graphic objects present on the Stage at a given time, just like you could always get any graphics object nested inside another. Now, however, the way that you work with the display list is simplified dramatically and with the new APIs introduced in ActionScript 3.0 you have to know a lot more about what's going on under the hood of your applications. Ultimately this is a good thing; when you know what's going on, you can work with it more efficiently. One of my favorite rules of simplicity is that knowing more makes things simpler. With that in mind let's take a look at the hierarchy of the display list, shown in Figure 12-1.

The hierarchy of the Flash Player display list

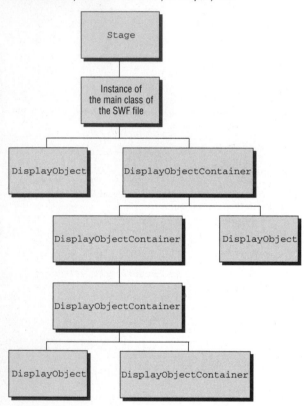

At the very top of your list is the Stage. As you attach DisplayObjects to the Stage you create the additional branches off of the main root. As you attach additional DisplayObjects to those already present on the Stage you create additional branches and leaves. For anyone who has used `attachMovie()` this might be familiar to you. You're still creating MovieClip-like objects with display properties and attaching them to the Stage or to each other in order to allow the user to see them. However, the way that you're navigating the display list and changing the properties and calling the methods of the objects with it has changed drastically. If you never wrote any ActionScript 2.0 don't worry, you're uncontaminated by the past, a blank slate upon which to write the goodness of the ActionScript 3.0 display APIs.

So why completely overhaul the way that Flash works with graphics? In a nutshell: speed and simplicity. The new display list is simpler to work with, both for you and Flash Player, which translates into improved performance. Before the display list everything was a `MovieClip`. Now, we as programmers can pick the appropriate class for what we need, keeping the memory footprint small and the performance of the player optimal. Just need a circle? Then make a `Shape` object. Need multiple frames? Then use a `MovieClip`. Need something that can have children but don't need any frames? Then use a `Sprite`. This approach requires a little more learning at first but vastly reduces the amount of little tricks you'll need to learn to master programming your graphics. Anything in the display list is accessible to you, including vector shapes, text fields, objects with nothing in them, all via index-based accessors (like an array) or by name (a string). Without getting too far into the details, keeping the children of a display object inside an array is a real performance enhancer. You'll look at how to take advantage of all these new features throughout this chapter.

At its heart the display list is a list of what needs to be rendered at a given time. Things that don't need to be displayed or accounted for aren't on the display list. So you can create a display object, load an image into it, and not need to do any rendering until you've added it to another display object. This saves resources in the player and gives you as the designer a lot more control over optimizing your code. When you put a new object on the display list it automatically goes on the top of the list. If I have a parent object with a child object inside of it and add another object, the parent automatically places the new object beneath the old one. Figure 12-2 shows an example using the `DisplayObjectContainer`, the base class that can contain other clips.

FIGURE 12-2

A DisplayObjectContainer with a DisplayObject added to it

245

Adding another object to that `DisplayObjectContainer` and the parent automatically places the child in the next available spot within its array of children as shown in Figure 12-3.

FIGURE 12-3

A DisplayObjectContainer with two DisplayObjects added to it

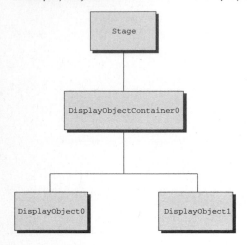

Contrast this to all the problems with handling levels in ActionScript 2.0 and you'll see what a time, sanity, and energy saver this is. Moving a display object from one parent to another, another thing that was slightly less than intuitive in ActionScript 2.0, is a breeze with ActionScript 3.0. Simply get a reference to the display object and use it to add that reference to a different display object. Voilà! Display object moved. No creating new MovieClips, no `createEmptyMovieClip()`. Just get the reference, either the variable name, or via `getChildAt(index:int)` or `getChildByName(name:String)`, and pass it to an object that can contain display objects.

Okay, so what holds the display list? Well, the Stage. You may remember the stage as `_root` in ActionScript 2.0. It's still in ActionScript 3.0, it's just simplified slightly. The Stage is built from the size and properties of the `Sprite` or `MovieClip` that is instantiated when the SWF file starts. Thinking of this as the root might help you conceptually, but it isn't what actually is going on. When the SWF file starts up the Stage takes all the display properties of the class that you've passed to the compiler. As you change that `DisplayObject`, adding or removing elements from it, the Stage and the display list change as well. Here is a class which will be passed to the compiler. For the sake of brevity the `GreenRectangle` class is omitted.

```
public class StageDemonstration extends Sprite
{
    public function StageDemonstration ()
    {
        trace(stage.width);
        //create a 100px wide rectangle
        var greenRectangle1:GreenRectangle = new GreenRectangle ();
        addChild(greenRectangle1);
        trace(stage.width);//traces 100
        //create a 100px wide rectangle
        var greenRectangle2:GreenRectangle = new GreenRectangle ();
        addChild(greenRectangle2);
        greenRectangle2.x = 200;
        trace(stage.width); //traces 300
        //create a 100px wide rectangle
        var greenRectangle3:GreenRectangle = new GreenRectangle ();
        addChild(greenRectangle3);
        greenRectangle3.x = 400;
        trace(stage.width); //traces 500
        //create a 100px wide rectangle
        var greenRectangle4:GreenRectangle = new GreenRectangle ();
        addChild(greenRectangle4);
        greenRectangle4.x = 600;
        trace(stage.width); //traces 700

    }
}
```

Each time the width of the Stage is checked, it will return the width of all the DisplayObjects that are *currently* on the Stage. After adding the first GreenRectangle the width is 100 pixels, because the width of the GreenRectangle is 100 pixels. After adding the second GreenRectangle object *and* moving it over 200 pixels the width of the stage is the distance from the left of the Stage to the right of the furthest object on the Stage, which is at this point 300 pixels. By the time you've added the fourth GreenRectangle, the Stage is 500 pixels wide and adding the fourth with an x position of 600 means that the total width of the Stage is the x position of the last GreenRectangle plus it's width of 100 pixels. The Stage is like a rubber band in this way, constantly stretching and sizing to fit whatever is placed inside of it. All DisplayObjects that can contain other DisplayObjects are called DisplayObjectContainer objects and their height and width all function this way. The Stage is important because all DisplayObjects reference the same stage and can use it to ensure that they are where they are supposed to be. Every display object knows where its stage is, which makes accessing it a lot easier and neater, but what is more important is that the Stage is at the top of the display list. The Stage is referenced through something that's already on the display list, which should tell you that although the Stage is really important, the display list is a far more fundamental concept.

The core of the display list is the DisplayObject, a simple object that acts as an abstract class (but isn't because ActionScript doesn't support those, instead it throws an error if you try to make a new one). Everything that gets displayed anywhere in Flash Player 9 inherits from DisplayObject, including the Stage and the core `DisplayObject` that is the main class of your application. The `DisplayObject` and its subclasses all have the ability to be added to anything that can contain a `DisplayObject`. This concept of adding `DisplayObjects`, and removing them when you're done with them, is the core of `DisplayList` programming. Now you found out that anything that can be added to the display list must inherit from `DisplayObject` but you haven't learned what can have children added to it, until now: `DisplayObjectContainer`. Nice logical name, eh? That is precisely what it does, contains a number of `DisplayObjects`, allowing them to be added and removed, keeping track of them for access, and allowing them to be positioned within it. Take a look at the following example:

```
var sprite:Sprite = new Sprite();
sprite.addChild(someDisplayObject);
```

Now in order to get this code to work you'll need an instance of a `DisplayObject`, but you can't instantiate a `DisplayObject`, so you'll need to subclass it, which I'll get to shortly. First, look into some more of the properties of the `DisplayObjectContainer` and all its subclasses that you're going to leverage when building your ActionScript 3.0 applications. This will help you understand the display list.

```
// you create new objects simply by calling their constructors
var parent:Sprite = new Sprite();
var child:Sprite = new Sprite();
var anotherChild:Sprite = new Sprite();
// you can give any DisplayObject a name to identify it for easier
//access
anotherChild.name = "favoriteChildren";
// this is where the magic happens
// you just add the childDoc to the parent
parent.addChild(child);

parent.getChildAt(0); // will return childDoc
parent.addChild(child);
parent.swapChildren(child, anotherChild);
parent.getChildAt(0); //will return anotherChild
anotherChild.x = 100;
//places anotherChild at 100 pixels right relative to parent 0, 0 point
anotherChild.y = 100;
//places anotherChild at 100 pixels lower relative to parent 0, 0 point
parent.removeChild(parent.getChildByName("favoriteChildren"));
```

As you can see, you're able to get access to any display objects that you've added to your `DisplayObjectContainer` using `getChildAt(index:int)` and `getChildByName(name:String)`. If the variables are within scope, you can manipulate them using their instance name, changing their position relative to their parent, and modifying any of their other properties or calling any of their methods. Most of the classes you're going to work with in the display list API extend from `DisplayObjectContainer`, because it's handy to be able to add and get children out of things.

To sum up quickly: the display list is a list of all `DisplayObjects` that have been attached to a `DisplayObjectContainer`. This means that as soon as the object is added it has access to the Stage and through the Stage access to any other display object in the display list hierarchy. All `DisplayObjectContainer` objects (that is, all objects that can be a parent to a `DisplayObject`) have a `numChildren` property. All `DisplayObjects` also have a `parent` property that can be used to find whatever clip is currently containing the clip. Take a quick look at this:

```
var firstContainer:Sprite = new Sprite();
var secondContainer:Sprite = new Sprite();
//nothing is visible right now on the stage
secondContainer.addChild(firstContainer);
//still nothing visible, because you've added the firstContainer to the
//secondContainer but not put either container on the main display list
addChild(secondContainer);
//now they're both visible.
var thirdContainer: Sprite = new Sprite();
//add the thirdContainer
firstContainer.addChild(thirdContainer);
trace(firstContainer.numChildren);//traces "2"
//double them all in size, so you'll use the numChildren to count through them
for(var i:int = 0; i<firstContainer.numChildren; i++)
{
//and use getChildAt(index) to get the child and change its properties
    firstContainer.getChildAt(i).width *= 2;
}
```

All the classes that make up the display list API extend from `DisplayObject` and are all contained within the `flash.display` package. They all have a great deal in common, although they were all designed with distinct sets of responsibilities and characteristics. Next, go through and look at the different types, potential uses for each type, and start to put together some simple examples that will show you how to put the new display list API to use.

DisplayObject and DisplayObjectContainer

As the base object for all objects that will appear on the display list, the `DisplayObject` represents all the fundamental properties and methods for anything that can be put onto the display list. It dispatches events when it is added to the Stage, when the Stage enters a new frame, when it is rendered, and when it is removed from the Stage. The `DisplayObject` class implements the `IBitmapDrawable` interface also implemented by the `BitmapData` class. This hints at the `DisplayObject`'s true roots: a simple software bitmapped graphics object. The `DisplayObject` as mentioned earlier, cannot be instantiated, only sub-classed. This may seem strange at first, but consider it a clarifying act by the Adobe engineers; it's the root, not the branch.

The `DisplayObjectContainer` is the base class that all display objects that can have child objects extend. It provides the base functionality for adding, indexing, accessing, and removing children `DisplayObjects`. Like the `DisplayObject`, it also is an abstract class and cannot be instantiated. When you work with a `DisplayObjectContainer` object you are most often working with the `Sprite` class. You'll look at the `Sprite` in greater depth later in this chapter. For now, al you need to know is that it's the building block for graphical objects that need to contain other objects and graphics.

What is an abstract class?

The abstract class is a language construct that the language designers decide on in order to ensure that base classes cannot be instantiated. This guarantees that the class's responsibilities are not contaminated by unnecessary clutter that may be associated with common usages for that group of classes. That's a convoluted way of saying that the frame of a car is great for building a car on, not for driving cross-country. Making an abstract class enables you to ensure that the blueprint for your frame will be used to build the frame and that extraneous concerns won't get rolled onto your original intention. One of the central concerns of object-oriented programming is keeping the responsibilities of any class to their minimal logical parts. Abstract classes allow us to define functionality that can be implemented in the future for users to build upon, without needing to worry about what they'll do with that class itself. They aren't widely used in ActionScript 3.0, but they are present in the core API and in the Display API in particular. So if you understand what they are and why they're used, you'll have a clearer understanding of what the designers of ActionScript had in mind when they designed it.

Understanding the x and y position of a DisplayObject

The x and y position are always relative to the `DisplayObject` that contains it, so when you try to get or set the coordinate positions you need to keep that in mind. If you need the global position of the `DisplayObject`, you can use `localToGlobal()` to get or set the position of the `DisplayObject` in relation to the Stage. You can also do the inverse with `globalToLocal()` to pass a point from the Stage into a `DisplayObject` to get a local position, relative to the local objects x and y position. Here's an example using the `Sprite` class:

```
var parentSprite:Sprite = new Sprite();
addChild(parentSprite);
var childSprite:Sprite = new Sprite();
parentSprite.addChild(childSprite);
childSprite.x = 100;
parentSprite.x = 100;
childSprite.y = 100;
var pt:Point = childSprite.localToGlobal(new Point(50, 50));
trace(pt); //traces x=250, y=150
pt = parentSprite.localToGlobal(new Point(0, 0));
trace(pt); //traces x=100, y=0
pt = childSprite.globalToLocal(new Point(100, 100));
trace(pt); //traces x=-100, y=0
```

The DisplayObjects stage

The `DisplayObject` has a `stage` property that you can use to get a reference to the Stage. All `DisplayObjects` that are on the display list have this property. Those that are not on the display list do not. Here's an example to help you understand the concept better. First a class that will be added to the display list of another class:

```
package
{
    import flash.display.Sprite;
    import flash.events.Event;

    public class StageListenerSprite extends Sprite
    {
        public function StageListenerSprite()
        {
            trace(" after the constructor is called the stage = "+stage);
            addEventListener(Event.ADDED_TO_STAGE, traceStage);
            addEventListener(Event.REMOVED_FROM_STAGE, traceStage);
        }

        private function traceStage(event:Event):void
        {
            trace(stage.width);
        }
    }
}
```

Here is a `Sprite` object that can add your StageListenerSprite so that the `ADDED_TO_STAGE` and `REMOVED_FROM_STAGE` events will be called.

```
    public class StageTestProject extends Sprite
    {
        public function StageTestProject()
        {

            var stageListenerSprite:StageListenerSprite = ↵
new StageListenerSprite();
            addChild(stageListenerSprite);
            removeChild(stageListenerSprite);

        }
    }
```

When you run the example, you'll see the `ADDED_TO_STAGE` event means that the stage object is set to the stage of the application. When the `REMOVED_FROM_STAGE` event is dispatched, your stage object will still refer to the same `DisplayObjectContainer` that contained your

Sprite. This is important to remember because any information that you want to know about the Stage or any other object on the display list isn't accessible until your object has been added to the display list. After it has been added to the display list, your `DisplayObject` can access any other object on the display list.

Transform

The `DisplayObject` contains a transform property that gives information about its matrix, color transform, and pixel bounds. This is useful for grabbing information about the `DisplayObject` for comparison with other `DisplayObjects`, as a part of a graphics routine. Suppose that you have multiple `DisplayObjects` and need to find which ones have had a certain color transformation. Here's what you need to do:

```
private function checkTransform(do:DisplayObject):void
{
    for(var prop:String in do.transform)
    {
        trace("prop "+do.transform[prop]);
    }
}
```

Sizing the DisplayObject

There are four distinct properties that control the size of any `DisplayObject`. The `scaleX` property indicates the horizontal scale of the `DisplayObject` from the registration point, which is by default the upper left corner, from the time that it was first added to the display list. If your `DisplayObject` was originally 300 pixels wide and it has been scaled to be 150 pixels wide, then your `scaleX` property will be 0.5. If you then scale the `DisplayObject` to 600 pixels, the `scaleX` property will be 2.0. The `scaleY` property indicates the vertical scale of the `DisplayObject` from the registration point. The width is the width in pixels, whereas the height is height in pixels at the current time. As you change the width or height, the scale will change to reflect the relationship of the current size to the size when the `DisplayObject` was first added to the Stage.

It's important to remember that until there is something in a `DisplayObject`, it has no height or width, so calls to `height` or `width`, when there is no graphics object or something else filling the object, are meaningless.

Using the blend mode

The blend modes should be familiar to all users of Photoshop, After Effects, Illustrator, or other graphics programs. When you set the blend mode of a `DisplayObject` you're specifying how it reacts with objects that are below it in the z order (depth order) of the parent container. The blend mode is set using strings, and is by default set to "normal" or `BlendMode.NORMAL`. When you change the blend mode Flash Player looks through every pixel in your `DisplayObject` to determine how it will appear. When evaluating the colors Flash Player looks at the red, green, and blue values of each pixel and makes separate decisions for each of them.

Here is a short list of the different blend modes:

- **BlendMode.NORMAL** makes the `DisplayObject` show in front of the background. Only in places where the display object is transparent can you see the background.

- **BlendMode.MULTIPLY** multiplies the values of the colors in the top `DisplayObject` by the colors of the background making the colors darker. Multiplying the hexadecimal numbers that represent the colors of each pixel accomplishes this.

- **BlendMode.SCREEN** multiplies the inverse of the pixel by the complement of the background color making a much lighter color. This tends to "bleach" the appearance of the top `DisplayObject`, and makes the background appear.

- **BlendMode.LIGHTEN** simply picks the brighter of the two pixel values for each red, green, and blue value, background and foreground, and displays that one. Selects the lighter of the constituent colors of the `DisplayObject` and the color of the background (the colors with the larger values). This setting is commonly used for superimposing type.

- **BlendMode.DARKEN** works in the reverse of the LIGHTEN mode, selecting the darker of each value for each pixel.

- **BlendMode.DIFFERENCE** compares the red, green, and blue values for the `DisplayObject` and its background, and subtracts whichever is darker from whichever is higher, and then displays that color. This makes colors much brighter and vibrant and tends to remove tonal subtlety.

- **BlendMode.ADD** simply adds the values together, making colors much lighter.

- **BlendMode.SUBTRACT** subtracts the values of each pixel, making the image darker.

- **BlendMode.INVERT** inverts the background and displays it.

- **BlendMode.OVERLAY** overlays the top `DisplayObject` onto the background. Where the background is lighter, the colors are screened so that both top and background are blended. Where the background is darker the colors are multiplied. This generally makes the background and `DisplayObject` blend together while allowing more of the background to show.

- **BlendMode.HARDLIGHT** inverts the OVERLAY filters logic. Where the `DisplayObject` is lighter, the colors are screened so that both top and background are blended. Where the `DisplayObject` is darker the colors are multiplied. This generally makes the background and `DisplayObject` blend together while allowing more of the `DisplayObject` to show.

- **BlendMode.LAYER** allows the display object to use more complex layering effects, and in particular means that a parent can have complex Blends applied to its children.

- **BlendMode.ALPHA** applies the alpha value of each pixel of the `DisplayObject` to the background, so where the alpha of the top `DisplayObject` is 0, the `DisplayObject` will not appear. The parent's `blendMode` must be set to `BlendMode.LAYER`.

- **BlendMode.ERASE** erases the background based on the alpha value of the display object, so where the alpha of the top `DisplayObject` is not 0, the background will not appear. The parents' `blendMode` must be set to `BlendMode.LAYER`.

Introducing the Graphics Object

The Graphics class contains a set of methods that you can use to create a vector shape within another DisplayObject such as a Sprite or a Shape. You can't actually create a Graphics object or it will throw an error, but you will use them quite a bit. The Graphics object comes with a few built-in functions that are very helpful (compared to creating them yourself): drawRect(), drawRoundRect(), drawCircle(), and drawEllipse(). The following simple Sprite example uses the Graphics object to give your Sprite some graphical properties:

```
public function createSprite()
{
  var spr:Sprite = new Sprite();
  spr.graphics.beginFill(0x00ff00, 1.0);
  spr.graphics.drawRect(0, 0, 50, 50);
  spr.graphics.endFill();
  addChild(spr);
}
```

This will create a simple Sprite class and uses its graphics object to create a green rectangle within it. Keep in mind that the addChild() function has to be used within a class that extends DisplayObjectContainer in order to work properly.

Creating fills

Notice the line in the example above that reads beginFill(0x00ff00, 1.0). When you create a graphic, one of the first things you want to define is how the background is going to appear. This is called the fill of the vector, and it represents what goes inside of any points defined by the drawing routine. Creating a simple fill consists of three steps. First, set what the fill is going to be in terms of a hexadecimal color and an alpha value (1 is opaque, 0 is transparent), then draw a shape, and finally call endFill() so that Flash knows that you're done adding to the fill and that it can go ahead and render the shape you've drawn.

```
spr.graphics.beginFill(0xff00ff, 0.5);//our fill will be yellow
spr.graphics.drawCircle(0, 0, 50);//fill a circle with our fill
spr.graphics.endFill();//we're done with this graphic
```

Drawing lines in a graphics object

In order to draw in your graphics object, you must first provide a lineStyle() for the drawing API to use and then you can begin to draw using lineTo(), providing x and y coordinates for your line. The line begins from 0, 0 unless you specify a location to begin drawing from using moveTo().

```
var spr:Sprite = new Sprite();
spr.graphics.lineStyle(1, 0x0000ff);
spr.graphics.moveTo(30, 30);
spr.graphics.lineTo(100, 30);
```

```
spr.graphics.lineTo(100, 100);
spr.graphics.lineTo(30, 100);
spr.graphics.lineTo(30, 30);
spr.graphics.endFill();

addChild(spr);
```

Drawing curves in a graphics object

In order to draw curves, you use the same procedure as above except that you draw using curveTo, providing x and y coordinates for your line to end at as well as an anchor x and y positions that the line will curve towards. The line begins from 0, 0 unless you specify a location to begin drawing from using moveTo().

```
var spr:Sprite = new Sprite();
spr.graphics.beginFill(0x0000ff, 1.0);
spr.graphics.lineStyle(1, 0x0000ff);
spr.graphics.moveTo(30, 30);
spr.graphics.curveTo(180, 20, 250, 30);
spr.graphics.endFill();
addChild(spr);
```

This is a very brief introduction to creating graphics using the Graphics object. Creating lines and fills is covered in far greater detail in Chapter 30.

Working with the Stage

The Stage is where all the action takes place. It extends DisplayObjectContainer and has a few of its own properties related to the way that the application appears inside of its main container. The following section takes a quick look at setting up the Stage with a certain alignment and listening to resize events if the user decides to resize the window.

Using the stageResize event

Here's an example of how you can use the stageResize event:

```
package{
  import flash.display.Sprite;
  import flash.display.Stage;
  import flash.display.StageAlign;
  import flash.display.StageScaleMode;
  import flash.display.DisplayObjectContainer;
  import flash.events.Event;

  public class Simple extends Sprite
  {
```

```
        public function Simple()
        {

                this.graphics.beginFill(0xff0000, 1);
                this.graphics.drawRect(0, 0, stage.stageWidth/2, ↵
stage.stageHeight/2);
                this.graphics.endFill();
                //set what part of the browser the stage will set itself in
                this.stage.align = StageAlign.TOP_LEFT;
                //set how the stage scales itself
                this.stage.scaleMode = StageScaleMode.NO_SCALE;
                //add an event listener for the stages resized event
                stage.addEventListener(Event.RESIZE, stageResized);

        }

        private function stageResized(event:Event):void
        {
                trace(stage.stageHeight+"  "+stage.stageWidth);

                this.graphics.clear();
                this.graphics.beginFill(0xff0000, 1);
                this.graphics.drawRect(0, 0, stage.stageWidth/2, ↵
stage.stageWidth/2);
                this.graphics.endFill();
        }
    }
}
```

The stage does have a lot of the same properties as the `DisplayObjectContainer`, but many of them cannot be set. For example, if you try to set the x, y, alpha, or rotation (among others) of the Stage you'll see errors informing you that you've attempted to set a read-only property. The width and height of the Stage are dependent on the information set in the HTML page wrapping it (if there is one), so if your embed statement says `width="100%"` you'll see "100" when you try to access the SWF file. Notice too that you're accessing the Stage property via the main `DisplayObject` of your application. Among the many properties that all `DisplayObjects` possess is a reference to the Stage.

Setting the Stage alignment and scale mode

When you publish a SWF file, the Stage is centered by default and the SWF file scales to the size of the browser window. You can change this easily, however, using the `align` and `scaleMode` of the Stage, accessible through any child on the display list. There are two utility classes `flash.display` `.StageScaleMode` and `flash.display.StageAlign` that provide constant values you can use to set these properties, or you can simply write them out.

```
this.stage.scaleMode = StageScaleMode.NO_SCALE;
/*same as this.stage.scaleMode = "noScale"; */
this.stage.align = StageAlign.TOP_LEFT;
/* same as this.stage.align = "TL"; */
```

InteractiveObject and SimpleButton

The `InteractiveObject` is the base abstract class for all `DisplayObjects` that will interact with the mouse and keyboard, which means that it adds events to notify listeners of tab events, mouse events, and keyboard events. Since `InteractiveObject` is an abstract class, you'll be working with the `SimpleButton` class to make some simple examples of the functionality that these two objects provide.

SimpleButton

`SimpleButton` is a class that enables you to quickly create a button object with an up, over, down, and `hitTest` state. Each of these states is a `DisplayObject` that defines the look of that particular state.

The up state sets the `DisplayObject` that is used when the mouse is not positioned over the button. The down state sets the display object that is used when the user clicks the `htTestState` object. The over state specifies a display object that is used when the mouse is positioned over the button. The `hitTestState` sets the display object that is used as the hit testing object for the button.

You can pass all these properties into the `SimpleButton` in its constructor as follows:

```
/* the over state will be red, this will show when the user
hovers over the button */
var overSprite:Sprite = new Sprite();
  overSprite.graphics.beginFill(0xff0000, 1);
  overSprite.graphics.drawRect(0, 0, 100, 100);
  overSprite.graphics.endFill();
  /* the up state will be green, this will show when the user is not interacting
  with the button */
  var upSprite:Sprite = new Sprite();
  upSprite.graphics.beginFill(0x00ff00, 1);
  upSprite.graphics.drawRect(0, 0, 100, 100);
  upSprite.graphics.endFill();
  /* this is the down state sprite which will show when the user clicks on the
  button */
  var downSprite:Sprite - new Sprite();
  downSprite.graphics.beginFill(0xffffff, 1);
  downSprite.graphics.drawRect(0, 0, 100, 100);
```

```
    downSprite.graphics.endFill();
    /* now we just pass the sprites into the SimpleButton so that it has all of its
    states immediately, the last parameter describes the hitTestState, that is, the
    area that can be moused over or clicked on */
    var btnOne:SimpleButton = new SimpleButton(upSprite, overSprite, downSprite, ↵
    overSprite);
```

The `SimpleButton` also possesses an `enabled` property, when a button is disabled (the `enabled` property is set to false). The button is visible but cannot be clicked. By default the value is true. In addition the `SimpleButton` possesses a `useHandCursor` property that determines whether Flash Player shows the hand cursor when the mouse is over a `SimpleButton`.

Tab-enabled interactive objects

You can set objects to be tab enabled simply by setting their `tabEnabled` property to true. What does this mean? Think of a form where you tab through the fields starting, usually, in the upper left-hand corner and working down to the lower right. If you set an `InteractiveObject`'s tab-enabled property to true, then, when the user clicks the tab button, the object will be among the items that are selected. The `tabIndex` property of the object is where that object is within the array of "tab-able" objects. By default this is a list of all the objects from the upper left to the lower right. However, if you want a certain item to be in a different location, you simply set the index to the integer that you want and the array will be reorganized. The objects are ordered according to their `tabIndex` properties, in ascending order. An object with a `tabIndex` value of 1 precedes an object with a `tabIndex` value of 2.

The other tab-related property is `focusRect`. If you pass in a null object then the `InteractiveObject` doesn't display a focus rectangle when it receives focus. This means that if you were to tab through a list of items that had focus rectangles enabled, then you would see a box around whichever was selected. With `focusRect` set to null, the box does not appear.

Focus and Tab Events

Focus is very important in the Flash Player display list architecture. The object that has focus is the one that will receive events that are being passed up, like changes in the mouse or keyboard, and it generally represents the object that the user is interested in. It's important to keep track of what object has focus and to help you do that the `InteractiveObject` defines a few focus events that you can listen for.

■ `focusIn` or `flash.events.FocusEvent.FOCUS_IN` is the event that notifies you that an `InteractiveObject` has been made the focus object. Only one object can have focus at a given time. This can get tricky when you have lots of things inside of one another, like in a form of sorts, but if you think of focus as going *down* the display list it becomes easier. If you want to know when something has focus, you simply listen for this event.

■ focusOut or `flash.events.FocusEvent.FOCUS_OUT` is dispatched after a display object loses focus. This happens when a user highlights a different object with a pointing device or keyboard navigation. The object that loses focus is called the target object of this event, while the corresponding `InteractiveObject` instance that receives focus is called the related object. A reference to the related object is stored in the target object's `relatedObject` property. The `shiftKey` property is not used. This event precedes the dispatch of the `focusIn` event by the related object.

Events are covered more fully in Chapter 16. However, for the sake of understanding the focus event and the way the `InteractiveObject` gets and loses focus, check out this example.

```
public class SimpleFocus extends Sprite
    {
        public function SimpleFocus()
        {

            var spr:Sprite = new Sprite();
            var sprTwo:Sprite = new Sprite();
            spr.graphics.beginFill(0x00ff00, 1);
            spr.graphics.drawRect(0, 0, 100, 100);
            spr.graphics.endFill();
            sprTwo.graphics.beginFill(0x0000ff, 1);
            sprTwo.graphics.drawRect(0, 0, 100, 100);
            sprTwo.graphics.endFill();

            var btnOne:SimpleButton = new SimpleButton(spr, spr, spr, spr);
            var btnTwo:SimpleButton = new SimpleButton(sprTwo, sprTwo, ↵
    sprTwo, sprTwo);

            addChild(btnOne);
            addChild(btnTwo);

            sprTwo.x = 300;

            btnOne.addEventListener(MouseEvent.MOUSE_OVER, focusMe);
            btnTwo.addEventListener(MouseEvent.MOUSE_OVER, focusMe);

            btnOne.addEventListener(FocusEvent.FOCUS_IN, fin);
            btnOne.addEventListener(FocusEvent.FOCUS_OUT, fout);
            btnTwo.addEventListener(FocusEvent.FOCUS_IN, fin);
            btnTwo.addEventListener(FocusEvent.FOCUS_OUT, fout);

        }

        private function fin(focusEvent:FocusEvent):void
        {
```

```
                              trace(' focus in '+focusEvent.target+' related object ↵
           '+focusEvent.relatedObject);
                 }

               private function fout(focusEvent:FocusEvent):void
               {
                     trace(' focus out '+focusEvent.target+' related object ↵
           '+focusEvent.relatedObject);
                 }

               private function focusMe(mouseEvent:MouseEvent):void
               {
                   trace(" stage focus ");
                   stage.focus = (mouseEvent.target as InteractiveObject);
                 }
           }
```

tabChildrenChange or flash.events.Event.TAB_CHILDREN_CHANGE is dispatched
when the value of the object's tabChildren flag changes. tabEnabledChange or flash
.events.Event.TAB_ENABLED_CHANGE is dispatched when the object's tabEnabled flag
changes. tabIndexChange or flash.events.Event.TAB_INDEX_CHANGE is dispatched
when the value of the object's tabIndex property changes.

Mouse properties

The InteractiveObject, being interactive, defines methods for working with the mouse as well.
The DisplayObject, in the interest of keeping it simple, doesn't define any mouse interactivity.
That is left up to the InteractiveObject to define. The mouse properties added in here are:

- mouseEnabled, which specifies whether the object receives any mouse messages, like
  "mouseOver", "mouseDown", "mouseMove". By default this is true, but if
  mouseEnabled is set to false, the instance doesn't receive any mouseEvents, which
  means that listening for mouseEvents on the object won't work.

- doubleClickEnabled means, well, what it says, that the InteractiveObject can
  receive double-click mouse events. We can enable or disable this property.

Events that the InteractiveObject receives

The InteractiveObject defines most of the Mouse and Keyboard events that we work with.
They are all listed here for reference, but you should also refer to Chapter 17 for more information
on these events and how to listen for them.

- click or flash.events.MouseEvent.CLICK is dispatched when the user clicks *over*
  the InteractiveObject, if the mouse is not currently over the InteractiveObject
  the event is not dispatched.

- `doubleClick` or `flash.events.MouseEvent.DOUBLE_CLICK` is dispatched when the user double-clicks on the `InteractiveObject` and the object's `doubleClickEnabled` property is set to true.

- `keyDown` or `flash.events.KeyboardEvent.KEY_DOWN` is dispatched whenever the user clicks a key and the `InteractiveObject` has focus.

- `keyFocusChange` or `flash.events.FocusEvent.KEY_FOCUS_CHANGE` is dispatched when the user changes focus using the keyboard. This usually happens when using the tab key, although this could be other keys if you've created custom focus behavior.

- `keyUp` or `flash.events.KeyboardEvent.KEY_UP` is dispatched whenever the user releases a key after pressing it down.

- `mouseDown` or `flash.events.MouseEvent.MOUSE_DOWN` is dispatched when the user triggers the `mouseDown` event *over* the `InteractiveObject`.

- `mouseFocusChange` or `flash.events.FocusEvent.MOUSE_FOCUS_CHANGE` is dispatched when the user changes the focus using the mouse.

- `mouseMove` or `flash.events.MouseEvent.MOUSE_MOVE` is dispatched whenever the user moves the mouse and the `InteractiveObject` has focus.

- `mouseOut` or `flash.events.MouseEvent.MOUSE_OUT` is dispatched whenever the mouse was over the `InteractiveObject` and then leaves the boundaries of the `InteractiveObject`.

- `mouseOver` or `flash.events.MouseEvent.MOUSE_OVER` is dispatched when the mouse was not over the `InteractiveObject` object but moves over it.

- `mouseUp` or `flash.events.MouseEvent.MOUSE_UP` is dispatched whenever the mouse button is released and the `InteractiveObject` has focus.

- `mouseWheel` or `flash.events.MouseEvent.MOUSE_WHEEL` is dispatched when the user moves the mouse wheel and the `InteractiveObject` has focus.

- `rollOut` or `flash.events.MouseEvent.ROLL_OUT` is dispatched whenever the user moves the mouse off of the `InteractiveObject` *and* any of its children.

- `rollOver` or `flash.events.MouseEvent.ROLL_OVER` is dispatched whenever the user moves the mouse onto the `InteractiveObject` *or* any of its children.

Shape

What's the `Shape` class good for? Think of all the times when you need something simple — a circle, a rectangle, a line — but nothing else. You could draw in a `MovieClip` like you did in ActionScript 2.0, but at what expense? You don't need frames, you don't need to be able to add more children to it, so why would you want to add all the overhead that the `MovieClip` will require? It's going to greatly increase the speed of our application at runtime and reduce the size of it to use only what you need; judiciousness pays its dividends in all things, especially in drawing routines.

The Shape is at its core, a wrapper for the graphics object that is contained in all the DisplayObject subclasses. Of all the DisplayObjects though, it is the most lightweight. It contains a reference to a graphics object that can be used for any vector drawing.

```
import flash.display.Sprite;
import flash.display.Shape;

public class ShapeInstance extends Sprite
{
    public function ShapeInstance()
    {
        var shape:Shape = new Shape();
        shape.graphics.beginFill(0x00ff00, 1.0);
        shape.graphics.drawRect(10, 10, 50, 50);
        shape.graphics.endFill();
        addChild(shape);
    }
}
```

Use of the Shape provides you with access to drawing routines with the least possible amount of overhead.

Creating User Interface Elements with Sprite

The Sprite class is the perfect DisplayObject to begin building user interface (UI) components with. It's light, doesn't make use of frames and the associated overhead, provides drag-and-drop support, acts as a DropTarget for other DisplayObjects, and has a button mode property. It extends the DisplayObjectContainer and has all the associated methods of that class, while adding a few more. For all those times in ActionScript 2.0 that you used a MovieClip to create UI components that did not require frames, you were wishing (even if you didn't know it) to have a Sprite class to work with.

Dragging and dropping

Dragging support in particular sets the Sprite class apart from its superclass and makes it a great candidate to build the moveable parts of a UI component with. Here's how dragging works in ActionScript 3.0:

```
    package
{
import flash.display.Sprite;
import flash.events.MouseEvent;
public class CodeSample extends Sprite
{
    private var draggableSprite:Sprite;
    private var droppableSprite:Sprite;
    private var nonDroppableSprite:Sprite;
```

```
public function CodeSample()
{
    draggableSprite = new Sprite();
    draggableSprite.graphics.beginFill(0xff0000, 1);
    draggableSprite.graphics.drawCircle(0, 0, 10);
    draggableSprite.graphics.endFill();
    droppableSprite = new Sprite();
    droppableSprite.graphics.beginFill(0x0000ff, 1);
    droppableSprite.graphics.drawRect(0, 0, 100, 100);
    droppableSprite.graphics.endFill();
    nonDroppableSprite = new Sprite();
    nonDroppableSprite.graphics.beginFill(0xff0000, 1);
    nonDroppableSprite.graphics.drawRect(0, 0, 100, 100);
    nonDroppableSprite.graphics.endFill();
    addChild(nonDroppableSprite);
    addChild(droppableSprite);
    addChild(draggableSprite);

    nonDroppableSprite.x = 200;
    droppableSprite.x = 500;
    nonDroppableSprite.y = 100;
    droppableSprite.y = 100;
    draggableSprite.y = 100;

    draggableSprite.addEventListener(MouseEvent.MOUSE_DOWN, ↵
        startDragSprite);
    draggableSprite.addEventListener(MouseEvent.MOUSE_UP, ↵
        stopDragSprite);
}

private function startDragSprite(mouseEvent:MouseEvent):void
{
    (mouseEvent.target as Sprite).startDrag();
}

private function stopDragSprite(mouseEvent:MouseEvent):void
{
    var target:Sprite = mouseEvent.target as Sprite;
    if (target.dropTarget == droppableSprite)
    {
        target.stopDrag();
    } else {
        target.x = 0;
    }
}
}
}
```

Now, this creates some familiar functionality where you define a drop area where a draggable `Sprite` can be dropped. If you don't drop it there, it just goes back to where it came from. To make this really nice I'd like to make an easing function that puts it back in a "pretty way" but for a quick and dirty example this does the trick. Remember how the new event-handling scheme works in ActionScript 3.0. Take a look at the line where you've defined the event handler for the mouse down to the draggable `Sprite`.

Are you confused as to why it doesn't have the following line?

```
draggableSprite.addEventListener(MouseEvent.MOUSE_DOWN,
draggableSprite.startDrag());
```

Well, `startDrag()` doesn't take a `MouseEvent` and remember that methods that can't accept `Event` objects as parameters can't be used as `EventListeners`. It helps you keep your event handling code and event listening separate and clean and that's a good thing.

Using the buttonMode of the Sprite

Let's take a look at another really cool property of the `Sprite` that is introduced in this class:

```
var foo:Sprite = new Sprite();
foo.graphics.beginFill(0xff0000, 1);
foo.graphics.drawRect(0, 0, 100, 100);
foo.graphics.endFill();
foo.buttonMode = true;
addChild(foo);
```

Setting the `buttonMode` to true means that any time the mouse passes over the `Sprite` it changes from a pointer to a hand and invites the user to click. Use some `MouseEvent` handlers on that `Sprite` and off you go, a fully functional, incredibly lightweight button. It is better to use the `SimpleButton` class for creating fully functional buttons. However, the `Sprite` will do when you don't need as much interactivity for the button, or when you want to script it all yourself.

Using the hitArea

The `Sprite` class provides a `hitArea` that determines what part of the `Sprite` can be clicked to dispatch the `MouseDown` event for the `Sprite`, by default this is the `Sprite` itself, though it can be specified as another `Sprite` or `DisplayObject`.

```
package
{
public class CodeProject extends Sprite
{
    public function CodeProject()
    {
        var notHitArea:Sprite = new Sprite();
```

```
        notHitArea.graphics.beginFill(0x00FF00, 1.0);
        notHitArea.graphics.drawRect(0, 0, 30, 30);
        notHitArea.graphics.endFill();
        addChild(notHitArea);
        notHitArea.x = 100;
        notHitArea.y = 200;
        //create a new sprite to use as the hit area for the new sprite
        //this sprite will serve as the hit area for our 'notHitArea' sprite
        var hitAreaSprite:Sprite = new Sprite();
        hitAreaSprite.graphics.beginFill(0x0000FF, 1.0);
        hitAreaSprite.graphics.drawRect(0, 0, 30, 30);
        hitAreaSprite.graphics.endFill();
        addChild(hitAreaSprite);
        //what we've set as the hit area for our 'notHitArea' sprite
        notHitArea.hitArea = hitAreaSprite;
        //we have to set the hitAreaSprite to mouseEnabled = false
        //otherwise our hitAreaSprite will be throwing its own mouseEvents
        hitAreaSprite.mouseEnabled = false;
        //add the event listener for the MOUSE_DOWN event, it will fire
        //if we click on the 'hitAreaSprite' sprite
        notHitArea.addEventListener(MouseEvent.MOUSE_DOWN, clickHandler);
    }
    /* the clickHandler for the MOUSE_EVENT which will only fire when you click
     * on the hitAreaSprites */
    private function clickHandler(mouseEvent:MouseEvent):void
    {
        trace(" clickHandler ");
    }
}
}
```

Using hitTestPoint

The `Sprite` class provides a method to test whether a given set of Cartesian coordinates is within its bounds that returns true if the point is within its bounds and false if not.

```
        var pt:Point = new Point(20, 30);

        var temp:Sprite = new Sprite();
        temp.graphics.beginFill(0x00ff00, 1.0);
        temp.graphics.drawRect(0, 0, 30, 30);
        temp.graphics.endFill();
        addChild(temp);

        if (temp.hitTestPoint(pt.x, pt.y))
        {
            trace("Point within bounds");
        }
```

Swapping the depths of children

Setting the depths of children is much simpler in ActionScript 3.0 than it has been in the past, thanks to the DisplayObjectContainer's numChildren property and swapChildren() method. Since the children are stored in an array you count from 0 and the numChildren property starts from 1, you always need to subtract 1 from the numChildren property in order to retrieve the correct child but this is easily enough done.

```
package
{
import flash.display.Sprite;
import flash.events.Event;
public class DepthSwapping extends Sprite
{
    public function DepthSwapping()
    {
        super();

        var aSpr:Sprite = new Sprite();
        var bSpr:Sprite = new Sprite();
        var cSpr:Sprite = new Sprite();
        var dSpr:Sprite = new Sprite();

        aSpr.addEventListener(MouseEvent.MOUSE_DOWN, swapSprites);
        bSpr.addEventListener(MouseEvent.MOUSE_DOWN, swapSprites);
        cSpr.addEventListener(MouseEvent.MOUSE_DOWN, swapSprites);
        dSpr.addEventListener(MouseEvent.MOUSE_DOWN, swapSprites);

        addChild(aSpr);
        addChild(bSpr);
        addChild(cSpr);
        addChild(dSpr);
    }

    private function swapSprites(evt:Event):void
    {
        swapChildren((evt.target as Sprite), getChildAt(numChildren - 1));
    }
}
}
```

Reparenting display objects

When you do `addChild()` you're adding a *specific* instance of a `DisplayObject` to a `DisplayObjectContainer`. This means that a single `DisplayObject` cannot exist inside of two other clips at the same time. Let's look at this a little more closely to see what happens when we try to do this:

```
package {
    mport flash.display.*;
    import flash.events.*;

    public class Simple extends Sprite
    {
        var squareOne:Sprite = new Sprite();
        var squareTwo:Sprite = new Sprite();

        var shapeInst:ShapeInstance = new ShapeInstance();

        public function Simple()
        {
        squareOne.graphics.beginFill(0x00ff00, 1);
        squareOne.graphics.drawRect(0, 0, 200, 200);
        squareOne.graphics.endFill();

        squareTwo.graphics.beginFill(0x00ff00, 1);
        squareTwo.graphics.drawRect(0, 0, 200, 200);
        squareTwo.graphics.endFill();

        addChild(squareOne);
        addChild(squareTwo);

        squareTwo.x = 300;

        squareOne.addEventListener(MouseEvent.MOUSE_DOWN, addShape);
        squareTwo.addEventListener(MouseEvent.MOUSE_DOWN, addShape);
        }

        private function addShape(event:Event):void
        {
            event.target.addChild(shapeInst);
        }
    }
}
```

If what you intended to do was to add a new instance of your `ShapeInstance` class then changing the `addChild` method in the `addShape` function to the following would work:

```
event.target.addChild(new ShapeInstance());
```

You'll need to create a new instance of the `ShapeInstance` class every time you want to attach it to something. This indicates what the underlying structure of the display list is like, references to individual graphics drawing objects held by the parent clip. Any time you create a new object and add it, you add a new leaf to the tree of the display list; any time you move a `DisplayObject` you un-parent and then re-parent that object within the display list.

Working with the MovieClip

The `MovieClip` class is, in contrast to its treatment in ActionScript 2.0, now a specialized class for graphical objects that contain frame-based animations. `MovieClip`, unlike the other `DisplayObjects` you've explored, contains a frame and frame rate reference, scene references, which refer to the scenes contained inside a clip, and timeline methods. These timeline methods include the familiar `gotoAndPlay()` and `gotoAndStop()` methods as well as `nextScene()`, `nextFrame()`, `previousFrame()`, and `previousScene()`. These enable you to control Scenes and Frames created in the Flash CS3 Professional IDE.

Each `MovieClip` has a frame rate that the frames of the animation will pass, expressed in *frames per second*. You can set a `MovieClip` frame rate individually. If you have multiple `MovieClips` in an application, you can set their frame rates individually. Or you can set the frame rate of all `MovieClips` in the application using `stage.framerate`. Be aware if you're putting any code on any frame of a movie clip that the `MovieClip` won't advance until all the code on the first frame has completed.

Using stop() and gotoAndPlay()

Suppose you need to load a movie from an external source and then tell it to play from a certain frame, but stop at frame 30. To do that you'll make use of `gotoAndPlay()` and `stop()`, as well as listening to the `MovieClip`'s `onEnterFrame` event and checking its progress in frames. You'll use the `Loader` class to do this, even though you haven't encountered it yet, but you will soon enough (if you're curious now, skip ahead to Chapter 29).

```
package {
import flash.display.*;
import flash.net.URLRequest;
import flash.events.Event;
public class Movies extends Sprite
{
    public function Movies()
    {
        var loader:Loader = new Loader();
        loader.load(new URLRequest("movie.swf"));
        loader.contentLoaderInfo.addEventListener(Event.COMPLETE, makeMovie);
```

```
    }
    private function makeMovie(event:Event):void
    {
        var mc:MovieClip = (event.target.content as MovieClip);
        mc.gotoAndPlay("intro");
        mc.addEventListener(Event.ENTER_FRAME, stopMovie);
    }
    private function stopMovie(event:Event):void
    {
        try
        {
            if (MovieClip(event.target).currentFrame == 30)
                MovieClip(event.target).stop();
        } catch(err:Error) {
            trace("oops...");
        }
    }
}
}
```

Checking totalFrames and framesLoaded

The `MovieClip` has a `framesLoaded` and `totalFrames` property that are very helpful when loading a SWF file. To check these properties simply compare `framesLoaded` and `totalFrames` on some interval. The following example checks on the `onEnterFrame` event and uses it to draw into a simple `preloader`.

```
private var _mc:MovieClip;

public function LoaderTest()
{
    super();
    this.addEventListener(Event.ENTER_FRAME, drawPreLoader);
}

public function set mc(movieClip:MovieClip):void
{
    _mc = movieClip;
}

private function drawPreLoader(event:Event):void
{

    var framesLoaded:Number = (_mc.framesLoaded/_mc.totalFrames)*100;
    this.graphics.clear();
    this.graphics.beginFill(0x0000FF, 1.0);
    this.graphics.drawRect(0, 0, framesLoaded, 6);
    this.graphics.endFill();
}
```

Examples using the Display List

In ActionScript development, we frequently find ourselves doing the same sorts of things with slight variations over and over. The language designers who put together the APIs and language constructs of ActionScript appreciated this and tried to help us out by making a lot of these tasks easier to do. One of the best ways to learn about a difficult subject like the display list is to look at some common tasks and see how they're done.

Creating an item renderer

One of the most common tasks facing ActionScript developers is to create an item renderer that will create display objects for each item in an `Array`. The following example does just that. You'll need to create an iterating function in order to loop over all the items in the `Array` and within that create new `DisplayObjects`, add properties to them, and then add them to the display list as children of your parent clip. Read through the code below and follow along.

```
package
{
import flash.display.Sprite;
import flash.text.TextField;
public class ItemRenderer extends Sprite
{
    /* this is the array that we're going to use to populate our list. Fill
     * it with strings so that we'll have something easy to use though it
     * could be anything really */
    private var array:Array = ["one", "two", "three", "four", "five"];

    public function ItemRenderer()
    {
        super();
        for(var i:int = 0; i < array.length; i++)
        {
            // make a sprite for each item in the array
            var spr:Sprite = new Sprite();
            // put a graphic in the sprite
            spr.graphics.beginFill(0x880088, 1);
            spr.graphics.drawRect(0, 0, 100, 30);
            spr.graphics.endFill();
            // create a text field
            var txt:TextField = new TextField();
            // put the string from the array into the text field
            txt.text = String(array[i]);
            // add the text field to the new sprite
            spr.addChild(txt);
            // add the sprite to our main sprite
            addChild(spr);
            // move it down a little bit so that we can see
```

```
                              //all the renderers at once
                              spr.y = i * 32;
                      }
                  }
             }
         }
```

The example is greatly simplified by being able to create the `DisplayObjects` through the use of a constructor, calling the constructor, setting the properties of the `DisplayObject`, and then adding them to the display list and manipulating their positions.

Creating a bouncing ball

Here is another classic example: animating a bouncing ball. Again, nothing mind-expanding, but touching on enough important subjects that it isn't completely trivial to demonstrate. You're going to create a few objects and then attach event listeners to their `onEnterFrame` events so that you can change their x and y positions.

```
package
{
import flash.display.Sprite;
import flash.events.Event;
public class BouncingBall extends Sprite
{
    private var ballOne:Sprite;
    private var ballTwo:Sprite;
    //a flag to determine whether we should be going up or down
    private var direction:int = 1;

    public function BouncingBall()
    {
        //create the Sprites and draw a ball in each of them
        ballOne = new Sprite();
        ballOne.graphics.beginFill(0xff0000, 1);
        ballOne.graphics.drawCircle(0, 0, 30);
        ballOne.graphics.endFill();
        ballTwo = new Sprite();
        ballTwo.graphics.beginFill(0x0000ff, 1);
        ballTwo.graphics.drawCircle(0, 0, 30);
        ballTwo.graphics.endFill();
```

```
        //add the balls to the display list
        addChild(ballOne);
        addChild(ballTwo);

        //start the balls at some initial positions
        ballTwo.x = 200;
        ballOne.x = 300;
        ballTwo.y = 5;
        ballOne.y = 5;

        //add the event listeners you'll use to actually move
        //the sprites on the stage
        ballTwo.addEventListener(Event.ENTER_FRAME, bounce);
        ballOne.addEventListener(Event.ENTER_FRAME, bounce);
    }

    private function bounce(event:Event):void
    {
        var target:Sprite = event.target as Sprite;
        try
        {
            //since you're incrementing by 1 each time
            //you know you'll always hit 199
            if (target.y == 199)
            {
                //if the ball is about to go too far
                //change the direction to negative
                direction = -1;
            }

            if (target.y == 1)
            {
                //if the ball is about to go too far
                //change the direction to positive
                direction = 1;
            }

            //add whatever the direction is (either 1 or -1)
            //to the y position of whatever dispatched the event
            if (target.y < 200 && target.y > 0)
            {
                trace(target.y + "  :  " + direction);
                target.y += direction;
            }
```

```
        } catch(err:Error) {
            trace("ooops....");
        }
    }
}
}
```

Checking for collisions

In games, user interfaces, and many other types of applications you frequently want to know whether a certain clip is on top of another clip. The Sprite class provides a convenient hitTest method which we can pass another DisplayObject into to check whether the two are overlapping at any point.

```
package
{
import flash.display.Sprite;
import flash.events.Event;
import flash.geom.Point;

public class CollidingBalls extends Sprite
{
    private var firstBall:Sprite;
    private var secondBall:Sprite;

    private var direction:int;
    private var firstX:int = 3;
    private var firstY:int = 2;
    private var secondX:int = -2;
    private var secondY:int = -3;

    public function CollidingBalls()
    {
        super();

        firstBall = new Sprite();
        secondBall = new Sprite();

        firstBall.graphics.beginFill(0x00FF00, 1.0);
        firstBall.graphics.drawCircle(0, 0, 20);
        firstBall.graphics.endFill();

        secondBall.graphics.beginFill(0x0000FF, 1.0);
        secondBall.graphics.drawCircle(0, 0, 20);
        secondBall.graphics.endFill();
```

```
        addChild(firstBall);
        addChild(secondBall);

        firstBall.x = 10;
        firstBall.y = 10;
        secondBall.x = 190;
        secondBall.y = 190;

        firstBall.addEventListener(Event.ENTER_FRAME, collide);
        secondBall.addEventListener(Event.ENTER_FRAME, collide);

        addEventListener(Event.ENTER_FRAME, moveSprites);
    }

    private function collide(event:Event):void
    {
        if (firstBall.hitTestObject(secondBall))
        {
            trace("first hit second ");
        }
        if (secondBall.hitTestObject(firstBall))
        {
            trace("second hit first ");
        }
    }

    private function moveSprites(evt:Event):void
    {
        if (!inXBounds(firstBall))
        {
            firstX *= -1;
        }
        if (!inYBounds(firstBall))
        {
            firstY *= -1;
        }
        firstBall.x += firstX;
        firstBall.y += firstY;

        if (!inXBounds(secondBall))
        {
            secondX *= -1;
        }
        if (!inYBounds(secondBall))
        {
```

```
            secondY *= -1;
        }

        secondBall.x += secondX;
        secondBall.y += secondY;
    }

    private function inXBounds(spr:Sprite):Boolean
    {
        var glPoint:Point =↵
            localToGlobal(new Point(spr.x, spr.y));
        if (glPoint.x < 200 && glPoint.x > 1)
        {
            return true;
        }
        return false;
    }

    private function inYBounds(spr:Sprite):Boolean
    {
        var glPoint:Point =↵
            localToGlobal(new Point(spr.x, spr.y));
        if (glPoint.y < 200 && glPoint.y > 1)
        {
            return true;
        }
        return false;
    }
}
}
```

Summary

- The display list is one of the more complex topics in ActionScript. At its core, the display list is a list of all `DisplayObject` classes currently on the Stage. When a `DisplayObject` is attached to the Stage, all `DisplayObject` classes that are children within that `DisplayObject` are also on the display list and visible. The x and y position of any object in the display list is relative to its parent.

- The two base classes of the display list, the `DisplayObject` and `DisplayObject-Container`, are both abstract classes that cannot be instantiated. We use the methods and properties of these classes by using classes that extend them, `Sprite`, `Shape`, `MovieClip`

- `Shape` is a lightweight class that contains a `Graphics` object that we can use to do vector drawing. It can be added to any `DisplayObjectContainer` class.

- `Sprite` is a more robust class that posses drag, drop, and interactive methods that can be used to create UI controls. It inherits all the methods of the `InteractiveObject` class and hence dispatches mouse and focus events.

- The `SimpleButton` class is a utility class that allows you to use multiple Sprites to create a Button that has Up, Down, Over, and Hit states.

- The `MovieClip` possesses frames and scenes, as well as a frame rate, and specific methods to control and access frames and scenes.

Chapter 13

Working with DisplayObjects in Flash CS3

Despite AS3's improved display list and drawing capabilities, in most cases, drawing graphics from scratch using code is far too tedious to be practical. Likewise, loading graphics from external files can be complicated and may be too much trouble for smaller applications. In fact, for many situations, you will likely be working with Flash CS3's timeline and drawing tools and Flash and Flex's ability to embed graphic and SWF files into classes for use in code.

While embedding assets allows you to load them at the same time as your SWF and work with them directly, all embedded assets will add to the total file size of your program. In ActionScript 3.0, embedded assets are stored as classes and can be accessed and instantiated in your code. Flash CS3 has improved the way that DisplayObjects are handled in code even on the timeline. The new abilities of the display list allow you to create symbols that use the classes in the `flash.display` package or a custom subclass.

IN THIS CHAPTER

Embedding images and vector graphics with Flash CS3 and Flex

Setting up linkages to automatically generated and custom classes

Accessing embedded graphics from your code

Creating Symbols Within Flash CS3

A symbol is a reusable piece of graphics, sound, animation, or other media stored within your Flash file. In timeline-based Flash, symbols are used to create the visual aspects of your program. Creating symbols in Flash CS3 works very much the same as it did in Flash 8 and earlier versions. The main difference is in the linkage for a symbol. In Flash CS3, all of the symbols linked into your ActionScript are stored in special classes. The linkage window allows you to choose which `flash.display` class you want to use for the base. These classes can be accessed in your code to create new copies of the symbol. Let's take a look at a simple example.

Figure 13-1 shows a drawing of a dog on the stage. In order to use this in ActionScript, you need to first convert it into a symbol. To do that, first select the drawing and then click Modify ➪ Convert to Symbol (or press F8). This opens the Convert to Symbol dialog box, shown in Figure 13-2.

A drawing of a dog in Flash CS3

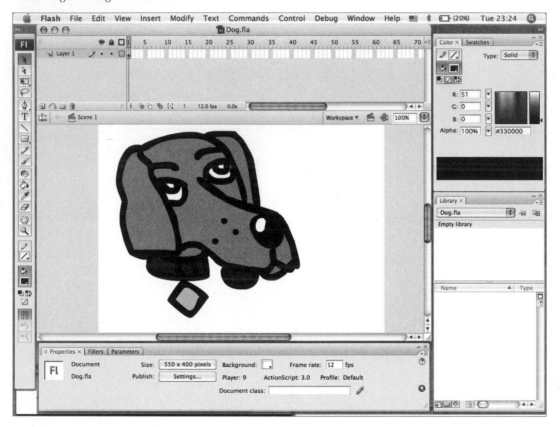

First, click the Advanced button to show the entire menu. For the Name field, you can use any name you want. This example uses "dog." This is the name that will appear in the symbol library. It has no bearing on the ActionScript.

In order to use this symbol in ActionScript, you have to choose Movie clip for the type. You also need to click Export for ActionScript in the Linkage section. This will cause the rest of the Linkage section to activate.

FIGURE 13-2

Converting a drawing into a symbol

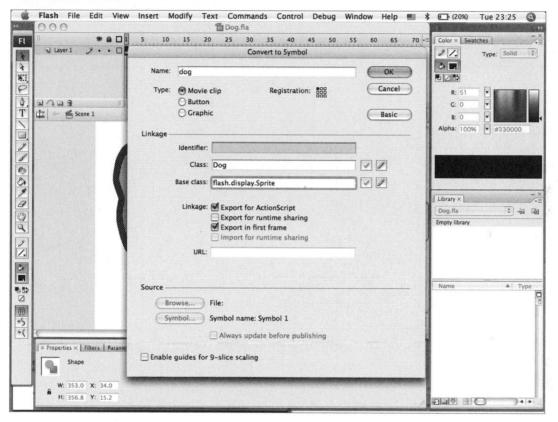

> **NOTE** Although you're making this symbol a Movie clip, you do not have to use `flash .display.MovieClip` as the superclass for this symbol. This is a name left over from previous versions of Flash but in this context it simply means it will be ActionScript-enabled.

Here we see something new for users of Flash 8 — a Class field and a Base Class field both with two buttons next to them. The class field allows you to specify what class name you want to use for this symbol. In this case, use "Dog." The Base Class lets you choose which class you will inherit from. This example uses `flash.display.Sprite`. You can also add a custom class that you've written as long as it is a subclass of `DisplayObject`. If you put an invalid class name here, Flash defaults to `flash.display.MovieClip`. The checkbox buttons verify whether the classes you specified can be found while the pencil buttons open the classes for editing.

Now click OK. Before returning to the stage, a dialog box pops up warning you that the specified class cannot be found. That's okay! If Flash can't find the class you specify (in this case Dog.as), the class will be automatically generated within your SWF file when you export it as demonstrated by Figure 13-3.

It's not necessary that the class be present when setting the linkage.
If Flash can't find your class it will generate one for you.

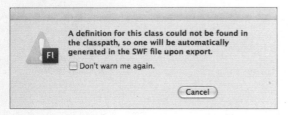

From here you can use the new symbol you created on the stage and drag new ones from the library to the stage.

Setting the variable name of your symbol on the stage

If you're working with elements in the timeline, you'll be able to access each instance of them by providing an instance name. Just select the instance of your symbol on the stage and add a name to the Properties inspector in the <Instance Name> field, as shown in Figure 13-4.

In your ActionScript code, you can access this Sprite by referring to it by its instance name as though it was the name of a variable. For example:

```
rover.rotation = 180; // play dead!
```

Using a custom class for your symbol

If we wanted to add additional functionality to all of the dog symbols, we could create an actual class to use for the symbol instead of the internally generated one. Let's create a new class called Dog.as that will be saved in the same folder as the Dog.fla file. You won't need to update the linkage because it's already set to use Dog as the class.

```
package {
    import flash.display.Sprite;
    import flash.utils.Timer;
    import flash.events.TimerEvent;

    public class Dog extends Sprite {
```

```
        var timer:Timer;
        public function Dog () {
            super();
            timer = new Timer(1000);
            timer.addEventListener(TimerEvent.TIMER, bark);
            timer.start();
        }

        public function bark(event:TimerEvent = null):void {
            trace("Woof!");
        }
    }
}
```

Now when we export the SWF file, we should see a picture of a dog with the word "Woof!" written to the output window every second.

Add a name to the doggie in the Properties inspector.

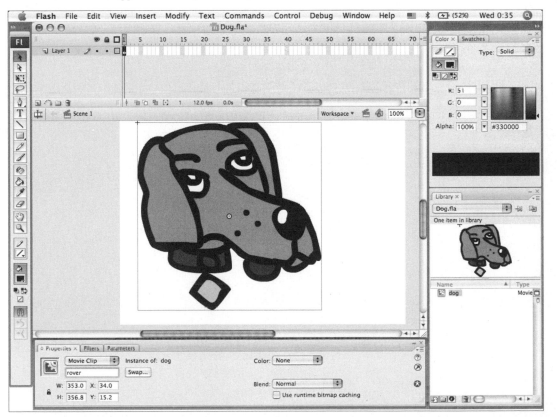

Embedding bitmap graphics assets into your program

Embedding bitmaps works along the same principles as vector graphics. The difference here is that we'll use the File ➪ Import command to load the graphics files, and instead of `MovieClip`, the graphics will be a subclass of `BitmapData`. Another new thing is that in Flash CS3, you can apply linkage to the bitmap symbol directly without making it a `MovieClip` first. Here's how you might import a bitmap.

1. In your Flash file, go to File ➪ Import ➪ Import to Stage (you can also import to library).

2. If you wish to use ActionScript to control your bitmap, you need to export the bitmap for ActionScript. To do this, right-click on the bitmap asset and choose Linkage.

3. Make sure the Export for ActionScript box is checked.

4. Give the bitmap a fully qualified class name. This will be used to identify your bitmap. If no class exists, one will be automatically created internally when you compile your SWF.

5. From this point, the bitmap object will be accessible to the ActionScript code you write in Flash. To use a specific graphic, you use the class name for the asset instead of the `BitmapData` class. For example:

```
var dogBitmap:DogBitmap = new DogBitmap();
addChild(dogBitmap);
```

Using Flex to embed graphics

When using the Flex framework, you can embed your own graphics by using the Embed tag, which requires the location of the graphics source file. The embed tag must be placed near to the definition of the Class variable that holds the embedded image.

```
[Embed(source="dog.jpg")]
public var Dog:Class;
```

Flex embedding supports the following graphics file types:

- GIF
- JPEG
- PNG
- SVG
- SWF

For more information on this topic, please refer to the Flex Developers Guide.

Accessing Embedded Graphic Classes

Whether you use Flash or Flex, to utilize the embedded graphics in your code, simply use the class for the symbol or image to create a new display object. If we were to create a new instance of the Dog class, we might do something like this:

```
var rex:Sprite = new Dog();
addChild(rex);
```

This is the equivalent of dragging the dog onto the stage and placing it at position 0,0.

Summary

- ActionScript 3.0 stores graphics in class objects. Creating new graphics is as easy as instantiating the class.
- Movie clip symbols bind graphics to a class. This can be a customized class or one that's automatically generated when the SWF is compiled.

Chapter 14

Printing

I n this chapter, you learn how to manage the printing of Flash content using the `flash.printing.PrintJob` class. With ActionScript, you can control what portions of your movie are printable, and you can even specify the way those portions print.

Why Print from Flash?

Even though you don't need to print everything, some things are still better printed, such as driving maps (until everyone has mobile devices with GPS units), coupons, and purchase receipts. In this section, you explore some printing features that work with Flash movies.

Most Web browsers simply can't print *any* plug-in content. Some browsers print a gray area where the plug-in content should be, or they leave it empty. Therefore, if you do want to print from the Flash Player plug-in, you should use ActionScript's `PrintJob` class to do the work. You'll learn the specifics of the `PrintJob` class later in this chapter.

It can be difficult to predict how regular HTML Web pages print, even with traditional layouts without plug-in content. Each browser defines page margins differently, and prints unique header and footer information. Have you ever gone to a Web site that offers driving directions, and printed a map that just barely bled off the edge of the printed version? You can avoid frustrating situations such as this by using the print capabilities of Flash Player, which gives you a greater degree of control over the printable area of your movie's content. You can define what area of the stage prints for each frame, if necessary. More important, however, you can control the relationship of the Flash movie's stage size to the printed size.

IN THIS CHAPTER

Controlling print output

Avoiding problems with print functionality

Optimizing artwork for grayscale printers

Printing multiple pages of text

Of course, you also have the normal benefits of using Flash for any type of output, whether it is for the computer screen or the printed page:

- **Embedded fonts:** Although many Web pages use the same Web fonts, such as Verdana or Georgia, you can design Flash movies that use whatever fonts you want your visitors to see. These fonts can be used on printed output from Flash movies as well.

- **Easy and precise layout tools:** You can create Flash artwork and elements very easily, and place the content without using frames, tables, and DHTML layers.

- **Incredibly small file sizes:** Compared to equivalent Acrobat PDF files or HTML pages, Flash movies with graphics and text intended for print can download very quickly. The native vector format of Flash movies makes them ideal for printing anything with logo and branding elements.

Given the preceding points, there is the radical notion that Flash content can be a reasonable substitute for PDF documents. Seem far-fetched? Well, with embedded fonts and precision layout, Flash movies can offer many of the same features that PDF documents do. However, PDF files still offer some advantages. The following list details some of the benefits of PDF files. If Flash movies offer a similar benefit then that is listed as well.

- PDF files are an industry standard for printable documents on the Web. Just about every major company on the Web, from Adobe to Sony, provides downloadable and printable information in the PDF format. However, with FlashPaper technology (www.adobe.com/products/flashpaper) it's possible to deploy SWF-based printable documents. Flash Player is all that is required to view FlashPaper documents, and Flash Player generally takes less time to start than Acrobat Reader.

- PDF files have a more standardized structure than Flash content. For example, PDF files can have a table of contents (Bookmarks) that does not require the content developer to invent his or her own system of indexing. Creating an index of a printable Flash movie involves much more time and planning.

- Some search engines such as Google.com can index (and therefore search) the content of PDF files on the Web. As of this writing, such services for Flash content are not as developed. (Google can index static text within .swf files, but it does not currently have the capacity to index dynamic content.)

- Several Web sites use server-side technology that can convert PDF documents to HTML pages on-the-fly. Because PDF files have a standard structure, these server-side applications to render HTML layouts are very similar to the PDF original. The Adobe Document Server is just one of several applications that create such HTML documents from PDF files. However, it's worth noting that one of the reasons to convert PDF files to HTML is for the benefit of readers without Acrobat Reader or for those that don't want to wait for Acrobat Reader to start. Because Flash-based documents require Flash Player, it's far more likely that a reader will be able to view the document in the Flash format, and Flash Player start time is minimal. Furthermore, the Acrobat Reader application and plug-in are much larger downloads (in excess of 8MB!) than the Flash Player plug-in. So even if a reader doesn't have Flash Player, it's not too difficult to download and install when compared with Acrobat Reader.

- PDF files can be encrypted and password-protected. There's currently no similar option for SWF-based documents.

- The full version of Adobe Acrobat installs the Acrobat PDFWriter or Distiller printer driver, which enables you to print just about any document (for example, Microsoft Word documents) to a PDF file. FlashPaper lets you convert any document to an SWF.

While Flash movies aren't appropriate for every printing scenario, they are often the best option. As noted in some of the preceding points, FlashPaper technology can convert documents to Flash movies. FlashPaper documents have built-in printing capabilities. As such, there's no need to add any additional ActionScript code to enable printing. However, for standard, non-FlashPaper Flash movies you'll have to write some ActionScript code to manage printing. Let's take a look at the ActionScript PrintJob class next.

Controlling Printer Output from Flash

With the `flash.printing.PrintJob` class, you can define how pages are constructed and sent to the printer. This section describes each of the methods and properties of the PrintJob class, collectively known as the `PrintJob` API (application programming interface), and explains how each works. If you want to see the `PrintJob` API in action, continue to the section "Adding Print Functionality to Applications."

Introducing the PrintJob class

On the surface, there isn't too much to the `PrintJob` class. In fact, there are only three methods for the class. To create a new instance of the `PrintJob` class, you use the constructor in a new statement:

```
var printJob:PrintJob = new PrintJob();
```

You do not specify any parameters with the constructor. Once you have a `PrintJob` object, you initiate the three methods of the object, in the following order:

- `start()`: This method opens the Print dialog box on the user's operating system. If the user clicks the Print (or OK) button in the Print dialog box, the method returns a `true` value. If the user cancels the dialog box, the method returns a `false` value. You should use the other two methods only if the `start()` method returns a `true` value.

- `addPage()`: This method tells the `PrintJob` object which sprite to print from your Flash application. You can invoke several `addPage()` methods. Each method call will add one page to the printer's output. This method uses several complex arguments, which are discussed in the following sections.

- `send()`: This method finalizes the output and sends the data to the printer's spooler.

Once you have sent the output to the printer with the `send()` method, it's usually a good idea to delete the `PrintJob` object. Let's take a closer look at the `start()` and `addPage()` methods.

Starting a print request

When you call the start() method, Flash opens a new print dialog box that prompts the user to accept or cancel the print request. It also enables the Flash movie to retrieve the user's print settings — such as the printer to which to send the document, the page size, and page orientation — and lets the user adjust them.

The following properties are set on the PrintJob object if the user clicks OK to a print dialog box initiated from a Flash application. Some of the properties use a unit of measurement called a *point,* abbreviated as *pt*. There are 72 points to one inch.

- paperHeight: This property returns the height (in points) of the paper size that the user has selected. For example, if the user has selected a paper size of 8.5″ × 11″, paperHeight returns a value of 792 points (11″ × 72 pt/inch = 792 pt).

- paperWidth: This property returns the width (in points) of the paper size that the user has selected. If you use the previous example, an 8.5″ × 11″ paper size returns a paperWidth value of 612 points.

- pageHeight: Perhaps the more useful of the height-based properties, the pageHeight property returns the height (in points) of actual printable area. Most printers can print to only a certain portion of the paper size, leaving a margin around the edges of the paper. For example, on an 8.5″ × 11″ piece of paper, most printers can print only an area sized 8.17″ × 10.67". If you are trying to size output to the page, you should use this property over paperHeight.

- pageWidth: As mentioned with the pageHeight property, this property is likely to be more useful to you than the paperWidth property. This property returns the width (in points) of the actual printable area on the paper.

> **NOTE** The data type of all width and height properties is int.

- orientation: This property returns a string value of either portrait or landscape, based on the user's setting in the Print dialog box. The width and height properties will simply flip-flop from one orientation to the next.

The start() method is synchronous. That means that it effectively pauses Flash until the user clicks the OK or Cancel button in the Print dialog box.

> **NOTE** You must have a print driver installed to print from Flash or any other application. If you don't have a printer, you can still install a print driver to print to a file. There are many commercial and even free drivers that print to a file.

Determining the print target and its formatting options

Perhaps the most difficult aspect of Flash printing involves using the `addPage()` method. The `addPage()` method uses the following syntax, where `printJob` represents a `PrintJob` instance:

```
printJob.addPage(target, printArea, printOptions, frame);
```

The parameters are as follows:

- `target`: The `Sprite` that you want to print.

- `printArea`: A `Rectangle` instance whose properties determine the margins of the printable target. This parameter is optional; if it is omitted, the entire area of the target sprite is printed.

> **NOTE** The print area's coordinates are determined from the registration point of the target sprite you are printing.

- `printOptions`: A `flash.printing.PrintJobOptions` instance that determines how the target's contents are sent to the printer. By default, all contents are sent as vector artwork. However, if you specify a `PrintJobOptions` value, you can toggle whether or not the page is printed as a bitmap. The `PrintJobOptions` constructor accepts a Boolean parameter. If the property is set to `true`, the artwork is rendered as a bitmap and then sent to the printer. If the property is set to `false`, the artwork is rendered in vectors and then sent to the printer. See the sections "Printing targets as vectors" and "Printing targets as bitmaps" for more information.

- `frame`: The frame number of the target movie clip (`MovieClip` is a subclass of `Sprite`, so you can specify a `MovieClip` instance as the target) to print. If you want to print a specific frame of the target, you can use this optional parameter. If you omit this parameter, the current frame of the target is printed. Note that any ActionScript code on the specified frame will not be executed. As such, if you have any code that you want to affect the look of your printed target, you should make sure that code is invoked before using the `addPage()` method.

You apply these parameters in later examples of this chapter. In the next sections, you learn more specifics of the `addPage()` parameters and how they affect the printed output from the Flash application.

Printing targets as vectors

The `PrintJobOptions` instance should be constructed with a value of `false` for the print options parameter for the `addPage()` method when you are printing the following vector artwork elements in a sprite, including the main timeline (`root`):

- Text contained within Static, Dynamic, or Input text fields.

- Artwork created with Flash tools, or imported from an illustration application such as Adobe Illustrator.

- Symbol instances *without* any alpha, brightness, tint, or advanced color effects. If you've used the Color menu options in the Property inspector for an instance, you've automatically ruled out printing the content as vector artwork. (This rule also applies to instances that have had color transforms applied using ActionScript code.)

If your Flash content is limited to these considerations, you can safely construct a `PrintJobOptions` object with a value of `false` in order to print high-quality output. If the output is directed to a high-quality printer, all lines and artwork print "clean," with very smooth edges.

CAUTION Any alpha or color settings for symbol instances or artwork are ignored when printing as vectors. Bitmap images also print with more aliasing (that is, rough, pixelated edges) if printed as vector artwork. Printing as vector artwork also fills alpha channels of any bitmap images with solid white.

Printing targets as bitmaps

The `PrintJobOptions` parameter should be constructed with a value of `true` when you are using a variety of sources for your artwork and content. If you have a Flash movie with a mixture of the elements listed in the previous section *and* the following items, you should set the target to print as bitmap content when calling `addPage()`.

- Symbol instances using alpha, brightness, tint, or advanced color effects. If you have used the Property inspector or a Color object in ActionScript to modify the appearance of a symbol instance, you should print as bitmap artwork.

- Artwork or symbol instances containing imported bitmap images. Although bitmap images can be printed as vector artwork, they appear sharper when printed as bitmaps. More important, bitmap images with alpha channels print correctly if the transparent areas of the alpha channel overlap other artwork.

What happens to vector artwork (including text) that is printed as bitmaps? This setting still prints vector artwork, but it won't be as crisp as artwork output with the vector setting. However, you might find the differences between bitmap and vector settings with vector artwork negligible — if you're ever in doubt, test your specific artwork with both settings and compare the output. The bitmap setting is usually the safest bet if you are using bitmap images and any alpha or color effects.

NOTE Colors with alpha settings in the Color Mixer panel used as fills or strokes print perfectly fine with the bitmap setting but not with the vector setting.

Controlling the printable area of the target

Perhaps the most difficult concept to grasp with the `addPage()` method is how the target is sized to the printed page. Using a conversion formula, you can determine how large your target will print on the printer's paper:

1 pixel = 1 point = $\frac{1}{72}$ inch

Therefore, if you have a sprite containing a 400 × 400–pixel square, that artwork will print at roughly 5.5″ × 5.5″ on the printed page. You can keep this formula in mind if you're planning to print on standard page sizes such as 8.5″ × 11″ — as long as your target's size uses the same aspect ratio (roughly 1:1.3), your target can be resized to fill the page.

Potential issues with the Flash-printed output

Watch out for the two following pitfalls with the `addPage()` method parameters, which can cause unpredictable or undesirable output from a printer:

- **Device fonts:** If at all possible, avoid using device fonts with the printed output. Make sure all text is embedded for each text field used for printable content. Text that uses device fonts will print — however, if you have several elements in addition to device font text, the device text may not properly align with other elements on the page.

- **Background colors:** If you are using a dark background color make sure you account for how that will affect the printing. If necessary, you can add a filled rectangle behind your printable content within the targeted sprite instance. For example, if you want to print black text on white, you can temporarily add a white rectangle behind the text within the printable sprite as you send it to the printer.

Be sure to check your applications for these problems before you test your printed output from a Flash application.

Printing Issues with Flash: Color, Grayscale, and PostScript

Although this book focuses on the development side of Flash movies, you want to make sure that your artwork prints reasonably well on a wide range of printers. Not everyone has a high-quality color inkjet or laser printer connected to her or his computer. As such, you want to test your Flash application output to a couple of different printers or ask another associate to test the output on his or her printer. The artwork might not have the same contrast ratios when converted to grayscale.

How can you help correct the problem of not-so-great-looking black-and-white print output from a color original? You can try two things to help alleviate poor grayscale translations of colored artwork: Choose colors that have greater tint variation, or make "hidden" grayscale equivalents of artwork directly in Flash. For the former method, as an example, don't use red and green colors that are close in lightness or brightness values. Rather, choose a darkly tinted red and a lightly tinted green. For the latter method, create a separate Movie Clip symbol of a grayscale version of the artwork. Just duplicate its symbol in the Library, and use the Paint Bucket and Ink Bottle tools to quickly fill with grayscale colors.

continued

Adding Print Functionality to Applications

In the following exercise you add printing functionality to Flash applications:

1. Open a new Flash document, and save it as printing001.fla.
2. Set the document class for the Flash document as `com.wiley.as3bible.printing` `.Printing`.
3. Define a new class file as follows:

```
package com.wiley.as3bible.printing {
    import flash.display.Sprite;
    import flash.text.TextField;
    import flash.text.TextFieldAutoSize;
    import flash.net.URLLoader;
    import flash.net.URLRequest;
    import flash.events.Event;
    import flash.printing.PrintJob;

    public class Printing extends Sprite {

        private var _printableContent:Sprite;
        private var _textField:TextField;
        private var _loader:URLLoader;

        public function Printing() {

            // Load the text from a text file.
            _loader = new URLLoader();
            _loader.load(new URLRequest( ↵
"http://www.rightactionscript.com/samplefiles/lorem_ipsum.txt"));
            _loader.addEventListener(Event.COMPLETE, completeHandler);
            // Create a multiline text field that auto-sizes.
            _textField = new TextField();
```

```
            _textField.width = 400;
            _textField.multiline = true;
            _textField.wordWrap = true;
            _textField.autoSize = TextFieldAutoSize.LEFT;

            // Create a sprite container for the text field,
            // and add the text field to it.
            _printableContent = new Sprite();
            addChild(_printableContent);
            _printableContent.addChild(_textField);

        }

        // When the text loads add it to the text field and
        // then print the text.
        private function completeHandler(event:Event):void {

            _textField.text = _loader.data;

            var printJob:PrintJob = new PrintJob();
            if(printJob.start()) {
                printJob.addPage(_printableContent);
                printJob.send();
            }
        }
    }
}
```

4. Test the application.

When you click OK in the Print dialog box, one page prints. That one page will be the first page of text. The following example shows a way to print the entire text.

1. Open printing001.fla, and save it as printing002.fla.

2. Edit the class as follows. The changes are bolded.

```
package com.wiley.as3bible.printing {

    import flash.display.Sprite;
    import flash.text.TextField;
    import flash.text.TextFieldAutoSize;
    import flash.net.URLLoader;
    import flash.net.URLRequest;
    import flash.events.Event;
    import flash.printing.PrintJob;

    public class Printing extends Sprite {

        private var _printableContent:Sprite;
        private var _textField:TextField;
```

```
        private var _loader:URLLoader;

    public function Printing() {

        _loader = new URLLoader();
        _loader.load(new URLRequest("http://www.rightactionscript.com/ ↵
samplefiles/lorem_ipsum.txt"));
        _loader.addEventListener(Event.COMPLETE, completeHandler);

        _textField = new TextField();
        _textField.width = 400;
        _textField.multiline = true;
        _textField.wordWrap = true;
        _textField.autoSize = TextFieldAutoSize.LEFT;

        _printableContent = new Sprite();
        addChild(_printableContent);
        _printableContent.addChild(_textField);
    }

    private function completeHandler(event:Event):void {

        _textField.text = _loader.data;

        var printJob:PrintJob = new PrintJob();
        if(printJob.start()) {

            // Scale the text field to fit the page.
            _textField.scaleY = printJob.pageHeight / _textField.height;
            _textField.scaleX = _textField.scaleY;
            printJob.addPage(_printableContent);
            printJob.send();

            // Scale the text field back to the original
            // size once printed.
            _textField.scaleY = 1;
            _textField.scaleX = 1;
        }
    }
}
}
```

Note that when you print from the movie this time, it prints the entire text on one page. The text is scaled down, but while it fits on one page, it's not legible. In the next example, rather than scale the text, we set the width of the text so it will print at the same width of the page.

1. Open printing002.fla, and save it as printing003.fla.

2. Edit the code on frame 1. The changes are bolded.

```
package com.wiley.as3bible.printing {
    import flash.display.Sprite;
    import flash.text.TextField;
    import flash.text.TextFieldAutoSize;
    import flash.net.URLLoader;
    import flash.net.URLRequest;
    import flash.events.Event;
    import flash.printing.PrintJob;
    public class Printing extends Sprite {
        private var _printableContent:Sprite;
        private var _textField:TextField;
        private var _loader:URLLoader;

        public function Printing() {

            _loader = new URLLoader();
            _loader.load(new URLRequest( ↵
"http://www.rightactionscript.com/samplefiles/lorem_ipsum.txt"));
            _loader.addEventListener(Event.COMPLETE, completeHandler);

            _textField = new TextField();
            _textField.width = 400;
            _textField.multiline = true;
            _textField.wordWrap = true;
            _textField.autoSize = TextFieldAutoSize.LEFT;

            _printableContent = new Sprite();
            addChild(_printableContent);
            _printableContent.addChild(_textField);

        }

        private function completeHandler(event:Event):void {

            _textField.text = _loader.data;

            var printJob:PrintJob = new PrintJob();
            if(printJob.start()) {

                // Adjust the width of the text field to
                // match the page.
                _textField.width = printJob.pageWidth;
                printJob.addPage(_printableContent);
                printJob.send();

                // Reset the text field width once printed.
                _textField.width = 400;
            }
        }
    }
}
```

This time the text prints legibly so it fits to the width of the page. However, it still prints only one page. Next, we look at how to print the text over many pages:

1. Open printing003.fla, and save it as printing004.fla.

2. Edit the class, as shown in the following code. The changes are bolded.

```
package com.wiley.as3bible.printing {

    import flash.display.Sprite;
    import flash.text.TextField;
    import flash.text.TextFieldAutoSize;
    import flash.net.URLLoader;
    import flash.net.URLRequest;
    import flash.events.Event;
    import flash.printing.PrintJob;
    import flash.geom.Rectangle;
    public class Printing extends Sprite {

        private var _printableContent:Sprite;
        private var _textField:TextField;
        private var _loader:URLLoader;

        public function Printing() {

            _loader = new URLLoader();
            _loader.load(new URLRequest( ↵
"http://www.rightactionscript.com/samplefiles/lorem_ipsum.txt"));
            _loader.addEventListener(Event.COMPLETE, completeHandler);

            _textField = new TextField();
            _textField.width = 400;
            _textField.multiline = true;
            _textField.wordWrap = true;
            _textField.autoSize = TextFieldAutoSize.LEFT;

            _printableContent = new Sprite();
            addChild(_printableContent);
            _printableContent.addChild(_textField);

        }

        private function completeHandler(event:Event):void {

            _textField.text = _loader.data;
            var printJob:PrintJob = new PrintJob();
            if(printJob.start()) {

                // Determine the number of pages.
                var pages:Number = Math.ceil(_textField.height / ↵
printJob.pageHeight);
```

```
            _textField.width = printJob.pageWidth;

            // Loop through each page.
            for(var i:Number = 0; i < pages; i++) {
                    printJob.addPage(_printableContent, new Rectangle(0, i * ↵
printJob.pageHeight, printJob.pageWidth, printJob.pageHeight));
            }
            printJob.send();
            _textField.width = 400;
        }
    }
  }
}
```

When you test printing this time, the Flash application will print as many pages as necessary to print the entire text. Although it's a marked improvement over the first few stages, there is still one major text-printing issue. You'll notice that the page breaks can occur in the middle of a line of text such that the top of a line of text can appear on one page, and the bottom of that line of text appears on the next page.

Summary

- You can print many useful items from Flash movies, such as purchase receipts, artwork, and product catalogs or datasheets.
- The `PrintJob` class has all of the methods and properties necessary to print Flash content.
- The `addPage()` method of the `PrintJob` class enables you to control which sprite is printed and how it should be printed.
- Avoid the use of device fonts or dark background colors for Flash content that you intend to print.

Chapter 15

Working with Text and Fonts

ext is an indispensable aspect of any web application and the TextField is the base object for dealing with text anywhere in Flash Player 9. It handles both text fields that a user can put text into, like a form, or it can display text simply by setting its type to either `input` or `dynamic`. We discuss these types later on, but for right now, just understand that a TextField is still a TextField if it's taking user input or just displaying some text.

To display our `TextField` objects, we'll add and remove them from the stage or parent object like any other `DisplayObject`. Because `TextField` extends `flash.display.InteractiveObject`, it has methods to deal with mouse interaction, many interactive events it can throw, as well as many of the methods we are familiar with from Chapter 13. Sizing, scaling, moving, and reparenting a TextField is all handled in the same way as any other `DisplayObject`, which shortens the learning curve.

Unique to the `TextField` are methods and properties to control the appearance of text within it with `TextFormat` objects or CSS styles or with a subset of HTML. Using the `TextFormat` class, we can set properties for the entire `TextField` or just for certain groups of characters within the `TextField`. We put this to good use for handling user selections of characters. We'll also look at how to embed system fonts and how to control the way that those fonts appear in the `TextField` with some advanced scaling methods.

Introducing TextFields

The TextField is used everywhere you need text displayed. In this chapter, we look at creating TextField objects and applying formatting to them both with a StyleSheet object and TextFormat objects and investigate some of the problems and tricks to working with text formatting in ActionScript 3.0.

Creating a new TextField

Like all objects that extend DisplayObject, in order to create a TextField we give it a variable name and then call its constructor. When we're ready to add the TextField to the Display List we use addChild() to add it to any class that extends DisplayObjectContainer. The default for the TextField is to be a dynamic text field. Later in the chapter, we look at how to work with input TextFields.

```
var txt:TextField = new TextField();
addChild(txt);
```

The preceding code snippet assumes that the TextField is being created within an object that DisplayObjectContainer and therefore has a definition for addChild().

Adding new text to a TextField

Once we have some text in the TextField, we can either append the String object that is the text of the TextField() or we can use the appendText() method of the TextField class, as follows.

```
var txt:TextField = new TextField();
txt.text = "Hello World.";
addChild(txt);
txt.text += "Hello again. ";
txt.appendText("Last hello, I promise. ");
```

The appendText() method generally runs faster than += and so is preferred.

Setting a TextField's size

The TextField has an autoSize property that by default is set to true. This means that the TextField sizes to the amount of text within it. However, when we set either the height or width or both, the TextField will display text only within those boundaries. This can work to your advantage if we're making multiline TextField objects, which we look at later, but for right now, let's say that we need to be careful when setting the width and height. Here we will manually set the width of the TextField.

```
var txt:TextField = new TextField();
txt.width = 100; // not all the text below will appear
```

```
txt.text = "Gaius Marius (157 BCE-January 13, 86 BCE) was a Roman general ↵
and politician";
txt.width = 800; // now it will all show up
addChild(txt);
```

We have another option that we can use to control sizing: `autoSize`. The `autoSize` property of the `TextField` allows you to set which direction you wish to align the text within the `TextField` and tells the `TextField` to resize accordingly. The acceptable parameters for `autoSize` are `right`, `left`, and `center`. Using `autoSize = "left"` means that the text is treated as left-justified text, and the left margin of the text field stays in place while the right margin in resized to fit all of the text. Using `autoSize = "right"` means that the text is treated as right-justified text, while the left margin is resized to fit all of the text. Using `center` means that the text is treated as center-justified text, and resizing is equal for both the right and left margins. If the text includes a line break (for example, `\n` or `\r`), the bottom is also resized to fit the next line of text.

```
var txt:TextField = new TextField();
txt.autoSize = "left";
addChild(txt);
txt.text = "Hi";
//we'll automatically be about 15 pixels wide
txt.text = "Gaius Marius (157 BCE - January 13, 86 BCE) was a ↵
Roman general and politician";
//we'll automatically be about 400 pixels wide
```

Now our `TextField` automatically resizes itself to fit whatever text is placed into it, which is great if you're not working within fixed boundaries like on a form, but not so great if you are. Using a mixture of `autoSize` and fixed-width `TextFields` will let you do whatever you need to do.

Setting a TextField's scaling and rotation

When we set both the `scaleX` and `scaleY` of a `TextField` we change the width and height values of the `TextField` itself, but not that of the text inside of it. That is to say, changing your `TextField` won't change (scale) your font:

```
var txt:TextField = new TextField();
txt.scaleX = 2;
txt.autoSize = "left";
addChild(txt);
txt.text = "Gaius Marius (157 BCE-January 13, 86 BCE) was a ↵
Roman general and politician";
```

To set the `TextField` rotation property, which it inherits from the `DisplayObject`, simply set the rotation property to a `Number`, which represents the degrees you wish the `TextField` to be turned. Keep in mind, however, that unless you use an embedded font, the `TextField` will disappear because the Flash Player can't display device fonts (non-embedded fonts) when they're rotated.

Retrieving strings from a TextField

The text property of the TextField also allows you to get the text that is currently displayed in the TextField. This works for both input TextField objects and dynamic TextField objects. There are three additional methods that you can use to retrieve text from a text field in more specific ways than simply getting all the text within the TextField. These methods are listed here, with a brief description of each:

- getCharIndexAtPoint(x:Number, y:Number):int — Returns the zero-based index value of the character at the point specified by the x and y parameters.

- getFirstCharInParagraph(charIndex:int):int — Given a character index, returns the index of the first character in the same paragraph.

- replaceText(beginIndex:int, endIndex:int, newText:String):void — Replaces the range of characters that the beginIndex and endIndex parameters specified with the your newText parameter. This method will not work if a style sheet is applied to the text field.

Let's look at using the getCharIndexAtPoint() method:

```
package {

import flash.text.TextField;
import flash.events.MouseEvent;
import flash.display.Sprite;

public class WidthHeightTest extends Sprite
{
    private var txt:TextField;
    public function WidthHeightTest()
    {
        txt = new TextField();
        txt.autoSize = "left";
        addChild(txt);
        txt.text = "Gustav Mahler (July 7, 1860 - May 18, 1911) ↵
was a Bohemian-Austrian composer and conductor.";
        txt.addEventListener(MouseEvent.MOUSE_MOVE, ↵
getTextUnderMouse);
    }

    private function getTextUnderMouse(mouseEvent:MouseEvent):void
    {
        var charInt:int = ↵
txt.getCharIndexAtPoint(mouseEvent.stageX, mouseEvent.stageY);
        trace(txt.text.charAt(charInt));
    }
}
}
```

Displaying HTML

Flash supports a limited subset of HTML that can be displayed in the TextField. The following is a quick list of all the tags and what they do in Flash:

- The <a> tag creates a hypertext link.

- The <b> tag renders text as bold. A bold typeface must be available for the font used.

- The <br> tag creates a line break in the text field. You must set the text field to be a multiline text field to use this tag.

- The <font> tag specifies a font or list of fonts to display the text.

- The <img> tag lets you embed external image files (JPEG, GIF, PNG), SWF files, and movie clips inside text fields. Text automatically flows around images you embed in text fields. To use this tag, you must set the text field to be multiline and to wrap text.

- The <i> tag displays the tagged text in italics. An italic typeface must be available for the font used.

- The <li> tag places a bullet in front of the text that it encloses. Note: Because Flash Player does not recognize ordered and unordered list tags (<ol> and <ul>) they do not modify how your list is rendered. All lists are unordered and all list items use bullets.

- The <p> tag creates a new paragraph. You must set the text field to be a multiline text field to use this tag.

- The <span> tag, which performs the same function as it does on an HTML page, is available only for use with CSS text styles. You can use the span to specify a class for a section of htmlText.

- The <textformat> tag lets you use some of the paragraph formatting properties of the TextFormat class within text fields. We cover this in greater detail later in the chapter.

- The underline tag, <u>, underlines the tagged text.

- To add HTML to a TextField, we use the htmlText property of the TextField:

```
private function addText():void
{
   var txt:TextField = new TextField();
   txt.height = 300;
   txt.width = 300;
   txt.multiline = true;

   txt.htmlText = "<p>List of books I've started and not finished ↵
and why. <br> <li>Finnegans Wake - incoherent</li><li>Atlas ↵
Shrugged - boring</li><li>Programming Perl - don't like ↵
Perl</li><li>Remembrance of Things Past - too long</li></p>";
   addChild(txt);
}
```

This renders an `htmlText` field that contains an unordered list with bullets next to each item. Notice that we aren't using a `<ul>` or `<ol>` tag to delimit our list because the `TextField` can't create an ordered list, so there isn't much point in specifying which kind of list we want. When you want to use characters such as <, &, >, ", and ' in your `htmlText` you need to use HTML entities in order to have them displayed properly, for example to display a <br /> tag, we'd need to do the following:

```
txt.htmlText = "&lt;br /&gt; is a break tag";
```

Adding images or SWF files to a TextField with <img>

The `img` tag that you may know from HTML can be used to embed images or SWF files in Flash Player 9. This lets you use HTML with images in it just the same as you would in any HTML page, including SWF files. If you're going to embed SWF files, there are a few additional properties you can use. Let's look at an example and walk through some of the new properties for the `img` tag.

- `src`: Specifies the URL to an image or SWF file, or the linkage identifier for a movie clip symbol in the library. This attribute is required; all other attributes are optional. External files (JPEG, GIF, PNG, and SWF files) do not show until they are downloaded completely.

- `width`: The width of the image, SWF file, or movie clip being inserted, in pixels.

- `height`: The height of the image, SWF file, or movie clip being inserted, in pixels.

- `align`: Specifies the horizontal alignment of the embedded image within the text field. Valid values are `left` and `right`. The default value is `left`.

- `hspace`: Specifies the amount of horizontal space that surrounds the image where no text appears. By default this is 8 pixels.

- `vspace`: Specifies the amount of vertical space that surrounds the image where no text appears. By default this is 8 pixels.

- `id`: Specifies the name for the movie clip instance (created by Flash Player) that contains the embedded image file, SWF file, or movie clip. This is useful if you want to control the embedded content with ActionScript.

- `checkPolicyFile`: Specifies that Flash Player will check for a cross-domain policy file on the server associated with the image's domain.

```
var txt:TextField = new TextField();
txt.wordWrap = true;
txt.multiline = true;
txt.width = 200;
txt.height = 200;
txt.htmlText = '<img src="assets/text.png" width="100" ↵
height="100" /> And now we\'ll add some text around our image ↵
and we\'ve got an exciting TextField';
addChild(txt);
```

Now that we have an `img` object embedded through our `htmlText`, let's go ahead and embed a SWF file.

```
txt.htmlText = '<img src="assets/TextMovie.swf" id="textMovie" ↵
width="100" height="100" /> And now we\'ll add some text around ↵
our image and we\'ve got an exciting TextField';
addChild(txt);
```

Using the StyleSheet with a TextField

You can use CSS styles to set properties of the `htmlText` of a `TextField`, in much the same way that you're accustomed to using CSS with standard HTML. You can write styles and define classes that can be applied to objects in your TextField. To do this, you use an instance of the `StyleSheet` class, which we instantiate and define properties for. Once you've done this, you simply set the `stylesheet` property of the `TextField` to add the styles to the `TextField`. To access those style classes you simply use the style class within the `htmlText` you assign to the `TextField`.

```
var txt:TextField = new TextField();
txt.multiline = true;
txt.wordWrap = true;
var cssString:String = ".redStyle{color:#FF0000; font- ↵
family:Arial;}.blueStyle{color:#0000FF; font-family:Courier;}";
var styles:StyleSheet = new StyleSheet();
styles.parseCSS(cssString);
txt.styleSheet = styles;
txt.htmlText = '<span class="redStyle">This will show up ↵
red</span> And this will not. <span class="blueStyle">This will ↵
show up blue</span>';
addChild(txt);
```

You can also load the `StyleSheet` string at runtime from an external file, parse it into a `StyleSheet` object, and then apply it to a `TextField`. The great advantage of this is that it allows you to change the appearance of a single or multiple TextFields without recompiling the SWF file. Later, we look at another way to format text using the `TextFormat` object.

Creating backgrounds for a TextField

`TextField` objects have Shape objects in their background that can be set using the `backgroundColor` and `hasBackground` properties. By default, the background of the `TextField` has an alpha of 0. In order to change that, you need to set two properties, the background Boolean property that, if true, means the `TextField` has a background, and then the `backgroundColor`. This should be a hexadecimal value in the format of 0xFFFFFF:

```
var txt:TextField = new TextField();
txt.backgroundColor = 0x0000FF;
txt.background = true;
```

You can also create a border for the TextField by simply setting border and then setting a borderColor. If you don't specify a border color in hexadecimal format, then it appears black. Here we'll set the border of the TextField to a dark blue.

```
txt.borderColor = 0x000099;
txt.border = true;
```

Using TextFormat

The TextFormat object is another way to give text in your TextField a specific look that is slightly different than the StyleSheet object. While you can specify specific ranges of characters for the TextFormat to control, if you're using HTML, you may find it easier to use the StyleSheet object. If you're formatting arbitrary ranges of text—for example, a line, or the first 100 characters—then the TextFormat object makes much more sense to use. TextFormat is an object with properties that you set to describe a group of characteristics that you want to apply to a TextField or to specific characters.

Creating and applying a TextFormat to a TextField

To use a TextFormat object, you need to create a new TextFormat object and then add all of the properties that we would like to use to that object. To apply the TextFormat object to the TextField, you use either setDefaultFormat to apply the styles to any text added to the TextField, or setTextFormat to apply the format to text currently in the TextField.

```
var textFormat:TextFormat = new TextFormat();
textFormat.font = "Arial";
textFormat.color = 0x4444FF;
textFormat.size = 18;
var nameField:TextField = new TextField();
nameField.text = "Josh Noble";
nameField.setTextFormat(textFormat);
addChild(nameField);
```

You can also apply the TextFormat to specific characters in the TextField, using setTextFormat and passing in integers to mark the first character that you want to receive the formatting and the last. If you don't specify a last, then the format is applied to all the rest of the characters:

```
nameField.setTextFormat(textFormat, 5, 10);
```

You also can set a default TextFormat that you want to use and then override it in specific places:

```
var blueFormat:TextFormat = new TextFormat();
blueFormat.font = "Arial";
blueFormat.color = 0x4444FF;
```

```
blueFormat.size = 18;
var redFormat:TextFormat = new TextFormat();
redFormat.font = "Courier";
redFormat.color = 0xFF0000;
redFormat.size = 14;
var nameField:TextField = new TextField();
nameField.text = "Josh Noble";
nameField.defaultTextFormat = blueFormat;
nameField.setTextFormat(redFormat, 0, 5);
addChild(nameField);
```

The `TextFormat` object is a very convenient and powerful way to control the appearance and layout of text that is not `htmlText`. By assigning `TextFormat` objects to specific parts of a `TextField` based on user interaction, you have very precise control over the appearance of your text.

The `TextFormat` class has 16 properties that you can use to apply various formatting to `TextField` object content. The following sections detail each of these properties.

align

You can use the `align` property to place the text relative to the right and left edges of the `TextField` object's bounding box. The property can have the following values:

- `left`: This value places the text such that the left side of the text is against the left side of the bounding box.

- `right`: This value places the text such that the right side of the text is against the right side of the bounding box.

- `center`: This value places the text such that the center of the text is aligned with the center of the bounding box.

- `justify`: You can use a value of `justify` so that the text fits the width of each line, adjusting spacing per line as necessary.

- `null`: The `null` value is the default value and it resolves to the same thing as a value of `left`.

The following code creates text aligned to the center:

```
var tContent:TextField = new TextField();
tContent.multiline = true;
tContent.border = true;
tContent.wordWrap = true;
tContent.text = "center-aligned text";
var tfFormatter:TextFormat = new TextFormat();
tfFormatter.align = "center";
tContent.setTextFormat(tfFormatter);
```

blockIndent

The blockIndent property has an effect on text only when the text is aligned left. In that case, the blockIndent property indents the entire block of text inward relative to the left margin. The value should be a number indicating the points value by which you want to indent the text.

The following code creates text that is indented as a block:

```
var tContent:TextField = new TextField();
tContent.multiline = true;
tContent.border = true;
tContent.wordWrap = true;
tContent.text = "a few lines\nof text\nthat are indented\nas a block";
var tfFormatter:TextFormat = new TextFormat();
tfFormatter.blockIndent = 10;
tContent.setTextFormat(tfFormatter);

addChild(tContent);
```

bold

The bold property applies faux bold formatting to the targeted text. To turn bold formatting on, use a Boolean value of true. To turn bold off, use a Boolean value of false. By default, this property is defined with a null value, which produces the same effect as false.

bullet

The bullet property adds a bullet character (•) in front of the text if the property's value is set to true. You can turn off bullet formatting by assigning a false value to the property. By default, this property has a value of null. The font face used for the bullet character is the same as that defined for other text in the TextFormat object (via the font property, discussed later). The bullet points are placed 19 pixels from the left margin of the field, affected only by the left margin settings. (Properties such as blockIndent don't have an effect when bullet points are used.) The bulleted text is spaced 15 pixels to the right of the bullet point.

The following code displays a list of bulleted text:

```
var tContent:TextField = new TextField();
tContent.multiline = true;
tContent.border = true;
tContent.wordWrap = true;
tContent.text = "a\nb\nc\nd";
var tfFormatter:TextFormat = new TextFormat();
tfFormatter.bullet = true;
tContent.setTextFormat(tfFormatter);
addChild(tContent);
```

color

This property controls the font color of the targeted text. The value for this property should be numeric. The following code displays red text:

```
var tContent:TextField = new TextField();
tContent.multiline = true;
tContent.border = true;
tContent.wordWrap = true;
tContent.text = "red text";
var tfFormatter:TextFormat = new TextFormat();
tfFormatter.color = 0xFF0000;
tContent.setTextFormat(tfFormatter);
addChild(tContent);
```

font

The font property controls the font face used for the text. This property uses a string value, indicating the name of the font. The name that you use can depend on how you are working with the font in Flash. By default, the font property has a value of null, which results in the default font being used. The font face can be applied only if the user has the font installed on his/her system, or if the font has been embedded or shared with the Flash movie.

The following code displays the text formatted with the Verdana font face:

```
var tContent:TextField = new TextField();
tContent.multiline = true;
tContent.border = true;
tContent.wordWrap = true;
tContent.text = "Verdana text";
var tfFormatter:TextFormat = new TextFormat();
tfFormatter.font = "Verdana";
tContent.setTextFormat(tfFormatter);
addChild(tContent);
```

You might want to use the TextField.getFontList() method in conjunction with the font property of a TextFormat object. The TextField.getFontList() method is a static method that returns an array of the fonts available on the client computer.

Indent

The indent property controls the spacing applied from the left margin to the first line of text within a paragraph. A *paragraph* is defined as any text that precedes a carriage return (such as \r). This property uses pixel units. The default value is null. The following code indents the text by 10 pixels:

```
var tContent:TextField = new TextField();
tContent.multiline = true;
tContent.border = true;
tContent.wordWrap = true;
tContent.text = "When you have several lines of text, ";
```

```
tContent.text += "and you have set the indent value to a positive ";
tContent.text += "integer, the first line will appear indented."
var tfFormatter:TextFormat = new TextFormat();
tfFormatter.indent = 10;
tContent.setTextFormat(tfFormatter);
addChild(tContent);
```

italic

The `italic` property controls whether the targeted text uses faux italic formatting. If the property is set to `true`, the text appears in italic. If the property is set to `false`, the text appears normal. By default, this property has a value of `null`, which achieves the same effect as a value of `false`.

Leading

The `leading` property controls the spacing inserted between each line of text. The values for this property are pixel-based. By default, the value of this property is `null`. You cannot programmatically set the leading value to be a negative number.

The following code inserts 10 pixels of space between each line of text:

```
var tContent:TextField = new TextField();
tContent.multiline = true;
tContent.border = true;
tContent.wordWrap = true;
tContent.text = "When you have several lines of text, ";
tContent.text += "and you have set the leading value to a positive ";
tContent.text += "integer, the spacing between the lines changes."
var tfFormatter:TextFormat = new TextFormat();
tfFormatter.leading = 10;
tContent.setTextFormat(tfFormatter);
addChild(tContent);
```

leftMargin

The `leftMargin` property determines the spacing (in pixels) inserted between the text and the left border of the `TextField` object. By default, the value of this property is `null`, which achieves the same effect as a value of 0. The following code creates a left margin of 10 pixels.

```
var tContent:TextField = new TextField();
tContent.multiline = true;
tContent.border = true;
tContent.wordWrap = true;
tContent.text = "Left margin";
var tfFormatter:TextFormat = new TextFormat();
tfFormatter.leftMargin = 10;
tContent.setTextFormat(tfFormatter);
addChild(tContent);
```

The `blockIndent` and `leftMargin` properties affect the text offset on the left side in a cumulative manner.

rightMargin

The `rightMargin` property controls the spacing (in pixels) inserted between the text and the right border of the `TextField` object. By default, the value of this property is `null`.

The following code illustrates the effect of the `rightMargin` property:

```
var tContent:TextField = new TextField();
tContent.multiline = true;
tContent.border = true;
tContent.wordWrap = true;
tContent.text = "Right margin text that wraps to the next line";
var tfFormatter:TextFormat = new TextFormat();
tfFormatter.rightMargin = 10;
tContent.setTextFormat(tfFormatter);
addChild(tContent);
```

size

The `size` property determines the size (in points) of the text. Remember that when a value is given in points, it will display differently depending on the font face used. Therefore, the actual pixel size for two font faces can differ even if the point size is the same.

The following code creates text that displays with a point size of 20:

```
var tContent:TextField = new TextField();
tContent.multiline = true;
tContent.border = true;
tContent.wordWrap = true;
tContent.text = "Some text";
var tfFormatter:TextFormat = new TextFormat();
tfFormatter.size = 20;
tContent.setTextFormat(tfFormatter);
addChild(tContent);
```

tabStops

The `tabStops` property defines a custom array specifying the values used by tabs within the text. The first element of the array specifies the spacing (in points) to use for the first tab character in succession. The second element specifies the spacing to use for the second tab character in succession, and so on. The value of the last element in the array is used for all subsequent tab characters. The default value for `tabStops` is `null`. When the property has a value of `null`, the default value of four points is used between each successive tab character. However, using the `tabStops` property you can specify how ordered tabs are spaced within text.

For example, you can create a `TextFormat` object that uses a tab spacing of 10 pixels for the first tab, a tab spacing of 50 pixels for the second tab (in succession), and a tab spacing of 150 pixels for the third tab. The following code does just that:

```
var tContent:TextField = new TextField();
tContent.multiline = true;
tContent.border = true;
tContent.wordWrap = true;
tContent.text = "\ta\n";
tContent.text += "\t\tb\n";
tContent.text += "\t\t\tc";
var tfFormatter:TextFormat = new TextFormat();
tfFormatter.tabStops = [10, 50, 150];
tfFormatter.align = "left";
tContent.setTextFormat(tfFormatter);
```

target

The `target` property works in conjunction with the `url` property (discussed later in this section). You can specify a string value for the `target` property that indicates the name of the browser window (or frame) where the URL specified in the `url` property should appear. You can use the predefined target values of `"_blank"` (new empty browser window), `"_self"` (the current frame or window), `"_parent"` (the parent frame or window), or `"_top"` (the outermost frame or window), or you can use a custom browser window or frame name (as assigned in the HTML document or JavaScript). If you use the `url` property without specifying a value for the `target` property, the URL loads into the current frame or window (`"_self"`).

underline

The `underline` property can add an underline to text. When this property is set to `true`, an underline appears with the text. When it is set to `false`, any underlines are removed. By default, the value of this property is `null`, which has the same effect as a value of `false`.

url

The `url` property allows you to add a hyperlink to text. The Flash Player does not provide any immediate indication that the `url` property is in use for a given range of text — you may want to change the color and add an underline to the affected text to make the link more apparent to the user. However, the mouse pointer automatically changes to the hand icon when the mouse rolls over the linked text.

In order to use the `url` property, you must make sure the `html` property is set to `true` for the `TextField`. Otherwise, the hyperlink is not applied properly.

The following code applies a hyperlink to a portion of the text:

```
var tContent:TextField = new TextField();
tContent.multiline = true;
```

```
tContent.border = true;
tContent.wordWrap = true;
tContent.text = "Visit the Web site";
tContent.html = true;
var tfFormatter:TextFormat = new TextFormat();
tfFormatter.url = "http://thefactoryfactoryfactory.com/wordpress";
tfFormatter.target = "_blank";
tfFormatter.underline = true;
tContent.setTextFormat(10, 18, tfFormatter);
addChild(tContent);
```

More Advanced Control Over Text

In addition to what you can do with the TextFormat and StyleSheet objects, you can control
how the text within your TextField appears to a very fine degree if you're using embedded fonts.
Now keep in mind that embedding fonts adds a lot of bulk to your generated SWF file so it's something you need to consider carefully, but if you want the control over the pixellation of your fonts,
it's there for you to use.

Embedding fonts and using AntiAlias

If you want to use an embedded font, you'll need to use the metadata property and pass in the
location of a TTF file. The extension .ttf marks a TrueType font file and is compatible with Mac
and PC. By pointing to one of these files, you're able to embed all the information about that font
into the SWF file itself. Fonts that aren't normally available in the Flash Player are suddenly available to you. The caveat to this is that you expand the size of your compiled or published SWF file
by quite a bit. The amount isn't totally consistent but it's usually a few dozen extra kilobytes and it's
something to keep in mind if you're going to embed multiple fonts in a movie. To embed a font
using Flex Builder, use the following code:

```
[Embed (source="C:\Windows\Fonts\AwesomeFont.ttf",
fontName="AwesomeFont", mimeType="application/x-font-truetype")]
```

Once you've done this, you've embedded the font into the SWF movie, which means that you can
now set the TextField's embedFonts to true:

```
textField.embedFonts = true;
```

Now you can set the TextField object's font property to the fontName that you specified in
the embed statement. Just like that you've brought in fonts from your computer to embed into a
Flash application. Once you've embedded fonts, there are additional things you can do with the
TextField, including rotating it and setting the anti-alias type. Anti-aliasing a font means that you
try to determine, for each pixel in your character, how much of that pixel is occupied by the font,
and the Flash Player draws that pixel with a little bit less opacity. The characters of your font will
seem less pixellated and slightly smoother. Figures 15-1 and 15-2 show the difference in the text's
appearance with and without anti-aliasing.

FIGURE 15-1

Without anti-aliasing

sample

FIGURE 15-2

With anti-aliasing

sample

sample

The TextField's anti-aliasing comes in two varieties, normal and advanced. The essential difference is that advanced anti-aliasing is better for smaller font sizes, whereas normal is recommended for larger font sizes. Let's look at a simple example of embedding a font into an application and using that embedded font and applying anti-aliasing to that TextField. The Embed metadata tag is used with Flex Builder only:

```
package
{
import flash.text.TextField;
import flash.text.TextFormat;
import flash.display.Sprite;
public class TextProject extends Sprite
{
    [Embed(source="C:\\WINDOWS\\Fonts\\verdana.TTF", fontName="Verdana")]
    private var verdana_str:String;

    public function TextProject()
    {
        var format:TextFormat = new TextFormat();
        format.font = "Verdana";
        format.size = 40;

        var txt:TextField = new TextField();
        txt.defaultTextFormat = format;

        //since we want to use the antiAliasType property we have to remember
```

```
        //to use the embedFonts property
        txt.embedFonts = true;
        txt.antiAliasType = flash.text.AntiAliasType.ADVANCED;

        //also, we want to make sure that we've got the TextFormat assigned
        //and the antiAliasType set *before* we set the text
        txt.text = "This Arial is embedded";
        addChild(txt);
    }
}
}
```

Now you have an embedded font that will be available for you to use anywhere via a `TextFormat` object.

Using gridFitType

The type of grid fitting used for this text field, this property applies only if the `AntiAliasType` property of the text field is set to "advanced." The type of grid fitting used determines whether Flash Player forces strong horizontal and vertical lines to fit to a pixel or subpixel grid, or not at all. For the `flash.text.GridFitType` property, you can set it to the following values:

- `flash.text.GridFitType.SUBPIXEL`: This indicates that you want your lines to fit to the subpixel grid available on LCD monitors. The `flash.text.AntiAliasType` property of the text field has to be set to `flash.text.AntiAliasType.ADVANCED`. This is often good for right-aligned or centered dynamic text, and it is sometimes a useful tradeoff for animation versus text quality.

- `flash.text.GridFitType.PIXEL`: This specifies that strong horizontal and vertical lines are fit to the pixel grid. This setting works only for left-aligned text fields. The `flash.text.AntiAliasType` property of the text field has to be set to `flash.text.AntiAliasType.ADVANCED`.

Using the numLines and wordwrap properties

The `numLines` property indicates the number of lines in a multiline `TextField`. It is a read-only property so you cannot set it. From a multiline `TextField`, you also can get very specific information about the characters and strings within specific lines within the `TextField`:

```
var lines:int = txt.numLines;
trace(lines);
```

The `getLineIndexOfChar()` method allows you to find the line that contains a specific character within the `TextField`. The `getLineLength()` method allows you to get the length in characters in a specified line. You can also get the metrics of a specific line, as well as the text within a specified line. By using the `getLineOffset()` method, you can get the first character in a line of a multiline `TextField`. Let's quickly look at putting all these to use with a search input field that will allow you to search a second `TextField` and highlight the line where a character is found:

```
package
{
import flash.display.Sprite;
import flash.text.TextField;
import flash.text.TextFormat;
import flash.events.TextEvent;
public class SearchField extends Sprite
{
    private var input:TextField;
    private var text:TextField;
    private var regex:RegExp;
    private var selectedFormat:TextFormat;
    private var defaultFormat:TextFormat;

    public function SearchField()
    {

        defaultFormat = new TextFormat();
        defaultFormat.bold = false;
        defaultFormat.color = 0x00000;

        selectedFormat = new TextFormat();
        selectedFormat.color = 0xFF0000;
        selectedFormat.bold = true;

        input = new TextField();
        input.type = "input";
        input.border = true;
        input.height = 20;
        addChild(input);
        input.addEventListener(TextEvent.TEXT_INPUT, checkInput);

        text = new TextField();
        text.text = "Arnold Franz Walter Schoenberg (September 13, 1874 - ↵
July 13, 1951) was an Austrian and later American composer. Many of ↵
Schoenberg's works are associated with the expressionist movements in ↵
early 20th-century German poetry and art, and he was among the first ↵
composers to embrace atonal motivic development.";
        text.wordWrap = true;
        text.multiline = true;
        addChild(text);
        text.y = 200;
    }
```

```
        private function checkInput(textEvent:TextEvent):void
        {
            text.setTextFormat(defaultFormat);

            var indexOfInt:int;
            var lineIndex:int;
            var firstChar:int;
            var lastChar:int;
            if((indexOfInt = text.text.indexOf(input.text)) != -1)
            {
                lineIndex = text.getLineIndexOfChar(indexOfInt);
                firstChar = text.getLineOffset(lineIndex);
                lastChar = firstChar + text.getLineLength(lineIndex);
                text.setTextFormat(selectedFormat, firstChar, lastChar);
            }
        }
    }
}
```

Altering or restricting characters for a text field

What if you want to control the characters that a user can put into a `TextField`? Well, there is a pretty simple way to control the characters that can be entered. The first is to set the characters that can be put into the `TextField` itself. If you were to have a `TextField` where your users enter their phone numbers, you would want to prevent them from entering letters. You can do this using the restrict characters property of the TextField. When you set the restrict characters property, it restricts user interaction only; a script may put any text into the text field.

The string you pass in is scanned from left to right, and you allow a range by using a hyphen:

```
textField.restrict = "0-9";
```

The preceding code allows all numbers and nothing else. The next snippet of code allows all numbers and uppercase letters from A to F, which would be handy if you were trying to keep your text field to valid hexadecimal colors.

```
textField.restrict = "0-9 A-F";
```

So what if you want to specify characters you don't want? You use the caret (^), which marks anything after the caret as disallowed and anything before it or not listed as acceptable:

```
textField.restrict = "0-9 A-F ^ a-z";
```

This allows the same range as before, but disallows all lowercase characters. So far so good, but what if you want to allow the hyphen because you want users to be able to enter their phone number? You can't just throw it in there because it's expected that you're specifying a range when you use it. You can escape it by prefacing it with two backslashes "\\".

```
textField.restrict = "0-9 \\-";
```

Now users can enter numbers and dashes and nothing else. The other control that you have over the user's input into the input TextField is the `maxChars` property. This allows you to set the maximum number of characters that a TextField can contain. You may recall the phone number example from earlier in the chapter. In that instance, you would limit your TextField to ten numbers and there is the possibility of two hyphens, so you would use the following:

```
textField.maxChars = 12;
```

Using the scroll properties

By default the user can scroll through the text in a TextField using the arrow keys. If you want to allow the mouse wheel to scroll as well, simply set `mouseWheelEnabled` to `true`. Often, however, you'll want to give the user more indication of what they can do with the text in front of them, especially if there's a lot of it. The TextField defines a few different scrolling properties that correlate to the current amount of scrolling in the TextField and maximum amount of scrolling that can be allowed:

- `maxScrollH`: The maximum amount of horizontal scroll allowed by the bounds of the TextField. This is a read-only property.
- `maxScrollV`: The maximum amount of vertical scroll allowed by the bounds of the TextField. This is a read-only property.
- `scrollH`: The current horizontal scrolling position.
- `scrollV`: The vertical position of text in a text field.

The `scrollV` and `maxScrollV` properties are in lines. This means that if you have a TextField with 20 lines, 10 of which are visible at a given time, your `maxScrollV` will be 10. This means that the maximum value for the line currently at the top of the TextField is 10. The `scrollH` and `maxScrollH` properties are in pixels. So if your line is 300 pixels wide and your TextField is 200 pixels wide, your `maxScrollH` will be 100. Let's look at making a simple auto-scrolling TextField:

```
package
{
import flash.text.TextField;
import flash.events.MouseEvent;
import flash.display.Sprite;
public class ScrollText extends Sprite
{
```

```
        private var txt:TextField;

        public function ScrollText()
        {
            txt = new TextField();
            txt.multiline = true;
            txt.wordWrap = true;
            txt.text = "Arnold Franz Walter Schoenberg (September 13, 1874 -
July 13, 1951) was an Austrian and later American composer. Many of
Schoenberg's works are associated with the expressionist movements in
early 20th-century German poetry and art, and he was among the first
composers to embrace atonal motivic development.";
            txt.height = 100
            txt.width = 50;
            addChild(txt);
            txt.addEventListener(MouseEvent.MOUSE_MOVE, scrollTextField);
        }

        private function scrollTextField(mouseEvent:MouseEvent):void
        {
            if (mouseEvent.stageY < 30)
            {
                txt.scrollV--;
            }

            if (mouseEvent.stageY > 70)
            {
                txt.scrollV++;
            }
        }
    }
}
```

Using multiline and TextMetrics

When you want your `TextField` to have multiple lines, you simply set the `multiLine` property to `true` and the `wordWrap` property to `true`. Once you've done this, a great number of properties and methods become available to you to enable you to determine which line the user has selected, which line is at a particular x and y point, and what the metrics of your `TextField` are.

Let's look at an example in which we want to set the characters in the line underneath the user's mouse to red. We use a multiline `TextField` that we've set to use a `wordWrap` so that we have distinct lines we can set properties for. Look through the code and we'll explain some of the new methods in the text that follows:

```
package
{
import flash.display.Sprite;
```

```
import flash.text.TextField;
import flash.events.MouseEvent;
import flash.text.TextFormat;
import flash.display.StageAlign;
import flash.display.StageScaleMode;
public class MultilineTextExample extends Sprite
{
    private var multilineField:TextField;
    private var redFormat:TextFormat;
    private var blackFormat:TextFormat;

    public function MultilineTextExample()
    {
        stage.align = StageAlign.TOP_LEFT;
        stage.scaleMode = StageScaleMode.NO_SCALE;

        redFormat = new TextFormat();
        redFormat.color = 0xFF0000;

        blackFormat = new TextFormat();
        blackFormat.color = 0x000000;

        multilineField = new TextField();
        multilineField.multiline = true;
        multilineField.wordWrap = true;
        multilineField.height = 400;
        multilineField.width = 400;
        multilineField.mouseEnabled = true;
        multilineField.addEventListener(MouseEvent.MOUSE_MOVE, ↵
            getMouseOverLine);
        multilineField.addEventListener(MouseEvent.MOUSE_OUT, ↵
            getMouseOutLine);
        multilineField.text = "Returns metrics information about a given↵
text line. Parameters lineIndex:int The line number for which you want↵
metrics information. Returns TextLineMetrics A TextLineMetrics object. ↵
Throws RangeError: The line number specified is out of range.";

        addChild(multilineField);
    }

    private function getMouseOverLine(mouseEvent:MouseEvent):void
    {

        var characterInLine:int = ↵
            multilineField.getCharIndexAtPoint(10, mouseEvent.stageY);
        if(characterInLine != -1)
```

```
        {
            var lineIndex:int =⏎
                multilineField.getLineIndexOfChar(characterInLine);

            var firstCharIndex:int = multilineField.getLineOffset(lineIndex);

            var lastCharIndex:int = firstCharIndex⏎
                + multilineField.getLineLength(lineIndex);

            //we want to set all the TextField to black except
            //the text underneath the mouse
            multilineField.setTextFormat(blackFormat);⏎
            multilineField.setTextFormat(redFormat,
                firstCharIndex, lastCharIndex);
        }
    }

    private function getMouseOutLine(mouseEvent:MouseEvent):void
    {
        multilineField.setTextFormat(blackFormat);
    }
}
}
```

The method doing most of the work is `getCharIndexAtPoint()`, which takes an x coordinate and y coordinate to determine what character is under that point. Earlier we mentioned using the `TextFormat` object to set the `TextFormat` for either the entire `TextField`, or for just a specified range of characters. Now, by using the width of your `TextField` to get the character at the right index and 0 to get the character at the left index, we pass the `MouseEvent` y coordinate into `getCharIndexAtPoint()` to find the beginning character and ending character for each line. Then we set the `TextFormat` object for that line. Here's the signature for `getCharIndexAtPoint()`:

```
public function getCharIndexAtPoint(x:Number, y:Number):int
```

Another property of the TextField when it is in multiline mode is that it can return `TextLineMetrics` about a given line if you wish. The `TextLineMetrics` object contains properties that allow you to look deep into the layout of a particular line. The properties of the `TextLineMetrics` object are as follows:

- `x:Number`: The left position of the first character in pixels.
- `width:Number`: The width of the text of the selected lines (not necessarily the complete text) in pixels.
- `height:Number`: The height of the text of the selected lines (not necessarily the complete text) in pixels.
- `ascent:Number`: The length from the baseline to the top of the line height in pixels.

- `descent:Number`: The length from the baseline to the bottom depth of the line in pixels.
- `leading:Number`: The measurement of the vertical distance between the lines of text.

Figure 15-3 will clarify a lot more than any explanation.

FIGURE 15-3

How Text Metrics measure a character and font

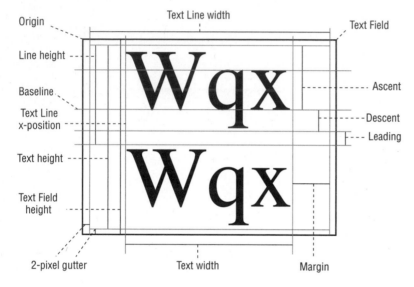

Displaying Unicode

To display Unicode text, for example Chinese or Arabic characters, or special symbols such as the copyright symbol or the Euro, we use the Unicode code for the character and set the TextFields text property with it as a string. You can find a list of all Unicode escape sequences here:

```
http://en.wikibooks.org/wiki/Windows_Programming/Unicode/
    Character_reference/0000-0FFF
```

Other references can be found by searching for "Unicode characters list." If you want to use the Greek letter Delta, you add it like so:

```
txt.text = "The greek letter delta looks like so: \u0395";
```

Creating Text Input fields

The `TextField` has a `type` property that allows you to create an input `TextField`. The default for the `TextField` is to be a dynamic `TextField`, which means its text can be altered at run-time, but not altered by the user. The input `TextField` can have text in it when it first appears or not, and can be altered by the user.

Making a TextField an input field

As we mentioned earlier, to make a `TextField` into an input `TextField` you simply set the `TextField` object's `type` property to `"input"`. Once you've done that, you've got an input `TextField`. Any text that you specify will appear at the beginning of the field and will be editable by the user.

```
var txt:TextField = new TextField();
txt.type = "input";
txt.text = "Enter your name here";
txt.border = true;
txt.borderColor = 0x0000FF;
```

As soon as the user begins typing in your input `TextField`, she can add onto our original text.

Using tabs with an input TextField

One of the things to keep in mind when designing a user interface, no matter how simple, is what the user is accustomed to doing. Many people are used to being able to tab through a group of `TextField` to change focus from one TextField to another. If you're on the `TextField` at the top of the page, you tab to get the next lowest. If you're in the `TextField` at the bottom of the page, you tab to go to the Submit button. Because some users are accustomed to it, they might be pleasantly surprised to find that they can tab through the `TextField` object, although more likely than not they won't notice. Because they assume that your app is tab-enabled they'll notice only if it isn't. Such is the lot of a UI designer.

To tab-enable your text fields, set `tabEnabled = true`. This means that our `TextField` will be in the array of `tabEnabled DisplayObjects` on the stage at a given time. The `tabIndex` is the position of your `TextField` within the `tabEnabled` array. The array is determined by looking across the screen from top left to bottom right. So as you tab through the screen, you're just selecting the next item in the array of `tabEnabled DisplayObjects`. You can also explicitly set the `tabIndex` of your `DisplayObject` if you want it to be in a different position within this array. In the following code snippet the tab index of the two `TextField` objects:

```
this.jobField.tabEnabled = true;
this.jobField.tabIndex - 1;
this.nameField.tabEnabled = true;
this.nameField.tabIndex = 0;
```

Listening to TextField events

The TextField defines three events that it dispatches, in addition to the events that it inherits from DisplayObject. We look at each of these and examine how to use the focusIn and focusOut events with the TextField.

textInput event

The textInput event extends flash.events.Event and is fired off any time the user changes text within a TextField that is of type input. This means that anything that the user does to alter the text that is within the TextField will fire off this event. Since this provides access to text input into a TextField as soon as it is entereed. This can be used to create a predictive text input. We've all seen these before — you type "fla", it predicts "flash." Before you get started, you'll want to think about what you want the event to do. If you've made a prediction and the user has accepted it, then you want to move on to the next prediction, but if you've given users a prediction that they don't want, you want to try a different prediction. After they've typed something in — for example "flash" — if it's not in your little dictionary then you want to add it. Sounds simple right? Well, we'll see:

```
package
{
    import flash.text.TextField;
    import flash.display.Sprite;
    import flash.events.TextEvent;
    public class InputExample extends Sprite
    {
        private var inputText:TextField;
        private var regex:RegExp;
        private var dict:Array;

        public function InputExample()
        {

            dict = new Array("flash", "java", "C#", "python", "ruby", "C++");
            inputText = new TextField();
            inputText.type = "input";
            inputText.addEventListener(TextEvent.TEXT_INPUT, predictText);
            inputText.border = true;
            addChild(inputText);
        }

        private function predictText(textEvent:TextEvent):void
        {
            this.regex = new RegExp(textEvent.text, "i");
            for each(var term:String in dict)
```

```
                            {
                                if(regex.test(term))
                                {
                                    inputText.text = term.substring(textEvent.text.length);
                                }
                            }
                        }
                    }
                }
```

By attaching an event listener for the text input event, you can get the character that the user just entered and try to suggest possible programming languages for them. Now, of course, to make this more complete you would want to add any terms that have been input into the TextField, but for now, it's a start.

change and scroll event

The change event is dispatched every time that the TextField object's value is changed. That means that every time the user presses a key while the TextField has focus, the change event is broadcast. The textInput event is broadcast before the value of the text has changed. The scroll event is dispatched *after* the user has scrolled the TextField.

focusIn and focusOut events

The focusIn and focusOut events are inherited from DisplayObject. This event is broadcast any time that the TextField receives focus from the user. Let's look at a small example listening for TextField events and changing the background color to indicate the current event:

```
package
{
    import flash.text.TextField;
    import flash.events.*;
    import flash.display.Sprite;
    public class FocusIn extends Sprite
    {
        var primaryText:TextField;
        var secondaryText:TextField;

        public function FocusIn()
        {

            primaryText = new TextField();
            secondaryText = new TextField();

            primaryText.text = "This is the primary TextField.";
```

```
                    secondaryText.text = "This is the secondary TextField";

                    primaryText.addEventListener(FocusEvent.FOCUS_IN, setFocus);
                    secondaryText.addEventListener(FocusEvent.FOCUS_IN, setFocus);
                    primaryText.addEventListener(FocusEvent.FOCUS_OUT, loseFocus);
                    secondaryText.addEventListener(FocusEvent.FOCUS_OUT, loseFocus);

                    primaryText.background = true;
                    secondaryText.background = true;

                    primaryText.backgroundColor = 0xFFFFFF;
                    secondaryText.backgroundColor = 0xFFFFFF;

                    addChild(this.primaryText);
                    addChild(this.secondaryText);

                    secondaryText.x = 500;
                }

                private function setFocus(focus:FocusEvent):void
                {
                    (focus.target as TextField).backgroundColor = 0xFF0000;
                }

                private function loseFocus(focus:FocusEvent):void
                {
                    (focus.target as TextField).backgroundColor = 0xFFFFFF;
                }
            }
        }
```

link events

One of the coolest new features in ActionScript 3 is the capability to listen to the events from any link tags within `htmlText` contained within a `TextField`. An event is dispatched when a user clicks a hyperlink in an HTML-enabled text field, where the URL begins with `event:`. The remainder of the URL after `event:` will be placed in the text property of the `link` event. This allows you to handle links in the same way that an HTML page would and makes handling HTML text much more useful to developers.

```
        var tf:TextField = new TextField();
        tf.addEventListener(TextEvent.link, linkClicked);

        private function linkClicked(event:TextFieldEvent):void
        {
            trace(event.text);
        }
```

Now, of course, a much more reasonable thing to do is to listen to the event and have the TextField send over the URL it wants to go to. Let's make a link to Wiley:

```
TextField.htmlText = "<a url=\"event:http://www.wiley.com\">go ↵
to Wiley.</a>";
```

Notice that we needed to escape the quotes around the url attribute. Now we'll set up the event listener to take this value and actually go to that URL:

```
private function textEventListner(event:Event):void
{
    flash.net.navigateToURL(event.text);
}
```

Just like that, we've set up a listener to use the navigateToURL function; we'll be sent off to the URL we specify in our HTML.

Summary

- We use a TextField wherever we want text to be displayed within our application.
- The TextField is either dynamic TextFields by default, or they can have their type set to "input" to make them input TextFields.
- The TextField contains properties to control whether they are multiline or wordwrap, and whether they have a border and background colors.
- TextField extends the DisplayObject class and has all the properties, methods, and events inherited.
- TextField objects that are multiline have scroll properties that allow you to scroll up and down through the lines in the TextField.
- You can use a TextFormat object to control the appearance of text in the TextField.
- If the TextField has htmlText, you can use a StyleSheet object to apply CSS classes to HTML.
- TextField objects dispatch distinct TextEvents to indicate when the user has entered text if the TextField is an input field, or a link event if the TextField has htmlText with links within it.

Part IV

Understanding the Event Framework

Chapter 16

Understanding Events

ctionScript 3.0 adds a powerful framework for handling internal communication known as the *event framework*. *Events* are messages that are sent between objects when an action, such as a button click, has taken place. This enables you to create functionality that occurs sequentially without the need for the Flash Timeline or for complicated method calls to other classes.

The Flash Player 9 API uses events for many different purposes that were formerly handled in loose and inconsistent ways. Mouse actions, timers, networking, and asynchronous errors are all examples. We'll talk about how these subsystems use the event framework.

We'll take a look at how EventDispatcher objects communicate and the structure of the new Event objects. We'll also look at some of the more advanced features of the event framework, including how to create your own custom events and how to use the new event bubbling feature.

Introducing Events

What exactly is an event? At its core, an event is an object that represents an occurrence and describes the conditions surrounding that occurrence, including but not limited to, a description of the event, called the *event type*, and the origin of the event, also known as the *event target*.

This is by no means a new concept. In the past, ActionScript users have had access to callback functions such as onClipEvent handlers and button actions. ActionScript 2.0 users might have used the elusive and poorly documented mx.events.EventDispatcher class — or perhaps the even more elusive and even less documented `ASBroadcaster` class. Java users are, no doubt, familiar with the `Observer/Observable` combo. And all of these use the principles defined in the Observer design pattern. What is new about the event system in ActionScript 3.0 is the way it's implemented across many different areas of the API with a consistent and robust design.

Events and the Observer design pattern allow one object, called an *event dispatcher*, to trigger the actions of one or more other objects, called *event listeners*, without having to know anything about the structure of the other objects. Because the object broadcasting the event doesn't need to know what methods to call on the receiving objects, listeners can be added and taken away at any time without altering code. That is what makes them so powerful.

To understand this better, let's take a look at an example of how events work by using a real-world example.

Saturday morning events

The relationship between an event dispatcher and an event listener is like that of a person who subscribes to a magazine or newspaper. Imagine it's a laid-back Saturday morning, your opportunity to wake up late, have a cup of coffee, and read the Saturday paper. Each Saturday, the paperboy delivers the paper to me and my neighbors Anja and Jim. Personally, I like the City section, Anja loves Style, and Jim checks the Arts section for gallery openings. If you were to draw a diagram, it would look something like Figure 16-1.

FIGURE 16-1

The paperboy delivers the paper to all the subscribers. Everybody's happy!

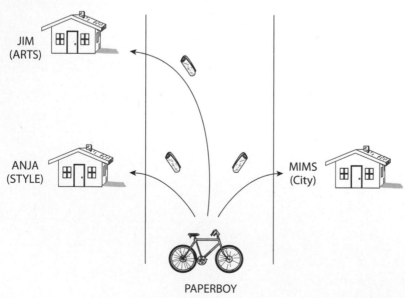

This diagram shows almost the same thing that happens when an event is dispatched to its listeners. In fact, it's often said that a listener subscribes to an event dispatcher. Let's imagine this scene a little differently.

If we were describing this scenario with ActionScript, we might think of the paperboy as an event dispatcher, the newspaper subscribers as event listeners, and the newspaper as an event (or as a property of an event if you prefer). The action triggering the event in this case would be the delivery of the paper. Like the newspaper example, each subscriber can choose how to respond to that event by reading a different section of the paper.

So, let's assume that the paperboy is an event dispatcher who fires off an event of type `paperDelivered`. Each person uses the `addEventListener()` method to subscribe to the delivery event and sets up his or her own version of the event handler `onPaperDelivered()`. When the `dispatchEvent()` method is called by the paperboy, every listener receives notice and is passed an Event object, as shown in Figure 16-2.

FIGURE 16-2

The paperboy object sends a paperDelivered event to all the listeners. Everybody.happy = true;

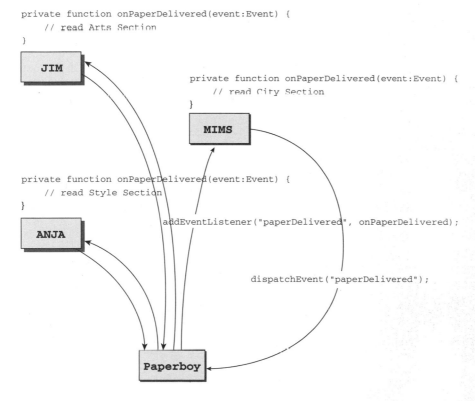

```
private function onPaperDelivered(event:Event) {
    // read Arts Section
}
```

JIM

```
private function onPaperDelivered(event:Event) {
    // read City Section
}
```

MIMS

```
private function onPaperDelivered(event:Event) {
    // read Style Section
}
```

ANJA

`addEventListener("paperDelivered", onPaperDelivered);`

`dispatchEvent("paperDelivered");`

Paperboy

With a real newspaper subscription, if one of the subscribers decides she isn't interested in keeping up with the news anymore, she can easily unsubscribe by phoning the newspaper. The same thing works for event listeners. By using the `removeEventListener()` method, it's easy to unsubscribe from the events.

Let's take a closer look at the different players and the terminology surrounding events.

Event terminology

It will be easier to talk about event dispatchers once you have the terminology surrounding events down. The following sections provide important terms and what they refer to or what roles they play.

event

This could either be an occurrence that is associated with a call to `dispatchEvent()` such as a mouse click or the end of a load sequence, or it could refer to the `Event` object that is dispatched during a `dispatchEvent()` call such as an instance of the `MouseEvent` class.

type

This describes the event being broadcast. You might also think of this as being the title or name of the event. All calls to `dispatchEvent()` and `addEventListener()` must include a specific event type. Each Event class can have several types — for example, a `MouseEvent` class has a `"click"` type and a `"mouseMove"` type.

target

When an event is broadcast, the target is the object that called `dispatchEvent()`. This is a slightly confusing term because the source of the event is called a target. It is this way because technically, the Flash Player dispatches the event to the target object. A reference to the target object is always sent out as part of the event so any event handler will have access to the dispatcher.

dispatcher

This term also refers to the object calling the `dispatchEvent()` method. Dispatch, fire, and broadcast are all terms used to describe the action of sending out an event.

listener

A listener is an object that registers with a dispatcher to receive events. A listener might also be said to listen for or subscribe to events. A single dispatcher may have several listeners.

handler

A function that is invoked when an event is received is called an event handler. It's also called a listener function.

flow

The event system in ActionScript 3.0 is different from previous versions. When dealing with objects in the display list (such as sprites) some events are sent through every parent object of a given display object until reaching the target. After reaching the target, the event is sometimes sent back through every parent object until reaching the stage. This behavior is called the event flow. Event flow allows you to assign event listeners to groups of display objects such as a set of buttons. It may sound very confusing at first but we'll cover it later in the chapter in the section "Understanding Event Flow."

phase

The trip down to the target object and the trip back up to the stage are each separate phases of the event flow. They are known as the capture phase and the bubble phase respectively.

Now that you have a better understanding of all the working parts, let's dive into the Event classes.

Understanding EventDispatcher

At the root of event dispatching is the EventDispatcher class. You'll find that many classes in AS3 (including all display objects and many networking classes) already extend EventDispatcher, making the logistics of sending events quite convenient.

Using EventDispatcher

In most situations you're going to be using a class that inherits from EventDispatcher. Let's walk through the process of triggering, dispatching, and receiving events.

The first thing you need is an event dispatcher. Let's create a subclass of EventDispatcher for this demo called Thermometer. You'll use this to measure a temperature. (In this case, you're going to set the temperature manually.) Let's add a public setter function for changing the temperature. In this setter, you're going to add a dispatchEvent() call so that other objects can be notified when the temperature changes:

```
package {
    import flash.events.*;
    public class Thermometer extends EventDispatcher {
        private var _temp:Number = 32;
        public static const TEMP_CHANGED:String = "tempChanged";

        public function set temp(newTemp:Number):void {
            _temp = newTemp;
            trace("Fired TEMP_CHANGED event");
            dispatchEvent(new Event(TEMP_CHANGED));
        }

        public function get temp():Number {
```

```
            return _temp;
        }
    }
}
```

Let's walk through some of the key lines more carefully.

```
private var _temp:Number = 32;
```

`_temp` stores the temperature value. The default is 32 (degrees Fahrenheit).

```
public static const TEMP_CHANGED:String = "tempChanged";
```

`TEMP_CHANGED` is a simple string that you're going to use to define the type of event you're broadcasting. This string can be anything just as long as your event listeners are listening for the same string. The easiest way to do this is to store the string in a static constant; that way, it's always publicly available and can't be changed.

> **TIP**　You will often see event types defined as static constants of specific `Event` classes such as `MouseEvent.CLICK`. **This is a good practice to use, but to keep things simple, let's define the event type in the** `Thermometer` **class for now.**

```
dispatchEvent(new Event(TEMP_CHANGED));
```

This is where your event is being fired out to the listeners. The `dispatchEvent()` method takes a single argument, which is an `Event` object. That event object contains information about the event. In this case, you're creating a new `Event` with type `TEMP_CHANGED` and passing it directly to the `dispatchEvent()` call.

This class is pretty straightforward. Whenever the temperature changes, an event is fired out.

Now let's create some listeners for this dispatcher:

```
package {
    import Thermometer;
    import flash.events.*;
    public class TempDisplay {
        public function TempDisplay (thermometer:Thermometer) {
            thermometer.addEventListener(Thermometer.TEMP_CHANGED, onTempChanged);
        }
        protected function onTempChanged(event:Event):void {
            var thermometer:Thermometer = Thermometer(event.target);
            trace(thermometer.temp + "F");
        }
    }
}
```

Let's step through the `TempDisplay` class now.

```
public function TempDisplay (thermometer:Thermometer) {
```

In the constructor, you're passing a thermometer object to the new `TempDisplay`. This allows you to reference it for adding listeners.

```
thermometer.addEventListener(Thermometer.TEMP_CHANGED, onTempChanged);
```

Speaking of adding listeners . . . Here you tell the `thermometer` object to invoke the `onTempChanged()` function when the `TEMP_CHANGED` event is dispatched.

NOTE In ActionScript 3.0, methods remember the object they're associated with, unlike previous versions of ActionScript where delegates were required in some situations to execute methods belonging to an outside object. That means that you no longer need to pass the listener object to an event dispatcher, only the function that you wish to use as the callback. The correct function will be called when the event is fired without the need for a delegate.

```
public function onTempChanged(event:Event):void {
```

You define `onTempChanged` as a function that takes one argument, an Event object. You'll use this object to gather data about the event and then act on it.

TIP In all cases, the only argument an event handler should have is the event object and nothing else. Sometimes you will actually use this event object and other times you won't. If you know that the event won't be used, you might find it helpful to set it to `null` by default:

```
function onEvent (event:Event = null):void { ... }
```

That way, you will be able to call the function with or without an event object making it more versatile.

```
var thermometer:Thermometer = Thermometer(event.target);
```

By using the `event.target` property, you can get the original sender of the event. The target property has the type `Object`, so you are also casting that object to type `Thermometer` so you can access its `temp` property.

```
trace(thermometer.temp + "F");
```

Finally, you trace out the value of the thermometer's temperature and add an `"F"` for Fahrenheit.

The last step is to set up your main application class to run this code:

```
package {
    import flash.display.*;
    public class TemperatureMonitor extends Sprite {
        protected var thermometer:Thermometer;
        protected var tempDisplayF:TempDisplay;
        public function TemperatureMonitor () {
            thermometer = new Thermometer();
```

```
        tempDisplayF = new TempDisplay(thermometer);

        thermometer.temp = 57;
        thermometer.temp = 98.6;
        thermometer.temp = -12;
    }
  }
}
```

This class is very straightforward. You simply set up a `Thermometer` object and a `TempDisplay` object and change the temperature a few times. If you compile all of this code, you get the following output:

```
Fired TEMP_CHANGED event
57F
Fired TEMP_CHANGED event
98.6F
Fired TEMP_CHANGED event
-12F
```

The event was passed from `thermometer` to `tempDisplayF` causing it to display the temperature. Yay!

Not impressed?

We can't say we blame you. Why do you need to pass an event just to display the temperature? Well, this is a simplified setup for demonstration purposes, but as you'll see, events can become quite powerful.

Let's say you want to make your TemperatureMonitor international by adding Celsius to the readouts. This is as simple as adding another event listener to the `Thermometer`. First, you'll need to know the formula for converting Fahrenheit to Celsius:

$$C = (F - 32) \times 5/9$$

In order to monitor the temperature in two different systems, let's create another type of TempDisplay and add it as an event listener. In this class, you're keeping the same setup as TempDisplay but doing a conversion on the number before displaying it:

```
package {
   import flash.events.*;
   public class TempDisplayCelsius extends TempDisplay {
      public function TempDisplayCelsius (thermometer:Thermometer) {
         super(thermometer); // call the parent class' constructor
      }
```

```
    // write over the onTempChanged handler from the parent class and ↵
replace it with this.
    override protected function onTempChanged(event:Event):void {
        var f:Number = Thermometer(event.target).temp;
        var c:Number = Math.round((f - 32) * 5 / 9);
        trace(c + "C");
    }
  }
}
```

Now edit your application class slightly so it looks like this:

```
package {
    import flash.display.*;
    public class TemperatureMonitor extends Sprite {
        protected var thermometer:Thermometer;
        protected var tempDisplayF:TempDisplay;
        protected var tempDisplayC:TempDisplay;

        public function TemperatureMonitor () {
            thermometer = new Thermometer();
            tempDisplayF = new TempDisplay(thermometer);
            tempDisplayC = new TempDisplayCelsius(thermometer);

            thermometer.temp = 57;
            thermometer.temp = 98.6;
            thermometer.temp = -12;
        }
    }
}
```

If you ran this new modified version, the output would be:

```
Fired TEMP_CHANGED event
57F
14C
Fired TEMP_CHANGED event
98.6F
37C
Fired TEMP_CHANGED event
-12F
-24C
```

The event is sent to both TempDisplay objects. Notice that the code for Thermometer didn't have to change at all. This will become a crucial feature as your applications become more complex. You'll find that unlike using callback functions or storing a reference to all the objects that need to be informed, using events to communicate between objects is a very scalable solution.

Using EventDispatcher by composition

`IEventDispatcher`, an interface found in the `flash.events` package, identifies a class as being capable of dispatching events. `EventDispatcher` implements `IEventDispatcher`. It's important to distinguish from `EventDispatcher` because by providing the interface, AS3 provides the means to create your own system for dispatching events that still conforms to the specifications expected.

> **TIP** Remember that an interface defines the functionality that must be in a class without defining the specifics of how it is implemented.

Perhaps more useful is the ability to make something an event dispatcher without actually sub-classing `EventDispatcher`. Say you have a class called `Sprocket` that must extend a custom class written by your client called `Widget` (`Widget` can be any class that does not inherit from `EventDispatcher`). So you would have:

```
class Sprocket extends Widget {
    //...
}
```

How would you add the ability to dispatch events to `Sprocket` (assuming that you cannot go back and edit `Widget`)? Remember that each class can extend only one other class.

The answer is that you add the event dispatching behavior by composition. That is, you compose the class to include an event dispatcher. By combining this with the `IEventDispatcher`, you can get the same functionality as an `EventDispatcher` by implementing the methods and passing the calls onto the dispatcher object. This is easier to understand by executing it:

```
class Sprocket extends Widget implements IEventDispatcher {
    private var dispatcher:EventDispatcher = new EventDispatcher();

    override public function dispatchEvent(event:Event):Boolean {
        return dispatcher.dispatchEvent(event);
    }
    // implement other methods the same way here.
}
```

As you can see, by doing this you can get a `Sprocket` with all the benefits of `Widgets` and `EventDispatchers`!

Working with Event Objects

When an event occurs in ActionScript 3.0 and a `dispatchEvent()` call is triggered, a message is sent out to all the recipients of the event. That message comes in the form of an `Event` object. `flash.events.Event` is a new class in AS3 that contains any pertinent data relating to an occurrence in your script. It's a replacement for the generic objects used for the older event broadcasting models from earlier versions of ActionScript. The new class offers a much more reliable way to transmit data than a plain object.

The `Event` class is a base class for all other types of events. It can be subclassed and customized to fit your needs. The Flash Player 9 API comes with several subclasses of `Event` already defined. Each one may contain specific information about the kind of event it describes. For example, a `MouseEvent` contains information such as the event type as well as information about the position of the mouse and state of its buttons; a `ProgressEvent` contains information such as the number of bytes in a file that have been loaded. A list of all of these classes can be found in the AS3 documentation.

Creating a new event

Before dispatching any message, you'll need to create a new Event object. Typically, using the `Event` class will be sufficient. Occasionally, you might need to subclass `Event` and create a customized event that contains more data specific to your needs. We'll focus on creating a basic event for now.

Here's the function signature for the Event constructor:

```
public function Event(type:String, bubbles:Boolean = false, ↵
cancelable:Boolean = false)
```

First is the `type` parameter. We've seen this before in this chapter — it's a string that describes the event taking place such as `"click"` or `"load"`.

Next, `bubbles` is a flag you can pass to your event to indicate whether it should participate in the bubbling phase of the event flow. We discuss what the event flow is later in this chapter.

Finally, `cancelable` states whether a default behavior can be cancelled. This parameter is mostly for internal use by the Flash Player API and, again, we'll talk about default behaviors later also.

So to review, the Event constructor has a required `type` parameter, one parameter that is rarely used, and one that is used internally only. Let's create a new Event object.

```
var event:Event = new Event("dance");
```

We just created a `dance` event! Firing this event is just as easy.

```
dispatchEvent(event);
```

Many times you'll see these lines combined:

```
dispatchEvent(new Event("dance"));
```

One more thing — it's not a very good practice to use raw strings such as `"dance"` in your code for a number of reasons. First, strings and other literals are difficult to change. If you needed to make this `"tango"` instead, you would have to search for every listener and make changes there as well. It's also more prone to typos because you can't use code hinting — when working with constants, the compiler is able to check for errors at compile time while string errors might pass through unchecked.

To get around these issues, it's common practice to use a static constant for every event type you want to include. By convention, this constant is defined in the Event class but if you don't want to create a subclass of the Event class, you can define the constant in the class that's dispatching the event:

```
public static const DANCE:String = "dance"; // add this to your class
dispatchEvent(new Event(DANCE));
```

Adding and Removing Event Listeners

You've already taken a look at some examples that use addEventDispatcher(). Now we'll go over how listeners are added and removed in more detail. First, the following is the full method signature for addEventListener():

```
addEventListener(type:String, listener:Function, ↵
useCapture:Boolean = false, priority:int = 0, ↵
useWeakReference:Boolean = false):void
```

Whoa. There's a lot going on here.

type

The first object you pass to the function is the type (in the previous example, the type was "dance"). You can think of the type as the frequency on which the event is broadcast the same way a radio station uses a particular frequency to broadcast music. Most of the time, the type you pass in will be stored as a static string in the Event class that you are using. Built-in Event classes have several of these predefined.

listener

Next comes the listener function. This is the function that will be invoked when the event is fired.

NOTE   So far, we've referred to the object containing the handler function as the listener. This isn't completely accurate. The real listener is the handler function itself! It's a subtle difference but important. Remember that in ActionScript 3.0, a method retains its class scope even when run from another scope, which eliminates the need for Delegates and allows the function to stand alone as the listener. However, I've always found it easier to think of the object as being the listener and people tend to talk about it that way, albeit incorrectly.

Furthermore, to be technically accurate, events originate from the Flash Player and are passed to the target object (hence the name) but for simplicity's sake, we'll keep it simple and consider the target object the source of the event.

useCapture

The useCapture flag determines whether you will listen for the event on the capture phase or on the target and bubble phases. This is used only for events that use the event flow, which we discuss later in the chapter.

priority

Even though all event listeners appear to execute simultaneously, there is a distinct order in which the code is executed. Sometimes, event handlers might conflict with each other. Say for example, you have two different listener functions called onLoad in two different objects. If the first one changes the loaded data before the second one reads it, you might have an unexpected conflict that can be very hard to troubleshoot. This is where the priority parameter comes in. This value is an integer that can be set only while adding the listener. A higher number listener gets executed before lower numbers. If two listeners' priorities are the same, they're executed in the order they were added to the event dispatcher. In most cases, the default value, zero, can be used.

There may be cases where you wish to abort the handling of events. For example, you might want to use a single event listener to validate data before allowing the event to propagate to other listeners, canceling the event if the data is bad. This can be done using the stopImmediatePropogation() method of the Event class. Calling this method cancels all event handlers that haven't already been invoked. This isn't permanent; the effects last only until the next time the event is dispatched.

useWeakReference

In many cases, you will not need to use this parameter (whose default is false), but for the sake of memory management, it's always a good idea.

ActionScript 3.0 introduces the concept of weak and strong memory references. Typically, an object will be garbage collected if there are no references to the object. That is, when no objects are using a variable, it gets thrown out. Weak references allow you to reference an object, but the object will still be eligible for garbage collection unless another object holds a strong reference to the object. By setting the useWeakReference flag to true, you will create a weak link between the event broadcaster and the event listener. That way, if an event listener is deleted while still listening to the event broadcaster, the weak reference will allow it to be garbage collected. This helps to prevent memory leaks when you forget to unsubscribe from events. However, useWeakReference can cause premature collection if you don't keep your own references to the dispatchers, stopping events from functioning properly.

Removing a listener from a dispatcher

Removing an event listener is as easy as adding one and the syntax is very similar:

```
dispatcher.addEventListener("eventType", onEvent);
dispatcher.removeEventListener("eventType", onEvent);
```

Use this method when you no longer wish your listener to respond to events. Also, it's a good idea to remove all event listeners (or use weak references) when you destroy an EventDispatcher object so that there aren't references to the dispatcher holding it in memory.

 If you set the `useCapture` flag to `true` when you add the event listener, you'll need to set it to `true` when removing it as well.

Understanding Event Flow

When working with Display List objects, events take on a behavior that may be new to many ActionScript developers. Instead of simply being fired from a single object, the event dispatching process steps through every parent `DisplayObject` in the chain starting with the Stage and working up to the target object that called `dispatchEvent()`. This is called the *event flow* and as strange as it may sound, it's a W3C recommendation for dealing with events.

If you retain nothing else, remember the purpose of event flow is to allow events dispatched by child display objects to appear to come from the parent object as well. For example, say you had a sprite containing several buttons. Typically, listening for click events on all buttons would require you to call `addEventListener()` for each button. But, because events in AS3 are dispatched from every parent display object in the chain leading up to the target, you could listen for button clicks just once on the parent sprite.

The event flow allows you to listen for events that occur within a system without understanding the details of how the system functions. And obscuring the details of complicated systems is generally considered a good thing when it comes to object-oriented software design. Armed with a sense of purpose, let's delve into how event flow works

The phases of event flow

When the `dispatchEvent()` method is called from any DisplayObject in the Display List, the event goes through three phases. These are called the capture phase, the target phase, and the bubble phase. You might think of an elevator where each floor is a parent display object on the way to the target. The elevator stops and dispatches an event on every floor it passes, as shown in Figure 16-3.

Capture phase

In the capture phase, Flash Player steps through every parent display object starting with the Stage and working up to the object that called `dispatchEvent()` and treats each one as though it was the event target. The effect is that the event is broadcast from every level of the Display List that is a parent of the display object that called `dispatchEvent()`. Display objects that are not ancestors (or parent objects) of the target object do not dispatch events. In order to listen for events in the capture phase, you will have to set the `useCapture` flag to `true` when adding the event listener.

Target phase

During this phase, the event is dispatched from the target object. For events outside of the display list event flow, this is the only phase that you will see.

FIGURE 16-3

The three phases of event flow

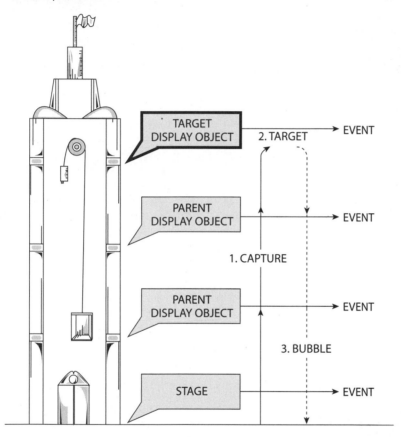

Bubble phase

Optionally, the event might bubble back up dispatching from each parent display object until the stage is reached. Whether an event bubbles is set when creating a new Event object. The default setting depends on the class of the Event, but it is used for mouse and key events as well as other events dispatched by the Flash Player API. It is useful if you ever need to ensure that the target is reached before handling events.

NOTE By default, the target and bubble phases are used when calling addEventListener(). By setting useCapture to true, the capture phase will be used instead. If you want to use all three phases, you'll have to add two separate event listeners, one with useCapture set to true and one with it set to false.

Because the Stage is the parent object for all display objects in the display list, events that use event flow will always pass through the Stage. Therefore, it's possible to listen for *any* event coming from within the display list by simply adding event listeners to the Stage. Remember that you can always use the type property of an event to filter your responses from within an event handler.

The current phase of an event in the flow can be determined from the eventPhase property. The values returned will be one of the following constants: EventPhase.CAPTURING_PHASE, EventPhase.AT_TARGET, or EventPhase.BUBBLING_PHASE. You can use a check like the one that follows to determine where in the event flow an event is and respond differently depending on which phase it's in. If you put this listener on the Stage, you would see every event fired by any DisplayObjects in the Display List.

```
private function onEvent(event:Event):void {
    if (event.eventPhase == EventPhase.CAPTURING_PHASE) {
        trace("Capture Phase");
        trace("Event is at " + event.currentTarget);
    }
    else if (event.eventPhase == EventPhase.AT_TARGET) {
        trace("Target Phase");
        trace("Event target is " + event.target);
    }
    else if (event.eventPhase == EventPhase.BUBBLING_PHASE) {
        trace("Bubble Phase");
        trace("Event is at " + event.currentTarget);
    }
}
```

Notice that we're using both event.target and a new property, event.currentTarget. This property will return the display object that is currently being targeted within the event flow while the target property remains the same and is always the object from which the event was dispatched.

At any time, the events in the event flow might be terminated by a listener function by using stopPropagation() or stopImmediatePropagation(). Overriding propagation can be useful to prevent other listeners from receiving the event.

Event flow in action

The best way to understand the event flow is to see it in action. In this example, you create a set of several buttons contained within a button container. To emphasize how the event bubbling affects all of the parent classes, you'll also place the button container inside a larger UI container, which is in turn placed on the Stage. Even though you'll create three buttons, only one listener is needed to handle all of the click events.

Let's start by defining a new Button class. This button will simply contain a rectangle and a TextField with the button's name:

```
package {
    import flash.display.Sprite;
```

```
import flash.text.TextField;

public class Button extends Sprite {
    private var labelField:TextField;

    public function Button (label:String = "button") {
        // draw the background for the button.
        graphics.beginFill(0x3366CC);
        graphics.drawRect(0, 0, 100, 30);

        // store the label as the button's name.
        name = label;

        // create a TextField to display the button label.
        labelField = new TextField();
        // ensure clicks are sent from labelField rather than the button.
        labelField.mouseEnabled = false;
        labelField.selectable = false;
        labelField.text = label;
        labelField.x = 10;
        labelField.y = 10;
        labelField.width = 80;
        labelField.height = 20;
        addChild(labelField);
    }
}
}
```

Next, you'll set up the EventFlow class, which will run the application:

```
package {
    import flash.display.Sprite;
    import flash.text.TextField;
    import flash.events.MouseEvent;
    import flash.display.DisplayObject;

    public class EventFlow extends Sprite {
        private var uiContainer:Sprite;
        private var buttonContainer:Sprite;
        private var uiLabel:TextField;
        private var stopButton:Button;
        private var playButton:Button;
        private var pauseButton:Button;

        public function EventFlow() {
            // create the UI container and add it to the stage.
            uiContainer = new Sprite();
            uiContainer.name = "uiContainer";
            addChild(uiContainer);

            // create the button container and add it to the UI container.
```

```
            buttonContainer = new Sprite();
            buttonContainer.graphics.beginFill(0x666666);
            buttonContainer.graphics.drawRect(0, 0, 420, 50);
            buttonContainer.name = "buttonContainer";
            buttonContainer.y = 20;
            uiContainer.addChild(buttonContainer);

            // create the UI label and add it to the UI container.
            uiLabel = new TextField();
            uiLabel.name = "uiLabel";
            uiLabel.text = "Audio Controls";
            uiLabel.width = 80;
            uiLabel.height = 15;
            uiContainer.addChild(uiLabel);

            // create three buttons and add them to the button container.
            stopButton = new Button("Stop");
            stopButton.x = 10;
            stopButton.y = 10;
            buttonContainer.addChild(stopButton);

            playButton = new Button("Play");
            playButton.x = 160;
            playButton.y = 10;
            buttonContainer.addChild(playButton);

            pauseButton = new Button("Pause");
            pauseButton.x = 310;
            pauseButton.y = 10;
            buttonContainer.addChild(pauseButton);

            uiContainer.addEventListener(MouseEvent.CLICK, onClick);
        }

    private function onClick(event:MouseEvent):void {
        trace("Click received.");
        trace("Event Target:", DisplayObject(event.target).name);
        trace("Current Target:", DisplayObject(event.currentTarget).name);
    }
  }
}
```

Notice that the only place where you added an event listener was on `uiContainer`. The UI container is near the top of the display list ancestry because it contains the button container, which in turn contains all of the buttons. Because every parent display object dispatches the events, this is the only listener you need to capture clicks from the buttons. In fact, you may notice that this captures clicks from not only the buttons, but from the `uiLabel TextField` and from the gray `buttonContainer` as well.

Clicking each of the buttons will trigger the `onClick` handler and produce the following results:

```
Click received.
Event Target: Stop
Current Target: uiContainer
Click received.
Event Target: Play
Current Target: uiContainer
Click received.
Event Target: Pause
Current Target: uiContainer
```

Again, you're using the event's `target` property to get the original DisplayObject that received the click and the `currentTarget` property to get the DisplayObject that's being listened to (in this case `uiContainer`).

Preventing Default Behaviors

Many events are so commonplace in ActionScript programming that they are taken for granted. For example, when text is input by the user into a text field, the letters appear onscreen. You may not realize it, but that is the result of an event handler being invoked behind the scenes. Handlers like this one — where there is an expected, predictable result — are called *default behaviors*.

Only events defined in the Flash Player 9 API are able to have default behaviors associated with them. Your custom events will never use them.

The event framework allows you to stop some of these default behaviors from occurring. Each Event object has a property called `cancelable`, a read-only flag you can set in the constructor that lets you know whether the default can be cancelled. If this flag is set to `true`, as it is by default in `TextEvent.TEXT_INPUT`, then the default behavior can be prevented using the method `preventDefault()`. Events have one more flag, which is set by calling `preventDefault()` — `isDefaultPrevented` will let you know whether default behavior has been called.

In the real world of programming, you will probably not do much with canceling default behaviors. Indeed, most of the default behaviors in the API are not cancelable anyway. Nevertheless, you may find that an understanding of what is going on under the hood is helpful in understanding the entire system.

Summary

Events can be an amazingly useful tool when creating your ActionScript programs. By making the entire system more integrated than previous versions of ActionScript, you are more likely to encounter events and therefore more likely to use them and become familiar with them. You'll see a dramatic difference in the way your objects communicate.

In this chapter, you learned the following:

- The terminology surrounding events.
- The basic relationship between event dispatcher, event object, and event listener.
- How to create a new event object and dispatch it. Also how to set up a listener for that event.
- How to use event dispatchers by composition by implementing `IEventDispatcher`.
- Events dispatched from DisplayObjects travel through the ancestral chain in a process known as the event flow.

Chapter 17

Working with Mouse and Keyboard Events

Any time you want to capture user interaction, you're probably going to deal with the mouse and the keyboard. You do this by capturing MouseEvent events and KeyboardEvent events. These two classes and their properties are the workhorses of user-driven Flash applications. The class that you're going to deal with the most in working with mouse and keyboard events is the InteractiveObject class found in the flash.display package. InteractiveObject is an abstract class and cannot be instantiated, but it provides event dispatching on all mouse and keyboard events to its subclasses. It also has several properties that you can use to define whether or not it is listening to these mouse and keyboard events.

MouseEvent Basics

Flash Player sends a mouse event to all listeners any time that the user clicks a mouse button, moves the mouse, or scrolls the mouse over an object. Moving the mouse and scrolling the mouse are similar cases, and that is one of the tricks of working with the MouseEvent class. The MouseEvent is relative to the InteractiveObject dispatching it.

Any object that inherits from InteractiveObject can listen for a MouseEvent. However, when an InteractiveObject listens for a MouseEvent that event must be within that object's scope. If you have a Sprite that is listening for a mouse click, that event will be caught only when the user clicks on *that* Sprite. Nothing will happen if the user clicks on a different sprite, off-screen, or anywhere that is not within your Sprite. Let's take a look at a quick example:

```
package
{
import flash.display.Sprite;
import flash.events.MouseEvent;
public class MouseEventExample extends Sprite
{
    public function MouseEventExample()
    {
        var listener:Sprite = new Sprite();
        listener.graphics.beginFill(0x0000ff, 1);
        listener.graphics.drawRect(0, 0, 200, 200);
        listener.graphics.endFill();

        listener.doubleClickEnabled = true;
        addChild(listener);

        listener.addEventListener(MouseEvent.MOUSE_DOWN, mouseDownHandler);
        listener.addEventListener(MouseEvent.MOUSE_MOVE, mouseMoveHandler);
        listener.addEventListener(MouseEvent.MOUSE_OUT, mouseOutHandler);
        listener.addEventListener(MouseEvent.MOUSE_UP, mouseUpHandler);
        listener.addEventListener(MouseEvent.MOUSE_WHEEL, mouseWheelHandler);
        listener.addEventListener(MouseEvent.MOUSE_OVER, mouseOverHandler);
        listener.addEventListener(MouseEvent.DOUBLE_CLICK, doubleClickHandler);
    }

    private function mouseDownHandler(mouseEvent:MouseEvent):void
    {
        trace("mouseDownHandler");
    }

    private function mouseMoveHandler(mouseEvent:MouseEvent):void
    {
        trace("mouseMoveHandler");
    }

    private function mouseOutHandler(mouseEvent:MouseEvent):void
    {
        trace("mouseOutHandler");
    }

    private function mouseUpHandler(mouseEvent:MouseEvent):void
    {
        trace("mouseUpHandler");
    }

    private function mouseWheelHandler(mouseEvent:MouseEvent):void
    {
        trace("mouseWheelHandler");
```

```
        }

        private function mouseOverHandler(mouseEvent:MouseEvent):void
        {
            trace("mouseOverHandler");
        }

        private function doubleClickHandler(mouseEvent:MouseEvent):void
        {
            trace("doubleClickHandler");
        }
    }
}
```

This is a good example to run because it will show you when each event is getting fired. Notice that the MouseEvent.MOUSE_MOVE event does not get fired when you move the mouse around outside of the Sprite. The only MouseEvent that occurs off of the Sprite itself is the MOUSE_OUT event, which tells you that the Mouse has left the Sprite. Once the mouse isn't over the Sprite, you don't hear anything from it. The InteractiveObject listening to the events catches them only when the MouseEvent occurs relative to that InteractiveObject.

So how do you catch all MouseEvents in a movie? Well, let's rephrase that. How do you catch all MouseEvents in an *empty* movie? Easy, you listen to the stage. How do you listen to every MouseEvent.MOUSE_MOVE event? Again, listen to the stage, like so:

```
    this.stage.addEventListener(MouseEvent.MOUSE_MOVE, listenToMovement);
```

Keep in mind that this code snippet must be placed inside of a DisplayObject. Now, as a word of warning, because a DisplayObject doesn't have a stage object when it isn't attached to the display list, your event won't fire until your DisplayObject has been added to the display list.

How do you listen for every MouseEvent.MOUSE_DOWN event? Well, this is slightly different. You need to listen for MouseEvent.MOUSE_DOWN on *every* InteractiveObject on the stage *or* you can listen on the stage. The MouseEvent event percolates up the chain of InteractiveObjects looking for the object that *isn't* affected by the event. The stage, however, always listens for the MouseEvent.MOUSE_DOWN event. Let's look at an example:

```
    package
    {
    import flash.display.Sprite;
    import flash.events.MouseEvent;
    public class MouseEventHierarchy extends Sprite
    {
        private var firstListener:Sprite;
        private var secondListener:Sprite;

        public function MouseEventHierarchy()
```

```
        {
            firstListener = new Sprite();
            firstListener.graphics.beginFill(0x0000ff, 1);
            firstListener.graphics.drawCircle(0, 0, 100);
            firstListener.graphics.endFill();
            secondListener = new Sprite();
            secondListener.graphics.beginFill(0x00ff00, 1);
            secondListener.graphics.drawCircle(0, 0, 30);
            secondListener.graphics.endFill();
            addChild(firstListener);
            addChild(secondListener);
            firstListener.y = 300;
            secondListener.y = 250;
            this.stage.addEventListener(MouseEvent.MOUSE_DOWN, mainMouseDown);
            firstListener.addEventListener(MouseEvent.MOUSE_DOWN, firstMouseDown);
            secondListener.addEventListener(MouseEvent.MOUSE_DOWN, secondMouseDown);

            this.stage.addEventListener(MouseEvent.MOUSE_MOVE, mainMouseMove);
            firstListener.addEventListener(MouseEvent.MOUSE_MOVE, firstMouseMove);
            secondListener.addEventListener(MouseEvent.MOUSE_MOVE, secondMouseMove);
        }

        private function mainMouseMove(me:MouseEvent):void
        {
            trace(" stage move ");
        }

        private function firstMouseMove(me:MouseEvent):void
        {
            trace("first move ");
        }

        private function secondMouseMove(me:MouseEvent):void
        {
            trace("second move");
        }

        private function mainMouseDown(me:MouseEvent):void
        {
            trace(" stage down ");
        }

        private function firstMouseDown(me:MouseEvent):void
        {
            trace("first down ");
        }

        private function secondMouseDown(me:MouseEvent):void
        {
```

```
        trace("second down ");
    }
}
}
```

As you'll notice, the stage catches all the MouseEvents, whereas the two Sprites catch only the events that are actually within their scope, i.e., when the mouse is actually over them. Clicking on the smaller secondListener Sprite doesn't throw the firstListener event but it does throw the event for the stage.

Local and Stage Coordinates

The MouseEvent object defines stageX, stageY, localX, and localY properties. These represent a big potential headache because *where* the mouse is at a given point in time is pretty interesting, but knowing what to do with the numbers that you get back from that event is potentially very difficult:

- stageX:Number: The x position at which the event occurred in relationship to the global Stage coordinates. This is determined when the localX property is set.

- stageY:Number: The y position at which the event occurred in relationship to the global Stage coordinates. This is determined when the localY property is set.

- localX:Number: The x position at which the event occurred in relationship to the display object catching the event.

- localY:Number: The y position at which the event occurred in relationship to the display object catching the event.

Let's look at a quick example in order to see how these work:

```
package
{
    import flash.display.Sprite;
    import flash.events.MouseEvent;
    public class LocalGlobalSample extends Sprite
    {
        public function LocalGlobalSample()
        {

            this.stage.scaleMode = "noScale";
            this.stage.align = "tl";

            var localSprite:Sprite = new Sprite();
            localSprite.graphics.beginFill(0x00ffCC, 1);
            localSprite.graphics.drawCircle(0, 0, 50);
```

```
                    localSprite.graphics.endFill();

                    addChild(localSprite);
                    localSprite.x = 200;
                    localSprite.y = 200;

                    localSprite.addEventListener(MouseEvent.MOUSE_MOVE, moving);
                }

                private function moving(mouseEvent:MouseEvent):void
                {
                    trace(' local ' + mouseEvent.localX + ' ' + mouseEvent.localY);
                    trace(' stage ' + mouseEvent.stageX + ' ' + mouseEvent.stageY);
                }
            }
        }
```

Again, although you don't have to run this example to see what's going on, it doesn't hurt to do so. Because the Sprite that we're catching events with is a circle, it draws from its center outwards, which means that 0, 0 is at the circle's center. So given that we've moved the Sprite to 200, 200, when the mouse is directly over the circle's center, what will we see for the different properties? For localX and localY we'll see 0 and 0, and for stageX and stageY, we'll see, you guessed it, 200 and 200. Once Flash Player figures out where the mouse is in relation to the InteractiveObject that's listening to it, it makes a globalToLocal() call on the point and evaluates what that would be in relation to the rest of the stage. It's very helpful that we have these four distinct properties to help us understand where our MouseEvents are coming from at all times.

Other MouseEvent Properties

The delta property of the Mouse was a big deal when it was first introduced five years ago. Today, it's not so exciting, but useful nonetheless. The delta is the amount that the MouseWheel, or the scroll wheel on your mouse, has scrolled. It purports to indicate how many lines in a TextField should be scrolled through. A little odd, but it's a useful notation. A positive delta means an upward scroll; a negative means a downward scroll. Now, this property applies only to the MouseEvent.MOUSE_WHEEL event, so unless we're listening for that specific event, the delta will be null.

The MouseEvent also defines a ctrlKey Boolean property that indicates whether the Control key is active (true) or inactive (false). If you are on a Mac, this property represents the Command key. This is very handy if you want to implement control-click combinations that are distinct from normal mouse clicks. This is very similar to the shiftKey Boolean property, which lets us know whether the Shift key is active or inactive. In the same spirit, we also have an altKey Boolean property, which behaves in the same fashion. Last, we have a mouseButton Boolean property, which indicates whether the primary mouse button — the left one on a two-button mouse — is depressed at the time the `MouseEvent` is fired.

The last property to discuss for the `MouseEvent` is the `relatedObject` property. The `relatedObject` is the `InteractiveObject` related to the event so if, for example, you're listening for a `mouseOut` `MouseEvent`, then the `relatedObject` is the object that the mouse has rolled onto after leaving the object you're listening on. In the case of a `mouseOver` `MouseEvent`, the `relatedObject` is the `InteractiveObject` that was just rolled off.

MouseEvent Types

Okay, so let's look at all of the types of `MouseEvents` for Flash Player 9. One thing to note about all these is that like most events in ActionScript, they have public static constants to represent their string values. This is to prevent typos and make life easier on you, the programmer. You will see the public static constant variable name and also see its string value to help you become familiar with both. The constant name can always be accessed using `MouseEvent.`*`CONSTANT_VALUE`* like so:

```
this.addEventListener(MouseEvent.MOUSE_OVER, mouseOverHandler);
```

while the string value can be passed in like so:

```
this.addEventListener("mouseOver", mouseOverHandler);
```

MouseEvent.CLICK

The `click` event is dispatched when a user presses and releases the main button of the user's pointing device over the same InteractiveObject. To create a click event, there has to be both a `mouseDown` event and then `mouseUp` from the same object (both events will be defined later in this section). Clicking down and then moving the mouse off the object before you release the button doesn't create a click event.

MouseEvent.DOUBLE_CLICK

The `doubleClick` event functions much the same as the double-click in any desktop application, with one key difference: `InteractiveObjects` must have their `doubleClickEnabled` flag set to `true` in order for this event to be dispatched. By default, the `doubleClickEnabled` property of an `InteractiveObject` is set to `false`. The difference between two clicks and a double-click is determined by your system. If your target is a TextField, then the default behavior of the double-click is to select the word that the mouse is currently over, so if you want to do something else with the event you'll need to cancel the default behavior. One thing to keep in mind is that `doubleClickEnabled` properties are different for `InteractiveObjects` than for `DisplayObjects`. We cover canceling default behaviors later in this chapter.

MouseEvent.MOUSE_DOWN

The `mouseDown` event is dispatched when a user presses the mouse down on an `InteractiveObject`. If the target is a `SimpleButton` instance, the `SimpleButton` instance displays its down state. TextFields, if they have their `selectable` property set to `true`, insert a caret to select text as the default behavior.

MouseEvent.MOUSE_MOVE

The `mouseMove` event is dispatched when the user moves the mouse anywhere over an `InteractiveObject`. Remember that the event is not dispatched if the mouse is not over the object you're listening for the event on. The only way to listen to events on the entire movie is to listen to events on the stage. If the target is a text field that the user is selecting, the selection is updated as the default behavior.

MouseEvent.MOUSE_OUT

The `mouseOut` event is dispatched when the mouse moves outside of the bounds of an `InteractiveObject` instance. Whatever `InteractiveObject` the mouse was previously over is the object that throws this event. The `relatedObject` is the object the pointing device has moved to. If the target is a `SimpleButton` instance, the button displays its up state as the default behavior.

MouseEvent.MOUSE_OVER

Also known as `mouseOver`, this lets you know that the user has dragged the mouse over the boundary of an `InteractiveObject`. If your target is an instance of `SimpleButton`, the object displays its over state by default.

MouseEvent.MOUSE_UP

The `mouseUp` event lets you know that the user has released the mouse button over an `InteractiveObject` instance in the Flash Player window. If this is a `SimpleButton` instance, the `SimpleButton` displays its up state by default. If the target is a selectable text field, the text field ends selection as the default behavior.

MouseEvent.MOUSE_WHEEL

The `mouseWheel` event is dispatched when a mouse wheel is spun over an `InteractiveObject` instance in the Flash Player window. For `TextField` objects, the text scrolls as the default.

MouseEvent.ROLL_OUT

The `rollOut` `MouseEvent` is very similar to the `mouseOut` `MouseEvent`, but makes coding rollout behaviors much easier for instances of the `DisplayObjectContainer` class that have children. When the mouse leaves the area of a display object or the area of any of its children to go to an object that is not one of its children, the `InteractiveObject` dispatches the `rollOut` event. The `mouseOut` event, in contrast, is thrown each time the mouse leaves the area of any child object of the display object container, even if you're still over another child object of the `DisplayObjectContainer`. Internally, this works by having `rollOut` events dispatched farther and farther up the parent chain of the object, starting with the object and ending with the highest parent that is neither the root nor an ancestor of the `relatedObject`.

MouseEvent.ROLL_OVER

Very similar to the `rollOut` is the `rollOver`. The `rollOver` event makes rollover behaviors easier. When the mouse enters the area of a display object or the area of any of its children, the `InteractiveObject` dispatches the `rollOver` event. The `mouseOver` event, in contrast, is thrown each time the mouse enters the area of any child object of the display object container, even if you're still over another child object of the `DisplayObjectContainer`.

FocusEvent.MOUSE_FOCUS_CHANGE

Now, there is one event pertaining to `MouseEvents` that is *not* a `MouseEvent` yet has a lot to do with the mouse and fits nicely here, and that is the `mouseFocusChange` event. This is actually a type of `FocusEvent` that is dispatched when the user changes focus with a mouse. By default behavior, the event changes the focus and dispatches the corresponding `focusIn` and `focusOut` events. `mouseFocusChange` is dispatched to the object that currently has focus, so as you move out of a `TextField` with the mouse and try to select a different control, this event will be dispatched to the `TextField`. You can prevent the change in focus by calling `preventDefault()` in an event listener. Let's take a look at this quickly:

```
package
{
    import flash.display.Sprite;
    import flash.text.TextField;
    import flash.events.FocusEvent;

    public class FocusChange extends Sprite
    {
        public function FocusChange()
        {
            var tf1:TextField = new TextField();
            tf1.type = "input";
            tf1.height = 20;
            tf1.width = 100;
            tf1.border = true;
```

```
                    addChild(tf1);
                    tf1.addEventListener(FocusEvent.MOUSE_FOCUS_CHANGE, checkFocus);

                    var tf2:TextField = new TextField();
                    tf2.type = "input";
                    tf2.height = 20;
                    tf2.width = 100;
                    tf2.border = true;
                    addChild(tf2);
                    tf2.x = 200;
                }

                private function checkFocus(focusEvent:FocusEvent):void
                {
                    if ((focusEvent.target as TextField).text == "")
                    {
                        focusEvent.preventDefault();
                    }
                }
            }
        }
```

If you run this, you'll see how the first `TextField` doesn't lose focus if there's no text entered in it. We know this isn't a `MouseEvent`, but it's relevant to the `InteractiveObject` and to the mouse and demonstrates `preventDefault()`.

Using MouseEvent in Conjunction with the Mouse

Let's look at an example that changes the pointer that the mouse uses when you roll over certain Sprites. We'll use the `flash.ui.Mouse` class to hide and show the default mouse arrow:

```
package
{
    import flash.display.Sprite;
    import flash.events.MouseEvent;
    import flash.ui.Mouse;
    public class SwitchOutPointer extends Sprite
    {
        private var circleMouse:Sprite;
        private var squareMouse:Sprite;
        private var currentMouse:Sprite;
```

```
private var useSquareField:Sprite;
private var useCircleField:Sprite;

public function SwitchOutPointer()
{
    super();
    useSquareField = new Sprite();
    useSquareField.graphics.beginFill(0xFFFFFF, 1);
    useSquareField.graphics.drawRect(0, 0, 100, 100);
    useSquareField.graphics.endFill();
    useSquareField.name = "square";
    useSquareField.x = 200;
    useCircleField = new Sprite();
    useCircleField.graphics.beginFill(0xFFFFFF, 1);
    useCircleField.graphics.drawRect(0, 0, 100, 100);
    useCircleField.name = "circle";
    useCircleField.graphics.endFill();
    addChild(useCircleField);
    addChild(useSquareField);
    //here I add my event listeners to the respective sprites
    useCircleField.addEventListener(MouseEvent.ROLL_OVER, useCircle);
    useSquareField.addEventListener(MouseEvent.ROLL_OVER, useSquare);
    useCircleField.addEventListener(MouseEvent.ROLL_OUT, showMouse);
    useSquareField.addEventListener(MouseEvent.ROLL_OUT, showMouse);
    //now I'm creating the object that's going to replace
    //my mouse when we're over certain sprites
    circleMouse = new Sprite();
    circleMouse.graphics.beginFill(0x00ff00, 1);
    circleMouse.graphics.drawCircle(0, 0, 5);
    circleMouse.graphics.endFill();
    currentMouse = new Sprite();

    squareMouse = new Sprite();
    squareMouse.graphics.beginFill(0xff0000, 1);
    squareMouse.graphics.drawRect(0, 0, 10, 10);
    squareMouse.graphics.endFill();
    //now I want to listen to ALL mouse movement events
    //so that I can reposition the mouse
    this.stage.addEventListener(MouseEvent.MOUSE_MOVE, moveNewMouse);
}

/* move whatever mouse is the current mouse to the mouse's stage
 * position. note how I offset the position slightly this is because
 * the rollOff event of the useSquareField and useCircleField will be
 * fired if the circleMouse or squareMouse object is in between the
 * mouse and the useSquareField or useCircleField object. */
private function moveNewMouse(mouseEvent:MouseEvent):void
```

```
        {
            currentMouse.x = mouseEvent.stageX + 5;
            currentMouse.y = mouseEvent.stageY + 5;
            mouseEvent.updateAfterEvent();
        }

        private function useSquare(mouseEvent:MouseEvent):void
        {
            Mouse.hide();
            addChild(squareMouse);
            currentMouse = squareMouse;
        }

        private function useCircle(mouseEvent:MouseEvent):void
        {
            Mouse.hide();
            addChild(circleMouse);
            currentMouse = circleMouse;
        }

        /* if we roll off, then go ahead and remove respective icon
         * for the mouse using the target property to figure out which
         * one it was and show the normal mouse icon. */
        private function showMouse(mouseEvent:MouseEvent):void
        {
            if((mouseEvent.target as Sprite) == useSquareField)
            {
                removeChild(squareMouse);
            }
            else {
                removeChild(circleMouse);
            }
            currentMouse = new Sprite();
            Mouse.show();
        }
    }
}
```

KeyboardEvent Basics

What's a KeyboardEvent? It's any time you press on a key, of course. The keyboard event, like the MouseEvent, is dispatched by an object that inherits from InteractiveObject. This object must have focus in order to hear the event, so if you want global KeyboardEvent notification, listen to the Stage; otherwise listen to the InteractiveObject you're interested in.

The `KeyboardEvent` defines a `KeyCode` property that returns the key pressed by the user. There is a similar property, `charCode`, which contains the character code value of the key pressed or released. The character code values are English language keyboard values. For example, if you press Shift+3, `charCode` is # on a Japanese keyboard, just as it is on an English language keyboard.

You use the `keyCode` and `charCode` properties to find out what key was pressed. The `keyCode` property is a number representing a key on the keyboard whereas the `charCode` property is the number representing the key within the current character set, which is, by default, UTF-8. Now, a key code value represents a particular key on the keyboard, so 8 and * are the same while the character value represents a particular character that the computer can read or render, for instance, B and b. The mapping between keys and key codes is device- and operating system–dependent. UTF-8 values. on the other hand, retain their value across operating systems and machines.

Using the `charCode()` method is a real convenience when working with KeyboardEvents. When you want to check for a certain key combination — Ctrl+P for Print, for example — you would need to either look up the different keyboard codes for the letter *p* (not terrible but not the most convenient) or would use the `charCodeAt()` method of a String and the `charCode` property of a KeyboardEvent like so:

```
private function keyListener(keyEvent:KeyboardEvent):void
{

   if(keyEvent.charCode == String("p").charCodeAt(0) &&
keyEvent.ctrlKey)
   {
       trace("Let's get printing, Gutenberg");
   }
}
```

KeyboardEvent Types

The KeyboardEvent comes in two types: KEY_DOWN, dispatched when the user has pressed a key, and KEY_UP, dispatched when the user has released a key. Like the `MouseEvent`, the KeyboardEvent is scoped to the object that is listening for it; therefore, if you want to capture all keypress events you must listen to the stage. If you want to capture key events when only a certain object has focus, listen on that object. Related to the KeyboardEvent is `FocusEvent.KEY_FOCUS_CHANGE`, which is broadcast when the user changes the focus using the keyboard. The two types of the KeyboardEvent are:

- KEY_DOWN or "keyDown": Fired when a key is pressed down. This event occurs before the keyUp event.

- KEY_UP or "keyUp": Fired when a key is released. The KeyboardEvent.KEY_UP event happens after the keyDown event, unless the user doesn't let go of the key, of course.

Both of these events have the following properties:

- `charCode`: Contains the character code value of the key pressed or released.
- `ctrlKey`: true if the Control key is active; `false` if it is inactive.
- `keyCode`: The key code value of the key pressed or released.
- `keyLocation`: The location of the key on the keyboard, used to differentiate between modifier keys included on both sides of a keyboard (such as left shift and right shift).
- `shiftKey`: true if the Shift key is active; `false` if it is inactive.

FocusEvent.KEY_FOCUS_CHANGE

As you saw earlier, there is a keyboard-related event that is not a KeyboardEvent per se, but correlates quite closely to the keyboard and to UI event handling around the keyboard. This is the `keyFocusChange` event. This is dispatched when the user changes focus to a different object using the keyboard. The related object for this event is the `InteractiveObject` instance that receives focus if you do not prevent the default behavior. You can prevent the change in focus by calling the `preventDefault()` method in an event listener that is properly registered with the target object. Flash Player changes the focus and dispatches `focusIn` and `focusOut` events as the default behavior.

Understanding keyCodes

Let's look at a quick example of reading the `keyCode` property of a `KeyboardEvent` and using it to move a Sprite around on the stage. The key codes for the arrow keys are Left 37, Up 38, Right 39, Down 40. Look at the switch/case statement in the event handler and you'll see this put to use:

```
package
{
    import flash.display.Sprite;
    import flash.events.KeyboardEvent;
    public class KeyboardEventExample extends Sprite
    {
        private var sprite:Sprite;

        public function KeyboardEventExample()
        {
            sprite = new Sprite();
            sprite.graphics.beginFill(0xFF0000, 1);
            sprite.graphics.drawRect(0, 0, 20, 20);
            sprite.graphics.endFill();
            addChild(sprite);
```

```
            this.stage.addEventListener(KeyboardEvent.KEY_UP,
moveSprite);
        }

        private function moveSprite(keyEvent:KeyboardEvent):void
        {
            switch (keyEvent.keyCode)
            {
                case 37:
                    sprite.x--;
                    break;
                case 38:
                    sprite.y--;
                    break;
                case 39:
                    sprite.x++
                    break;
                case 40:
                    sprite.y++;
                    break;
                default:
                    break;
            }
        }
    }
}
```

Now keep in mind that because the keyCode is dependent on the system and keyboard being used, this example may work on our Windows machine, but it may not work on other machines (this example does, but others might not).

IMEEvents

What's an IME? A better question would be, "What does a Chinese typewriter look like?" Well, having lived in China for a few years, let me tell you, it looks just like our keyboard, but with a program to map the keys to an editor that will allow the user to pick the correct characters. Flash Player refers to these as Input Method Editors and they exist for non–Roman alphabet languages such as Japanese, Chinese, and Korean. To deal with the IMEEvent, Flash has a special IMEEvent object that is dispatched when the user enters text using an Input Method Editor. This correlates to the flash.system.IME object that helps determine which combination of keys has been pressed in an alternate keyboard system. The primary property of the IMEEvent is the text property, which it inherits from flash.events.TextEvent (we know, we know, yet another non-keyboard or mouse event class). This will return a String in the particular encoding being used at the time that will allow you to process the user's input.

Summary

- MouseEvents are broadcast by the display objects to which they apply, and all subclasses of `InteractiveObject` can dispatch them.

- If you want to listen to MouseEvents independent of particular InteractiveObjects and listen instead to all instances of mouse activity, you can subscribe to the `MouseEvents` broadcast by the stage. This won't work with `rollOut` and `rollOver` because the player loses focus when the stage is rolled off.

- `KeyboardEvents` are broadcast when keys are pressed by the user. They are also broadcast by whatever object currently has focus.

- `IMEEvents` are broadcast by Input Method Editors that users speaking Japanese, Chinese, and Korean frequently use to input characters. They inherit from `flash.events` `.TextEvent` and possess a text property you can use to get the encoded character or ideograph the user has entered.

Chapter 18

Using Timers

The timer is an important and valuable tool used for triggering time-based events in AS3. Nearly any application that involves real-world time will use a timer. Timers can be useful for delaying an action, timing out when an asynchronous action takes too long to execute, triggering an action repeatedly or after a delay, or synchronizing several actions.

If you're familiar with ActionScript 2.0, you've probably used the `setInterval()` function. In ActionScript 3.0, `setInterval()` has been replaced with the `Timer` class. Instead of relying on a single function being fired after a set interval, AS3 timers use the new event framework.

Each instance of a timer will repeatedly fire events spaced out by a set amount of time using the AS3 event framework. Using events rather than callback functions not only makes them more consistent and easy to use, but also allows you to trigger multiple functions with a single timer (or with multiple timers).

Timers are similar in some ways to `for` loops in that both structures can be used to repeat a bit of code several times, but are otherwise quite different. `for` loops attempt to execute every iteration immediately using as much processing power as needed. No other code is executed until the `for` loop is finished. Timers, on the other hand, always space out the execution of their scripts with some type of delay and other code can execute even if a timer is running.

In this chapter, we discuss how to set up your own timers, and we offer a few tricks to help you get the most out of them.

Timer Basics

For working with intervals, we'll be using the `Timer` class found at `flash.utils.Timer`. You must add the line `import flash.utils.Timer;` to your program to use the `Timer` class.

Creating a timer

To create a timer, we'll use the Timer constructor, which takes two arguments:

- `delay`: This is the number of milliseconds between each time the timer event fires.

- `repeatCount`: This is the number of times the timer event will be fired. The default value, zero, will cause the timer to fire indefinitely until the timer is stopped or the program ends.

> **TIP** All variables related to delay or time in ActionScript use milliseconds — that is, thousandths of a second. So, the number 1,000 represents one second. If you are working with values in seconds — for example, 120 seconds — it might be easier to read if you write the numbers as `120 * 1000` instead of `120000`.

Let's go ahead and create a `TimerDemo` program to test out the timer functionality. The following code creates a timer that fires every second and ends after ten iterations:

```
package com.wiley.as3bible {
    import flash.display.Sprite;
    import flash.utils.*;
    import flash.events.*;
    public class TimerDemo extends Sprite {
        public static const TIMER_DELAY:Number = 1 * 1000;
        public var timer:Timer;

        public function TimerDemo() {
            timer = new Timer(TIMER_DELAY, 10);
        }
    }
}
```

If you run this program, you'll notice that the timer doesn't do anything yet. That's because we still need to add event listeners to it.

Listening for timer events

Every time the timer delay elapses, an event is fired from the timer object. These events use the class `TimerEvent`, which is a special type of event used only by timers. There are two different event types in the `TimerEvent` class:

- `TimerEvent.TIMER`: This event type is dispatched every time the timer delay has elapsed. In other words, it's the ticking of the timer's clock.

- `TimerEvent.TIMER_COMPLETE`: This event type is dispatched when the `repeatCount` is reached. In cases where the `repeatCount` is zero, this event is never dispatched at all.

Let's add listeners for both of these events to our `TimerDemo`:

```
package com.wiley.as3bible {
    import flash.display.Sprite;
    import flash.utils.*;
    import flash.events.*;
    public class TimerDemo extends Sprite {
        public static const TIMER_DELAY:Number = 1 * 1000;
        public var timer:Timer;

        public function TimerDemo() {
            timer = new Timer(TIMER_DELAY, 10);
            timer.addEventListener(TimerEvent.TIMER, onTimer);
            timer.addEventListener(TimerEvent.TIMER_COMPLETE, ↵
                onTimerComplete);
        }
        private function onTimer(event:TimerEvent):void {
            trace("Tick.");
        }
        private function onTimerComplete(event:TimerEvent):void {
            trace("Ding!");
        }
    }
}
```

Running this code still doesn't do anything, and that's because we need to start the timer!

Starting, stopping, and resetting the timer

Once your timer is instantiated and your event listeners are added, it's time to start your timer. The `Timer` class offers three methods for controlling the timer:

- `start()` — Starts the timer counting. When the timer is running, the timer's read-only property `running` will be set to `true`.

- `stop()` — Stops the timer counting. When the timer is stopped, the `running` property is set to `false`.

- `reset()` — This resets the number of times the timer has repeated since it was started. The `currentCount` property is set back to zero.

TIP It's easy to forget to start your timer. If you're having trouble, make sure you've called the `start()` method.

Once we add the start() method to our program, things start happening:

```
package com.wiley.as3bible {
    import flash.display.Sprite;
    import flash.utils.*;
    import flash.events.*;
    public class TimerDemo extends Sprite {
        public static const TIMER_DELAY:Number = 1 * 1000;
        public var timer:Timer;

        public function TimerDemo() {
            timer = new Timer(TIMER_DELAY, 10);
            timer.addEventListener(TimerEvent.TIMER, onTimer);
            timer.addEventListener(TimerEvent.TIMER_COMPLETE, ↵
                onTimerComplete);
            timer.start();
        }
        private function onTimer(event:TimerEvent):void {
            trace("Tick.");
        }
        private function onTimerComplete(event:TimerEvent):void {
            trace("Ding!");
        }
    }
}
```

Running this program should show the following output over the course of 10 seconds.

```
Tick.
Tick.
Tick.
Tick.
Tick.
Tick.
Tick.
Tick.
Tick.
Tick.
Ding!
```

Handling the TimerEvent

Now that we've looked at how to set up a timer and listen to the events it dispatches, let's take a look at some practical ways to use these events.

Getting a reference to the timer

As stated earlier, the `Timer` class fires off `TimerEvent` objects. These events are ultimately not much different from the base `Event` class. No additional information is stored within a `TimerEvent` that's not in a regular `Event`. However, the timer object itself can be used within your event handler to access timing information. To get a reference to the timer, just use the event's `target` property and type cast it to a Timer by using `Timer()`.

From this point you can access information about the counting such as the number of times the timer has fired since it was started or the amount of time between each tick:

```
private function onTimer(event:TimerEvent):void {
    var timer:Timer = Timer(event.target);
    var timeElapsed:Number = timer.currentCount * timer.delay;
    var remainingCount:Number=timer.repeatCount- timer.currentCount;
    trace("Time elapsed :", (timeElapsed / 1000), "seconds.");
    if (remainingCount > 0) {
        trace("There are", remainingCount, "ticks remaining.");
    }
}
```

The handler prints out the time elapsed in seconds every time the TIMER event is fired. If used on a timer that fires five times every 500ms, it should look something like this:

```
Time elapsed : 0.5 seconds
There are 4 ticks remaining.
Time elapsed : 1.0 seconds
There are 3 ticks remaining.
Time elapsed : 1.5 seconds
There are 2 ticks remaining.
Time elapsed : 2.0 seconds
There are 1 ticks remaining.
Time elapsed : 2.5 seconds
There are 0 ticks remaining.
```

As you can see, it makes use of three properties of the `Timer` class:

- `timer.currentCount` — This is the number of times that the timer has fired since it was started. If you use the `reset()` command, this number will be reset to 0. This is a read-only property so it can't be changed directly.

- `timer.repeatCount` — This is the number of times the timer event will be fired. The default value, zero, will cause the timer to fire indefinitely until the timer is stopped or the program ends. This is the same value that is defined when you create the timer instance. `repeatCount` is a read/write property so it can be changed on-the-fly.

- `timer.delay` — This is the number of milliseconds between each firing of the timer event. This is the same value that is defined when you create the timer instance. `delay` is a read/write property so it can be changed on-the-fly.

Delaying the execution of a function

Timers make it easy to delay the execution of a function. Simply set up a timer that fires only once and set the delay for the time you'd like to wait before firing. A common application for this is creating a *timeout*, a predetermined time allotted for an action to take place, such as a server response, after which the action is aborted.

We'll now use a timer to create something you're no doubt familiar with from browsing the Internet, a redirect script. First we'll create our Redirect class, which will handle the timer and navigation.

```
package com.wiley.as3bible {
    import flash.net.*;
    import flash.utils.*;
    import flash.events.*;

    public class Redirect {

        private var redirectTimer:Timer;
        private var redirectURL:URLRequest;
        private static const REDIRECT_DELAY:int = 5000;

        public function Redirect(url:String, delay:Number=REDIRECT_DELAY) {
            redirectURL = new URLRequest(url);
            redirectTimer = new Timer(delay, 1);
            redirectTimer.addEventListener(TimerEvent.TIMER,onRedirect);
            redirectTimer.start();
        }

        private function onRedirect(event:Event = null):void {
            navigateToURL(redirectURL, "_self");
        }
    }
}
```

This class takes a URL as a string and redirects the user there after the specified delay. Next we set up a class to test the new redirect class:

```
package {
    import flash.display.Sprite;
    import flash.net.*;
    import flash.text.*;
    import com.wiley.as3bible.Redirect;
    public class RedirectTest extends Sprite {
```

```
        private var redirectURL:String = "http://www.mimswright.com";
        private var redirectDelay:Number = 5 * 1000;
        public function RedirectTest() {
            var redirect:Redirect = new Redirect(redirectURL, redirectDelay);

            var tf:TextField = new TextField();
            tf.autoSize = TextFieldAutoSize.LEFT;
            tf.text = "This page no longer exists. You will be redirected to ↵
" + redirectURL + " after " + redirectDelay/1000 + " seconds.";
            addChild(tf);
        }
    }
}
```

The result should be a page with the redirect message that navigates away after 5 seconds.

Creating a World Clock

Let's try a quick and easy example that makes use of the `Timer` class's ability to send timing events to multiple recipients. We'll create a very simple world clock that shows the time in multiple time zones.

First let's create the clock class. Make a new ActionScript file called `LocalClock.as`:

```
package com.wiley.as3bible{
    import flash.utils.*;
    import flash.events.*;

    public class LocalClock {
        private var location:String;
        private var date:Date;
        private var timezoneOffset:int;
        public function LocalClock(timer:Timer, location:String, ↵
timezoneOffset:int = 0) {
            this.location = location;
            this.timezoneOffset = timezoneOffset;
            timer.addEventListener(TimerEvent.TIMER, onTimer);
        }

        private function onTimer(event:TimerEvent = null):void {
            date = new Date();
            date.setUTCHours(date.getUTCHours()+timezoneOffset);
```

```
                    updateDisplay();
        }

        private function updateDisplay():void {
            trace(location, "-", date.getUTCHours() + ":" + ↵
                date.getUTCMinutes() + ":" + date.getUTCSeconds());
        }
    }
}
```

Each clock is set up with a timer object as a seed, which triggers a tick every second. The location and time zone offset are saved and used to create the readout. Each time the TIMER event fires, the date is updated and the time zone offset is applied. Then the local time is displayed in the trace window.

Now we'll create a class to run the world clocks. You can edit the time zone code to show whatever cities are most useful for you. Notice that all three clocks are able to use the same timing seed.

```
package {
    import flash.display.*;
    import flash.utils.*;
    import com.wiley.as3bible.*;

    public class WorldClockTest extends Sprite {
        private var timer:Timer;
        private var nyc:LocalClock, paris:LocalClock, tokyo:LocalClock;

        public function WorldClockTest() {
            timer = new Timer (1000);

            nyc = new LocalClock(timer, "New York City, USA", -5);
            paris = new LocalClock(timer, "Paris, France", 1);
            tokyo = new LocalClock(timer, "Tokyo, Japan", 10);

            timer.start();
            trace("Start world clock");
        }
    }
}
```

Running this as an application should give you a time readout similar to this one:

```
New York City, USA - 21:32:57
Paris, France - 3:32:57
Tokyo, Japan - 12:32:57
```

Bonus

If you're feeling extra ambitious, try creating a display object to show the readout for the clocks. You can make a digital clock using the `TextField` class or, for a real challenge, try an analog clock.

Legacy Timer Functions

For the sake of backwards-compatibility, the older AS2 interval functions have been included in the `flash.utils` package; however, we recommend that you use the `Timer` class instead. It may take a little time to get used to it, but we think you'll find it to be much more useful than these functions.

The following functions are replaced by the `Timer` class:

- `setInterval()`
- `setTimeout()`
- `clearInterval()`
- `clearTimeout()`

Because these functions are deprecated, we won't discuss them here. However, they can be found in the ActionScript 3.0 help files (`http://livedocs.adobe.com/flex/2/langref/flash/utils/package-detail.html`).

Using getTimer()

The `flash.utils` package also contains `getTimer()`. This is another legacy function (and incidentally, has nothing to do with the `Timer` class) that returns the number of milliseconds that have elapsed since the program was initialized. `getTimer()` can be a useful tool when you simply need to measure the duration of an action, such as an external XML file loading, without dealing with the overhead of the `Timer` class.

To find an elapsed time, you can store one value from `getTimer()` as your starting time and subtract it from another time when the action is finished:

```
var startTime:Number = getTimer();
// Do some action that might take a while
var endTime:Number = getTimer();
var elapsedTime:Number = endTime - startTime;
```

Notice that a new time is returned every time you use `getTimer()`.

Summary

- The Timer class is a much needed improvement over the setInterval() methods of AS2. Using the AS3 event framework makes the timer more versatile and consistent.

- Timers are useful for a number of things including delaying a function, repeating a function, and synchronizing several functions.

- Timers have a delay time and a repeat count. Setting the repeat count to zero causes them to continue firing indefinitely.

- Event handlers can be added as listeners to a timer. The events fired are TIMER and TIMER_COMPLETE. Both are of type TimerEvent.

- The timer can be accessed by the listener by using the target property of the TimerEvent.

Part V

Working with Error Handling

Chapter 19

Understanding Errors

Despite our best intentions and wishes, programs sometimes fail. In Chapter 5, you learned about ways that the compiler can catch your typos and invalid requests: syntax errors and type mismatches. These are kinds of compile-time errors. But there are countless kinds of errors that can happen while your program is running, which may be the result of a logical error in your code, or just the result of unexpected circumstances out of your control. Whichever is the case, ActionScript 3.0 gives you the opportunity to handle these errors at runtime. This chapter gives you the tools to understand runtime errors and keep them from affecting the end user.

IN THIS CHAPTER

Understanding failure states

Using exceptions

Handling asynchronous errors

Comparing Ways to Fail

If a certain function fails, there are a few ways for it to signal this failure. Some functions return a value that indicates it did not complete successfully. Code that uses this function must then check to make sure all went as planned before continuing. There are a few problems with this approach.

First, returning a Boolean signifying if the function call was successful is not always possible. What if the function is already supposed to return a value? If you are returning a complex object, setting the value of this returned object to `null` is one option. If you are returning an `int`, you must decide on a reserved number to signify failure, such as `-1`. But these values might actually be valid responses, and this also means that different functions might return different values for a failure state. Checking for failure becomes more and more complex this way.

The increasing complexity of checking return values of these functions is another good reason to avoid this approach. If you have to wrap every function call in an `if` statement to check its results, your code starts becoming very ugly, and unnecessarily complex.

So, most programmers respond to this dilemma by skipping these checks, assuming that when things go wrong, they can insert the checks only where really necessary. In fact, it's sometimes not obvious that the function is supposed to return a particular value if it fails. It's not entirely the programmer's fault for being negligent here: It's very difficult to keep track of every single possible failure point.

The ultimate result of this kind of error reporting is a problem that might be familiar to you. Say you have a sequence of operations: You call a function, assign the returned value to some variable, use that variable in a different context, pass it around, and do some more things to it. Eventually, way down the line, something truly fatal happens. When you finally catch it, you have no way to know that the problem is that seven steps ago, a function returned `null`, which was automatically converted to `false`, or an empty string, or the number 0, and the program went on assuming this was the intended value. It becomes your job to painstakingly tease out what went wrong and where.

That's why this kind of error reporting is known as *failing silently*. Unless you put in those checks yourself, the program will keep on truckin', attempting to use your failure value as a real value, as long as it's nonfatal. And when everything fails silently, everything is nonfatal, so you really don't find out what went wrong until much later. As a general strategy, you should make your code, like code in the Flash Player API, very noisy. Be alarmist! Run in circles, scream and shout! In code, as in life, the sooner you become aware of a potential problem, the easier it is to fix it.

We should draw a distinction between ActionScript language features and application design. Returning `null` and using exceptions are two ways to signal and handle errors. These are part of ActionScript's error handling capabilities. Knowing what to do when a runtime error occurs is part of an error handling *strategy*, and is part of your application design. In this chapter, we cover low-level error handling, and once you have this as a foundation, you learn how to employ these practices in an error-handling strategy in Chapter 21.

Understanding Exceptions

Exceptions are another way to signal, transmit information about, and capture errors at runtime. They are a language feature made explicitly for this purpose, so they won't interfere with your code's normal activities: They don't prevent you from returning certain values or limit anything your code can do.

Exceptions are both ordinary and extraordinary. Exceptions are objects that exist in the virtual machine and can be manipulated like any other object. But when you use exceptions, you also alter the control flow of your program.

Because exceptions are objects, you can consider them nouns. To understand them better, let's examine what verbs you can apply to them. You might say that exceptions are like baseballs. You can throw them and catch them, but if nobody catches them you're out. You can *throw* an exception, and you can *catch* an exception. There are also *uncaught* exceptions, which are unarguably a bad thing.

Throwing exceptions

Errors at runtime are represented by exceptions; throwing an exception is the way in which you signal an error. Confusingly, there is no `Exception` class. Rather, all exceptions are represented by instances of `Error` or its subclasses. Further, there is special syntax for throwing an exception. You are performing a verb and have a noun, so you might expect this to look like the following:

```
var myException:Error = new Error();
myException.throw();
```

But we have the actor here wrong. Really, the exception represents the error, and the virtual machine handles propagating it; the exception is passive, much like an event object. The syntax for throwing an exception is:

```
throw new Error("oh noes!! i already eated the cookie", 512);
```

You can use two lines, as in the first snippet, to create and then throw the exception, but using one line as in the preceding code is more common. As shown in the preceding code, `Error` objects are allowed to carry a human-friendly message describing what went wrong in more detail, and a more computer-friendly error code that you can use in your error handling strategy. In addition, the type of the exception encodes information about what went wrong. There are several subclasses of `Error`, and you can define your own. Both of the exception's descriptors, the `message` and the `id`, are optional. In this snippet, an exception is thrown without any description, but its type communicates some information:

```
throw new ArgumentError();
```

> **NOTE** The implementation of exceptions in ActionScript 3.0 is very similar to that in Java, but methods that throw errors do not explicitly say so in the method signature as they do in Java.

Catching exceptions

When you're handling errors with exceptions, you can handle errors and do whatever is necessary to recover, by catching the appropriate exception. There's more to catching exceptions than a single-line catch method, however. Handling exceptions involves surrounding the dangerous code in a special kind of construct. This construct has at least two parts: first, the code that might generate exceptions, and next, one or more blocks to handle certain kinds of exceptions; and optionally a block to run whether there were exceptions or not.

These three units make up a `try/catch/finally` block, or simply a `try/catch` block. One of the benefits of exceptions is the way in which exceptions can break out of the normal flow of a program. When an expression results in a thrown exception, everything stops, and the virtual machine starts looking for an appropriate `catch` block to handle the exception. This is in stark contrast to handling errors by returning `null`, in which case the code will keep executing, making it more likely to lose track of where the error occurred. This also enables you to write code that otherwise assumes that everything went well, confident that the lines after an error will not be executed.

You encapsulate potentially exception-generating code and the instructions that depend on it in its own `try` block. Everything that does not depend on the potentially error-prone operation, and has no chance of failure, can go outside the block. Everything that might cause an error, and the code that depends on an error not happening, goes inside the block. Here's an example of a `try` block, but note that it is not complete (it won't even compile) without the `catch` block, which we cover next:

```
var foo:Array = [1, 2, 3];
try
{
    var a:int = potentiallyUnsafeOperation(foo[0]);
    a += 10;
    trace(a);
}
//TODO: catch goes here
var b:int = 1 << 10;
```

Before and after the `try` block, we do operations completely unrelated to the potentially unsafe function, which might throw an exception. Inside the `try` block, however, we include everything that depends on that function executing properly: anything that uses its return value a. If `potentiallyUnsafeOperation()` threw an exception, it would never store the return value into a because the exception would have interrupted execution.

We use `try` blocks not just to contain an error, but also to define where it should be handled. Each `try` block must go with one or more `catch` blocks. If the exception is generated in a `try` block and handled in a subsequent `catch` block, execution can resume after the block is over. Thus, the exception is generated and handled, and then the program keeps going. *Voilà!* Furthermore, with multiple `catch` blocks, you can handle multiple types of errors differently within a single `try/catch` block, allowing your `try` block to contain a whole series of actions, each action depending on the success of the one before it, even if they all throw different kinds of errors.

Let's add a `catch` block to the preceding snippet:

```
var foo:Array = [1, 2, 3];
try
{
  var a:int = potentiallyUnsafeOperation(foo[0]);
  a += 10;
  trace(a);
} catch (error:Error) {
  trace("An error occurred", error.message);
}
var b:int = 1 << 10;
```

If the potentially unsafe function call ends up throwing an exception, flow proceeds immediately to the `catch` block. There, the system traces out an error message, including the message defined in the `Error` object. Finally, execution continues with the first line outside the block, assigning 1024 to b.

The exception flow

When you throw an exception, it follows a well-defined flow, much like events do. Exceptions bubble up through the call stack until they find themselves in a `try` block. For each one of these, the exception compares its type to the types of the errors the associated `catch` blocks are looking for, top to bottom. If no `catch` block catches that type of exception, it continues its way up the call stack. If it reaches the top of the call stack without being caught, it becomes an uncaught exception.

This means that not only do you have a choice of where to catch exceptions, but that choice makes a difference in how your program behaves. Take, for example, this class, which computes ten square roots of whole numbers between –50 and 50.

```
package
{
    import flash.display.Sprite;

    public class ExceptionTester extends Sprite
    {
        public function ExceptionTester()
        {
            try
            {
                for (var i:int = 0; i < 10; i++)
                {
                    var n:Number = Math.round(Math.random() * 100 - 50);
                    trace(squareRoot(n));
                }
            } catch (err:ArgumentError) {
                trace("ERROR: " + err.message);
            }
        }

        protected function squareRoot(n:Number):Number
        {
            if (n < 0)
            {
                throw new ArgumentError("squareRoot() does not ↵
support imaginary numbers.");
            }
            return Math.sqrt(n);
        }
    }
}
```

The squareRoot() method checks its input and considers an attempt to calculate the square root of a negative number an error. Checking your inputs for validity is one important part of an overall error-handling strategy. The virtual machine and compiler can ensure your arguments are of the right type, but sometimes your preconditions must be more specific. In this case, the best the type system can do is ensure that a Number is passed to squareRoot(), but it can't verify that the number is positive with types alone. An ArgumentError is an Error subclass designated for exceptions relating to arguments passed to a method.

In any case, this version of the example will terminate the loop the first time a negative number is chosen. You might receive only three square roots before an error message, or seven, or none, depending on your luck. This says that the entire loop is predicated on all of the iterations finishing successfully.

However, you can change this behavior by simply moving the try block. By putting the try block inside the loop body, the program will always print out ten results or errors rather than quitting after the first error. The flow of control in your program is affected by exception handling, and changes in your exceptions can change the outcome of your program.

The catch blocks specify what kind of error is being handled. Because all exceptions are either an instance of Error or a subclass thereof, catching an Error type will handle *any* kind of exception. You can use this in the same way you would use default in a switch statement. This example shows an error being handled further up the call stack, and with multi-tiered catch blocks:

```
package
{
    import flash.display.Sprite;

    public class CatchBlocksExample extends Sprite
    {
        public function CatchBlocksExample()
        {
            try
            {
                var n:int = sumSomeNumbers();
                trace(n);
            } catch (e:UnrelatedError) {
                trace("something unrelated happened.");
            } catch (e:DispleasingNumberError) {
                trace("somewhere, a number is displeasing.");
            } catch (e:Error) {
                trace("something bad happened");
            }
        }

        protected function sumSomeNumbers():int
        {
            var sum:int = 0;
```

```
        for (var i:int = 0; i < 10; i++)
        {
            sum += someNumber();
        }
        return sum;
    }

    protected function someNumber():int
    {
        var n:int = Math.round(Math.random() * 10);
        if (n < 2)
        {
            throw new PatheticallySmallNumberError();
        }
        return n;
    }
  }
}
class DispleasingNumberError extends Error {}
class PatheticallySmallNumberError extends DispleasingNumberError {}
class UnrelatedError extends Error {}
```

With any luck, this example will eventually throw a `PatheticallySmallNumberError` as it is
displeased with encountering the number 0 or 1. This exception originates in `someNumber()`, goes
unhandled to the code which called it in `sumSomeNumbers()`, which again is not in a `try` block,
and finally goes up to where the call originated, when the constructor `CatchBlocksExample()`
called `sumSomeNumbers()`. This is inside a `try` block, so the exception compares itself with the
handled exception types in the associated `catch` blocks in order. Because it's comparing an object
to classes to see if it is an instance of that class or its subclasses, you can think of this comparison
as using the `is` operator. The `PatheticallySmallNumberError` is not an `UnrelatedError`,
but it is a `DispleasingNumberError`, so the second `catch` block will handle it, and "somewhere, a number is displeasing" is traced out. If neither of these `catch` blocks had caught the
exception, again, the third would have, as all exceptions are `Error`s.

Uncaught exceptions

When an exception is thrown without being caught anywhere, it is an *uncaught exception*. All of
your chances to intercept and handle it, by definition, have passed, and it is up to Flash Player
to decide what to do with the error. Different versions of Flash Player treat uncaught exceptions
differently.

If you're developing applications, you are probably running SWF files in the debug version of
Flash Player. When an uncaught exception occurs in the debug version of Flash Player, execution
halts and you are presented with a dialog box giving you information about the error, as shown in
Figure 19-1.

FIGURE 19-1

An uncaught exception using the Debug Flash Player

Even better, if you are running a SWF compiled for debugging, and you have connected to a debugger using either Flash CS3 Professional or Flex Builder 2, instead of the dialog box you will enter an interactive debugging mode. Debugging applications this way is covered in greater detail in Chapter 20. Suffice to say, this gives you an excellent way to identify bugs immediately, and at their source.

If you are running the production or release distribution of Flash Player, unhandled exceptions are silent. No dialog box is displayed, the currently executing code is immediately terminated, and the next frame is rendered, at which point further code might be triggered. This means that if you should somehow let a bug slip into your program unhandled, and that program is deployed, the end users will not see a glaring "Error" dialog box as you do. The program might not work correctly, but that's not nearly as worrisome as a giant error dialog box. When this happens to you — and it will — explain this to your boss, customer, or client, tell them everything is going to be all right, and go fix that bug.

finally

Finally, we come to `finally`. The optional `finally` clause can appear after the `catch` blocks, and code inside it will execute after the `try` block successfully completes or after the relevant `catch` block finishes. If the `try` block depends on certain objects that need to be set up and created, use the `finally` block to break them down and clean them up. They should be properly disposed of whether you had an error or not.

Most of the examples that necessitate a `finally` block involve creating a file handle or stream object, trying to read from it, and then closing it whether there was an error or not, because these kinds of objects need you to explicitly clean up after them. However, most of these accesses are asynchronous in ActionScript 3.0, and `try/catch/finally` helps you catch synchronous errors only.

```
package
{
    import flash.display.Sprite;
    import flash.errors.IOError;
    import flash.net.Socket;

    public class FinallyExample extends Sprite
```

```
    {
        public function FinallyExample()
        {
            try
            {
                var s:Socket = new Socket();
                s.connect("http://www.cmu.edu/", 80);
                //TODO: add asynchronous error handling;
                //see Handling Asynchronous Errors below.
            } catch(error:IOError) {
                trace("I/O Error:", error.message);
            } catch(error:SecurityError) {
                trace("Security Error:", error.message);
            } finally {
                s.close();
            }
        }
    }
}
```

This is a good example of an object that needs to be cleaned up after, and thus a good use of `finally`. However, even this is not entirely realistic because you'd usually do many (asynchronous) accesses on the socket before closing it, so you wouldn't have the opportunity to wrap the entire session in a single block.

Rethrowing exceptions

If the baseball analogy holds true, then you can also pass the ball: catch it and throw it on to another teammate. If you catch an exception and determine, by examining the id of the Error, perhaps, that a higher authority needs to handle the exception, you can re-throw the same Error object that was passed to you in the first place. This puts the exception back in the flow up the call stack, as you can see in the following code:

```
try
{
    try
    {
        throw new Error();
    } catch (error:Error) {
        trace("inner handler");
        throw error;
    }
} catch (error:Error) {
    trace("outer handler");
}
//inner handler
//outer handler
```

Catching Errors Generated by Flash

In ActionScript 3.0, many of the built-in methods throw exceptions to signal errors. This is a god-send because it helps you track down bugs immediately as they surface: If you don't handle them you will be alerted via the uncaught exception handler (the error dialog box or debugger).

You can catch these errors in the same way you catch any other exception. Wrap the potentially error-causing code and any dependent code in a `try` block, and create `catch` blocks for the kinds of errors that may arise.

A common time to generate errors is when downcasting objects. If you try to convert a type to an incompatible type using an explicit cast, a `TypeError` exception is thrown:

```
var object:Object = "Definitely Not a Display Object";
try
{
    var displayObject:DisplayObject = DisplayObject(object);
} catch (error:TypeError) {
    trace("Incompatible cast!");
    displayObject = new Sprite();
}
addChild(displayObject);
```

In this case, an incompatible cast would recover by creating a new, empty `Sprite` to add into the display list. This way, the code can continue executing.

To find out what kinds of exceptions a certain method can throw, look up its definition in the ActionScript 3.0 Language Reference, and look for the "Throws" header. The documentation includes all exceptions that each method can throw, and descriptions of the errors. An exhaustive list would be difficult to reproduce here and of little use. However, it is useful to enumerate some of the most common types of exceptions. You can find this in Table 19-1.

TABLE 19-1

Built-in Exception Types

Exception Type	Description	Potential Cause & Notes
Error	Base exception type.	Custom errors without custom subclasses. Not abstract, can be used for actual errors.
EvalError	Errors in eval().	Any call to eval(), which is provided for ECMAScript compatibility, but not implemented.

Exception Type	Description	Potential Cause & Notes
RangeError	A number is out of the valid range.	Converting numeric types, getting display object children at invalid indices, creating `Array`s of invalid sizes, writing bytes as characters when they are not in the range of acceptable characters, and so on.
ReferenceError	Attempt to access an undefined property of an object.	Looking up a property that doesn't exist on a sealed class.
SyntaxError	Code is not syntactically valid.	Usually compiler catches syntax errors, but they can arise with invalid `RegExps`.
TypeError	Mismatched types.	The type of an argument is incompatible with the expected type, as a parameter to a function, operator, assignment, and so on.
URIError	Malformed URI.	You will never get this. Theoretically for incredibly invalid Unicode characters in URIs.
ArgumentError	Error with arguments passed to a function.	Common in methods with variable argument lists or flexibly typed arguments such as `Object` or `*`. Occurs when function does its own validation manually.
SecurityError	Violation of Flash Player's security policy.	When access is denied to a URL, server, or system hardware, either by the security sandbox or the user.
VerifyError	Malformed SWF encountered.	Attempting to load a corrupt SWF into the program.
flash.error.EOFError	Attempted to read beyond the end of the stream/file.	When reading more bytes than are available from a `URLStream`, `ByteArray`, or `Socket`.
flash.error.IllegalOperationError	A method call exists but is not supported.	Calling certain `DisplayObjectContainer` methods on stage, `FileReference` methods called in the wrong order, `Accessibility` methods are called when the SWF is not compiled with accessibility support, and so on
flash.error.IOError	Error reading or writing to a resource.	Can happen to any network access, as networks are inherently unreliable.

continued

TABLE 19-1 *(continued)*

Exception Type	Description	Potential Cause & Notes
`flash.error.MemoryError`	Memory was requested that cannot be provided.	Requesting more memory than can be addressed. More common on embedded devices where addresses might be shorter. When more memory is requested than is available, a different Error (#1000) is thrown.
`flash.error.ScriptTimeoutError`	Code executes beyond a set duration before completing and allowing Flash Player to draw the next frame.	The script timeout duration can be written into the SWF. By default, it is 15 seconds. Can be caught only once; otherwise it is an uncatchable error.
`flash.error.StackOverflowError`	The execution stack exceeds its maximum depth.	A recursive function is probably not reaching the intended end conditions and recurses infinitely.

Custom Exceptions

Because `catch` blocks depend on the type of the exception object to match and handle exceptions, you should use the appropriate kind of `Error` object for each error. For some errors that you might encounter in your own code, the built-in `Error` classes are appropriate, such as throwing `ArgumentErrors` and `RangeErrors` when arguments are invalid or out of range.

You should use custom `Error` subclasses when you are throwing errors specific to your program that you are going to handle. As you have already seen in this chapter, this is as simple as creating an otherwise empty subclass of the `Error` class. Additionally, you can create more specific exceptions by further extending `Error` subclasses. This hierarchy can be used to `catch` with more specificity.

Handling Asynchronous Errors

Not all errors occur immediately, just as not all functions can return a result immediately. In ActionScript 3.0 there are many functions that perform their task asynchronously, reporting back their result by firing an event. Unfortunately, as exceptions are tied into the control flow, they cannot handle asynchronous operations that result in failure.

Instead, asynchronous operations signal failure using the same method as they return a valid result: by broadcasting an event. These error events are broadcast and subscribed to in exactly the same way as any other event. For a review of events, please reference Chapter 16.

Because asynchronous errors are just events, they are not subject to the exception flow. You must subscribe to the error events of asynchronous methods if you wish to handle them. An uncaught asynchronous error event gets the same treatment in the debug Flash Player as an uncaught exception: an alarming dialog box. However, because these errors are asynchronous, the debug player won't break into the debugger to show you where your error is; the error is where you forgot to add a handler for the error event.

To see what asynchronous errors are dispatched by built-in methods, check the ActionScript 3.0 Language Reference for that method and look under the Events header. Asynchronous error events typically have names ending in ErrorEvent, such as IOErrorEvent:

```
package
{
    import flash.display.Sprite;
    import flash.net.Socket;
    import flash.events.Event;
    import flash.events.IOErrorEvent;

    public class AsynchronousErrorExample extends Sprite
    {
        protected var sock:Socket;

        public function AsynchronousErrorExample()
        {
            super();
            sock = new Socket();
            sock.addEventListener(Event.CONNECT, onSocketOpen);
            sock.addEventListener(IOErrorEvent.IO_ERROR, onIOError);
            sock.connect("www.cmu.edu", 80);
        }

        protected function onSocketOpen(event:Event):void
        {
            trace("Connected succesfully!");
            sock.close();
        }

        protected function onIOError(event:IOErrorEvent):void
        {
            trace(event.text);
            //Error #2031: Socket Error. URL: www.cmu.edu
            sock.close();
        }
    }
}
```

391

This example attempts to connect to a web server, an asynchronous operation. Failure is signaled by broadcasting the IOErrorEvent.IO_ERROR event, which is captured and handled by onIOError().

Summary

- Returning a special value to represent errors is an approach with severe limitations.
- Exceptions are a better way to report and handle errors.
- Exception objects represent an error.
- Exceptions can be thrown, caught, re-thrown, or uncaught.
- Exceptions interrupt the flow of control of your program.
- Exceptions travel up through the call stack, until they find themselves in a try block, and match the first catch block which handles exceptions of the same type.
- Error is the base class for exceptions and the catch-all type for catch blocks.
- The type of exceptions denotes the kind of error, and its id and message transmit more information.
- Uncaught exceptions will be caught in the debugger, display an error dialog box in the debug Flash Player, or stop all frame scripts in the release Flash Player.
- You can create your own Error subtypes to use as custom exceptions.
- Flash Player defines many built-in types of exceptions.
- Asynchronous errors are just events.

Chapter 20

Using the AVM2 Debugger

Every builder needs the right tools for the job, and with ActionScript 3.0 comes a much improved tool for correcting problems, an interactive debugger. With effective use of the debugger, you can locate and correct problems in your code intelligently, without hunting or head-scratching.

Introducing Debugging

An interactive debugger performs lots of different jobs. The net effect is that you can run your program in a controlled environment and interactively follow its execution. Without a debugger, executing code is like running an experiment with tiny particles: Because you can't see them, you have to rely on secondary or tertiary effects of your experiment to determine what's really going on. You must carefully craft situations in which you can measure the outcome and attempt to support your theory with the data. When you have a debugger, it's like having a powerful microscope: You can see everything in perfect detail and there is no mystery to your code.

When you compile your ActionScript 3.0 program, it turns into a series of very simple instructions called bytecodes that are interpreted by the ActionScript Virtual Machine 2, or AVM2. When you run the program in Flash Player, it's those bytecodes that are being interpreted: The system doesn't know or care what you originally wrote in AS3 code. But when you are using a debugger, you can watch the program being run by the AVM2 as if the virtual machine were running your original code and not the bytecodes. You wrote the code, and the bugs are in your code, so you get to see your code. The debugger helps you visualize your code in action.

Running your program in the debugger is like stepping in as the director and cameraman for a dress rehearsal of your program. You have the script — the source code — in your hand. But now, you can call the shots. You can start and stop the production. You can stop at a specific scene, or a specific line, and have your actors read the scene line by line. You can automatically cut the production when a catastrophe occurs. And you have a camera that lets you focus in on any actor. You can always find where the production is in the script, and you can always find out how it got there. Using your powers as director, you can interactively run through your production and work out the kinks in the script.

You'll see how this metaphor applies as you learn about the features of the debugger in ActionScript 3.0.

Launching the Debugger

The first thing you need to do to debug your program is to get the debugger running. Different products that use ActionScript 3.0 have different options for debugging, which we cover in this section. At a minimum, to start a debugging session, you need three things:

- A SWF compiled specifically for debugging
- The debugger version of Flash Player
- A version of the AVM2 debugger

These requirements mean that you can debug programs in a variety of situations. You can debug a program running inside your browser from a remote web site, for instance, as long as your browser is running the debugger version of Flash Player, the remote SWF has been compiled for debugging, and you are running a debugger locally.

> **TIP** It's possible to have different versions of the Flash Player installed in different browsers, as well as to have a different version of the standalone SWF player. If you are having trouble starting a debugging session, double-check the installed version of Flash Player in the environment you are attempting to debug the SWF in.

When you're developing an application on your computer and you run into a problem, you can usually run a debugging session locally, and if you're using Flash CS3 Professional or Flex Builder 2, you can do this with one click or keystroke. So while there are a multitude of ways you can set up a debugging session, for most purposes it's a very simple affair.

Each development environment for ActionScript 3.0 has its own debugger. If you are building your applications in Flash CS3 Professional, you will use the AVM2 debugger in Flash. If you are using Flex Builder 2, you will use the Flex Debugging perspective in Flex Builder. If you are using the Flex 2 SDK, you can use the command line Flash Player Debugger, fdb. To get started, let's take a look at how to launch a debugging session in Flash CS3 and Flex Builder 2.

Starting and stopping the Flash CS3 debugger

You can start debugging a project in Flash by choosing Debug Movie from the Debug menu, as shown in Figure 20-1, or by pressing Cmd+Shift+Return or Control+Shift+Enter.

FIGURE 20-1

Starting a debugging session in Flash CS3 Professional

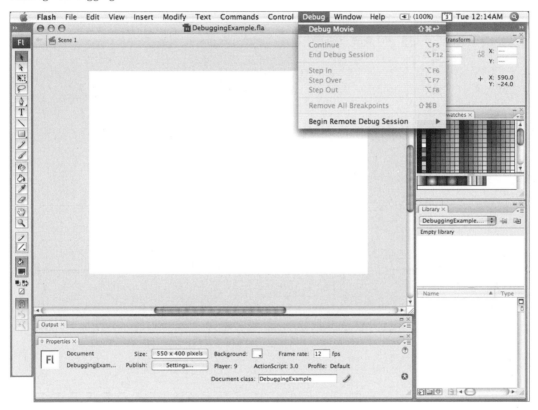

Doing this will compile your application with debugging information, launch the SWF in the debugger version of the Standalone Flash Player, and open panels associated with debugging. You should be able to see and use the following panels: Debug Console, Variables, and Output. If any of these fail to appear, you can re-enable them by finding them in the Window ⇨ Debug Panels menu. It may help you to organize the panels so that you can see all of them, as shown in Figure 20-2.

FIGURE 20-2

Debugging in Flash CS3 Professional

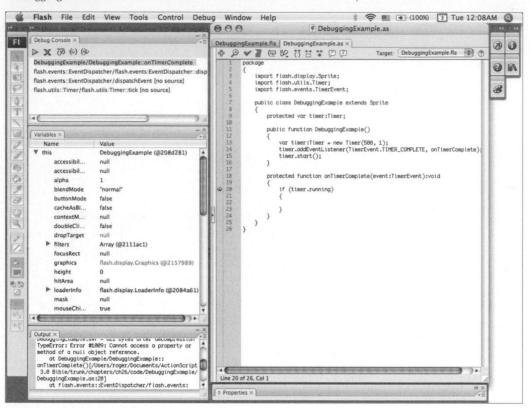

To stop a debugging session in Flash, select End Debug Session, either as the red X button in the Debug Console, or under the Debug menu.

Starting and stopping the Flex Builder 2 debugger

You can debug a project in Flex Builder 2 by choosing Debug [*name of the application*] in the Run menu, by clicking the debug button (a green bug icon in the toolbar), by setting up a custom debug configuration (choose Debug ➪ Other), or by pressing an associated keyboard command. Depending on your project's configuration, your project will launch in either a browser or a stand-alone Flash Player. If you want to debug in-browser, it's important to make sure that your browser has a debugging version of the Flash Player plug-in installed.

Once the debugging session starts, you may automatically be taken into the Flex Debugging perspective. If not, click the Flex Debugging button in the perspective bar (by default in the upper-right toolbar). In Figure 20-3, a debugging session is about to be initiated in Flex Builder 2.

FIGURE 20-3

Starting the debugger in Flex Builder 2

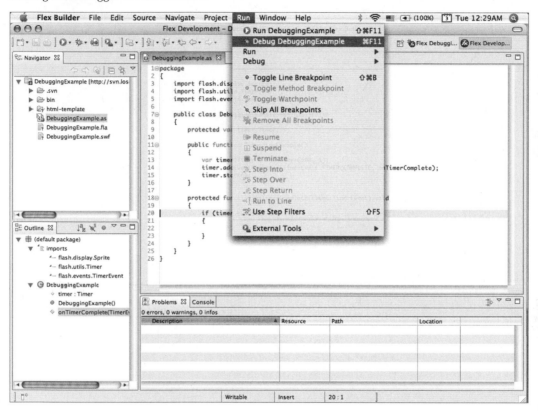

In the Flex Debugging perspective, you should be presented with a few views: Debug, Variables, Console, Breakpoints, and Expressions. The Debug view is analogous to Flash's Debug Console, the Variables view to Flash's Variables panel, and the Console view to Flash's Output panel. If these views are not visible, you can enable them in the Window menu. Figure 20-4 shows the Flex Debugging perspective in action.

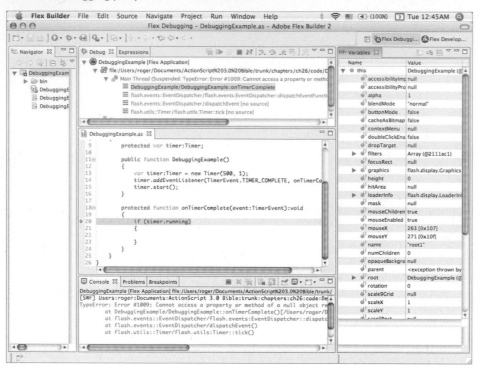

FIGURE 20-4

The Flex Debugging perspective in Flex Builder 2

To stop a debugging session in Flex Builder 2, select Terminate in the Run menu or on the Debug view's toolbar (the red square icon). You can also disconnect the debugger from the Flash Player without terminating it by selecting Disconnect in the Debug view's toolbar.

Debuggers compared

The Flex Builder 2 debugger is, while essentially the same debugger as the Flash debugger, easier to use and has a few additional useful features such as temporarily toggling all breakpoints. If you have the choice, you might find it easier to debug your programs using the Flex 2 debugger.

Throughout the rest of this chapter, we use the Flash CS3 Professional debugger to illustrate debugging concepts. The interactive debuggers, even the command-line debugger `fdb`, are all operated in the same manner and support the same kind of actions.

CAUTION While the debugger is running, either Flash Player or the browser remains in suspended animation, so it may appear to be an unresponsive program to the system. Instead of forcibly terminating the player or your browser, terminate the debugging session first.

If you are debugging in a browser and you need to use the browser normally while debugging, use a browser that can run windows in separate processes, or debug in a different browser than you use for browsing.

Taking Control of Execution

When you start a debugging session, you compile a SWF, launch it in a debugger version of the Flash Player, and connect a debugger to it. While you're all set to debug now, nothing might happen. By default, the program runs normally. As the director, you need an opportunity to step in and yell "cut!" before you can start working on a particular bug. This is called breaking the program (break as in "taking a break" more than "Honey, I broke all the good china"), or halting execution. There are three ways to transfer control between normal execution and interactive debugging.

Stopping at an uncaught exception

If your debugging session started properly, when things go catastrophically wrong, you will be handed the director's bullhorn and have an opportunity to step in. Uncaught exceptions, which without a debugger connected might pop up a dialog box, will now automatically break the execution of the program right where the error occurs. Figure 20-2 shows a program halted because of an uncaught exception.

Halting everything when an uncaught exception occurs allows you to get to the bottom of the cause of the error immediately, so with little effort, you can fix runtime errors as quickly as they crop up. The combination of an API that utilizes exceptions fully and a debugging environment that halts automatically on uncaught exceptions is great for finding and solving small bugs before they become big bugs.

In the remainder of this chapter, we look at how to use the tools the debugger gives you. For now let's take a sneak peek and see how you can use the debugger to resolve an uncaught exception. In Figure 20-2, we see the debugger immediately after an uncaught exception halted execution. The source code of this program follows:

```
package
{
    import flash.display.Sprite;
    import flash.utils.Timer;
    import flash.events.TimerEvent;

    public class DebuggingExample extends Sprite
    {
        protected var timer:Timer;

        public function DebuggingExample()
        {
            var timer:Timer = new Timer(500, 1);
```

```
                timer.addEventListener(TimerEvent.TIMER_COMPLETE, onTimerComplete);
                timer.start();
        }

        protected function onTimerComplete(event:TimerEvent):void
        {
            if (timer.running)
            {
            }
        }
    }
}
```

The arrow in the source editor in Figure 20-2 points to where the program was halted: This is where the exception must have originated. This line is displayed in bold in the preceding listing. The Output panel gives you the kind of error that occurred: "Cannot access a property or method of a null object reference." We can put these two bits of information together: We tried to access a property or method of `null`, and it happened on a line where we check `timer.running`. At this point you might suspect that the timer reference is `null`, and you would be correct. In Pulling Back the Curtain, you'll see how to use the Variables panel to verify this hunch.

This runtime error, raised when you try to access a child of a null reference, is a reminder for the programmer. You're likely to see this error when you assumed that an object existed in the variable you're accessing, but for some reason there is none. In some cases, `null` is a valid value for the variable, in which case your error was assuming the value was not `null`. In other cases, it points to a logical error you made elsewhere. Here, we fully expect `timer` to exist — after all, it's created in the constructor. The debugger alerted us to a scoping error: When we set `timer` in the constructor, it was to a local `timer` variable, which shadowed the `timer` instance variable. By simply removing the local variable in the constructor, we can fix our error:

```
//var timer:Timer = new Timer(500, 1); //original line with error
timer = new Timer(500, 1); //corrected line
```

Stopping at a breakpoint

An essential technique for interactive debugging is setting breakpoints. A breakpoint is, literally, a point in the code at which normal execution will break and you can debug. In the stage rehearsal analogy, setting a breakpoint is like telling the actors that when they get to a certain point in the script, you're going to start directing them. You don't necessarily have to choose a line where an error occurs, either. You can set the breakpoint a few lines earlier so you can get some context, or you can set a breakpoint just to make sure a piece of code is behaving as you expect it to. Breakpoints are the gateways between normal execution and debugging.

To set a breakpoint in an ActionScript file in Flash, just click once on the left gutter (the gray vertical bar to the left of the line numbers) of the line you wish to stop at. The breakpoint will appear as a red octagon, like a stop sign. To toggle it off, just click it again. You may also use Debug ⇨ Toggle

Breakpoint or its associated keystroke. To clear all breakpoints at once, Flash provides Debug ⇨ Remove Breakpoints in This File and Debug ⇨ Remove Breakpoints in All AS Files.

To set a breakpoint in Flex Builder, double-click the gutter of the line you wish to break at. The breakpoint will appear as a blue circle. To toggle it off, double-click the blue circle and it will disappear. You may also use the menu item Run ⇨ Toggle Line Breakpoint or its associated key command. You can manage breakpoints in Flex Builder with the Breakpoints view. This allows you to see all the breakpoints in one spot, selectively remove or disable them, and clear all of them at once.

> **TIP** You may not set a breakpoint at a line where there is no executable code. You might also decide to break up a long expression into multiple lines so that you can set a breakpoint somewhere in the middle.

When you start a debugging session with breakpoints set, the program will execute normally without interaction until it reaches a breakpoint. In Figure 20-5, a breakpoint has been set on line 33. A debugging session was then started. Because the line that the breakpoint is on is triggered by a click on the button, the program will execute normally, showing a button, until you click it. At that time, the program is halted and the debugging windows come to the front. Figure 20-5 shows the Flash CS3 Professional debugger right after the button was clicked.

FIGURE 20-5

The debugger becoming active at a breakpoint

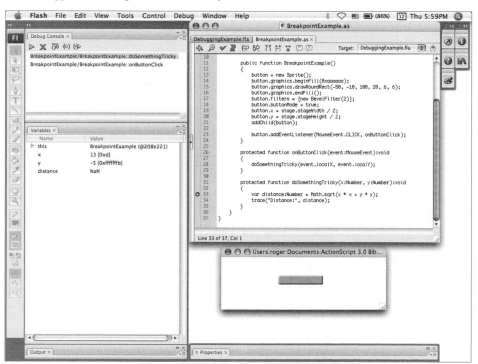

Breakpoints are great for when a program misbehaves in a way that doesn't throw errors. If you are getting unexpected results and you have an idea where they might be originating, you can break there, investigate, and confirm your suspicion.

Stopping on demand

Finally, you can halt execution manually, like just grabbing the bullhorn and yelling "cut!" This method of gaining control over debugging is more difficult to control, but it can be used to catch infrequent bugs that don't throw exceptions and manifest themselves in a way you can see. When you halt the program manually, it's rarely in a useful place, like the beginning of a frame or a timer tick. But you can take the opportunity to set new breakpoints and then continue normal execution until they are hit.

In Flex Builder, you can stop execution at the next line of source code to be run by selecting Suspend from the Run menu or the Debug view. In fdb, when the program is running normally, press Return and confirm the prompt to break normal execution at the next line of ActionScript.

In Flash CS3 Professional, there is no way to force execution to halt immediately. However, in all three debuggers, you can add a breakpoint while the program is running, which you can exploit in much the same way to break the program when you see something you want to investigate further.

All in all, this method of halting execution is not as useful as setting breakpoints, and often is used as a means to set breakpoints.

Pulling Back the Curtain

You can gain a complete understanding of your program by tightly controlling its execution, and by examining the state at any step. This section teaches you how to see inside Flash Player, and the next one covers how to control execution.

Using the Variables panel in Flash, the Variables view in Flex Builder, and the `print` or `p` command in fdb, you can examine the value of any variable in scope at the current line.

ActionScript developers may be used to adding `trace` statements to find out the value of a variable. Logging is still available and a possible debugging technique, but examining the variables interactively while execution is halted enables you to spot things you weren't looking for, gives you feedback instantly, and lets you investigate whatever you want without adding code or recompiling.

> **TIP** Logging a value can be more effective than inspecting variables in certain cases. Remember to always use the tool that is best suited to the task! When you have to see what range of values a variable can take, or you want to collect a large sample of possible values, it's better not to have to stop execution for every measurement. In these cases, logging the values and analyzing the results afterward may be a better technique.

Interpreting the Variables panel

The Variables panel is a tree view in two columns. The left column shows the name of the variable or property, and the right column shows its value. Because types are maintained at runtime, the debugger can format these appropriately: `Strings` will appear in quotes, `ints` will appear as numbers and optionally with a hexadecimal interpretation, and `Booleans` appear as `true` or `false`. Complex types and `Arrays` and `Objects` that are non-null display their type and their location in memory, and you can expand them to see, in turn, their properties.

In Figure 20-5, the Variables panel is visible. The code being executed is shown in the figure and listed here:

```
package
{
    import flash.display.*;
    import flash.filters.BevelFilter;
    import flash.events.MouseEvent;

    public class BreakpointExample extends Sprite
    {
        protected var button:Sprite;

        public function BreakpointExample()
        {
            button = new Sprite();
            button.graphics.beginFill(0xaaaaaa);
            button.graphics.drawRoundRect(-50, -10, 100, 20, 6, 6);
            button.graphics.endFill();
            button.filters = [new BevelFilter(2)];
            button.buttonMode = true;
            button.x = stage.stageWidth / 2;
            button.y = stage.stageHeight / 2;
            addChild(button);

            button.addEventListener(MouseEvent.CLICK, onButtonClick);
        }

        protected function onButtonClick(event:MouseEvent):void
        {
            doSomethingTricky(event.localX, event.localY);
        }

        protected function doSomethingTricky(x:Number, y:Number):void
        {
            var distance:Number = Math.sqrt(x * x + y * y);
            trace("Distance:", distance);
        }
    }
}
```

The debugger is halted at a breakpoint set at the line presented in bold in the preceding code. The panel in Figure 20-5 displays all variables in scope. This includes local variables bound to the arguments of a method, such as x and y; local variables created with var, such as distance; and instance variables of the class the code is executing in the scope of — in other words, everything under this. If you were to expand the view of this, you would find the instance variable button, but also all the properties of a Sprite such as scaleX and visible, because the example extends Sprite.

The variables in scope depend on where in the code you're looking, and they represent the variables' state at the very moment in time you are looking at. The line that your program is about to run is marked with an arrow, which in Figure 20-5 is superimposed over the breakpoint symbol because the program is halted exactly at the breakpoint. You can see that the variable distance is NaN, the default value for unassigned Numbers. That's because the current line calculates distance, and it has not run yet. You can see the values of x and y, and you can see that this is a BreakpointExample, so you know this code is executing in the scope of a BreakpointExample.

You can configure the Variables panel to show all the fields of a class, including its private instance variables, implicit getter functions and derived properties, constants, and static variables, by changing the options of the Variables panel.

Flex Builder Variables panel and watches

The Variables view in Flex Builder has some convenient options not present in the Flash debugger. Flex Builder gives you more temporal feedback on variables: When variables change or are assigned new values, they flash red momentarily. The Flex Builder Variables view enables you to see the currently selected variable in a detail pane, which uses text wrapping so you can see long strings, XML, and other verbose variables in detail.

In addition, Flex Builder's Flex Debugging perspective adds an Expressions view to the Variables view. This is similar to the Variables view, but it lets you watch just the values you are looking for, and it lets you construct simple expressions that are evaluated at the current line in the debugger. This is handy for keeping an eye on certain values, or watching for a specific situation that you can write an expression to test for. You add and remove watch expressions from this view manually.

TIP   Often, expressions you write can be evaluated only in a certain scope. Outside this scope, your watch expression will display in red as <errors during evaluation>. Don't let this stop you from creating the watch expressions that will help you in a particular scope.

In the command line debugger fdb, you can add and remove watch expressions with the display and undisplay commands.

Navigating Through Code

With an interactive debugger, you can drive the execution of your program. Once you break normal execution of the code, you can take over, moving and jumping ahead in your program (unfortunately, you can't jump back).

Continue

You can resume normal execution of a suspended program by continuing. You will give up debugging control over the program until execution is again halted by another breakpoint or uncaught exception.

You can use a combination of continue and breakpoints to jump a long distance forward in your program. When execution is halted, you can set a new breakpoint, and then click Continue to jump right to it, provided Flash Player doesn't hit another breakpoint or uncaught exception first.

You can continue a suspended program in Flash CS3 Professional by choosing Debug ➪ Continue, or by clicking the green right-facing triangle button in the Debug Console panel.

In Flex Builder 2, the command is called Resume, and it is found in Run ➪ Resume or as a yellow bar and green triangle button, reminiscent of the Frame Advance button on a VCR, in the Debug view.

In fdb, type **c** or **continue** to continue a suspended program.

Continue can be very useful if you have a breakpoint set on a function triggered multiple times or by user interaction, and you are interested in it only in certain cases. When the program breaks and you don't have anything to debug in this particular case, you can click Continue and wait for the code to be invoked again.

> **TIP** If you are using Flex Builder's Debugging perspective, as an alternative to setting a breakpoint and continuing multiple times when it's not relevant, you can set a breakpoint and toggle whether it is active or not using the Breakpoints view. This way, you can keep your breakpoints set, but ignore them until you're ready to trigger the case you want to debug. An inactive breakpoint will not break the program when it is reached.

The call stack

As the ActionScript virtual machine executes your code, it has to shift gears all the time. Every time you call a function, the AVM must remember what it was doing, what the scope was, what all the local variables were immediately before the function call. With this information secured away, it can start with a clean slate in the new function, which may be running in a different scope (as a bound method) and with a new set of local variables. Similarly, once it reaches a return statement, it must grab that return value, go back to whatever it was doing before, with all the scope and local variables restored, use the returned value as the evaluation of the function call, and continue executing.

Every time the AVM enters a function, it adds a new stack frame onto the call stack. This frame represents the new environment: the scope, the local variables, and the location in the code. The new stack frame is added on the top of previous frames, which provide a trail of crumbs back to where the outermost method was invoked. When the function returns, that executing frame is complete, and it pops off the top of the stack. Finally, the AVM returns to the calling function and its stack frame, which is the new top of the stack. Therefore, the top of the stack always represents the currently executing environment.

In the following example, if you create a new A, the stack will build up as the constructor for A calls the constructor for B, and the constructor for B calls the method c(). As each function returns, however, it returns control to the line that called that function, and so on until the end of the constructor of A is reached, and the work of making a new A is over.

```
class A
{
    var b:B;
    public function A()
    {
        //1. call stack is A::A
        b = new B();
        //6. call stack is A::A. Now return and stack is empty.
    }
}
class B
{
    public function B()
    {
        //2. call stack is B::B, A::A
        c();
        //5. call stack is B::B, A::A
    }
    protected function c():void
    {
        //3. call stack is B::c, B::B, A::A
        return;
        //4. start going back up
    }
}
```

The call stack gives context to the code that's being executed. When you view the contents of the call stack, you're looking at a *stack trace*. While you might be looking at a line somewhere in a class, that line is executing as the result of a chain reaction of method calls, which the stack trace is documentation for.

The Debug Console panel in Flash CS3 Professional and the Debug view in Flex Builder 2 both give you an interactive view of the call stack. You can use it as a stack trace, to see why the current line of code is being run. In Figure 20-5, you can see that the current method is doSomethingTricky() because it is at the top of the call stack, and it was called by the entry below it, onButtonClick().

In fdb, use `bt` to print a *backtrace*, another term for a stack trace.

The call stack in the graphical debuggers is interactive: If you click a stack frame below the current one (which is, again, always on top), the code view, current line, and variables view will refresh to show you the state of the suspended stack frame. You can see the code that called the method you're currently debugging, and the state of the scope and locals in that frame when it invoked the function.

Step into

You can move a line forward in your program with ease. When you do this repeatedly, you are *stepping through* your code. In general, a step takes you forward one line of the program. But even this definition has some ambiguity, and there are three kinds of steps you can take to step forward. Step Into takes you to the next line of code to execute, drilling into any calls the current line might make.

For example, if this line of code were up next:

```
→      var name:String = getName();
       name = "Mr. " + name;
```

Step Into would transport you to the first line of the `getName()` function, rather than to the line that adds "Mr."

Step Into drills its way into accessor functions, even if they are implicit. So when you see an innocuous assignment such as the following:

```
       color = child.color;
```

you may end up stepping first into the implicit getter function for `color` (on `child`) and then into the implicit setter function for `color` on `this`. A single line like this, when executing, can end up jumping to many different parts of a program before finishing. Step Into will follow every line that the ActionScript Virtual Machine executes without sparing you any details.

CAUTION While stepping into, the AVM2 debugger will not enter any Flash Player API calls. These are part of the Flash Player software itself and not written in ActionScript, nor do their internals become part of your program. The debugger steps through lines of code that are compiled into your program from ActionScript or SWCs. However, the Flex 2 framework is written in ActionScript, and the AVM2 debugger *will* attempt to step into the framework's internals if you step into a Flex 2 API call.

Stepping through code while inspecting variables gives you a perfect view of how your program actually works (or fails to work). It is the ultimate in virtual machine voyeurism.

Step over

Step Into might provide you with more excruciating detail than you need. If you find yourself impatiently clicking Step Into over and over, you should either jump ahead to another breakpoint, or use Step Over. Step Over lets you jump to the next line in the current scope, if it exists, jumping over any function calls that exist in the current line. These calls are performed and completed, but you don't have to see them step by step; just as when you continue until the next breakpoint, all code in between is executed normally.

Use Step Over when you're interested in the behavior of a certain block of code or algorithm, and want to track it without shifting perspective into other stack frames. Step Over may be the most useful kind of step.

Step out/return

Step Out (in the Flash CS3 Professional debugger) and Step Return (in Flex Builder's Debugging perspective) are used to jump out of the current stack frame. They execute everything in the current function until the function returns, and leave you at the previous stack frame, where the function was called from.

Step Out is useful for when you accidentally step in to a function, or when, in looking at code in the debugger, you develop a suspicion that the problem lies in a calling function rather than the current one. You can somewhat preview a step out operation by examining the stack frame that you would return to by actually stepping out, but that won't do anything to actually move the current line or step forward in the execution of the code.

Debugging a Simple Example

In this example, we tried to make a rocket ship point toward your mouse cursor. But we left in an error that we can use the debugger to help find. First, the code:

```
package
{
    import flash.display.*;
    import flash.events.Event;
    import flash.geom.Point;

    public class RocketshipExample extends Sprite
    {
        protected var ship:MovieClip;

        public function RocketshipExample()
        {
            ship = getChildByName("rocketshipMovieClip") as MovieClip;
            addEventListener(Event.ENTER_FRAME, onEnterFrame);
        }

        protected function onEnterFrame(event:Event):void
        {
            var p:Point = new Point(stage.mouseX, stage.mouseY);
            p.subtract(ship.localToGlobal(new Point()));
            var rad:Number = Math.atan2(p.y, p.x);
```

```
        ship.rotation = rad * 180 / Math.PI;
      }
    }
  }
```

This class was set as the document class of a new Flash file. We drew a rocket ship, made it a movie clip symbol with the registration point at the center, and set its instance name on the stage to `rocketshipMovieClip`.

On every frame, the class changes the `rotation` of the `ship` so that its nose points toward the mouse cursor. It does this by constructing a vector that points from the center of the ship (the `MovieClip`'s registration point) to the current position of the mouse. Then it takes the arctangent of this vector to get its angle, and assigns that rotation to the ship, converting from radians to degrees along the way.

Or, that's the way it should work. But when you run this, the spaceship only seems to point between right and down (0 to 90 degrees). There's something wrong, but no errors are thrown, so it's up to us to figure out where the error is. The angle that's produced is incorrect, so we know that the error must be somewhere in the lines that produce that angle (lines 19–22, as shown in Figure 20-6).

FIGURE 20-6

Debugging the rocket ship example

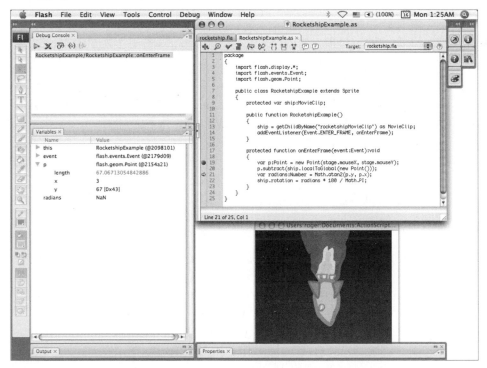

We'll figure out what is going wrong with the angle calculation by looking at the variables involved. We set a breakpoint at the beginning of the calculation, line 19. When we start debugging, the program immediately breaks before we can see what's going on. This might be a good opportunity to add a breakpoint at runtime, so you can try removing the breakpoint, seeing how the rocket ship reacts to the mouse, and adding the breakpoint during the debug session when you're ready to dive in. Because code runs every frame, adding a breakpoint inside onEnterFrame while the program is running will suspend execution on the very next frame.

The first two lines create a Point object that defines the vector between the rocket ship and the mouse, or, to think of it another way, the location of the mouse with the origin placed at the center of the ship. First, the point p is set to the absolute position of the mouse. To see this assignment, you can step into or step over after the breakpoint. This executes the line we were at (the breakpoint, line 19). In the Variables panel, p turns from null into a flash.geom.Point. We use the Variables panel to examine the contents of this object by clicking the disclosure triangle (plus/minus box on Windows). The Point contains properties x, y, and length. In Figure 20-6, you can see that p.x is 3 and p.y is 67.

The next line shifts that point so that it's relative to the position of the rocket ship rather than absolute. It gets a new Point, which is initialized to (0, 0), and converts that location on the rocket ship to a global location. By converting the origin of the rocket ship to the global coordinate space, we find the absolute location of the ship. Then, that location is subtracted from the position of the mouse to find the position of the mouse relative to the ship. Again, we step in or step over to execute the line. Note that because the inner function calls in this line are calls to the Flash Player API, Step Into does not drill into them. After you execute this line, keeping your eye on the Variables panel, you should notice that the properties of p don't change. This means that either the rocket ship is at the origin of the global coordinate space — because subtracting (0, 0) wouldn't do anything) — or that there is an error in this line. If you want to eliminate the possibility of the first case, you can stop debugging to create an intermediate variable that you can then monitor, as discussed in the next section. However, if you check that line more carefully with the knowledge that p doesn't change, you should be able to realize the error in this code.

Calling subtract() on p doesn't change the value of p. Why? Because Point.subtract() is a non-destructive method. It returns the result of the subtraction, rather than performing it on this. Mixing up destructive methods with non-destructive methods is a common programming slip-up, especially when the method name doesn't hint at whether it is destructive or not.

To fix the example, you simply change line 20 to read:

```
p = p.subtract(ship.localToGlobal(new Point()));
```

Interactive debugging is an investigative science. You have to use the tools in the debugger together to collect facts or run tests that confirm or disprove hypotheses. The most important tool in debugging is your brain. The debugger doesn't debug your programs — you do.

Using the Debugger Effectively

We've covered all of the basic techniques you can employ to debug programs in ActionScript 3.0. As you use the debugger, you can develop your own combinations of techniques that help you figure out different kinds of problems. Here are a few techniques that can help you get started.

When you encounter an uncaught exception, the call stack is especially useful in figuring out why it happened. In these cases, you have no control over where the program breaks, so rather than go back in time, which you can't do, you can go up the call stack, examining the Variables view in previous stack frames to, at a minimum, build up a case that can replicate the error, or at best, determine the problem off the bat.

You should use the Variables panel or Variables view liberally to not just see what variables are at a certain line, but to watch them as the code executes. However, you can also use it to assign new values to variables at runtime. You can use this to see how your program will deal with invalid input or exceptional cases, and you can use it to instigate rare errors manually, if you know what situation leads to that kind of error.

When you have complex expressions that you can't step into, you might consider — at least temporarily — splitting the expression up into intermediate variables. This way, you can debug the expression piece by piece when you could not otherwise. For example, you might break up

```
return (Math.sqrt(x * x + y * y));
```

into

```
var x2:Number = x * x;
var y2:Number = y * y;
var sum:Number = x2 + y2;
var ret:Number = Math.sqrt(sum);
return ret;
```

This way, you can use the Variables panel to examine all the constituents of the expression one by one.

A similar technique is to use the Variables panel to try out several different options for evaluating an expression if things aren't working right one way. Again, create several local variables and some temporary code that assigns the options to them. You can then set a breakpoint after they're evaluated and check them out in the Variables panel. This is a lot better than tracing out their values because you can dig into their references if they are complex objects.

At the top of a function, you might notice that all the local variables are already populated in the Variables view, but with unassigned values (null for objects, NaN for Numbers, and so on), even if you don't declare these local variables until later. This is because the ActionScript 3.0 compiler uses variable hoisting: All the declarations for local variables are moved to the top of the function even if they don't get an assignment until later. It should not affect your program.

You can use Continue as a kind of code stepping for loops. Set a breakpoint at the first line of the body of a loop, and click Continue to step to the next iteration of the loop body.

With an interactive debugger, some techniques for utilizing it, and a forensic approach, you should be able to fix bugs in your code quickly, effectively, and without resorting to trial-and-error.

Summary

- The AVM2 debugger is an interactive tool that helps you fix problems in your program.
- There is a version of the AVM2 debugger for each product that uses ActionScript 3.0.
- The debugger must be launched with a SWF compiled for debugging, and using a debugger version of Flash Player.
- Flash CS3 Professional and Flex Builder 2 let you launch debugging sessions in one click.
- The program executes normally until the debugger takes over.
- The debugger can take over at an uncaught exception or a breakpoint.
- You can use the debugger to examine, and even change, properties of any variable in scope.
- You can follow any reference in the debugger to reach nested or associated objects.
- You can watch the variables change as you move through the program.
- The call stack allows you to see what called the current code.
- The call stack enables you to switch perspective through all the lines that called methods to get to the current line.
- You can examine local variables at other depths of the call stack.
- You can move through the program with Step Into, Step Over, Step Out/Return, and Continue.
- The debugger is a set of tools, but the real debugger is you. Set up experiments and test cases that can help you get to the bottom of a bug.

Chapter 21

Making Your Application Fault-Tolerant

IN THIS CHAPTER

Handling errors

Logging

Giving feedback to users

Y ou can call it many things: fault-tolerant, bulletproof, robust. However you describe it, an application that doesn't shatter when things go wrong is a joy to use. These kinds of applications behave well not through luck or coding practices, but because an extensive error handling strategy was devised and applied. This chapter introduces the kinds of errors that can occur and general strategies for handling them.

Developing a Strategy

Why does your application need an error handling strategy? Despite the best efforts of the smartest people, things will always, always, *always* go wrong. If you do nothing to recover from errors, your program can appear to malfunction to the end user. In Chapter 19, you learned that uncaught exceptions in the release versions of the Flash Player will terminate all code executing on the frame. While this might not sound so bad — at least the program keeps going on the next frame, right? — terminating all code for a frame can be disastrous, skipping vital code and leaving the internals of your program in an invalid state. Imagine if one day, without warning, you were transported forward in time a full year. You would find your taxes have not been paid; you haven't showed up to work; and you haven't answered your spouse's calls. Things would probably not be so great for you. Just like life, most programs have to finish things up in an expected way before moving forward so you can't rely on the default behavior of uncaught exceptions.

Handling failures is not as simple a topic as it might seem. Especially for large applications, it's important that you develop (and even document) a strategy for handling failures. In order to do this, you need to determine what kinds of failures you should handle, how you should handle them, and what kind of information to collect and display about them.

Determining What Errors to Handle

Catching exceptions is only the beginning of an error handling strategy. Any kind of input that you are expecting from outside your program, especially from the Internet or a user, should be validated. You should be prepared for any request from a network to fail, including both multimedia content and server requests. Not only could the resource you are looking for have been moved, but it's possible that the server hosting it is down or unavailable, or the user's computer's connection is terminated or disrupted.

If your project has a server-side component, code on the server might fail. When this happens, the request might complete successfully from a networking perspective, but the result might not be a valid response. For example, you might make a request expecting an XML file to be served in response, but receive an error from the web server or the script's interpreter. If you go to `http://example.com/doSomething.php?make=measammich` and expect something like:

```
<?xml version="1.0"?>
<response>
    <banhmi/>
</response>
```

there may be a chance that an error in the server code will result in a response that isn't valid XML:

```
<b>Notice</b>:  ARGGH i died! in
<b>c:\apache\www\tmp\dosomething.php</b> on line <b>1</b>
```

You should always ensure that server-side failures are communicated to your program in a way that you can capture that information. You need to be able to determine that an error happened on the server side, and you have to prevent your program from interpreting the error message as it would normal data.

Even if you include measures that validate security concerns, it's possible that your requests might still fail if the user specifically denies them. You should handle denied requests, even when they should be accepted by default. For example, requests to store information locally with a `SharedObject` (see Chapter 24) or capture audio from the user's microphone (see Chapter 28) may require permission from the user. Users can also use software or their browser preferences to deny storing cookies or opening popup windows.

It's not possible to list every thing your particular program should handle, but here is a partial list:

- Loading XML/text
- Strings/XML not formatted as you expect
- Loading images/video/sound/SWFs

- Events coming from unexpected targets
- Functions that return error codes or null
- Functions that raise exceptions
- Server-side errors
- Timeouts in network requests
- Security sandbox violations

In addition, keep your eyes open to the kinds of errors you get when developing your program. An error that occurs to you once in a freak accident can point you to a weakness in your error-handling strategy.

Categorizing Failures

After identifying the kinds of errors that might occur in your program, you can determine how to react to them. For each potential error, there might be steps you can take to alleviate the problem. For some errors, however, there may be no way to recover. In determining how to handle an error, you must first decide if it is possible to recover from it. These kinds of decisions affect how the application works for the end user, and they should be made with the end user's experience in mind.

For example, if an image fails to load, you can draw a "broken image" icon or placeholder image in its place. But think about how it will make your program behave. In some cases, drawing a placeholder image might not be appropriate, for example if the image is a CAPTCHA image. CAPTCHA images are simple queries that theoretically prove that there is a human user interacting with the computer, by requiring some trivial task that is difficult for a computer, typically recognizing a distorted word, as demonstrated in Figure 21-1. If this image fails to load, showing a replacement image won't be an acceptable solution, as Figure 21-2 makes evident. This example illustrates the need to react to errors based on the user's experience. A good strategy in one case can be unacceptable in another case.

FIGURE 21-1

A program using a CAPTCHA image

Enter the code shown: w58z

A program using an error-handling strategy for images that fail to load

Enter the code shown: w58z

There's no way to list every possible response to an error. However, your intent should depend on the severity of the failure. If the error is nonfatal, your intent should be to return the program to a state in which everything else can continue normally. If the error is fatal, your intent should be to try again, or gracefully terminate the program.

Returning the program to a normal state can be difficult, especially if other areas of the program depend on something that failed. You must also ensure that even if a runtime error disrupts the flow of control of your application, you can resume and perform necessary cleanup code. In other words, make sure you utilize the `catch` and `finally` blocks when handling runtime errors.

In addition to your primary goal of returning the program to normalcy, there are two actions that are useful to any error handling strategy: logging errors and reporting failures to the user.

Logging Errors

Why should you log errors? When developing an application, these logs can be vital to your own development and bug-fixing process. Once the application is deployed, the logs can help you collect and fix bugs that appear in the wild. For instance, if the person who paid for the software you developed has some problem with it on his or her computer at home, the hope is that you will still be able to investigate the causes of that failure.

Logging, although it technically doesn't help you handle an error once the error occurs, is an essential part of any long-term error handling strategy. Without logging, you won't be able to tell the difference between a program that is handling lots of faults correctly and a program that is having no trouble at all. Error logs help you start identifying problems without using a debugger, and they let your program complain about errors without completely breaking.

Logging can be tricky because there are many different ways to get information out of a running SWF. Your approach can greatly depend on how your program is deployed, as well. Therefore, the implementation details of different logging methods are beyond the scope of this book. Some different ways you can log information, in brief, are:

- **Using `trace()` output:** This method can be viewed only if you have the debugging version of Flash Player, and have it configured correctly for logging. This approach takes no effort to write code for, but can be complicated to set up properly, especially if you need to capture logs from a SWF running in a browser. Mark Walters explains how in his post at `www.digitalflipbook.com/archives/2005/07/trace_from_the.php`.

- **To a separate application through sockets or a** `LocalConnection`**:** This approach doesn't require special setup of the Flash Player, but does require an external application to capture the logs. Several third-party products provide the external log viewer and the framework to log to it. One popular external logger is SOS, which you can find at `http://sos.powerflasher.de/english/english.html`.

- **To the browser or enclosing web page using JavaScript:** One example of this is logging to FireBug, a debugging extension to the Firefox browser. This approach requires that specific browser and extension, but it is very easy to set up. One implementation of this idea is hosted at `http://foobr.co.uk/2007/02/debug_flash_with_firebug/`.

- **To a file, if the program is running on the desktop with Adobe AIR:** One approach is described at `www.partlyhuman.com/blog/roger/logging-to-a-file-in-apollo`.

- **To a server:** You should be very careful of both network overhead and privacy concerns if you choose this method. You should let the user know exactly what is being transferred, and avoid logging personal or sensitive information at any cost.

In all of these cases, you should log information that will help you debug problems if they arise. A message in the log that says "Something went wrong!" is useless. Log a description of what went wrong, and where. The following snippet shows very specific messages depending on the kind of error that happened:

```
public function displayText():void
{
    try {
        var tf:TextField = TextField(getChildAt(0));
        tf.htmlText = "Hello World!";
    } catch (error:RangeError) {
        Console.log("displayText(): No display child found at position 0!");
    } catch (error:TypeError) {
        Console.log("displayText(): The display child at position 0 is not a ↵
TextField!");
    }
}
```

All of the preceding logging methods require you to write slightly different code, so in place of `Console.log()` you might see `trace()` or `Log.getLogger().log()`, or something entirely different. The concept is always the same, however: Get a message out of the program in a semi-hidden way.

Along with a message, it is typical to log the severity of the error. Table 21-1 explains the canonical error severities.

TABLE 21-1

Error Severities

Severity	Meaning
info	Not an error, just information. You should remove most of these before deploying your program for general use.
warn	A warning. Something is atypical and might cause an error later, or an easily recoverable error was handled.
error	Some kind of error. Should be recoverable.
fatal	An error that can't be recovered from. The program must terminate.

A severity is sent along with a logging message in some way similar to this:

```
Log.getLogger("com.wiley.as3bible.Shell").fatal("Can't load main SWF!");
```

ActionScript 3.0 doesn't specify how logging should work, or the syntax for logging errors. However, if you are using Flex, it has a good logging framework that you should employ. The preceding example shows the syntax used in the Flex 2 logging framework. The class name com.wiley.as3bible.Shell is used here as a logging category to help us identify where the error came from.

Whichever way you choose to log errors, having a record of those errors will benefit you.

Messaging the User

An important component of handling errors, both ones that can be recovered from, and especially fatal ones, is messaging the user. In some cases, this can be implied, such as using a "broken image" icon. In other cases you can reuse a general error dialog, like the one shown in Figure 21-3, to communicate explicitly.

FIGURE 21-3

A reusable message dialog box

If you are doing something that might take a while, you should definitely warn the user. For example, if a server call fails to return, you could wait a moment and try it again. If this is going to take more than a second or two, it might be good to let the user know that there is some network trouble.

If the server fails outright when the user requests some action, the expectation that the request was fulfilled is not just your program's but the user's as well. You should let the user know if a request she initiated was not completed normally. For example, if she presses the Save button, but the server can't save the file, you should be a pal and tell her that her document wasn't actually saved. Otherwise, she might close your program, lose her changes, and probably be very unhappy when she finds out much later what happened.

Of course, you want to limit the amount of feedback you give users, as well. We all know how irritating it can be to be assaulted with dozens of confirmation dialog boxes that you don't care about. If the user doesn't need to know that you recovered from an error successfully, just log it.

In the case of a completely fatal error, the best thing you can do is inform the user and, depending on who the audience is, consider providing an explanation as well. We've all had the experience of staring at a stalled, or blank, or messed-up screen, wondering if we should just keep waiting, or give up and reboot. Not knowing makes the experience even more harrowing. Although you should do everything in your power to avoid the situation in the first place, making a complete failure into an elegant, apologetic event can parlay a user's frustration into some measure of appreciation.

Degrading Styles: An Example

The following example shows a text field that tries to display a message with some styling. Because the style isn't as important as the message, failing to load the style sheet isn't treated as fatal. In all failure cases, a bare-bones style, which is compiled into the program, is used. Additionally, a timer stops the stylesheet from loading if it takes more than 2 seconds.

```
package
{
    import com.partlyhuman.debug.Console;

    import flash.display.Sprite;
    import flash.events.*;
    import flash.net.URLLoader;
    import flash.net.URLRequest;
    import flash.text.StyleSheet;
    import flash.text.TextField;
    import flash.utils.Timer;

    public class DegradingStyles extends Sprite
    {
        protected const STYLESHEET_LOCATION:String =
            "http://localhost/tmp/style.css";
```

```
protected const BASIC_STYLE:String = ↵
    "a {text-decoration: underline; color: #0000ff}";
protected const TIMEOUT:int = 2000;

protected var timer:Timer;
protected var loader:URLLoader;
protected var tf:TextField;

public function DegradingStyles()
{
    makeTextField();
    loadStyleSheet();
}

protected function makeTextField():void
{
    tf = new TextField();
    tf.width = stage.stageWidth;
    tf.height = stage.stageHeight;
    tf.multiline = true;
    tf.wordWrap = true;
    addChild(tf);
}

protected function loadStyleSheet():void
{
    loader = new URLLoader();
    loader.addEventListener(IOErrorEvent.IO_ERROR, onLoadError);
    loader.addEventListener(SecurityErrorEvent.SECURITY_ERROR, ↵
onLoadError);
    loader.addEventListener(Event.COMPLETE, onLoadSuccess);

    loader.load(new URLRequest(STYLESHEET_LOCATION));

    timer = new Timer(TIMEOUT, 1);
    timer.addEventListener(TimerEvent.TIMER, onTimeout);
    timer.start();
}

protected function onLoadError(event:Event):void
{
    removeEventListeners();
    Console.warn("Error loading CSS:", event.type, ". Using basic ↵
style.");
    setDefaultStyle();
}
```

```
protected function onLoadSuccess(event:Event):void
{
    removeEventListeners();
    try {
        var cssText:String = loader.data;
        var styleSheet:StyleSheet = new StyleSheet();
        styleSheet.parseCSS(cssText);
        setStyle(styleSheet);
    } catch (error:Error) {
        Console.warn("Error parsing CSS. Using basic style.");
        setDefaultStyle();
    }
}


protected function onTimeout(event:TimerEvent):void
{
    Console.warn("CSS loading timed out. Using basic style.");
    loader.close();
    removeEventListeners();
    setDefaultStyle();
}


protected function removeEventListeners():void
{
    timer.stop();
    timer.removeEventListener(TimerEvent.TIMER, onTimeout);
    loader.removeEventListener(IOErrorEvent.IO_ERROR, onLoadError);
    loader.removeEventListener(SecurityErrorEvent.SECURITY_ERROR, ↵
onLoadError);
    loader.removeEventListener(Event.COMPLETE, onLoadSuccess);
}


protected function setDefaultStyle():void
{
    var styleSheet:StyleSheet = new StyleSheet();
    styleSheet.parseCSS(BASIC_STYLE);
    setStyle(styleSheet);
}


protected function setStyle(styleSheet:StyleSheet):void
{
    tf.styleSheet = styleSheet;
    tf.htmlText = '<p>Welcome to the <span class="title">AS3 ↵
Bible</span>! Go <a href="http://www.partlyhuman.com/">here</a>.</p>';
    }
  }
}
```

Another approach to this problem is to add the text into the text field at the very beginning, and redraw the text with the appropriate style after the stylesheet loads successfully. This way, the user can see the content without delay. On the other hand, it might produce a visible flicker as the text is redrawn. These considerations are the core of an error-handling strategy.

Summary

- It's necessary to come up with a comprehensive error-handling strategy.
- Error handling isn't just about `try/catch` blocks.
- You should handle errors that occur from a variety of sources, including from any remote or unverified source.
- Some errors you can recover from; others are fatal.
- Think of errors from the user's standpoint: How does the program behave?
- When you handle an error, your job is to return the program to a normal state, and make sure that dependent code will be okay.
- When errors occur, log them.
- Logging can be done many different ways, each with its pros and cons, depending on the environment your program executes in.
- When errors affect the user, let the user know with some kind of feedback.
- When errors are fatal, let the user know.

Part VI

Working with External Data

Chapter 22

Understanding Networking Basics

A time will come where you, like Leif Eriksson before you, will yearn to leave the fjords of Iceland, which you're accustomed to, and explore the great unknown across the Atlantic. Now, replace "fjords of Iceland" with "Flash Player" and "the Atlantic" with "the rest of the Internet" and we've got something to talk about. So what's out there? Well, for starters there's the page your SWF is embedded in, beyond that, the server your SWF file resides on, and finally, the rest of the Internet. Much like the experience of crossing the sea differs for each who crosses it, the manner in which you can communicate with these myriad locations is different: load XML, call to scripts, read AMF data, read binary information . . . the choice is yours. In the next few chapters, you explore all this.

To those of you with previous Flash experience, the `LoadVars` class that you were familiar with has been replaced by a much richer and more powerful set of classes that allow you more flexibility and functionality.

For starters let's talk about the basics of communicating with external files. The central concept of this basic external communication is that you create a request that contains the information about what you want to talk to — either the Uniform Resource Identifier (URI) or Uniform Resource Locator (URL) — and then pass that to something that will do the communicating. How you set up that communication is entirely up to you, depending on the class that you choose and the parameters that you pass to the object of that class. The browser handles data about pages through the use of HTTP or HyperText Transfer Protocol, which you can think of as being the sea in which your Flash movie swims. All HTML pages, including those in which your Flash Movie is embedded, are sent via HTTP, from a server in response to a client request.

An example of a simple HTTP request and response is the user sitting at her laptop and telling the server "Give me file A." The server answers, "I have it. Here is the content of file A: (...content of file A...)." HTTP uses its own simplified language: `GET /fileA` gets answered by `200 OK` (`...content of file A...`) or `404 File Not Found` or `500 Internal Server Error`. What we're going to be doing is using the Flash Player network API to send our own requests that will get handled by different servers, either our own or others'.

Enough overview — let's get to some specifics. Let's look at the first and simplest example of communicating with the outside world: opening up an HTML page. You know the drill — you want to link to an HTML page, a different SWF file, you need to give the user a link to click. In ActionScript 3.0, the first thing you do is create an instance of a `URLRequest`. Then you pass that `URLRequest` object to the `flash.net.navigateToURL()` function. This `navigateToURL()` method is a static function within the `flash.net` package, available for all to use. Let's walk through the `URLRequest` class and then see how to navigate to another page.

URLRequest

The `URLRequest` represents all the information about a call to the browser that you'd like to make. This includes the URL you want to use; any data you'd like to send, such as GET and POST variables, which we look at later; and the content type of any information you're sending to the browser. The most important of these right now is the `URL` property. To create a new `URLRequest` object, you make sure you import the `flash.net.URLRequest` class into your file and then instantiate it. The signature of the constructor states that the `URL` parameter is optional. Usually, you'll pass the URL in, although you certainly don't need to:

```
var request:URLRequest = new URLRequest("http://example.com/");
```

So now you have a `URLRequest` that will head off to the web site passed in and do what you want it to do. In our case, we want to have this redirect the browser to this URL:

```
var request:URLRequest = new URLRequest("http://example.com/");
flash.net.navigateToURL(request);
```

For something this simple, you can use the following shorthand:

```
flash.net.navigateToURL(new URLRequest("http://example.com/"));
```

This works fine because we're still creating a new instance of the `URLRequest` object to pass to the method. However it doesn't allow us to use any of the other attributes that the `URLRequest` possesses. If we need our request to do more, we'll need to create the object on its own and pass it into the method. Like what? Well, like sending `GET` and `POST` data for one. We go over what these are and what they do in the "URLLoader" section.

navigateToURL()

As you already learned, `navigateToURL()` is a public static method that takes two parameters. The first is the `URLRequest` that contains the URL you wish to navigate to and the second is the window that you wish to open this in. This second parameter can be either `_self`, meaning the current window; `_blank`, meaning a new window; `_parent`, which means the parent frame if your page is using frames; or `_top`, meaning the top-level frame in the window. By default, `navigateToURL()` creates a new window. The `navigateToURL()` method takes the following parameters:

- `request:URLRequest` — A `URLRequest` object that specifies the URL to navigate to.
- `window:String` — The browser window or frame to display the URL into.

So if we want to open the previous example in the same frame we're currently viewing the SWF file in, we would use:

```
var request:URLRequest = new URLRequest("http://server.com");
flash.net.navigateToURL(request, "_self");
```

This would be sent off to the web site in the same window we're currently using.

GET and POST

GET and POST are two ways of sending information between web pages via the browser. This is nice for us as people who make things on the web because we can have the user's browser do a lot of the work for us. Let's look at a GET variable first:

```
http://server.com?user=josh&login=true
```

What this is telling us is to not only go to this page, but also to take along with us two GET variables, one called `user`, which is set to `josh`, and one called `login`, which is set to `true`. The actual HTTP request for this looks like this:

```
GET /index.html?user=josh&login=true HTTP/1.1
Host: server.com
User-Agent: Mozilla/4.0
```

The one thing to always remember about GET is that it is *not* safe from prying eyes. Anyone can see the information sent in a GET, which hopefully would not be someone's credit card number or other valuable information. This is also true with POST. In any event, anything really important or even somewhat important should be encrypted, but that's another topic and another book. We're going to talk a lot more about the different things we can do with this in the next chapter, but for right now, let's move onto POST variables.

A POST doesn't show up in the URL; it gets hidden in the actual HTTP request that the browser sends and looks like this:

```
POST /login.jsp HTTP/1.1
Host: server.com
User-Agent: Mozilla/4.0
Content-Length: 21
Content-Type: application/x-www-form-urlencoded
user=josh&login=true
```

As you can see, the information is the same, but the method that we're sending it in is not. We set the method that we want to use in the `method` property of our URLRequest.

```
var request:URLRequest = new URLRequest("http://server.com");
request.method = "GET";
```

Now that we've established that we're using a GET parameter, we can set some data to go over with this request.

```
request.data = "name=josh&login=true";
flash.net.navigateToURL(request);
```

When we run this, we see the following in our address bar:

```
http://server.com/?name=josh&login=true
```

Which means that it worked. Were we to change our method to POST, we wouldn't see anything, although if the page were expecting POST variables to be sent it would receive and be able to process them.

All variables sent through GET and POST use *URL encoding*. This means that they are encoded so as not to confuse the browser. Multiple variables are always joined using the ampersand (&) and no quotes are used to mark strings. In order to use a character that already has a specific meaning, we need to encode it. The following is a list of encodings:

```
space         %20
!             %21
"             %22
#             %23
$             %24
%             %25
&             %26
'             %27
(             %28
)             %29
*             %2A
+             %2B
,             %2C
```

–	%2D
.	%2E
?	%3F
[	%5B
\	%5C
]	%5D
^	%5E
_	%5F
`	%60
{	%7B
|	%7C
}	%7D
~	%7E
¢	%A2
£	%A3
¥	%A5
¦	%A6
§	%A7
«	%AB
¬	%AC
	%AD

To include some of these characters in a POST variable, you would use the URL encoded value like so:

```
name=josh&question=Wasn%27t%20Leif%20Eriksson%20born%20in%20Iceland%3F
```

This would read: "Wasn't Leif Eriksson born in Iceland?" In fact, he was.

URLLoader

So what if we can pass data to the outside world? We want to be able to get data from the outside world into our SWF. For that, we need to use the URLLoader class.

URLLoader basics

The URLLoader takes a URLRequest object and allows you to load information from that location or send and load information from that location. The URLLoader is an EventDispatcher, so it uses events to notify any listeners when it begins loading data, if there's an error, what the status of the http request is, when there's any progress and finally, when it's complete. Let's create a simple URLLoader first:

```
var request:URLRequest = new URLRequest("http://server.com");
flash.net.navigateToURL(request, "_self");
```

Now, in order to begin loading this data, all we need to do is call load, but we want to attach some event listeners to let us know what's going on. We'll attach one to most commonly used events so that the URLLoader can dispatch it for the sake of demonstration:

```
package
{
import flash.display.Sprite;
import flash.events.*;
import flash.net.*;
public class NetworkProject extends Sprite
{
    private var loader:URLLoader;

    public function NetworkProject()
    {
        var request:URLRequest = new URLRequest("http://example.com/test.xml");
        loader = new URLLoader(request);
        loader.addEventListener(Event.ACTIVATE, activatedListener);
        loader.addEventListener(Event.COMPLETE, completeListener);
        loader.addEventListener(ProgressEvent.PROGRESS, progressListener);
    }

    private function activatedListener(event:Event):void
    {
        trace(" activated " + loader.bytesLoaded +↵
            " but nothing loaded yet ");
    }

    private function completeListener(event:Event):void
    {
        trace(" all done loading " + loader.data +↵
            " and here's the xml file we loaded ");
    }

    private function progressListener(event:Event):void
    {
        trace(" we're in progress, we've loaded " + loader.bytesLoaded +↵
            " out of " + loader.bytesTotal + " bytes ");
    }
}
}
```

This is an excellent one to try and run on your own because it will show you the order that the URLLoader performs its actions in. First, we open the URLLoader by calling load(); then we check the progress. Because this file is so small, we get it all at once, which means that the bytesLoaded will be the same as the bytesTotal: 70. Finally, the complete event is broadcast and we access the data that we've loaded through the data property of the URLLoader. Let's break each of these down a little:

- load(): This method sends and loads data from the URL in the URLRequest object passed to the URLLoader.

- data: This is data received from the load operation. This property is null until the downloading has completed. The data is of type wildcard, which is represented by the asterisk (*) symbol. This means that it can be anything — a Number, String, Array, XML, Object, and so on. We simply need to cast it to do what we want with it.

  There is a related property that you can set on the URLLoader, the dataFormat property.

- dataFormat: This determines what you do with the data when you get it. By default this is text, but if you know it's going to be something else, you can declare it as such and the Flash Player will treat it that way. If this is text, the received data is a string containing the text of the loaded file. If this is "binary", the received data is a ByteArray object containing the raw binary data. This will be discussed in a later chapter. If this is set to "variables", the received data is a URLVariables object containing the URL-encoded variables. We cover this later in the chapter.

- bytesLoaded: This indicates the number of bytes that have been loaded thus far during the load operation.

- bytesTotal: This indicates the total number of bytes in the downloaded data. This property contains 0 while the load operation is in progress and is populated when the operation is complete.

Now there is one thing to be aware of: By default, the URL you load must be in exactly the same domain as the calling SWF file. A SWF file on server1.com can load files from server2.com only if there is a crossdomain.xml file on server2.com that lists all the servers that may load files from it, and the list contains server1.com. Also note that if you're trying to load files from a local folder, you'll likely get security errors until you change the settings on your particular instance of the Flash Player to allow you communicate with the folder that you're trying to use.

The URLLoader also dispatches the following events:

- flash.events.Event.COMPLETE or "complete": Dispatched after all the received data is decoded and placed in the data property of the URLLoader object. The received data may be accessed once this event has been dispatched.

- flash.events.HTTPStatusEvent.HTTP_STATUS or "httpStatus": Dispatched if a call to URLLoader.load() attempts to access data over HTTP and the current Flash Player environment is able to detect and return the status code for the request. (Some browser environments may not be able to provide this information.) Note that the `httpStatus` event (if any) is sent before (and in addition to) any complete or error event.

- `flash.events.IOErrorEvent.IO_ERROR` or `"ioError"`: Dispatched if a call to `URLLoader.load()` results in a fatal error that terminates the download.

- `flash.events.Event.OPEN` or `"open"`: Dispatched when the download operation commences following a call to the `URLLoader.load()` method.

- `flash.events.ProgressEvent.PROGRESS` or `"progress"`: Dispatched when data is received as the download operation progresses. Note that with a `URLLoader` object, it is not possible to access the data until it has been received completely. So, the progress event serves only as a notification of how far the download has progressed. To access the data before it's entirely downloaded, use a `URLStream` object.

- `flash.events.SecurityErrorEvent.SECURITY_ERROR` or `"securityError"`: Dispatched if a call to `URLLoader.load()` attempts to load data from a server outside the security sandbox. It also contains a text property that defines the text to be displayed as an error message.

The `close()` method closes the load operation in progress. Any load operation in progress is terminated immediately. This is useful if you time out (the server not responding) or if you give users the ability to quit loading something if they get bored or change their minds.

Doing more with the URLLoader

Now that you understand the basics of the `URLLoader`, let's look at some slightly more advanced topics. With the `URLLoader`, you can create a simple preloader that you'll use to monitor the progress of a very large XML file. You'll do this using the `bytesLoaded` and `bytesTotal` properties of the `URLLoader`, so that as you download you'll check the progress and give the user some indication of his progress. In the following code snippet, the progress of the downloading is checked and reported.

```
package
{
import flash.display.Sprite;
import flash.events.*;
import flash.net.*;
public class DisplayLoadBar extends Sprite
{
    private var loader:URLLoader;
    private var total:Sprite;
    private var loaded:Sprite;

    public function DisplayLoadBar()
    {
```

```
        var request:URLRequest = new URLRequest("http://example.com/huge.xml");
        loader = new URLLoader(request);

        //sprite that represents the total amount of data that we need to load
        total = new Sprite();
        total.graphics.beginFill(0xff0000, 1);
        total.graphics.drawRect(0, 0, 200, 10);
        total.graphics.endFill();
        addChild(total);
        total.y = 200;
        total.x = 100;

        //sprite that represents the amount loaded
        loaded = new Sprite();
        addChild(loaded);
        loaded.y = 200;
        loaded.x = 100;

        loader.addEventListener(Event.OPEN, openListener);
        loader.addEventListener(Event.COMPLETE, completeListener);
        loader.addEventListener(ProgressEvent.PROGRESS, progressListener);
    }

    private function openListener(event:Event):void
    {
        trace(" opened " + loader.bytesLoaded +↵
            " but nothing loaded yet ");
    }

    private function completeListener(event:Event):void
    {
        trace(" all done loading " + loader.data +↵
            " and here's the xml file we loaded ");
    }

    private function progressListener(event:Event):void
    {
        var amount:Number = (loader.bytesLoaded / loader.bytesTotal) * 200;
        loaded.graphics.clear();
        loaded.graphics.beginFill(0x00ff00, 1);
        loaded.graphics.drawRect(0, 0, amount, 10);
        loaded.graphics.endFill();
    }
}
}
```

Now, in addition to loading information from external sources, we can send information to external sources that will allow us to receive data back based on what we sent. We'll look much more deeply into this in the next chapter, but let's look at the basics now.

The same way that we used the `URLRequest` object to send some data along with the browser redirect that we called using `navigateToURL()`, we can send data along with an instance of `URLLoader`:

```
var request:URLRequest = ↵
    new URLRequest("http://example.com/simple_response.php");
request.method = "GET";
request.data = "name=user&request=xml";
```

This will allow us to send the GET information that we specify in the request; all we need to do now is pass it through a `URLLoader`, which will also load the data that we receive:

```
var loader:URLLoader = new URLLoader();
loader.addEventListener(IOErrorEvent.IO_ERROR, errorLoading);
loader.addEventListener(Event.COMPLETE, dataLoaded);
loader.load(request);
```

We want to make sure that we're always listening for potential errors when we're loading data because you never know what might go wrong: a server down, an ISP conking out, a tree falling on a power line somewhere, or any number of potential disasters. It's best to be able to say "Something went wrong" rather than just leaving the user to wonder if you know what you're doing.

We can communicate with many different kinds of server-side scripts using GET and POST and loading the results, and later we're going to cover many more specifics. For now, however, we understand the basics of this communication. We know how to send data and we know how to listen for the response and that's a powerful thing to know.

Introducing URLVariables

In addition to loading XML or text files, we can load `URLVariables`. Look at the data that we're sending in the GET and POST statements:

```
name=josh&hometown=Columbus&homestate=Ohio
```

These name-value pairs are known as `URLVariables`. When we know we're loading `URLVariables`, we can set the property of the `URLLoader.dataFormat` to `"variable"` so that Flash allows us to treat the data that we receive as name-value pairs. This allows us to loop through them, greatly simplifying our data handling code:

```
private function loadingComplete(event:Event):void
{
    for each(var prop:String in loader.data)
    {
        trace("The property "+prop+"" = "+loader.data[prop]");
    }
}
```

The `URLVariables` object contains two methods:

- `decode()`: This method converts the source to properties of the specified `URLVariables` object. Because this method is used internally by the `URLVariables`, you don't need to call this method directly.

- `toString()`: This returns the string of the `URLVariable` that have been loaded into a `URLVariables` instance.

`URLVariables` objects use the same encoding as discussed with GET and POST variables. You can also use the `URLVariables` object to send data to a server with a `URLRequest`. Let's send the same data to a server using the `URLVariables` object:

```
var request:URLRequest = ↵
    new URLRequest("http://example.com/script.php");
var urlVars:URLVariables = new URLVariables();
urlVars.name = "josh";
urlVars.hometown = "Columbus";
urlVars.homestate = "Ohio";
request.data = urlVars;
var loader:URLLoader = new URLLoader(request);
```

Usually, if you're building up many requests dynamically, using `URLVariables` is much simpler and less bug-prone than building up strings separated by & symbols.

URLStream

In some rare cases, you'll need to get access to the data that you're downloading before it's done downloading. To do so, you use a `URLStream` object in place of a `URLLoader`. We should stress, however, that most times the `URLLoader` is good enough. The only situations in which you should consider using a `URLStream` are those where you have very large amounts of data and where you know a lot about what that data is. The methods that the `URLStream` uses allow you to read the data as it's being downloaded in a binary format. This means that most object handling functionality is disabled. You're looking at raw bytes.

It is also important to remember that we're trying to inspect bytes as they are downloaded; we need to make sure we're not trying to read bytes that do not exist. More information on byte handling in ActionScript 3.0 is provided in Chapter 34, so we won't go too deeply into the byte methods here.

```
package
{
    import flash.net.URLStream;
    import flash.net.URLRequest;
    import flash.events.Event;
    import flash.events.ProgressEvent;
    public class URLStreamDemo
    {
        private var streamer:URLStream;
```

```
    public function URLStreamDemo()
    {
        var request:URLRequest =↵
            new URLRequest("http://example.com/binary_data.bin");
        streamer = new URLStream(request);
        streamer.addEventListener(ProgressEvent.PROGRESS, progressListener);
    }

    private function progressListener(event:Event):void
    {
        if(streamer.bytesAvailable != 0)
        {
            trace(streamer.readByte());
        }
    }
}
}
```

As you can see, we're reading a byte out of the data stream every time a progress event is thrown. Again, this method is very advanced, and in all likelihood, you won't need access to data as it's loading because most XML, variables, and text files take very short amounts of time to load.

sendToURL()

Along with `navigateToURL`, the `flash.net` package defines a public static function called `sendToURL()` that sends information to the URL defined in the `URLRequest` passed to it, without actually redirecting the browser. Think of it as doing everything *but* actually going there. You send the information, but you don't redirect and because you're not redirecting, you don't actually care what the site says back to you. Now, most times, you want to at least know that what you just did worked, and you'll need to use a `URLLoader` in order to get that notification.

```
var request:URLRequest = new URLRequest("http://example.com");
flash.net.sendToURL(request)
```

Using the Loader

There's one aspect of loading data that we haven't discussed, and that is loading images or SWF files into a movie. The Loader object is a `DisplayObject` that possesses the ability to take a `URLRequest` object and load binary data, pictures or SWF files, from that request, and display the result.

Let's take a quick look at loading a JPG file from the local filesystem:

```
var loader:Loader = new Loader();
loader.load(new URLRequest("http://example.com/image.jpg"));
addChild(loader);
```

We create the `Loader` object, create a `URLRequest`, and pass that to the `load()` method, and then add the child to the display list. This code assumes that it is within a `DisplayObjectContainer` object. As mentioned earlier, the `Loader` object is a `DisplayObject`, although it cannot have children added or removed, other than the external object loaded in. The `Loader` object possesses a `content` property, which is the loaded image or SWF file. This content property is null until the content finishes loading. To find out when the content object is fully loaded, we listen for events on the `contentLoaderInfo` property of the Loader:

```
package
{
import flash.display.Sprite;
import flash.display.Loader;
import flash.net.URLRequest;
import flash.events.Event;
public class LoaderDemo extends Sprite
{
    private var loader:Loader;

    public function LoaderDemo()
    {
        loader = new Loader();
        loader.load(new URLRequest("image.jpg "));
        loader.contentLoaderInfo.addEventListener(Event.COMPLETE, ↵
            contentComplete);
        addChild(loader);
    }

    private function contentComplete(event:Event):void
    {
        trace(loader.content);
    }
}
}
```

The `Loader` object also possesses an `unload()` method that will allow you to remove the content object from the `Loader`. We can also use the Loader to load SWF files that we can then access and control programmatically.

First we create a simple class to load and then call methods on:

```
public class LoadedSample extends Sprite
{
    public function LoadedSample()
    {
        super();
    }

    public function addCircle():void
    {
        graphics.beginFill(0x00ff00, 0.5);
        graphics.drawCircle(0, 0, 30);
```

```
    }

    public function addSquare():void
    {
        graphics.beginFill(0x0000ff, 0.5);
        graphics.drawRect(60, 60, 50, 50);
    }
}
```

Then we load the created SWF file and call methods on it. Notice that instead of waiting for the
`Event.COMPLETE` event we're waiting for the `Event.INIT` event that informs us that the SWF
file has completely loaded into the containing SWF file:

```
package
{
import flash.display.Sprite;
import flash.display.Loader;
import flash.net.URLRequest;
import flash.events.Event;
public class LoaderDemo extends Sprite
{
    private var loader:Loader;

    public function LoaderDemo()
    {
        loader = new Loader();
        loader.contentLoaderInfo.addEventListener(Event.INIT, contentComplete);
        loader.load(new URLRequest("LoadedSample.swf"));
    }

    private function contentComplete(event:Event):void
    {
        trace(loader.content);
        addChild(loader);
        var loadedSample:LoadedSample = (loader.content as LoadedSample);
        loadedSample.addCircle();
        loadedSample.addSquare();
    }
}
}
```

While we can load pre–ActionScript 3.0 (Flash Player 8 or earlier) SWF files and allow them to play,
we cannot communicate directly with them because of the differences between the ActionScript
Virtual Machine 2 or AVM2 (used for Flash Player 9) and the ActionScript Virtual Machine 1, or
AVM, which is used by all versions of Flash Player previous to Flash Player 9.

The following paragraph lists security concerns you should consider when loading SWF files.

You can't load a SWF if the calling SWF file is local (i.e., on the Desktop of a local machine), and the
file to be loaded is local (i.e., also on the Desktop). This can be remedied by setting its security settings
in the embed statement of the HTML page the file lives in or by attempting to set the correct System

settings. If the loaded content is a SWF file written with ActionScript 3.0, it cannot be cross-scripted by a SWF file in another security sandbox unless that cross-scripting arrangement was approved through a call to the `System.security.allowDomain()` or the `System.security .allowInsecureDomain()` methods in the loaded content file. This is bringing us very nicely into discussing the security mechanisms in the Flash Player, so without delay, let's look at that.

Understanding Flash Player Security

Flash Player, because it is downloaded and installed on system, and because it downloads what are essentially executable files in the form of SWFs, has the potential to do incredible damage to your computer. However, many safeguards are in place to prevent that from happening. The first is that Flash Player is limited by your OS to certain behavior, much like what your OS does to other scripts or applications running in your browser. You wouldn't want someone else's JavaScript going and running shell scripts on your computer and neither would you want Flash Player doing that. The good news is, it can't. That part is quite solid and doesn't affect us much in day-to-day development. The part that does affect us in day-to-day development is the security sandbox, which affects where we can load files from and where we cannot.

The security sandbox exists to ensure that you and only you can specify the locations where content will be loaded into the SWF file that you're hosting. When you put a SWF file on your server and a user downloads it, the Flash Player makes note of the domain where that SWF is coming from and creates a security sandbox defined by that domain. That means that if the user goes and downloads SWF files from my web site with the name `http://www.mysite.com`, the Flash Player will define a security sandbox for `http://www.mysite.com` that all content and data for that player must originate from. It's important to note that `http://www.mysite.com` is not the same as `http://mysite.com` or `http://82.39.28.182`, even if `http://82.39.28.182` is the IP address of your web site. This is nice because it greatly decreases the likelihood that someone will get a virus or something somehow malevolent from viewing Flash content on your site, but it can be a nuisance when you're trying to load XML files or pictures from another site. The Flash Player raises a security sandbox exception and halts the execution of your program until the user agrees to continue. The way around this is to define a crossdomain.xml file that lists all the IP addresses and domain names that you plan on accessing content from for your SWF file. This crossdomain.xml file should sit at the server root so the Flash Player can access it and needs to be nothing more than a list of acceptable domains. An example crossdomain.xml file might look like this:

```
<?xml version="1.0"?>
<cross-domain-policy>
    <allow-access-from domain="*.mysite.com" />
    <allow access from domain="www.anotherofmysites.com" />
    <allow-access-from domain="282.39.28.182" />
</cross-domain-policy>
```

Now we can load PNG files, SWF files, or XML from any of these three sites in addition to the original URL that our SWF file was downloaded from without trouble. This file can be kept at the server root or it can be loaded in your SWF file by using `Security.loadPolicyFile()`. This is a good idea when you have multiple SWF files with different sandbox requirements.

439

If you want to know what the current security settings of a SWF file are, you need only to call `Security.sandboxType()` and see the string that is returned. The possible values are:

- `Security.REMOTE`: The SWF file is from an Internet URL, and operates under domain-based sandbox rules.

- `Security.LOCAL_WITH_FILE`: The SWF file is a local file, but it has not been trusted by the user and was not published with a networking designation. The SWF file can read from local data sources but cannot communicate with the Internet.

- `Security.LOCAL_WITH_NETWORK`: The SWF file is a local file and has not been trusted by the user, but it was published with a networking designation. The SWF can communicate with the Internet but cannot read from local data sources.

- `Security.LOCAL_TRUSTED`: The SWF file is a local file and has been trusted by the user, using either the Settings Manager or a Flash Player trust configuration file. The SWF file can both read from local data sources and communicate with the Internet.

In addition to restricting the URLs from which the Flash Player may access content, the security mechanism may also restrict what content that is loaded can access or load. When you load a SWF file, you can set the context parameter of the `load()` method of the Loader object that is used to load the file. This parameter takes a `LoaderContext` object. When you set the `securityDomain` property of this `LoaderContext` object to `Security.currentDomain`, Flash Player trusts the loaded SWF exactly as much as it already trusts the executing SWF. In other words, it applies the security settings of the current SWF to the loaded SWF. If `securityDomain` is not set (this is the default), the loaded SWF is loaded in a fresh sandbox and its actions must be approved anew.

Additionally, by setting the `applicationContext` parameter of the `LoaderContext` object, you can load the SWF file as imported media. In this way, the file doing the loading can access objects and classes in the application domain of the loaded SWF. The following code snippet shows loading a SWF file and setting that SWF file's `ApplicationDomain` to be the domain of the loading SWF:

```
public function load(lib:String):void
{
    var loader:Loader = new Loader();
    var request:URLRequest = new URLRequest(swfLib);
    var context:LoaderContext = new LoaderContext();
    context.applicationDomain = ApplicationDomain.currentDomain;
    loader.load(request, context);
}
```

Additionally, the `Security.allowDomain()` method allows the loaded SWF to do things within the domain of the loading SWF file. Call the `Security.allowDomain()` method in the constructor method of the main class of the loaded SWF file, and then have the loading SWF file add an event listener to respond to the `init` event dispatched by the `contentLoaderInfo` property of the `Loader` object. When this event is dispatched, the loaded SWF file has called the `Security.allowDomain()` method in the constructor method, and classes in the loaded SWF file are available to the loading SWF file. The loading SWF file can retrieve classes from the loaded SWF file by calling `Loader.contentLoaderInfo.applicationDomain` `.getDefinition()`. The following example shows how a SWF loaded into another SWF can use `Security.allowDomain()` to allow the domain of the loading SWF:

```
public function ExampleConstructor()
{
    Security.allowDomain("http://www.newdomain.com");
}
```

Summary

- The `URLRequest` class is used to store information about a URL you might want to navigate to, send information to, or get information from, or data that you might want to send.

- To redirect the browser, you use `flash.net.navigateToURL()` and pass in a URLRequest object that has the URL that you wish to redirect to.

- You can also set GET and POST variables to be used by the URLRequest. These need to be URL encoded.

- To load data from a URL, you use a `URLLoader` object. `URLLoaders` dispatch events when they are opened, when they make progress in downloading, when there is an error in downloading, and when they are completed.

- To access the information downloaded by the `URLLoader`, you access the `URLLoader`'s data property. You can access this only when the downloading is complete. You determine when a URLLoader is finished downloading by listening to the `flash.events` `.Event.COMPLETE` event.

- If you are downloading text or XML, you want the `URLLoader`'s `dataFormat` to be set to text, which is the default. If you are downloading `URLVariables`, you want the `URLLoaders` dataFormat to be set to `"variables"`. This creates a `URLVariables` object that you can loop through to access all of its properties and data.

- If you aren't interested in any response to your `URLRequest`, you can use the `sendToURL()` method, which sends the request, but doesn't listen for any information from the user.

Chapter 23

Communicating with Server-Side Technologies

I n the parlance of the Web, we refer to anything that happens on the user's computer as client-side and anything that happens on the server as server-side. Flash Player itself is a client-side technology because the movie is downloaded onto the user's machine before it is viewed. HTML, CSS, and AJAX are all client-side technologies that are run locally; however, they frequently communicate with a server-side technology to request data in the form of text, images, or video. The range of client-side technologies is quite vast and pretty much any problem has a solution in each different technology. Which technology you choose is up to you, as is the fashion in which your SWF file communicates with the server. In this chapter, you look at some of the different ways that Flash can communicate with a server, and some of the different ways that server-side technologies can send information to the Flash Player.

Communicating via URLLoader

The simplest way of communicating with a server is via the `URLLoader` class. From the server-side perspective, something sends the server a request, the server processes it, and then the server writes everything out to the page that was requested. From the perspective of the SWF file, the SWF sends information to a URL and waits for it to have something written out to it. Once something is written out, the SWF fires the event notifying any listeners that the data has been loaded from the URL and can be stored in the `loaderContent`.

For a simple example, let's say that you want to send a username to a PHP script that will return information in XML format. Let's look at the ActionScript that you'll be using first:

```
package
{
    import flash.display.Sprite;
    import flash.net.URLLoader;
    import flash.net.URLRequest;
    import flash.events.Event;
public class PHPCommunication extends Sprite
{
    private var _username:String = "josh";
    private var _id:String = "143";
    private var loader:URLLoader;

    public function PHPCommunication()
    {
        loader = new URLLoader();
        loader.addEventListener(Event.COMPLETE, dataLoaded);
        var request:URLRequest = new URLRequest("http://localhost:8888/↵
as3bible/ch23/PHPScript.php?username=" + _username + "&id=" + _id);
        loader.load(request);
    }

    public function dataLoaded(event:Event):void
    {
        var xmlResponse:XML = XML((event.target as URLLoader).data);
        trace(xmlResponse);
    }
}
}
```

In the preceding example, you're simply passing the values that you want to be processed on the server via GET variables. You can also do this using the URLVariables class:

```
var variables:URLVariables = new URLVariables();
var request:URLRequest = new URLRequest();
variables.id = "143";
request.method = "GET";
request.data = variables;
```

Using PHP to communicate with Flash

PHP is a very powerful server-side scripting language that has gained many admirers for its power and flexibility. Here, you're using it to read the values passed via the request to the server, compared to a hash value, and then returned. To write XML, the script simply prints it.

```php
<?php
    $name = $_GET['username'];
    $id = $_GET['id'];
    $programmers['143'] = "<programmer><hometown>Boston</hometown>@to<skill>↵
    Actionscript</skill></programmer>";
    $programmers['121'] = "<programmer><hometown>Boca Raton</hometown><skill>↵
    PHP</skill></programmer>";
    $returnxml = $programmers[$id];
    echo $returnxml;
?>
```

The PHP script writes out the values and the Flash Player receives them as XML. The same approach can be applied to many other server-side languages. You can send variables to the server side using either the URLVariables class or by simply appending them to the URL string that you pass to the URLRequest object.

Sending data without loading it

If you're not interested in getting a response that a particular server-side script sends as a response to a URLRequest you've sent out, you can simply send variables using sendToURL() instead of using the URLLoader class as we did in the previous example. Let's say that you have a simple voting tabulator in your application and you need to send the vote to a script that will process it but you don't need to update the application with any new information from the server. Here is an example of using sendToURL():

```actionscript
package
{
    import flash.display.Sprite;
    import flash.net.URLRequest;
    import flash.net.sendToURL;
public class SendVote extends Sprite
{
    private var _videoID:String = "23929";
    private var vote:int = 1;

    public function SendVote()
    {
        var request:URLRequest = new URLRequest("http://↵
example.com/script.php?videoid=" + _videoID + "&vote=" + vote);
        sendToURL(request);
    }
}
}
```

XMLSocket

An XML socket server is a special server that receives and sends XML to Flash Player via a socket connection. The socket on the server is identified by an IP address or a domain name and frequently by a port number such as the following:

```
http://example.com:8080
```

The XMLSocket class, which makes communication with an XML socket server simple, is at its most useful in client-server applications that need to update frequently, such as chats or multiplayer games. If you were to use HTTP in these situations you would need to *poll* the server, or request data from the server at set intervals. An XMLSocket chat solution maintains an open connection to the server, which lets the server immediately send incoming messages without a request from the client.

Setting up an application to serve as an XML socket server on your server is not the easiest thing to do and isn't really appropriate to use if you don't need real-time interactivity. In many cases, you should use the URLLoader class instead of the XMLSocket class.

Creating an XMLSocket object

To communicate with an XML socket server, you need to create a new XMLSocket object, add event listeners for the connect event, and add data events to notify you when the application has connected to the server and when the server has sent data to the application.

```
var socket:XMLSocket = new XMLSocket();
socket.addEventListener(Event.CONNECT, connected);
socket.addEventListener(DataEvent.DATA, dataReceived);
```

You then define methods to handle these events:

```
private function connected(event:Event):void
{
    socket.send("hi");
}
private function dataReceived(dataEvent:DataEvent):void
{
    trace(dataEvent.data);
    var xml:XML = new XML(dataEvent.data);
}
```

The only thing left to do is to connect to the server. When you connect, you pass in the name of the server, either as the host name or an IP address, and the port that you will connect to the server on:

```
socket.connect("localhost", 8989);
```

Each XML message is a complete XML document, terminated by a zero (\0) byte. This is how Flash Player knows that the message has concluded. An unlimited number of XML messages can be sent and received over a single XMLSocket connection.

The server side of an XMLSocket

The following code lists two simple sockets that return XML. Both of these could, with some extra work on your part, function as an XMLSocket for the Flash Player to use.

For example in Python, an XMLSocket would look like so:

```
from socket import *
host = "localhost"
port = 8989
buf = 1024
addr = (host, port)

python_socket = socket(AF_INET, SOCK_STREAM)
python_socket.bind((host, port))
python_socket.listen(3) #allow 3 connections

while 1:
    connection, address = python_socket.accept()
    print 'python_socket connection on ', address
    while 1:
        data = connection.recv(1024)
        if not data: break
        print data
        if data == 'hi\0':
            connection.send('<?xml version="1.0"↵
encoding="|ISO-8859-1|"?><response>hello!</response>\0')
        if data == 'bye\0':
            connection.send('<?xml version="1.0"↵
encoding="|ISO-8859-1|"?><response>bye!</response>\0')
        connection.close()
```

In Ruby, a similar server would look like the following:

```
require 'socket'
server = TCPServer.new('127.0.0.1', 8989)
while (session = server.accept)
  request = session.gets
  puts request
  session.print "<data>Your request was #{request}</data>"
  session.close
end
```

These sockets utilize very similar mechanisms, and the code, beyond syntactic differences, is very similar as well. Sockets in most languages are implemented in a similar fashion.

To communicate with these sockets you would use the `XMLSocket` class and understand that you're expecting top-level XML node data and then move from there. One challenge with XML sockets is that it's frequently difficult to handle unexpected return values. However, it is simple enough with some planning ahead to create a simple schema to use in these cases.

Flash Remoting

As you learned earlier, Flash Remoting is a powerful way of allowing a Flash application to communicate with a server. It allows you to use AMF (ActionScript Message Format), a binary format, to send information from the server. AMF is a very powerful tool for Flash developers because it is so lightweight and is processed so quickly. Objects that are returned in AMF format are typed; that is, their properties are Strings or Numbers, and this makes processing data returned from Flash Remoting much easier.

Remoting is not limited to any particular middle-tier language or configuration; in fact, Flash Remoting solutions are available for Java, Perl, ColdFusion, Ruby, .NET, and PHP middle tiers. This means that Flash can integrate with nearly any environment.

NetConnection

The `NetConnection` class defines everything the Flash Player needs to know about connecting to an external server and sending and receiving information with the server. Generally, the URL that you connect to is referred to as the Remoting Gateway:

```
var nc:NetConnection = new NetConnection();
nc.connect("http://server.com");
```

You should use one `NetConnection` object per Remoting gateway that you would like to connect to. The `NetConnection` object is also used to call methods on the server. The `NetConnection` class contains methods and properties related to RTMP or video streaming and methods and properties related to AMF and Flash Remoting. We explore aspects of the `NetConnection` related to Flash Remoting here:

- `objectEncoding`: This determines the type of AMF that the `NetConnection` instance is using. One of the most powerful aspects of using the AMF format is that it has a close relationship to ActionScript. You can use either AMF3, or the ActionScript 3.0 version, or AMF0, the ActionScript 1.0 and 2.0 version. Unless you need to communicate with a server that is supporting legacy components that need to continue to be served in AMF0, you'll most likely be using AMF3. You can't set the `objectEncoding` of a `NetConnection` after you have connected to a server. Once you try to connect, if the `objectEncoding` you've selected is incorrect, you'll receive an event of type `NetStatusEvent`, which will contain an info property with a code property of `NetConnection.Connect.Failed`. You can listen for it like this:

```
var nc:NetConnection = new NetConnection();
nc.addEventListener(NetConnection.NET_STATUS, status);
```

```
private function status(netStatusEvent:NetStatusEvent):void
{
   if(netStatusEvent.info.code == NetConnection.Connect.Failed)
   {
      trace(" wrong encoding ");
   }
}
```

■ connect: This opens the connection to a server. There are a few security considerations to take into account. By default, the file can call only a server that it has been downloaded from. If you want to call a server that the SWF does not reside on, you will need to define a cross-domain.xml file on the server that you're attempting to contact. If the allowNetworking parameter of the embed statement used to embed the SWF file in an HTML page is set to false then NetConnections cannot be used.

■ call: The call method of the NetConnection object invokes the command or function on the server that you want to invoke. The method takes a required parameter, the name of the method, and then the responder to handle the response from the server, and then an array of additional parameters that are the arguments that you want to pass to the server. So, for example, if you have a method on your server called getAuthorInfo that requires an author name and a book name, you would call it like this:

```
nc.call("getAuthorInfo", responder, "Joshua Noble",
"ActionScript 3 Bible");
```

This snippet assumes that you have a Responder object named responder defined within the scope of this method call.

■ close: When you're finished working with a NetConnection object but aren't going to close the application, you should call the close method to close the connection to the server. Any queued data that hasn't yet been sent to the server will be discarded, and any data that the server has yet to send to the application will not be received. To reconnect, you don't need to create a new NetConnection object; you can simply call connect on an object previously created and go from there.

Responder

The Responder is what it says it is, an object that is used to get any response from the server from a NetConnection call that is not a Fault. When you call a Remoting method, you're usually, but not always, interested in what data will be returned from that Remoting method. The Responder is used as a parameter in the NetConnection.call method to indicate that whatever comes back from the server should be handled by that particular Responder. The constructor for a Responder has two parameters: the function that will be called when the server returns a method, and the method to be called whenever the server updates its status. Here is a code snippet that shows creating a Responder with appropriate handler methods.

```
import flash.net.Responder;
var responder:Responder = new Responder(resultHandler, errorHandler);
```

```
function resultHandler(result:Object):void
{
    for (var property:String in result)
    {
        trace(property + " : " + result[property]);
    }
}
function errorHandler(error:Object):void
{
    trace(error.description);
}
```

Notice that the objects sent in the result and error events from the Remoting method are not a subclass of the `flash.events.Event` but instead are typed as `Object`. The result handling method should be typed to handle whatever you're expecting from the server. If it's a single integer, then the method signature should expect an integer. More often, you'll be receiving associative arrays, or an object with multiple properties.

Flash Remoting server solutions

Flash Remoting comes in many different flavors, as mentioned earlier. Here, let's look at AMFPHP, which is an open source and free Flash Remoting solution written in PHP. To run it, you simply need a server with PHP 4+ installed on it. The libraries and installation can be found at www.amfphp.org, along with tutorials, documentation, and support.

Let's assume that you have a database that contains a table of developers and a table of projects. The developers have names, ages, years of experience, and one or more skills, whereas the projects each have one or more developers and more skills being utilized in the project. You want to provide two ways for your Flash application to request data from this database: all developers on a project, and all projects that a developer is currently on.

For those of you interested in SQL, let's assume that you have a MySQL database that contains three tables, DEVELOPERS, PROJECTS, and DEVELOPER_PROJECT_MAP. Following good database design, you have a table to define all the projects and all the developers, and because developers can be on many projects and projects can have many developers, you define a table that maps those relationships to one another. For the sake of argument, let's say that all the DEVELOPERS table contains is a string for the developer's name and an ID. In the PROJECTS table, there is simply a name for the project and an ID as well. The DEVELOPER_PROJECT_MAP consists of pairs of developer IDs and project IDs. For those of you not interested in SQL, don't worry about it — you're not missing a thing. The important thing is to note the two methods that are being defined: `getDevelopersByProject()` and `getProjectByDevelopers()`. You'll look at the ActionScript code to call these after you take a look at the code that creates the methods:

```
<?php
class ProgrammerService
{
    var $project_table = "projects";
```

```
var $dev_table = "developers";

function ProgrammerService()
{
    /* we set up the connection to our database */
    $this->db = mysql_connect("localhost", "user", "password");
    /* and select the database that we'll be using */
    mysql_select_db("amfphp");
    $this->methodTable = array(
      "getDevelopersByProject" => array(
          "access" => "remote",
          "description" => "Get a list of developers",
          "returntype" => "Array"
      ),
      "getProjectsByDeveloper" => array(
          "access" => "remote",
          "description" => "Get a list of projects",
          "returntype" => "Array"
      )
    );
}

/* mysql_connect and mysql_select_db are in the constructor */
function getDevelopersByProject($id)
{
    $sql = "select distinct name from developers d join ↵
(select * from developer_project_map where project_id = ".$id.") dpa ↵
on d.id = dpa.developer_id";
    return mysql_query($sql);
}

function getProjectsByDeveloper($id)
{
    $sql = "select distinct name from projects p join ↵
(select * from developer_project_map where developer_id = ".$id.") dpa ↵
on p.id = dpa.project_id";
    return mysql_query($sql);
}
}
?>
```

The two functions that you're defining both query the database and then return information to the ActionScript application as an AMF-encoded object. In both of these cases, an array of strings is returned, in the first method the names of the developers, and in the second, the names of the projects

```
//first we create a new nc
var nc:NetConnection = new NetConnection();
// then we set the URL we're going to call
```

```
var gatewayUrl:String = "http://example.com/remoting/gateway.php";
// then we connect to that URL
nc.connect(gatewayURL);
// now we set up the responders
var devResponder:Responder = new Responder(handleDevelopers, errorHandler);
var projResponder:Responder = new Responder(handleProjects, errorHandler);
//now we can call the methods, passing the name of the service and
//method, the responder that will handle the response, and the
//parameters.
nc.call("ProgrammerService.getDevelopersByProject", devResponder, 1);
nc.call("ProgrammerService.getProjectsByDeveloper", projResponder, 2);
```

A `NetConnection` object is defined to connect to the server and `Responders` are defined to handle the results or errors of the calls that you're making on that `NetConnection`, so now the actual service methods that map to the functions defined earlier in our PHP file can be called. Now that handlers have been defined for the service, these methods need to be added to handle the results of those Flash Remoting calls and an error handler to send an alert if anything goes wrong.

```
private function handleDevelopers(object:Object):void
{
    for(var s:String in object)
    {
        trace("property: "+s+" value: "+object[s]);
    }
}
private function handleProjects(object:Object):void
{
    for(var s:String in object)
    {
        trace("property: "+s+" value: "+object[s]);
    }
}
private function errorHandler(error:Object):void
{
    trace("error "+error.description);
}
```

One of the great conveniences of working with Flash Remoting is that whether you're calling a ColdFusion, Java, PHP, Ruby, or .NET service, your Flash Remoting code will look very similar, if not identical, allowing you to feel assured that your code will be portable and reusable.

For more information on different Flash Remoting solutions, visit http://osflash.org/documentation/ for general information on Flash Remoting, and http://osflash.org/projects for more information on different Flash Remoting solutions.

Summary

- You can use the URLLoader class to communicate with server-side scripts by passing parameters via the URL string in the URLRequest or by using the URLVariables class.

- If you don't need to load a response from the server about a server-side scripts then you can send parameters via sendToURL.

- XMLSockets are servers that can return XML via a constant stream. XML socket servers don't require polling or requesting data from the server; instead, the application is notified whenever data has been sent from the server via the XMLSockets instance.

- XML socket servers can be written in most scripting languages and are usually connected to from the Flash Player via an HTTP port.

- Flash Remoting is a method of communicating with a server and requesting information via a NetConnection instance.

- Flash Remoting uses AMF or ActionScript Message Format to encode the data it sends back. This means that the data is usually more lightweight and uses ActionScript native types.

Chapter 24

Saving Data to a Local Machine Using SharedObject

When you're building programs in ActionScript that run inside a browser, you don't have access to the user's hard drive. But using local shared objects, you can easily store all kinds of information that can be retrieved when the program runs again, even after the user shuts down the browser, or her computer. Using `SharedObjects`, you can allow users to personalize your programs, retain those preferences, and improve their experience.

Comparing Approaches to Persistent Storage

There are several ways that SWFs playing in the browser can attain persistent storage. Here, by persistent storage, we mean the ability to store data, close the browser, and then come back later and retrieve the data. The approaches all have different strengths and weaknesses, so let's compare them briefly.

Storing information in a local shared object

Using `SharedObjects` to persistently store data from ActionScript is as cheap, painless, and efficient as instant noodles for dinner, and probably better for you, too. However, `SharedObjects` have some limitations in terms of size of the information you can store, persistence, and their dependence on the host computer. Through the remainder of the chapter, you will see the details of these claims.

The last claim, that SharedObject data is associated with a machine, is probably the biggest limitation. When you store information in a local shared object, it is saved on the computer. When you use the program again from the same computer, you'll have access to that information; when you use it from another user's account or another computer, you won't. On shared computers that use a single guest account rather than registered user accounts, like those in some libraries and schools, the shared objects' data will also be shared. For instance, if you remember the user's name, address, and phone number on a public computer, there's a chance that the next user of the terminal will have access to that information, presenting a clear privacy concern.

Storing information on a server

If you're building a client-server application, you can always send things you need to be stored to the server. This is commonly the only acceptable approach when you need to store any sizable amount of data. You should utilize the server's storage if you need to retain any kind of multimedia or files. It is also the only approach for which you control the security. You can require authentication to get to information on a server, and you can transmit it across secure connections. Finally, using a server, you can control the longevity of and guarantee the persistence of the information stored on it.

However, using a server to maintain information from a SWF means a lot of additional work. You must develop code on the server that can accept and retrieve the requested information. You must develop a way in which sessions can be tracked and you can verify that the same user is retrieving his own information. Without authentication, you might have to use a cookie in combination with this technique. You must determine and implement a way to serialize and deserialize information sent to and from the server.

A server that stores information can be made secure and can handle bigger loads of data, but it is far from the convenience of using a SharedObject.

Storing information in a browser cookie

Web browsers allow a kind of persistent storage through cookies. Cookies are very limited in terms of size, and they can be string values only, so if you want to encode more complex types, you will have to encode them as strings as well. As they are part of the browser's API in JavaScript, you have to interface with JavaScript code in order to use browser cookies. You can read more about interfacing with JavaScript in Chapter 36.

Cookies are subject to the same limitations as SharedObjects as far as being associated with a physical computer and system account rather than with the user himself. A further limitation is that cookies are also associated with the browser that created them. SharedObjects can store information for a SWF regardless of the version of Flash Player used to create them and which browser they were running in, but a cookie created while browsing in Firefox won't be available in Opera, even on the same computer. Additionally, many savvy users clear their cookies frequently, so they may be more volatile than SharedObject storage.

Table 24-1 summarizes some of the issues inherent in using these three approaches to persistent storage.

TABLE 24-1

Solutions for persistent storage from ActionScript

	Local Shared Objects	Cookies	Servers
Ease of Implementation in ActionScript 3.0	Easy	Intermediate	Intermediate to difficult
Additional Work to Use	None	Some	Some to lots
Privacy	Low	Low	High
Persistence	Medium	Low	High
Storing Typed Data	Easy to intermediate	Difficult	Intermediate to difficult
Default Size Limit	100 kilobytes	4 kilobytes	None

Identifying Useful Situations for Shared Objects

Using local shared objects is great when you need to store small to medium amounts of non–mission-critical information that is not private. They are excellent for storing preferences of users without requiring them to sign in. You can use local shared objects to:

- Keep bookmarks in text, audio, and video, so that the user can come back to long media and continue right from where he left off.

- Remember the text size picked by the user, so that she can read text in a way that is comfortable to her.

- Save the user's preference to hear music and/or sound effects on a site that provides them.

- Persist any kind of theme customizations such as colors and background images.

- Remember which parts of your program have been used or visited.

- Present help or intro animations only once.

- Remember the user's connection speed to present optimized content without asking about or measuring bandwidth a second time.

Returning to an application that remembers these kinds of small details without asking can be a very positive experience. These are good examples because they are not personal or private; they help a user in tangible ways when the user has already expressed a preference that is not likely to change, and they are small features that it would be frustrating to authenticate just to retrieve.

Using SharedObjects

Using SharedObjects is about as simple as it can get. You retrieve a SharedObject, and then read and write to it. Things you put in it, stay in it.

Retrieving a SharedObject

Before you can start storing information in a SharedObject, you must get one. Your program can create and use as many as it needs, until it exceeds the space limitation set for the domain you host it on. More on that later, however. Because you can create lots of SharedObjects, you have to identify them by a unique name. To get a SharedObject, use the static SharedObject.getLocal() method. The full class name is flash.net.SharedObject so don't forget to include an import statement.

 **The name of the shared object may not contain spaces, or these characters:**
~ % & \ ; : " ' , < > ? #

In the following example, no matter what you call the variable, it will retain the data stored in the SharedObject named hiscores. Furthermore, the first time you try to get the SharedObject with this name, it will be created for you, so you don't have to worry if a SharedObject already exists or not.

```
import flash.net.SharedObject;
var hiscores:SharedObject = SharedObject.getLocal("hiscores");
```

 **Do not use** new **to construct a** SharedObject. **Use the static method** SharedObject.getLocal().

Reading from, and writing to, a SharedObject

Once you have retrieved a SharedObject, also called a local shared object or LSO, use its data property as an associative array. Any property you add to the data object will be stored and available in later sessions.

You can set and retrieve properties of data, like any other Object, using either dot notation or array access notation. To read from the SharedObject, just access the desired property of the data object. If you try to access a property that has not yet been defined, you will get undefined. For more information on using Objects, please see Chapter 9.

```
//write to the SharedObject
hiscores.data.highest = 999999;
//read from the SharedObject
if (hiscores.data.scores)
{
```

```
for (var i:int = 0; i < hiscores.data.scores.length; i++)
{
    trace(i + ": " + hiscores.data.scores[i]);
}
}
```

CAUTION You can't assign a value to data itself. You may add only properties to the data object.

And that's it! There is no step three. Values you put into the data property of a SharedObject will be there when you retrieve it next time with getLocal().

Deleting information from a SharedObject

Because the data property of a SharedObject is an Object, just as you can read and write to the shared object as you would to an Object, you can delete properties as you would delete them from an Object. Just use the delete operator with the property you want to clear from the data property, as the following snippet shows:

```
var so:SharedObject = SharedObject.getLocal("storage");
delete so.data.bookmark; //remove the bookmark
```

Removing properties from a SharedObject will ensure that they won't be available the next time you attempt to retrieve them. Additionally, the space available to SharedObjects is fairly limited, so it's a good idea to clear out larger structures if they are no longer needed.

To totally wipe out the entire SharedObject, use its clear() method. This will not only remove all the stored data, but the SharedObject file itself.

```
var so:SharedObject = SharedObject.getLocal("storage");
so.clear(); //nuke the LSO named "storage"
```

After using clear(), the next time you request a local SharedObject with the same name, it won't be found and a new one will be created for you and returned.

Saving information

You don't have to do anything special to ensure that the local shared object's information is stored for later reference. The LSO will be synchronized to disk when the SWF is unloaded, or when the SharedObject is no longer used and your program retains no more references to it.

However, you can force the SharedObject to save to disk by calling its flush() method. With no arguments, the method simply forces the LSO to write itself to the shared object file.

```
var so:SharedObject = SharedObject.getLocal("storage");
so.data.username = "Roger";
so.flush(); //make sure this is saved right away
```

When passed an argument, the flush() method is useful for reserving space for large objects, so we will revisit it soon.

Sharing Information Between SWFs

By default, when you save information to a local shared object, it is associated with the SWF that created it. The SWF is identified by the location from which it was loaded, so that each SWF gets its own whole namespace of possible SharedObject names. This means you don't have to worry if another SWF on the Internet wants to use the name storage for its SharedObject.

To understand this better, let's lift back the hood of Flash Player and find how SharedObjects are stored on your local drive. Somewhere in your drive, under your username, is a folder that stores all those SharedObjects. Let's call this directory #SharedObjects. When you create an LSO named storage in a file hosted at http://example.com/examples/sharedobjects .swf, information stored in that shared object will end up in a file named:

    #SharedObjects/example.com/examples/sharedobjects.swf/storage.sol

This literal mapping between the name of the SharedObject and a file on the filesystem explains why you are prevented from using specific characters when naming an LSO.

This scheme of storing shared object files also allows you to share shared objects between SWFs hosted in different locations on the same domain. You can, for example, store a central set of preferences that are implemented across several modules seamlessly.

To be able to share local shared objects, you must ensure that the shared object file is stored in a place that is accessible to SWFs in both locations. If you placed the shared object file at:

    #SharedObjects/example.com/storage.sol

it would be accessible to any SWF stored on http://example.com/. Likewise, storing it in the examples/ directory would make it accessible to any SWF stored in the examples directory or its subdirectories, but not in other directories or other domains.

In order to modify the location of the local shared object, you can pass a second parameter to the SharedObject.getLocal() method. This optional parameter defines the path (relative to the domain) under which the local shared object file will be stored, and by extension defines which SWFs can share data stored in it. The parameter defaults to the location of the SWF, as in the following example:

```
//in code run by http://DOMAIN/ORIGINAL/PATH/test.swf ...

SharedObject.getLocal("NAME");
//creates or retrieves #SharedObjects/DOMAIN/ORIGINAL/PATH/test.swf/NAME.sol
```

```
SharedObject.getLocal("NAME", "/");
//creates or retrieves #SharedObjects/DOMAIN/NAME.sol

SharedObject.getLocal("NAME","/NEW/PATH");
//creates or retrieves #SharedObjects/DOMAIN/NEW/PATH/NAME.sol
```

By targeting all your SWFs on the same domain to use a shared object file at the same location, and choosing that location so that it is accessible to all your SWFs, you can share one set of data persistently between multiple programs or multiple parts of a program.

CAUTION It is not possible to move the LSO file outside of the domain name directory. The highest directory you can set for the `localPath` parameter is `/`, which maps to the root of the domain. Using this value for `localPath` allows any SWF in the domain to access the `SharedObject`. Be aware that Flash Player's security sandbox restrictions still apply in addition to the `localPath` parameter.

Requiring a secure connection

You can add a further layer of security by creating local shared objects that are available only from SWFs served through a secured (HTTPS) connection. Pass `true` as the optional parameter `security` of `SharedObject.getLocal()` to retrieve a `SharedObject` that is only valid for SWFs served from secured connections.

This is the final parameter that `getLocal()` can accept, so let's review its full method signature:

```
static function getLocal(name:String, localPath:String = null,
                         security:Boolean = false);
```

When you retrieve a `SharedObject` from a SWF served over HTTPS, a `SharedObject` will be retrieved or created that can't be accessed from non-HTTPS locations. Attempting to retrieve a secure `SharedObject` from an HTTP connection returns `null`.

```
//from https://example.com/shortbread.swf
var so:SharedObject = SharedObject.getLocal("desserts", "/", true);
so.data.cookies = 100;

//from https://example.com/frozen/icecream.swf
var so:SharedObject = SharedObject.getLocal("desserts", "/", true);
trace(so.data.cookies); //100
so.data.icecreams = [{flavor: "chocolate", rating: 5}];

//from http://example.com/hot/pie.swf
var so:SharedObject = SharedObject.getLocal("desserts", "/", true);
//returns null
```

```
//from http://example.com/hot/pie.swf
var so:SharedObject = SharedObject.getLocal("desserts", "/");
trace(so.data.cookies); //undefined
trace(so.data.icecreams); //undefined
```

In the preceding example, the `desserts` `SharedObject` can exist both as a secured `SharedObject` and an insecure one. These two will live independently, but SWFs served from insecure connections such as `pie.swf` won't have access to the secure versions.

> **CAUTION**   Storing local shared objects as secured guarantees only the ability or inability of Flash movies to access the data in them. However, any information you store in them will be stored unencrypted on the user's computer in an accessible directory. Again, do not use local shared objects to store sensitive or private information, especially without the user's consent.

Sharing with ActionScript 1.0 and 2.0 SWFs

ActionScript 3.0 uses the new AMF3 format for serializing data to local shared objects. However, SWFs that use prior versions of ActionScript use AMF0. By default, this means that a SWF written in AS3 can access shared objects saved by SWFs written in AS1 or AS2. But, those older SWFs won't be able to access shared objects saved by SWFs that use ActionScript 3.0.

In order to retain compatibility in both directions, you can explicitly instruct `SharedObjects` to use AMF0 or AMF3 when encoding data. To do so, use the static `SharedObject.defaultObjectEncoding` property or the instance variable `objectEncoding`.

> **NEW IN AS3**   These properties of `SharedObject` are available only in ActionScript 3.0.

```
static function set defaultObjectEncoding(value:uint):void;
static function get defaultObjectEncoding():uint;
function set objectEncoding(value:uint):void;
function get objectEncoding():uint;
```

If you want to pick one format to use for the entire program, just set `SharedObject` `.defaultObjectEncoding` once during your program's initialization. If you need more fine control, you can set the `objectEncoding` property on each `SharedObject` instance as you require.

These properties accept `uint`s. The value 0 represents AMF0, and 3 represents AMF3, but you should instead use the static properties `AMF0` and `AMF3` of `flash.net.ObjectEncoding`, as shown in the following snippet:

```
import flash.net.ObjectEncoding;
SharedObject.defaultObjectEncoding = ObjectEncoding.AMF0;
```

If you choose to use AMF0, types new to ActionScript 3.0 such as `ByteArray`, `int`, and `XML` will be stored incorrectly. You also won't be able to work with custom classes that use `IExternalizable` while using AMF0.

Working with Size Constraints

Ultimately, the user has control over whether your program can store data locally or not, and how much. Therefore, technically you can't rely on local shared objects for your application to work correctly. However, the vast majority of users have local shared objects enabled, and in reality, you can make this a requirement without shutting out more than a handful of users. The same limitations hold true for browser cookies, and there are a great number of web applications that require cookies. In fact, local shared objects have an advantage here because you have the ability to query the user for more space when you need it.

User settings

You, and any Flash Player user, can control the Flash Player's policies on local storage by accessing the Flash Player Settings Manager. The Settings Manager is an embedded control panel that you can find by accessing `www.macromedia.com/support/documentation/en/flashplayer/ help/settings_manager.html`.

There are two relevant panels for controlling local shared object storage. You can set how much space is allotted by default for sites using the Global Storage Settings panel, as shown in Figure 24-1. You can control the space allotted to sites on a site-by-site basis, examine disk usage, and clear individual sites' local shared objects by using the Website Storage Settings panel, as shown in Figure 24-2.

FIGURE 24-1

The Flash Player Global Storage Settings panel

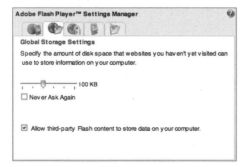

FIGURE 24-2

The Flash Player Website Storage Settings panel

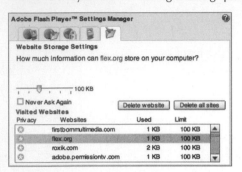

It's worth repeating that a great majority of users will use your program with the default settings: 100KB allotted by default per site.

User requests

When your program uses more than its allotment of space, rather than failing to save the requested information, the user is prompted to allow this action. A dialog box is opened automatically by Flash Player with this prompt, showing the amount of space requested and the amount of space currently allocated. You don't have to provide this dialog box yourself, but you also can't customize it. A sample dialog box is shown in Figure 24-3.

FIGURE 24-3

Flash Player requesting additional space

CAUTION Any SWF that might display this kind of prompt must be at least 215 pixels wide by 138 pixels high or bigger, in order to accommodate this prompt. If it is sized smaller, the request will be automatically denied and the user will see no prompt.

This kind of prompting means that you can have the chance to store as much information as you want in a shared object, but also that it is never guaranteed. Furthermore, for many applications, allowing the user to see this dialog box might be entirely unacceptable, and you might have to plan for a limit of 100KB and hope for the best.

When this kind of dialog box appears, you will have to wait asynchronously for the user to interact with it, as well, which can complicate the control flow of your program.

Asking for space before it's too late

Earlier you learned that SharedObjects are synchronized to disk automatically as the SWF unloads, so you don't have to use flush(). However, if your assignments to the LSO require it to ask the user to expand in size, it is too late to display this dialog box if the SWF is closing.

If you are using SharedObjects to casually store a tiny bit of non-critical information, this should be no problem and you may choose not to manually synchronize the shared object to disk with flush(). In this case, popping up a dialog box isn't even preferable to losing the information if the information is so unimportant.

However, if you need to know if the data was successfully stored or not, you should explicitly use flush().

Asking for space up front

The flush() method can take an optional parameter that represents the amount of disk space you anticipate needing. By using this parameter, you can limit user-facing dialog boxes to a single request.

For example, say you store 150KB, flush, store another 150KB, flush, and store a final 50KB and flush. With a default limit of 100KB, this will result in three dialog boxes, first to expand from 100KB to 150KB, then to expand from 150KB to 300KB, and finally to expand from 300KB to 350KB.

Instead, you could — even before storing any data to the SharedObject — flush while requesting 350KB of space. This would present a dialog box, but then (assuming the user accepts) the rest of the flush operations would proceed without requiring user intervention, as the total space of 350KB was already allocated.

Using flush()

The signature of the SharedObject's flush() method is:

```
function flush(minDiskSpace:int = 0):String
```

Use the minDiskSpace argument to request the total amount of space you anticipate needing, in bytes.

The return type lets you know if you need to wait for the user to accept or deny the request, or if the operation failed. `flush()` may also throw an `Error` or dispatch an asynchronous `NetStatusEvent` error if the user specified to globally deny these requests or the dialog box can't be shown.

The possible return types are defined by static properties of the `flash.net` `.SharedObjectFlushStatus` class:

- `SharedObjectFlushStatus.PENDING` is returned if the user has been presented with a dialog box requiring his approval.

- `SharedObjectFlushStatus.FLUSHED` is returned if the shared object has been successfully written to disk.

When calling `flush()`, you can check to see if user verification is necessary, and if so, subscribe to the `SharedObject` to be notified if the request is approved or denied. The following example shows how to do this by requesting space up front with the `minDiskSpace` parameter of `flush()`:

```
package
{
    import flash.display.Sprite;
    import flash.events.NetStatusEvent;
    import flash.net.SharedObject;
    import flash.net.SharedObjectFlushStatus;

    public class OverflowTest extends Sprite
    {
        protected var so:SharedObject;

        public function OverflowTest()
        {
            so = SharedObject.getLocal("storage");

            //request 1 MB up front
            if (so.flush(1024 * 1024) == SharedObjectFlushStatus.PENDING)
            {
                so.addEventListener(NetStatusEvent.NET_STATUS, onUserAction);
                trace("User approval pending...");
            }
        }

        public function onUserAction(event:NetStatusEvent):void
        {
            so.removeEventListener(NetStatusEvent.NET_STATUS, onUserAction);
            switch (event.info.code)
            {
                case "SharedObject.Flush.Success":
                    trace("Accepted");
                    break;
```

```
            case "SharedObject.Flush.Failed":
                trace("Denied");
                //do error recovery
                break;
        }
    }
}
```

Unlike most events in which the type of the event is communicated fully by its `type` parameter, the `NetStatusEvent.NET_STATUS` event can signal many different kinds of events, so you must inspect the event's `info` object to determine what really happened.

Viewing used space

You can check the amount of disk space already in use by a `SharedObject` by accessing its `size` implicit getter. This returns the size of the particular local shared object in bytes. However, it calculates this by measuring every object inside it, so it can be processor-intensive.

Storing Custom Classes

Using a `SharedObject`, you can store any native type in ActionScript 3.0 persistently. You can also store your own custom classes as well, with a little bit of extra work. The extra work has to do with the process of encoding objects into bytes so that they can be written to the local shared object file. Encoding objects into a flat binary representation is called *serialization*, and restoring them into their original form as runtime objects is called *deserialization*. You've already seen that Flash Player uses AMF to serialize and deserialize objects for storage in shared objects.

Storing custom classes without modification

Certain kinds of classes can be serialized and deserialized in AMF with no problem. If you create classes that follow these restrictions, you will be able to retrieve and store them in shared objects without additional code:

- All properties of the class must be public.
- The class's constructor must take no arguments, or all arguments to the constructor must have default values.

Classes that are structured like this are essentially `Object`s with methods attached: AMF can serialize `Object`s, and methods are not serialized. Of course, all of the object's properties must also be of serializable types for the object to be serialized.

The following is a custom class that can be natively serialized in AMF3. Because it uses an `int` type, you should use AMF3 as the encoding method (again, this is the default when programming in ActionScript 3.0):

```
package com.wiley.as3bible
{
    public class Bookmark
    {
        public var page:int;

        public function Bookmark()
        {
        }

        public function toString():String
        {
            return "[Bookmark at page " + page + "]";
        }
    }
}
```

Note that the `Bookmark` class has only public properties, and its constructor takes no arguments. Let's see how you can use and persistently store this custom class.

In order for Flash Player to know what class to associate an object with when it comes out of a serialized format, it must also know what class the bytes originally represented. So in order to use custom classes in a shared object, you must give the class a name that will be stored along with it. This must be done in both directions: to ensure that a name is saved along with a class's representation, and to know what class to create from the class's name when it is reconstituted. This is performed rather simply by one operation: `flash.net.registerClassAlias()`. This function registers a class definition with a `String` identifier. You must ensure that this is called before any `SharedObject` that contains custom classes is retrieved or created.

Then, to get the type back when retrieving an instance of a custom class, retrieve the property from the shared object's `data` property and cast it to the type that it should be, as shown in the following example:

```
package
{
    import flash.display.Sprite;
    import flash.net.ObjectEncoding;
    import flash.net.SharedObject;
    import flash.net.registerClassAlias;
    import com.wiley.as3bible.Bookmark;

    public class CustomClassTest extends Sprite
    {
        protected const TOTAL_PAGES:int = 1024;
        protected var currentPage:int;
```

```
        protected var so:SharedObject;

        public function CustomClassTest()
        {
            registerClassAlias("com.wiley.as3bible.Bookmark", Bookmark);
            so = SharedObject.getLocal("storage");
            if (so.data.bookmark)
            {
                //go to the stored bookmark
                var b:Bookmark = Bookmark(so.data.bookmark);
                trace("found", b);
                gotoPage(b.page);
            } else {
                //bookmark a random page.
                gotoPage(int(Math.random() * TOTAL_PAGES));
            }
        }

        public function setBookmark():void
        {
            var b:Bookmark = new Bookmark();
            b.page = currentPage;
            so.data.bookmark = b;
            trace("setting", so.data.bookmark);
        }

        public function gotoPage(page:int):void
        {
            currentPage = page;
            setBookmark();
        }
    }
}
```

In order to make sure there are no name collisions, it is customary to use the fully qualified class name as the alias name in `registerClassAlias()`.

Creating self-serializing classes

You can get around the public variable restriction by using AMF3 and implementing the interface `flash.utils.IExternalizable` in your custom classes. By implementing this interface, you define how your class is turned into bytes and how it restores itself from bytes. In other words, if you elect to figure out how to do the serialization and deserialization of your class, Flash Player will simply rely on the encoding methods you provide.

The `IExternalizable` interface includes two functions, which you must implement:

```
function readExternal(input:IDataInput):void
function writeExternal(output:IDataOutput):void
```

These methods, when implemented, deserialize your class from, and serialize your class to, binary data. The IDataInput and IDataOutput interfaces are implemented by ByteArray; see Chapter 34 for more information on how to use these interfaces.

Internally, you can take advantage of AMF3 by using IDataInput.readObject() and IDataOutput.writeObject(), which perform AMF3 serialization and deserialization. For instance, you might simply construct an Object of your non-public properties, and use AMF3 to serialize that Object for you. This way, you don't have to worry exactly how your instance collapses into bytes; you can control the serialization at a higher level and use AMF encoding to do the grunt work.

The following extended Bookmark class shows this approach in action. Note that you can protect your properties this way, which is important to maintain encapsulation.

```
package com.wiley.as3bible
{
    import flash.utils.IDataOutput;
    import flash.utils.IDataInput;
    import flash.utils.IExternalizable;

    public class Bookmark implements IExternalizable
    {
        protected var page:int;
        protected var color:uint;
        protected var name:String;

        public function Bookmark(page:int = 0, color:uint = 0, ↵
                                 name:String = null)
        {
            this.page = page;
            this.color = color;
            this.name = name;
        }

        public function getPage():int
        {
            return this.page;
        }

        public function readExternal(input:IDataInput):void
        {
            var props:Object = input.readObject();
            page = props.page;
            color = props.color;
            name = props.name;
        }

        public function writeExternal(output:IDataOutput):void
        {
```

```
        var props:Object = {page: page, color: color, name: name};
        output.writeObject(props);
    }

    public function toString():String
    {
        return "[Bookmark at page " + page ↵
            + " color=" + color.toString(16) ↵
            + " name=" + name + "]";
    }
  }
}
```

By implementing IExternalizable and providing your own serialization and deserialization methods, you can store and retrieve custom classes that contain complex types without breaking encapsulation.

Using Serialization Concepts for Remoting

The methods used in this chapter to encode custom types for saving in locally shared objects are even more applicable to remoting, or remote method invocation, or remote procedure calls, or whatever your favored technology calls it. It's incredibly useful to be able to deal with real class instances on either side of a client-server application, rather than always converting from XML, JSON, or another transport format. Beyond being able to store typed data, AMF is binary, compressed, and fast. So, consider applying these serialization and deserialization strategies to support Flash Remoting in your client-server program. For more information, see Chapter 23.

Additionally, SharedObject may be used to create and represent *remote shared objects*. In contrast to local shared objects, remote shared objects are data containers that stay in synch with their representations on a server. You can take advantage of remote shared objects with technologies such as Flash Media Server and Flex Data Services. The SharedObject class is used for both remote and local shared objects. Some of its methods — send(), connect(), close(), setDirty(), and setProperty() — are applicable only to remote shared objects.

Summary

- Using SharedObject for locally shared objects is painless in ActionScript 3.0.
- SharedObjects give you a decent amount of storage.
- Local SharedObjects are comparable to browser cookies but have more persistence, security, and size, and require no bridge to JavaScript.
- Storing information on a server is, in most cases, more secure and more appropriate for media or other large data.

- `SharedObjects` are tied to an account on a computer rather than an actual user.

- You can share information in a `SharedObject` between SWFs in different locations on the same domain by constructing an appropriate `localPath` argument.

- You can create local shared objects that are used only in SWFs hosted from secure connections.

- The user ultimately has control over the available size for shared objects.

- When requesting more data than available, the user is prompted.

- You can find out if prompts to expand the available `SharedObject` size were successful or not.

- You can store custom classes in `SharedObject` instances with `registerClassAlias()` and, if necessary, `IExternalizable`.

Chapter 25

Managing File Uploads and Downloads

File upload and download is important for many applications. By enabling users to upload files, you allow them to contribute content such as images, audio, and video, which is crucial in a Web 2.0 world. By adding file download features to an application you allow users to save content locally on their computers. Flash Player supports both file upload and download using the `flash.net.FileReference` and `flash.net.FileReferenceList` classes.

Introducing FileReference

The `flash.net.FileReference` class enables users to browse for a file to upload or select a location to save a downloaded file to using a system dialog box. The `flash.net.FileReferenceList` class lets users select one or more files to upload. In this chapter, you learn to work with the `FileReference` class and the `FileReferenceList` class.

Except when returned from a `FileReferenceList`, `FileReference` objects are constructed using the constructor in a new statement. The constructor does not require any parameters:

```
var fileToUpload:FileReference = new FileReference();
```

Optionally, if you want the user to be able to select many files at once, you can use a `FileReferenceList` object. Like `FileReference`, the `FileReferenceList` constructor requires no parameters:

```
var fileListToUpload:FileReferenceList = new
FileReferenceList();
```

Uploading Files

The following sections explain how to upload files using `FileReference` and `FileReferenceList`.

Selecting a file to upload

To upload a file, the user must first select the file. You can prompt the user to select a file by calling the `browse()` method. The `browse()` method has an optional parameter, so that you can call it with no parameters or one parameter. When you call `browse()` with no parameters, it opens a new browse dialog box from which the user can select a file.

```
fileToUpload.browse();
```

By default, the browse dialog box displays all file types. However, you can specify which file types the user can select by passing an optional parameter to the `browse()` method. The parameter must be an array of `flash.net.FileFilter` objects. `FileFilter` objects allow you to specify a description for the type that will display in the browse dialog box, a list of allowable file extensions, and optionally a list of Macintosh file filters. The `FileFilter` constructor allows the following parameters:

- `description`: A string describing the file type.
- `extension`: A list of file extensions with wildcards. The list items must be delimited by semicolons.
- `macType`: A list of Macintosh file types delimited by semicolons. This parameter is optional.

The `macType` parameter is optional. If it is not specified, the file extensions specified by the `extension` property are used for Macintoshes as well.

Here's an example that opens a browse dialog with two filters. One filter displays only images of type .jpg, .gif, and .png, and the second filter displays only QuickTime movie files.

```
fileToUpload.browse([new FileFilter("Image Files", 
"*.jpg;*.gif;*.png"), new FileFilter("Quicktime Movies", 
"*.mov")]);
```

Here's the same example but with Macintosh types specified as well.

```
fileToUpload.browse([new FileFilter("Image Files", 
"*.jpg;*.gif;*.png", "JPEG;jp2_;GIFF"), 
new FileFilter("Quicktime Movies", "*.mov", 
"MooV")]);
```

The `FileReferenceList` class also defines a `browse()` method that uses identical syntax to the `FileReference` method of the same name. The only difference is that the browse dialog box opened from a `FileReferenceList` object allows the user to select more than one file.

Determining when a file is selected

Calling `browse()` causes the browse dialog box to open. However, it doesn't guarantee that the user will select a file. The browse dialog box has two buttons from which the user can select — Open and Cancel. If the user selects Open, the selected file data is sent to Flash Player before the browse dialog closes. If the user selects Cancel, the browse dialog closes without the file data getting sent to Flash Player. To build a good application, you need to be able to determine which option the user has selected, and you can accomplish that goal using a listener object with the `FileReference` or `FileReferenceList` object from which you've called `browse()`.

`FileReference` or `FileReferenceList` objects dispatch select (`Event.SELECT`) and cancel (`Event.CANCEL`) events when the user clicks the Open and Cancel buttons, respectively. The following example illustrates how these events work. When the user clicks the browse files text, the application launches a browse dialog. If the user selects a file then the output text displays `Selected File`, but if the user cancels the file selection then the output text displays `Canceled`.

```
package com.wiley.as3bible.files {

import flash.display.Sprite;
import flash.text.TextField;
import flash.events.Event;
import flash.events.MouseEvent;
import flash.net.FileReference;

    public class Files extends Sprite {

        private var _browse:TextField;
        private var _output:TextField;
        private var _fileReference:FileReference;

        public function Files() {

            _browse = new TextField();
            _browse.htmlText = "<u>click to browse files</u>";
            _browse.addEventListener(MouseEvent.CLICK, clickHandler);
            addChild(_browse);
            _output = new TextField();
            _output.width = 400;
            _output.height = 400;
            _output.y = 50;
            addChild(_output);

            _fileReference = new FileReference();
            _fileReference.addEventListener(Event.SELECT, selectHandler);
            _fileReference.addEventListener(Event.CANCEL, cancelHandler);
        }

        private function clickHandler(event:MouseEvent):void {
            _fileReference.browse();
        }

        private function selectHandler(event:Event):void {
```

```
                    _output.text = "Selected File";
            }

            private function cancelHandler(event:Event):void {
                _output.text = "Canceled";
            }
        }
    }
```

Retrieving file properties

Once the user has selected a file via the browse dialog box, that file's properties are sent to Flash Player, and they are accessible via the `FileReference` object from which the `browse()` method was called or from an array of `FileReference` objects stored in the `fileList` property of the `FileReferenceList` object. The `FileReference` class defines the following properties that describe the file to which it is associated:

- `name`: The name of the file.

- `size`: The size of the file in bytes.

- `type`: The file extension (Windows) or Macintosh file type.

- `creationDate`: A Date object representing the date on which the file was created.

- `modificationDate`: A Date object representing the date on which the file was last modified.

- `creator`: On Macintosh, the property is a string value specifying the user type of the user that created the file. On Windows the property returns null.

The following example builds on the preceding example. This example displays the file properties in the output text field if the user selects a file. Changes are shown in bold:

```
package com.wiley.as3bible.files {

    import flash.display.Sprite;
    import flash.text.TextField;
    import flash.events.Event;
    import flash.events.MouseEvent;
    import flash.net.FileReference;

    public class Files extends Sprite {

        private var _browse:TextField;
        private var _output:TextField;
        private var _fileReference:FileReference;

        public function Files() {

            _browse = new TextField();
            _browse.htmlText = "<u>click to browse files</u>";
            _browse.addEventListener(MouseEvent.CLICK, clickHandler);
```

```
        addChild(_browse);
        _output = new TextField();
        _output.width = 400;
        _output.height = 400;
        _output.y = 50;
        addChild(_output);

        _fileReference = new FileReference();
        _fileReference.addEventListener(Event.SELECT, selectHandler);
        _fileReference.addEventListener(Event.CANCEL, cancelHandler);

    }

    private function clickHandler(event:MouseEvent):void {
        _fileReference.browse();

    }

    private function selectHandler(event:Event):void {
        _output.text = "Selected File";
        _output.appendText("\nName: " + _fileReference.name);
        _output.appendText("\nSize: " + _fileReference.size);
        _output.appendText("\nCreated On: " + _fileReference.creationDate);
        _output.appendText("\nModified On: " + ↵
_fileReference.modificationDate);
    }

    private function cancelHandler(event:Event):void {
        _output.text = "Canceled";
    }
  }

}
```

The following code is a modification of the preceding example. This example uses a
`FileReferenceList` and displays the details of each file that was selected:

```
package com.wiley.as3bible.files {

    import flash.display.Sprite;
    import flash.text.TextField;
    import flash.events.Event;
    import flash.events.MouseEvent;
    import flash.net.FileReference;
    import flash.net.FileReferenceList;

    public class Files extends Sprite {

        private var _browse:TextField;
        private var _output:TextField;
        private var _fileReferenceList:FileReferenceList;

        public function Files() {
```

```
        _browse = new TextField();
        _browse.htmlText = "<u>click to browse files</u>";
        _browse.addEventListener(MouseEvent.CLICK, clickHandler);
        addChild(_browse);

        _output = new TextField();
        _output.width = 400;
        _output.height = 400;
        _output.y = 50;
        addChild(_output);

        _fileReferenceList = new FileReferenceList();
        _fileReferenceList.addEventListener(Event.SELECT, selectHandler);
        _fileReferenceList.addEventListener(Event.CANCEL, cancelHandler);

    }

    private function clickHandler(event:MouseEvent):void {
        _fileReferenceList.browse();

    }

    private function selectHandler(event:Event):void {
        _output.text = "Selected Files";
        var file:FileReference;
        for(var i:Number = 0; i < _fileReferenceList.fileList.length; i++) {
            file = _fileReferenceList.fileList[i];
            _output.appendText("\nName: " + file.name);
            _output.appendText("\nSize: " + file.size);
            _output.appendText("\nCreated On: " + file.creationDate);
            _output.appendText("\nModified On: " + file.modificationDate);
            _output.appendText("\n--------------------------------");
        }
    }

    private function cancelHandler(event:Event):void {
        _output.text = "Canceled";
    }

    }
}
```

Uploading a file

Once the user has selected a file or files, you can upload the file via the `upload()` method of the `FileReference` object you want to upload to the server. If you used a `FileReferenceList` object to let the user select more than one file, you have to call `upload()` for each element in the `fileList` array.

The `upload()` method requires one parameter — a `URLRequest` object specifying the script to which you want to upload the file. The `URLRequest` object must point to a resource that can handle HTTP file upload requests such as a PHP script like the one used in the exercise in the following section. When the file data is uploaded, it is sent via HTTP POST with a content type of multipart/form-data. By default, the content name (by which you can reference the file data from the script) is Filedata. Therefore, to the server resource handling the upload it is as though the file is being uploaded via an HTML form with a file input named Filedata. If you prefer to use a custom name, you can specify a second, optional parameter to the upload() method.

```
fileReference.upload(new URLRequest("script.php"), "CustomFile");
```

FileReference objects dispatch events as you attempt to upload files. The following are the uploading events:

- httpStatus: There was an HTTP error. The event is of type HTTPStatusEvent, which has a property called status indicating the HTTP error type (for example, 404).

- ioError: A network error occurred, the URL is invalid, or the server requires authentication that the current player does not support. The event is of type IOErrorEvent.

- securityError: An error occurred related to the Flash Player security model. For example, the requested URL may be inaccessible to Flash Player because of differing domains and no cross-domain policy file being found. This event is of type SecurityErrorEvent.

- open: The file has successfully started to upload. The event is of type Event.

- progress: Some portion of the file has uploaded. The event is of type ProgressEvent. Event objects of this type have bytesLoaded and bytesTotal properties.

- complete: The file has successfully uploaded. The event is of type Event.

Uploading files is subject to the same security model as any other HTTP request from Flash Player. Either the URL must be in the same exact domain as the SWF, or the server must have a policy file. You can read more about Flash Player security and policy files in Chapter 22.

If the server resource to which the file is uploaded requires authentication, Flash Player will prompt the user for authentication only when the SWF file is loaded in the browser. Otherwise, in any non-browser environment the upload will fail.

Adding Uploading Capabilities to an Application

In this exercise, you build a simple application that lets users upload files to a server from Flash Player utilizing a PHP script on the server. To run the exercise, you'll need access to a web server that runs PHP. PHP is fairly standard on most shared web hosts. If your web host does have PHP installed, then it's recommended that you use that web server. However, in the event that your web host does not have PHP installed, you can download and install PHP for free on your own computer. You can download PHP from www.php.net. PHP runs on Windows, Macintosh, and

Linux, to name a few operating systems, so you shouldn't have difficulty installing PHP on your computer. If you opt to run PHP on your computer, you'll also have to run a web server such as IIS or Apache. It's beyond the scope of this book to instruct you how to install a web server or PHP, but you should have no difficulty locating helpful resources for those topics on the Web.

1. Create a new text file called simpleFileUpload.php, and add the following code to the file:

```php
<?php
move_uploaded_file($_FILES['Filedata']['tmp_name'], ↵
'./'.time().$_FILES['Filedata']['name']);
?>
```

2. Copy the file to a PHP-enabled directory on your web server that is accessible via HTTP.

3. Open a new Flash document, and save it as fileUploader.fla. Set the document class to com.wiley.as3bible.files.FileUpload.

4. Create a new class, and add the following code to it:

```
package com.wiley.as3bible.files {

import flash.display.Sprite;
import flash.text.TextField;
import flash.events.Event;
import flash.events.MouseEvent;
import flash.events.IOErrorEvent;
import flash.events.ProgressEvent;
import flash.events.SecurityErrorEvent;
import flash.net.FileReference;
import flash.net.URLRequest;

public class FileUpload extends Sprite {

    private var _browse:TextField;
    private var _upload:TextField;
    private var _output:TextField;
    private var _fileReference:FileReference;

    public function FileUpload() {

        _browse = new TextField();
        _browse.htmlText = "<u>click to browse file</u>";
        _browse.addEventListener(MouseEvent.CLICK, browseHandler);
        addChild(_browse);

        _upload = new TextField();
        _upload.htmlText = "<u>click to upload file</u>";
        _upload.addEventListener(MouseEvent.CLICK, uploadHandler);
        _upload.x = 200;
        _upload.visible = false;
        addChild(_upload);
```

```
            _output = new TextField();
            _output.width = 400;
            _output.height = 400;
            _output.y = 50;
            addChild(_output);

            _fileReference = new FileReference();
            _fileReference.addEventListener(Event.SELECT, selectHandler);
            _fileReference.addEventListener(Event.CANCEL, cancelHandler);
            _fileReference.addEventListener(ProgressEvent.PROGRESS, ↵
progressHandler);
            _fileReference.addEventListener(IOErrorEvent.IO_ERROR, ↵
ioErrorHandler);
            _fileReference.addEventListener(SecurityErrorEvent.SECURITY_ERROR,↵
securityHandler);
            _fileReference.addEventListener(Event.COMPLETE, completeHandler);

    }

    private function browseHandler(event:MouseEvent):void {
        _fileReference.browse();
    }
    private function selectHandler(event:Event):void {
        _output.text = "Selected File";
        _output.appendText("\nName: " + _fileReference.name);
        _output.appendText("\nSize: " + _fileReference.size);
        _output.appendText("\nCreated On: " + _fileReference.creationDate);
        _output.appendText("\nModified On: " + ↵
_fileReference.modificationDate);
        _upload.visible = true;
    }

    private function cancelHandler(event:Event):void {
        _output.text = "Canceled";
    }

    private function uploadHandler(event:MouseEvent):void {
        _fileReference.upload(new URLRequest("simpleFileUpload.php"));
    }

    private function progressHandler(event:ProgressEvent):void {
        _output.text = "file uploading\noprogress (bytes): " + ↵
event.bytesLoaded + " / " + event.bytesTotal;
    }

    private function ioErrorHandler(event:IOErrorEvent):void {
        _output.text = "an IO error occurred";
    }
    private function securityHandler(event:SecurityErrorEvent):void {
        _output.text = "a security error occurred";
    }
```

```
        private function completeHandler(event:Event):void {
            _output.text = "the file has uploaded";
        }
    }
}
```

5. Test the application.

When you test the application, you should be able to browse to a file, select it, and then click the link to upload it. A copy of the selected file should appear on the server in the same directory as the PHP script.

Downloading a File

Using the download() method of FileReference, you can download a file from a URL to the user's computer. However, the user has to grant permission. When the download() method is called, a new dialog box is opened, and the user is prompted to save the file. The user has the choice to click Save or Cancel.

The download() method requires one parameter. The first parameter is a URLRequest object pointing to an HTTP resource to download:

```
fileToDownload.download(new URLRequest("http://server/file"));
```

Optionally, you can specify a second parameter, which determines the default name of the file as it appears in the download dialog box:

```
fileToDownload.download(new URLRequest("http://server/file", "a_file.txt"));
```

If the user clicks Cancel, the object dispatches a cancel event. If the user clicks Save, the object dispatches an open event. As the file downloads, the object dispatches progress events. And when the file has downloaded, the object dispatches a complete event. If there are any errors, the appropriate error events get dispatched (httpError, ioError, or securityError).

Summary

- Flash Player 9 allows for file upload and download functionality.

- Using the FileReference or FileReferenceList classes, you can prompt users to browse to and select a file or files from their local drive in order to upload the file(s).

- The FileReference class defines methods for uploading and downloading files.

Part VII

Enriching Your Program with Sound and Video

Chapter 26

Working with Sound

I n this section, you look at ways to integrate sound into your program. A little bit of sound goes a long way in adding depth and character to your Flash program. Although sound has been a part of every previous version of Flash, developers now have more control over sound than ever before. The ability to work with MP3 files locally or over the network and to access metadata makes Flash an ideal platform for cross-platform custom audio interfaces. As with many other areas of the API, the sound classes work with the AS3 event framework. Perhaps most important, the ability to compute an analysis of the sound spectrum will allow you to provide visual feedback controlled by the playing sound.

How Sound Works in AS3

The sound system works a little bit differently than previous versions of Flash. Here's an overview of how everything fits together.

Learning the AS3 sound classes

There are five major sound-related classes in ActionScript 3.0. Together, they work to make up the Flash Player 9 sound system. The Sound class, along with SoundLoaderContext, handles the loading of the sound file. Playing that Sound object creates a new SoundChannel, which can be used to control the playback of the sound. A SoundTransform can be attached to the SoundChannel to alter its volume or to the SoundMixer, which affects all sounds being played. Here they are, along with a brief description of each one's responsibilities:

- Sound: A Sound object is the basis for working with sound in Flash. It holds the audio data for a sound and is responsible for loading any external sound files. It's possible to play back sounds in your ActionScript program using only this class.

- SoundMixer: The SoundMixer is a manager for all the sounds being played back in the Flash Player. It represents the master control over all the channels of audio. The SoundMixer also is responsible for computing the spectrum byte array of all the sounds playing back.

- SoundChannel: When a sound is played, the audio is sent to a channel of the sound mixer. The sound channel represents the sound's playback. This way, the same sound can be played on multiple channels. A maximum of 32 channels of audio can be playing at any time — going over that limit will cause Sound.play() to return null instead of a SoundChannel object.

> **NOTE**   In the world of audio production, the left and right sides of a stereo sound are usually thought of as two separate channels. In Flash, each SoundChannel object contains both left and right tracks in a single channel.

- SoundTransform: SoundTransform allows you to control sound volume and panning for a SoundChannel or for the SoundMixer, which affects all sounds.

- SoundLoaderContext: SoundLoaderContext allows you to set the buffer time that a sound will load before it begins playing. It also handles the security settings when loading a sound over the network.

Figure 26-1 shows how they all work together.

Working with sound events

Sounds in ActionScript 3.0 use the Flash Player 9 event framework to broadcast information about their current status. The following is a list of events, all fired by a Sound object except for SOUND_COMPLETE, which is fired by a SoundChannel:

- flash.events.Event.OPEN: The open event fires when the loading begins.

- flash.events.ProgressEvent.PROGRESS: Progress events are fired continuously while the file is loading.

- flash.events.Event.COMPLETE: Successfully loading the sound will fire a complete event.

- flash.events.IOErrorEvent.IO_ERROR: If any disk or network errors occur while attempting to load the file, there will be an IO error event.

- flash.events.Event.ID3: When ID3 metadata for an MP3 file is done loading and becomes available, this event will be fired.

- flash.events.Event.SOUND_COMPLETE: When a SoundChannel is finished playing, a sound complete event is fired.

FIGURE 26-1

Sound uses SoundLoaderContext to load and play audio. SoundChannel tracks playback. SoundTransform alters the character of the sound. SoundMixer is the master control over all the sounds.

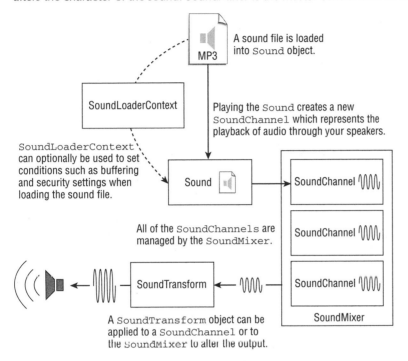

NOTE Of all the previous events listed, SOUND_COMPLETE is the only one that deals specifically with sound playback — the rest are used for loading the sound. There are no other events dispatched at the beginning of or during the playback of a sound.

Creating a Sound Object

The audio files associated with the Sound objects in Flash Player 9 can come from different sources — either from a local file in your asset folder or from a remote URL, or they can be embedded into your SWF file.

Loading a sound from an external file or URL

Loading audio files, holding onto audio data, and playing sound are all handled by the Sound class. While loading sound, a Sound object can behave much like a URLLoader object. Loading a sound from a local URL is fairly simple — just pass a URLRequest object to the Sound object's load() method.

The Sound object can load only audio files encoded in the MP3 format. In the following examples, you can assume that there is an MP3 file with the name sound.mp3 stored in the same folder as the SWF file.

```
var sound:Sound = new Sound();
var url:String = "sound.mp3";
var urlRequest:URLRequest = new URLRequest(url);
sound.load(urlRequest);
```

You can also pass the URLRequest directly to the constructor for a Sound object, thus saving a step.

Once your sound is loaded, playing it back is very easy — just use the play() method of the Sound object. The simplest way to play a sound is this:

```
var sound:Sound = new Sound(new URLRequest("sound.mp3"));
sound.play();
```

This will work for most cases when you need to quickly load and play a song.

Loading sounds from an external URL works the same way. Just replace the local filename with the remote URL. The sound will start streaming.

```
var song:Sound = new Sound(new URLRequest( ↵
"http://losdesigns.com/music/robotPicksFlowers.mp3"));
song.play();
```

NOTE   All the rules for Flash Player Security apply to the Sound object. If you're having trouble getting sounds to load, you may want to check out the sections on Security in "Programming ActionScript 3.0" or the "Flash Player 9 Security White Paper," which are both available from Adobe.

Buffering a streaming sound

When working with streaming audio, sounds sent to the client's computer may begin playing before the entire sound is loaded. On slower connections, you can help keep the client from running out of audio to play by setting a buffer time. This time is the amount of audio in milliseconds that will be pre-loaded before the song starts playing.

To do this, we'll create a new SoundLoaderContext file that, along with network security settings, will allow you to change the buffer time for the sound:

```
var context:SoundLoaderContext = new SoundLoaderContext();
context.bufferTime = 10000; // set buffer time to 10 seconds.
var song:Sound = new Sound(new URLRequest( ↵
"http://losdesigns.com/music/robotPicksFlowers.mp3"), context);
song.play();
```

The preceding code will wait for 10 seconds worth of the sound to be loaded before the playback begins.

Embedding sounds into your program

Embedding sounds allows you to use them without loading, but there is a tradeoff. Embedded sounds add to the overall file size for your SWF file. Sounds (and other assets) embedded in a SWF are stored as classes. The classes containing your embedded sound will be a subclass of the Sound class. Referencing these classes is like referencing a Sound object with the audio data already loaded for you.

Using Flash CS3 to embed sounds

Embedding sound in Flash CS3 is done through the Library. Follow these steps:

1. In your Flash file, go to File ➪ Import ➪ Import to Stage (you can also import to Library).

2. If you wish to use ActionScript to control your Sound, you'll need to export the Sound for ActionScript. To do this, right-click on the sound asset and choose Linkage. Figure 26-2 shows this window.

3. Make sure the Export for ActionScript box is checked.

4. Give the sound a fully qualified class name. This will be used to identify your sound. If no class exists, one will be automatically created internally when you compile your SWF.

5. From this point, the sound object will be accessible to the ActionScript code you write in Flash. To use a specific sound, you would use the class name for the asset instead of the Sound class.

FIGURE 26-2

Be sure Export for ActionScript is selected and provide a class for your sound asset.

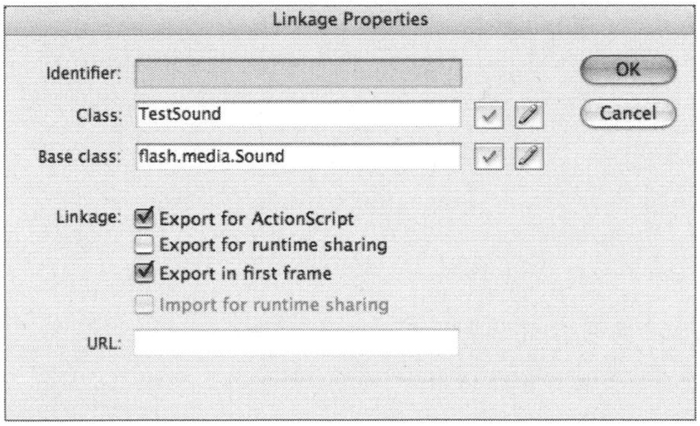

Using Flex to embed sounds

When using Flex Builder or mxmlc, you can embed your own Sounds by using the Embed tag, which requires the location of the audio's source file. The embed tag must be placed near to the definition of the Class variable that holds the embedded sound.

```
[Embed(source="sound.mp3")]
public var TestSound:Class;
```

Accessing embedded sounds

Regardless of which method you use to embed sound, to utilize the embedded sounds in your code, simply use the class that the sound is embedded in to create a new Sound object. In this case, we're using a sound whose class was called TestSound. The Sound object will be instantiated with the TestSound data already loaded.

```
var sound:Sound = new TestSound();
sound.play();
```

 The old process of attaching sound has been eliminated. ActionScript 3.0 takes a wholly class-based approach to embedding audio.

Controlling Playback of a Sound

By working with the play position and the methods for starting and stopping sound you can achieve a more granular control over the sound playback. You'll take a look at some of the functions and techniques used for more advanced playback.

Playing and stopping a sound

You've already looked at how to play a sound by calling play(); stopping the playback of a sound is just as easy. Simply call the stop() method for the SoundChannel object. This stops the song and resets the position to zero. In the following code sample, we'll load a song from a local URL, play it, and stop it after 5000 milliseconds have elapsed:

```
var jazz:Sound = new Sound(new URLRequest("MyFunnyValentine.mp3"));
var jazzChannel:SoundChannel = jazz.play(); // sound is playing
var timer = new Timer(5000, 1);
timer.addEventListener(TimerEvent.TIMER, onTimeout);
timer.start();
function onTimeout() {
    jazzChannel.stop(); // sound stops playing
}
```

Once the SoundChannel is stopped, you will have to use the Sound object's play() method to start it again.

If you are streaming an audio file, you can also stop it from playing back by using the Sound object's `clear()` method. This not only causes the sound to stop but it also stops the download of the streamed audio file. If you wish to play the sound again, you'll have to first re-initiate the loading of the sound file before you can play it.

In some cases, you'll want to quickly stop all audio playback. To handle this, you can use the `SoundMixer.stopAll()` static method. All currently playing sounds will be stopped.

Setting the start point and number of loops of a sound

The quickest way to get a sound started is by using the `play()` method. However, if you want more control over the playback, there are three optional parameters you can use. The function signature for `play()` looks like this:

```
play(startTime:Number = 0, loops:int = 0, ↵
sndTransform:SoundTransform = null):SoundChannel
```

Let's look at each of the three optional parameters:

- `startTime`: This is the number of milliseconds where you would like the sound to begin playback. Default is 0.

  ```
  sound.play(1000); // causes the sound to start 1 second in.
  ```

- `loops`: This is an integer for the number of times that your sound will repeat when it's played. The minimum is one time and any value less than one will still play once. The default is 0 and the maximum is `int.MAX_VALUE`. (There's not a built-in way to loop forever but MAX_VALUE, or about 2.1 billion, should last for several years.)

  ```
  sound.play(0, 99); // causes the sound to play 99 times.
  ```

- `sndTransform`: The `play()` method also takes an optional SoundTransform object that changes the panning and volume of your sound. We'll discuss how to use these later on in the chapter.

These parameters are fairly straightforward. Let's take a look at some ways to use them in context.

Fast-forwarding, rewinding, pausing, and restarting a sound

Using just the `startTime` parameter of the `play()` method and the `position` property of the SoundChannel object, you can get many of the standard audio player controls that one is used to seeing. You already know play and stop; here's how you might do fast forward and rewind.

With fast forward or rewind, the goal is to jump forward or backward from the currently playing portion of the sound. To do this, we'll use the `position` property to get the current playhead position, add or subtract some value to that, and then restart the song from the new position.

Pausing a sound is a bit more complicated. Because the `stop()` method causes the position to be lost, we'll need to keep track of the playback position during the time that the sound is paused. We can store this in an instance variable called `pausePosition`. Later, when the song is replayed, we can use the `pausePosition` to pick up where we left off.

Here's a simple sound player example with four buttons — rewind, pause, play, and fast forward — that make use of the position parameter in the `play()` method. There is also a text field that shows the current position and the overall time in seconds. Pay close attention to the methods for `play()`, `pause()`, `rewind()`, and `fastForward()`, and the `_playPosition` property.

```
package {
    import flash.display.*;
    import flash.media.*;
    import flash.net.*;
    import flash.text.*;
    import flash.events.*;

    public class SimpleSoundPlayer extends Sprite {
        private var _sound:Sound;
        private var _channel:SoundChannel;
        private var _pausePosition:Number;

        private var _rewButton:Sprite;
        private var _pauseButton:Sprite;
        private var _replayButton:Sprite;
        private var _ffButton:Sprite;
        private var _positionDisplay:TextField;

        private const SONG_URL:String = "song.mp3";
        private const SEARCH_RATE:int = 2000; // The ammount of FF or Rew for ↵
each click.

        public function SimpleSoundPlayer() {
            _sound = new Sound(new URLRequest(SONG_URL));
            play();

            _positionDisplay = new TextField();
            _positionDisplay.y = 50;
            addChild(_positionDisplay);

            _rewButton = new Sprite();
            _rewButton.graphics.beginFill(0x66CCFFFF);
            _rewButton.graphics.drawRect(0, 0, 20, 20);
            addChild(_rewButton);
```

```
        var rewLabel:TextField = new TextField();
        rewLabel.text = "<<";
        rewLabel.selectable = false;
        _rewButton.addChild(rewLabel);

        _pauseButton = new Sprite();
        _pauseButton.x = 30;
        _pauseButton.graphics.beginFill(0x66CCFFFF);
        _pauseButton.graphics.drawRect(0, 0, 20, 20);
        addChild(_pauseButton);

        var pauseLabel:TextField = new TextField();
        pauseLabel.text = "||";
        pauseLabel.selectable = false;
        _pauseButton.addChild(pauseLabel);

        _replayButton = new Sprite();
        _replayButton.x = 60;
        _replayButton.graphics.beginFill(0x66CCFFFF);
        _replayButton.graphics.drawRect(0, 0, 20, 20);
        addChild(_replayButton);

        var replayLabel:TextField = new TextField();
        replayLabel.text = ">";
        replayLabel.selectable = false;
        _replayButton.addChild(replayLabel);

        _ffButton = new Sprite();
        _ffButton.x = 90;
        _ffButton.graphics.beginFill(0x66CCFFFF);
        _ffButton.graphics.drawRect(0, 0, 20, 20);
        addChild(_ffButton);

        var ffLabel:TextField = new TextField();
        ffLabel.text = ">>";
        ffLabel.selectable = false;
        _ffButton.addChild(ffLabel);

        _rewButton.addEventListener(MouseEvent.CLICK, rewind);
        _pauseButton.addEventListener(MouseEvent.CLICK, pause);
        _replayButton.addEventListener(MouseEvent.CLICK, replay);
        _ffButton.addEventListener(MouseEvent.CLICK, fastForward);
        this.addEventListener(Event.ENTER_FRAME, updatePositionDisplay);
    }

public function play(position:int = 0):void {
    if (_channel) {
```

```
            _channel.stop();
        }
        _channel = _sound.play(position);
    }

    public function rewind(event:Event = null):void {
        if (_channel) {
            var newPosition:int = _channel.position - SEARCH_RATE;
            newPosition = Math.max(0, newPosition);
            play(newPosition);
        }
    }

    public function fastForward(event:Event = null):void {
        if (_channel) {
            var newPosition:int = _channel.position + SEARCH_RATE;
            newPosition = Math.min(_sound.length, newPosition);
            play(newPosition);
        }
    }

    public function pause(event:MouseEvent):void {
        _pausePosition = _channel.position;
        _channel.stop();
    }

    public function replay(event:MouseEvent):void {
        play(_pausePosition);
    }

    /**
     * Update the position display text with the current position
     * over the total length of the song in seconds.
     */
    public function updatePositionDisplay(event:Event = null):void {
        var currentPosition:Number = Math.round(_channel.position / 1000);
        var totalLength:Number = Math.round(_sound.length / 1000);
        _positionDisplay.text =  currentPosition + " / " + totalLength;
    }

    }
}
```

Make sure you stop the channel that's playing before playing again at a different position. If you don't stop the channel, you will hear a second instance of the sound playing on a different overlapping channel.

For an extra challenge, try to rewrite this code so that the fast forward button causes the song to play back at double speed. Hint: Use a timer.

Applying Sound Transformations

SoundTransforms are objects whose sole purpose is to store volume and panning controls for a sound. The name SoundTransform might make it sound more complicated than it really is. Within each sound control object are six properties — one for controlling volume, one for panning, and four for fine-tuning the mix between the left and right channels. When a SoundTransform object is applied to a SoundChannel or other audio object, the sound takes on the characteristics defined in the SoundTransform object, changing the output's volume and/or panning.

ActionScript 2.0 featured the ability to set a sound's transform information by using a generic object containing transformation data. The ActionScript 3.0 implementation takes this a step further by encapsulating the process in a separate class.

Changing the volume and panning of a sound

With SoundTransform objects, you can change the character of a sound by changing one of six properties:

- `volume`: The loudness of the sound represented as a number from 0.0 to 1.0.
- `pan`: The balance of whether the sound comes from the left or right speaker, represented as a number where −1.0 is all the way left, 1.0 is all the way right, and 0.0 causes no changes to the panning.
- `leftToRight`
- `leftToLeft`
- `rightToRight`
- `rightToLeft`

The last four properties in the list control the mix of the source channels to the output channels as a number from 0.0 to 1.0. For example, `leftToRight` controls the amount of sound from the left channel that plays on the right speaker (normally 0.0), whereas `rightToRight` controls how much of the right channel plays on the right speaker (normally 1.0). These allow you to fine-tune the panning for each channel.

Working with a Sound's Metadata

The Sound class in ActionScript 3.0 provides you with loads of data about the network status or song. You'll be able to track sound file loading, as well as get information about the artist, genre, and other details if the file is a song.

Checking the file size of a sound

Similar to the URLLoader class, Sound objects have public properties for getting the number of bytes that have been downloaded for an audio file as well as the total number of bytes. These are, of course, the bytesLoaded and bytesTotal properties. By using these values, you can provide much needed information to the user about the status of the audio file being downloaded. As with a URLLoader, you can get a percentage of completion by dividing the bytesLoaded by the bytesTotal.

Getting a song's ID3 data

One of the fantastic things about using MP3 files is the amount of metadata they can potentially store, known collectively as the ID3 tag. Flash Player 9 supports ID3 up to version 2.4 spec for song metadata, which is the same song information you see whenever you use your iPod, iTunes, WinAmp, and most other mp3 software and hardware.

You can watch for the ID3 data for a song to load by adding an event listener to the Event.ID3 event. This will be called when ID3 information becomes available. From there, you can access the data by using the id3 property of the song object, which is an object of the class ID3Info. The id3 object contains information about the song stored in properties within the object.

ID3 tags use four-letter codes to reference data that are not always easily readable by humans — for example, the code for artist is TPE1. To help out, some of the most common ones are referenced by ActionScript properties such as album, artist, genre, and songName. However, to keep things open-ended in case the spec changes in the future, the rest of the properties can be referenced by using the four-letter code — for example, use song.id3.TPUB to get the publisher name for a song. A complete list of supported codes can be found in the ActionScript 3.0 Language Reference.

Here's an example where we create a simple text field and populate it with ID3 data. You can replace the SONG_URL with any MP3 you like.

```
package {
    import flash.display.*;
    import flash.media.*;
    import flash.events.*;
    import flash.net.*;
    import flash.text.*;

    public class ID3Demo extends Sprite {
        private var _id3Display:TextField;
```

```
          private static const SONG_URL:String =
      http://www.wiley.com/go/as3bible/graveyardepiphany.mp3

          public function ID3Demo () {
              _id3Display = new TextField();
              _id3Display.width = 300;
              _id3Display.height = 400;
              addChild(_id3Display);

              var sound:Sound = new Sound ();
              sound.addEventListener(Event.ID3, onID3);
              sound.load(new URLRequest(SONG_URL));
              sound.play();
          }
          private function onID3(event:Event):void {
              var sound:Sound = event.target as Sound;
              _id3Display.text = sound.id3.songName + "\n";
              _id3Display.appendText("by " + sound.id3.artist + "\n");
              _id3Display.appendText("from the album " + sound.id3.album);
          }
      }
  }
```

The previous code will display a text field with the following output:

```
Graveyard Epiphany
by Carde
from the album Hubert Gould
```

Calculating Spectrum Data

The SoundMixer class's ability to compute the spectrum data of the sound being played instantaneously at any moment during a sound's playback allows for many new possibilities for visualizing audio. For this we use the SoundMixer.computeSpectrum() static method. This function analyzes the sound spectrum at 256 points and returns the data as a ByteArray, a type of object used for manipulating binary data. If you're not familiar with how ByteArrays work, you may want to check out Chapter 34.

The important thing to know for this chapter is that the byte array for a sound spectrum contains 256 values from −1.0 to 1.0 showing the sound's amplitude.

There are three parameters for the computeSpectrum() method. The first is outputArray, which is the empty ByteArray object to which the spectrum data will be written. There are 256 values for the left channel and 256 for the right, totaling 512.

> **NOTE** The `computeSpectrum()` method does not return a new ByteArray object as many other methods do. You must pass the output ByteArray object into the function as the first parameter.

The values created make up a raw sound wave for all the combined sounds playing in the Flash program at the moment that the method is called. By setting the second parameter in the method call, `FFTMode`, to `true`, the data output will be a list of amplitudes sorted by frequency rather than the combined soundwave.

The third parameter, `stretchFactor`, enables you to change the sample resolution of the spectrum. A value of 0 will sample every frequency band at 44.1 KHz. At 1, the sample resolution is halved to 22.05 KHz, at 2 quartered to 11.025 KHz, and so forth. You can usually leave this value at the default 0.

In this example, we use `computeSpectrum()` along with the `BitmapData` class, covered in Chapter 33, to create a real-time visualization of a song. You can replace the song URL with one of your favorite songs:

```
package {
    import flash.utils.ByteArray;
    import flash.events.*;
    import flash.net.*;
    import flash.display.*;
    import flash.media.*;
    import flash.geom.*;

    public class SpectrumDisplay extends Sprite {
        // The url of the sound to load
        private const SOUND_URL:String = ↵
http://www.wiley.com/go/as3bible/graveyardepiphany.mp3
        // The number of values in the spectrum graph
        private const SPECTRUM_WIDTH:int = 256;
        // The height and width of the bitmap to create
        private const BMP_HEIGHT:int = 200;
        private const BMP_WIDTH:int = 256;

        private var sound:Sound;
        // soundData will hold the spectrum ByteArray
        private var soundData:ByteArray;
        // bitmapData holds the graphic information while bitmapDisplay
        // is part of the display list.
        private var bitmapData:BitmapData;
        private var bitmapDisplay:Bitmap;

        public function SpectrumDisplay () {
            sound = new Sound(new URLRequest(SOUND_URL));
```

```
            sound.play();

            // Create the new bitmap data and add the bitmap to the display ↵
    list.
            bitmapData = new BitmapData(BMP_WIDTH, BMP_HEIGHT, true, ↵
    0x00000000);
            bitmapDisplay = new Bitmap(bitmapData);
            addChild(bitmapDisplay);

            this.addEventListener(Event.ENTER_FRAME, onEnterFrame);
        }

        public function onEnterFrame (event:Event):void {
            // Create an empty ByteArray to hold the spectrum data.
            soundData = new ByteArray();
            SoundMixer.computeSpectrum(soundData);

            // Erase the previous contents of the rectangle
            bitmapData.fillRect(bitmapData.rect, 0xFF000000);

            // for each step in the left channel...
            for (var i:int=0; i < SPECTRUM_WIDTH; i++) {
                // get the aplitude of that portion of the spectrum as a number
                var amplitude:Number = soundData.readFloat();

                // get the height of the band drawn in the bitmap
                var ampHeight:Number = BMP_HEIGHT/2 * (amplitude + 1);
                // create a rectangle for the band
                var rect:Rectangle = new Rectangle(i, BMP_HEIGHT - ampHeight, ↵
    1, ampHeight);
                // draw the rectangle on the bitmap
                bitmapData.fillRect(rect, 0xffffffff);
            }
        }
    }
}
```

Try copying this code and playing around with some of the values. If you want a challenge, try coming up with your own examples. There are several examples on the Internet if you search for "computeSpectrum." One blog (http://theflashblog.com/?p=197) even had a contest for the best sound visualization.

Detecting Audio Capabilities

Thanks to the Flash Player `Capabilities` class, you have the ability to check if the client's computer will support audio playback. The `hasAudio` and `hasStreamingAudio` properties will tell you if the client can support sound or streaming sound files. Here's a simple check:

```
package {
    import flash.display.Sprite;
    import flash.system.Capabilities;
    public class SoundCheck extends Sprite {
        public function SoundCheck() {
            if (Capabilities.hasAudio) {
                trace ("Audio OK!");
            } else {
                trace("Audio not available");
            }
            if (Capabilities.hasStreamingAudio) {
                trace ("Streaming OK!");
            } else {
                trace("Streaming not available");
            }
        }
    }
}
```

> **NOTE** If you attempt to play sounds on a computer that does not have audio support, the `Sound.play()` function will return `null` instead of a SoundChannel object.

Summary

- The sound system is made up of several classes that work together. The Flash Player event system is used to communicate status of sounds loading and playing.

- A Sound object contains the sound data and the ability to load the sound. SoundChannel represents the audio output from a Sound object. The SoundMixer controls the overall output of all the sounds.

- Sounds can be embedded, loaded from local files, or streamed from external files over the Web.

- ID3 data contains detailed information about an MP3 song such as artist, genre, and song name. Access this information through a sound's `id3` property.

- The SoundMixer contains the `computeSpectrum()` method for calculating sound information as an array of values. It's useful for creating sound visualizations.

Chapter 27

Adding Video

Flash is the most popular format for delivering video on the Web and will stay that way for at least the foreseeable future. This is due not only to the prevalence of the Flash plug-in, but also to the lightweight nature of the plug-in and the codecs (short for compression-decompression) and the ease of creating Flash applications that integrate video.

When you are displaying video within a Flash application, you have two basic options: load all the video data into the player when it is compiled, called embedding, or load the video data into the player via a request. The second of these options is covered in this chapter.

Working with Flash Video files

Understanding the Video and NetStream classes

Building an FLVPlayback application

Working with Flash Video Files

In this section, you learn how to make a FLV file from an existing digital video file. You also learn the different ways in which you can access a Flash Video file in a Flash movie. Later in this chapter, you learn how to load the FLV file into a movie using ActionScript.

Making an FLV file with the Flash Video Encoder

If you're using Flash CS3 Professional then you already have the Flash Video Encoder installed. By default, Flash Video Encoder is installed in a directory called Adobe Flash CS3 9 Video Encoder that is placed in the Adobe directory in the default location for program files. For example, on Windows, the application is installed at `C:\Program Files\Adobe\Adobe Flash CS3 Video Encoder\`.

Once you've started the Flash Video Encoder, you can add a video file to the queue to encode by clicking the Add button on the right side of the window. That brings up a dialog box that prompts you to select the video file you want to encode. The Flash Video Encoder can encode quite a few video formats — Active Streaming Format (.asf), AVI, DV Stream, QuickTime, MPEG, MPEG-4, and Windows Media. Using the dialog box, you can add one or more video files to encode.

For each video in the queue, you can apply settings by selecting the video from the queue list and pressing the Settings button. The settings dialog box lets you specify an output filename. Otherwise, the new filename is the same as the source filename, but with the .flv file extension. Optionally, you can click the Show Advanced Settings button, and then modify the encoding settings in more detail.

You can also trim the video using the in and out point slider controls on the video preview in the upper-right portion of the dialog box. The advanced settings also enable you to add cue points and key-value parameters for each cue point, and crop the video and export an XML file containing information about all the cue points. Flash CS3 Professional offers two different types of cue points: navigation cue points that the user can seek forward or backward to, much like the tracks on a CD, and event cue points that dispatch the onCuePoint event that the player can use to synchronize the video with other aspects of the player.

Once you've added the videos to the queue and applied the correct settings, simply click the Start Queue button to start the encoding.

Using RTMP to access FLV files

Flash Video (FLV) files were originally designed to be streamed in real time from Macromedia Flash Media Server. This media server technology can serve audio/video streams to multiple users simultaneously, record audio/video streams from a user's Webcam, edit together videos on-the-fly, and much more. Flash Media Server uses a proprietary protocol called RTMP, or Real Time Messaging Protocol, to connect Flash movies (SWF files) to Flash Media Server applications. When FLV files are streamed with Flash Media Server, the FLV file is never stored locally in the browser's cache folder and only the current frames being played are stored in the Flash Player's buffer.

You might want to use a Flash Media Server to deliver audio/video streams (from your FLV files) for the following reasons:

- **Digital Rights Management (DRM):** If you have a business client that is protective of its content, the use of Flash Media Server can make it harder for users to copy audio/video content. FLV files are stored in a protected area of the server and can be delivered by the Flash Media Server only. When viewed by a user, the FLV file is never downloaded in its entirety, nor is it stored as a local file in the browser's cache.

- **True streaming:** With Flash Media Server, the user will be able to begin watching the video sooner, and the video can begin playback at any point within the FLV file. The user does not have to wait until the entire stream has downloaded up to the point that is requested.

- **Minimize bandwidth consumption:** Regardless of a Flash Video file's length (or duration), Flash Media Server serves only what the user is currently watching. Therefore, if you have a 45-minute video file but the user wants to watch only 5 minutes, your server's connection will not be burdened with sending the entire video file to the user.

■ **Extended options:** With Flash Media Server, you can record ActionScript data to a stream (FLV file), retrieve a stream's length (in seconds), and make new copies of the stream (with different in/out points) on the server.

However, there's always a cost for such things. The following list covers some of these drawbacks:

■ **Licensing:** You have to purchase a license for Flash Media Server. Licensing costs vary depending on your connection and user needs.

■ **Learning curve:** You have to learn how to build and script Flash movies and Flash Media Server applications to work with real-time streams.

■ **Port and protocol restrictions:** If your target audience is using a computer that's behind a tight firewall or proxy server, Flash movies (SWF files) might be unable to connect to a Flash Media Server to view audio/video streams.

■ **Server installation:** You need to install and maintain Flash Media Server independently of your Web server. Although you can have a web server and the Flash Media Server software running on the same computer, you'll likely want to purchase a dedicated machine for serving and connecting clients with Flash Media Server.

There is another option for creating an RTMP streaming server as well — Red5, which is an open source project built in Java that provides some of the functionality of the Flash Media Server as well as allowing further configurability for a very wide variety of uses. More information is available at http://osflash.org/red5.

Using HTTP to access FLV files

If you don't want to use Flash Media Server to deliver FLV files to your audience, you're in luck. Flash Player 7+ enables Flash movies (SWF files) to directly load FLV files at runtime, over a standard HTTP (HyperText Transfer Protocol) connection. HTTP is the same protocol used to view regular web pages and content. You simply upload your FLV file to your Web server and point your Flash movie to the FLV file's location, and viewers can watch progressively downloaded FLV content. The following list provides some reasons why you might want to deliver FLV files over HTTP:

■ **Cost effective:** If you're making Flash content for the Web, you already have a web server that you can use to deliver FLV files.

■ **Easy to implement:** Once you learn how to load an FLV file into a Flash movie with ActionScript (as discussed in the next section), you do not need to learn a new server-side language to serve the video file (as Flash Communication may require, depending on the complexity of your application).

However, there are some drawbacks, including the following:

■ **Potential bandwidth overhead:** When you load an FLV file from a web server, the entire file is downloaded to the user's machine. It doesn't matter if the user watches only a portion of it. Once a web server receives a request for a resource, it can deliver only the whole resource, not just a portion of it.

> **NOTE**   When you serve an FLV file over HTTP, you are not technically streaming the content into the Flash movie. Media assets served over HTTP are progressive downloads. Although it's possible to begin playback before the entire file has downloaded, you can't prematurely pause the downloading process. Once it's started, the only way to stop it is to exit your web browser and/or Flash movie.

- **Digital Rights Management (DRM):** Because the FLV file is delivered over HTTP, it must be in a public location. Users can potentially load and save the FLV file separately from your Flash movie (SWF file), or they can search the browser cache for the FLV file.

Regardless of which protocol or server technology you use to deliver FLV files, keep the following points in mind:

- Audio/video content is rarely a small download for the user. Serving audio/video content can rack up bandwidth charges on your server hosting account.

- Make sure you have the rights to showcase the audio/video content. If you didn't shoot or record the content yourself, chances are that you'll need to obtain written consent to use the material on your own site.

- Don't use HTTP solely because it's perceived to be less of a financial hit. Thoroughly analyze the requirements for the audio/video content usage, and provide an overview of HTTP versus RTMP concerns to your business client.

Understanding the Video and NetStream Classes

The `Video` object is what you use to display any non-embedded video, video from a camera, or video that you've loaded via HTTP or RTMP. The `Video` class inherits from `DisplayObject` and so must be added to the Display List before it is visible and can be scaled, moved, or given a blend mode, filters, and an alpha setting. It is not, however, an `InteractiveObject` and so does not dispatch any `MouseEvents`.

The `Video` object has a very close relationship with the `NetStream` class when streaming video because all the data displayed in the `Video` object is controlled through the `NetStream` class. To play video from an external source, you first instantiate a `Video` object and pass it a `NetStream` object. In this case, we'll say that we're planning on displaying the video using progressive downloading over HTTP, which means that the video is not truly streaming:

```
var video:Video = new Video();
addChild(video);
//we pass a null object to the NetConnection because we're not
connecting to a server
```

```
var connection:NetConnection = new NetConnection(null);
var stream:NetStream = new NetStream(connection);
video.attachNetStream(stream);
```

At this point, we're ready to tell the video to begin playing. We do this through the `NetStream`. This may seem a little counterintuitive at first, but remember that because we're downloading the video from the server as we're playing it, when we want to begin playing we need to begin loading the video. The method we want to call is `NetStream.play(URL)`. We pass the URL of the video that we want to play as a required parameter to the `NetStream`:

```
stream.play("http://example.net/videos/video.flv");
```

The video itself doesn't play, start, pause, or resume the video. All this is done through the `NetStream` object. Again, this is because we're stopping and starting the flow of data that makes up the video itself. To pause the video we would call the following:

```
stream.pause();
```

To restart the video after pausing, or to play the video from the last location, we call `resume`:

```
stream.resume();
```

The `Video` class also defines the following methods:

- `attachCamera(camera:Camera)`: To display video being captured by a camera, pass a functional camera to the `attachCamera()` method of a Video object.

- `attachNetStream(netStream:NetStream)`: To display the video downloaded in a NetStream, pass the NetStream object to the `attachNetStream()` method of the `Video` object. The video stream is either an FLV file being displayed by means of the `NetStream.play()` command, a `Camera` object, or null. If the value of the `netStream` parameter is null, video is no longer played within the object.

- `clear()`: This method clears the image in the Video object, for example if you want to display something else in the area where the video is without hiding or removing the Video object.

As mentioned earlier, the `NetStream` class is a connection between a server and Flash Player that goes one way: from the server to the player. Its properties are as follows:

- `bufferLength`: The number of seconds of data currently in the buffer.

- `bufferTime`: Allows you to specify the number of seconds of video that you would like to download before the video begins playing.

- `bytesLoaded`: The number of bytes loaded into the player by this NetStream instance.

- `bytesTotal`: The number of bytes in the file being loaded from the server into the player.

- `client`: The object listening for the `onMetaData` and `onCuePoint` events. We'll look at this more later in the chapter.

- `soundTransform`: Allows you to add a `SoundTransform` object to the `NetStream`, allowing you to increase the volume of the video played or pan the Sound.

- `time`: Indicates the timecode, in seconds, of the video currently being displayed in the `Video`.

The NetStream object also defines the following methods:

- `close()`: The `close()` method closes the connection between `NetStream` and the server. It sets the time property to 0, and makes the stream available for another use. This command also deletes the local copy of an FLV file that was downloaded through HTTP.

- `pause()`: Pauses the playback of the `NetStream`.

- `play(url:String)`: Begins playback of external audio or a video (FLV) file. To view video data, you must create a `Video` object and call the `Video.attachNetStream()` method; audio being streamed with the video, or an FLV file that contains only audio, is played automatically.

- `resume()`: Resumes playback of a video stream that is paused.

- `seek(offset:Number)`: Seeks the keyframe closest to the specified location (an offset, in seconds, from the beginning of the stream). The stream resumes playing when that location is reached. This means that if you try to seek to a position that has not been loaded, this method will not have the desired effect.

Loading FLV Files into a Flash Movie

After you make an FLV file, you're ready to load it into a Flash movie (SWF file). Although you can load FLV content without displaying it, most frequently you'll want to use a `Video` object to render the video. You can then use a `NetStream` object to load the FLV content, and associate the data with the `Video` object. The next few sections discuss how to accomplish that.

Building an HTTP connection to an FLV file

To play back progressive download FLV files, you need to do the following:

1. Construct a new NetConnection object. The NetConnection constructor doesn't require any parameters.

   ```
   var ncFLVConnection:NetConnection = new NetConnection();
   ```

2. Call the `connect()` method for the NetConnection object. The `connect()` method is normally used when connecting to a Flash Media Server application. In those cases, you pass the method the URL of the application. For progressive download video, specify `null`:

```
ncFLVConnection.connect(null);
```

3. Construct a new NetStream object that is linked to the NetConnection object. Use the NetStream constructor in a new statement, and pass the NetConnection object to the constructor:

```
var nsVideo:NetStream = new NetStream(ncFLVConnection);
```

4. Call the `play()` method of the NetStream object, specifying the URL to the FLV file:

```
nsVideo.play("video.flv");
```

Displaying the NetStream data in a Video object

Once you've added a Video object and used the `NetConnection` and `NetStream` classes to start the playback of the FLV video, you next need to tell Flash how to display the video. You can do that by way of the `attachVideo()` method of the `Video` class. The `attachVideo()` method requires one parameter — a reference to the NetStream object:

```
vFLVDisplay.attachVideo(nsVideo);
```

Checking status messages from the NetStream class

The `NetStream` class has an `onStatus()` event handler, which can be used to monitor the activity occurring on the NetStream instance. A NetStream object gets notified as events such as buffering, starting, and stopping occur. The `onStatus()` method gets passed one parameter. That parameter is an associative array with a property called `code`. The `code` property contains a string value that indicates what event has just occurred.

- When a stream begins to play, the `onStatus()` handler receives a code property of `NetStream.Play.Start`.

- When enough of the FLV file has downloaded into Flash Player's buffer, the `NetStream.Buffer.Full` message is sent to the `onStatus()` handler.

- When the stream playback reaches the end of the FLV file, the code property `NetStream.Play.Stop` is sent to the `onStatus()` handler.

- When all of the stream data has emptied from the Flash Player's buffer, the code property of `NetStream.Buffer.Empty` is sent to the `onStatus()` handler.

- For FLV files served over HTTP, there is also a code property of `NetStream.Play` `.StreamNotFound`. This value is returned to the `onStatus()` handler if the URL is invalid. This message can also occur if Flash Player does not have a working Internet connection.

There are other code values for FLV files served over an RTMP connection to a Flash Media Server application, such as `NetStream.Pause.Notify`.

The following is an example of an `onStatus()` method definition for a NetStream object called `videoStream`.

```
videoStream.addEventListener(NetStatusEvent.NET_STATUS, onStatus);
private function onStatus(oData:Object):void
{
  trace(oData.code);
}
```

Retrieving metadata

FLV files contain metadata that Flash Player retrieves when the FLV starts to download. The metadata contains an array of data. Arguably the most useful datum of the metadata is the duration of the FLV. The `NetStream` class doesn't define a property that tells you what the total playback time of the FLV is. However, you can retrieve the duration from the metadata for the FLV. As you'll see, the duration is critical if you want the user to be able to scrub the playback or if you want to display accurate playback progress.

When the metadata is read from an FLV, the `onMetaData()` callback method is called for the NetStream object playing back the FLV. Note that this method is called directly by the NetStream object, without using ActionScript 3.0's event model. The `onMetaData()` method is passed one parameter — an associative array. The keys of the associative array are the metadata. The duration metadatum is stored with a key of duration.

Earlier we discussed the `client` object property that can be assigned to the NetStream. In the code that follows, we define a client object as an Object and then define event listeners that listen to those events.

```
var clientObject:Object = new Object();
client.onMetaData = metaDataListener;
netStream.client = clientObject;

private function metaDataListener(object:Object):void
{
  var duration:int = object.duration;
  trace("the duration of the video is "+duration);
}
```

Depending on the video and the amount of metadata that has been inserted into the FLV file, the metadata object can contain the size of the video, its datarate, its framerate, and other information about the video.

For example, the default height and width of the Video object are 320 pixels by 240 pixels. We can set the size of the player at compile time by setting the height and width, or at runtime using the height and width properties of the metadata. The dimensions of a Video object determine the dimensions at which the video will get played back. For example, if a video is encoded at 320 × 240 pixels but the Video object is 160 × 120 pixels, the video will play back at 160 × 120 pixels. The following `onMetaData()` event handler method assigns the new width and height to the `width` and `height` properties of the Video object.

```
private function onMetaData(metadata:Object):void
{
  vFLV.width = metadata.width;
  vFLV.height = metadata.height;
}
```

Now that you've seen how to create a Video object and a NetStream, begin downloading video, and listen for the events dispatched by the NetStream, we'll begin building an FLV Playback application.

Building an FLV Playback Application

Generally speaking, the features expected of a video player are set by some of the more famous and familiar video players out there. We expect a play button, a pause button, a timeline with a scrollable playhead, and some sort of time indicator. Let's go ahead and look through the code to create a simple video application.

First, we need a timeline with a playhead that can be dragged by the user to scrub the video:

```
package
{
    import flash.display.Sprite;
    import flash.events.Event;
    import flash.events.MouseEvent;
    import flash.geom.Rectangle;
    public class Timeline extends Sprite
    {
        public static const SEEKING:String = "seeking";
        public static const FINISHED_SEEKING:String = "finishedSeeking";
        public var playhead:Sprite;

        public function Timeline()
        {
            this.graphics.beginFill(0xCCCCCC, 1);
            this.graphics.drawRect(0, 0, 100, 20);
```

```
            playhead = new Sprite();
            playhead.graphics.beginFill(0x0000ff, 1);
            playhead.graphics.drawRect(0, 0, 20, 20);
            addChild(playhead);
            playhead.x = -10;
            playhead.addEventListener(MouseEvent.MOUSE_DOWN, beginDrag);
        }

        private function beginDrag(mouseEvent:MouseEvent):void
        {
            playhead.startDrag(false, new Rectangle(0, 0, width, height));
            playhead.addEventListener(MouseEvent.MOUSE_UP, stopDragPlayhead);
            var event:Event = new Event("seeking");
            dispatchEvent(event);
        }

        private function stopDragPlayhead(mouseEvent:MouseEvent):void
        {
            playhead.stopDrag();
            var event:Event = new Event("finishedSeeking");
            dispatchEvent(event);
        }

        public function updatePlayhead(number:Number):void
        {
            playhead.x = number;
        }
    }
}
```

Our playhead needs to do two things: to show the current time of the NetStream and to be draggable so that the user can seek using the playhead. The first requirement is handled by the updatePlayhead() method. This will be called from the main application via the use of a Timer. The Timeline dispatches two events, one to indicate that we've begun seeking, which is triggered by the MouseEvent.MOUSE_DOWN event on the playhead, and one to indicate that we've finished seeking, which is triggered by the MouseEvent.MOUSE_UP event. Now let's look at the main application class:

```
package
{
import flash.display.Sprite;
import flash.events.Event;
```

```
import flash.events.TimerEvent;
import flash.media.Video;
import flash.net.NetConnection;
import flash.net.NetStream;
import flash.text.TextField;
import flash.utils.Timer;
public class SimpleVideo extends Sprite
{
    private var nDuration:Number = 0;
    private var nsVideo:NetStream;
    private var vFLV:Video;
    private var ncVideo:NetConnection;
    private var playBtn:VideoButton;
    private var stopBtn:VideoButton;
    private var timeline:Timeline;
    private var timer:Timer;
    private var isPlaying:Boolean = true;
    private var isDragging:Boolean = false;
    private var currentTimeTxt:TextField;

    public function SimpleVideo()
    {
        stage.scaleMode = "noScale";
        var ncVideo:NetConnection = new NetConnection();
        ncVideo.connect(null);
        nsVideo = new NetStream(ncVideo);
        nsVideo.play("video.flv");
        currentTimeTxt = new TextField();
        addChild(currentTimeTxt);
        currentTimeTxt.y = 360;
        currentTimeTxt.height = 20;
        vFLV = new Video();
        addChild(vFLV);
        vFLV.attachNetStream(nsVideo);
        var clientObject:Object = new Object();
        clientObject.onMetaData = onMetaData;
        nsVideo.client = clientObject;
        playBtn = new VideoButton("play");
        stopBtn = new VideoButton("stop");
        addChild(playBtn);
        addChild(stopBtn);
        stopBtn.x = 200;

        playBtn.addEventListener(VideoButton.CLICKED, play);
        stopBtn.addEventListener(VideoButton.CLICKED, stop);

        timer = new Timer(100);
        timer.addEventListener(TimerEvent.TIMER, updateProgress);
        timeline = new Timeline();
```

511

```
        timeline.addEventListener(Timeline.SEEKING, beginSeek);
        timeline.addEventListener(Timeline.FINISHED_SEEKING, finishedSeek);
        addChild(timeline);
        timeline.y = 420;
    }

    private function beginSeek(event:Event):void
    {
        nsVideo.pause();
        isPlaying = false;
        isDragging = true;
    }

    private function finishedSeek(event:Event):void
    {
        nsVideo.resume();
        nsVideo.seek(nDuration * ((timeline.playhead.x + 10) / 100));
        isDragging = false;
        isPlaying = true;
    }

    private function onMetaData(oMetaData:Object):void
    {
        nDuration = oMetaData.duration;
        timeline.updatePlayhead(nDuration);
        timer.start();
    }

    private function play(event:Event):void
    {
        if (isPlaying)
        {
            isPlaying = false;
            nsVideo.pause();
        } else {
            isPlaying = true;
            nsVideo.resume();
        }
    }

    private function stop(event:Event):void
    {
        nsVideo.pause();
        nsVideo.seek(0);
    }
```

```
private function updateProgress(timerEvent:TimerEvent):void
{
    var nPercent:Number = 100 * nsVideo.time / nDuration;
    currentTimeTxt.text = nsVideo.time.toString();
    if (!isDragging)
    {
        timeline.updatePlayhead(nPercent);
    }
}
}
}
```

Let's break this down into smaller pieces. First, in the constructor, we initialize the NetConnection and NetStream objects:

```
var ncVideo:NetConnection = new NetConnection();
ncVideo.connect(null);
nsVideo = new NetStream(ncVideo);
nsVideo.play("video.flv");
```

We then add a TextField to display the current time of the NetStream. Then we initialize the Video and attach the NetStream to the Video.

```
addChild(vFLV);
vFLV.attachNetStream(nsVideo);
```

Next, we need to be able to listen for the metadata object because the length of the video file we're going to play will be very important to our ability to accurately represent the playhead position and allow the user to scrub the video.

```
var clientObject:Object = new Object();
clientObject.onMetaData = onMetaData;
nsVideo.client = clientObject;
```

This assigns the handler for the onMetaData event to the onMetaData() method of this class. Within that method, we store the length of the video and then start the timer that will position the playhead correctly.

```
private function onMetaData(oMetaData:Object):void
{
    nDuration = oMetaData.duration;
    timeline.updatePlayhead(nDuration);
    timer.start();
}
```

Next, we need to account for the play and stop buttons that we've created, which is done easily enough by pausing and resuming the NetStream. We also need to add event listeners to our

Timeline object to listen for the SEEKING and FINISHED_SEEKING events. These make use of the NetStream's Seek method to move the video being played to an approximation of the location of the playhead with the Timeline.

```
private function finishedSeek(event:Event):void
{
    nsVideo.resume();
    nsVideo.seek(nDuration * ((timeline.playhead.x+10)/100));
    isDragging = false;
    isPlaying = true;
}
```

With this fairly simple application we can scrub video, stop and start, and see the progress of the video itself. If we wanted to build it out further we could add the ability to see the video in full screen, change the volume, show the video in slow motion, or any other number of features, but we'll leave it to you to discover those.

Summary

- Flash Video (FLV) files can be played in Flash Player and can be either streamed using Flash Media Server or by using progressive downloading. Using the Flash Media Server allows you to access true streaming media but has several disadvantages, whereas progressive downloading does not allow you to access video that you have not already downloaded.

- The NetStream class works in conjunction with the NetConnection and Video classes. A Video object displays the visual portion of a NetStream instance playing an FLV file.

- The onStatus() handler of a NetStream instance receives an information object with a code property. The code property specifies which particular event is occurring on a NetStream instance.

- Create a client object and assign that client object's onMetaData() method to a method in your application to read the metadata from an FLV file.

- You can use the play(), pause(), and seek() methods of the NetStream class to control the playback of an FLV file. You can also use the time property of the NetStream class to report the current playback time of the FLV file, and the duration metadatum to determine the total playback time.

Accessing Microphones and Cameras

T oo often, Flash Player is viewed strictly as a way to *show* things to the user, instead of as a communicative tool. One of the most powerful ways to use Flash Player is as a tool that the user can communicate *with* to use microphones or cameras attached to the computer. Flash provides a `Camera` and a `Microphone` class to allow you to access these peripherals, as well as a safeguard mechanism to ensure that users share only what they want to share.

Introducing the Camera

To create a camera object, you call the `getCamera()` method. This returns an array of all the cameras currently attached to the user's computer and, if you haven't specified a camera to use, selects the first camera that the Flash Player comes across.

When a SWF file tries to access the camera returned by `getCamera()`, Flash Player displays a dialog box that lets the user choose whether to allow or deny access to the camera, as shown in Figure 28-1. Make sure your application window size is at least 215 × 138 pixels; this is the minimum size Flash Player requires to display the dialog box. The user may also utilize the Flash Player Settings Manager to allow or deny access to his camera and microphone globally, in which case this dialog will not appear.

When the user responds to this dialog box, Flash Player returns an information object in the status event that indicates the user's response: `Camera.muted` indicates the user denied access to a camera; `Camera.unmuted` indicates the user allowed access to a camera. To determine whether the user has denied or allowed access to the camera without handling the status event, use the `muted` property.

FIGURE 28-1

Allow Camera Access dialog

To ensure that our `Camera` object is working, we'll create a monitor by using a Video object and passing it the Camera object that we've just acquired.

To set the width and height of the image that we're capturing, the `Camera` class provides a `setMode()` method because the height and width properties of the camera are read-only.

When we set the height and width of the camera using the `setMode()` method, Flash tries to accommodate the parameters that you pass in. However, if the parameters cannot be accommodated by the hardware of the camera, the player tries to match the ratio of height to width:

```
public function setMode(width:int, height:int, fps:Number,
favorArea:Boolean = true):void
```

The `favorArea` parameter defines whether or not you prefer Flash Player to fulfill the size of the player over the frame rate in the event that our camera cannot match the parameters that we've passed in. The default value is `true`; to maximize frame rate at the expense of camera height and width, pass `false` for the `favorArea` parameter.

The camera also defines a method to set the amount of motion that will trigger the camera's activity event: `Camera.setMotionLevel()`. This allows us to turn the camera stream off if there is no activity and on if there is. This can be of great importance when streaming video. We discuss camera streams later in this chapter. Related to the `motionLevel` is the `activityLevel` property, which defines the amount of motion that the camera is currently registering.

Attaching the camera to a video

To attach the camera feed to a video so that we can monitor it we simply pass that default instance of the Camera to an instance of a Video object. Let's take a quick look:

```
var cam:Camera = flash.media.Camera.getCamera();
var vid:Video = new Video();
vid.attachCamera(cam);
```

This will display the camera's video in the Video object that we've just created:

```
package
{
    import flash.display.Sprite;
    import flash.media.Video;
    import flash.media.Camera;
    import flash.events.Event;
    import flash.events.ActivityEvent;
    import flash.text.TextField;
    public class CameraViewer extends Sprite
    {
        private var cam:Camera;
        private var vid:Video;
        private var hasCamera:Boolean = true;
        private var text:TextField;

        public function CameraViewer()
        {
            cam = flash.media.Camera.getCamera();
            vid = new Video();
            vid.attachCamera(cam);
            addChild(vid);
            cam.setMotionLevel(20);
            this.addEventListener("enterFrame", enterFrame);
            cam.addEventListener(ActivityEvent.ACTIVITY, active);
            text = new TextField();
            addChild(text);
            text.x = 300;
        }

        private function active(evt:ActivityEvent):void
        {
            trace(cam.activityLevel + " " + cam.motionLevel + " " + cam.name);
        }

        private function enterFrame(event:Event):void
        {
            if(cam.activityLevel < 10)
            {
                text.text = "No activity detected";
            }
            if(cam.activityLevel > 12)
            {
                text.text = "Motion!";
            }
        }
    }
}
```

If we wanted to expand this example we could display the video only when the camera detects motion, set up a connection to a Flash Media Server to record whenever there's motion, or grab the frames with motion, cache them as bitmaps, and manipulate them using the Bitmap API.

Introducing the Microphone

The microphone is accessed in much the same way that you access the camera, by using a call to the Flash Player that attempts to access any microphone attached to the user's computer.

To create or reference a microphone attached to the user's computer, use `Microphone.getMicrophone()` to get the current microphone. There is an optional parameter to pass an index to the `getMicrophone()` method, although this isn't recommended as the behavior is unpredictable depending on the user's system configuration. This code snippet displays how to create a `Microphone` object:

```
var mic:Microphone = Microphone.getMicrophone();
```

After the `Microphone` is initialized, it dispatches a `StatusEvent` where the `Microphone` reports whether or not the user will allow the SWF access to the microphone that is attached to their computer. If the value of the `code` property is `Microphone.muted`, then the user didn't allow the SWF access to the microphone. The value `Microphone.unmuted` means that the user allowed the microphone access.

The microphone also defines a read-only `silenceLevel` property that reports what the silence level of the microphone is. This can be set using `setSilenceLevel()`, which sets the minimum input level that should be considered sound and (optionally) the amount of silent time signifying that silence has actually begun. Silence values correspond directly to activity values. Complete silence is an activity value of 0. Constant loud noise (as loud as can be registered based on the current gain setting) is an activity value of 100. After gain is appropriately adjusted, your activity value is less than your silence value when you're not talking; when you are talking, the activity value exceeds your silence value. The higher the silence level, the less sound Flash Player detects. To prevent the microphone from detecting sound at all, pass a value of 100 for `silenceLevel`; the activity event will not be dispatched.

To determine the amount of sound the microphone is currently detecting, use `Microphone.activityLevel`. Activity detection is the capability to detect when the microphone is detecting the appropriate amount of sound. For example, in creating a chat or broadcast application, when no one is talking, bandwidth can be saved because there is no need to send the associated audio stream. This information can also be used for visual feedback so that users know they (or others) are silent.

This method is similar in purpose to `Camera.setMotionLevel()`; both methods are used to specify when the activity event is dispatched. However, these methods have a significantly different impact on publishing streams:

- `Camera.setMotionLevel()` is designed to detect motion and does not affect bandwidth usage. Even if a video stream does not detect motion, video is still sent.

- `Microphone.setSilenceLevel()` is designed to optimize bandwidth. When an audio stream is considered silent, no audio data is sent. Instead, a single message is sent, indicating that silence has started.

To set the silence level, you pass the level that you want as well as the timeout that you wish to wait before dispatching the activity event. Here the `silenceLevel` of the `Microphone` object is set with the sound level and the length of time in milliseconds before dispatching the silence event:

```
mic.setSilenceLevel(20, 5);
```

Working with the microphone

Now that we've created a microphone and we've covered the basic properties and methods it provides, let's look at an example of getting a reference to the microphone and listening for events on it:

```
package
{
    import flash.display.Sprite;
    import flash.events.*;
    import flash.media.Microphone;
    import flash.system.Security;
    public class MicrophoneExample extends Sprite
    {
        public function MicrophoneExample()
        {
            var mic:Microphone = Microphone.getMicrophone();
            Security.showSettings("2");
            mic.setLoopBack(true);

            if (mic != null)
            {
                mic.setUseEchoSuppression(true);
                mic.addEventListener(ActivityEvent.ACTIVITY, activityHandler);
                mic.addEventListener(StatusEvent.STATUS, statusHandler);
            }
        }

        private function activityHandler(event:ActivityEvent):void
        {
            trace("activityHandler: " + event);
        }

        private function statusHandler(event:StatusEvent):void
        {
            trace("statusHandler: " + event);
        }
    }
}
```

Now, while that is somewhat interesting, we can't really *see* what the microphone *hears* yet. Using the activity property will allow us to do that, however. Because the activity level is a number representing the amount of sound that the microphone is hearing, we can make a simple level display that will show our user how much sound she's making:

```
package
{
```

```actionscript
import flash.display.Sprite;
import flash.events.ActivityEvent;
import flash.events.Event;
import flash.events.StatusEvent;
import flash.media.Microphone;
public class MicLevel extends Sprite
{
    public var mic:Microphone;
    public var level:Sprite;

    public function MicLevel()
    {
        mic = Microphone.getMicrophone();
        mic.setLoopBack(true);
        mic.addEventListener(ActivityEvent.ACTIVITY, activity);
        mic.addEventListener(StatusEvent.STATUS, status);
        mic.addEventListener(Event.ACTIVATE, active);
        addEventListener(Event.ENTER_FRAME, showMicLevel);
        level = new Sprite();
        addChild(level);
        level.y = 200;
        level.x = 100;
    }

    private function active(event:Event):void
    {
        trace("active");
    }

    private function status(event:StatusEvent):void
    {
        trace("status");
    }

    private function activity(event:ActivityEvent):void
    {
        trace("activity");
    }

    private function showMicLevel(event:Event):void
    {
        trace(mic.gain
                + " " + mic.activityLevel
                + " " + mic.silenceLevel
                + " " + mic.index
                + " " + mic.rate);
        level.graphics.beginFill(0xccccff, 1);
        level.graphics.drawRect(0, 0, (mic.activityLevel * 3), 100);
        level.graphics.endFill();
    }
}
}
```

Media Servers

Cameras and microphones become even more powerful tools when they are paired with a media server. When the camera or microphone is paired with a media server, you can create video- and audio-enabled chat applications, video that can be saved on a server, and a wealth of other options. There are two options for working with media servers. The first is the Flash Media Server (FMS) created by Adobe for precisely this purpose. A developer edition of FMS 2, which supports up to five connections, is available for free; anything above and beyond that is meant only for enterprise use and is priced accordingly. Another option is Red5, an open source media server and general all-around Flash communication server. Red5 is written in Java, and free to anyone. Detailed information is available at www.adobe.com/products/flashmediaserver/ for information on Flash Media Server, and at www.osflash.org/red5/ for Red5.

Media servers allow you to stream data from the user's cameras and microphone to the server for recording or for relay to other users, as in a video chat application. While the code on the server side to record or share the user's video is beyond the scope of this book, you can look at how you would stream that data to the server here:

```
package
{
    import flash.display.Sprite;
    import flash.events.ActivityEvent;
    import flash.events.Event;
    import flash.events.StatusEvent;
    import flash.media.Microphone;
    public class MicLevel extends Sprite
    {
        public var mic:Microphone;
        public var level:Sprite;

        public function MicLevel()
        {
            mic = Microphone.getMicrophone();
            mic.setLoopBack(true);
            mic.addEventListener(ActivityEvent.ACTIVITY, activity);
            mic.addEventListener(StatusEvent.STATUS, status);
            mic.addEventListener(Event.ACTIVATE, active);
            addEventListener(Event.ENTER_FRAME, showMicLevel);
            level = new Sprite();
            addChild(level);
            level.y = 200;
            level.x = 100;
        }

        private function active(event:Event):void
        {
            trace("active");
        }
```

```
        private function status(event:StatusEvent):void
        {
            trace("status");
        }

        private function activity(event:ActivityEvent):void
        {
            trace("activity");
        }

        private function showMicLevel(event:Event):void
        {
            trace(mic.gain
                    + " " + mic.activityLevel
                    + " " + mic.silenceLevel
                    + " " + mic.index
                    + " " + mic.rate);
            level.graphics.beginFill(0xccccff, 1);
            level.graphics.drawRect(0, 0, (mic.activityLevel * 3), 100);
            level.graphics.endFill();
        }
    }
}
```

The media server will contain methods to handle the published stream, which is a stream from the user to the server that the server will handle.

Summary

- To create a Camera object, you call the static method `Camera.getCamera()`, which returns the first working camera attached to the user's computer that the Flash Player has access to.

- To view the video that the camera is currently viewing, you attach the camera to a `flash.media.Video` instance.

- To create a Microphone object, you call the static method `Microphone .getMicrophone()`, which returns the first working microphone attached to the user's computer that Flash Player has access to.

- To monitor the sound level on the microphone, you use `Microphone.activityLevel`, which returns the volume of the microphone being used.

- If you are working with a media server such as Flash Media Server or Red5, you can stream information from a user's camera to the server using `flash.media.NetStream`.

- To attach a camera or microphone to a NetStream, you call `attachNetStream()` on the camera or microphone.

Part VIII

Programming Graphics and Motion

Chapter 29

Applying Filters to Your Graphics

Want to add some Photoshop-like effects to your `DisplayObjects`? Perhaps you'd like to create a photo blur, or create a beveled edge, or add a glow to a `Sprite`, or perhaps you want to distort an image. Whatever it is that you'd like to do, it's more than likely that if it can be done in Flash, you'll be doing it with some of the filters in the `flash .filters` package.

Filters are built-in effects you can apply to any `DisplayObject`: `Sprite`, `MovieClip`, or `TextField`. The filters in Flash Player 9 are built into the player, and they use native bitmap functionality to create their effects; that means that the filters can render filters quickly. Under the hood of Flash Player, when you apply a filter to a `DisplayObject`, Flash Player renders a bitmap surface with the related effect. Any time you apply a filter to a `DisplayObject`, its `cacheAsBitmap` property is set to `true`. `DisplayObjects` that contain simple vector graphics can be cached simply as vectors to save resources in the player. However, once you apply a filter to a `DisplayObject` it is more efficient to save it as a bitmap.

The filters available in Flash Player 9 are as follows:

- `BevelFilter`
- `BlurFilter`
- `ColorMatrixFilter`
- `ConvolutionFilter`
- `DisplacementMapFilter`
- `DropShadowFilter`
- `GlowFilter`
- `GradientBevelFilter`
- `GradientGlowFilter`

In this chapter, we look at each of the filters, and how to apply filters to display objects.

Introducing Filters

Every `DisplayObject` instance has a `filters` property. The `filters` property is an array of filter objects applied to the instance. If you apply a filter at authoring time, that filter object is accessible during runtime via the `filters` property. For example, if you applied a bevel filter to a `DisplayObject` object named `clip` during authoring time, the bevel filter object will be found in `clip.filters[0]`.

However, when you read elements from the filters array, it returns *copies* rather than references to the actual filter objects. That means that any changes you make to the properties of the filter object won't get applied to the display object automatically.

When you want to apply a filter to an object programmatically, you must assign an array of filter objects to the `filters` property. Not only does the filters array return copies of the filter objects, but when you read the `filters` property, it returns a copy of the array rather than a reference. So it won't work to use standard array methods such as `push()`, and you cannot overwrite elements of the array and have the updates affect the display object automatically. If you're still uncertain of how to apply a filter object, some examples will help make things clearer. In subsequent sections you'll learn more about each of the different types of filter classes. For the next few examples, however, you construct very basic filter objects. For example, the following code constructs a basic `DropShadowFilter` object:

```
var dsfInstance:DropShadowFilter = new DropShadowFilter();
```

Once the filter object is constructed, you can apply it to a `DisplayObject` by adding it as an element of an array and assigning that array to the `filters` property of the `DisplayObject`. In the case of the example, the array has just one element: the `DropShadowFilter` object. Let's apply the drop shadow to a `DisplayObject` named `circle`:

```
circle.filters = [dsfInstance];
```

Not only does the `filters` property return copies of the filter object applied to a `DisplayObject` when you read it, but it also applies a copy of the filter when you assign the filter object. That means that if you change a property of the filter object after you assign it to the filters array of a display object, it will have no effect on the display object. For example, `DropShadowFilter` objects have a distance property that determines the displacement of the shadow in pixels. The default is 4 pixels. If you set the property before assigning the object to the filters array, there will be a visible effect:

```
dsfInstance.distance = 100;
circle.filters = [dsfInstance];
```

However, if you change the property after assigning the object to the filters array, it won't affect the display object:

```
circle.filters = [dsfInstance];
dsfInstance.distance = 100;
```

If you want to reapply a filter after making changes to the properties, as in the preceding example, you need to then reassign the filters array. For example, the following retrieves a filter from the filters array, makes a change to it, and reassigns the filter:

```
var dsfInstance:DropShadowFilter = new
DropShadowFilter(circle.filters[0]);
dsfInstance.distance = 0;
circle.filters = [dsfInstance];
```

As mentioned earlier, when you apply a filter to a display object, the `cacheAsBitmap` property of the display object is set to `true`. If you clear all filters, the original value of `cacheAsBitmap` reverts to `false`. If `cacheAsBitmap` is set to `true`, Flash Player caches an internal bitmap representation of the display object. This caching can increase performance for display objects that contain complex vector content. All vector data for a display object that has a cached bitmap is drawn to the bitmap instead of the main display. The bitmap is then copied to the main display as unstretched, unrotated pixels snapped to the nearest pixel boundaries. Pixels are mapped 1 to 1 with the parent object. If the bounds of the bitmap change, the bitmap is recreated instead of being stretched. No internal bitmap is created unless the `cacheAsBitmap` property is set to `true`. After you set the `cacheAsBitmap` property to `true`, the rendering does not change, but the display object performs pixel snapping automatically. The animation speed can be significantly faster depending on the complexity of the vector content.

Applying Filters

Let's now look more closely at each of the different filters and examine the parameters that each filter accepts and possible uses for each.

Blur filters

You can add blur effects to display objects using BlurFilter objects. The `BlurFilter` class has three properties:

- `blurX`: The number of pixels to blur in the x direction. The default is 4.
- `blurY`: The number of pixels to blur in the y direction. The default is 4.
- `quality`: The number of times to run the blur. The range is from 0 to 15. The default value is 1.

You can make a new `BlurFilter` instance using the `BlurFilter` constructor. The constructor accepts from 0 to 3 parameters. The parameters are in the same order as they appear in the preceding list. The following code constructs a `BlurFilter` instance with default settings:

```
var blfInstance:BlurFilter = new BlurFilter();
```

The following constructs a new `BlurFilter` instance that blurs 100 pixels in the x direction but no pixels in the y direction. It uses a quality setting of 15 to achieve a very smooth blur.

```
var blfInstance:BlurFilter = new BlurFilter(100, 0, 15);
```

As with any other filter, you can change the properties of a `BlurFilter` object after it has been instantiated.

Figure 29-1 shows the effect of the following code:

```
var bfInstance:BlurFilter = new BlurFilter(10, 40);
circle.filters = [bfInstance];
```

FIGURE 29-1

A blur filter applied to an image

Adding the drop shadow filter

You can use `DropShadowFilter` objects to apply drop shadows to display objects. The class has the following properties:

- `distance`: The number of pixels from the display object to offset the shadow. The default is 4.
- `angle`: The angle of the light source in degrees where 0 is directly to the left of the object. The default value is 45.

- `color`: The color of the shadow specified as an unsigned integer from 0x000000 to 0xFFFFFF. The default value is 0x000000.

- `alpha`: The alpha of the shadow from 0 to 1. The default is 1.

- `blurX`: The amount to blur the shadow in the x direction from 0 to 255. The default is 4.

- `blurY`: The amount to blur the shadow in the y direction from 0 to 255. The default is 4.

- `strength`: The punch strength of the shadow from 0 to 255. The default is 1.

- `quality`: The number of times to run the blur on the shadow. The range is from 0 to 15. The higher the number, the smoother the blur of the shadow will appear. The default is 1.

- `inner`: A Boolean value indicating whether or not the shadow should be applied to the inside of the object. The default value is `false`, which means the shadow is applied outside the object.

- `knockout`: A Boolean value indicating whether or not the original display object contents should be transparent. If `true`, that section of the object is transparent (the background or whatever is underneath the object is visible) and the drop shadow is visible around the edges of that area. The default value is `false`.

- `hideObject`: A Boolean value indicating whether or not to hide the contents of the display object. If `true`, the contents of the display object are hidden, and the drop shadow is visible. The default value is `false`.

The `DropShadowFilter` constructor accepts between 0 and 11 parameters. The parameters are in the order they appear in the preceding list. The following constructs a `DropShadowFilter` object with the default settings:

```
var dsfInstance:DropShadowFilter = new DropShadowFilter();
```

The following constructs a `DropShadowFilter` object with a distance of 20, an angle of 0, and a color of 0xFF0000:

```
var dsfInstance:DropShadowFilter = new DropShadowFilter(20, 0, ↵
0xFF0000);
```

As with other filter objects, you can change the properties of a `DropShadowFilter` instance after it's constructed. The following constructs an instance with the default settings, and then changes the drop shadow to an inner shadow.

```
var dsfInstance:DropShadowFilter = new DropShadowFilter();
dsfInstance.inner = true;
```

Figure 29-2 shows the effect of the following code:

```
var dsfInstance:DropShadowFilter = new DropShadowFilter(10, 0, ↵
0x000000, 1, 10, 10);
circle.filters = [dsfInstance];
```

FIGURE 29-2

A drop-shadow filter applied to an image

Bevel filters

Bevel filters are instances of the `BevelFilter` class. `BevelFilter` instances have the following properties:

- `distance`: The offset of the bevel in pixels. The greater the number, the more pronounced the bevel. The default is 4.

- `angle`: The angle of the light source to the object in degrees. A value of 0 makes the light source directly to the left, while a value of 180 makes the light source directly to the right. The default is 45.

- `highlightColor`: The highlight color specified as an unsigned integer from 0x000000 to 0xFFFFFF. The default value is 0xFFFFFF.

- `highlightAlpha`: The alpha of the highlight. The range is from 0 to 1. The default is 1.

- `shadowColor`: The shadow color specified as an unsigned integer from 0x000000 to 0xFFFFFF. The default value is 0x000000.

- `shadowAlpha`: The alpha of the shadow. The range is from 0 to 1. The default is 1.

- `blurX`: The number of pixels to blur the bevel in the horizontal direction. The greater the number, the softer the bevel appears. The default is 4.

- `blurY`: The number of pixels to blur the bevel in the vertical direction. The greater the number, the softer the bevel appears. The default is 4.

- `strength`: The punch strength of the bevel. The greater the number, the more visible the shadow and highlight will be when the blur properties are set to greater numbers. The default is 1.

- `quality`: The number of times to run the blur. The range is from 1 to 15. The greater the number, the smoother the bevel appears. The default is 1.
- `type`: The type can be one of the `flash.filters.BitmapFilter.Type` constants: `inner`, `outer`, or `full`. The default is `inner`.
- `knockout`: Whether or not to knock out the contents of the object. The default is `false`.

The `BevelFilter` constructor accepts between 0 and 12 parameters. Parameters are in the same order they appear in the preceding list. For example, the following instantiates a `BevelFilter` object with a distance of 10 and an angle of 0:

```
var bvfInstance:BevelFilter = new BevelFilter(10, 0);
```

The following instantiates a new BevelFilter object with each of the 12 parameters:

```
var bvfInstance:BevelFilter = new BevelFilter(10, 0,↵
0xFF0000, .5, 0xCCCCCC, .5, 10, 10, 5, 15, ↵
BitmapFilterType.INNER, true);
```

You can adjust any of the properties of a `BevelFilter` object once it's instantiated. The following makes a new `BevelFiter` object with the default settings, and then sets the type to `outer`:

```
var bvfInstance:BevelFilter = new BevelFilter();
bvfInstance.type = "outer";
```

Figure 29-3 shows the effect of the following code on a `DisplayObject` called `image`.

```
import flash.filters.BevelFilter;

var bvfInstance:BevelFilter = new BevelFilter(5, 45, 0xFFCCCC, ↵
1, 0x000000, 1, 10, 10, 5, 15, "inner");
image.filters = [bvfInstance];
```

FIGURE 29-3

A bevel filter applied to an image

Glow filtering

You can use instances of the GlowFilter class to apply glows to display objects. The GlowFilter class has the following properties:

- color: The color of the glow specified as an unsigned integer from 0x000000 to 0xFFFFFF. The default value is 0xFF0000.

- alpha: The alpha of the glow from 0 to 1. The default is 1.

- blurX: The amount to blur the glow in the x direction from 0 to 255. The default is 6.

- blurY: The amount to blur the glow in the y direction from 0 to 255. The default is 6.

- strength: The punch strength of the glow from 0 to 255. The default is 2.

- quality: The number of times to run the blur on the glow. The range is from 0 to 15. The higher the number, the smoother the blur of the glow will appear. The default is 1.

- inner: A Boolean value indicating whether or not the glow should be applied to the inside of the object. The default value is false, which means the glow is applied outside the object.

- knockout: A Boolean value indicating whether or not the original display object contents should be transparent. If true, that section of the object is transparent (the background or whatever is underneath the object is visible) and the glow is visible around the edges of that area. The default value is false.

The GlowFilter constructor accepts from 0 to 8 parameters. The parameters are in the order they appear in the preceding list. The following code constructs a GlowFilter object with the default settings:

```
var gfInstance:GlowFilter = new GlowFilter();
```

The following code constructs a GlowFilter object with a color of 0x00FFFF and an alpha of 0.5:

```
var gfInstance:GlowFilter = new GlowFilter(0x00FFFF, 0.5);
```

As with other filter objects, you can change the properties of a GlowFilter object after it has been constructed. The following constructs a GlowFilter object with default settings, and then makes it an inner glow.

```
var gfInstance:GlowFilter = new GlowFilter();
gfInstance.inner = true;
```

Figure 29-4 shows the effect of the following code:

```
import flash.filters.GlowFilter;

var gfInstance:GlowFilter = new GlowFilter(0x000000, .5, 40, 20);
image.filters = [gfInstance];
```

FIGURE 29-4

A glow filter applied to an image

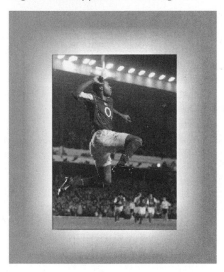

Adding the gradient bevel filter

The GradientBevelFilter class is much like the BevelFilter class except that you can specify more control over the colors. The class defines the following properties:

- distance: The number of pixels from the edge of the display object to offset the bevel. The default is 4.

- angle: The angle of the light source in degrees where 0 is directly to the left of the object. The default value is 45.

- colors: The colors of the bevel specified as an array of an unsigned integer from 0x000000 to 0xFFFFFF.

- alphas: The alphas of the bevel specified as an array of values from 0 to 100 such that each element corresponds to an element in the colors array. The default is null.

- ratios: The ratios to use when distributing the colors across the bevel specified as an array of values from 0 to 255. Each element of the array corresponds to an element of the colors array. Each color in the colors array blends into the next, and so each color appears at 100 percent at just one point in the continuum.

- blurX: The amount to blur the bevel in the x direction from 0 to 255. The default is 4.

- blurY: The amount to blur the bevel in the y direction from 0 to 255. The default is 4.

- strength: The punch strength of the bevel from 0 to 255. The default is 1.

- quality: The number of times to run the blur on the bevel. The range is from 0 to 15. The higher the number, the smoother the blur of the bevel will appear. The default is 1.

- type: The type can be one of the following BitmapFilterType values: inner, outer, or full. The default value is inner.

- knockout: A Boolean value indicating whether or not the original display object contents should be transparent. If true, that section of the object is transparent (the background or whatever is underneath the object is visible). The default value is false.

The GradientBevelFilter constructor accepts between 0 to 11 parameters. The parameters are in the order they appear in the preceding list. The following code constructs a new GradientBevelFilter with the default values:

```
var gbfInstance:GradientBevelFilter = new GradientBevelFilter();
```

However, unlike many other filter types, the GradientBevelFilter default values don't have any visible effect because the defaults for the three array parameters are undefined. Therefore, in order for there to be some visible effect, you need to somehow specify values for at least the three array parameters. The following code constructs a new GradientBevelFilter object with blue, white, and black colors:

```
var aColors:Array = [0x0000FF, 0xFFFFFF, 0xFFFFFF, 0xFFFFFF,
0x000000];
var aAlphas:Array = [100, 20, 0, 20, 100];
var aRatios:Array = [0, 255 / 4, 2 * 255 / 4, 3 * 255 / 4, 255];
var gbfInstance:GradientBevelFilter = new GradientBevelFilter(10, 45, ↵
aColors, aAlphas, aRatios);
```

You can also construct an instance with default settings, and then assign values to the properties:

```
var gbfInstance:GradientBevelFilter = new GradientBevelFilter();
gbfInstance.colors = aColors;
gbfInstance.alphas = aAlphas;
gbfInstance.ratios = aRatios;
```

Unlike the BevelFilter type, GradientBevelFilter automatically fills the entire object with the gradient bevel. That means that the middle element(s) in the colors array fills the main contents of the object. For example, in the preceding examples, the colors array has five elements. The third element is used to fill the shape of the display object inside the bevel. Normally the alpha of the element is set to 0, as in the preceding examples.

Convolution filtering

For basic color operations, the `ColorTransform` class will work. However, for more complex color transformations such as changes in color saturation, hue, and so forth, you can apply a `ColorMatrixFilter`.

The `ColorMatrixFilter` class has one property: `matrix`. The matrix property is an array that defines a 4 × 5 (4 rows and 5 columns) grid of values, as shown here:

```
| a b c d e |
| f g h i j |
| k l m n o |
| p q r s t |
```

The default matrix is an identity matrix, and it looks something like the following:

```
| 1 0 0 0 0 |
| 0 1 0 0 0 |
| 0 0 1 0 0 |
| 0 0 0 1 0 |
```

The default identity matrix means that no color transformation is applied. Applying the identity matrix at any point resets the colors.

The matrix is used in a matrix multiplication operation with color vectors representing the colors of the display object. The color vectors look something like the following:

```
| red   |
| green |
| blue  |
| alpha |
```

The matrix multiplication product is a new 4 × 1 matrix that represents the updated color.

```
| updated red   |
| updated green |
| updated blue  |
| updated alpha |
```

If you're not familiar with matrix multiplication, you can calculate the product vector using the following equations:

```
updated red = red * a + green * b + blue * c + alpha * d + e
updated green = red * f + green * g + blue * h + alpha * i + j
updated blue = red * k + green * l + blue * m + alpha * n + o
updated alpha = red * p + green * q + blue * r + alpha * s + t
```

There are many color transformations that you can apply using a `ColorMatrixFilter`. Some of the most common include the following:

- Digital negative
- Grayscale
- Saturation
- Tint
- Brightness
- Contrast
- Hue

The following sections address each of these.

Applying a digital negative

A digital negative substitutes the complementary color for each pixel in the original. A complementary color is the color that, when paired with the original color, adds to `0xFFFFFF`. You can calculate the complementary color by subtracting the red, blue, and green parts each from 255, and then compositing them. It would require quite a few lines of code in order to calculate and apply the complementary color to each pixel in a display object using conventional means. However, using a color matrix, you can apply the change in as little as one line of code. The matrix that converts a display object to its digital negative is as follows:

```
| -1  0  0 0 255 |
|  0 -1  0 0 255 |
|  0  0 -1 0 255 |
|  0  0  0 1 0   |
```

Therefore, if you want to simply apply a digital negative effect to a display object, you can use the following `ColorMatrixFilter` object:

```
var cmfDigitalNegative:ColorMatrixFilter = new ColorMatrixFilter([-1, 0, 0, ↵
0, 255, 0,-1, 0, 0, 255, 0, 0,-1, 0, 255, 0, 0, 0, 1, 0]);
```

Then, apply the filter using the `filters` property of the display object:

```
photograph.filters = [cmfDigitalNegative];
```

Figure 29-5 shows the effect of the following code on a `DisplayObject` containing an image.

```
var cmfInstance:ColorMatrixFilter = new ColorMatrixFilter( ↵
[-1, 0, 0, 0, 255, 0, -1, 0, 0, 255, 0, 0, -1, 0, 255, 0, ↵
0, 0, 1, 0]);
image.filters = [cmfInstance];
```

FIGURE 29-5

An image with colors inverted

Applying a grayscale

While areas of color images are distinguished by variations in both color values and luminance, grayscale images vary only in luminance. That means that it is possible to convert a color image to grayscale by determining the luminance at each point.

A non-technical way of understanding luminance is as a measurement of brightness. It is possible to determine the luminance of a color by multiplying the red, green, and blue parts by constants of 0.3086, 0.6094, and 0.0820, respectively. You can use a color matrix to aid in making those calculations. Doing so simplifies things significantly. You can use the following color matrix to convert an image to grayscale:

```
| 0.3086 0.6094 0.0820 0 0 |
| 0.3086 0.6094 0.0820 0 0 |
| 0.3086 0.6094 0.0820 0 0 |
| 0      0      0      1 0 |
```

The following code constructs a `ColorMatrixFilter` object that will convert an image to grayscale:

```
var cmfGrayscale:ColorMatrixFilter = new ColorMatrixFilter([0.3086, 0.6094,
0.0820, 0, 0, 0.3086, 0.6094, 0.0820, 0, 0, 0.3086, 0.6094, 0.0820, 0, 0, 0,
0, 0, 1, 0]);
```

Then, apply the filter using the `filters` property of the display object:

```
mPhotograph.filters = [cmfGrayscale];
```

Applying saturation changes

You can change the saturation of colors using a matrix that looks like the following:

```
| a b c 0 0 |
| d e f 0 0 |
| g h i 0 0 |
```

In the preceding matrix, *a* through *i* are calculated as shown in the following code, where rw, gw, and bw are the luminance constants discussed in the preceding section, and level is a saturation level generally in the range of 0 to 3.

```
a = (1 - level) * rw + level
b = (1 - level) * gw
c = (1 - level) * bw
d = (1 - level) * rw
e = (1 - level) * gw + level
f = (1 - level) * bw
g = (1 - level) * rw
h = (1 - level) * gw
i = (1 - level) * bw
```

As you may notice, when the level is 0, the matrix formed by *a* through *i* is equivalent to the grayscale matrix. Therefore, when the saturation level is set to 0, the effect is to convert the display object to grayscale. A value of 1 for the level forms an identity matrix, so the effect is that the colors are set to the defaults. The higher the level, the more saturated the colors appear. Beyond a level of 3, the colors start to blend together so much as to make the display object's contents indistinguishable.

The following code makes a `ColorMatrixFilter` object with a matrix that increases the color saturation slightly to boost the vibrancy of the colors in a Sprite called `photograph`, as shown in Figure 29-6:

```
var nRed:Number = 0.3086;
var nGreen:Number = 0.6094;
var nBlue:Number = 0.0820;
var nLevel:Number = 1.5;
var nA:Number = (1 - nLevel) * nRed + nLevel;
var nB:Number = (1 - nLevel) * nGreen;
var nC:Number = (1 - nLevel) * nBlue;
var nD:Number = (1 - nLevel) * nRed;
var nE:Number = (1 - nLevel) * nGreen + nLevel;
var nF:Number = (1 - nLevel) * nBlue;
var nG:Number = (1 - nLevel) * nRed;
var nH:Number = (1 - nLevel) * nGreen;
var nI:Number = (1 - nLevel) * nBlue + nLevel;
var aSaturation:Array = [nA, nB, nC, 0, 0,
                         nD, nE, nF, 0, 0,
                         nG, nH, nI, 0, 0,
                          0,  0,  0, 1, 0];
photograph.filters = [new ColorMatrixFilter(aSaturation)];
```

FIGURE 29-6

An image with a ColorMatrixFilter applied to increase saturation

Applying tint

You can use a color matrix to tint an image. There are two ways to apply the tint, and they corre-spond to the two ways of tinting via a `ColorTransform` object: multipliers and offsets. Using a `ColorMatrixFilter` object, the multipliers are the diagonal elements represented by r, g, b, and a in the following matrix.

```
| r 0 0 0 0 |
| 0 g 0 0 0 |
| 0 0 b 0 0 |
| 0 0 0 a 0 |
```

The range that is typically useful for the multipliers is from –1 to 1. The following code applies a `ColorMatrixFilter` to a `DisplayObject` such that it halves the green and blue components so that the effect is a red tint:

```
var aRedTint:Array = [1, 0, 0, 0, 0,
                      0, .5, 0, 0, 0,
                      0, 0, .5, 0, 0,
                      0, 0, 0, 1, 0];
photograph.filters = [new ColorMatrixFilter(aRedTint)];
```

Changing the multipliers in a matrix that otherwise looks like an identity matrix is called *scaling* the color because the effect of such a matrix is that it simply multiplies one or more of the color components (red, blue, green, or alpha).

You can also apply offsets to each of the color components via a matrix such as the following. In the following matrix, r, g, b, and a represent the red, green, blue, and alpha offsets.

```
| 1 0 0 0 r |
| 0 1 0 0 g |
| 0 0 1 0 b |
| 0 0 0 1 a |
```

The range that is typically useful for offsets is from –255 to 255. The following code applies a `ColorMatrixFilter` object to a `DisplayObject` such that the red component is offset by 255. That applies a strong red tint to the display object.

```
var aRedTint:Array = [1, 0, 0, 0, 255,
                      0, 1, 0, 0, 0,
                      0, 0, 1, 0, 0,
                      0, 0, 0, 1, 0];
photograph.filters = [new ColorMatrixFilter(aRedTint)];
```

Of course, you can combine both multipliers and offsets in one matrix, just as you can combine multipliers and offsets in a `ColorTransform` object.

Applying brightness

You can apply brightness effects by either scaling or offsetting the color uniformly with the red, green, and blue multipliers or offsets. The following example scales each of the red, green, and blue values uniformly with a multiplier of 2, which causes the display object to appear brighter:

```
var aBrighten:Array = [2, 0, 0, 0, 0,
                       0, 2, 0, 0, 0,
                       0, 0, 2, 0, 0,
                       0, 0, 0, 1, 0];
photograph.filters = [new ColorMatrixFilter(aBrighten)];
```

Similarly, the following code brightens the display object by applying a `ColorMatrixFilter` in which the red, green, and blue offsets are uniformly adjusted:

```
var aBrighten:Array = [1, 0, 0, 0, 100,
                       0, 1, 0, 0, 100,
                       0, 0, 1, 0, 100,
                       0, 0, 0, 1, 0];
photograph.filters = [new ColorMatrixFilter(aBrighten)];
```

If you combine both multiplier and offset matrices, you'll change the contrast rather than the brightness.

Applying contrast

You can adjust the contrast of a display object by applying a `ColorMatrixFilter` object that both scales and offsets the red, green, and blue values. The Adjust Color filter available from the Property inspector at authoring time in Flash CS3 Professional uses the `ColorMatrixFilter` class to manage the color effects, and for contrast effects it uses the following matrix ranges:

- Multiplier range from 0 to 11
- Offset range from 63.5 to −635

If you want contrast effects that match those from the Adjust Color filter, you can use calculations such as those in the following code. Note that you'll want to change `nContrast`, which has a practical range from 0 to 1, to affect the amount of contrast. The closer `nContrast` is to 0, the less contrast. You can see the effect of this code in Figure 29-7.

```
var nContrast:Number = .5;
var nScale:Number = nContrast * 11;
var nOffset:Number = 63.5 - (0.2 * 698.5);
var aContrast:Array = [nScale, 0, 0, 0, nOffset,
                       0, nScale, 0, 0, nOffset,
                       0, 0, nScale, 0, nOffset,
                       0, 0, 0, 1, 0];
photograph.filters = [new ColorMatrixFilter(aContrast)];
```

FIGURE 29-7

An image with a ColorMatrixFilter applied to increase contrast

Adding the convolution filter

The convolution filter does not have an authoring time interface. It can be applied only at runtime. You can apply a convolution filter by way of a ConvolutionFilter object. The `ConvolutionFilter` class defines the following properties.

- `matrixX`: The number of columns in the convolution matrix.

- `matrixY`: The number of rows in the convolution matrix.

- `matrix`: An array defining the elements of the convolution matrix.

- `divisor`: The divisor is applied to the values calculated after the matrix has been applied. The default is 1.

- `bias`: The bias is a number that is added to the values after the matrix has been applied. The default is 0.

- `preserveAlpha`: By default, the value is `true`, which means that the convolution matrix is applied only to the red, green, and blue channels. If `false`, the convolution matrix is applied to the alpha channel as well.

- `clamp`: Convolution transformations are applied by applying a matrix transformation to all the pixels that surround each pixel. Therefore, by necessity the pixels along the edges will have to use some non-existent values for the pixels that are off the edge of the image. By default, the value of `clamp` is set to `true`, which means that the edge pixels' values are duplicated for those calculations. A value of `false` means that an alternate color value is used.

- `color`: If clamp is set to `false`, then color is used to specify the alternate color value.

- `alpha`: The alpha value corresponding to the alternate color.

Convolution matrix transforms enable advanced effects such as edge detection, embossing, and sharpening. Because the use of `ConvolutionFilter` is so specialized, we won't discuss it in too much detail. However, you may find some of the following matrices to be useful guides.

For edge detection use the following matrix;

```
|  0   1   0  |
|  1  -3   1  |
|  0   1   0  |
```

For sharpen effects use the following matrix;

```
|  0  -1   0  |
| -1   5  -1  |
|  0  -1   0  |
```

For an emboss effect use the following matrix:

```
| -2 -1  0 |
| -1  1  1 |
|  0  1  2 |
```

The following example code applies an emboss effect to mPhotograph:

```
mPhotograph.filters = [new ConvolutionFilter(3, 3, [-2, -1,↵
0, -1, 1, 1, 0, 1, 2])];
```

Gradient glow filtering

Gradient glows are applied using GradientGlowFilter objects. The properties of the GradientGlowFilter class are identical to those of GradientBevelFilter. Similarly, the GradientGlowFilter constructor accepts the parameters in the same order as the GradientBevelFilter constructor does. Refer to the preceding section for more information.

Displacement filtering

The DisplacementMapFilter class lets you apply distortion and texture effects to display objects. For example, using DisplacementMapFilter, you can apply a magnifying lens effect or make an image look like it's reflecting in a pool of rippling water. The DisplacmentMapFilter class has the following properties:

- mapBitmap: A BitmapData object (see Chapter 12) to use as the displacement map

- mapPoint: A flash.geom.Point object to use to map the BitmapData object to a point on the coordinate space of the display object.

- componentX: A color channel to use from the BitmapData object in order to map to the display object in the x direction. Possible values are 1 for red, 2 for green, 4 for blue, and 8 for alpha.

- componentY: A color channel to use from the BitmapData object to map to the display object in the y direction. Possible values are the same as for componentX.

- scaleX: The multiplier to use when scaling the displacement in the x direction. A value of 0 causes no displacement.

- scaleY: The multiplier to use when scaling the displacement in the y direction

- mode: How to displace pixels along the edges. When the filter is applied, part of the display object is shifted by an amount determined by the scaleX and scaleY proper ties. Options for mode are the IGNORE, WRAP, CLAMP, and COLOR constants from the flash.filters.DisplacementMapFilter.Mode class. IGNORE causes the adjacent edges to repeat. WRAP causes the displaced pixels from the opposite edges to wrap to the other side. CLAMP causes the edge pixels to extend outward. COLOR uses a solid color.

- color: If COLOR is specified for mode, then the color property determines the color to use. The default is 0xFFFFFF.

- alpha: If COLOR is specified for mode, then the alpha property determines the alpha of the color. The default is 100.

Adding More Than One Filter

You can add more than one filter to an object by simply placing each filter object as an element in the filters array. For example, the following code applies a bevel and a drop shadow to a Sprite named circle:

```
var bvfInstance:BevelFilter = new BevelFilter();
var dsfInstance:DropShadowFilter = new DropShadowFilter();
circle.filters = [bvfInstance, dsfInstance];
```

The filters have cumulative effects. Each filter is applied in the order in which it appears in the array. For example, in the preceding code the bevel is applied before the drop shadow. The sequence in which the filters are applied can be important. Because the effects are cumulative, it makes a difference whether a drop shadow or a bevel filter was applied first.

In some cases, you may want to apply more than one filter to a display object, but you may not want the effects to be cumulative. For example, if you apply a glow to a display object, and then a drop shadow, the shadow will apply not only to the original shape of the display object, but also to the glow. If you want the drop shadow to apply only to the original shape of the display object, you can use duplicateDisplayObject() to make a duplicate of the original DisplayObject, and then apply the glow filter to one instance and the drop shadow to the other. The following code illustrates the difference. The code assumes there are two Sprite objects on the stage: circleA and circleB:

```
package
{
    import flash.display.Sprite;
    import flash.filters.DropShadowFilter;
    import flash.filters.GlowFilter;
    public class SpriteOverlay extends Sprite
    {
        private var circleA:Sprite;
        private var circleB:Sprite;

        public function SpriteOverlay()
        {
            circleA = new Sprite();
            circleB = new Sprite();

            circleA.graphics.beginFill(0x00ff00, 1);
```

```
circleA.graphics.drawCircle(0, 0, 15);
circleA.graphics.endFill();

circleB.graphics.beginFill(0x00ff00, 1);
circleB.graphics.drawCircle(0, 0, 15);
circleB.graphics.endFill();

circleA.filters = [new DropShadowFilter(100),
                   new GlowFilter(0xFF0000, .5, 100, 100)];

circleB.filters = [new DropShadowFilter(100)];
var circleGlow:Sprite = new Sprite();
circleGlow.addChild(circleA);
circleGlow.addChild(circleB);
circleGlow.y = 100;
addChild(circleGlow);
circleGlow.filters = [new GlowFilter(0xFF0000, .5, 100, 100)];
    }
  }
}
```

Figure 29-8 shows the effects of the preceding code on two circle `DisplayObjects`. The `circleA DisplayObject` is on the left.

Multiple filters applied to DisplayObjects

Rotating Objects with Filters

As noted earlier in this chapter, filters are applied as bitmap surfaces. That means that anything that causes a bitmap surface to redraw will also cause the filter to get reapplied. This has implications with regard to rotation. For example, consider a circle `DisplayObject` to which a blur has been applied. The blur has a `blurX` property set to 40 and a `blurY` property set to 10. That means that the blur is taller than it is wide. As you rotate the `DisplayObject`, you'd likely expect the blur to rotate as well, so that when it is rotated 90 degrees the blur is wider than it is tall. However, because the filter is reapplied each time the object is rotated, the blur always appears taller than it is wide.

To achieve a proper rotation effect, you can use the `BitmapData` class. With the `BitmapData` class, you can draw the contents of a `DisplayObject` to a `BitmapData` object. You can then display that object in a `DisplayObject`, and rotate that `DisplayObject`. The following code illustrates how it works:

```
package
{
import flash.display.Bitmap;
import flash.display.BitmapData;
import flash.display.Sprite;
import flash.events.MouseEvent;
import flash.filters.BlurFilter;
import flash.geom.Matrix;
public class FilterRotation extends Sprite
{
    private var circle:Sprite;
    private var circleCopy:Sprite;

    public function FilterRotation()
    {
        addEventListener(MouseEvent.MOUSE_MOVE, onMouseMove);
        circle = new Sprite();
        circle.graphics.beginFill(0x00FF00, 1);
        circle.graphics.drawCircle(0, 0, 15);
        circle.graphics.endFill();
        addChild(circle);
        var bfInstance:BlurFilter = new BlurFilter(10, 40);
        circle.filters = [bfInstance];
        var bmpDataCircle:BitmapData = new BitmapData(circle.width + 20, ↵
circle.height + 80);
        bmpDataCircle.draw(circle, new Matrix(1, 0, 0, 1, 10, 40));
        var bmpCircle:Bitmap = new Bitmap(bmpDataCircle);
        circle.visible = false;
        circleCopy = new Sprite();
        circleCopy.addChild(bmpCircle);
        addChild(circleCopy);
```

```
        }

        private function onMouseMove(mouseEvent:MouseEvent):void
        {
            circleCopy.rotation = (mouseX / 550) * 360;
        }
    }
}
```

Summary

- Filters let you apply bitmap effects to display objects.

- You can apply a filter to a display object via the `filters` array property that every `DisplayObject` possesses.

- Filter effects are cumulative. If you want to apply more than one filter in a non-cumulative fashion, you can make duplicates of the display object and apply each filter individually.

- Filter effects are reapplied each time an object rotates. You can use a `BitmapData` object to apply rotating filter effects.

Chapter 30

Drawing Vector Graphics Programmatically

Drawing programmatically allows you much greater freedom in creating and modifying your graphics at runtime, enabling you to create rich and exciting interactivity. Whenever you're drawing programmatically you're creating vector graphics. You do this using lines and fills, where lines define a vector that has at least two points and no fill, and fills define colors bounded by lines. To anyone who has used any image manipulation tool, a vector graphic is probably familiar. Whenever you've used circle or rectangle drawing tools, you've created vector graphics.

If you used the Drawing API in previous versions of Flash then many of the methods and properties we explore here will be somewhat familiar to you. However, the object in which the graphics are drawn has changed, and several new methods have been added.

All `DisplayObjects` possess a `graphics` object and a series of methods, which you can use to draw vector `graphics`. This graphics object is, in fact, an instance of `flash.display.Graphics` and it is that class that we will investigate. Because any `DisplayObject` can be used for drawing, in our examples here we use Sprite objects or Shape objects, depending on whether we want to listen for mouse events on that object.

Lines and LineStyles

We'll start our graphics exploration with the line. I've always found it easy to think of the line as a pen. You put the pen down at a certain point, you draw a line to a certain point and then you pick the pen up, which ends the line.

Setting a line style

Before you can do anything with a pen, you have to first tell it what kind of lines to draw. This is kind of like selecting among a set of different pens before drawing on a piece of paper. You want to choose the right pen for the job. Do you want a thin or thick line? What color should the line be? Each Graphics object has its own pen. So you have to set the line style for each `DisplayObject` before you can draw in it. To set the line style, you can use the `lineStyle()` method. This method accepts eight parameters. All but the line thickness are optional parameters with default values.

```
lineStyle(thickness:Number, color:uint = 0, alpha:Number = 1.0, ↵
pixelHinting:Boolean = false, scaleMode:String = "normal", ↵
caps:String = null, joints:String = null, ↵
miterLimit:Number = 3):void
```

The following lists the parameters in the order in which the method expects them:

- `thickness`: This numeric value can range from 0 (hairline) to 255. This value indicates how many pixels wide the line should be. The parameter is required.

- `color`: This numeric value should be the color for the line. Typically it is convenient to work with hexadecimal representation for this value, but it is not required. For example, to draw a blue line you can use the value 0x0000FF. The default value is 0x000000 or black.

- `alpha`: This is a value from 0 to 1 indicating the alpha of the line. Typically a value of 0 is used only when you want to create a filled shape that displays no outline. The default value is 1.

- `pixelSnapping`: This optional Boolean parameter lets you instruct the line to snap to whole pixel values. The default value is `false`.

- `scaleType`: You can optionally specify how a line thickness scales. By default, the value is `"normal"`, which means the line scales as the `MovieClip` scales. For example, a 1 pixel line within a MovieClip that is scaled to 200 percent will appear 2 pixels wide. Setting the value to `"vertical"` means it scales only if the display object is scaled vertically, and setting the value to `"horizontal"` means it scales only if the display object is scaled horizontally. Setting the value to `"none"` means the line does not scale. These properties are available as static constant properties of the `flash.display` `.LineScaleMode` class.

- `endCaps`: You can specify what type of end cap to apply to the line. The default is `"round"`. You can also specify `"square"` or `"none"`.

- `joinStyle`: You can specify how lines join to one another. If two lines share a common endpoint, then Flash Player applies a join style. By default, the join style is `"round"`. You can also specify `"none"` or `"miter"`, which can cause a pointed or blunted join. These properties are available as static constants of the `flash.display.JoinStyle` class.

- `miterLimit`: If you specify a `"miter"` join style, you can also specify a number to use as the miter limit. The miter limit specifies the number of pixels from the line join point the join is cut off. The default value is 3, and the valid range is from 0 to 255.

Here is an example in which we create a new `Shape` and set the line style on the `Graphics` object that it contains. We'll use a hairline, red line with 1.0 alpha (implicit because no value is specified).

```
var shape:Shape = new Shape();
shape.graphics.lineStyle(0, 0xFF0000);
```

You can change the line style at any point as well. For example, you may want to draw one red line and then one green line. You take a look at the `lineTo()` method in more detail in a moment, but for right now, here is a simple example that demonstrates how you can change the line style:

```
shape.graphics.lineStyle(0, 0xFF0000);
shape.graphics.lineTo(100, 0);
shape.graphics.lineStyle(0,0x00FF00);
shape.graphics.lineTo(100, 100);
```

The following code illustrates the pixel snapping functionality. The code draws two rectangles using almost identical parameters. The only difference is that one uses pixel snapping in the line style, and the other does not. When you test the code, you'll notice that the first rectangle has jagged lines while the second has square, smooth lines. The effect is shown in Figure 30-1.

```
rectangleA.graphics.lineStyle(1, 0x000000, 100, false);
rectangleA.graphics.lineTo(100, 0.4);
rectangleA.graphics.lineTo(100.4, 50);
rectangleA.graphics.lineTo(0, 50.4);
rectangleA.graphics.lineTo(0.4, 0)

rectangleB.graphics.lineStyle(1, 0x000000, 100, true);
rectangleB.graphics.lineTo(100, 0.4);
rectangleB.graphics.lineTo(100.4, 50);
rectangleB.graphics.lineTo(0, 50.4);
rectangleB.graphics.lineTo(0.4, 0);
rectangleB.x = 200;
```

FIGURE 30-1

The pixel snapping parameter can cause lines to straighten.

The following code illustrates the scale type parameter. Both rectangles are scaled to four times their original size in the x direction. However, while the line thickness in the first rectangle scales, the line thickness in the second does not. The effect is shown in Figure 30-2.

```
rectangleA.graphics.lineStyle(1, 0, 100);
rectangleA.graphics.lineTo(100, 0);
rectangleA.graphics.lineTo(100, 50);
rectangleA.graphics.lineTo(0, 50);
rectangleA.graphics.lineTo(0, 0);
rectangleA.scaleX = 4;
```

```
rectangleB.graphics.lineStyle(1, 0, 100, false, "none");
rectangleB.graphics.lineTo(100, 0);
rectangleB.graphics.lineTo(100, 50);
rectangleB.graphics.lineTo(0, 50);
rectangleB.graphics.lineTo(0, 0);
rectangleB.y = 1;
rectangleB.scaleX = 400;
```

FIGURE 30-2

Setting the scale type parameter determines how lines scale.

The following code illustrates the types of line end caps. The effect is shown in Figure 30-3.

```
var lineA:Shape = new Shape();
var lineB:Shape = new Shape();
var lineC:Shape = new Shape();
lineA.x = 100;
lineA.y = 100;
lineA.graphics.lineStyle(20, 0, 1, false, "none", "round");
lineA.graphics.lineTo(100, 0);

lineB.x = 100;
lineB.y = 150;
lineB.graphics.lineStyle(20, 0, 1, false, "none", "square");
lineB.graphics.lineTo(100, 0);

lineC.x = 100;
lineC.y = 200;
lineC.graphics.lineStyle(20, 0, 1, false, "none", "none");
lineC.graphics.lineTo(100, 0);
```

FIGURE 30-3

The line cap styles

The following code illustrates the join styles and miter limits. The effect is shown in Figure 30-4.

```
linesA.x = 100;
linesA.y = 100;
linesA.graphics.lineStyle(20, 0, 100, false, "none", "none", "round");
linesA.graphics.lineTo(100, 0);
linesA.graphics.lineTo(0, 50);

linesB.x = 250;
linesB.y = 100;
linesB.graphics.lineStyle(20, 0, 100, false, "none", "none", "none");
linesB.graphics.lineTo(100, 0);
linesB.graphics.lineTo(0, 50);

linesC.x = 100;
linesC.y = 200;
linesC.graphics.lineStyle(20, 0, 100, false, "none", "none", "miter");
linesC.graphics.lineTo(100, 0);
linesC.graphics.lineTo(0, 50);

linesD.x = 250;
linesD.y = 200;
linesD.graphics.lineStyle(20, 0, 100, false, "none", "none", "miter", 10);
linesD.graphics.lineTo(100, 0);
linesD.graphics.lineTo(0, 50);
```

FIGURE 30-4

Joint styles

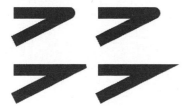

Moving the pen without drawing

If you've ever worked with an Etch-a-Sketch, you know how limiting it is to not be able to lift the pen in order to move it without drawing a line. Fortunately, the Flash Drawing API does not have this limitation. You can use the moveTo() method to instruct the pen to move to a specific point within the Sprite's coordinate system without drawing a line. The moveTo() method requires two parameters: the x and y coordinate values. The following example creates a Shape object, sets the line style, and then moves the pen to 100, 100 without drawing a line yet:

```
var shape:Shape = new Shape();
shape.graphics.lineStyle(0, 0xFF0000);
shape.moveTo(100, 100);
```

Remember that the point to which you are moving is a coordinate within the coordinate space of the display object.

Drawing a straight line

The simplest type of drawing in ActionScript is a line. You can create a straight line with the lineTo() method. The lineTo() method, like the moveTo() method, requires that you specify the x and y coordinates to which you want to move the pen. The difference is that unlike moveTo(), the lineTo() method actually draws a line to that point. The line is always drawn from the current coordinate of the pen. If you have not otherwise moved the pen within a DisplayObject object, the pen rests at 0, 0. Once you have moved the pen using moveTo(), lineTo(), or the curveTo() method (which you look at in just a moment), the pen rests at the destination point you specified in the method call. The following example creates a Shape object, sets the line style, and then draws a line to 100, 0:

```
var shape:Shape = new Shape ();
shape.graphics.lineStyle(0, 0xFF0000);
shape.graphics.lineTo(100, 0);
```

Now that you have drawn one line, if you add another call to the graphics.lineTo() method that draws a line to 100, 100, the second line will be drawn starting from 100, 0, the previous resting place for the pen:

```
shape.graphics.lineTo(100, 100);
```

Of course, if you don't want to start drawing from 0, 0, or if you want to draw a line and then draw another line that is not immediately adjacent to the first, you can use lineTo() in conjunction with moveTo(). Here is an example:

```
shape.graphics.lineStyle(0, 0xFF0000);
shape.graphics.moveTo(100, 100);
shape.graphics.lineTo(150, 100);
shape.graphics.moveTo(200, 100);
shape.graphics.lineTo(250, 100);
shape.graphics.moveTo(125, 200);
shape.graphics.lineTo(225, 200);
```

Drawing a curve

Okay. You've mastered drawing straight lines, and you're anxiously awaiting the next exciting drawing method. Your anticipation is not in vain. The next method looks at the curveTo() method — it's leaps and bounds more exciting than drawing simple lines. Now you can tell Flash to draw a *curved* line.

To draw a curved line, Flash needs several pieces of information: the starting point (which it already knows without you having to tell it), the destination point, and a control point. A control point is a point that is not on the curve. Rather, it is the point at which the tangents to the curve at the starting and ending points of the curve will intersect. Figure 30-5 illustrates this concept.

FIGURE 30-5

A curve and its control point

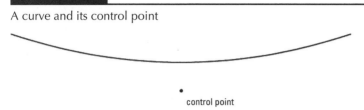

control point

The curveTo() method, therefore, requires four parameters: the x and y coordinates for the control point and the x and y coordinates for the destination point. The current position of the "pen" is used as the starting point. Here is an example that draws a curve starting at 0, 0 to 100, 0. The curve has a control point of 50, 100.

```
shape.graphics.lineStyle(0, 0xFF0000, 100);
shape.graphics.curveTo(50, 100, 100, 0);
```

Adding a simple one-color fill

When you draw closed shapes, you can have Flash Player fill the shape with either a solid color or a gradient. The solid color fill is much simpler, so let's look at that first.

The beginFill() and endFill() methods should always be used in conjunction with one another. The beginFill() method should be called just prior to the lineTo() and/or curveTo() methods that draw a closed shape. The endFill() method should be called just after those methods. The beginFill() method requires one parameter — the numeric color value you want to use to fill the shape. The endFill() method does not require any parameters. Here is an example that draws a 100 by 100–pixel square with a red outline and a yellow fill. Figure 30-6 shows the square.

```
shape.graphics.lineStyle(0, 0xFF0000);
shape.graphics.beginFill(0xFFFF00,100);
```

```
shape.graphics.lineTo(100, 0);
shape.graphics.lineTo(100, 100);
shape.graphics.lineTo(0, 100);
shape.graphics.lineTo(0, 0);
shape.graphics.endFill();
```

FIGURE 30-6

A square with a fill applied using beginFill()

If you call the `beginFill()` method before a sequence of `graphics.lineTo()` and/or `curveTo()` methods that do not create a closed shape, Flash Player will automatically add a line to close the shape if possible.

```
shape.graphics.lineStyle(0, 0xFF0000, 100);
shape.graphics.beginFill(0xFFFF00,100);
shape.graphics.curveTo(50, 100, 100, 0);
shape.graphics.endFill();
```

Notice that the code creates only a single curve. However, if you test this code, you will discover that Flash automatically adds another line to create a closed shape, as shown in Figure 30-7.

FIGURE 30-7

Flash Player will attempt to close a shape if possible.

Adding a bitmap fill

You can add a bitmap fill to any shape using a `BitmapData` object in conjunction with the `beginBitmapFill()` method. The `beginBitmapFill()` method requires a single parameter, a `BitmapData` object, and accepts up to three additional parameters — a `Matrix` object (see Chapter 32 for more details regarding the `flash.geom.Matrix` class) to transform the bitmap, a Boolean value to determine whether or not to clip the bitmap (in other words, prevent the bitmap from tiling), and another Boolean value to determine whether or not to apply smoothing to bitmap if it's scaled.

Let's look at an example. The following code uses a Loader object to load a JPEG into a `DisplayObject` instance. It then uses that `DisplayObject` to draw the bitmap data into a `BitmapData` object. At that point it draws a shape, and uses the `BitmapData` object as a bitmap fill for the shape:

```
package
{
import flash.display.*;
import flash.events.Event;
import flash.net.URLRequest;
public class BitmapDataFillExample extends Sprite
{
    private var shape:Sprite;
    private var loader:Loader;
    private var bmpImage:BitmapData;
    private var mShape:Sprite;

    public function BitmapDataFillExample()
    {
        loader = new Loader();
        loader.contentLoaderInfo.addEventListener(Event.COMPLETE, picLoaded);
        loader.load(new URLRequest("image1.jpg"));
        // Make a sprite into which to draw the shape.
        mShape = new Sprite();
        // Move the sprite so it's visible on stage.
        mShape.x = 100;
        mShape.y = 200;
    }

    private function picLoaded(event:Event):void
    {
        // Define a BitmapData object with dimensions identical to the movie
        // clip with the image.
        bmpImage = new BitmapData(loader.width, loader.height);
        // Draw the image into the BitmapData object.
        bmpImage.draw(loader);
        // Draw a shape, and use the BitmapData object as the bitmap fill.
        mShape.graphics.lineStyle(10);
        mShape.graphics.beginBitmapFill(bmpImage);
        mShape.graphics.curveTo(100, -50, 200, 0);
        mShape.graphics.lineTo(200, 100);
        mShape.graphics.lineTo(0, 100);
```

```
        mShape.graphics.lineTo(0, 0);
        mShape.graphics.endFill();
        addChild(mShape);
    }
}
}
```

Figure 30-8 shows the bitmap fill from the preceding code.

A shape with a bitmap fill applied

Next, check what happens when using the optional parameters with the `beginBitmapFill()` method. Using the same code as in the preceding example, update the `beginBitmapFill()` statement to the following:

```
shape.graphics.beginBitmapFill(bmpImage, new Matrix(0.1, 0, 0, 0.1));
```

The matrix used in the preceding line of code scales the bitmap to one-tenth. You'll notice that the scaled bitmap fill tiles within the shape, as shown in Figure 30-9.

If you omit the third parameter, it's the equivalent of specifying a value of `true`. However, if you specify `false`, the bitmap will not tile. Instead, the edge pixels will extend to the edges of the shape. You can see an example of that by using the following line of code in place of the previous `beginBitmapFill()` line. Figure 30-10 shows the effect.

```
shape.graphics.beginBitmapFill(bmpImage, new Matrix(0.1, 0, 0, 0.1), false);
```

FIGURE 30-9

A bitmap fill with a matrix transform applied

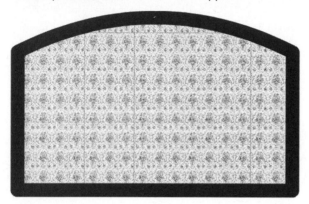

FIGURE 30-10

Specifying false for the third parameter causes the bitmap not to tile.

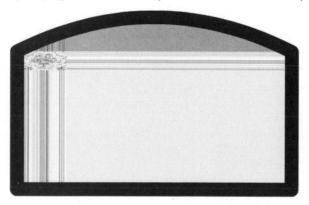

The fourth parameter, if omitted, is the equivalent to specifying `false`. When the parameter is omitted or `false`, and if the bitmap is scaled greater than 100 percent, it may appear blocky. Use the following line of code in place of the previous `beginBitmapFill()` statement to see a bitmap tile scaled up without smoothing.

```
shape.beginBitmapFill(bmpImage, new Matrix(10, 0, 0, 10));
```

Then, use the following line of code to see how it appears with smoothing.

```
shape.beginBitmapFill(bmpImage, new Matrix(10, 0, 0, 10), true, true);
```

Working with gradients

There are two types of gradients that you can apply using the Drawing API — gradient lines and gradient fills. Gradient lines are new to Flash Player 9, while gradient fills have been around for several versions. Each works in a very similar fashion, so once you learn one, the other will be quite simple to learn. Additionally, the `Matrix` class provides a method, `createGradientBox()`, that assists in building the necessary matrix when applying gradients. That makes your work that much simpler in comparison to previous versions of ActionScript, in which you had to construct the matrix manually.

Applying gradients to lines

With Flash Player 9, you can apply gradient styles to lines using the `lineGradientStyle()` method. The `lineGradientStyle()` method is not a substitute for the `lineStyle()` method. The `lineStyle()` method is still necessary to set the basic line style parameters. However, once you've set that, you can also use the `lineGradientStyle()` method to instruct Flash Player to draw a line using a gradient. The method requires the following parameter data:

- `type`: Specifies whether the gradient is to be *linear* (the color changes gradually along a line) or *radial* (the color changes gradually from a central point and moves outward).

- `colors`: ActionScript expects you to specify an array of numeric color values. For linear gradients, the colors gradate from left to right. For radial gradients, the colors gradate from the center out.

- `alphas`: For each color value, you must include an accompanying alpha value. Again, ActionScript expects an array for these values. Each element of the `alphas` array should correspond to an element of the `colors` array. The alpha values should be from 0 to 100.

- `ratios`: Flash also needs to know what ratios to use for the colors. Where along the spectrum of the gradient should Flash center each color from the colors array? Flash uses values from 0 to 255 to indicate the ratios. A value of 0 means that the corresponding color's center should be located at the far left (linear) or center (radial) of the gradient. A value of 255 indicates that the corresponding color's center should be located at the far right (linear) or outside (radial) of the gradient.

- `matrix`: The default gradient used by Flash is a 1 pixel by 1 pixel gradient. Obviously that is not going to fill most lines or shapes. Therefore, Flash needs to know how to transform this unit gradient to fill the line or shape in the way that you want. In order to accomplish this, Flash uses a transformation matrix, which you can construct using a Matrix object as discussed shortly.

- `spreadMethod`: The spread method is a string value of either `"pad"` (default), `"reflect"`, or `"repeat"`. The `pad` option means that if the gradient dimensions are less than those of the line or shape, it pads the remainder of the line or shape using the last color in the colors array. Reflect means that it will reverse the gradient repeatedly as necessary. For example, if the gradient gradually goes from red to blue, if necessary it will then go from blue to red. When the repeat option is selected, the same gradient simply repeats as necessary.

- interpolationMethod: The interpolation method is a string value of either "RGB" (default) or "linearRGB". If the "linearRGB" option is specified, the colors are distributed linearly.

- focalPointRatio: The focal point ratio can range from –1 to 1, with the default being 0. It has an effect only when the gradient type is radial, as it shifts the focus (the center of the gradient) from left (–1) to right (1) within the ellipse.

That's a lot of parameters, so let's look at a few examples. First, however, let's briefly discuss how to construct a matrix using the Matrix class. You can construct a standard Matrix object, and then use the createGradientBox() method. The createGradientBox() method accepts up to five parameters — width, height, rotation (in radians), amount to translate in the x direction, and amount to translate in the y direction. The width and height parameters are required. The remaining parameters have default values of 0. The following code creates a Matrix object that you can use with the lineGradientStyle() method to apply a gradient that has dimensions of 200 by 100 pixels:

```
var mxBox:Matrix = new Matrix();
mxBox.createGradientBox(200, 100);
```

Next, let's look at some examples. The following draws a shape, and applies a gradient to the line that uses a linear gradient that ranges from yellow to cyan, as shown in Figure 30-11:

```
package
{
import flash.display.*;
import flash.geom.Matrix;
public class SpreadMethodTest extends Sprite
{
    public function SpreadMethodTest()
    {
        var shape:Sprite = new Sprite();
        shape.x = 100;
        shape.y = 100;
        // Define a matrix that will scale the gradient to 200 by 200 pixels.
        var mxBox:Matrix = new Matrix();
        mxBox.createGradientBox(200, 200);
        // Set the line style.
        shape.graphics.lineStyle(25);
        // Set the line gradient style to apply a linear gradient that goes from
        // yellow to cyan with yellow at the left edge and cyan at the right
        // edge.
```

```
shape.graphics.lineGradientStyle(GradientType.LINEAR,
    [0xFFFF00, 0x00FFFF], [100, 100], [0x00, 0xFF], mxBox);
shape.graphics.curveTo(200, -100, 400, 0);
shape.graphics.lineTo(400, 200);
shape.graphics.lineTo(0, 200);
shape.graphics.lineTo(0, 0);
shape.graphics.endFill();
addChild(shape);
        }
    }
}
```

FIGURE 30-11

A line with a gradient applied

You'll notice that when you test the code, the gradient is not evenly distributed across the entire shape. The cyan is at 100 percent at halfway across the shape. That is because the matrix scales the gradient to 200 by 200 pixels, but the shape is 400 pixels across. Because the default spread method is pad, the cyan pads the rest of the shape. Next take a look at the effects of the optional parameters. We'll start by updating the preceding code by specifying a value for the spread method parameter. Update the lineGradientStyle() line to the following:

```
shape.graphics.lineGradientStyle("linear", [0xFFFF00, 0x00FFFF], ↵
[100, 100], [0x00, 0xFF], mxBox, "reflect");
```

When you do that, you'll notice that the gradient goes from yellow on the left to cyan in the middle, and then back to yellow on the right. If you use a value of repeat instead, the same gradient will repeat so that it will go from yellow to cyan and then yellow to cyan again.

The next parameter determines how Flash Player interpolates the colors as they gradate. So far, you've seen the effects of the standard interpolation algorithm. Update the lineGradientStyle() line as follows to use the linear interpolation algorithm. The effects are rather subtle, particularly because the gradient is applied to a 10-point line.

```
shape.graphics.lineGradientStyle("linear", [0xFFFF00, 0x00FFFF], ↵
[100, 100], [0x00, 0xFF], mxBox, "reflect", "linearRGB");
```

In order for the focal point ratio parameter to have a noticeable effect, let's use a radial gradient for the next few updates to the example. If you update the lineGradientStyle() method as follows, it will tell Flash Player to use a radial gradient instead of a linear one. Notice that we're also setting the spread method to pad.

```
shape.graphics.lineGradientStyle("radial", [0xFFFF00, 0x00FFFF], ↵
[100, 100], [0x00, 0xFF], mxBox, "pad", "linearRGB");
```

When you test the code, you'll likely see what appears to be a solid cyan line. That's because the yellow portion is located within the shape, and it radiates outward toward the cyan edges. In order to be able to see some of the yellow portion of the gradient, update the line style to draw a 100-point line instead of a 10-point line:

```
shape.graphics.lineStyle(100);
```

Then, when you test the code, you'll see the edges of the yellow radiating outward. Let's next adjust the focal point:

```
shape.graphics.lineGradientStyle("radial", [0xFFFF00, 0x00FFFF], ↵
[100, 100], [0x00, 0xFF], mxBox, "pad", "linearRGB", 1);
```

You can set the ratio to anything from –1 to 1. Check out the effect with different values.

Applying gradient fills

You can apply gradient fills using the beginGradientFill() method. The beginGradientFill() method works similarly to the beginFill() method in that you call it just prior to drawing the shape, and you call endFill() once you've drawn the shape. The beginGradientFill() method accepts the same parameters as does lineGradientStyle(), so refer to the preceding section for more details about the parameters. The following code illustrates how to use the beginGradientFill() method. Figure 30-12 shows the effect.

```
var shape: Shape = new Shape ();
shape.x = 100;
shape.y = 100;

var mxBox:Matrix = new Matrix();
mxBox.createGradientBox(200, 200);

shape.graphics.lineStyle(10);
```

```
shape.graphics.beginGradientFill("radial", [0xFFFF00, 0x00FFFF], ↵
[100, 100], [0x00, 0xFF], mxBox, "reflect", "RGB", 1);
shape.graphics.curveTo(200, -100, 400, 0);
shape.graphics.lineTo(400, 200);
shape.graphics.lineTo(0, 200);
shape.graphics.lineTo(0, 0);
shape.graphics.endFill();
```

FIGURE 30-12

A gradient fill

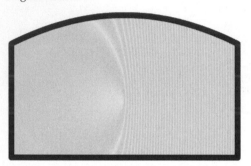

Clearing previously drawn graphics

Of course, even the trusty Etch-a-Sketch allows you to clear what you have drawn so that you can draw again. The Graphics object, not to be shamed by Etch-a-Sketch, also provides you the means by which you can clear what you have drawn. The clear() method removes all lines, curves, and fills that have been drawn within a Graphics object:

```
shape.graphics.clear();
```

Creating Shapes

Now that we've created simple lines and fills, it's time to begin creating more complex shapes. The Graphics object provides simple methods to create circles, ellipses, rectangles, and rounded rectangles. All of these methods have a somewhat similar signature, and similar steps are required in order to use them. First we create a Sprite object and set either its fill or line style using either the linestyle(), lineGradientStyle(), beginFill(), beginGradientFill(), or beginBitmapFill() methods; then we invoke the drawing method, and call endFill() to finish.

```
var rectangleShape:Sprite = new Sprite();
rectangleShape.graphics.beginFill(0xff0000, 1);
```

```
rectangleShape.graphics.drawRect(0, 0, 100, 100);
rectangleShape.graphics.endFill();
```

This will draw a red rectangle within the sprite positioned at 0, 0 and 100 pixels high and wide. If you're just drawing shapes, you can omit the endFill() method. However, if you want to draw a rectangle and then draw lines over top of it, you'll need to call endFill() unless you want the area bounded by your lines to have the same fill. The parameters of the drawRect() method are as follows:

- x: A number indicating the horizontal position relative to the registration point of the parent display object (in pixels).

- y: A number indicating the vertical position relative to the registration point of the parent display object (in pixels).

- width: The width of the rectangle (in pixels).

- height: The height of the rectangle (in pixels).

Drawing circles

A circle is drawn using the "Graphics drawCircle()" method, which takes the following parameters.

- x: The x location of the center of the circle relative to the registration point of the parent display object (in pixels).

- y: The y location of the center of the circle relative to the registration point of the parent display object (in pixels).

- radius: The radius of the circle (in pixels).

```
shape.graphics.beginFill(0x000000, 1);
shape.graphics.drawCircle(0, 0, 40);
```

If you run this code, you'll notice that the circle is drawn with the center of the circle at the 0, 0 point of the Graphics object. This can lead to surprising results:

```
package
{
    import flash.display.Sprite;
    import flash.display.Shape;
    import flash.display.StageScaleMode;
    import flash.display.StageAlign;
    public class ShapeTest extends Sprite
    {
        private var shape:Shape;

        public function ShapeTest()
        {
            stage.scaleMode = StageScaleMode.NO_SCALE;
```

```
        stage.align = StageAlign.TOP_LEFT;
        shape = new Shape();
        addChild(shape);
        shape.x = 100;
        shape.y = 100;
        shape.graphics.beginFill(0x000000, 1);
        shape.graphics.drawCircle(0, 0, 100);
        shape.graphics.endFill();
        shape.graphics.lineStyle(1, 0xFFFFFF);
        shape.graphics.moveTo(0, 0);
        shape.graphics.lineTo(0, 300);
        shape.graphics.moveTo(0, 0);
        shape.graphics.lineTo(300, 0);
    }
  }
}
```

If you want your circle centered so that its edges touch the lines defined at shape.x = 0 and shape.y = 0, then you simply set the x and y points of the drawCircle method to the radius of the circle:

```
shape.graphics.drawCircle(100, 100, 100);
```

This places the circle within the boundaries of the shape.

Drawing ellipses

The drawEllipse() method is very similar to the drawCircle() method except that instead of the radius of the circle you pass a width and height to define the ellipse. The method accepts the following parameters in order:

- x: A number indicating the horizontal position relative to the registration point of the parent display object (in pixels).

- y: A number indicating the vertical position relative to the registration point of the parent display object (in pixels).

- width: The width of the ellipse (in pixels).

- height: The height of the ellipse (in pixels).

Drawing rounded rectangles

The Graphics object has two methods to draw rounded rectangles. The first is the drawRoundRect() method, which defines a rectangle and ellipse within it, with the rectangle masking the ellipse. This allows corners to appear rounded while giving you greater control over the angle at which they round.

Remember that before you can use any of the drawing methods, the fill or line style of your graphics must be set using `beginFill()` or `lineStyle()`. The following method defines a shape where the corners are not evenly rounded:

```
shape.graphics.drawRoundRect(0, 0, 100, 100, 10, 20);
```

The following method defines a shape with evenly rounded corners:

```
shape.graphics.drawRoundRect(0, 0, 100, 100, 10, 20);
```

The `drawRoundRect` method accepts the following parameters:

- `x`: A number indicating the horizontal position relative to the registration point of the parent display object (in pixels).
- `y`: A number indicating the vertical position relative to the registration point of the parent display object (in pixels).
- `width`: The width of the round rectangle (in pixels).
- `height`: The height of the round rectangle (in pixels).
- `ellipseWidth`: The width of the ellipse used to draw the rounded corners (in pixels).
- `ellipseHeight`: The height of the ellipse used to draw the rounded corners (in pixels). Optional; if no value is specified, the default value matches that provided for the `ellipseWidth` parameter.

The second way of drawing a rounded rectangle is to use the `drawRoundRectComplex()` method, which allows you to define the "rounded-ness" of each of the four corners of your rectangle independently:

```
shape.graphics.drawRoundRectComplex(0, 0, 300, 300, 100, 0, 0, 0);
```

This would draw your rectangle with the upper-left corner rounded and all of the others square. The `drawRoundRectComplex` method accepts the following parameters.

- `x`: A number indicating the horizontal position relative to the registration point of the parent display object (in pixels).
- `y`: A number indicating the vertical position relative to the registration point of the parent display object (in pixels).
- `width`: The width of the rectangle (in pixels).
- `height`: The height of the rectangle (in pixels).
- `upperLeftRadius`: The radius that the upper-left corner of the rectangle will display.
- `bottomLeftRadius`: The radius that the bottom-left corner of the rectangle will display.
- `upperRightRadius`: The radius that the upper-right corner of the rectangle will display.
- `bottomRightRadius`: The radius that the bottom-right corner of the rectangle will display.

Filling shapes

You can fill shapes using the same method you use to fill the concave area of a curve. Here we add a bitmap fill to a rectangle drawn with a gradient line style:

```
package
{
import flash.display.*;
import flash.events.Event;
import flash.geom.Matrix;
public class BitmapDataRect extends Sprite
{
    private var shape:Sprite;
    private var loader:Loader;
    private var bmpImage:BitmapData;

    public function BitmapDataRect()
    {
        loader = new Loader();
        loader.loaderInfo.addEventListener(Event.COMPLETE, picLoaded)
        loader.load("image1.jpg");
        // Make a sprite into which to draw the shape.
        shape = new Sprite();
        // Move the sprite so it's visible on stage.
        shape.x = 100;
        shape.y = 200;
    }

    private function picLoaded(event:Event):void
    {
        // Define a BitmapData object with dimensions identical to the sprite
        bmpImage = new BitmapData(loader.width, loader.height);
        // Draw the image into the BitmapData object.
        bmpImage.draw(loader);
        // Draw a shape, and use the BitmapData object as the bitmap fill.
        shape.graphics.lineStyle(25);
        shape.graphics.lineGradientStyle(
            GradientType.LINEAR, [0x00ff00, 0xff0000], [100, 100], [150, 255]);

        // Set the line gradient style to apply a linear gradient that goes from
```

```
            // yellow to cyan with yellow at the left edge and cyan at the right
            // edge.
            var mxBox:Matrix = new Matrix();
            mxBox.createGradientBox(200, 200);
            shape.graphics.lineGradientStyle(GradientType.LINEAR,
                [0xFFFF00, 0x00FFFF], [100, 100], [0x00, 0xFF], mxBox);
            shape.graphics.beginBitmapFill(bmpImage);
            shape.graphics.drawRect(0, 0, 200, 200);
            shape.graphics.endFill();
        }
    }
}
```

You apply gradient fills in the same fashion, both to lines and shapes. You can also clear and redraw the lines at any time you'd like.

Masks

A mask defines the area of a `Graphics` object that Flash Player will draw. When you apply a mask to a `Graphics` object, you will see only the part of that object that exists within the mask; everything else will be invisible. You define a shape by creating a `DisplayObject` and setting it to be the mask of a second `DisplayObject` like so:

```
gettingMasked.mask = maskShape;
```

This enables `gettingMasked` to be seen where it intersects with `maskShape`. Let's look at a different example where you draw a circle, mask it with a box, and scroll down to reveal the entire circle:

```
package
{
    import flash.display.*;
    import flash.events.Event;
    public class ShapeMasking extends Sprite
    {
        private var circle:Shape;
        private var vBox:Shape;
        private var up:Boolean = false;

        public function ShapeMasking()
        {
            super();
            stage.scaleMode = "noScale";
            circle - new Shape();
            circle.graphics.beginFill(0xFF6600, 1);
```

```
                              circle.graphics.drawCircle(250, 250, 250);
                              vBox = new Shape();
                              vBox.graphics.beginFill(0x000000, 1);
                              vBox.graphics.drawRect(0, 0, 1000, 20);
                              circle.mask = vBox;
                              addChild(vBox);
                              addChild(circle);

                              addEventListener(Event.ENTER_FRAME, scrollVertBox);
                          }

                          private function scrollVertBox(event:Event):void
                          {
                              if(up)
                              {
                                  vBox.y -= 2;
                              } else {
                                  vBox.y += 2;
                              }

                              if(vBox.y > 520)
                              {
                                  up = true;
                              }
                              if(vBox.y < 0)
                              {
                                  up = true;
                              }
                          }
                      }
                  }
```

Notice that we added the masking object to the Stage. The shape will work as expected if the mask is not added to the Display List, but changing its attributes at runtime, when you're using the scrollVertBox() method, won't actually change any properties of the mask.

Advanced masks

In the following code, two Sprite objects will be created, the maskingSprite that will be used to mask another Sprite object and the maskedSprite which has its mask property set to be the maskingSprite.

```
      package
      {
          import flash.display.Sprite;
          import flash.events.MouseEvent;
          public class MaskDemo extends Sprite
          {
```

```
private var maskingSprite:Sprite;
private var maskedSprite:Sprite;
private var maskHolder:Sprite;

public function MaskDemo()
{

    stage.scaleMode = "noScale";
    stage.align = "TL";
    maskingSprite = new Sprite();
    maskedSprite = new Sprite();

    maskedSprite.graphics.beginFill(0xFFCC00, 1);
    maskedSprite.graphics.drawRect(0, 0, 1000, 600);
    maskedSprite.graphics.lineStyle(20, 0x000000);
    maskedSprite.graphics.lineTo(1000, 600);
    maskedSprite.graphics.moveTo(1000, 0);
    maskedSprite.graphics.lineTo(0, 600);
    addChild(maskedSprite);

    maskHolder = new Sprite();
    maskHolder.graphics.beginFill(0x000000, 1);
    maskHolder.graphics.drawRect(0, 0, 120, 120);

    maskingSprite.graphics.beginFill(0x000000, 1);
    maskingSprite.graphics.drawRect(0, 0, 100, 100);
    maskingSprite.graphics.endFill();
    addChild(maskingSprite);
    maskedSprite.addEventListener(MouseEvent.MOUSE_DOWN, dragMask);
    maskedSprite.addEventListener(MouseEvent.MOUSE_UP, stopDragMask);
    maskedSprite.mask = maskingSprite;
}

private function dragMask(mouseEvent:MouseEvent):void
{
    trace(" drag ");
    maskingSprite.startDrag();
}

private function stopDragMask(mouseEvent:MouseEvent):void
{
    maskingSprite.stopDrag();
}
    }
}
```

Notice that we're adding the masking Sprite to the stage. If we don't add the Sprite to the stage, we won't be able to change its attributes at runtime. Also, we're listening to the MouseEvents on the sprite that is being masked, so we can't listen for mouse events on the Sprite that is masking.

Making a Drawing Application

Let's put all of our vector drawing to use with a drawing application. This simple application will consist of three classes: the ColorPicker, the ToolSet, and the DrawingCanvas.

Alright, here's the main class of the application, which you'll call DrawingCanvas. You'll find that the drawing canvas defines a _stage object that you will do all of your drawing on, and then several properties to define the vector graphics you'll be creating, and finally ToolSet and ColorPicker objects.

```
package
{
import flash.display.Shape;
import flash.display.Sprite;
import flash.events.DataEvent;
import flash.events.MouseEvent;
import flash.geom.Point;
public class DrawingCanvas extends Sprite
{
    private var _stage:Sprite;
    private var toolState:String = "line";
    private var drawingShape:Shape;
    private var currentColor:uint;
    private var currentShape:Shape;
    private var lineThickness:Number = 4;
    private var colorPicker:ColorPicker;
    private var toolSet:ToolSet;
    private var startPoint:Point = new Point(0, 0);

    public function DrawingCanvas()
    {
        stage.scaleMode = "noScale";
        stage.align = "TL";
        _stage = new Sprite();
        _stage.graphics.beginFill(0xFFFFFF, 1);
        _stage.graphics.drawRect(0, 0, 500, 500);
        _stage.graphics.endFill();
        addChild(_stage);
        _stage.addEventListener(MouseEvent.MOUSE_DOWN, startDraw);
```

```
    _stage.addEventListener(MouseEvent.MOUSE_UP, stopDraw);
    colorPicker = new ColorPicker();
    addChild(colorPicker);
    colorPicker.x = 0;
    colorPicker.addEventListener("colorSelected", changeColor);
    toolSet = new ToolSet();
    addChild(toolSet);
    toolSet.y = 150;
    toolSet.x = 20;
    toolSet.addEventListener("toolSelected", changeTool);
    drawingShape = new Shape();
}

private function stopDraw(mouseEvent:MouseEvent):void
{
    _stage.removeEventListener(MouseEvent.MOUSE_MOVE, draw);
}

private function startDraw(mouseEvent:MouseEvent):void
{
    var newShape:Shape = new Shape();
    startPoint.x = _stage.mouseX;
    startPoint.y = _stage.mouseY;
    drawingShape = newShape;
    _stage.addEventListener(MouseEvent.MOUSE_MOVE, draw);
    if(toolState == "line" || toolState == "eraser")
    {
        drawingShape.graphics.moveTo(mouseEvent.stageX, mouseEvent.stageY);
    }
}

private function draw(mouseEvent:MouseEvent):void
{
    switch(toolState)
    {
        case "line":
            drawingShape.graphics.lineStyle(lineThickness, currentColor);
            drawingShape.graphics.lineTo(mouseEvent.stageX, ↵
mouseEvent.stageY);
            addChild(drawingShape);
```

```
                  break;
              case "circle":
                  drawingShape.graphics.clear();
                  drawingShape.graphics.beginFill(currentColor, 1);
                  drawingShape.graphics.drawCircle(startPoint.x, ↵
startPoint.y, findDistance(mouseEvent));
                  addChild(drawingShape);
                  break;
              case "square":
                  drawingShape.graphics.clear();
                  drawingShape.graphics.beginFill(currentColor, 1);
                  drawingShape.graphics.drawRect(startPoint.x, ↵
startPoint.y, _stage.mouseX - startPoint.x, _stage.mouseY - startPoint.y);
                  addChild(drawingShape);
                  break;
              case "eraser":
                  drawingShape.graphics.lineStyle(lineThickness, currentColor);
                  drawingShape.graphics.lineTo(mouseEvent.stageX, ↵
mouseEvent.stageY);
                  addChild(drawingShape);
                  break;
          }
      }

      private function changeTool(evt:DataEvent):void
      {
          toolState = evt.data;
          if(toolState == "eraser")
          {
              currentColor = 0xFFFFFF;
          }
      }

      private function changeColor(dataEvent:DataEvent):void
      {
          currentColor = parseInt(dataEvent.data, 16);
          drawingShape.graphics.lineStyle(lineThickness, currentColor);
          if(toolState == "eraser")
          {
              toolState = "line";
          }
      }
```

```
        private function findDistance(mouseEvent:MouseEvent):Number
        {
            var dist:Number = Math.sqrt(Math.pow(_stage.mouseX - startPoint.x, 2) +
                Math.pow(_stage.mouseY - startPoint.y, 2));
            return dist;
        }
    }
}
```

The `ColorPicker` class creates the familiar color picker using a little bit of `Bitmap` trickery so that our users can select what color they want to use in their drawings.

```
package
{
import flash.display.*;
import flash.geom.ColorTransform;
import flash.events.MouseEvent;
import flash.events.DataEvent;
public class ColorPicker extends Sprite
{
    private var k:int = 255;

    public function ColorPicker()
    {
        for(var i:int = 0;i < 256; i += 48)
        {
            for(var j:int = 0;j < 256; j += 48)
            {
                var spr:Sprite = new Sprite();
                spr.graphics.beginFill(0xFFFFFF, 1);
                spr.graphics.drawRect(0, 0, 20, 20);
                spr.graphics.endFill();
                //apply color transofrm
                var trans:ColorTransform = new ColorTransform();
                var red:uint = i << 16;
                trans.color = red + green + blue;
                var green:uint = j << 8;
                var blue:uint = k;
                trace(red + " " + blue + " " + green + " " + trans.color);
                spr.transform.colorTransform = trans;
                addChild(spr);
                spr.addEventListener(MouseEvent.CLICK, dispatchColorPicked);
                spr.x = i / 2;
```

```
                        spr.y = j / 2;
                        k -= 48;
                    }
                }
            }

        private function dispatchColorPicked(mouseEvent:MouseEvent):void
        {
            var target:Sprite = mouseEvent.target as Sprite;
            var trans:ColorTransform = target.transform.colorTransform;
            var color:uint = trans.color;
            var dataEvent:DataEvent = new DataEvent("colorSelected",
                false, false, trans.color.toString(16));
            dispatchEvent(dataEvent);
        }
    }
}
```

Finally, the ToolSet class defines a few simple tools that the user can select by clicking on them. You'll notice that when the user clicks on the tool an event is dispatched from the ToolSet indicating what tool has been selected. This event will be listened to by the main application class.

```
package
{
    import flash.display.Sprite;
    import flash.events.MouseEvent;
    import flash.events.DataEvent;
    public class ToolSet extends Sprite
    {
        public var circle:Sprite;
        public var square:Sprite;
        public var line:Sprite;
        public var eraser:Sprite;

        public function ToolSet()
        {
            line = new Sprite();
            line.graphics.lineStyle(5, 0x000000);
            line.graphics.lineTo(30, 30);

            circle = new Sprite();
            circle.graphics.beginFill(0x000000, 1)
            circle.graphics.drawCircle(0, 0, 15);

            square = new Sprite();
            square.graphics.beginFill(0x000000, 1);
            square.graphics.drawRect(0, 0, 30, 30);
```

```
        eraser = new Sprite();
        eraser.graphics.lineStyle(5, 0x000000);
        eraser.graphics.lineTo(30, 30);
        eraser.graphics.moveTo(30, 0);
        eraser.graphics.lineTo(0, 30);

        addChild(square);
        addChild(circle);
        addChild(line);
        addChild(eraser);
        square.addEventListener(MouseEvent.MOUSE_DOWN, toolClicked);
        line.addEventListener(MouseEvent.MOUSE_DOWN, toolClicked);
        circle.addEventListener(MouseEvent.MOUSE_DOWN, toolClicked);
        eraser.addEventListener(MouseEvent.MOUSE_DOWN, toolClicked);
        circle.y = 15;
        square.x = 25;
        line.x = 60;
        eraser.x = 95;
    }

    private function toolClicked(mouseEvent:MouseEvent):void
    {
        var tool:String;
        switch(mouseEvent.target)
        {

            case square:
                tool = "square";
                break;
            case line:
                tool = "line";
                break;
            case circle:
                tool = "circle";
                break;
            case eraser:
                tool = "eraser";
                break;
        }
        dispatchEvent(new DataEvent("toolSelected", false, false, tool));
    }
}
}
```

That sure is a lot of code so let's break it down and look at the important parts. In the `DrawingProject.as` file, you created a variable called `drawingShape`, which is a shape, and a `_stage`, which is a Sprite. The `drawingShape` is always the shape that you're currently drawing and the stage is the Sprite that the `drawingShape` will get added to. This is how you ensure that you're always going to have the newest drawing on top of all the previous ones.

The main work of the application is done in this method:

```
private function draw(mouseEvent:MouseEvent):void
{
    switch(toolState)
    {
        case "line":
            drawingShape.graphics.lineStyle(lineThickness, currentColor);
            drawingShape.graphics.lineTo(mouseEvent.stageX, mouseEvent.stageY);
            addChild(drawingShape);
            break;
        case "circle":
            drawingShape.graphics.clear();
            drawingShape.graphics.beginFill(currentColor, 1);
            drawingShape.graphics.drawCircle(startingPoint.x, ↵
startingPoint.y, findDistance(mouseEvent));
            addChild(drawingShape);
            break;
        case "square":
            drawingShape.graphics.clear();
            drawingShape.graphics.beginFill(currentColor, 1);
            drawingShape.graphics.drawRect(startingPoint.x, startingPoint.y,↵
_stage.mouseX-startingPoint.x, _stage.mouseY-startingPoint.y);
            addChild(drawingShape);
            break;
        case "eraser":
            drawingShape.graphics.lineStyle(lineThickness, currentColor);
            drawingShape.graphics.lineTo(mouseEvent.stageX, mouseEvent.stageY);
            addChild(drawingShape);
            break;
    }
}
```

This method is called by a `MouseEvent` listener when the user has the mouse down and the mouse is moving. The class keeps the state of the tool that the user has selected via the `toolState` variable and uses that to determine what kind of drawing you should be doing. The `drawingShape` is drawn until the user releases the mouse button, sending the `MOUSE_UP` event.

The `startDraw()` method is called when the mouse button is pressed and takes care of creating a new Shape object that we will draw into. We set the `drawingShape` object for our application equal to that new shape so that we can provide application-wide access to the shape and then add the new shape to the display list.

```
private function startDraw(mouseEvent:MouseEvent):void
{
    var newShape:Shape = new Shape();
    startingPoint.x = _stage.mouseX;
    startingPoint.y = _stage.mouseY;
    drawingShape = newShape;
    _stage.addEventListener(MouseEvent.MOUSE_MOVE, draw);
    if(toolState == "line" || toolState == "eraser")
    {
        drawingShape.graphics.moveTo(mouseEvent.stageX, mouseEvent.stageY);
    }
}
```

If we're creating lines, we want to move the initial point of the line to the current location of the user's mouse. When we've finished drawing our current object, when the user releases the mouse button, we're done drawing and we want to remove the event listener:

```
private function stopDraw(mouseEvent:MouseEvent):void
{
    _stage.removeEventListener(MouseEvent.MOUSE_MOVE, draw);
}
```

You may notice something tricky looking in the `ColorPicker` class:

```
public function ColorPicker()
{
    for(var i:int = 0; i < 256; i+=48)
    {
        for(var j:int = 0; j < 256; j+=48)
        {
            var spr:Sprite = new Sprite();
            spr.graphics.beginFill(0xFFFFFF, 1);
```

```
                    spr.graphics.drawRect(0, 0, 20, 20);
                    spr.graphics.endFill();
                    //apply color transofrm
                    var trans:ColorTransform = new ColorTransform();
                    var red:uint = i << 16;
                    trans.color = red+green+blue;
                    var green:uint = j << 8;
                    var blue:uint = k;
                    trace(red+" "+blue+" "+green+" "+trans.color);
                    spr.transform.colorTransform = trans;
                    addChild(spr);
                    spr.addEventListener(MouseEvent.CLICK, dispatchColorPicked);
                    spr.x = i/2;
                    spr.y = j/2;
                    k-=48;
                }
            }
        }
```

Although this looks really tricky, all we're doing is getting some values that will make good hexa-decimal color values and bitshifting them to the right values.

Go ahead and run the application and play around with it a bit; then come back to the code and look carefully at the draw() method from the DrawingCanvas class.

Summary

- All DisplayObjects possess an instance of the Graphics class that can be used to draw vector graphics.

- Vector graphics are a combination of lines and fills.

- To create a line, you must first set the lineStyle(); then you can move the drawing point to anywhere within the containing DisplayObject, and draw your line with lineTo().

- To fill your lines, you set a fill to be used by calling beginFill().

- To create a shape, you must first set a fill to be used to fill an area within your shape, even if the fill is invisible, and you then draw your shape.

- Any Shape object can be used to mask another Shape object by setting the masking object to be the masked object's mask.

Chapter 31

Scripting Animation

Animation is one of the serious strong points of the Flash platform. Flash evolved out of an animation tool, and it continues to be used to animate everything from web comics to popular television shows and advertisements. There has always been a big gap between using the Flash IDE to animate by hand and creating animations in ActionScript 3.0. New functionality in Flash CS3 Professional helps to bridge this gap. In addition, Flex sports its own animation framework and there are a number of freely available third-party animation frameworks for ActionScript 3.0.

Understanding Flash Player and Animation

Intuitively, you know that animation is movement. Specifically, animation is movement achieved by sequencing individual still pictures. Your eyes and your brain conspire to interpret these separate pictures, or *frames*, as one fluid motion, through persistence of vision.

Frame rate

Flash Player, like all things running on a computer, displays static frames in sequence. It attempts to display these frames as fast as the *frame rate* of the movie, which is measured in frames per second. Motion at 30 frames per second (fps) appears fluid, but presenting even more frames per second can help — although the brain might not be able to distinguish these frames as individual pictures, their image is factored into the perception of motion overall, like motion blurring. In both Flex and Flash you have control over the frame rate of the SWF you publish, and we recommend using at least 30 fps unless you have a compelling reason not to.

 **The default frame rate for new Flash movies created in Flash CS3 Professional is 12 frames per second.**

If video is playing in your SWF, the video will still play at its source frame rate regardless of the frame rate of the host SWF. However, a subordinate SWF loaded into your own SWF will play in the master SWF's frame rate regardless of its own.

For comparison, films play at 24 fps. Television in the United States plays at about 30 fps. However, the motion perceived in television is much greater because the image is interlaced, so you see half of a new picture about 60 times a second. Computer displays can be driven at a great variety of actual refresh rates, but when designing your application, target it for whatever speed you desire.

Flash Player operation

Flash Player will not always display new frames at exactly the rate you request. The frame rate you set is a goal that Flash Player will try to achieve. The actual frame rate is limited by many variables.

In order to render a frame, Flash Player must utilize enough CPU time to render the new frame before it is scheduled to display. This can be limited by the complexity of the animation and ActionScript code that is running, the speed of the CPU and other hardware factors (bus speed, memory available, cache misses, and so on), as well as by the operating system and browser. It's a lamented fact that no SWF file running in a browser will run as fast as it does in the standalone Flash Player application. The plug-in architectures available on the various browsers limit the plug-in Flash Player's access to and allotment of resources. The browser and operating system sometimes take further chunks of performance away from plug-ins like Flash Player for the sake of power consumption and other first-class applications.

Executing ActionScript is just part of what goes into rendering a frame. Flash Player must also put together the image you will see. As of Flash Player 9, Flash Player uses purely software rendering to ensure that images will look the same on all computers, as opposed to 3D games and newer operating systems which offload much of this work onto your graphics card. Because the images that you see are composed using your CPU, composing any one frame can take up a lot of time in addition to any ActionScript running.

If you set the frame rate of a SWF file to 60 fps, Flash Player has just $\frac{1}{60}$ of a second to draw each frame, or 16.67 milliseconds. If the system takes 25 milliseconds to render one of these frames, it's going to show up as soon as it can, around 8 milliseconds late. Already, with one frame late, Flash Player isn't truly playing at 60 fps. If a few frames come in late, you might see that the player's true frame rate is fluctuating. And if every frame takes 25 milliseconds to render, then Flash Player will play at 40 fps, regardless of the fact that you asked for 60 fps. In conclusion, the frame rate is not a guarantee, and it is not fixed. It controls how often Flash Player *tries* to render new frames.

Flash Player juggles two kinds of control flow: while it's rendering frames, it's also running ActionScript. It's important to understand that for any given frame to render, all ActionScript for that frame must be completed. If, for example, you ran the following code:

```
for (var i:int = 0; i < 500; i++)
{
    myBlueShape.x = i;
}
```

The display object `myBlueShape` would *not* appear to move from the left edge of the stage to 500 pixels to the right. Instead, it would appear suddenly at 500 pixels. Since all available ActionScript code is executed before you see the next frame, you can't use synchronous code to make anything move. Flash Player does execute all 500 iterations of this loop, and each assignment is made in order (x holds the value 0, then 1, then 2 and so on), but nothing makes its way to the screen until all the code is completed. Because Flash Player works this way, you have to be aware of the order that things occur. Although action B might occur far after action A in code, the user will not be able to see this gap in time represented on the screen. And if you set a variable to something in reaction to an event, there may be frames that execute for which that variable is not yet set.

A side effect of the order in which Flash Player operates is that involved computation can slow down or halt the rendering of new frames. This is also the reason that when an uncaught exception aborts all ActionScript on a frame, the results can be fatal. Skipping to ActionScript executed in the next frame can ignore hundreds or thousands of lines of code.

ActionScript that you write isn't concurrent. It can't be threaded or fork off processes. It executes from top to bottom. However, native Flash Player API calls may execute in parallel behind the scenes, like network accesses. You can use some asynchronous events like those broadcast by `Timer` (see Chapter 18) and the `enterFrame` event to schedule ActionScript to execute after one or more frames are rendered. Correspondingly, you can use `updateAfterEvent()` methods to request a frame to draw immediately after ActionScript processing finishes, regardless of when the next frame is scheduled to render.

These asynchronous events are the primary way that ActionScript gets executed in frames after the first one, and as such, they can make things animate.

Animating with Pure ActionScript

At the core of any programmatic animation is some event that is fired at regular intervals. This enables ActionScript to be executed repeatedly across time, rather than all at once. If you can move an object a tiny bit at a time at regular intervals, you have achieved animation. We will show simple examples of building animation from scratch using only `enterFrame` or a `Timer`.

Creating these examples yourself will give you an understanding of what's happening behind the scenes, and enable you to create your own animation code when pre-made animation packages do not suffice.

Animating by time

Animating using a `Timer` object gives you some distinct benefits. When you are using a `Timer` object, you can set the frequency at which new frames are drawn completely independently of the published frame rate of the SWF. You can employ this to change the frame rate of programmed animations without interfering with timeline animations created by the Flash authoring tool, or to run two animations at different frame rates. For example, you could animate the main characters of a game at 30 fps, but save some CPU time by animating the background at 15 fps.

It's possible for events from a `Timer` object to fire more frequently than the published frame rate of a movie, and you can ensure that the results of these events are made visible by calling `updateAfterEvent()` on the event object. This can actually make Flash Player play faster than the published frame rate. However, updating more frequently than the frame rate without showing the results visually is a waste.

NEW IN AS3 The `updateAfterEvent()` **method is now a method of certain event classes:** `KeyboardEvent`, `TimerEvent`, **and** `MouseEvent`. **It is not a global function, as it was in ActionScript 2.0.**

The following class, when used as a Document class with at least one object on the Stage, will animate moving the object to the right at whatever frame rate is assigned to the `fps` variable (here, it is 60).

```
package
{
    import flash.display.*;
    import flash.events.TimerEvent;
    import flash.utils.Timer;

    public class TimerAnimation extends Sprite
    {
        protected var myShape:DisplayObject;

        public function TimerAnimation()
        {
            // fps = frames/second
            var fps:int = 60;
            // 1/fps = seconds/frame, 1/fps*1000 = milliseconds/frame
            var mspf:int = Math.round(1 / fps * 1000);

            var t:Timer = new Timer(mspf);
            t.addEventListener(TimerEvent.TIMER, onTimer);
            t.start();

            myShape = getChildAt(0);
        }

        protected function onTimer(event:TimerEvent):void
        {
            myShape.x += 0.5;
```

```
                    event.updateAfterEvent();
            }
        }
    }
```

The `onTimer()` method will be called every 17 milliseconds, or about 60 times a second, or as close to that as Flash Player can manage. After the method modifies the `x` property of the display object, it asks Flash Player to redraw the screen.

Even if you use this code in a SWF published at 12 fps, the animation will play at 60 fps. We could modify the preceding example to redraw at the rate of its host SWF with this line:

```
    var fps:int = stage.frameRate;
```

Animating by frames

You can tie the frame rate of programmatic animation to the frame rate of the movie by using the `enterFrame` event broadcast by display objects when Flash Player advances to the next frame. This is a less invasive way of scheduling animations: it lets the host SWF determine the frame rate, and it doesn't force frames to be drawn when they wouldn't normally be drawn.

The following code animates the first display object inside it toward the right.

```
package
{
    import flash.display.*;
    import flash.events.Event;

    public class FrameAnimation extends Sprite
    {
        protected var myShape:DisplayObject;

        public function FrameAnimation()
        {
            addEventListener(Event.ENTER_FRAME, onEnterFrame);
            myShape = getChildAt(0);
        }

        protected function onEnterFrame(event:Event):void
        {
            myShape.x += 0.5;
        }
    }
}
```

Animation and speed

Both of the previous examples move the display object at a particular frequency: 1 pixel every 2 frames. But in both approaches, the speed of the motion depends on the frame rate. To determine how fast the object will appear to be moving, we can factor frames out of the equality:

pixels / second = pixels / frame × frames / second

585

Applying this equality, the object will move at 30 pixels per second at 60 fps, and 15 pixels per second at 30 fps. Again, the number of frames per second determines how fluid motion is; pixels per second is an absolute measure of speed.

The formula above tells us why it can be dangerous to program animation in terms of frames. In the timer example, changing the SWF's frame rate won't actually change the frame rate of the programmatic animation, and the object should appear to move at the same speed. In the `enterFrame` example, changing the SWF's frame rate will directly change the speed of the animation. In both cases, when Flash Player can't keep up with the requested frame rate, the speed of the animation will be affected.

A better approach is to construct an update function that moves the target at the desired speed, by linking the amount of motion to the amount of time that actually elapsed since the last frame was rendered. If you ignore the frame rate of the SWF and the frequency of the `Timer` interval, and measure the time yourself, you can adjust for inadequate or changing frame rates. Although you can never guarantee that the frame rate will keep up, you can guarantee that if it doesn't, the speed of the motion will remain the same.

You can use the function `flash.utils.getTimer()` to measure real elapsed time. The function will return the number of milliseconds since the SWF started playing. Remember that:

$$v = \quad \Delta d\,/\,\Delta t$$

Or, velocity equals the change in distance over the change in time. To animate at a constant velocity you must determine how far to move the object at every frame. To find that out, simply rearrange the equation:

$$\Delta d = v \times \Delta t$$

NEW IN AS3   The `getTimer()` method works the same as in earlier versions of ActionScript, but it has been moved to the `flash.utils` package and must be imported to be used.

The following example keeps track of the change in time in order to move the object a constant speed regardless of frame rate:

```
package
{
    import flash.display.*;
    import flash.events.Event;
    import flash.utils.getTimer;

    public class AdaptiveFrameAnimation extends Sprite
    {
        protected const SPEED:Number = 50; //50 pixels per second
        protected var myShape:DisplayObject;
        protected var lastTime:int;

        public function AdaptiveFrameAnimation()
        {
```

```
                addEventListener(Event.ENTER_FRAME, onEnterFrame);
                lastTime = getTimer();
                myShape = getChildAt(0);
            }

            protected function onEnterFrame(event:Event):void
            {
                var time:int = getTimer();
                myShape.x += SPEED * (time - lastTime) / 1000;
                lastTime = time;
            }
        }
    }
```

You should apply this principle, especially in games and simulations, to keep differences in computers' speed from affecting the gameplay or visual feedback. Even when things aren't moving at constant speeds, it's a great idea to move them based on actual time elapsed rather than time derived from a frame rate which may not be accurate.

Animating Using Flash

The Flash authoring tool enables you to create timeline animations that are compiled into the SWF and play out without any ActionScript code. You can find out how to use the Flash authoring tool to create timeline animations in any Flash book such as *Adobe Flash CS3 Professional Bible*. Timeline animations are easy to create, but in the context of an ActionScript driven project, they are inflexible.

By using code to create your animations, you can modify animations on-the-fly, make them more interactive, apply them to different kinds of targets, even load them externally.

Flash CS3 Professional comes with a new animation framework that can represent animations as chunks of XML, called *motion XML*. With the addition of E4X, this means you can construct and modify complex animations deftly. It also makes animations convenient to store and load. The icing on the cake is a set of Flash Commands that bridge animations you create on the timeline with motion XML. You can create an animation on the timeline, convert it into XML, optionally modify it in ActionScript to meet your needs, play the animation back without any timeline using the Flash motion package, and you can even go round-trip, converting motion XML back into timeline animations. These commands are found in the Commands menu of Flash CS3 Professional.

Of course, you can also create animations using motion XML you create by hand. You can also create animations using the classes that the motion XML maps to, but it is far easier and more efficient to work in XML and then use the Animator class to consume the XML.

Preliminarily, we will review some animation terminology as it relates to Flash animation. Then, we will introduce the structure of motion XML, and finally we'll investigate how to use the fl.motion package.

Review: tweens, keyframes, and easing

Two important terms are used consistently to describe animations. Since this terminology carries over into motion XML and ActionScript, it begs a small review.

The pioneers of animation quickly discovered a concept that carries through to all modern animation processes: you have to draw a *lot* of pictures, and some aren't as important as others. For example, picture Bugs Bunny sneezing. His face goes from normal, to all twisted up, to forcefully expelling air and spittle. You can, in your mind's eye (hey, he's still under copyright), picture these three key states. But if the act of sneezing takes a whole second of film, then in addition to those three key frames, you will have to draw all 21 other pictures that go in between: the frames that move his face at the right speed through those key positions.

The key frames are called *keyframes*, and the in-between frames are called *tweens*. Animation is a ton of work, so early on in animation studios, it became the lead animator's responsibility to draw those key frames, and it was up to the junior animators to fill in the in-between frames. Nowadays, animation is still a ton of work, and in-between frames are often sent to third parties to finish. (And if you really have a good, trusting relationship with your contract animators, you might only send them animatics.) Now, computers have made things easier for everyone. With Flash CS3 Professional and other animation packages, you can set up two keyframes, and have the system tween between them. No interns necessary!

Our brains have adapted to intuitively recognize the effects of Newton's laws. Due to inertia, things in our experience always accelerate and decelerate rather than instantly switching speeds. Thus, a linear tween between two positions will almost always look unnatural. Although it can move an object from point A to point B smoothly, it does so at a constant speed; so at the beginning of the tween the object instantly changes from no speed to the average speed, and at the end of the tween, the object instantly stops. Thankfully, you can ease into and ease out of tweens, accelerating at the beginning and decelerating at the end, to make the motion look more natural, as shown in Figure 31-1. The change in speed through a tween is called its *easing*, and it can be set by the Flash authoring tool as well as animations created in ActionScript.

Introducing motion XML

Motion XML is comprised of a few simple elements in a predictable structure. Although animating in the timeline can provide for some awkwardly precise decimal values, motion XML should be on the whole easy to read and modify.

Each capitalized tag found in motion XML corresponds to a class, usually one from the `fl.motion` package. In the root tag, `<Motion>`, XML namespaces are imported that help you identify where the classes come from. Lower case tags indicate that the child of the tag is assigned to a property on the parent object. Attributes of a tag also become properties of the object that tag will create. For example,

```
<Sandwich layers="4">
    <toppings>
        <Lettuce/>
        <VeggieMeat/>
    </toppings>
</Sandwich>
```

FIGURE 31-1

Three animations: one with no tweening, one with easing out at the end, and one with easing in and out.

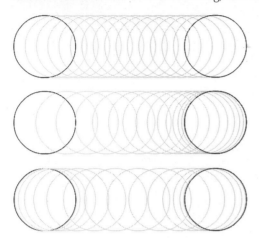

would create a `Lettuce` object and a `VeggieMeat` object inside the `toppings` property of a `Sandwich` object, like:

```
var sandwich:Sandwich = new Sandwich();
sandwich.layers = 4;
sandwich.toppings = [new Lettuce(), new VeggieMeat()];
```

This naming convention should be familiar to Flex users. We'll call nodes that correspond to objects *object nodes*, and nodes that correspond to properties *property nodes*. This structure should help you understand how motion XML is converted into objects in the `fl.motion` package, but you don't have to understand it to create and use motion XML. In fact, you can simply use the Flash authoring environment to generate motion XML for you. The package adapts to many different styles of use.

The basic structure of motion XML is as follows. Namespaces and attributes are omitted for clarity, and all optional nodes are shown.

```
<Motion>
    <source>
        <Source>
            <dimensions>
                <Rectangle/>
            </dimensions>
            <transformationPoint>
                <Point/>
            </transformationPoint>
        </Source>
    </source>
    <Keyframe>
        <color>
```

```
            <Color/>
        </color>
        <tweens>
            <ITween/>
        </tweens>
        <filters>
            <BitmapFilter/>
        </filters>
    </Keyframe>
</Motion>
```

Before we go into the details of each node, an overview. All motion XML is contained inside a root `Motion` node. The `Motion` node optionally contains a `source` property node containing a `Source` object node. Following the `source` property node is the bulk of the motion XML, a series of any number of `Keyframe` object nodes.

Each `Keyframe` can set any combination of transformation properties, color transformations, and filters. The color transformations are encoded in the `color` property node and the `Color` object node, and the filter settings for a given keyframe are encoded as object nodes inside a `filters` property node. The node name of a filter object node is equivalent to the name of the filter class.

A `Keyframe` also defines the easing applied to the keyframe, by including tween object nodes in a `tweens` parameter node. All tweens implement `ITween`. You can theoretically include more than one tween object node in order to tween different properties separately (a situation you can't replicate using timeline tweens).

The Motion object

The root node of any motion XML, the `<Motion>` node sets up the XML's namespaces, associating each namespace with a package so that child nodes scoped to a namespace can be mapped to valid classes within the package. Additionally, the `Motion` object defines the duration of the animation in frames.

```
<Motion duration="14" xmlns="fl.motion.*" xmlns:geom="flash.geom.*" ↵
xmlns:filters="flash.filters.*"></Motion>
```

This sample node defines an animation that will last 14 frames. It also scopes itself and all child nodes with no explicit namespace to the `"fl.motion.*"` namespace. This helps the animation framework know that when you write a `<Keyframe>` node, it describes an instance of the class `fl.motion.Keyframe` in the package `fl.motion`. For more information about XML namespaces, see Chapter 10.

Running motion XML you create is covered below in "Using the Flash motion package." To follow along with the examples, create an object to animate, and use a new `Animator` object to execute the motion XML you create. Remember that thanks to E4X, you can type XML directly into your code:

```
var ball:Sprite = new Sprite();
ball.graphics.beginFill(0xff0000);
ball.graphics.drawCircle(0, 0, 20);
ball.graphics.endFill();
addChild(ball);

var motionXML:XML = <Motion duration="14" xmlns="fl.motion.*" ↵
xmlns:geom="flash.geom.*" xmlns:filters="flash.filters.*"></Motion>;

var animator:Animator = new Animator(motionXML, ball);
animator.play();
```

This particular example doesn't do anything but set up the motion XML, so it won't animate the ball. But you can apply this example snippet to the following motion XML examples to see them in action.

The Source object

Stored in the `source` property of the `Motion` object, The `fl.motion.Source` object is a comprehensive record of the context in which motion XML was created. It can help Flash CS3 Professional map imported XML back on to display object instances. For custom motion XML, it can be omitted with no ill effect.

Properties that a `Source` object stores about its contents include the display object's type, instance name, and symbol in the library; the frame rate of the containing document; and the initial position, scale, rotation, and skew of the display object.

The most useful property of a `Source` object, and the main reason to use a `Source` node in custom motion XML, is the `transformationPoint` property. This property stores a `Point` object which represents the location around which transformations in the animation will happen; it is equivalent to the position of the transformation point (the white circle with a black stroke) in Flash CS3 Professional. Setting this can drastically change the outcome of rotation, scaling, and skewing, as you can see in Figure 31-2.

FIGURE 31-2

The effect of rotating a box 45 degrees with different transformation points

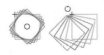

The `Point` object in the `transformationPoint` property is normalized, or scaled to a unit square. Regardless of the size of the object you are animating, (0, 0) will correspond to the upper-left corner, and (1, 1) will correspond to the lower right corner. When normalized, the two transformation points shown in Figure 31-2 are (0.5, 0.5) and (-0.16, -0.2) from left to right.

Below is an example motion XML with only a `source` property.

```
<Motion duration="5" xmlns="fl.motion.*"
        xmlns:geom="flash.geom.*" xmlns:filters="flash.filters.*">
    <source>
        <Source frameRate="12" x="145" y="81" scaleX="1" scaleY="1"
         rotation="0" elementType="movie clip" symbolName="Square">
            <dimensions>
                <geom:Rectangle left="0" top="0" width="44" height="44"/>
            </dimensions>
            <transformationPoint>
                <geom:Point x="0.5" y="0.5"/>
            </transformationPoint>
        </Source>
    </source>
</Motion>
```

Notice that the `<geom:Point>` and `<geom:Rectangle>` nodes are in the `geom` namespace, which refers to `"flash.geom.*"`. This lets the animation framework know to convert the nodes into a `flash.geom.Point` and a `flash.geom.Rectangle`.

Again, the `source` attribute node is optional, and you can leave it out, or include a `Source` node with only a `transformationPoint` attribute node.

The Keyframe Object

The `<Keyframe>` node corresponds to the `fl.motion.Keyframe` class. These objects represent a single keyframe. At any keyframe, you can set a slew of properties, and the change in these properties will be tweened when the animation plays.

A simple `Keyframe` might be represented in motion XML as:

```
<Keyframe index="13" x="100" y="78" scaleY="1" rotation="70"/>
```

Attributes of the `<Keyframe>` node, shown in Table 31-1, determine the time at which the keyframe is set, the basic transformations of a display object at that point in time, and various special behaviors.

Additionally, there are several attributes which provide finer control for Graphic symbols, motion paths, and other flags which are particular to the Flash authoring environment.

The `Keyframe` object can also contain a `color` property, a `filters` array, and a `tweens` array. These are represented in motion XML as child nodes.

TABLE 31-1

Attributes of the <Keyframe> Node

Attribute Name(s)	Type	Usage
index	int	The frame at which this keyframe is set.
label	String	Sets an accessible frame label at this keyframe.
x, y	Number	Position of the target at this keyframe.
scaleX, scaleY	Number	The horizontal and vertical scale of the target at this keyframe.
skewX, skewY	Number	The horizontal and vertical skew of the target at this keyframe.
rotation	Number	The rotation, in degrees, of the target at this keyframe.
rotateTimes	uint	Sets rotation by number of revolutions.
rotateDirection	String	Determines direction of rotation ("auto" by default). Defined by constants in fl.motion.RotateDirection.
blank	Boolean	If set to true, hides the target at this keyframe.
blendMode	String	Changes the blend mode of the target at this keyframe.

The Color Object

The fl.motion.Color class, stored in the color attribute of a Keyframe, is used to tween colors and transparency. A Color object encodes a color transform at a point in time in much the same way that a flash.geom.ColorTransform object does. In fact, Color extends ColorTransform, adding the ability to easily construct color transformations that match the brightness and tint controls in the Flash authoring environment.

To set a control point for any of the properties of a color transform, set the corresponding attribute on the <Color> node. For example, this motion XML turns an object's brightness all the way down, then fades it out.

```
<Motion duration="90" xmlns="fl.motion.*"
xmlns:geom="flash.geom.*" xmlns:filters="flash.filters.*">

    <Keyframe index="0">
        <tweens>
            <SimpleEase/>
        </tweens>
    </Keyframe>

    <Keyframe index="45">
        <color>
            <Color brightness="-1"/>
        </color>
        <tweens>
            <SimpleEase/>
```

```
          </tweens>
      </Keyframe>

      <Keyframe index="90">
          <color>
              <Color alphaMultiplier="0"/>
          </color>
      </Keyframe>

  </Motion>
```

The following attributes are supported from `ColorTransform`:

- `redMultiplier`
- `greenMultiplier`
- `blueMultiplier`
- `alphaMultiplier`
- `redOffset`
- `greenOffset`
- `blueOffset`
- `alphaOffset`

For more detail on those properties, see Chapter 32. The `Color` class adds the following properties to the above:

- `brightness:Number` — A percentage of brightness between –1 and 1.
- `tintColor:uint` — A color to tint to.
- `tintMultiplier:Number` — The amount of tint to apply, between 0 and 1.

These properties control the color of the target like the Brightness and Tint controls in the Color area of the Properties panel in Flash CS3 Professional.

Filter Objects

Filters can be set on any keyframe by adding the appropriate filter objects to the `filters` property of the `Keyframe` object. In motion XML, this consists of creating a tag in the `filters` namespace with the name of the filter you want, and the properties of the filter encoded in attributes. If you have the same kind of filter in two or more adjacent keyframes, you can animate properties of the filter. However, you must always include *all* properties of the filter: default values for omitted properties are picked up from the defaults of the filter class rather than the last keyframe in which they were set.

```
  <Keyframe index="4">
      <tweens>
          <SimpleEase ease="0"/>
      </tweens>
```

```
<filters>
    <filters:GlowFilter blurX="12" blurY="12"
        color="0xFFFFFF" alpha="1" strength="1" quality="2"
        inner="false" knockout="false"/>
</filters>
</Keyframe>
```

The ITween Objects

For the properties you set on a Keyframe object to be automatically interpolated, the Keyframe must contain at least one ITween object that defines how to tween the values into the next keyframe. These tweens come in four types: SimpleEase, CustomEase, FunctionEase, and BezierEase.

A SimpleEase tween can be linear, an ease in, or an ease out, depending on the value assigned to its ease property. When omitted, this property defaults to 0, a linear tween with no easing. This kind of tween is the same as the one created by the Ease slider in the Flash authoring environment.

- <SimpleEase/> linear easing, constant speed throughout the tween.

- <SimpleEase ease="-1"/> 100% ease in, quadratic acceleration in the beginning of the tween.

- <SimpleEase ease="1"/> 100% ease out, quadratic deceleration at the end of the tween.

A CustomEase tween follows a Bezier curve to interpolate values between the two keyframes. You can declare any curve you want starting at (0, 0) and ending at (1, 1). The x axis represents time, where 0 is exactly at the keyframe whose ease you are declaring, and 1 is at the time of the following keyframe. The y axis represents the progress of the tween, where 0 is all the values as set at the first keyframe, and 1 is the end values as they are set in the next keyframe. If you draw a straight line from (0, 0) to (1, 1), that's a linear ease. The steep vertical parts of your curve will animate very fast (lots of value change over little time change), and flat parts of your curve will slow down or freeze the animation (very little change over lots of time).

You can draw these curves using the Custom Ease In / Ease Out panel in the Flash authoring environment, and export them to motion XML. Because this enables you to visually draw and preview the curve, it's much easier than writing CustomEases manually. Below is a simple example of a keyframe that eases in at the beginning of a tween and eases out at the end of it:

```
<Keyframe index="4">
    <tweens>
        <CustomEase>
            <geom:Point x="0.5" y="0"/>
            <geom:Point x="0.5" y="1"/>
        </CustomEase>
    </tweens>
</Keyframe>
```

Note that the control points are defined with `Point` object nodes. Also, the first (0, 0) and last (1, 1) points are implied. The two points are not control points themselves, but the right handle of the control point at (0, 0), and the left handle of the control point at (1, 1). The curve defined by this `CustomEase` is shown in Figure 31-3.

FIGURE 31-3

Curve of a CustomEase that eases in and out

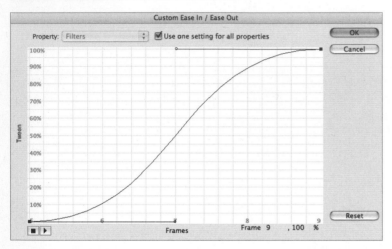

Other than the first and last point, each control point in a `CustomEase` curve is defined by three `Point` objects: the location of the incoming handle, the location of the point itself, and the location of the outgoing handle. So a more complex curve with three control points in the middle would be defined by eleven `Point` objects: three for each of the control points, one for the outgoing handle of (0, 0), and one for the incoming handle of (1, 1).

A `FunctionEase` tween uses a formula to determine the easing of the tween. All of the well-known easing functions by Robert Penner are included in the animation framework in the `fl.motion.easing` package. Simply assign the fully qualified name of a function with the correct signature to this object's `functionName` property to apply it:

```
<FunctionEase functionName="fl.motion.easing.Bounce.easeIn"/>
```

NOTE   You can read more about Robert Penner's easing equations on his site at www.robertpenner.com/easing/.

For the motion XML to be able to find the function, you must also remember to import the easing class and ensure it's compiled in. You can do this simply by referencing it:

```
import fl.motion.easing.Bounce;
Bounce; //force the Bounce class to compile into the SWF
```

A `BezierEase` tween is very similar to a `CustomEase` tween. They both depend on a user-supplied Bezier curve to fully define the value at every point of time. The `BezierEase` tween, however, uses unscaled values of y: the y axis represents the literal value that the tweened property will take on, rather than the interpolation between the values set out in the keyframes. Therefore, you can use this kind of tween to blow the value out of the range that would otherwise be defined by the endpoints.

Like the `CustomEase`, however, the first and last points are still implied, and the x axis is still scaled to unit time between the current keyframe (0) and the next (1).

Using the Flash motion package

In order to use the motion XML which you write or copy from the timeline, you need to use the Flash motion package. You can use the classes in this package by themselves, or describe animations entirely in motion XML and let the motion package automatically instantiate all the objects you described in XML. For this approach, the main entry point to the motion package is the `fl.motion.Animator` class.

CAUTION The Flash motion package, when compiled into your SWF, adds a little more than 12 KB to the size of the SWF. This is fairly heavy for an animation toolkit, so if size is a great concern, you might want to consider alternatives.

The Flash motion package requires Flash Player version 9.0.28.0 or above.

To create a new animation from motion XML, pass the motion XML and the display object you wish to animate to the `Animator` constructor:

```
var anim:Animator = new Animator(myMotionXML, myDisplayObject);
```

When you have an `Animator`, you're set. You can use some intuitively named methods to control the playback of your new animation, detailed in Table 31-2.

TABLE 31-2

Methods of the Animator Class

Method	Function
`play():void`	Starts playing the animation.
`stop():void`	Stops playing the animation and returns to the first frame.
`end():void`	Stops playing the animation and moves to the last frame.
`pause():void`	Pauses the animation until `resume()` is called.
`resume():void`	Resumes a paused animation.
`nextFrame():void`	Proceeds to the next frame in the animation.
`rewind():void`	Jumps to the first frame in the animation.

Additionally, there is a static method, `Animator.fromXMLString()`, that creates new `Animator` objects without using the constructor. It accepts a `String` containing XML rather than an `XML` object.

You can set the transformation point of the target display object by assigning it to the `transformationPoint` property of the `Animator` object itself, allowing you to avoid using the `Source` object entirely.

The `time` property of an `Animator` object not only lets you check the current progress of an animation in frames, but lets you skip to a specific frame by writing to the property.

The `autoRewind` property and the `repeatCount` property can be used to set up a looping animation.

The `Animator` object also broadcasts some very useful events, described in Table 31-3. These events are all of the type `fl.motion.MotionEvent`.

TABLE 31-3

MotionEvent Events

Event Name	Constant	Purpose
`"motionStart"`	`MotionEvent.MOTION_START`	The motion has started playing.
`"motionEnd"`	`MotionEvent.MOTION_END`	The motion has ended, of its own accord or by a call to `stop()` or `end()`.
`"timeChange"`	`MotionEvent.TIME_CHANGE`	The animation is about to work on the next frame. The `time` property has been updated.
`"motionUpdate"`	`MotionEvent.MOTION_UPDATE`	The animation finished working on a frame and updated the screen.

Any animation structure that you could build in motion XML, you can build by creating and composing classes, but doing so is painfully verbose. Instead, use E4X to set up those relationships in XML. This isn't to say that there is no reason to use the classes in the `fl.motion` package by themselves. You can exploit some of the work that the motion package has to do internally, in order to save yourself some time. For instance, the `Color` class has a method, `interpolateColor()`, which can blend any two colors.

The real gem is `MatrixTransformer`, a class which does some of the heavy lifting for the motion package. You can use this class to set skews, transform objects around points other than their registration point, and work in radians, all with ease. This is a nice bonus, even if your project doesn't use the rest of the `fl.motion` package to animate.

Animating Using Flex

Flex 2 has an effects system which works brilliantly with styles and states. It enables you to create one-off effects or reusable ones, in ActionScript 3.0 or MXML. Unlike the Flash motion package, the effects package provides support for sequential and parallel animations. It also comes with a few base effect types that you can easily customize. Creating entirely custom effects using the Flex 2 effects framework is less intuitive, however.

If you are using Flex 2, we recommend you tie into the `mx.effects` package. More information about effects in Flex 2 can be found in the Flex documentation or a book such as *Programming Flex 2*, by Chafic Kazoun and Joey Lott (O'Reilly, 2007).

Choosing a Third-Party Animation Toolkit

In addition to the choices enumerated above, there are always a growing number of third-party animation packages. You should always choose the right tool for the job. Sometimes the built-in animation library is the right tool, and sometimes it's not. At the time of writing, there were two major third-party contenders in this category. There will likely be many more in the coming years, so keep up-to-date and try them all out, so that you know their pros and cons. Here I will present my *opinion* on the available options. This is not exhaustive, nor is it the last word on the subject.

Flash motion package

The Flash motion package is excellent for simulating and integrating with timeline animations. If you have a workflow that is tightly integrated with Flash animators or designers, this package wins hands-down. The ability to easily write custom easing is a huge plus. The built-in ability to tween skews and filters is a definite plus.

However, the package has a lot of drawbacks. Motion XML can get unnecessarily large, especially when you want to animate one property of a filter, or you want to write a very simple tween without a lot of code. There is no support for sequential or parallel animations. The package can only run on frames and not seconds. It's tightly integrated with `DisplayObject`: It's difficult to tween arbitrary properties of a class.

Tweener

The Tweener package, by Zeh Fernando, is available under the MIT license at `http://code .google.com/p/tweener/`. Tweener is lightweight and fast, and the syntax is compact and simple. It can operate on time as well as frames. And it can tween any property of any object with no tricks, which lets you use Tweener as the engine that drives your custom visuals.

Because Tweener is so adaptive, it might not catch typos. It doesn't let you store and use animations on new targets. It doesn't have built in syntax for sequential or parallel animations. And it doesn't give you a handle for newly created animations, so you have to provide criteria that match your animation to Tweener functions to specify which animation to operate on.

This simple example of Tweener fades out `cat` while moving it to the right:

```
Tweener.addTween(cat, {alpha: 0, x: cat.x + 500, time: 1});
```

AnimationPackage

Alex Uhlmann's ActionScript 3.0 version of AnimationPackage is, at the time of writing, in alpha at `www.alex-uhlmann.de/flash/animationpackage/ap3/`. AnimationPackage has a huge amount of great graphics code. It includes Bezier motion paths, skewing, filter animation, special effects like shake, motion trail, and color effects. It can compose animations in parallel and sequence. Furthermore, it's a very powerful vector drawing tool. It is very object oriented.

Although you can usually create animations using existing classes, creating your own involves some digging into the inner workings of AnimationPackage and a lot of boilerplate code. Composing classes manually is tedious when working with many-part animations. There are a ton of ways to set animation parameters that can get you lost.

Although AnimationPackage is a little unwieldy to use, it has a ton of features that you won't find in other packages. Here's a small snippet of AnimationPackage code that moves `cat` to the right and fades it out:

```
var anim:Parallel = new Parallel();
anim.addChild(new Move(cat, cat.x + 500, cat.y));
anim.addChild(new Alpha(cat, 0));
anim.animationStyle(1000, Linear.easeNone);
anim.animate(0, 100);
```

Summary

- Animation changes properties over time.
- Flash Player is running frames as well as ActionScript.
- Flash Player has to finish all the ActionScript on a frame before it can draw the next one.
- The frame rate of a SWF is not a guarantee.
- You can use asynchronous code to create motion.
- Two approaches are `enterFrame` events and `Timer`.
- `Timer` animation is more flexible, but it can be wasteful if you run faster than the frame rate and don't force screen updates.
- Use the actual time differential as reported by `getTimer()` to keep speed constant regardless of frame rate.

- Keyframes are the important frames, and tweens automatically fill the in-between frames.

- Easing can modulate the speed of tweens.

- Flash has a motion package that has feature parity with the timeline.

- The motion package lets you use motion XML, which can be exported from the timeline and imported to the timeline, as well as modified and written from scratch with E4X.

- Motion XML is translated into objects and properties with the same names as the nodes and attributes.

- `Motion` contains an optional `Source` and `Keyframes`.

- `Keyframe` objects can animate anything the timeline can: transformations, color, and filters.

- The motion package supports four ways to describe easing.

- Wrap motion XML in an `Animator` to use it.

- Flex 2 has a totally different approach to animation than the Flash motion package.

- There are third-party animation packages that might be better for the job, depending on your goals.

Chapter 32

Applying Transformations to Graphics

The `flash.geom.Transform` class lets you apply two sorts of transformations to display objects — geometric and color. A `Transform` object has a handful of properties, two of which are `matrix` and `colorTransform`. The `matrix` property is a `Matrix` object you can use to apply geometric transforms, as discussed in the section "Working with Matrix Transforms." The `colorTransform` property is a `ColorTransform` object you can use to apply color transforms, as discussed in the section "Working with Color Transforms."

Working with Matrix Transforms

You've already seen how you can transform a display object in basic ways using properties such as x, y, width, height, and so on. However, using matrices you can apply more complex transformations — not only offsetting the coordinates, scaling, or rotating the object, but also skewing/shearing the object.

A matrix is a representation of a set of linear equations. For example, the following equation determines a line in two-dimensional space:

```
2x + 10y = 5
```

That linear equation can be written as the following 1×3 matrix:

```
| 2  10  5 |
```

IN THIS CHAPTER

Understanding transforms

Using matrices to rotate, scale, translate, and shear MovieClip objects

Using color transforms

Applying solid colors

Applying tints

If you have more than one linear equation, you can group each of them into a single matrix. For example, consider the following three linear equations:

```
2x + 10y = 5
1x + 2y = 8
4x + 1y = 3
```

The preceding three equations can be written as the following matrix:

```
| 2   10   5 |
| 1    2   8 |
| 4    1   3 |
```

By plugging actual values for x and y into specific kinds of linear equations, you can achieve linear transformations like scaling, rotation, and skewing. The inputs of the formulas are specific points (x and y) and the outputs are the points after transformation. By representing the sets of linear equations as matrices, you can calculate the result of transforming a point by doing one matrix multiplication instead of several substitutions. This makes matrices an ideal way to represent transformations concisely. Matrix operations are frequently more efficient than their non-matrix counterparts. There is an entire branch of mathematics pertaining to working with matrices. However, even if you don't know much about matrix operations, you can still apply matrix transformation to display objects via the `flash.geom.Matrix` class.

Every display object has a `transform.matrix` property that is a `Matrix` instance specifying the transformations applied to it. The `Matrix` object represents a 3 x 3 matrix that can be denoted as follows:

```
| a   b   tx |
| c   d   ty |
| 0   0    1 |
```

When we multiply the matrix representing a point x, y by this matrix:

```
| x |   | a b tx |
| y |   | c d ty |
| 1 |   | 0 0  1 |
```

we can see that the transform is made up of two equations:

```
x' = a x + b y + tx
y' = c x + d y + ty
```

Different coefficients in these linear equations can have different effects on the transformation that they apply on input points. In its default state, the matrix values are as follows:

```
| 1 0 0 |
| 0 1 0 |
| 0 0 1 |
```

The default matrix is known as the *identity matrix*. Multiplying the matrix for x, y by this matrix shows us that the linear equations for these properties are:

```
x' = 1 x + 0 y + 0 = x
y' = 0 x + 1 y + 0 = y
```

In other words, the identity matrix transforms points to themselves.

Setting a display object's transformation matrix to the identity matrix resets any transformations to the default state.

The properties of the `Matrix` class are as follows:

- `a`: The scale amount in the x-direction. The default is 1, which means 100 percent. A value of 2 would scale the object in the x direction to 200 percent.

- `b`: The amount to shear the object in the y direction. A shear in the y direction is the amount by which the y pixels are shifted for every corresponding x pixel value. Another way of thinking of that in more mathematical terms is the slope of the horizontal lines. For example, a y shear of 1 means the horizontal lines are at a 45-degree angle (a slope of 1). The default value is 0, which means the horizontal lines are actually horizontal.

You may access any of these properties of the Matrix object. The properties a, b, c, d, tx, and ty are all read-write. These properties let you directly read and modify a transformation matrix.

Obviously there is a relationship between the matrix properties and some of the basic display object properties such as `x`, `y`, `width`, `height`, `scaleX`, `scaleY`, and `rotation`. The relationship between x and y and `tx` and `ty` is direct. If the object is moved to 100, 200 then the `tx` and `ty` properties of the matrix will have values of 100 and 200, respectively. Likewise, there is a relationship between the `width`, `height`, `scaleX`, and `scaleY` properties with the a and d properties of the matrix. The relationship between the `rotation` property and the matrix is not quite so apparent, but it does exist. A change in the `rotation` property affects the a, b, c, and d properties of the matrix.

Aside from setting the properties of a `Matrix` object, you can also use some of its methods to simplify things. For example, rather than setting the `tx` and `ty` properties directly, you can use the `translate()` method, as follows:

```
// The equivalent of setting tx to 100 and ty to 200
matrix.translate(100, 200);
```

And rather than setting a and d, you can call the `scale()` method:

```
// The equivalent of setting a to 2 and d to 3.
matrix.scale(2, 3);
```

Using some trigonometry, you can determine the proper values to assign to each of the matrix properties in order to rotate an object. However, it's much simpler to use the `rotate()` method.

The `rotate()` method expects an angle in radians. If you find it more convenient to use degrees, you can convert from degrees to radians by multiplying by `Math.PI/180`. The following code applies a rotation of 31 degrees by converting it to radians, and passing the value to the `rotate()` method of a `Matrix` object.

```
var radians:Number = 31 * Math.PI / 180;
matrix.rotate(radians);
```

Matrix methods are cumulative. Each method composes the new values with the existing values. For example, the following constructs a `Matrix`, translates it by 100 pixels to the right, then by 100 pixels to the right again. Notice that the effect is that the matrix is translated 200 pixels total rather than just 100 pixels:

```
var matrix:Matrix = new Matrix();
trace(matrix); // (a=1, b=0, c=0, d=1, tx=0, ty=0)
matrix.translate(100, 0);
trace(matrix); // (a=1, b=0, c=0, d=1, tx=100, ty=0)
matrix.translate(100, 0);
trace(matrix); // (a=1, b=0, c=0, d=1, tx=200, ty=0)
```

The same thing occurs with `scale()` and `rotate()`. While it may seem obvious, the effect can cause some unexpected behaviors if you accidentally assume it will work differently. That's not too difficult to do — especially when you're working with the `rotate()` method. You might want to rotate an object by `Math.PI/2` (90 degrees) total. However, if you already called `rotate()` for the same `Matrix` object previously, then the effect might be other than what you had anticipated. And it gets particularly complex when you start applying various transformations. For example, once you've rotated, scaled, and translated a `Matrix` object, it gets particularly difficult to then rotate it to an absolute value (non-cumulative).

So what if you want to apply more than one transformation effect? In such cases you can make new `Matrix` objects for each transformation effect (scale, rotate, translate, shear), and combine them using the `concat()` method. The `concat()` method combines the matrices using matrix multiplication. Matrix multiplication is a non-commutative operation, which means that matrixA * matrixB is not necessarily the same as matrixB * matrixA. Therefore, when you combine matrices using the `concat()` method, it may make a difference which order you use to concatenate them.

The `concat()` method requires a `Matrix` parameter. It then multiplies the calling matrix by the parameter, and it updates the properties of the calling matrix with the product. The following code is an example in which two matrices get concatenated.

```
var cumulative:Matrix = new Matrix();

// (a=1, b=0, c=0, d=1, tx=0, ty=0)
trace(cumulative);

var rotate:Matrix = new Matrix();
rotate.rotate(Math.PI/2);

// (a=6.12303176911189e-17, b=1, c=-1, d=6.12303176911189e-17, tx=0, ty=0)
trace(rotate);
```

```
var shear:Matrix = new Matrix(1, 1, 0, 1, 0, 0);

// (a=1, b=1, c=0, d=1, tx=0, ty=0)
trace(shear);

cumulative.concat(rotate);

cumulative.concat(shear);
// (a=6.12303176911189e-17, b=1, c=-1, d=-1, tx=0, ty=0)
trace(cumulative);
```

> **NOTE** As a result of rounding, the cumulative matrix may display –0.9999999 in place of –1 for the d property.

Notice what happens when the matrices are concatenated in the other order:

```
var cumulative:Matrix = new Matrix();

// (a=1, b=0, c=0, d=1, tx=0, ty=0)
trace(cumulative);

var rotate:Matrix = new Matrix();
rotate.rotate(Math.PI/2);

// (a=6.12303176911189e-17, b=1, c=-1, d=6.12303176911189e-17, tx=0, ty=0)
trace(rotate);

var shear:Matrix = new Matrix(1, 1, 0, 1, 0, 0);

// (a=1, b=1, c=0, d=1, tx=0, ty=0)
trace(shear);

cumulative.concat(shear);
cumulative.concat(rotate);

// (a=-1, b=1, c=-1, d=6.12303176911189e-17, tx=0, ty=0)
trace(cumulative);
```

Using matrix transformations

In the following simple exercise, you build a SWF that uses matrices to transform four rectangles using shearing, scaling, rotation, and translation transformations:

```
package com.wiley.as3bible.transforms {

    import flash.display.Sprite;
    import flash.display.Loader;
    import flash.net.URLRequest;
    import flash.events.Event;
    import flash.events.MouseEvent;
    import flash.geom.Matrix;
    public class MatrixTransform extends Sprite {
```

```
        private var _containerA:Sprite;
        private var _containerB:Sprite;
        private var _loaderA:Loader;
        private var _loaderB:Loader;
        private var _current:Sprite;
        private var _a:Sprite;
        private var _b:Sprite;

        public function MatrixTransform() {
            _loaderA = new Loader();
            _loaderA.contentLoaderInfo.addEventListener(Event.COMPLETE, ↵
completeHandler);
            _loaderA.load(new ↵
URLRequest("http://www.rightactionscript.com/samplefiles/image2.jpg"));
            _loaderA.scaleX = .5;
            _loaderA.scaleY = .5;
            _containerA = new Sprite();
            addChild(_containerA);
            _containerA.addChild(_loaderA);
            _loaderB = new Loader();
            _loaderB.contentLoaderInfo.addEventListener(Event.COMPLETE, ↵
completeHandler);
            _loaderB.load(new ↵
URLRequest("http://www.rightactionscript.com/samplefiles/image2.jpg"));
            _loaderB.scaleX = .5;
            _loaderB.scaleY = .5;
            _containerB = new Sprite();
            addChild(_containerB);
            _containerB.addChild(_loaderB);
            _containerB.x = 400;
        }

        private function completeHandler(event:Event):void {
            var loader:Loader = event.target.content.parent as Loader;
            if(loader == _loaderA) {
                _a = new Sprite();
                _a.graphics.lineStyle(0, 0, 1);
                _a.graphics.beginFill(0xFFFF00, .5);
                _a.graphics.drawRect(-5, -10, 10, 20);
                _a.graphics.endFill();
                _a.x = _loaderA.width;
                _a.y = _loaderA.height / 2 - 10;
                addChild(_a);
                _a.addEventListener(MouseEvent.MOUSE_DOWN, aMouseDownHandler);
            }
            else {
                _b = new Sprite();
                _b.graphics.lineStyle(0, 0, 1);
                _b.graphics.beginFill(0xFFFF00, .5);
```

```
            _b.graphics.drawRect(-10, -5, 20, 10);
            _b.graphics.endFill();
            _b.x = _loaderB.width / 2 - 10 + _containerB.x;
            _b.y = _loaderB.height;
            addChild(_b);
            _b.addEventListener(MouseEvent.MOUSE_DOWN, bMouseDownHandler)
        }
    }
    private function aMouseDownHandler(event:MouseEvent):void {
        addEventListener(MouseEvent.MOUSE_MOVE, verticalMouseMoveHandler);
        addEventListener(MouseEvent.MOUSE_UP, mouseUpHandler);
        _current = event.target as Sprite;
    }
    private function bMouseDownHandler(event:MouseEvent):void {
        addEventListener(MouseEvent.MOUSE_MOVE, horizontalMouseMoveHandler);
        addEventListener(MouseEvent.MOUSE_UP, mouseUpHandler);
    }
    private function verticalMouseMoveHandler(event:MouseEvent):void {
        _a.y = mouseY;
        _containerA.scaleX = 1;
        _containerA.scaleY = 1;
        var matrix:Matrix = new Matrix();
        matrix.b = ((_a.y - _containerA.y) / (_a.x - _containerA.x)) - ↵
((_loaderA.height / 2) / _loaderA.width);
        _containerA.transform.matrix = matrix;
    }

    private function horizontalMouseMoveHandler(event:MouseEvent):void {
        _b.x = mouseX;
        _containerB.scaleX = 1;
        _containerB.scaleY = 1;
        var matrix:Matrix = new Matrix();
        matrix.tx = _containerB.x;
        matrix.c = ((_b.x - _containerB.x) / (_b.y - _containerB.y)) - ↵
((_loaderB.width / 2) / _loaderB.height);
        _containerB.transform.matrix = matrix;
    }

    private function mouseUpHandler(event:MouseEvent):void {
        removeEventListener(MouseEvent.MOUSE_MOVE, ↵
verticalMouseMoveHandler);
        removeEventListener(MouseEvent.MOUSE_MOVE, ↵
horizontalMouseMoveHandler);
        removeEventListener(MouseEvent.MOUSE_UP, mouseUpHandler);
    }

    }
}
```

When you run the application you'll see two images with rectangular controllers on them. The image on the left has a controller that allows you to shear it vertically while the image on the right has a controller that allows you to shear it horizontally.

Working with Color Transforms

There are several ways to apply color changes to display objects — using the `transform` `.colorTransform` property (which is an instance of the `ColorTransform` class) or using a `ColorMatrixFilter` object. Using the `transform.colorTransform` property, you can quickly apply solid color fills and tints to display objects. For more complex color operations such as changing brightness, hue, and the like, use a `ColorMatrixFilter` object, as discussed in Chapter 33.

Applying color transforms

The `transform.colorTransform` property of a display object is a `flash.geom` `.ColorTransform` object. Each display object has a default `ColorTransform` object assigned to it. You can retrieve the color transform object already assigned to the display object, make changes to it, and reassign it, or you can construct a new `ColorTransform` object, and assign that to the `transform.colorTransform` property of the display object.

When retrieving the `transform.colorTransform` property of a display object, Flash Player returns a copy. That means that making changes to the copy won't affect the display object. You have to assign the object back to the `transform.colorTransform` property for any changes to take effect. Likewise, when you apply a `ColorTransform` object to the `transform` `.colorTransform` property of a display object, Flash Player applies a copy. Therefore, any updates to the object won't affect the display object unless you reassign it to the `transform` `.colorTransform` property.

Getting and setting the color

The `ColorTransform` class defines a `color` property that lets you apply and retrieve a solid color fill. The value of the `color` property is an unsigned integer value ranging from 0x000000 to 0xFFFFFF. The corresponding color is then applied to every pixel of the display object. The property applies a solid color fill, and not a tint. That means that any contrast of color that is visible in the actual contents of a display object is indistinguishable after the fill is applied. For example, if you apply a solid color fill to a object containing a rectangular photograph, the effect will be a rectangle filled with a solid color.

The following example constructs a new `ColorTransform` object, assigns a value of 0xFF0000 (red) to the `color` property, and then assigns the object to the `transform.colorTransform` property of a sprite instance named `circle`:

```
var colorTransform:ColorTransform = new ColorTransform();
colorTransform.color = 0xFF0000;
circle.transform.colorTransform = colorTransform;
```

You can also retrieve the color that is currently applied to a display object using the `color` property. The property returns the current color applied to the `ColorTransform` object (if any):

```
var colorTransform:ColorTransform = circle.transform.colorTransform;
trace(colorTransform.color);
```

However, a `ColorTransform` object does not report the color of the artwork within a display object. It reports only on the color transform applied to the instance. For example, if a display object instance has a yellow square within it, but no color transform applied to the instance, then the `transform.colorTransform.color` property will not return the number corresponding to yellow. It will return 0 because no color transformation has yet been applied.

Tinting a display object

The `ColorTransform` class defines the following properties for working color transformations with more control than is possible using the `color` property:

- `redMultiplier`
- `greenMultiplier`
- `blueMultiplier`
- `alphaMultiplier`
- `redOffset`
- `greenOffset`
- `blueOffset`
- `alphaOffset`

You can set the properties of a `ColorTransform` object using the constructor or you can set them once the object has already been constructed. The constructor accepts from zero to eight parameters matching the properties in the preceding list. The order of the parameters is the same as in the preceding list. The following code constructs a new `ColorTransform` object with the default properties:

```
var colorTransform:ColorTransform = new ColorTransform();
```

Each of the multiplier properties (`redMultiplier`, `greenMultiplier`, and so on) can range from –1 to 1, and determines the percentage of the color component that is applied to each pixel. Every color can be represented by a combination of red, green, and blue. Each pixel contains a color value ranging from 0x000000 to 0xFFFFFF. In hexadecimal format (such as 0xFFFFFF) each pair of digits represents a red, green, or blue value that comprises the entire value — 0xRRGGBB. Therefore, 0xFF0000 is pure red, 0x00FF00 is pure green, and 0x0000FF is pure blue. The multiplier properties default to 1, which means that each red, green, and blue component of each pixel's color is at 100 percent. By changing the multiplier properties, you can effectively apply a tint to a

display object. When the multiplier properties are changed, it doesn't remove the contrast and definition of the contents within a display object. For example, if a display object contains a photograph, applying changes to the multiplier properties will change the tint of the photograph, but the
subject of the photograph will likely still be distinguishable. The following code applies a green
tint (by reducing the red and blue components to 0) to a sprite object called photograph:

```
photograph.transform.colorTransform = new ColorTransform(0, 1, 0, 1, 0, 0, 0, ↵
0);
```

The offset properties (redOffset, greenOffset,and so on) add to and subtract from the red,
green, blue, and alpha components of the color. The ranges for the offset properties are from –255
to 255. The default values are 0. The following applies a red tint to a photograph by setting the
redOffset to 255:

```
var colorTransform:ColorTransform = new ColorTransform();
colorTransform.redOffset = 255;
photograph.transform.colorTransform = colorTransform;
```

The multiplier and offset properties of a ColorTransform object can work in conjunction with
one another. The difference is that the multiplier properties affect the percentage of a color component already present within each pixel, whereas the offset properties add or subtract to or from the
color component of the pixel. For example, if a pixel has a color of 0xFFFFFF (white) then setting
the redMultiplier to 0 or setting the redOffset to –255 has the same effect. However, if the
color is 0x000000 (black) then setting the redMultiplier property will not change the amount
of red in the color. 100 percent and 0 percent of 0 are both 0. But you can set the redOffset to
add red to the color.

> **NOTE** The color property and the offset properties are interconnected. When you set the
> color property, it sets the offset properties. When you set the offset properties, they
> affect the color property. The color property is simply a more convenient way to work with the
> offsets.

Resetting colors

You can reset the colors applied to a display object by applying a ColorTransform object with
the default properties as follows:

```
sprite.transform.colorTransform = new ColorTransform();
```

Transforming colors

In the following example, you'll load an image into the player, and then use a ColorTransform
object to tint it based on the location of the mouse. Each click of the mouse will cycle through
the multiplier properties (redMultiplier, greenMultiplier, blueMultiplier, and

alphaMultiplier) and each gets set to 0 as the mouse is at the far left and to 100 as the mouse is at the far right.

```
package com.wiley.as3bible.transforms {

    import flash.display.Sprite;
    import flash.display.Loader;
    import flash.net.URLRequest;
    import flash.events.Event;
    import flash.events.MouseEvent;
    import flash.geom.ColorTransform;

    public class Color extends Sprite {

        private var _loader:Loader;
        private var _current:int;

        public function Color () {
            _loader = new Loader();
            _loader.load(new ↵
URLRequest("http://www.rightactionscript.com/samplefiles/image2.jpg"));
            addChild(_loader);
            _loader.addEventListener(MouseEvent.CLICK, clickHandler);
            _loader.addEventListener(MouseEvent.MOUSE_MOVE, mouseMoveHandler);
        }

        private function mouseMoveHandler(event:MouseEvent):void {
            var value:Number = _loader.mouseX / _loader.width;
            var colorTransform:ColorTransform = ↵
_loader.transform.colorTransform;
            if(_current == 0) {
                colorTransform.redMultiplier = value;
            }
            else if(_current == 1) {
                colorTransform.greenMultiplier = value;
            }
            else if(_current == 2) {
                colorTransform.blueMultiplier = value;
            }
            else if(_current == 3) {
                colorTransform.alphaMultiplier = value;
            }
            _loader.transform.colorTransform = colorTransform;
        }
```

```
private function clickHandler(event:MouseEvent):void {
    _current++;
    if(_current == 4) {
        _current = 0;
    }
}


}

}
```

When you test the application, you can move the mouse from left to right to adjust the red, green, blue, and alpha multipliers for the image. Each time you click the mouse, it advances to the next color component.

Summary

- Each display object has a `transform` property from which you can access the `matrix` and `colorTransform` properties in order to apply transforms to the object.

- Using the `matrix` property, you can apply transforms such as rotation, translation, scaling, and shearing.

- Using the `colorTransform` property, you can apply colors and tints to display objects.

Chapter 33

Drawing Bitmap Graphics Programmatically

Flash Player 9 contains an API for working with bitmaps. The `flash.display.BitmapData` class is the main focus with regard to bitmaps, and it has methods for getting and setting pixels, applying pixel dissolves, setting threshold settings, applying filters, and more. In this chapter, you look at how to work with the new API to achieve a variety of effects.

Creating a BitmapData Object

There are several ways to construct or retrieve a new `BitmapData` object in ActionScript:

- You can use the constructor to make a new, blank `BitmapData` object with specific dimensions and background.

- If you have an embedded asset (embedded with the `[Embed]` tag in Flex Builder or with a library symbol in Flash authoring) you can construct a new `Bitmap` or `BitmapAsset` instance using the class name you assigned to the embedded asset, and retrieve the `bitmapData` property from it.

In the following sections, you look at how to use those ways to construct or retrieve `BitmapData` objects. No matter how you want to work with bitmaps via ActionScript, you'll need to use at least one of those ways to create and retrieve a reference to the object.

Using the constructor method

You can construct a new BitmapData object using the constructor method as part of a new state-ment. The constructor requires at least two parameters, and allows for up to four parameters (two optional). The parameters are as follows:

- width: The width of the bitmap in pixels.
- height: The height of the bitmap in pixels.
- transparent: Indicates whether or not the bitmap background is transparent. The default is true.
- fillColor: The color to use for the background if the background is not transparent. The value is specified as 0xAARRGGBB, where AA represents the alpha channel. The default is 0xFFFFFFFF (opaque white).

The following code constructs a new BitmapData object for a 500 × 200–pixel image. The back-ground is set to transparent:

```
var bmpRectangle:BitmapData = new BitmapData(500, 200);
```

The following code constructs the same BitmapData object, except the background is an opaque red:

```
var bmpRectangle:BitmapData = new BitmapData(500, 200, false,
0xFFFF0000);
```

 Simply constructing a BitmapData **object does not render it. To render the image, you have to use a** Bitmap **display object as discussed in the section "Displaying BitmapData** Images."

Typically you'll use the BitmapData constructor when you intend to create an object to which you will programmatically add content.

Creating instances of embedded assets

Embedded assets are those that get compiled into the SWF file. Flex and Flash use two different mechanisms to embed assets. However, once an asset is embedded you can create instances with ActionScript in the same way for both Flex and Flash.

In Flex and ActionScript projects built in Flex Builder, you can embed image assets using the [Embed] metadata tag. The [Embed] metadata tag requires that you specify a source attribute with a value of the path where the image asset can be found. Here's an example:

```
[Embed(source="exampleImage.png")]
```

Furthermore, the [Embed] tag should always appear just prior to a variable declaration of type Class. This syntax will embed the image asset, and it will make it available as a class with the name you give to the variable.

```
[Embed(source="exampleImage.png")]
private var ExampleImage:Class;
```

In Flash CS3 Professional, you can import an image asset into the Library using File ⇨ Import ⇨ Import to Library. This will create a new Bitmap symbol in the Library. In order to make the asset available to ActionScript, you must set the linkage properties for the Bitmap symbol. You can access the linkage properties by selecting the symbol in the Library and then selecting Linkage from the Library menu. In the Linkage Properties dialog box, you should select the Export for ActionScript option. You are then required to specify a value in the Class field. Here you should specify the name of the new class you want to use to create instances of the symbol. This class does not need to exist in your class path. Flash CS3 Professional will automatically create it for you when compiling the SWF file.

Once you've embedded a bitmap asset using these instructions, you can create an instance using the class name you assigned to the asset either as the variable name following the [Embed] tag (Flex) or in the linkage properties (Flash). Whereas in Flash the symbol becomes an actual class and valid type, in Flex the embedded image becomes a class variable. This class, like all runtime class references, is not available to the type system. Here's an example that creates an instance of an embedded asset that was assigned a class called ExampleImage in Flash:

```
var example:ExampleImage = new ExampleImage();
```

If you embedded this asset in Flex Builder and bound it to a variable named ExampleImage of type Class, you can't create instances with the type ExampleImage. The Class reference associated with the image extends BitmapAsset, so you could construct a new one like so:

```
[Embed(src="example.png")]
var ExampleImage:Class;

var example:BitmapAsset = new ExampleImage();
```

If you use Flash CS3 Professional and allow it to automatically create a class for you, then you will be required to specify values for the width and height parameters. You cannot actually affect the width and height of an instance of an embedded asset when constructing it using these parameters. That means that regardless of what values you pass to the constructor the actual width and height of the image will be used. Therefore, the following example will construct an instance with the actual image width and height even though values of 0 are used in the constructor:

```
var example:ExampleImage = new ExampleImage(0, 0);
```

Although there is nothing inherently problematic with this, you may prefer to be able to omit all the parameters for the constructor. If so, you can opt to create a subclass of BitmapData that does not require any of the parameters for the constructor. You can then specify this class as the value in the Base class field in the linkage properties for the Bitmap symbol. Here's an example of such a class:

```
package com.wiley.as3bible.display {
    import flash.display.BitmapData;
    public class EmbeddedBitmapData extends BitmapData {
        public function EmbeddedBitmapData(width:Number = 0, ↵
height:Number = 0, transparent:Boolean = true, ↵
fillColor:Number = 0xFFFFFFFF) {
            super(width, height, transparent, fillColor);
        }
    }
}
```

617

Displaying BitmapData images

Regardless of how you construct a BitmapData object, it exists only in the non-rendered state until you specifically instruct the player to render the data visually. You can render the data visually to a flash.display.Bitmap object. Bitmap objects are display objects designed specifically for the purpose of rendering BitmapData objects.

The Bitmap constructor does not require any parameters, but it accepts up to three parameters as follows:

- bitmapData: The BitmapData object.

- pixelSnapping: One of the following strings: "auto", "always", "never". The default is "auto". These strings are also available as static constants of the flash .display.PixelSnapping class.

- smoothing: Indicates whether or not to apply smoothing to the image as it is scaled beyond 100 percent. The default is true.

Frequently, when you construct a Bitmap object you will specify at least one parameter. However, you can also set the BitmapData object to be rendered using the bitmapData property after the Bitmap object has been constructed.

The following code makes a new BitmapData object with an opaque purple background, and renders it to a Bitmap object:

```
var squareData:BitmapData = new BitmapData(200, 200, false, 0xFFCC00CC);
var square:Bitmap = new Bitmap(squareData);
addChild(square);
```

Pixel snapping

If a bitmap rendering is not placed at integer coordinates, you can use pixel snapping to snap it to integer coordinates. As noted in the preceding section, the Bitmap constructor lets you optionally specify a pixel snapping setting. The default, "auto", means that any non-scaled, non-rotated bitmap rendering will snap to integer coordinates. The value of "always" means that the bitmap rendering will always snap to integer coordinates regardless of whether or not it is scaled or rotated. You can also specify "never" so that the bitmap rendering will not snap to integer coordinates. You can use the flash.display.PixelSnapping class constants of NEVER, AUTO, and ALWAYS for these values.

 A bitmap rendering will appear at non-integer coordinates if the parent display object is at non-integer coordinates.

The following example sets the pixel snapping settings when constructing the Bitmap object.

```
var bitmap:Bitmap = new Bitmap(bitmapData, PixelSnapping.ALWAYS);
```

You can also set pixel snapping settings after constructing a `Bitmap` object by setting the `pixelSnapping` property.

```
bitmap.pixelSnapping = PixelSnapping.NEVER;
```

Image smoothing

By default, rendered bitmaps apply smoothing when they are scaled beyond 100 percent. That prevents the image from rendering with a pixelated appearance. However, it also means that the image may appear blurry when scaled. If you prefer that Flash not apply smoothing you can specify a value of `false` for the third parameter of the `Bitmap` constructor.

```
var bitmap:Bitmap = new Bitmap(bitmapData, PixelSnapping.AUTO, false);
```

You can optionally set the `smoothing` property of the object after it has been constructed:

```
bitmap.smoothing = false;
```

Working with BitmapData Properties

`BitmapData` objects have the following read-only properties:

- `width`: The width of the `BitmapData` object in pixels.
- `height`: The height of the `BitmapData` object in pixels.
- `transparent`: A Boolean value indicating whether or not the background is transparent.
- `rect`: A Rectangle object representing the dimensions of the `BitmapData` object for use with methods that require a Rectangle object

The properties are read-only, so you cannot use them to make adjustments to the `BitmapData` object after it has been constructed.

Copying Images

The `BitmapData` class defines several methods for copying bitmap data from other ActionScript objects including other `BitmapData` objects as well as display objects. This is useful in a variety of situations including (but not limited to) the following:

- Creating screen captures of sections of the application
- Manipulating content at the pixel level such as applying dissolve effects on images loaded at runtime
- Creating several copies of existing content

There are various ways in which you can copy bitmap content depending on what you are trying to accomplish. These include the following:

- Copying content from display objects
- Creating a clone of all or part of an existing `BitmapData` object
- Creating a merged version of two bitmaps

Copying from display objects

The `BitmapData` class defines the `draw()` method for copying bitmap data from objects implementing the `IBitmapDrawable` interface, which includes all `DisplayObject` instances (including subclasses such as `Shape`, `Sprite`, `Loader`, and so on). The `draw()` method copies every pixel from a region of a source to the `BitmapData` object from which it is called.

The `draw()` method accepts the following parameters. Only the first parameter is required.

- `source`: A reference to the `IBitmapDrawable` object from which to copy the pixels.
- `matrix`: A Matrix object to use to apply any transformations. The default is an identity matrix that applies no transformations.
- `colorTransform`: A `ColorTransform` object that adjusts the colors as the pixels are copied. By default no color transformation is applied.
- `blendMode`: Indicates what, if any, blend mode to apply. The blend modes are specified using the `flash.display.BlendMode` constants.
- `clipRect`: A `Rectangle` object that specifies the region of the target BitmapData object into which to draw the pixels. By default the `Rectangle` x and y values are 0 and `width` and `height` are equal to the width and height of the source data.
- `smoothing`: A Boolean value indicating whether or not to smooth the content when it is drawn. The default is `false`.

The following code illustrates one use of the `draw()` method. In the example, you programmatically draw a design (two concentric circles with two crossed rectangles) within a `Shape` object. You then make four `BitmapData` objects, and use `draw()` to draw four quadrants of the design — one quadrant per `BitmapData` object.

```
var shape:Shape = new Shape();
shape.graphics.lineStyle(0, 0, 1);
shape.graphics.drawCircle(100, 100, 100);
shape.graphics.drawCircle(100, 100, 50);
shape.graphics.drawRect(25, 50, 150, 100);
shape.graphics.drawRect(50, 25, 100, 150);

// Make a BitmapData object with the same dimensions as the
// shape. Set the background to opaque, and set the color
// to a light red. That way we can differentiate between
```

```
// the BitmapData objects when they are rendered to the stage.
var bitmapDataA:BitmapData = new BitmapData(200, 200, false, 0xFFFFCCCC);

// Copy the pixels from shape to the new BitmapData object.
// Only copy to the upper left quadrant.
bitmapDataA.draw(shape, new Matrix(), null, null, new Rectangle(0, 0, 100, ↵
100));

// Make a Bitmap object, and render the BitmapData object.
var bitmapA:Bitmap = new Bitmap(bitmapDataA);
addChild(bitmapA);

// Make a BitmapData object for the second quadrant. Use
// a background color of light green.
var bitmapDataB:BitmapData = new BitmapData(200, 200, false, 0xFFCCFFCC);

// Copy only to the second quadrant.
bitmapDataB.draw(shape, new Matrix(), null, null, new Rectangle(100, 0, 100, ↵
100));

var bitmapB:Bitmap = new Bitmap(bitmapDataB);
addChild(bitmapB);
bitmapB.x = 200;

// Make a BitmapData object for the third quadrant. Use
// a background color of light blue.
var bitmapDataC:BitmapData = new BitmapData(200, 200, false, 0xFFCCCCFF);
// Copy only to the third quadrant.
bitmapDataC.draw(shape, new Matrix(), null, null, new Rectangle(0, 100, 100, ↵
100));
var bitmapC:Bitmap = new Bitmap(bitmapDataC);
addChild(bitmapC);
bitmapC.y = 200;
// Make a BitmapData object for the fourth quadrant. Use
// a background color of light yellow.
var bitmapDataD:BitmapData = new BitmapData(200, 200, false, 0xFFFFFFCC);
bitmapDataD.draw(shape, new Matrix(), null, null, new Rectangle(100, 100, ↵
100, 100));

var bitmapD:Bitmap = new Bitmap(bitmapDataD);
addChild(bitmapD);
bitmapD.x = 200;
bitmapD.y = 200;

// Add the shape to the display list so you can compare the original shape
// to the copies of the quandrants.
addChild(shape);
shape.x = 100;
shape.y = 100;
```

Figure 33-1 shows the effect.

FIGURE 33-1

Using the draw() method to copy regions of a design from a Shape to BitmapData objects

You'll likely notice in the preceding example that the quadrants are copied to the new BitmapData object with the same x and y coordinates as they appeared in the original Shape object. That means the new BitmapData objects have nothing drawn in the other quadrants. How about drawing the new BitmapData objects such that the object's dimensions are equal to the region you want to draw into it? That's possible, too. The next example looks at how you can accomplish that by simply moving the artwork within the source Shape before copying. The following code is nearly identical to the preceding example. The changes are bolded, and comments are added to indicate what the changes do. The effect is shown in Figure 33-2.

```
var shape:Shape = new Shape();
shape.graphics.lineStyle(0, 0, 1);
shape.graphics.drawCircle(100, 100, 100);
shape.graphics.drawCircle(100, 100, 50);
shape.graphics.drawRect(25, 50, 150, 100);
shape.graphics.drawRect(50, 25, 100, 150);
// Add a container object into which to place the shape.
var container:Sprite = new Sprite();
container.addChild(shape);

var bitmapDataA:BitmapData = new BitmapData(100, 100, false, 0xFFFFCCCC);
```

```
// Copy the pixels from the container now.
bitmapDataA.draw(container, new Matrix(), null, null, new Rectangle(0, 0,  ↵
100, 100));

var bitmapA:Bitmap = new Bitmap(bitmapDataA);
addChild(bitmapA);

var bitmapDataB:BitmapData = new BitmapData(100, 100, false, 0xFFCCFFCC);

// Move the shape to the left so the upper right quadrant is aligned to
// 0,0 in the container.
shape.x = -100;

bitmapDataB.draw(container, new Matrix(), null, null, new Rectangle(0, 0,  ↵
100, 100));

var bitmapB:Bitmap = new Bitmap(bitmapDataB);
addChild(bitmapB);
bitmapB.x = 200;

var bitmapDataC:BitmapData = new BitmapData(100, 100, false, 0xFFCCCCFF);
// Move the shape up and back to the right so the lower left quadrant
// is aligned to 0,0 in the container.
shape.x = 0;
shape.y = -100;

bitmapDataC.draw(container, new Matrix(), null, null, new Rectangle(0, 0,  ↵
100, 100));

var bitmapC:Bitmap = new Bitmap(bitmapDataC);
addChild(bitmapC);
bitmapC.y = 200;

var bitmapDataD:BitmapData = new BitmapData(100, 100, false, 0xFFFFFFCC);

// Move the shape to the left so the lower right quadrant is aligned to
// 0,0 in the container.
shape.x = -100;

bitmapDataD.draw(container, new Matrix(), null, null, new Rectangle(0, 0,  ↵
100, 100));

var bitmapD:Bitmap = new Bitmap(bitmapDataD);
addChild(bitmapD);
bitmapD.x = 200;
bitmapD.y = 200;

// Don't add the shape or the container to the display list.
```

FIGURE 33-2

The four quadrants drawn to BitmapData objects with correct dimensions

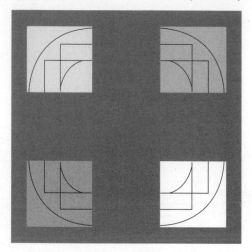

Loading BitmapData images

Although you cannot directly make a BitmapData object from an external image, you can use a Loader object as an intermediary. Using Loader, you can load the image at runtime. Then, you can construct a new BitmapData object using the constructor, and use the draw() method to copy the pixels from the Loader object to the BitmapData object. The following code uses the preceding technique to load an image and draw four quadrants into four BitmapData objects:

```
package com.wiley.as3bible.bitmaps {

    import flash.net.URLRequest;
    import flash.display.BitmapData;
    import flash.display.Bitmap;
    import flash.display.Sprite;
    import flash.display.Loader;
    import flash.geom.Matrix;
    import flash.geom.Rectangle;
    import flash.events.Event;

    public class RuntimeBitmap extends Sprite {

        private var _loader:Loader;

        public function RuntimeBitmap() {
```

```
        // Create a loader and load an image.
        _loader = new Loader();
        _loader.load(new URLRequest("http://www.rightactionscript.com/ ↵
samplefiles/image2.jpg"));
        _loader.contentLoaderInfo.addEventListener(Event.COMPLETE, ↵
completeHandler);
    }

    // This method handles the complete event when the image
    // has loaded into the application.
    private function completeHandler(event:Event):void {
        var w:Number = _loader.width;
        var h:Number = _loader.height;

        // Create a BitmapData object for the first quadrant
        // and draw just that section of the loader into the
        // object. Then display it using a Bitmap object.
        var bitmapDataA:BitmapData = new BitmapData(w/2, h/2);
        bitmapDataA.draw(_loader, new Matrix(), null, null, new ↵
Rectangle(0, 0, w/2, h/2));
        var bitmapA:Bitmap = new Bitmap(bitmapDataA);
        addChild(bitmapA);

        // Move the loader content so the upper right quadrant
        // is aligned to the center point of the loader. Then
        // do the same thing as previously to copy that quadrant
        // and display it.
        _loader.content.x = -w/2;
        var bitmapDataB:BitmapData = new BitmapData(w/2, h/2);
        bitmapDataB.draw(_loader, new Matrix(), null, null, new ↵
Rectangle(0, 0, w/2, h/2));
        var bitmapB:Bitmap = new Bitmap(bitmapDataB);
        addChild(bitmapB);
        bitmapB.x = w/2 + 10;

        // Move the loader content so the lower left quadrant
        // is aligned to the center point of the loader, and
        // copy that quadrant and display it.
        _loader.content.x = 0;
        _loader.content.y = -h/2;
        var bitmapDataC:BitmapData = new BitmapData(w/2, h/2);
        bitmapDataC.draw(_loader, new Matrix(), null, null, new ↵
Rectangle(0, 0, w/2, h/2));
        var bitmapC:Bitmap = new Bitmap(bitmapDataC);
        addChild(bitmapC);
        bitmapC.y = h/2 + 10;
```

```
            // Move the loader content so the lower right quadrant
            // is aligned to the center point of the loader, and
            // copy that quadrant and display it.
            _loader.content.x = -w/2;
            _loader.content.y = -h/2;
            var bitmapDataD:BitmapData = new BitmapData(w/2, h/2);
            bitmapDataD.draw(_loader, new Matrix(), null, null, new ↵
    Rectangle(0, 0, w/2, h/2));
            var bitmapD:Bitmap = new Bitmap(bitmapDataD);
            addChild(bitmapD);
            bitmapD.x = w/2 + 10;
            bitmapD.y = h/2 + 10;

        }

    }

}
```

Copying from BitmapData objects

You can copy pixels not only from display objects, but also from `BitmapData` objects. You can use the following methods to copy from a `BitmapData` object:

- `clone()`: Makes a new `BitmapData` object with an exact copy of the data of the original object.
- `draw()`: Works just like copying pixels from a display object.
- `copyPixels()`: Copies a region of pixels.
- `copyChannel()`: Copies the red, green, blue, or alpha channel.
- `merge()`: Merges images.
- `getPixel()`/`setPixel()`/`getPixel32()`/`setPixel32()`: Get and set pixels.

Cloning a BitmapData object

You can clone a `BitmapData` object using the `clone()` method. The method requires no parameters, and it makes a new `BitmapData` object with a copy of the data of the original:

```
var cloneBitmapData:BitmapData = originalBitmapData.clone();
```

Cloning `BitmapData` objects is useful when you want to create several independent versions of a bitmap data. Note that it's not necessary to create clones in order to display the same bitmap data several times since you can associate one `BitmapData` object with many Bitmap objects. However, clones of `BitmapData` objects are necessary if you want to make changes to the clones without affecting the original.

Drawing into a BitmapData object

Earlier in this chapter, you learned how to use the draw() method to copy pixels from a display object to a BitmapData object. You can use the draw() method in the same way to copy pixels from one BitmapData object to another BitmapData object. If you specify only one parameter, the draw() method makes a copy of the data into the new BitmapData object:

```
bitmapDataB.draw(bitmapDataA);
```

When you use the draw() method to copy pixels from a BitmapData object, you can specify one parameter more than when copying from a display object. The sixth (optional) parameter is a Boolean value that determines whether or not to smooth the image when it is scaled beyond 100 percent. The default is false. The following code illustrates how to use the smoothing parameter. The code loads an image, copies the pixels to a BitmapData object, and then copies that data to two BitmapData objects: one with smoothing and one without, as shown in Figure 33-3. You can see that the one on the left is pixelated while the one on the right is smoothed.

```
package com.wiley.as3bible.bitmaps {

    import flash.net.URLRequest;
    import flash.display.BitmapData;
    import flash.display.Bitmap;
    import flash.display.Sprite;
    import flash.display.Loader;
    import flash.geom.Matrix;
    import flash.events.Event;

    public class RuntimeBitmap extends Sprite {

        private var _loader:Loader;

        public function RuntimeBitmap() {

            _loader = new Loader();
            _loader.load(new URLRequest("http://www.rightactionscript.com/ ↵
samplefiles/image1.jpg"));
            _loader.contentLoaderInfo.addEventListener(Event.COMPLETE, ↵
completeHandler);
        }

        private function completeHandler(event:Event):void {
            var w:Number = _loader.width / 10;
            var h:Number = _loader.height / 10;
            var bitmapData:BitmapData = new BitmapData(w, h);
            bitmapData.draw(_loader);

            var copyA:BitmapData = new BitmapData(w, h);
            copyA.draw(bitmapData, new Matrix(10, 0, 0, 10));
            var bitmapA:Bitmap = new Bitmap(copyA);
            addChild(bitmapA);
            bitmapA.scaleX = 4;
```

```
            bitmapA.scaleY = 4;
            var copyB:BitmapData = new BitmapData(w, h);
            copyB.draw(bitmapData, new Matrix(10, 0, 0, 10), null, null, ↵
null, true);
            var bitmapB:Bitmap = new Bitmap(copyA);
            addChild(bitmapB);
            bitmapB.x = bitmapA.width;
            bitmapB.scaleX = 4;
            bitmapB.scaleY = 4;


        }
    }
}
```

FIGURE 33-3

The left image has no smoothing applied, while the right does.

Copying pixels

You can use the copyPixels() method to copy rectangular regions of a BitmapData object. From a practical perspective it is similar to the draw() method. However, the parameters are different, and the copyPixels() method allows you to copy pixels in a slightly different way. The parameters are:

- sourceBitmapData: The BitmapData object from which you want to copy pixels.

- sourceRect: A Rectangle object specifying the region of the source bitmap you want to copy.

- destPoint: A Point object specifying the point in the destination bitmap at which you want to start placing the copied pixels.

- alphaBitmapData: A BitmapData object from which you want to use the alpha channel. The parameter is optional. By default, the alpha channel of the source BitmapData object is used.

- `alphaPoint`: A `Point` object that specifies a point within the alpha `BitmapData` object that maps to the upper-left corner of the destination `BitmapData` object. The parameter is optional.

- `mergeAlpha`: A Boolean value indicating whether or not to merge the alpha channels of both the source `BitmapData` object and the alpha `BitmapData` object. If `false`, only the alpha `BitmapData` alpha channel is used. If true, both alpha channels are used. The parameter is optional.

As already stated, the `copyPixels()` method is often used in much the same way as the `draw()` method: to copy rectangular regions. The following code is a rewrite of a previous example from the "Loading BitmapData Images" section, using `copyPixels()` instead of `draw()`. While both accomplish the same effect, the logic is slightly different.

> **NOTE** The following code does still use `draw()` to copy the image data from a Loader object to a `BitmapData` object. However, it uses `copyPixels()` to make rectangular regions from the original bitmap.

```
package com.wiley.as3bible.bitmaps {

    import flash.net.URLRequest;
    import flash.display.BitmapData;
    import flash.display.Bitmap;
    import flash.display.Sprite;
    import flash.display.Loader;
    import flash.geom.Matrix;
    import flash.geom.Point;
    import flash.geom.Rectangle;
    import flash.events.Event;

    public class RuntimeBitmap extends Sprite {

        private var _loader:Loader;

        public function RuntimeBitmap() {

            // Create a loader and load an image.
            _loader = new Loader();
            _loader.load(new URLRequest("http://www.rightactionscript.com/ ↵
samplefiles/image2.jpg"));
            _loader.contentLoaderInfo.addEventListener(Event.COMPLETE, ↵
completeHandler);
        }

        // This method handles the complete event when the image
        // has loaded into the application.
        private function completeHandler(event:Event):void {
            var w:Number = _loader.width;
            var h:Number = _loader.height;
```

```
                      // Create a BitmapData object with a copy of the loaded image.
                      var bitmapData:BitmapData = new BitmapData(w, h);
                      bitmapData.draw(_loader);

                      // Create four BitmapData objects, copying the quandrants
                      // from the source image.
                      var bitmapDataA:BitmapData = new BitmapData(w/2, h/2);
                      bitmapDataA.copyPixels(bitmapData, new Rectangle(0, 0, w/2, ↵
             h/2), new Point(0, 0));
                      var bitmapA:Bitmap = new Bitmap(bitmapDataA);
                      addChild(bitmapA);

                      var bitmapDataB:BitmapData = new BitmapData(w/2, h/2);
                      bitmapDataB.copyPixels(bitmapData, new Rectangle(w/2, 0, w/2, ↵
             h/2), new Point(0, 0));
                      var bitmapB:Bitmap = new Bitmap(bitmapDataB);
                      addChild(bitmapB);
                      bitmapB.x = w/2 + 10;

                      var bitmapDataC:BitmapData = new BitmapData(w/2, h/2);
                      bitmapDataC.copyPixels(bitmapData, new Rectangle(0, h/2, w/2, ↵
             h/2), new Point(0, 0));
                      var bitmapC:Bitmap = new Bitmap(bitmapDataC);
                      addChild(bitmapC);
                      bitmapC.y = h/2 + 10;

                      var bitmapDataD:BitmapData = new BitmapData(w/2, h/2);
                      bitmapDataD.copyPixels(bitmapData, new Rectangle(w/2, h/2, w/2, ↵
             h/2), new Point(0, 0));
                      var bitmapD:Bitmap = new Bitmap(bitmapDataD);
                      addChild(bitmapD);
                      bitmapD.x = w/2 + 10;
                      bitmapD.y = h/2 + 10;

                 }
            }
       }
```

Copying channels

The copyChannel() method lets you copy the red, green, blue, and alpha channels from a BitmapData object. The parameters for copyChannel() are as follows:

- sourceBitmapData: The BitmapData object from which you want to copy pixels.

- sourceRect: A Rectangle object specifying the region of the source bitmap you want to copy.

- `destPoint`: A `Point` object specifying the point in the destination bitmap at which you want to start placing the copied pixels.

- `sourceChannel`: A number from the set of 1, 2, 4, and 8 representing red, green, blue, and alpha, respectively.

- `destChannel`: A number from the set of 1, 2, 4, and 8 representing red, green, blur, and alpha, respectively.

For each of the channel parameters you can use the RED, GREEN, BLUE, and ALPHA constants of the `flash.display.BitmapDataChannel` class.

The following code is very similar to the code in the previous section. However, rather than using `copyPixels()`, the following code uses `copyChannel()`. Each of the quadrants renders only specific channels from the original image so that they appear as blue, red, yellow, and green.

```
package com.wiley.as3bible.bitmaps {

    import flash.net.URLRequest;
    import flash.display.BitmapData;
    import flash.display.Bitmap;
    import flash.display.Sprite;
    import flash.display.Loader;
    import flash.geom.Matrix;
    import flash.geom.Point;
    import flash.geom.Rectangle;
    import flash.display.BitmapDataChannel;
    import flash.events.Event;

    public class RuntimeBitmap extends Sprite {

        private var _loader:Loader;

        public function RuntimeBitmap() {

            // Create a loader and load an image.
            _loader = new Loader();
            _loader.load(new URLRequest("http://www.rightactionscript.com/ ↵
samplefiles/image2.jpg"));
            _loader.contentLoaderInfo.addEventListener(Event.COMPLETE, ↵
completeHandler);
        }

        // This method handles the complete event when the image
        // has loaded into the application.
        private function completeHandler(event:Event):void {
            var w:Number = _loader.width;
            var h:Number = _loader.height;

            var bitmapData:BitmapData = new BitmapData(w, h);
            bitmapData.draw(_loader);
```

```
        var bitmapDataA:BitmapData = new BitmapData(w/2, h/2);
        bitmapDataA.copyChannel(bitmapData, new Rectangle(0, 0, w/2, ↵
h/2), new Point(0, 0), BitmapDataChannel.RED, BitmapDataChannel.RED);
        var bitmapA:Bitmap = new Bitmap(bitmapDataA);
        addChild(bitmapA);
        var bitmapDataB:BitmapData = new BitmapData(w/2, h/2);
        bitmapDataB.copyChannel(bitmapData, new Rectangle(w/2, 0, w/2, ↵
h/2), new Point(0, 0), BitmapDataChannel.GREEN, BitmapDataChannel.GREEN);
        var bitmapB:Bitmap = new Bitmap(bitmapDataB);
        addChild(bitmapB);
        bitmapB.x = w/2 + 10;

        var bitmapDataC:BitmapData = new BitmapData(w/2, h/2);
        bitmapDataC.copyChannel(bitmapData, new Rectangle(0, h/2, w/2, ↵
h/2), new Point(0, 0), BitmapDataChannel.BLUE, BitmapDataChannel.BLUE);
        var bitmapC:Bitmap = new Bitmap(bitmapDataC);
        addChild(bitmapC);
        bitmapC.y = h/2 + 10;

        var bitmapDataD:BitmapData = new BitmapData(w/2, h/2);
        bitmapDataD.copyChannel(bitmapData, new Rectangle(w/2, h/2, ↵
w/2, h/2), new Point(0, 0), BitmapDataChannel.RED, BitmapDataChannel.RED);
        bitmapDataD.copyChannel(bitmapData, new Rectangle(w/2, h/2, ↵
w/2, h/2), new Point(0, 0), BitmapDataChannel.BLUE, BitmapDataChannel.BLUE);
        var bitmapD:Bitmap = new Bitmap(bitmapDataD);
        addChild(bitmapD);
        bitmapD.x = w/2 + 10;
        bitmapD.y = h/2 + 10;


    }
  }
}
```

Merging BitmapData images

You can use the merge() method to merge the data from BitmapData objects. The method requires the following parameters:

- sourceBitmapData: The BitmapData object from which you want to copy pixels.
- sourceRect: A Rectangle object specifying the region of the source bitmap you want to copy.
- destPoint: A Point object specifying the point in the destination bitmap at which you want to start placing the copied pixels.
- redMultiplier: The amount by which to multiply the red value of the source bitmap. The range is from 0 to 256.
- greenMultiplier: The amount by which to multiply the green value of the source bitmap. The range is from 0 to 256.

- `blueMultiplier`: The amount by which to multiply the blue value of the source bitmap. The range is from 0 to 256.

- `alphaMultiplier`: The amount by which to multiply the alpha value of the source bitmap. The range is from 0 to 100.

The multiplier parameters may not seem immediately obvious in terms of how you can use them to achieve the effect you want. The formulas that Flash uses are:

```
red = (redSource * redMultiplier) + ↵
(redDestination * (256: redMultiplier)) / 256

green = (greenSource * greenMultiplier) + ↵
(greenDestination * (256: greenMultiplier)) / 256

blue = (blueSource * blueMultiplier) + ↵
(blueDestination * (256: blueMultiplier)) / 256

alpha = (alphaSource * alphaMultiplier) + ↵
(alphaDestination * (100: alphaMultiplier)) / 100
```

The following code loads two images, copies them to `BitmapData` objects, and then merges them:

```
package com.wiley.as3bible.bitmaps {

    import flash.net.URLRequest;
    import flash.display.BitmapData;
    import flash.display.Bitmap;
    import flash.display.Sprite;
    import flash.display.Loader;
    import flash.geom.Point;
    import flash.geom.Rectangle;
    import flash.events.Event;

    public class RuntimeBitmap extends Sprite {

        private var _loaderA:Loader;
        private var _loaderB:Loader;
        private var _loadCount:Number;

        public function RuntimeBitmap() {

            _loadCount = 0;

            // Create a loader and load the first image.
            _loaderA = new Loader();
```

```
        _loaderA.load(new URLRequest("http://www.rightactionscript.com/ ↵
samplefiles/image1.jpg"));
        _loaderA.contentLoaderInfo.addEventListener(Event.COMPLETE, ↵
completeHandler);
        // Create a loader and load the second image.
        _loaderB = new Loader();
        _loaderB.load(new
URLRequest("http://www.rightactionscript.com/samplefiles/image2.jpg"));
        _loaderB.contentLoaderInfo.addEventListener(Event.COMPLETE, ↵
completeHandler);
    }

    // This is the listener for the complete event dispatched by
    // the loaders. When both images have loaded call mergeImages().
    private function completeHandler(event:Event):void {
        _loadCount++;
        if(_loadCount == 2) {
          mergeImages();
        }
    }

    private function mergeImages():void {
        var w:Number = _loaderA.width;
        var h:Number = _loaderA.height;

        // Copy the first image to a BitmapData object.
        var bitmapDataA:BitmapData = new BitmapData(w, h);
        bitmapDataA.draw(_loaderA);

        // Copy the second image to a BitmapData object.
        var bitmapDataB:BitmapData = new BitmapData(w, h);
        bitmapDataB.draw(_loaderB);

        // Merge the second image with the first.
        bitmapDataA.merge(bitmapDataB, new Rectangle(0, 0, w, h), new ↵
Point(0, 0), 0, 256, 0, 100);

        var bitmap:Bitmap = new Bitmap(bitmapDataA);
        addChild(bitmap);
    }
  }
}
```

Getting and setting pixels

You can get and set pixels using the getPixel(), setPixel(), getPixel32(), and setPixel32() methods. The getPixel() method returns a number in the form of 0xRRGGBB for a pixel specified by x and y coordinates:

```
trace(bitmapData.getPixel(100, 100).toString(16));
```

The setPixel() method sets the color of a pixel. The parameters are the x coordinate, the y coordinate, and the color as a number in the form of 0xRRGGBB:

```
bitmapData.setPixel(100, 100, 0xRR0000);
```

The getPixel32() and setPixel32() methods work as the getPixel() and setPixel() methods. However, they work with colors in the format of 0xAARRGGBB.

Applying Color Transformations

You can use the colorTransform() method to apply color transformations to regions of a BitmapData object. The colorTransform() method requires two parameters: a Rectangle object defining the region to which to apply the color transform, and a ColorTransform object to use.

CROSS-REF Refer to Chapter 32 for more details on working with ColorTransform objects.

The following code downloads an image to the player, copies the image to a BitmapData object, and then applies four ColorTransform objects to four quadrants of the image:

```
package com.wiley.as3bible.bitmaps {

    import flash.net.URLRequest;
    import flash.display.BitmapData;
    import flash.display.Bitmap;
    import flash.display.Sprite;
    import flash.display.Loader;
    import flash.geom.Rectangle;
    import flash.events.Event;
    import flash.geom.ColorTransform;

    public class RuntimeBitmap extends Sprite {

        private var _loader:Loader;

        public function RuntimeBitmap() {

            _loader = new Loader();
            _loader.load(new URLRequest("http://www.rightactionscript.com/ ↵
samplefiles/image2.jpg"));
            _loader.contentLoaderInfo.addEventListener(Event.COMPLETE, ↵
completeHandler);
        }

        private function completeHandler(event:Event):void {
            var w:Number = _loader.width;
            var h:Number = _loader.height;
```

```
            var bitmapData:BitmapData = new BitmapData(w, h);
            bitmapData.draw(_loader);
            bitmapData.colorTransform(new Rectangle(0, 0, w/2, h/2), new ↵
    ColorTransform(1, 0, 0, 1, 0, 0, 0, 0));
            bitmapData.colorTransform(new Rectangle(w/2, 0, w/2, h/2), new ↵
    ColorTransform(0, 1, 0, 1, 0, 0, 0, 0));
            bitmapData.colorTransform(new Rectangle(0, h/2, w/2, h/2), new ↵
    ColorTransform(0, 0, 1, 1, 0, 0, 0, 0));
            bitmapData.colorTransform(new Rectangle(w/2, h/2, w/2, h/2), new ↵
    ColorTransform(1, 1, 0, 1, 0, 0, 0, 0));

            var bitmap:Bitmap = new Bitmap(bitmapData);
            addChild(bitmap);
        }
    }
}
```

Applying Fills

You can apply fills to `BitmapData` objects using the `fillRect()` and `floodFill()` methods.

Applying rectangular fills

You can apply fills to rectangular regions using the `fillRect()` method. The method requires two parameters: a Rectangle object defining the region to which to apply the fill, and a color as a number in the form of 0xAARRGGBB. The following example makes a `BitmapData` object, and then applies four fills:

```
var bitmapData:BitmapData = new BitmapData(200, 200);

bitmapData.fillRect(new Rectangle(0, 0, 100, 100), 0xFFFF0000);
bitmapData.fillRect(new Rectangle(100, 0, 100, 100), 0xFF00FF00);
bitmapData.fillRect(new Rectangle(0, 100, 100, 100), 0xFF0000FF);
bitmapData.fillRect(new Rectangle(100, 100, 100, 100), 0xFFFFFF00);

var bitmap:Bitmap = new Bitmap(bitmapData);
addChild(bitmap);
```

Applying flood fills

Flood fills are fills that get applied to a region based on the existing color of the region. A flood fill requires a destination point. It applies a color to the destination point as well as every adjoining point that has the same color as the pre-filled color of the destination point. You are likely most familiar with flood fills by way of the paint bucket tool in most drawing and painting applications (such as Flash).

You can programmatically apply flood fills to `BitmapData` objects using the `floodFill()` method. The method requires the following parameters: the x coordinate of the destination point, the y coordinate of the destination point, and the color in the form of 0xAARRGGBB. The following example uses the example from the preceding section as a starting point, and then adds an event handler that applies a flood fill to the `BitmapData` object at the mouse coordinates when the user clicks on the image:

```
package com.wiley.as3bible.bitmaps {

    import flash.display.BitmapData;
    import flash.display.Bitmap;
    import flash.display.Sprite;
    import flash.geom.Rectangle;
    import flash.events.MouseEvent;
    public class RuntimeBitmap extends Sprite {

        private var _bitmapData:BitmapData;

        public function RuntimeBitmap() {

            _bitmapData = new BitmapData(200, 200);
            _bitmapData.fillRect(new Rectangle(0, 0, 100, 100), 0xFFFF0000);
            _bitmapData.fillRect(new Rectangle(100, 0, 100, 100), 0xFF00FF00);
            _bitmapData.fillRect(new Rectangle(0, 100, 100, 100), 0xFF0000FF);
            _bitmapData.fillRect(new Rectangle(100, 100, 100, 100), 0xFFFFFF00);

            var container:Sprite = new Sprite();
            addChild(container);

            var bitmap:Bitmap = new Bitmap(_bitmapData);
            container.addChild(bitmap);

            container.addEventListener(MouseEvent.CLICK, clickHandler);
        }

        private function clickHandler(event:MouseEvent):void {
            _bitmapData.floodFill(mouseX, mouseY, 0xFF000000 | ↵
Math.random() * 0xFFFFFF);
        }
    }
}
```

Detecting Areas by Color

You can detect areas within a bitmap that contain a specific color using `getColorBoundsRect()`. The method accepts the following parameters:

- `mask`: The mask to use to determine which bits of a 32-bit color value to consider in the calculations. For example, 0xFFFFFFFF will consider all bits while 0xFF000000 will consider only the alpha values.

- `color`: The 32-bit color for which to find the bounds.

- `findColor`: A Boolean value indicating whether to find the area containing the color, or to find the area where the color does *not* exist. The default value is `true`.

The method returns a `Rectangle` object enclosing the section of the bitmap that contains the color. The following example loads an image and then draws a rectangular outline around the color bounds when the user clicks on the image:

```
package com.wiley.as3bible.bitmaps {

    import flash.display.Bitmap;
    import flash.display.BitmapData;
    import flash.display.Shape;
    import flash.display.Sprite;
    import flash.display.Loader;
    import flash.net.URLRequest;
    import flash.events.MouseEvent;
    import flash.events.Event;
    import flash.geom.Point;
    import flash.geom.Rectangle;

    public class RuntimeBitmap extends Sprite {

        private var _bitmapData:BitmapData;
        private var _loader:Loader;
        private var _outline:Shape;

        public function RuntimeBitmap() {
            _loader = new Loader();
            _loader.load(new URLRequest("http://www.rightactionscript.com/ ↵
samplefiles/image2.jpg"));
            _loader.contentLoaderInfo.addEventListener(Event.COMPLETE, ↵
completeHandler);

            addEventListener(MouseEvent.CLICK, clickHandler);

        }

        private function completeHandler(event:Event):void {

            var w:Number = _loader.width;
            var h:Number = _loader.height;

            _bitmapData = new BitmapData(w, h);
            _bitmapData.draw(_loader);

            var bitmap:Bitmap = new Bitmap(_bitmapData);
            var container:Sprite = new Sprite();
            addChild(container);
            container.addChild(bitmap);

            _outline = new Shape();
            addChild(_outline);

        }

        private function clickHandler(event:MouseEvent):void {
```

```
            var color:uint = _bitmapData.getPixel32(mouseX, mouseY);
            var rectangle:Rectangle = ↵
_bitmapData.getColorBoundsRect(0xFFFFFFFF, color);
            _outline.graphics.clear();
            _outline.graphics.lineStyle(0, 0x000000, 1);
            _outline.graphics.drawRect(rectangle.x, rectangle.y, ↵
rectangle.width, rectangle.height);
        }
    }
}
```

Applying Effects

The BitmapData class has methods that enable you to apply effects such as replacing colors, pixel dissolves, and remapping the color palette.

Replacing colors with threshold

The threshold() method enables you to replace colors within a BitmapData object using various operations. The method accepts the following parameters:

- sourceBitmapData: The BitmapData object from which you want to copy pixels.
- sourceRect: A Rectangle object specifying the region of the source bitmap you want to copy.
- destPoint. A Point object specifying the point in the destination bitmap at which you want to start placing the copied pixels.
- operation: One of the following as a string: <, >, <=, >=, !=, or ==.
- threshold: A number in the form of 0xAARRGGBB that specifies the threshold color.
- color: The color to use in place of anything that tests true to the threshold operation. The value is in the form of 0xAARRGGBB. The default is 0x00000000.
- mask: A color in the form of 0xAARRGGBB to use as a mask in the operation. The default is 0xFFFFFFFF.
- copySource: A Boolean value indicating whether or not to copy the source bitmap data that doesn't test true. The default is false.

Using the threshold() method, you can make transition effects, two-tone contrast versions of raster graphics, and more. The operation and threshold parameters work together to determine the operation to run. For example, if you use an operation parameter of < and a threshold parameter of 0xFF00FF00, Flash will use the color value for each of the pixels in the destination object that correspond to pixels in the source object with colors less than green. The following example code illustrates how you can use threshold() to apply an interesting transition effect:

```
package com.wiley.as3bible.bitmaps {

    import flash.net.URLRequest;
    import flash.display.BitmapData;
```

639

```
import flash.display.Bitmap;
import flash.display.Sprite;
import flash.display.Loader;
import flash.geom.Rectangle;
import flash.geom.Point;
import flash.events.Event;
import flash.events.TimerEvent;
import flash.utils.Timer;

public class RuntimeBitmap extends Sprite {

    private var _loader:Loader;
    private var _bitmapData:BitmapData;
    private var _bitmapDataThresholdCopy:BitmapData;
    private var _timer:Timer;
    private var _threshold:Number;
    private var _color:Number;
    private var _hide:Boolean;
    public function RuntimeBitmap() {

        _loader = new Loader();
        _loader.load(new ↵
URLRequest("http://www.rightactionscript.com/samplefiles/image2.jpg"));
        _loader.contentLoaderInfo.addEventListener(Event.COMPLETE, ↵
completeHandler);
        _threshold = 0xCCFF;

        _timer = new Timer(50);
        _timer.addEventListener(TimerEvent.TIMER, timerHandler);

        _color = 0xFFFFFF * Math.random() | 0xFF000000;

        _hide = true;

    }

    private function completeHandler(event:Event):void {
        var w:Number = _loader.width;
        var h:Number = _loader.height;

        _bitmapData = new BitmapData(w, h);
        _bitmapData.draw(_loader);
        _bitmapDataThresholdCopy = _bitmapData.clone();

        var bitmap:Bitmap = new Bitmap(_bitmapDataThresholdCopy);
        addChild(bitmap);

        _timer.start();

    }
    private function timerHandler(event:TimerEvent):void {
```

```
            _bitmapDataThresholdCopy.threshold(_bitmapData, new Rectangle(0, ↵
0, _bitmapData.width, _bitmapData.height), new Point(0, 0), "<=", ↵
0xFF000000 | _threshold, _color, 0xFFFFFFFF, true);
            if(_hide) {
                _threshold += (0xFFFFFF - _threshold)/5;
                if(_threshold >= 0xFFFFCC) {
                  _hide = !_hide;
                }
            }
            else {
                _threshold -= (0xFFFFFF - _threshold)/5;
                if(_threshold <= 0x00CCCC) {
                  _hide = !_hide;
                }
            }
        }


    }
}
```

Using pixel dissolves

The pixelDissolve() method does just what it says: dissolves pixels. The method accepts the following parameters:

- sourceBitmapData: The BitmapData object from which you want to copy pixels.

- sourceRect: A Rectangle object specifying the region of the source bitmap you want to copy.

- destPoint: A Point object specifying the point in the destination bitmap at which you want to start placing the copied pixels.

- randomSeed: A random number used by Flash Player to run the pixel dissolve. This can start at any random number. If you use the same number twice, the dissolve will look the same. When performing successive calls to pixelDissolve(), the value ought to be the value returned by the previous call to the pixelDissolve() method.

- numPixels: The number of pixels to dissolve. The default is ⅟₃₀ of the total pixels.

- fillColor: If you specify the destination as the source bitmap, it dissolves to a solid color. You can specify the color using the fillColor parameter with a number in the form of 0xAARRGGBB. The default is 0x00000000.

The pixelDissolve() method dissolves the number of pixels specified by the numPixels parameter from the source BitmapData object to the destination BitmapData object. It uses an algorithm to randomly select which pixels to dissolve. Therefore, it is possible that it could dissolve one or more pixels that had already been dissolved. However, the method returns a number that you can use in the next call to the method as the randomSeed parameter. If you do so, Flash will not dissolve a pixel that was already dissolved. That way, you can ensure that every pixel will get dissolved within a specific number of calls to the method.

The following example code illustrates how to use pixelDissolve(). It loads two images, copies them to BitmapData objects, and then uses a timer and pixelDissolve() to continually dissolve between the two images.

```
package com.wiley.as3bible.bitmaps {

    import flash.net.URLRequest;
    import flash.display.BitmapData;
    import flash.display.Bitmap;
    import flash.display.Sprite;
    import flash.display.Loader;
    import flash.geom.Point;
    import flash.geom.Rectangle;
    import flash.events.Event;
    import flash.utils.Timer;
    import flash.events.TimerEvent;

    public class RuntimeBitmap extends Sprite {

        private var _loaderA:Loader;
        private var _loaderB:Loader;
        private var _loadCount:Number;
        private var _bitmapDataA:BitmapData;
        private var _bitmapDataB:BitmapData;
        private var _bitmapDataToRender:BitmapData;
        private var _randomNumber:Number;
        private var _count:Number;
        private var _direction:Boolean;

        public function RuntimeBitmap() {

            _loadCount = 0;

             // Create a loader and load the first image.
            _loaderA = new Loader();
            _loaderA.load(new URLRequest("http://www.rightactionscript.com/ ↵
samplefiles/image1.jpg"));
            _loaderA.contentLoaderInfo.addEventListener(Event.COMPLETE, ↵
completeHandler);
            // Create a loader and load the second image.
            _loaderB = new Loader();
            _loaderB.load(new URLRequest("http://www.rightactionscript.com/ ↵
samplefiles/image2.jpg"));
            _loaderB.contentLoaderInfo.addEventListener(Event.COMPLETE, ↵
completeHandler);
            _direction = true;
            _randomNumber = 0;
            _count = 0;

        }
```

```
// This is the listener for the complete event dispatched by
// the loaders. When both images have loaded call renderBitmaps().
private function completeHandler(event:Event):void {
    _loadCount++;
    if(_loadCount == 2) {
      renderBitmaps();
    }
}

private function renderBitmaps():void {
    var w:Number = _loaderA.width;
    var h:Number = _loaderA.height;

    // Copy the first image to a BitmapData object.
    _bitmapDataA = new BitmapData(w, h);
    _bitmapDataA.draw(_loaderA);

    // Copy the second image to a BitmapData object.
    _bitmapDataB = new BitmapData(w, h);
    _bitmapDataB.draw(_loaderB);

    // Create a clone of the first BitmapData object.
    _bitmapDataToRender = _bitmapDataA.clone();

    var bitmap:Bitmap = new Bitmap(_bitmapDataToRender);
    addChild(bitmap);

    // Start a timer that dissolves the image.
    var timer:Timer = new Timer(50);
    timer.addEventListener(TimerEvent.TIMER, timerHandler);
    timer.start();
}

private function timerHandler(event:TimerEvent):void {
    // Based on the direction select one of the two images
    // to which to dissolve.
    var bitmapData:BitmapData = _direction ? _bitmapDataB : ↵
_bitmapDataA;

    // Determine the number of pixels by dividing the area by 20.

    // This means it will take 20 counts to dissolve between the
    // images.
    var pixels:Number = bitmapData.width * bitmapData.height / 20;
    // Dissolve.
    _randomNumber = _bitmapDataToRender.pixelDissolve(bitmapData, ↵
new Rectangle(0, 0, bitmapData.width, bitmapData.height), new Point(0, 0), ↵
_randomNumber, pixels);

    // Determine whether or not to change the direction.
    _count++;
```

```
            if(_count > 20) {
                _direction = !_direction;
                _count = 0;
            }
        }
    }
}
```

Remapping the color palette

You can remap the color palette of a BitmapData object using the paletteMap() method. For
example, you can tell it to convert every red pixel to green and every blue pixel to yellow. The
paletteMap() method accepts the following parameters:

- sourceBitmapData: The BitmapData object from which you want to copy pixels.

- sourceRect: A Rectangle object specifying the region of the source bitmap you want
  to copy.

- destPoint: A Point object specifying the point in the destination bitmap at which
  you want to start placing the copied pixels.

- redArray: An array of 256 numbers mapping reds.

- greenArray: An array of 256 numbers mapping greens.

- blueArray: An array of 256 numbers mapping blues.

- alphaArray: An array of 256 numbers mapping alphas.

Each of the array parameters is optional. If they are omitted or null then the corresponding color
channel map is not changed. The following example loads an image and then displays it using a
remapped color palette.

```
package com.wiley.as3bible.bitmaps {

    import flash.net.URLRequest;
    import flash.display.BitmapData;
    import flash.display.Bitmap;
    import flash.display.Sprite;
    import flash.display.Loader;
    import flash.geom.Point;
    import flash.geom.Rectangle;
    import flash.events.Event;

    public class RuntimeBitmap extends Sprite {

        private var _loader:Loader;

        public function RuntimeBitmap() {
```

```actionscript
            // Create a loader and load the image.
            _loader = new Loader();
            _loader.load(new ↵
URLRequest("http://www.rightactionscript.com/samplefiles/image2.jpg"));
            _loader.contentLoaderInfo.addEventListener(Event.COMPLETE, ↵
completeHandler);
        }

        // This is the listener for the complete event dispatched by
        // the loader.
        private function completeHandler(event:Event):void {
            var w:Number = _loader.width;
            var h:Number = _loader.height;

            // Copy the image to a BitmapData object.
            var bitmapData:BitmapData = new BitmapData(w, h);
            bitmapData.draw(_loader);

            // Create arrays for red, green, and blue which remap the
            // color values.
            var red:Array = new Array();
            for(var i:Number = 0; i < 256; i++) {
                red[i] = 0xFF00FFFF | (255 - i) << 16;
            }

            var green:Array = new Array();
            var i:Number;
            for(i = 0; i < 256; i++) {
                green[i] = 0xFFFF00FF | (255 - i) << 8;
            }

            var blue:Array = new Array();
            for(i = 0; i < 256; i++) {
                blue[i] = 0xFFFFFF00 | (255 - i);
            }

            // Remap the colors using paletteMap().
            bitmapData.paletteMap(bitmapData, new Rectangle(0, 0, w, h), new ↵
Point(0, 0), red, green, blue);

            var bitmap:Bitmap = new Bitmap(bitmapData);
            addChild(bitmap);

        }
    }
}
```

Making Noise

Noise typically refers to unintentional and random data interruptions that can cause specks or grain in images. However, there are many possible reasons for which you might want to *intentionally* introduce noise. For example, you can use noise to apply texture and randomness. The `noise()` and `perlinNoise()` methods enable you to do just that.

Adding noise

The `noise()` function lets you apply randomly distributed noise to a `BitmapData` object. The noise is applied to the entire `BitmapData` object, and is constructed by assigning a random value (within certain parameters) to each pixel. The `noise()` method accepts the following parameters:

- `randomSeed`: A number to use in order to generate the randomization factor.
- `low`: The lowest value to use for each channel (red, green, blue, and alpha). The default is 0.
- `high`: The highest value to use for each channel. The default is 255.
- `channelOptions`: Which channels to utilize. Use 1 for red, 2 for green, 4 for blue, and 8 for alpha. Combine channels by adding the numbers. For example, 5 is red and blue (1+4). The default value is 7, meaning red, green, and blue. You should use the `flash .display.BitmapDataChannel` constants for these values. The constants are called `RED`, `GREEN`, `BLUE`, and `ALPHA`.
- `grayScale`: A Boolean value indicating whether or not to convert the noise colors to grayscale. The default is `false`.

The following code makes a `BitmapData` object. It then uses a timer and `noise()` to continually reapply random noise. The effect appears like static.

```
package com.wiley.as3bible.bitmaps {

    import flash.display.BitmapData;
    import flash.display.Bitmap;
    import flash.display.Sprite;
    import flash.utils.Timer;
    import flash.events.TimerEvent;

    public class RuntimeBitmap extends Sprite {

        private var _bitmapData:BitmapData;

        public function RuntimeBitmap() {

            _bitmapData = new BitmapData(400, 400);
            var bitmap:Bitmap = new Bitmap(_bitmapData);
            addChild(bitmap);

            var timer:Timer = new Timer(50);
            timer.addEventListener(TimerEvent.TIMER, timerHandler);
```

```
            timer.start();

        }

        private function timerHandler(event:TimerEvent):void {
            _bitmapData.noise(Math.random() * 1000000);
        }

    }
}
```

The following code use the alpha channel as well as the color channels to make static that appears over an image:

```
package com.wiley.as3bible.bitmaps {

    import flash.display.BitmapData;
    import flash.display.Bitmap;
    import flash.display.Sprite;
    import flash.utils.Timer;
    import flash.events.TimerEvent;
    import flash.net.URLRequest;
    import flash.display.Loader;
    import flash.events.Event;
    import flash.display.BitmapDataChannel;

    public class RuntimeBitmap extends Sprite {

        private var _bitmapDataA:BitmapData;
        private var _bitmapDataB:BitmapData;
        private var _bitmapDataC:BitmapData;
        private var _bitmapDataD:BitmapData;
        private var _loader:Loader;

        public function RuntimeBitmap() {

            // Create a loader and load the image.
            _loader = new Loader();
            _loader.load(new ↵
URLRequest("http://www.rightactionscript.com/samplefiles/image2.jpg"));
            addChild(_loader);
            // Create four 200 by 200 BitmapData objects, add them
            // to the display list, and arrange them in a square.
            _bitmapDataA = new BitmapData(200, 200);
            var bitmapA:Bitmap = new Bitmap(_bitmapDataA);
            addChild(bitmapA);

            _bitmapDataB = new BitmapData(200, 200);
            var bitmapB:Bitmap = new Bitmap(_bitmapDataB);
            addChild(bitmapB);
            bitmapB.x = 200;

            _bitmapDataC = new BitmapData(200, 200);
```

```
            var bitmapC:Bitmap = new Bitmap(_bitmapDataC);
            addChild(bitmapC);
            bitmapC.y = 200;

            _bitmapDataD = new BitmapData(200, 200);
            var bitmapD:Bitmap = new Bitmap(_bitmapDataD);
            addChild(bitmapD);
            bitmapD.x = 200;
            bitmapD.y = 200;

            // Start a timer to animate static.
            var timer:Timer = new Timer(50);
            timer.addEventListener(TimerEvent.TIMER, timerHandler);
            timer.start();

        }

        private function timerHandler(event:TimerEvent):void {

            // Add noise to the four objects, each using the alpha
            // channel, and three also using another channel.
            _bitmapDataA.noise(Math.random() * 1000000, 10, 100, ↵
BitmapDataChannel.ALPHA);
            _bitmapDataB.noise(Math.random() * 1000000, 10, 100, ↵
BitmapDataChannel.ALPHA + BitmapDataChannel.RED);
            _bitmapDataC.noise(Math.random() * 1000000, 10, 100, ↵
BitmapDataChannel.ALPHA + BitmapDataChannel.GREEN);
            _bitmapDataD.noise(Math.random() * 1000000, 10, 100, ↵
BitmapDataChannel.ALPHA + BitmapDataChannel.BLUE);
        }
    }
}
```

Adding Perlin noise

Perlin noise is a specific type of noise named after Ken Perlin who invented the algorithm in order to make more realistic textures during the movie *Tron*. Perlin noise is not entirely random. It has a degree of randomness, but that randomness is controllable so that you can achieve effects that have an expected texture. While standard noise is good for making graininess or static, Perlin noise is good for making textures of many types. For example, using Perlin noise you can make water, clouds, fire, and other sorts of textures that would be difficult to otherwise mimic.

The perlinNoise() method accepts the following parameters:

■ baseX: The number of pixels in the x direction for the noise. Use the width of the
  BitmapData object as a standard of measurement. As the baseX decreases relative
  to the width of the BitmapData object, the effect will be a vertical zoom out.

■ baseY: The number of pixels in the y direction for the noise. Use the height of the
  BitmapData object as a standard of measurement. As the baseY decreases relative
  to the height of the BitmapData object, the effect will be a horizontal zoom out.

- numOctaves: Perlin noise layers noise. Each layer is called an octave. More octaves means greater detail. More octaves can also require more time to render. Use as few octaves as possible in order to achieve the effect you want. You can specify the number of octaves with the numOctaves parameter.

- randomSeed: A number the method uses to generate the randomness of the noise.

- stitch: A Boolean value indicating whether to smooth the edges of the bitmap in the event it is used as a tiling bitmap fill with the drawing API. The default value is false, which means that if it tiles, the edges are likely to be apparent. If stitch is set to true and the image tiles, the edges aren't likely to be apparent.

- fractalNoise: A Boolean specifying whether to make fractal noise (true) or turbulence (false). The default is false. Fractal noise is more continuous, whereas turbulence has more gaps. Each is more appropriate for various purposes.

- channelOptions: The channelOptions parameter works much like the channelOptions parameter for the noise() method. See the previous section for more details.

- grayscale: A Boolean indicating whether or not to make the noise grayscale. The default is false.

- offsets: An array of Point objects indicating the amount by which to offset each octave.

The perlinNoise() method may seem slightly difficult at first, but a few examples are likely to make it much more accessible to you. We'll use some code examples to highlight the effects of the parameters.

The following code applies Perlin noise to a 400 by 400–pixel BitmapData object. Using a timer, the noise is updated as the mouse moves, and the baseX and baseY values are set to the mouse coordinates so you can see the effect of the baseX and baseY parameters.

```
package com.wiley.as3bible.bitmaps {

    import flash.display.BitmapData;
    import flash.display.Bitmap;
    import flash.display.Sprite;
    import flash.utils.Timer;
    import flash.events.TimerEvent;

    public class RuntimeBitmap extends Sprite {

        private var _bitmapData:BitmapData;

        public function RuntimeBitmap() {

            _bitmapData = new BitmapData(400, 400);
            var bitmap:Bitmap = new Bitmap(_bitmapData);
            addChild(bitmap);

            var timer:Timer = new Timer(50);
            timer.addEventListener(TimerEvent.TIMER, timerHandler);
            timer.start();
```

649

```
                    }

        private function timerHandler(event:TimerEvent):void {
            _bitmapData.perlinNoise(mouseX, mouseY, 1, 1, false, false);
        }
    }
}
```

The following code snippet is similar to the `perlinNoise()` call in the preceding code. However, rather than continually updating the `baseX` and `baseY` parameters, the code updates the `octaves` parameter. The number of octaves ranges from 0 when the mouse is at the far left to 10 when the mouse is on the right side.

```
_bitmapData.perlinNoise(100, 100, mouseX * 10 / 400, 1, false, false);
```

The `randomSeed` parameter is responsible for the randomness of the noise. The following code snippet updates the parameter value using `Math.random()`:

```
_bitmapData.perlinNoise(100, 100, 1, Math.random() * 1000, false, false);
```

> **NOTE** The player will make different random values using the same `randomSeed` value if the application is reloaded. However, during the playback of an SWF the same `randomSeed` value will cause the same random value. The effect is that the Perlin noise will look the same if you use the same parameters during a single playback.

The following code makes a `BitmapData` object with Perlin noise, and then uses that object as a bitmap fill. Because the `stitch` parameter is `false`, the edges are visible as it tiles.

```
package com.wiley.as3bible.bitmaps {

    import flash.display.BitmapData;
    import flash.display.Shape;
    import flash.display.Sprite;
    import flash.utils.Timer;
    import flash.events.TimerEvent;

    public class RuntimeBitmap extends Sprite {

        private var _bitmapData:BitmapData;

        public function RuntimeBitmap() {

            _bitmapData = new BitmapData(200, 200);
            var shape:Shape = new Shape();
            shape.graphics.lineStyle(0, 0, 0);
            shape.graphics.beginBitmapFill(_bitmapData);
            shape.graphics.drawRect(0, 0, 600, 400);
            shape.graphics.endFill();
            addChild(shape);

            var timer:Timer = new Timer(1000);
            timer.addEventListener(TimerEvent.TIMER, timerHandler);
            timer.start();
```

```
            }

        private function timerHandler(event:TimerEvent):void {
            _bitmapData.perlinNoise(100, 100, 1, Math.random() * 100000, ↵
false, false);
        }

    }
}
```

However, notice what happens when you use the same code but set the stitch parameter to `true`. Then the tiling looks seamless.

You can also use the preceding example code to see the effects of the `fractalNoise` parameter. Use a value of `true` instead of `false`, and you'll notice that the effect is much smoother in appearance.

The only other parameter that is likely to need much explanation is the `offsets` parameter. The `offsets` parameter can make for some neat effects such as continuous scrolling of the noise. The following code uses the `offsets` parameter to continuously scroll the texture. Note that even though the noise is continually updated, the noise does not redistribute radically. That is because the same value is used each time for the `randomSeed` parameter.

```
package com.wiley.as3bible.bitmaps {

    import flash.display.BitmapData;
    import flash.display.Bitmap;
    import flash.display.Shape;
    import flash.display.Sprite;
    import flash.utils.Timer;
    import flash.events.TimerEvent;
    import flash.geom.Point;

    public class RuntimeBitmap extends Sprite {

        private var _bitmapData:BitmapData;
        private var _offset:Number;

        public function RuntimeBitmap() {

            _bitmapData = new BitmapData(200, 200);
            var bitmap:Bitmap = new Bitmap(_bitmapData);
            addChild(bitmap);

             offset = 0;

            var timer:Timer = new Timer(1000);
            timer.addEventListener(TimerEvent.TIMER, timerHandler);
            timer.start();

        }
```

```
        private function timerHandler(event:TimerEvent):void {
            _bitmapData.perlinNoise(100, 100, 1, 1, false, false, 1, false, ↵
[new Point(_offset++, 0)]);
        }


    }
}
```

Applying Filters

You can apply filters to `BitmapData` objects as well as display objects. You learned about applying filters to display objects in Chapter 29. The same filter types work with `BitmapData` objects as well. To apply a filter to a `BitmapData` object, use the `applyFilter()` method. The `applyFilter()` method accepts the following parameters:

- `sourceBitmapData`: The `BitmapData` object from which you want to copy pixels.

- `sourceRect`: A `Rectangle` object specifying the region of the source bitmap you want to copy.

- `destPoint`: A `Point` object specifying the point in the destination bitmap at which you want to start placing the copied pixels.

- `filter`: The filter object you want to apply.

The following code uses a `DisplacementMapFilter` object to apply a water ripple effect to an image drawn within a `BitmapData` object:

```
package com.wiley.as3bible.bitmaps {

    import flash.display.Bitmap;
    import flash.display.BitmapData;
    import flash.display.Shape;
    import flash.display.Sprite;
    import flash.display.Loader;
    import flash.net.URLRequest;
    import flash.utils.Timer;
    import flash.events.TimerEvent;
    import flash.events.Event;
    import flash.display.BitmapDataChannel;
    import flash.filters.DisplacementMapFilter;
    import flash.geom.Point;
    import flash.geom.Rectangle;

    public class RuntimeBitmap extends Sprite {
```

```
private var _bitmapDataSource:BitmapData;
private var _bitmapDataDisplay:BitmapData;
private var _noise:BitmapData;
private var _loader:Loader;

public function RuntimeBitmap() {

        _loader = new Loader();
        _loader.load(new URLRequest("http://www.rightactionscript.com/ ↵
samplefiles/image2.jpg"));
        _loader.contentLoaderInfo.addEventListener(Event.COMPLETE, ↵
completeHandler);

    }

    private function completeHandler(event:Event):void {

        var w:Number = _loader.width;
        var h:Number = _loader.height;

        _bitmapDataSource = new BitmapData(w, h);
        _bitmapDataSource.draw(_loader);

        _bitmapDataDisplay = _bitmapDataSource.clone();
        var bitmap:Bitmap = new Bitmap(_bitmapDataDisplay);
        addChild(bitmap);

        _noise = new BitmapData(w, h);

        var timer:Timer = new Timer(10);
        timer.addEventListener(TimerEvent.TIMER, timerHandler);
        timer.start();

    }

    private function timerHandler(event:TimerEvent):void {
        _noise.perlinNoise(50, 50, 10, Math.random() * 10000, false, ↵
false, BitmapDataChannel.RED + BitmapDataChannel.ALPHA);

        var filter:DisplacementMapFilter = new ↵
DisplacementMapFilter(_noise, new Point(0, 0), BitmapDataChannel.RED, 5, 5);
        _bitmapDataDisplay.applyFilter(_bitmapDataSource, new ↵
Rectangle(0, 0, _bitmapDataSource.width, _bitmapDataSource.height), new ↵
Point(0, 0), filter);
    }
  }
}
```

Summary

- You can construct new `BitmapData` objects using the `BitmapData` constructor method or by calling `clone()` on an existing object.

- Use a `Bitmap` object to render a `BitmapData` object.

- The `draw()` method lets you copy the pixels from a display object or another `BitmapData` object to a `BitmapData` object.

- You can use many different methods to copy from a `BitmapData` object. Some methods copy pixel regions while other methods copy channels or merge data.

- Apply color transforms using `colorTransform()`.

- You can use the `fillRect()` and `floodFill()` methods to apply fills to `BitmapData` objects.

- The `threshold()`, `pixelDissolve()`, and `paletteMap()` methods enable you to apply special effects.

- Apply noise using either the `noise()` or the `perlinNoise()` methods.

- Use filters with the `applyFilter()` method.

Part IX

Working with Binary Data

Chapter 34

Working with Binary Data

A byte array is an instance of the `flash.utils.ByteArray` class. As the name suggests, a byte array allows you to work with binary data by storing it in an array of bytes. A byte is unit of data comprised of 8 bits. A bit is the atomic unit of data used in your computer. A bit can contain only two possible values: 0 and 1. When you put 8 bits together to form a byte, the combined range is from 0 to 255. Although as humans we are more accustomed to working with a decimal counting system, all computer operations take place using binary behind the scenes. This means that a byte array is a convenient way to work with lower-level binary data for a variety of reasons. Most of the uses of byte arrays in ActionScript are fairly specialized, but an understanding of byte arrays and possible uses will help you to use a byte array appropriately when it would be useful.

Creating a Byte Array

You can create byte arrays in several ways. The most obvious is to use the constructor as follows:

```
var bytes:ByteArray = new ByteArray();
```

The other ways to create byte arrays rely on the built-in ActionScript methods that return new ByteArray objects. For example, the `BitmapData` class has a `getPixels()` method, which returns a `ByteArray` object.

Writing to a Byte Array

You can write data to a byte array in two basic ways: Use array-access notation (`[]`) to write to a specific index, and use the write methods: `writeBoolean()`, `writeInt()`, and so on. Array-access notation works exactly like writing to a standard array, as shown in the following example:

```
bytes[0] = 255;
```

The caveat with byte arrays is that each index in a byte array can store a value only up to 255. If you write a value greater than 255 then the modulo of that number and 256 will be used. For example, if you write 256 to an index, then the actual value written will be 0.

```
bytes[0] = 256;
trace(bytes[0]); // Outputs 0
```

Likely the most common way to write to byte arrays is to use the write methods. These methods are convenience methods which allow you to write all sorts of data to a byte array: `writeBoolean()`, `writeByte()`, `writeBytes()`, `writeDouble()`, `writeFloat()`, `writeInt()`, `writeMultiByte()`, `writeObject()`, `writeShort()`, `writeUnsignedInt()`, `writeUTF()`, and `writeUTFBytes()`. Each of these methods writes the appropriate number of bytes to the array depending on the type. For example, `writeInt()` writes a 32-bit integer to the array, which means it requires 4 bytes, as shown here:

```
bytes.writeInt(1);
trace(bytes[0] + " " + bytes[1] + " " + bytes[2] + " " + bytes[3]);
// Outputs 0 0 0 1
```

Reading from a Byte Array

You can read from a byte array in the same ways that you can write to it using either array-access notation or the convenience methods for reading data. You've already seen examples of reading data using array-access notation in the previous section (see `trace()` statements). Let's next look at the read methods.

The `ByteArray` class defines read methods that correspond to each of the write methods — for example, `readBoolean()`, `readByte()`, `readBytes()`, `readDouble()`, `readFloat()`, `readInt()`, `readMultiByte()`, `readObject()`, `readShort()`, `readUnsignedInt()`, `readUTF()`, and `readUTFBytes()`. In addition to all the corresponding methods, there are also `readUnsignedByte()` and `readUnsignedShort()` methods. Like the write methods, the read methods access the appropriate number of bytes for the type. That means that `readInt()` reads 4 bytes at a time, for example.

Common Uses of Byte Arrays

The simple fact is that the majority of use cases for byte arrays are very specialized, custom, and fairly advanced. However, there are a handful of fairly common uses for byte arrays in ActionScript:

- Computing sound spectrums
- Loading images
- Copying objects
- Serializing data
- Working with binary sockets

Computing sound spectrums

The `flash.media.SoundMixer` class has a `computeSpectrum()` method, which computes 512 (two 256 groups representing the left and right channels) floating-point values and stores them in a byte array that you pass to the method. You can then use those values to do things such as visually represent the sound spectrum on the screen, as you can see in the following example:

```
package {

    import flash.display.Sprite;
    import flash.utils.ByteArray;
    import flash.media.Sound;
    import flash.media.SoundChannel;
    import flash.media.SoundMixer;
    import flash.net.URLRequest;
    import flash.events.Event;
    import flash.system.Security;

    public class SoundExample extends Sprite {

        private var _channel:SoundChannel;
        private var _graph:Sprite;

        public function SoundExample() {
        Security.loadPolicyFile( "http://rightactionscript.com/ ↵
crossdomain.xml");
            var sound:Sound = new Sound();
            sound.load(new ↵
URLRequest("http://rightactionscript.com/samplefiles/Demo.mp3"), new ↵
SoundLoaderContext(1000, true));
            _channel = sound.play();
            _graph = new Sprite();
            _graph.y = 200;
            addChild(_graph);
            addEventListener(Event.ENTER_FRAME, enterFrameHandler);
        }
```

```
        private function enterFrameHandler(event:Event):void {
            var bytes:ByteArray = new ByteArray();
            SoundMixer.computeSpectrum(bytes);
            _graph.graphics.clear();
            _graph.graphics.lineStyle(0, 0, 1);
            var plotX:Number = 0;
            for(var i:Number = 0; i < 256; i++) {
                _graph.graphics.lineTo(plotX, bytes.readFloat() * ↵
stage.stageHeight / 2);
                plotX += stage.stageWidth / 256;
            }
        }
    }
}
```

Loading images

Although the standard way to load images is to use the `Loader` class as discussed in Chapter 22, you can optionally load the image as a byte array that you can then convert into an image for display. This is useful when you are loading an image from a socket as a byte stream, for example. In other cases you might want to load the image data as a byte array using a standard HTTP request via a `URLLoader` object. This second case doesn't offer much of an advantage over the preferred way of loading images using `Loader` objects except that if the data was encrypted by simply rearranging byte orders, this technique could allow you to reorder the bytes correctly before displaying the image. In any case, once you've loaded the byte array, you can display the image by passing the byte array to the `loadBytes()` method of a `Loader` object as the following example illustrates. Note that in this example the `URLLoader` object's `dataFormat` property is set to `binary` so that it automatically treats the loaded data as a byte array:

```
package {

    import flash.display.Sprite;
    import flash.utils.ByteArray;
    import flash.display.Loader;
    import flash.net.URLLoader;
    import flash.net.URLRequest;
    import flash.net.URLLoaderDataFormat;
    import flash.geom.Rectangle;
    import flash.events.Event;

    public class ImageExample extends Sprite {

        private var urlLoader:URLLoader;

        public function ImageExample() {
            urlLoader = new URLLoader();
            urlLoader.dataFormat = URLLoaderDataFormat.BINARY;
            urlLoader.load(new ↵
URLRequest("http://www.rightactionscript.com/samplefiles/image2.jpg"));
```

```
            urlLoader.addEventListener(Event.COMPLETE, completeHandler);
        }

        private function completeHandler(event:Event):void {
            var loader:Loader = new Loader();
            loader.loadBytes(urlLoader.data);
            addChild(loader);
        }


    }
}
```

Copying objects

When copying objects, you must consider several issues. One of the most common mistakes that beginning programmers make is to assume that a simple assignment statement will create a new copy of an object. Consider the following example:

```
var arrayA:Array = new Array("a", "b", "c", "d");
var arrayB:Array = arrayA;
```

This might appear to make a copy of arrayA, but all it really does is create a new reference to the same object. To see the implications of this, look at the following:

```
arrayB.push("e", "f", "g", "h");
trace(arrayA.length); // Outputs 8
```

In the preceding example, we add four more items to arrayB, but you can see that this actually affects arrayA as well. This is because both arrayA and arrayB merely point to the same object. If you want to create a copy of the array, you can create a new array and use a for statement to copy each item from arrayA to arrayB, as follows:

```
var arrayA:Array = new Array("a", "b", "c", "d");
var arrayB:Array = new Array();
for(var i:int = 0; i < arrayA.length; i++) {
    arrayB[i] = arrayA[i];
}
arrayB.push("e", "f", "g", "h");
trace(arrayA.length);   // Outputs 4
trace(arrayB.length);   // Outputs 8
```

This technique for copying the arrays works, although it is somewhat tedious. However, it gets unmanageable when you have nested objects. For example, consider what would be necessary if you wanted to copy an array of arrays. In such a case, you have to not only copy over each element one at a time, but you have to copy over the elements of each element one at a time.

You can use byte arrays to greatly simplify the copying of objects. You can use the writeObject() method of a byte array to first write the object to a byte array. You can then reset the position property to 0 and then use `readObject()` to read the object back from the byte array. Because `writeObject()` and `readObject()` actually make copies of each byte one at a time, this technique is much simpler than the earlier technique.

```
var arrayA:Array = new Array("a", "b", "c", "d");
var byteArray:ByteArray = new ByteArray();
byteArray.writeObject(arrayA);
byteArray.position = 0;
var arrayB:Array = byteArray.readObject() as Array;
arrayB.push("e", "f", "g", "h");
trace(arrayA.length);   // Outputs 4
trace(arrayB.length);   // Outputs 8
```

> **NOTE** The position property has to be reset to 0 because, otherwise, after you've written data to the byte array, the position will be at the last index at which data has been written. To read data from the start of the byte array you must reset the position to 0.

While this may not appear to be a great savings in lines of code initially, consider that the code to copy an object does not get more complex even as the object you are copying gets more complex.

There is one very important consideration when you are copying objects of custom types. Byte arrays write data using a format called AMF (action message format), which natively supports standard ActionScript data types. However, it does not natively support custom data types. That means that, by default, if you write an object of a custom type it will be written to the byte array correctly, but it will be stored as a generic object. Therefore, when you retrieve it from a byte array you will not be able to cast it back to the correct type. You can fix this by using the `flash.net.registerClassAlias()` function. The function requires two parameters specifying the identifier you want to use to register the class as well as a reference to the class. The following is an example that registers a class alias for a custom type and then makes a copy of an object of that type:

```
registerClassAlias("com.wiley.as3bible.ExampleType", ExampleType);
var a:ExampleType = new ExampleType();
var bytes:ByteArray = new ByteArray();
bytes.writeObject(a);
bytes.position = 0;
var b:ExampleType = bytes.readObject() as ExampleType;
```

Custom serialization of data

When you serialize data (which is what happens when you write to a byte array, for example), Flash Player attempts to write all data that is accessible via public properties (or getters and setters) for an object. However, it will not write private, protected, or internal data by default. The following example illustrates the implications of this. Consider the following class:

```
package com.wiley.as3bible {

    public class ExampleType {
```

```
        private var _a:Number;
        private var _b:Number;

        public function ExampleType(a:Number = -1, b:Number = -1) {
            if(a != -1) {
                _a = a;
            }
            if(b != -1) {
                _b = b;
            }
        }

        public function getA():Number {
            return _a;
        }

        public function getB():Number {
            return _b;
        }

    }

}
```

In this example, we have a very basic class that has no public properties or getters/setters, but it does have two private properties that are accessible via accessor methods only. By default, these values are not written when an object is serialized, as you can see in the following example:

```
package {
    import flash.display.Sprite;
    import flash.net.*;
    import flash.utils.ByteArray;
    import com.wiley.as3bible.ExampleType;

    public class CustomTypeExample extends Sprite {
        public function CustomTypeExample() {
            registerClassAlias("com.wiley.as3bible.ExampleType", ExampleType);
            var example1:ExampleType = new ExampleType(1, 2);
            var byteArray:ByteArray = new ByteArray();
            byteArray.writeObject(example1);
            byteArray.position = 0;
            var example2:ExampleType = byteArray.readObject() as ExampleType;
            trace(example2.getA());
            trace(example2.getB());
        }
    }
}
```

In this example, the two `trace()` statements output NaN because even though the object is correctly stored and retrieved as an `ExampleType` object, it does not write the private data to the byte array when it is serialized.

663

You can use the flash.net.IExternalizable interface to correct this. If a class implements the IExternalizable interface, then Flash Player automatically calls the writeExternal() method when trying to serialize the object and readExternal() when trying to deserialize the object. The writeExternal() method requires a parameter of type flash.net.IDataOutput while the readExternal() method requires a parameter of type flash.net.IDataInput. Both of these types (IDataOutput and IDataInput) are ByteArrays. In the writeExternal() method, you should use byte array methods to write all the data you want to serialize to the IDataOutput parameter, and in the readExternal() method you should read all the values from the IDataInput parameter and write them to properties. Here's the ExampleType class re-written so that it implements IExternalizable:

```
package com.wiley.as3bible {

    import flash.utils.IExternalizable;
    import flash.utils.IDataInput;
    import flash.utils.IDataOutput;

    public class ExampleType implements IExternalizable {

        private var _a:Number;
        private var _b:Number;

        public function ExampleType(a:Number = -1, b:Number = -1) {
            if(a != -1) {
                _a = a;
            }
            if(b != -1) {
                _b = b;
            }
        }

        public function getA():Number {
            return _a;
        }

        public function getB():Number {
            return _b;
        }

        public function writeExternal(output:IDataOutput):void {
            output.writeFloat(_a);
            output.writeFloat(_b);
        }

        public function readExternal(input:IDataInput):void {
            _a = input.readFloat();
            _b = input.readFloat();
        }
    }
}
```

With this change, the same code used before to copy the `ExampleType` object will also copy the private properties such that the subsequent calls to `getA()` and `getB()` return the correct values.

Working with binary sockets

Binary sockets allow you to create persistent connections between Flash Player and socket end points on a server. In contrast to this, consider how most network communications work with Flash Player. Whether you are using `URLLoader` or `NetConnection`, most network communications use HTTP, a protocol which requires that a socket connection be opened, data be sent, a response be returned, and the socket connection be immediately closed. That means that with standard network communications all communications from the server must be in response to requests from Flash Player. This is appropriate in many cases. Maintaining a persistent socket connection could be needlessly wasteful of available resources if it's not necessary. However, there are cases in which a persistent socket connection is either preferable or necessary.

Cases in which a persistent socket connection is preferable include low-latency applications such as multi-player games or instant message chat programs. Cases in which a persistent socket connection is necessary are those in which the server absolutely must be able to push messages and data to Flash Player. Furthermore, there are applications that require persistent socket connections by the very nature of how the server-side application works. Examples of these applications include those in which Flash Player interacts with an FTP server or a mail server.

Regardless of how you intend to use a persistent socket connection, you can use the `flash.net` `.Socket` class for this purpose. A `Socket` object allows you to create a persistent socket connection and then send and receive binary data over that connection. The basic steps in every case are the same:

1. Establish the connection.
2. Add a listener for events when messages are received from the server.
3. Send messages to the server.
4. Disconnect from the server when the connection is no longer needed.

Connection to the server

You can establish a persistent socket connection by constructing a `Socket` object and calling the `connect()` method. The `connect()` method requires two parameters: the address to the server and the port number on which to establish the socket connection:

```
var socket:Socket = new Socket();
socket.connect("localhost", 1234);
```

While the `connect()` method will attempt to connect to the server, you are not guaranteed that the connection will work correctly, nor are you able to send data until the connection is established. For this reason, you need to listen for events that the socket object might dispatch. The ioError event (`IOErrorEvent.IO_ERROR`) occurs if the server cannot be located or refuses the connection. The securityError (`SecurityErrorEvent.SECURITY_ERROR`) occurs if the server is outside the sandbox or the port number is too low (lower than 1024 is not permitted by default). On the other hand, if the connection is successful, then the socket will dispatch a connect (`Event.CONNECT`) event:

```
socket.addEventListener(IOErrorEvent.IO_ERROR, ioErrorHandler);
socket.addEventListener(SecurityErrorEvent.SECURITY_ERROR, ↵
securityErrorHandler);
socket.addEventListener(Event.CONNECT, connectHandler);
```

Listen for messages

You can listen for messages from the server by registering a listener for the socketData event (`ProgressEvent.SOCKET_DATA`):

```
socket.addEventListener(ProgressEvent.SOCKET_DATA, socketDataHandler);
```

When the socket data is received, you can then read it from the socket object using the same read methods as a byte array. In fact, `Socket` and `ByteArray` both implement `IDataOutput`, which is the interface requiring all the read methods. You should be careful not to read more bytes than are available. You can be sure to do this by testing that you're not reading more bytes than specified by `bytesAvailable`. Here's an example that uses a `while` statement to ensure that bytes are available before reading them:

```
private function socketDataHandler(event:ProgressEvent):void {
    while(socket.bytesAvailable) {
        trace(socket.readByte());
    }
}
```

Send messages to the server

You can send messages to the server by writing data to the socket object using the same write methods available to byte arrays. (`Socket` objects and `ByteArray` objects both implement the same `IDataInput` interface.)

```
socket.writeFloat(1.5);
socket.writeObject(exampleArray);
```

Once you've written data to the socket, you can call `flush()` to actually send it to the server:

```
socket.flush();
```

The `flush()` method sends the data to the server and clears the buffer in the socket.

Disconnect from the server

When you no longer need to maintain the connection to the server, you can disconnect using the `close()` method:

```
socket.close();
```

Building applications using sockets

Most applications that use binary sockets are fairly specialized and complex, and therefore they are outside the scope of this book. However, you can find several good examples of such applications on the Web. Here are a few examples:

- **AIM client:** A client for AOL Instant Messenger was written by Josh Tynjala, and is available at `www.zeuslabs.us/flex-2-instant-messenger-client`.

- **VNC client:** VNC stands for virtual network computing, and it allows for remote desktop sharing. FVNC is an open source VNC client written in ActionScript 3.0. The original work was done by Darron Schall. The project is available at `www.osflash.org/fvnc`.

Summary

- Byte arrays store binary data in sequences of bytes.
- Write to and read from byte arrays using either array-access notation or the read and write methods of the `ByteArray` class.
- You can use a byte array to compute sound spectrums.
- Byte arrays allow you to load images using a socket.
- Use byte arrays to create copies of objects.

Part X

Deploying Your Program

Chapter 35

Deploying Flash on the Web

Programming your creation in ActionScript 3.0 is the first, and most important, step. Any successful project must also deploy it correctly. In most cases, Flash content is seen on the World Wide Web, within your web browser. There are other possibilities for your content, such as a screensaver or a kiosk, that typically require third-party tools to implement. This chapter covers the important issues in preparing your Flash content for deployment over the Web.

Embedding Flash in a Page

If you are developing Flash content for the Web, at some point you will have to embed your SWF in an [X]HTML page. This process sounds like it should be a stroll in the park, but unfortunately the park is strewn with land mines.

Rendering Flash in a web page requires the Flash Player plug-in. And despite the fact that browsers have been around for many years, there are still differences in plug-in architectures and the HTML that should be used to embed them. To wit, Internet Explorer uses ActiveX controls, and Mozilla browsers use the NSPlugin architecture. Different tags have been used to embed content: the `<embed>` tag and the `<object>` tag. Browsers even implement these tags in slightly different ways. To complicate matters, writing valid [X]HTML is desirable, and often required, but the `<embed>` tag is not valid in HTML 4 or XHTML 1. To make things worse, the EOLAS patent suit against Microsoft in 2005 (`http://en.wikipedia.org/wiki/Eolas`) forced Internet Explorer to require a mouse click to activate plug-ins, and other browser vendors may face similar suits in the future.

671

In a utopian future, you will have to write just one standards-compliant <object> tag to embed Flash content. But at the present time, you have to choose a method of embedding SWFs that will provide your content to people with all kinds of browsers, without using invalid markup, that gets around the click-to-activate issue, that can display alternate content if the user does not have Flash, and that can detect the version of Flash Player that you are targeting.

CAUTION   **Without intervention, Flash Player tries to play SWFs published for any version of Flash Player. Flash Player 7 will try to display SWFs published for Flash Player 8. Backward compatibility should be perfect: Playing a SWF made for an older version of Flash Player should never be a problem. Not surprisingly, forward compatibility does not really exist. If you have any ActionScript in your Flash content at all, you should not allow older Flash Players to play your content. Accordingly, you should also publish your SWFs to the lowest version of Flash Player that supports the features you use.**

All ActionScript 3.0 programs require Flash Player 9 or above.

Fortunately, several methods and scripts have stepped up to fulfill these goals. The most comprehensive ones, Geoff Stearns's SWFObject (`http://blog.deconcept.com/swfobject/`) and Bobby van der Sluis's UFO (`www.bobbyvandersluis.com/ufo/`) are updated frequently to resolve bugs and even patch bugs in browsers and Flash Player. These solutions use JavaScript to embed Flash content. Flash CS3 Professional and Flex Builder 2 also ship with Adobe's ActiveContent JavaScript embedding solution.

Alternately, there are some HTML-only solutions that work with one or two exceptions to embed content cross-browser without additional features. The nested object solution and the Flash satay solution are both succinct and standards-compliant.

There has been a tremendous amount of debate over the last few years concerning the pros and cons of these approaches, but Bobby van der Sluis has summarized the state of the Flash embedding world in a very readable article on A List Apart (`www.alistapart.com/articles/flashembedcagematch/`). If you want to make an informed decision about which method to use to embed Flash content, start with this article and read the documentation on the SWFObject and UFO sites.

Until SWFFix (`www.swffix.org`), the collaboration between Stearns and van der Sluis, is released, we recommend that you use SWFObject wherever possible to embed Flash content. It's easy to use, meets all the goals laid out above, and the fact that it is constantly being updated to patch browser and Flash Player bugs enables you to concentrate on writing great ActionScript.

Furthermore, the web development community has produced some excellent extensions to SWFObject. For example, SWFAddress (`www.asual.com/swfaddress/`) makes it simple to provide browser history integration and deep linking, and SWFMacMouseWheel (`http://blog.pixelbreaker.com/2006/11/08/flash/swfmacmousewheel/`) uses JavaScript to add support for the mouse wheel on the Mac platform.

Embedding Flash Using SWFObject

While the ultimate destination for information about SWFObject is its home page at `http://blog` `.deconcept.com/swfobject/`, a quick introduction of the SWFObject syntax will provide context for the examples in the rest of this chapter. A simple HTML page that embeds Flash content using SWFObject might be written as follows:

```
<!DOCTYPE HTML PUBLIC "-//W3C//DTD HTML 4.0 Transitional//EN">

<html>
<head>
    <title>SWFObject Demo</title>
    <script type="text/javascript" src="swfobject.js"></script>
</head>
<body>

<div id="content">
    The HTML version of the Flash content.
</div>

<script type="text/javascript">
    var so = new SWFObject("demo.swf", "demo", "640", "480", "9", "#000000");
    so.addParam("wmode", "transparent");
    so.addVariable("age", "26");
    so.write("content");
</script>

</body>
</html>
```

When using SWFObject, you need to include the following three elements in your HTML page:

- A `<script>` tag to include the SWFObject code. Download `swfobject.js` from the SWFObject web page, upload it to your own site, and include it as in the preceding example.

- A `<div>` containing the HTML version of your Flash content, with an `id`. Think of this like an `alt` tag on an image. The HTML content will not be displayed if the user is capable of displaying the Flash content. It will appear to any search engine.

- A `<script>` block that creates a SWFObject and calls `write()` on it.

SWFObject replaces the content of the div named in `write()` with the HTML necessary to embed the Flash content as you specified using the SWFObject object. So we have a div named "content" in which `demo.swf` is embedded, replacing its HTML content.

The constructor is SWFObject's most important method. Its parameters, in the order in which they are set, are summarized in Table 35-1.

TABLE 35-1

SWFObject Constructor Arguments

SWFObject	Argument
swf	URL of the SWF file to load.
id	The id that will be assigned to the embed or object tag that holds your SWF. Remember that ids are unique: this can't be the id of any other HTML element.
width	Width of the Flash content. It is a CSS property, so percentages are allowed.
height	Height of the Flash content. It is a CSS property, so percentages are allowed.
version	The minimum required version of Flash Player for your content to show. Can be general, as in 9, or specific, as in 9.0.28.
background-color	The background color of your Flash content.
quality	[Optional, default is high] The Flash rendering quality as set on the embed or object tag written by SWFObject.
xiRedirectUrl	[Optional] A URL to redirect users to if they successfully upgrade Flash Player using Express Install.
redirectUrl	[Optional] A URL to redirect users to if they don't have a sufficient version of Flash Player, rather than displaying the content of the div.
detectKey	[Optional, default is detectflash] The name of a parameter which, if it is set to false in the query string when the HTML file is requested, will embed the Flash content without checking for the correct version of Flash Player.

The addParam() method and addVariable() methods are discussed in the next sections.

Enabling Flash Player Options

Regardless of which embedding technique you use, the tags used to embed Flash content can also convey a variety of options to Flash Player. These are fully documented in an Adobe TechNote at www.adobe.com/go/tn_12701.

When an <embed> tag is used, these options are set as attributes of the embed tag itself. When an <object> tag is used, the options are encoded as a sequence of child nodes of the form <param name="" value=""/>. Use this approach when writing [X]HTML by hand. For example, the following code sets the quality of a Flash movie using an embed tag in HTML:

```
<embed src="foo.swf" quality="high"></embed>
```

Or to set the same property using an object tag:

```
<object classid="clsid:D27CDB6E-AE6D-11cf-96B8-444553540000">
    <param name="movie" value="foo.swf">
    <param name="quality" value="high">
</object>
```

SWFObject lets you set any of these options with the `addParam()` method, which should be called before `write()`. Call this method as many times as needed to add single pairs of option names and values. This block of JavaScript would replace the div with an `id` of `flashcontent` with the Flash movie, and set the quality:

```
<script type="text/javascript">
    var so = new SWFObject("foo.swf");
    so.addParam("quality", "high");
    so.write("flashcontent");
</script>
```

There are two parameters that you can set on Flash embeds that are particularly useful. They are described in the sections that follow.

Transparent Flash

By default, the Flash Player plug-in renders your Flash content with an opaque background and without being composited against other elements in the browser. By setting the `wmode` parameter of the embedding code to `transparent`, you can make Flash content render without a background, composited with all other HTML elements in a page. This can be used to draw SWFs with irregular borders, expand Flash content by bleeding into an otherwise transparent region, and convincingly layer Flash content with transparent images.

> **CAUTION** Flash content embedded as transparent will take up more system resources and perform more slowly than its opaque counterpart. Use transparent Flash sparingly!

To set this parameter using SWFObject, simply use the `addParam()` method:

```
so.addParam("wmode", "transparent");
```

Full-Screen Flash

Starting in Flash Player 9.0.28, you can use ActionScript to put the Flash Player in full-screen mode, overtaking the user's entire screen with your content. You can even enable this behavior in a browser. This allows a Flash video player, for instance, to display in its normal size inside the browser window, or to fill the user's entire display.

For the Flash Player plug-in to enable full-screen mode, the `allowFullScreen` option of the embed code must be set to `true`. To set this parameter using SWFObject, simply use the `addParam()` method:

```
so.addParam("allowFullScreen", "true");
```

To switch between full-screen and normal windowed mode in ActionScript 3.0, change the `displayState` property of the `Stage` object as a reaction to mouse or keyboard input:

```
//somewhere in the code, listen to the click event from a button
button.addEventListener(MouseEvent.CLICK, onFullScreenButtonClick);

//add an event handler to react to the button click
protected function onFullScreenButtonClick(event:MouseEvent):void
{
    stage.displayState = StageDisplayState.FULL_SCREEN;
}
```

Because this feature requires Flash Player 9.0.28 or later, be sure to configure your Flash embed to require this version or later to ensure full-screen capability.

Passing Variables to a SWF

You can pass values from HTML into embedded Flash content. These variables are often inserted into the HTML by scripts or passed in via the URL query string. You can use this technique to enable one SWF to serve in many situations, to avoid adding a second network access to retrieve some value that is available at the time the HTML page is served, or to ensure that a value is set before the first frame of the SWF plays. For example, sIFR (www.mikeindustries.com/sifr/) uses one SWF file (per font) to display any given text in a specific typeface by passing the text to be rendered into the Flash content at embed time.

Passing values into embedded SWFs, in fact, is also achieved by setting an option on the embedding tags. The option name is `flashVars`, and its value is a URL-encoded set of name/value pairs. By using URL encoding, you can represent multiple variable names and values in one string so that you can use that string as the value of a single Flash embedding option. The following example illustrates this phenomenon. If you have the following variables:

```
var name = "Roger";
var age = 26;
var eyes = "brown";
```

you can send these to an embedded SWF by setting the `flashVars` option:

```
<param name="flashVars" value="name=Roger&age=26&eyes=brown"/>
```

Because of the URL encoding, all variables passed to an embedded SWF are encoded as strings. You can include as many variables as you want, but the whole URL-encoded string must be under 64KB or browsers may not accept it.

SWFObject lets you send variables into embedded SWFs without dealing with URL encoding or flashVars directly. Just call the addVariable() method on the SWFObject object once for every variable to pass in:

```
so.addVariable("name", "Roger");
so.addVariable("age", "26");
so.addVariable("eyes", "brown");
```

To access these variables in the embedded SWF, access the LoaderInfo object of the root class of that SWF. This is the Application file if you're using Flex Builder, or the class set to the Document Class if you're using Flash CS3 Professional. The parameters property of the LoaderInfo object is an Object in which you will find all the variables passed in at embed time. The following example, when used as the root class, will trace out all the variables passed in by the embed:

```
package
{
    import flash.display.*;

    public class FlashVarsTest extends Sprite
    {
        public function FlashVarsTest()
        {
            var flashVars:Object = this.loaderInfo.parameters;
            for (var variable:String in flashVars)
            {
                trace(variable + ": " + flashVars[variable]);
            }
        }
    }
}
```

NEW IN AS3 Variables passed in by an embed are stored in the parameters property of a LoaderInfo object. They are not added to the namespace of _root as in previous versions of ActionScript.

Automatically Upgrading Flash Player

To ensure that users see your content with an appropriate version of Flash Player, you must ask users with older versions to upgrade. However, you want to make this as easy as possible. Instead of redirecting users to Adobe's Flash Player install page, you can actually trigger Flash Player to upgrade itself without navigating away from the page using a technique called Express Install. Express Install will display a dialog box on the page where your SWF would normally display, asking only that you confirm the upgrade. Figure 35-1 shows what the user will see in place of the Flash content.

FIGURE 35-1

The Express Install interface

To follow an Express Install process, you must first determine that the user's Flash Player needs to be upgraded. Then, you typically pass off installation to an alternate SWF. This SWF, in order to be able to upgrade the oldest possible Flash Player version, should be compiled for the earliest version of Flash Player that supports Express Install, Flash Player 6.0.65. This SWF then loads in an upgrader SWF from Adobe: http://fpdownload.adobe.com/pub/flashplayer/ update/current/swf/autoUpdater.swf. Adobe's SWF will display a dialog box to the user requesting permission to upgrade the Flash Player, and if permission is granted, attempt to install the latest Flash Player. When it is complete, Adobe's updater SWF will signal a status back to your SWF, letting you know if the update was successful, failed, or was denied by the user.

SWFObject comes with a template FLA to customize your Express Install experience. Using Express Install with SWFObject is simple once you have the Express Install SWF created. Simply call useExpressInstall() on the SWFObject before writing it out. The parameter to this method should be the URL to a SWF that can be embedded in place of your content SWF when the user needs to upgrade.

```
so.useExpressInstall("expressinstall.swf");
```

Flex Builder 2 will export HTML that includes Express Install support if you check the Use Express Install option in a project's ActionScript Compiler properties panel.

To use Express Install, the user must have at least Flash Player 6.0.65, and the SWF it is running in must be at least 214 pixels wide by 137 pixels high. The user must also have access to install software on his or her own computer, which is often not the case for corporate or shared computers.

Summary

- There are many ways to embed Flash content on the Web.
- There are scripted solutions, and tag-only solutions.
- SWFObject is recommended.
- Flash content can be embedded with many options.
- Variables may be passed into embedded SWFs using `flashVars`.
- The Flash Player plug-in can attempt to update itself using Express Install.

Chapter 36

Interfacing with JavaScript

This chapter looks at Flash applications embedded in HTML pages and interfacing with JavaScript. We'll take a look at how you can communicate from Flash to JavaScript and vice versa.

Communicating Between JavaScript and Flash

When you deploy Flash content in a web browser, you may want to be able to communicate with the container HTML page. You may want to call JavaScript functions from the SWF, and you may want JavaScript functions to be able to call functions within the SWF. That lets you make integrated applications, of which the SWF is just one component.

The following sections take a look at the ways in which you can communicate between Flash and JavaScript.

Using ExternalInterface

You can use the `flash.external.ExternalInterface` class to both call JavaScript functions from Flash and to call ActionScript functions from JavaScript. The `ExternalInterface` class has been tested successfully in the following browsers:

- Internet Explorer 5.0 and above for Windows
- Netscape 8.0 and above for Windows and Macintosh
- Mozilla 1.7.5 and above for Windows and Macintosh
- Safari 1.3 and above for Macintosh
- Firefox 1.0 and above for Windows and Macintosh

681

Calling JavaScript functions from Flash

Using `ExternalInterface`, you can call JavaScript functions from within a Flash SWF. With `ExternalInterface`, the JavaScript function can return a value to Flash.

To call a JavaScript function from Flash, you simply use the static `ExternalInterface.call()` method. The `call()` method requires at least one parameter — the name of the function to call. You can also pass additional parameters, each of which is passed to the JavaScript function as a parameter. The following code calls the JavaScript `alert()` function with a parameter of `hello`:

```
ExternalInterface.call("alert", "hello");
```

If the JavaScript function returns a value, you can simply use the `call()` method as part of an expression such as an assignment statement. The following example code assigns the return value from a JavaScript function `getStringValue()` to a variable:

```
var value:String = ExternalInterface.call("getStringValue");
```

Calling ActionScript functions from JavaScript

You can also call ActionScript functions from JavaScript. To do so you must do two things — register the function in ActionScript so that it is accessible from JavaScript, and then call the function from JavaScript via the Flash object.

You can register an ActionScript function within Flash with the static `ExternalInterface .addCallback()` method. The method requires two parameters: the name of the function as you want to call it from JavaScript and the reference to the function/method that you want to register. The following example registers a function called `runScript()` so that you can call it from JavaScript as `runFlashScript()`:

```
ExternalInterface.addCallback("runFlashScript", runScript);
```

Once a function is registered, you can call it from within JavaScript. From JavaScript, you call the function as a method of the Flash object by referencing the ID of the plug-in or ActiveX object. The standard way to do this is with the `getElementById()` method, defined in HTML DOM Level 2. This is compatible with all modern browsers: Internet Explorer 5.0 and up, Mozilla 1.0 and up, Netscape 6.0 and up, Opera 7.0 and up, and Safari 1.0 and up. If your Flash content was embedded with an id of `"flashObjectID"`, you would retrieve a reference to the plug-in object like so:

```
document.getElementById("flashObjectID");
```

And you could call the registered ActionScript method from JavaScript with this code:

```
document.getElementById("flashObjectID").runFlashScript();
```

or

```
window.flashObjectID.runFlashScript();
```

You can pass parameters to the function. You can also use a function call in an expression if the ActionScript function returns a value.

Making an integrated HTML/Flash application with ExternalInterface

You've had a chance to read about the theory of `ExternalInterface`. Now you'll use the theory to put together a simple demonstration application. The application uses a Flash movie with a rotating rectangle, a start/stop button, and a text field. The Flash movie is placed within an HTML page with a text input and a button. The Flash movie requests that data, and displays it in the text field. When the user clicks the start/stop button in the Flash movie, it pauses and resumes the rotation of the rectangle, and it also sends a message to the HTML text input to display the current status of the rectangle. The HTML button makes a new random color and sends it to the Flash movie. The Flash movie then applies that color to the rectangle.

Create a new project, and write a main class in com/wiley/as3bible/ExternalInterfaceExample.as:

```
package com.wiley.as3bible {

    import flash.display.Sprite;
    import flash.text.TextField;
    import flash.utils.Timer;
    import flash.events.MouseEvent;
    import flash.events.TimerEvent;
    import flash.external.ExternalInterface;

    public class ExternalInterfaceExample extends Sprite {
        private var _rectangle:Sprite;
        private var _text:TextField;
        private var _isAnimating:Boolean;
        private var _timer:Timer;

        public function ExternalInterfaceExample() {

            _rectangle = new Sprite();
            _text = new TextField();
            _rectangle.graphics.lineStyle(0, 0, 1);
            _rectangle.graphics.drawRect(0, 0, 100, 100);
            _rectangle.y = 100;
            addChild(_rectangle);
            addChild(_text);
            _timer = new Timer(50);
            _timer.addEventListener(TimerEvent.TIMER, timerHandler);
            togglePlayback();
            ExternalInterface.addCallback("togglePlayback", togglePlayback);
            var browserData:Object = ExternalInterface.call("getBrowser");
            _text.text = browserData.browser + " " + browserData.browserVersion;
        }
```

```
        public function togglePlayback():void {
            if(_isAnimating) {
                _isAnimating = false;
                _timer.stop();
            }
            else {
                _isAnimating = true;
                _timer.start();
            }
        }

        private function timerHandler(event:TimerEvent):void {
            _rectangle.x += 5;
            if(_rectangle.x > stage.stageWidth) {
                _rectangle.x = 0;
            }
        }
    }
}
```

Publish the example as externalinterface.swf. Use SWFObject to embed the Flash content in an HTML page. You can learn more about using SWFObject in Chapter 35. If you don't already have the SWFObject JavaScript file then download it from blog.deconcept.com/swfobject and place the JS file in the same directory as the SWF file. In the same directory as the SWF and JS files, add a new HTML document called externalinterface.html with the following contents:

```
<!DOCTYPE html PUBLIC "-//W3C//DTD XHTML 1.0 Strict//EN"
"http://www.w3.org/TR/xhtml1/DTD/xhtml1-strict.dtd">
<!-- saved from url=(0014)about:internet -->
<html xmlns="http://www.w3.org/1999/xhtml" xml:lang="en" lang="en">
<head>
<meta http-equiv="Content-Type" content="text/html;
charset=utf-8" />
<title>Example ExternalInterface</title>
<script type="text/javascript" src="swfobject.js"></script>
<style type="text/css">

    body {
        background-color: #eeeeee;
        font: .8em verdana,arial,helvetica,sans-serif;
    }

    #buttons {
        width: 300px;
        overflow: auto;
    }
```

```
        #flashcontent {
            width: 550px;
            height: 400px;
            float: left;
            margin: 15px 20px;
        }

    </style>
    </head>
    <body>
        <div id="flashcontent">
            <strong>You need to upgrade your Flash Player</strong>
        </div>

        <script type="text/javascript">
            // <![CDATA[

            var so = new SWFObject("ExternalInterfaceExample.swf", "example", ↵
    "550", "400", "9", "#FFFFFF");
            so.addParam("allowScriptAccess", "always");
            so.write("flashcontent");

            // ]]>
        </script>

        <div id="buttons">
            <input type="button" onClick=↵
    "document.getElementById('example') .togglePlayback()" value="Toggle Playback"
    />
        </div>

    </body>
    </html>
```

Summary

- You can use `ExternalInterface` to create integrated applications in which Flash and JavaScript communicate synchronously.
- Use `ExternalInterface.call()` to call JavaScript functions from Flash.
- Use `ExternalInterface.addCallback()` to register an ActionScript function or method so that it can be called from JavaScript.

Chapter 37

Using Local Connections to Communicate Between Flash Applications

The `flash.net.LocalConnection` class allows for any Flash application in any player to communicate with any other Flash application in any other player on the same computer without needing any complicated JavaScript or other workarounds. All that is required is that the applications run on the same computer and that one is set up to broadcast messages and the other is set up to listen for messages. As an example of how you might use `LocalConnection`, consider that an application deployed on the Web could consist of several SWF files that need to work in conjunction with one another. With `LocalConnection`, the SWFs can communicate. There are many possibilities with `LocalConnection`. In this chapter, you learn how to work with the `LocalConnection` class.

> ### IN THIS CHAPTER
>
> **Creating local domain communication between Flash applications**
>
> ---
>
> **Creating communication between Flash applications across domains**

Creating a Sending Application

There are essentially two types of applications related to `LocalConnection` communication. The first of these is the *sending* application. Sending can be accomplished in as few as two steps. The first step is obviously to create a `LocalConnection` object. The `LocalConnection` constructor requires no parameters, so you can create an object like this:

```
var sender:LocalConnection = new LocalConnection();
```

After you have created the object, you need only to call the `send()` method in order to send to a receiving application. At a minimum, the `send()` method requires two parameters: the name of the connection over which you wish to send and the name of the method you want to invoke in the receiving application. The name of the connection is arbitrary and left up to you, but it must match the name of the connection over which the receiving

687

application is listening. Here is an example in which a `LocalConnection` object broadcasts a message over a connection named `aConnection`. The method invoked is named `someMethod`:

```
var sender:LocalConnection = new LocalConnection();
sender.send("aConnection", "someMethod");
```

Sending parameters

You can send parameters to the receiving application's method in addition to just calling the method. Any parameters that are added to the `send()` method after the required two (connection name and method name) are sent to the receiving application's method as parameters. The following example shows how three parameters can be sent to the `someMethod` method:

```
var sender:LocalConnection = new LocalConnection();
sender.send("aConnection", "someMethod", true, "two", 3);
```

In addition to primitive data types, objects and arrays can be sent as parameters:

```
var sender:LocalConnection = new LocalConnection();
var objectParameter:Object = {a: "one", b: "two", c: "three"};
var arrayParameter:Array = [1,2,3,4,5];
sender.send("aConnection", "someMethod", objectParameter, arrayParameter);
```

Checking the status of a send

Every time a `send()` method is invoked there is an accompanying event that the object dispatches. If the send failed because of invalid security permissions then the `LocalConnection` object dispatches a security error event. Therefore, if you want the application to properly handle security errors for local connections you should register a listener for the security error event, which is of type `SecurityErrorEvent.SECURITY_ERROR`.

```
sender.addEventListener(SecurityErrorEvent.SECURITY_ERROR, ↵
securityErrorHandler);
```

On the other hand, in most cases the `LocalConnection` object will dispatch a status event. The status event has a `level` property, which will have a value of either status or `error`. If the value is `status` it means that the send was successful, and the receiving application did handle the request. A value of `error` likely means that the receiving application refused the request. If you need to ensure proper receipt of the request, then you should register a listener for the status event. The status event is of type `StatusEvent.STATUS`:

```
sender.addEventListener(StatusEvent.STATUS, statusHandler);
```

Creating a Receiving Application

The receiving application is slightly more complex than the sending application, but not by much. The simplest receiving application has only four steps:

1. Create a new `LocalConnection` object.

2. Define the method that will get called by the sending application.

3. Tell the `LocalConnection` object what object should be used to handle the requests.

4. Instruct the application to listen for messages on a particular connection name.

The first step is the same as the first step in the sending application, replacing sender with receiver:

```
var receiver:LocalConnection = new LocalConnection();
```

The second step merely defines the method that will be called by the sending application:

```
public function methodName():void {
    // Code goes here
}
```

You then need to tell the `LocalConnection` object what object should handle the requests. The object that handles the requests is called the client, and you can simply assign a reference to the `client` property of the `LocalConnection` object. For example, if you define the method to be called within the same class in which you've defined the `LocalConnection` object you'd want to assign a reference of this to the `client` property of the `LocalConnection` object.

```
receiver.client = this;
```

And the last step is accomplished by the `connect()` method, which is invoked from the `LocalConnection` object you have created with a parameter of the name of the connection on which the application should listen:

```
receiver.connect(connectionName);
```

The method name must match the method name that is passed as the second parameter of the `send()` method in the sending application. And the connection name for the `connect()` method must match the connection name passed as the first parameter of the `send()` method of the sending application.

The receiving application continues to listen on a connection after the `connect()` method has been called, unless you instruct it not to. You can close a connection simply by calling the close() method from the `LocalConnection` object. For example:

```
receiver.close();
```

Sending and Receiving Across Domains

By default, `LocalConnection` objects attempt to communicate to the same domain. That is, if a sending application is being run from `www.rightactionscript.com`, it defaults to broadcasting to other applications on `www.rightactionscript.com`. With just a few changes, however, you can configure applications to send and receive messages across domains so that, for example, an application on `www.rightactionscript.com` can send to `www.themakers.com`.

The sending application

The sending application requires only one modification to send to another domain. The first parameter of the `send()` method (the connection name) can be modified in one of two ways. Either you can prefix the domain to which the command is to be sent, or you can use a connection name that starts with an underscore. Each works in a similar, but slightly different manner.

When a connection name neither prepends a domain nor starts with an underscore, Flash automatically converts the connection name to `localDomain:connection`. The domain is always the superdomain — the domain minus the subdomain such as www. For example, if the following is run from `www.rightactionscript.com`, Flash automatically converts the connection name to `rightactionscript.com:aConnection`.

```
sender.send("aConnection", "someMethod");
```

If you know you want to send the call to a Flash application running from `themakers.com`, you can prefix the connection name with `themakers.com` as follows.

```
sender.send("themakers.com:aConnection", "someMethod");
```

The preceding works well when you want to send only to Flash applications running on a specific domain. However, if you want to send the calls to applications running on any domain, it won't work. In those cases you can use a connection name that starts with an underscore. If the connection name starts with an underscore, Flash doesn't automatically prefix the domain. The following will send to any Flash application from any domain as long as it is listening on `_aConnection`:

```
sender.send("_aConnection", "someMethod");
```

The receiving application

The receiving application also requires a few modifications if you want it to receive calls from sending applications in different domains. Unlike the sending application, you cannot prefix the connection name of a receiving application with a different domain. Unless the connection name starts with an underscore, Flash automatically prepends the receiving application's domain to the connection name, and you cannot tell it to do otherwise. For example, if the receiving application is running from `www.rightactionscript.com`, the following connection is interpreted by Flash as `rightactionscript.com:aConnection`:

```
receiver.connect("aConnection");
```

As long as the sending application is running from `www.rightactionscript.com` as well or the sending application has a connection name of `rightactionscript.com:aConnection`, the calls will get picked up by the receiving application. If the sending application uses a connection name with an underscore as the first character, the receiving application must also use the same connection name with the starting underscore.

However, just because the receiving application receives the call, that doesn't mean it will then necessarily do what it was instructed by the sending application. By default, the application may receive calls, but it *accepts* calls only from the local domain. You can also allow other domains by using the `allowDomain()` method.

When a receiving application receives a communication from a sending application, Flash Player needs to decide whether or not to accept the request. It does so by consulting the `LocalConnection` object to see if the sending domain is in the list of allowable domains. By default, cross-domain requests are disallowed. However, you can use `allowDomain()` in the receiving application to specify one or more domains from which to accept requests. The following example accepts all requests from `rightactionscript.com`, `www.rightactionscript.com`, `themakers.com`, and `www.themakers.com`:

```
receiver.allowDomain("rightactionscript.com", ↩
"www.rightactionscript.com", "themakers.com", ↩
"www.themakers.com");
```

You can also use the * character as a wildcard meaning all domains:

```
receiver.allowDomain("*");
```

If the receiving SWF is served from a secure server using HTTPS and the sending SWF is using standard HTTP, then the request will not be accepted, even if `allowDomain()` is used. Instead, you must use `allowInsecureDomain()`. The `allowInsecureDomain()` method works just like the `allowDomain()` method except that it allows requests from HTTP when the receiving SWF is being served using HTTPS.

Summary

- Flash applications can communicate with other Flash applications with the `LocalConnection` class of objects. `LocalConnection` allows a sending application to call a method in a receiving application.

- By default, the `LocalConnection` object allows connections only between applications on the same domain. However, with some changes in the sending and receiving applications, communication can occur between applications on different domains.

Index

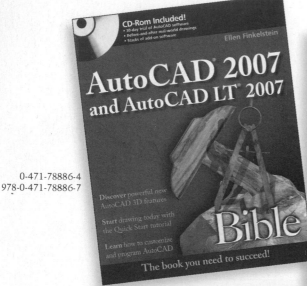

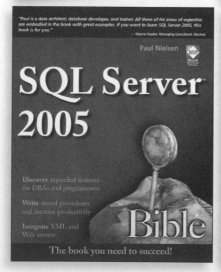